D1328056

The Quest for Authority and Honor in the American Professions, 1750–1900

THE QUEST FOR AUTHORITY AND HONOR
IN THE
AMERICAN PROFESSIONS, 1750–1900

Samuel Haber

The University of Chicago Press / Chicago and London

Samuel Haber, professor of history at the University of California, Berkeley, is the author of *Efficiency and Uplift* (University of Chicago Press, 1964).

The University of Chicago Press, Chicago 60637
The University of Chicago Press, Ltd., London
© 1991 by The University of Chicago
All rights reserved. Published 1991
Printed in the United States of America

00 99 98 97 96 95 94 93 92 91 5 4 3 2 1

Library of Congress Cataloging-in-Publication Data

Haber, Samuel.
    The quest for authority and honor in the American professions, 1750–1900 / Samuel Haber.
        p.   cm.
    Includes bibliographical references (p.   ) and index.
    ISBN 0-226-31173-2 (cloth)
    1. Professions—Social aspects—United States—History. 2. Social status—United States—History. 3. Occupational prestige—United States—History.   I. Title.
    HT687.H26   1991
    305.5′53′0973—dc20   90-46752
                                                          CIP

To Sara, Kate, Ruth
and to Celia

Contents

Illustrations

Preface

Many of those who consider the professions particularly important today see them as exemplary and up-to-date specimens of modernization, and there is much to be said for that view. However, the special secret of the professions is quite the opposite. What the professions do (and this helps account for much of their excitement and attainment) is to bring into the modern world ideals and standards that are premodern—both precapitalistic and predemocratic. A historical study is especially suited to uncover and explain such a secret, and that is what I endeavor to do in this book.[1]

One of my central arguments is that the American professions transmit, with some modifications, a distinctive sense of authority and honor that has its origins in the class position and occupational prescriptions of eighteenth-century English gentlemen. Such an argument has implications for the understanding of American society. For it underscores the cumulative and variegated nature of our culture, and it suggests the drawbacks of trying to describe our society as a system. It also accords with an endeavor to write a history that rescues for description and analysis mixed motives, composite conditions, as well as persons and parties acting upon contradictory explanatory schemes. The success of the American professions is in part a story of hybrid vigor, alloy strength, and amalgam adaptability—continuing presence of the past. It is precisely that kind of complex reality that neo-Weberian, ideal-type analysis often obscures, and that neo-Marxist efforts to dissolve history into theory usually ignore. The now familiar depiction of the growth of the professions as a movement toward economic monopoly or social modernization is clearly too limiting. Weber and Marx themselves provide more varied and richer alternatives. Weber, for example, often described monopolization or "closure" as arising from noneconomic motives and suggested that professional authority might frequently be benign. And Marx, when he wrote such forceful history as *The Eighteenth Brumaire of Louis Bonaparte*, portrayed men and groups as having ideal interests (though not necessarily benevolent or humane) as well as material ones, with the former not simply reflections of the latter but frequently antithetical and counteractive. This Weber and Marx might serve as a corrective to some of their followers who have written about the professions.[2]

My study also rests upon a particular way of defining professions. While learned men since Socrates have usually defined terms by isolating essential qualities, that is not a helpful way of dealing with the American professions. For they are, in the first place, social artifacts fashioned by public events and usage; and as Socrates quickly discovered, popular use and wont are generally oblivious to essences. The historian forfeits too much if he or she loses touch with popular use and wont. Historians must start with the self-understanding of the people they are studying, but of course they try to reach beyond it.[3]

A more advantageous method of definition, one which reflects the way in which Americans actually designated the professions in the eighteenth and nineteenth centuries, is much like the noting of family resemblances. The professions, as Americans characterized them, were occupations that had a complicated network of similarities but no necessarily common, essential feature for all. To push the borrowed metaphor further, the extended family of professions bore a special relation to a nuclear family consisting of the three long-esteemed professions—the ministry, law, and medicine. Here resemblances were sharper and easier to discern. For these three professions had appropriated the gentleman's authority and honor; they also betokened a liberal education, gratifying work, and a secure and comfortable income.[4]

Originally, a profession meant any work that afforded a livelihood. The word goes back to the practice of the Roman tax-gatherer requiring inhabitants to declare their occupations so that he might assess them properly. All occupations were professions then, as they still are in French usage and in a secondary sense in English usage as well. But by the mid-eighteenth century Dr. Johnson recorded in his dictionary a more specialized meaning, already widespread: "the term [profession] is particularly used of divinity, physic, and law." This elevation and contraction of meaning, using the word to indicate primarily the learned or liberal professions (those presupposing a classical education), brought with it the connotation that a profession was an upper-class occupation for a classical education was generally beyond the reach of the commonality. This joining of learning, class, and occupation made profession a name to conjure with. It also allowed for significant elisions. Officers of the army and navy, although not usually known for their learning, were clearly gentlemen, and their work was generally designated as a profession in the restricted and exalted sense. Fighting had once been the only work worthy of a gentleman. It was still an occupation by which a gentleman could "support his quality." Therefore a profession in the eighteenth century often came to mean an occupation that a gentleman could take up without demeaning himself, and more wondrously, an occupation that might make someone a gentleman simply by his taking it up.[5]

Of course the term gentleman itself had its turns and transformations. As the notion of profession became more circumscribed, the notion of the gentleman broadened somewhat. Eighteenth-century dictionaries still recorded the traditional notion that the gentleman must be well-born, yet such a requirement unmistakably had become moot. Defoe insisted that a "money-getting wretch, who amassed the estate" could not be a gentleman, for "he can no more leav the ravening after money, *Faus aut nefas,* than the old thief can leav off pilfering, or an old whore leav off procuring." Yet Defoe admitted that the "polite son" who inherited the estate and received a liberal education was not excluded from the title. Landed wealth, education, appropriate deportment and sentiments, at least in combination, provided access. Defoe also noted that captains of the army and navy, as well as clergymen, were gentlemen by right of their office, and other writers made claims for barristers and physicians.[6]

Though the lower boundaries of English gentility had become increasingly uncertain, nevertheless the undisputed standard bearer of gentlemanhood remained the landed proprietor living off the rents of his estates. His authority and honor were manifest and assured. He was accorded the right to command, direct, and advise his dependents and many of the common folk of his vicinage. His honor was the special regard given to rank; not to maintain that honor was to discredit the social order and weaken it. Yet the most important fact about the increasingly diverse body of gentlemen was their social position; they were that part of the nation that stood below the nobility but above the commonalty.[7]

The linking of the professions to gentlemanly standing meant that they were defined not only by resemblances but also by differences. A profession was definitely not a trade nor was it one of the mechanic arts. A tradesman bought and sold merchandise and an artisan took on manual labor. Neither was work befitting a gentleman. The tradesman and artisan dealt with customers in a somewhat unstructured relationship; by contrast, the professional dealt with clients and patients in a relationship that often suggested the professional's superior position. The tradesmen and artisans gave their customers what they wanted. The professional gave his clients and patients what he thought was good for them. Moreover, the linking of the professions to gentlemanly standing, when its lower boundaries were becoming increasingly uncertain, meant that the enterprise of self-definition took on considerable importance in the lives of would-be gentlemen and would-be professionals. Not that one could simply define oneself into either group. It was a much more complicated endeavor than that. Rather, the eager and adroit efforts of these striving for inclusion became significant for the history of both gentlemen and professionals. For the professions, resemblance, difference, and assertive self-depiction became primary elements of definition in the eighteenth century and remained important throughout the nineteenth.[8]

My story begins in the mid-eighteenth century, when the Atlantic Ocean as a barrier to the transit of culture from the mother country to the American colonies had shrunk. It was in this era that the British professions became naturalized along the Atlantic seaboard. In the American setting, the professions were granted some of the authority and honor of their British counterparts, and they also imbibed some of their aspirations. The American professions established associations, won honorific licensing legislation, achieved a remarkable cohesiveness, and developed a gentlemanly way of life that distinguished their practitioners from the workers in the less-esteemed occupations. The professional's gentlemanly right to command, direct, and advise was wielded not only in society at large but also within the work setting itself. Of course the professions were *occupations* and therefore had pressing economic interests as well. However, some sense of duty usually stood as a counterpoise to the simple maximizing of income, so that even the often announced aim of bringing duty and interest into accord usually meant a difficult trade-off. Such counterpoise was characteristically justified by the elevated purpose of the work.[9]

In the years roughly between 1830 and 1880, however, the professions came under a withering attack. They declined in stature and self-confidence and almost lapsed into indistinction. The licensing laws, that had endorsed the professions' separation between rightful and wrongful practitioners and had provided public recognition to the professions' claims, were stricken from the statute books. This onslaught, deriving much of its power from the vigorous growth of political democracy, market capitalism, and evangelical Protestantism, was actually part of a broader attack upon customary rankings in the society of the day. The years between 1830 and 1880 were also an era of rapid westward expansion and institutional decentralization. The professions in those years are best studied in their local habitats. The North/South division of the country became the most consequential differentiation in that era and even the professional values of authority and honor took on particular regional color. My chapters on Memphis and Cincinnati illustrate this.[10]

The last decades of the nineteenth century brought a more favorable setting for the professions. The leveling impetus of the previous era was largely dissipated, and the new hierarchies and constraints in society made the professional claims to authority and honor seem less anomalous. The professions grew rapidly, their associations thrived, and many of them again elicited advantages from the state legislatures in the form of licensing laws. From this privileged position, many professionals developed a social perspective unique to their circumstances. While some looked back upon the "golden age" of the late eighteenth century with nostalgia and appreciation, it became readily apparent to most that the specific perquisites of the traditional gentleman were no longer available. However, these professionals carried forward some of the most significant prepossessions and proclivities of that bygone gentlemanly class into the polarized industrial world of the late nineteenth century.[11]

The leading American professionals in the late nineteen-hundreds had once again worked out a self-regard and self-definition (enshrined in the great scholarly American reference work of the era, *The Century Dictionary* [1900]) that have persisted almost unchanged to the present day. What is striking about this self-definition is how the physicians, in particular, impend incognito in the background. This is not surprising, for physicians rose to a new preeminence among the professions in the late nineteenth century. The fortunes of the nuclear family of the professions, along with its slowly growing extended family, had risen in the late eighteenth century, declined in the mid-nineteenth, and risen once more in the late nineteenth century in response to shifting circumstances. Primacy within the family itself also had shifted, but this was in conjunction with even broader cultural considerations. In the late eighteenth century, law had overtaken the ministry as the leading profession; similarly, in the late nineteenth century, medicine surpassed law. The rise of law had been linked to the Enlightenment with its blurring of the sense of human sin and its sharpening of the sense of human rights. The rise of medicine was linked to a blurring of the sense of human rights and a sharpening of a sense of human needs. The preeminence of law had reflected the decline of Calvin and the rise of Locke as a guide to human affairs; the preeminence of medicine reflected the decline of Locke and the rise of Darwin as an interpreter of the human condition. The present study is an intellectual history, but it is an institutional history as well. My principal concern is with the way ideas enter into institutions, affect them, and are affected by them.[12]

In my attempt to tell this story fully and accurately, I have been led back to an appreciation of the aggregate nature of our society and the force of previous events on our own day and age. Surely we shed a new darkness on the present when we bring to our understanding of it only that which was born yesterday and disregard the accrued meanings and motives that come out of an earlier age. I have also been moved by an awareness that the history of the professions takes on a new importance for America today. With the decline in the size of our industrial work force and the rise of service occupations, the professions now stand out as models and guides for a special kind of success. The professions, with their almost prelapsarian privileges and prestige, seem to establish a precedent for the escape from vexing supervision at work as well as from some of the depersonalization and uncertainty of markets and bureaucracies. The hunger for professional status in the growing service industries is one of the central facts of our contemporary history. In this light, the history of the professions today demands at least the attention that we have given to the history of labor, agriculture, and business in the past.

Part I

The Gentlemanly Professions and the Atlantic Civilization, 1750–1830

The Reverend Thomas Bradbury Chandler, champion of the ascendancy of the Anglican clergy of colonial North America, in full wig and starched clerical bands. (*New England Historical and Genealogical Register*, 27 [1873]: 226)

Overview
of Part I

In 1750 much of colonial society in North America looked eastward. By then the earlier, formative era, when the loosened bonds between the colonies and the mother country allowed the diverse indigenous traditions and usages of the various colonies to take root and flourish, had come to an end. The centralizing, imperial policy and the rapidly expanding Atlantic commercial economy gave fresh impetus to the renewal and strengthening of ties with Britain. New common concerns, superimposed upon old and singular preoccupations, served to diminish the divergencies of the American colonies. Americans, however disparate their situation, felt some of the force of these new developments. Not only the inhabitants of the seaboard cities, but the tobacco planters on the Chesapeake, the wheat farmers of Pennsylvania, the fur traders on the Appalachian frontier, and the fishermen of New England were all drawn into the currents of imperial politics, economics, and administration. They often attended to Britain more readily than to their neighboring colonies. They came to share a common culture, in large part because they shared a common model and antagonist.[1]

It was the leading merchant and planter families in the colonies who looked most ardently to the mother country. The profits of overseas trade had brought prosperity and power to these notables, whose sentiments and social code might have seemed somewhat familiar to anyone who knew their counterparts in the English ports and countryside. Yet there was a crucial difference. The American merchants and planters stood at the head of societies that were becoming more and more self-assertive and even self-governing, and whose particular interests could not be ignored. Below these colonial leaders stretched a relatively affluent society that was becoming increasingly stratified, particularly in the seaport cities. In those cities, the eagerness for British ways and the impatience with seemingly outmoded local tradition was most apparent.[2]

America was a provincial society in 1750 and was to remain a provincial society in some measure, at least so far as the professions were concerned, almost until 1830. It was provincial in the fundamental sense of the word—America's most important standards were being defined elsewhere. No matter what the local achievements were, and in some instances those achievements might have surpassed those of the mother country, the criteria by which those achievements were measured were set overseas. Many leading Americans, and particularly many leading professionals, exhibited that unmistakable characteristic of provincialism, a sense of inferiority inextricably entwined with intense feelings of local pride. This mixture of feelings was to be a powerful impetus for institution building among the professions in America.[3]

To understand such accomplishments, it is necessary to glance at the professional traditions of London of the eighteenth century: the era in which the American colonies were being brought closer to Great Britain was also the era in which London rose to become the largest and perhaps the most powerful city in the Western world. In that bustling metropolis there were principally three learned professions: medicine, law, and the ministry. These were embedded in a sharply graded English society and were themselves graded. In medicine there were three ranks. The physician was a gentleman with a classical education and some medical training, which he might have acquired in various and seemingly casual ways. He attended to internal diseases and prescribed drugs; yet, as befitted a gentleman, he did not work with his hands. The surgeon, as the name indicates, did. His work was the treatment of injuries and external disorders and his training was simply through apprenticeship. He therefore could not assume the title of doctor nor usually the rank of a gentleman. The apothecary was simply a tradesman who bought and sold drugs.[4]

Owing to the fact that English lawyers were in part civil servants and had been granted, now and then, precedence for political purposes, the rankings in the legal profession were more intricate. There were three orders of gentlemen lawyers—king's counsel, serjeant, and barrister—all with training at the Inns of Court, university education, and different privileges of pleading at the various tribunals. The attorney and solicitor, instructed merely through apprenticeship, were not generally considered gentlemen and could not plead in any courts at Westminster. They prepared the cases and usually handed them on to the lawyers of higher rank for argument.[5]

The most ancient and rigid gradations in the professions were the orders within the Church: bishop, priest, and deacon. All had university educations and were generally considered gentlemen. Nevertheless, the range and disparity of esteem were greater among the clergy than within the other professions. The bishops were noblemen who sat in the House of Lords with power in the governing of the country as well as in the running of the Church. Their preeminence contrasted sharply with the wretchedness of the deacons, who earlier had been considered members of a probationary rank but in the eighteenth century had become a fixed "clerical proletariat." Although a few clergymen might rise to become bishops (some on merit alone but most chiefly through political skills), the topmost rank in the Church was largely the domain of the cadets of noble houses.[6]

The differences between the three professions should not be lost sight of, but their likenesses were of greater consequence. The clergy and the upper ranks of medicine and law were occupations of gentlemen, and one of the important marks of an eighteenth-century gentleman was a classical education. In that it was an almost exclusive privilege of the upper classes, classical learning usually conferred dignity and social status upon all who acquired it. Since the beginnings of Western thought, spirit had been customarily placed above matter, the intellectual above the animal parts of man. In addition, warriors, and subsequently gentlemen, had generally scorned manual labor. When, in the Renaissance, these intellectual and class traditions had come together, intellectual attainments and even intellectual work readily passed as marks of elevated social position. The universities had carried forward such claims. Their degrees were in the liberal arts, often placed in contrast to the servile arts. By the eighteenth century, educational handbooks argued that instruction in the Greek and Latin languages and authors engendered a refinement, embellishment, and enlargement of understanding (in contrast to the coarseness and narrowness that the experience of the tradesmen and mechanics stamped upon their minds). For a would-be gentleman, the classics nurtured the qualities and bearing suitable to that station.[7]

Technical training for professions was usually considered less important, but it was not considered demeaning if it followed a classical education. There were two ingredients in this technical training: its particular science and its craft. Both might be gained in an almost offhand way. The legal instruction in the Inns of Court in the eighteenth century meant, for the most part, paying the right fees and taking the right number of meals. The medical training at Oxford and Cambridge came largely through reading in the university library. Some doctors might then "walk" the London hospitals, but many did not. And while a few divinity students went on for higher degrees, most of them picked up their know-how in assistant curacies. Yet this did not mean a disregard for competence. Rather, it was assumed that competence was linked to class or to the breadth of outlook and education that came with class. A gentleman could easily acquire competence in his professional work.[8]

A profession's science bridged the character and dispositional training of the classics and the practical working knowledge of the profession's day-to-day tasks. It was a systemized knowledge based upon theoretical understanding. Though it might be acquired in an informal way, it was nevertheless a source of considerable pride for the profession. It was the profession's science, as well as its classical education, that lifted it above the menial occupations like surgery and attorneyship. Those occupations lacked theoretical understanding, and their practitioners learned their skills through apprenticeship. The professional societies ostensibly served as repositories and patrons of the professional sciences. These collegial bodies—the Royal College of Physicians, the Inns of Court, and the Convocation—offered the means of corporate action which, in varying degrees, included self-government, licensing, and some monopoly powers, although the latter were often ineffectual.[9]

Such were the usages and institutions of the professions in London and its immediate environs; in outlying regions various deviations and "corruptions" were abundant. However, for the colonies, London most often provided the example. "The incurvations of Practice," wrote Blackstone, flaunting a characteristic eighteenth-century attitude, "are then the most notorious when compared with the rectitude of the rule; and to elucidate the clearness of the spring, conveys the strongest satire on those who have polluted or disturbed it."[10]

The primary and all-inclusive "incurvation" of professional custom in America was the collapse of ranks. While the upper grades of the professions in England were the occupations of gentlemen, few gentlemen migrated to America and therefore the work of the professions was initially done chiefly by men following the usages of the lower ranks. America's first wave of professionalization, starting from about 1750, consisted largely of the assumption of the proprieties of the upper ranks of the British professions by men of lower standing. From the beginning, therefore, professionalization in America was linked with the "art of rising in life," with upward mobility. This was true to some extent in Britain as well. While a sprinkling of the cadets of noble houses and some of the sons of the gentry entered the professions, setting the tone and prescribing the usages for the professions, a sizable group of professionals came from more obscure origins. (Blackstone, for example, was an orphaned son of a tradesman from Cheapside.) But for American professionals it was not simply a matter of rising into the class of gentlemen; the Americans had to help create that class and maintain it.[11]

That prototype of the English gentlemanly class, the gentry living off the rents of their estates, had no exact counterpart in the colonies. With the relative availability of land in America, the prospects for that kind of gentry class were not promising. Nevertheless, there were two groups that might serve in its stead and in fact endeavored to do so. These were the Southern plantation owners and the wealthy urban mercantile families. Neither, however, could rely upon the comparative stability of family fortune available to the wealthy English landed classes under the "strict settlement." The plantation owners, particularly after the Revolution, when primogeniture and entail had been officially discarded, faced the danger that their large estates might easily become small ones, and they often pushed their sons out onto the frontier so that they might maintain their standing. American mercantile fortunes in this era were peculiarly unstable; moreover merchants, as wealthy as they might be, also came up against the anticommercial snobbery of the British gentlemanly tradition. Yet both these groups had access to the wealth, leisure, and economic positions of command that enabled them to ape British gentlemanly ways.[12]

Along with them were the professions, though the professions were less wealthy and leisured. Alexander Hamilton assumed that his society would be run by merchants, the landed interests, and the professions. Merchants, he thought, were "the natural representatives" of artisans and manufacturers who were commonly disposed to bestow their votes upon the mercantile leaders of society. As for the landed interest, here as his one-time associate James Madison explained, the opulent citizen will frequently guide others "to the objects of his choice." The professions, however, were unique. "They truly form no distinct interest in society," Hamilton thought, "and according to their situation and talents will be indiscriminately the objects of confidence and choice of each other and of other parts of the community." The professional was a gentleman of a special sort, "who will feel a neutrality to the rivalship between the different branches of industry, [and will] be likely to prove an impartial arbiter between them, ready to promote either, so far as it shall appear to him conducive to the general interests of society." [13]

Hamilton's extraordinary claim that a professional might be neutral and possibly an impartial arbiter was based on the supposition that professional work rested upon a science shaped by reason. Such science in the eighteenth century had taken on additional acclaim and commendation. Some of the most influential Enlightenment thinkers had projected an orderly universe that could be understood through reason and had suggested that such understanding might make men happy and perhaps even good. Reason seemed to be autonomous, for it had its own dictates; but it was not independent, for it was subject to the passions. Yet to the extent that such subjection could be escaped—and with the sciences in varying degrees that seemed possible—the sciences could provide an impartial understanding. Therefore, the judgment of the professional who had that understanding might be taken on trust. [14]

Yet for the professions such trust was never simply cognitive, nor was the professional's competence purely technical. Adam Smith, remarking on what seemed to be the handsome earnings of the professions, suggested that their income was a result of the great trust placed in them. "Such confidence could not be safely reposed in people of a very mean or low condition. Their reward must be such, therefore, as may give them the rank in society which so important a trust requires." This trust was more than a matter of special knowledge or of the reliability that the importance of their tasks required. Jewelers, locksmiths, shipwrights, and even mushroom gatherers, whose particular kind of expertise was relied upon in matters gravely affecting many lives and fortunes, were not granted the kind of trust Smith intended. Such trust implied a relation of authority and deference, honor and respect. And that relation owed as much to the rank of the men who customarily did the work as to the nature of the work itself. It was an important aspect of the demeanor of those practicing in the upper grades of medicine, law, and the ministry in England. Significantly, the competence of the professional described both his adequate skill and the adequate income that enabled him to support such skill. [15]

It is not surprising, therefore, that those who wished to bring British professional traditions to America proposed to set up distinct ranks within the occupations and, most important, to constitute the uppermost ranks. Their success was quite uneven; it was largely restricted to the seaboard cities. Even there, the rankings in medicine never took hold, and in law the grades were irregular and porous. The attempt to set up a cohesive elite of Anglican priests and to bring a bishop to America failed. Nonetheless, what was most important, many of the ideals and inclinations of the upper ranks were retained, and the very concept of a profession peculiar to those upper ranks in England prevailed, even in the more motley American professions. Moreover, those ideals and inclinations helped promote an era of notable professional achievement. The active spirit of professional organizations spread and was followed by the enactment of licensing laws to raise standards, esteem, and, more improbably, the incomes of practitioners. By 1800, three-quarters of the states had such laws for legal practice, and by 1830 only three states were without them for medicine. In some jurisdictions, the principal standard was a gentleman's education in the classics; later writers were to wonder at the many professionals of this era with academic degrees. More than ninety percent of Massachusetts lawyers between 1800 and 1830 were college graduates.[16]

The combined ideological and economic forces released by the American Revolution ultimately transformed the homemade American professional gentleman. That outcome, however, was not apparent until well into the nineteenth century, and even then some of the most important, distinctive traits of that earlier gentleman remained. Therefore it is necessary at this point, at least in a preliminary way, to look more broadly at those preeminent claims of the eighteenth-century gentleman: honor and authority.

Honor had once been the regard given to a warrior class as well as the code of behavior that justified such regard. This code was tempered and transformed by both Christianity and the rise of monarchal powers, but it maintained the marks of its origins. One of the principal themes of *Morte D'Arthur* was the conflict of standards: those of Carbonek, the Fortress of the Christian soul, and of Camelot, the palace of courtly honor. The mitigation of the conflict was one of the principal undertakings of the champions of honor, and their chief strategy was to claim that honor was the embodiment and reward of virtue. Of course the radical Christian virtues—forgiving injuries, loving enemies, blessing opponents—were unaccommodating for this. But the broader admonition to act for the glory of God (for His fame, splendor, and majesty—as if He Himself were a feudal lord) was more congenial. "No man can do anything for God's glory," wrote a Protestant divine, "but what will tend also to his own." Still, Christian teach-ings occasionally supplied a critique of the notion of honor as well as a support.[17]

The growing power of regal courts also tamed warriors. Mon-archs subdued ancient aristocratic families and co-opted their honor, which became primarily civil rather than military. At the same time, the kings gradually monopolized violence. Honor, therefore, became the reward of closeness to and assistance to the sovereign. The King, reported Blackstone, was "the Fountain of honor." He rewarded service to the state and even to learning; honor could be won as readily in political intrigue, in bureau-cratic machinations, and in scholarly disputation as on the field of battle. These avenues to honor, however, were still open mainly to men of superior rank. In eighteenth century England, honor came to mean principally the respect due to superior rank and the somewhat vague code of behavior, characteristic of that rank, that served to guide and counterbalance private advantage.[18]

Though the King was "the Fountain of honor" various subsid-iary fountains remained, and the most scandalous of these was sheer wealth. The lowest rank to which honor was attached, that of gentleman, was remarkably available. "In these days he is a gentleman, who is commonly so taken. And whosoever studieth the Laws of the Realm, who studieth in the University, who pro-fesseth the liberal sciences, and, to be short, who can live with-out manual labour, and will bear the Port, Charge, and Counte-nance of a gentleman, he shall be called Master, and shall be taken for a gentleman." Even such a gentleman, however, was expected to adhere to the "Principles of Honour," giving special attention to dignity, decorum, and beneficence—the last rather loosely construed. This civil honor also occasionally met with a Christian censure that reprehended "the fool of distinction," "the glorious impertinence of the state," and "the solemn farce of tit-ular greatness," for "we were all descended from Adam." More characteristically, however, the divines of the eighteenth century supported the claims of titular honor. Not to do so, they believed, was to disparage the social order and to enfeeble it; and the social order was God's instrument.[19]

Some inkling of what happened to gentlemanly honor when it was translated to American shores might be seen in one of the most widely popular didactic and moral tracts that reached the colonies from England. It was far better known and more widely praised here than in the mother country. This work was Phillip Doddridge's *The Life of Col. James Gardiner, who was slain at the Battle of Preston-Pans, September 21, 1745;* it was reprinted many times over the years and still thought edifying enough, as late as 1828, to be published in a new edition by the American Sunday School Union. Doddridge was among the leading eighteenth-century English nonconformist writers and educators who tried to stem the decline of nonconformity by moderating the clash of its factions and by emphasizing its harmony with the broader English culture. He was just the man to give the concept of honor an up-to-date Christian baptism.[20]

Doddridge's ostensible purpose in writing about his friend Gardiner was to demonstrate that Gardiner's true claim to honor lay in his spiritual loftiness, which arose from a God-sent and heartfelt conversion. Yet, specially striking about Gardiner was the fact that he somehow possessed many of the traditional claims to distinction as well: good family, education, soldierly heroism, royal favor, and official rank. Moreover, after his conversion (through which he learned to estimate his happiness by nearness to God rather than increase in honor), almost miraculously, his honor did just then increase manyfold. For Gardiner served "a gracious God, who hath promised that all things shall work together for good to those that love him." Doddridge did not hide the fact that Gardiner had once been an unblushing gallant, given to the pursuit "of animal pleasure, as a supreme good," and that he had once been envied by the multitude, who called him "by a dreadful kind of compliment, the happy rake." Moreover, Doddridge stressed the fact that, when Gardiner abandoned his profligate life after his spiritual rebirth, he did not lose "any one valuable friend by this change of character." He did not "withdraw himself from cheerful conversation; but on the contrary gave several hours every day to it, lest religion should be reproached as having made him morose." Even his refusal to duel did not forfeit the respect of other gentlemen of rank, because, along with this modification, he maintained the gentlemanly code of behavior that stressed personal independence, fidelity to king and duties, as well as the nurturing of courtesy and gracious benevolence.[21]

Of the various American responses to Doddridge's work, perhaps the most extraordinary and foreboding was the essay "On Honor" written by the young Aaron Burr while he was still a student at Princeton. It was a short literary composition revealing a fervid assortment of conflicting thoughts and feelings. The restraining force of his Presbyterian tutors and the rebellious exuberance of young Burr were both evident; and perhaps, also, there was some hint of the divergent paths of Northern and Southern honor in a later era.[22]

Burr made no mention of ancient families, titles, or royal appointments. His men of honor might hold high office or would be counselors to such men who did, but they owed their elevated positions to talents awarded by "the author of nature." They were a natural aristocracy that stood above "the herd of mankind," much as the human species was exalted above the rest of creation. Notions of natural aristocracy, usually less presumptuous than Burr's, were common in the colonies. However, even Burr's natural aristocrats were to use their superiority to contribute to the public good; they would "revive the languid spark of public spirit, raise oppressed states, [and] strengthen society with its wholesome rules." Their principles of honor were controlled by reason and Christianity. To illustrate this, Burr turned to Doddridge's Col. James Gardiner, who refused a duel, not because he feared feeble man but because he feared to sin against Almighty God. "There spake at once the Christian hero and the true, warlike man," explained Burr. "There spake that which reason dictates to all." But if the man of honor rejected the control of God and reason, then, the young Burr warned somewhat prophetically, he became a "meteor-like flame" and "like the raging winds that speed desolation through their vast career."[23]

Yet Burr himself seemed to let reason slip wondrously near the end of the essay. For "the man of honor," he then declared in rhapsodic transport, "is like a lamp lighted by the breath of God, the luster and brightness of which cannot be taken in or bounded by the thought of man . . . And how does the soul shoot away, as it were, with swiftness of imagination, to mingle with the spirits of men of honor, where all is grandeur, where all is greatness, where all is profusion of holiness, felicity, and joy." One can almost see sober, strait-laced old President Witherspoon swallowing hard.[24]

Doddridge's study of the life of Col. James Gardiner not only epitomized a Christianized honor but also a Christianized version of authority. Like honor, the notion of authority had its origins in classical civilizations. *Auctoritas* had been a technical term referring to the vote of the Roman Senate through which it registered its opinion, an opinion which had great influence although it was devoid of legal power. The fascination with such informal influence impressed many of those interested in human governance long after the Roman Senate had disappeared. Such influence had been connected to a relation of protection and dependence from the beginning. With little increase in statutory powers, the Senate had extended its sway owing to the fact that its membership included the great landowners of the republic, patrons in a system of clientage that gave the society much of its cohesion. By the eighteenth century, authority meant a right to command, direct, initiate, and advise; it ranged through various degrees of forcefulness, from the imperative to the merely consultative. It was distinct from power in that it was necessarily rightful, and one might have the right but not the power to command. Yet if that right were too long divorced from power, authority might disappear. When Col. Gardiner strode unarmed into the midst of mutinous troops, he quelled them "by his presence alone" because they somehow recognized his right to command. Yet if they had not been long accustomed to such recognition, the outcome might have been quite different.[25]

After his conversion, Gardiner held many positions of authority, and Doddridge used Gardiner's experiences to demonstrate the proper behavior of a Christian gentleman in those positions. Gardiner's authority was made Christian in that he considered all the children of Adam as standing upon a level before their great Creator, and had also a deeper sense of the dignity and worth of every immortal soul, "how meanly soever it might chance to be lodged." Though in society men could never stand upon a level, the awareness of this specific kind of spiritual equality was to qualify the relation between those on superior and inferior stations. This awareness was enjoined upon the family, the community, the church, and the relations and offices of state, both civil and military. Gardiner was a husband, father, master of a handsome estate, justice of the peace, and military officer. In all these relations, "he knew how to reconcile the tenderness with responsibility." As for his soldiers in particular, Gardiner sought to be a father to them in all interests temporal and spiritual, yet he distributed his preferments strictly according to merit. He generally chose to reside among the troops as much as he could, however when he was with them, he maintained a decorum and good manners, "which has always a great efficacy towards keeping inferiors at a proper distance." The calmness and steadiness of his behavior served the same purpose. Such equanimity was essential, for "how unfit they are to govern others who cannot govern themselves." The gentleman's dominion, therefore, was characteristically personal, mixing authority with a special type of intimacy that is perhaps difficult to understand and appreciate today.[26]

For the American gentleman after the Revolution, the mixture of authority and intimacy would be more difficult. To the ethereal, spiritual equality was now added a mundane political equality of men as citizens. The ramifications of that growing political equality gradually became more pervasive as the nineteenth century progressed. Yet, at least in the first third of that century, many American gentlemen—along with the renowned Elias Boudinot, for example—could feel comfortable in assuming positions of authority with all the appropriate distinctions that must be derived from "rational equality." Boudinot had been an ardent Revolutionary lawyer who had risen to a position of leadership in the Continental Congress, serving as its president and then as an influential member in the first three Congresses of the United States. In his much acclaimed Fourth of July address of 1793, Boudinot, a great admirer of Doddridge, discoursed carefully upon "rational equality."[27]

We are all "the workmanship of the same divine hand . . . abstractly considered," Boudinot explained, and in addition we were invested with equal rights as men and citizens. Yet men's different natural and moral character "will always make men different among themselves, and of course create preeminence and superiority one over another" in society at large. For "order is heaven's first law," and God has "made it essential to every good government, and necessary for the welfare of every community, that there should be distinctions among members of the same society." Moreover, the most capable were "stewards of His appointment," whom He designated to work "for the service, benefit, and best good as a whole." Relationships of protection and dependence must continue in a republic, and along with them the particular positions of authority and honor to be assumed by the society's worthy stewards. For a long while American gentlemen could see themselves as just such stewards.[28]

The professions in particular contrived to create and sustain such a gentlemanly vision and bearing in the eighteenth century and to preserve it, with some modifications and qualifications, into the increasingly inauspicious setting of the nineteenth century. How that was accomplished may be better understood if we follow their exploits at closer range.

1

The Ministers and the Moral Purpose of Religion

Even for Jeremiah Gridley, one of the leaders of the Massachusetts bar, it seemed to be a difficult case. He had been summoned by a learned and gentlemanly old minister, the reverend Solomon Lombard, who had been tossed out of a parsonage by his congregation and replaced by a less literate but more enthusiastic young preacher. Lombard had suffered two earlier legal defeats in his efforts to recover the home he had once called his own. Yet Gridley stood self-confidently before the judge and, calling upon the elaborate technical distinctions of eighteenth-century special pleading, in a rapid series of exchanges with the opposing counsel, won the case. When he told his client, "You have obtained your cause," the minister was astonished. "How sir?" the minister asked. "You can never know," Gridley replied with a slight smile, "till you get to heaven."[1]

This irreverent drollery captured the striking shift in social standing among the professions over the course of the eighteenth century in America. Ministers had lost their preeminence to lawyers. It had once been the great religious mysteries that New Englanders were told would be understood only in heaven. But now the learned minister, unsettled in his influence and prerogatives, had come up against, and had come to depend upon, the mysteries of the law—and the lawyer. Even in Connecticut, the heartland of orthodoxy, the shift was noticeable. In Massachusetts it was unmistakable. "How greatly elevated above the Common People, and above the Divines is this lawyer," scribbled John Adams in his diary.[2]

At the beginning of the eighteenth century, when the ministry had been foremost in the professions, it was generally assumed in the Northern and Middle colonies that the most capable young men of intellectual bent would seek careers in the ministry rather than in medicine and law. By the end of the century that was doubtful. In the interim the ministry had been shaken by a series of troublous events—the Anglican ascendance, the Great Awakening, the American Revolution—and had worked out new understandings and accords that enabled them to maintain some of their remarkable esteem and importance in American churches and culture, although the unique kind of preeminence that had once been theirs was now gone.[3]

The Anglicans, Congregationalists, and Presbyterians were the major churches of eighteenth-century America. They had the largest membership, with the Anglicans established in the South and the lower counties of New York, and the Congregationalists supported by civil authority in most of New England. It was the Anglican clergy in the North who were most ambitious and assertive in their efforts to elevate their standing and influence, and those efforts had considerable consequence even for ministers of much different allegiance and bearing. The primary component in the campaign to upgrade the Anglican clergy was the endeavor to establish a resident bishop in America. The desire for such a dignitary was linked to a sense of the integrity of their Church. Many Anglican priests had been attracted to the Church because of the religious majesty of its worship, yet in America its rites and regularity were defective.[4]

Without a resident bishop there could be no visitation nor confirmation, and ordination was possible only by way of a hazardous, transatlantic voyage. The encroachment of the laity, a vexation to which American society seemed conducive, could not be effectively resisted without such a prelate, nor could clergymen otherwise be freed of the demeaning jurisdiction of the civil courts. The bringing of a bishop, the rectification of Church observances, and the assumption by the Anglican priest of his rightful place were seen by American proponents as one and the same cause.[5]

Not only would the defectiveness of the Church and its priests be remedied, but this would also be a step toward remedying broader defects in society at large. The Church would serve as an exemplar of proper authority and honor. Among the arguments that the Reverend Thomas Bradbury Chandler advanced for bringing a bishop was one that would be difficult to understand today. Chandler wrote:

> Men's governing themselves by certain rules and laws (if the expression may be allowed of) and their being governed by others, who have proper authority, although according to the same

laws, are things that will ever be found to be different. In the former case some appearance of order may be maintained but the body is without strength and liable to be destroyed in innumerable accidents; whereas it is only in the later case, that health and vigour and permanency can be reasonably expected.

The premise of this argument was a graded society in which subordination was a virtue and a blessing. From that standpoint, "masterlessness" was a kind of nakedness both unbecoming and dangerous, while proper subordination was a type of cooperation that raised the subordinate in purpose and power by making him an agent of a higher and nobler intention outside himself. In such a society, authority and honor were usually attached to rank and therefore less perplexing than they would later become. Even law "always supposes some superior who is to make it," Blackstone explained. In America, however, where ranks seemed fragmentary, order was ad hoc and often voluntary. That was particularly dangerous, for if society were based merely upon agreement, then disagreement would dissolve it. Rather one must look to "proper authority," authority based upon the wisdom of ancient tradition and its legitimate interpreters. In submission to a bishop, priests could truly be lordly with the laity.[6]

Such traditionalism, it might seem, would readily find support in England and elicit influential patronage for the campaign to bring a bishop to America. Quite the contrary. In the eighteenth century such "high-flying" notions, particularly in Church matters, brought suspicions of lack of patriotism. It was the refractory nonjurors and the Jacobites—those who, after 1688, had scrupled to take the oath of allegiance to the new royal house on the grounds of the previous oaths to the Stuarts and their successors—who championed high conceptions of the Church. The reigning bishops of this era, like Hoadly and Tillotson, by contrast, were less interested in ritualism; they combined a belief in the clear submission of the Church to civil authority in all matters with the loosening of constraints on religious thought and behavior. Hoadly, a Court favorite, went so far as to preach that the laws and sanctions of the Church had little relevance to the affairs of this world and that Christianity "in its first simplicity" lay in unfettered private judgments. These preachments would seem to dissolve the Church as a corporate body and make sincerity, rather than religious truth, the proper test of appraisal. It was a doctrine that the American Anglicans who set about to bring a bishop to the colonies would not find attractive.[7]

Chandler, one of the chief strategists in that struggle, was strongly drawn to the doctrine of apostolic succession and to the belief that the Church was a spiritual society with absolute laws of its own. "The clergy have their commission from God Almighty, and by consequence their authority is no grant of the Crown," he wrote. Of course, they owed their temporal powers and rights to civil society. Yet, "if the consent of the King or the State is necessary, in order to permit a bishop's coming over to America, so is the consent of the master of the ship in which he comes over; and the former does not change the nature of his office or of his authority any more than the latter." While the American Anglican churchmen justly protested that no group preached subordination and dependence more heartily than their clergy in the colonies, nonetheless the very neglect of sending a bishop did bring some disaffection. Chandler berated his superiors in England for "irresolution and pusillanimity" and for "triming [sic] to a corrupt court." The Stamp Act crisis, he thought, was intended by Providence to punish the Government for neglect of the Church. There was need for "a missionary from us, in order to convert the guardians of the Church [in England] from the errors of their ways. I think our sending missionaries among them is almost as necessary as their sending missionaries to America. But I fear the difficulty of proselyting such a nation will be found greater than that of converting the American savages."[8]

Chandler's teacher and guide was the American Samuel Johnson, whose career helps us understand the upsurge of Anglicanism in eighteenth-century New England. It was in 1722 at Yale, the headquarters of Connecticut Calvinism, that the Rector Timothy Cutler, two tutors, and four neighboring ministers (Samuel Johnson among them) announced their doubts regarding the validity of presbyterian ordination (i.e., ordination at the hands of ministers) and their intention of joining the Church of England. Johnson's reading in the works of contemporary Anglican divines (as well as his experience as pastor of the church in West Haven, Connecticut) had made the doctrine of apostolic succession seem particularly attractive and persuasive to him. "I had hoped when I was ordained that I had sufficiently satisfied myself of the validity of Presbyterian ordination under circumstance," he confessed to his diary, "but alas I have ever since had growing suspicions that it is not right and that I am an usurper in the House of God." To doubt that type of ordination was to doubt, among other things, the role of the layman in the government of the Church, and to question indirectly the doctrine of the priesthood of all believers. Archbishop Potter, the foremost Anglican ecclesiologist of the eighteenth century, and one of Johnson's favorite authors, openly repudiated that basic Reformation doctrine.[9]

Samuel Johnson had come to dislike that part of New England piety that seemed to set loose the spontaneous self. The extemporary way in prayer meetings, for example, he thought nourished "self-conceit and spiritual pride," and the strain of invention it placed upon the congregation hindered "the offering up of our hearts with our words." The congregational form of church government was all too democratic and lent itself to the vagaries of "the unhedged psyche." Moreover, Johnson became dissatisfied with the "rigid Calvinistic notions in which he had been bred." When he came upon the works of the Anglican theologians all "this was like a flood of day to his low state and mind." [10]

Of course it was not to the latitudinarian bishops, who dominated the English Church, that Johnson and his friends looked. Rather it was to the opponents of enlightened religion, the nonjurors and now-forgotten sect called the Hutchinsonians—both of whom called for a return to more traditional doctrine, ceremony, and authority. By the early eighteenth century, the nonjurors had broadened their opposition by demanding freedom of the Church and its clergy from control by civil power, and by calling for an enrichment of the liturgy through the recovery of former usages. The Hutchinsonians provided a new, mystical testimony for old doctrines and ritual from a sectarian reading of the Hebrew Bible. They insisted that everything be derived from revelation rather than from the common-sensical fusion of reason and scripture prevalent in the Church at the time. [11]

It is not at all surprising, therefore, that Johnson considered the preaching of Bishop Hoadly almost as radical as deism itself. The latitudinarian Archbishop Tillotson, for Johnson, was a danger; for Cutler he was an anathema. Johnson disparaged "the well meaning but too conceited Mr. Locke." He also argued that the prodigious genius of Mr. Hutchinson seemed to be "superior to Sir Isaac [Newton] himself, and to have very much unhinged his [Newton's] main principles and proved his inconsistency." When Johnson embraced Berkeley's philosophy, it was as an antidote to natural science and as a support to traditional Christian dogmas. The Anglicanism that many American clergy in the Northern Colonies sought was a liturgical religion, with a Book of Common Prayer providing ornate ceremonies and a propitiatory Holy Communion service that preserved some of the mysterious aspects of the medieval Eucharist. The priest, by virtue of being master of such ecclesiastical ceremonies and necessary to their performance, was exalted when these ceremonies were exalted. His powers derived from the original apostles and not from the say-so of church members. In his hands alone was placed the "power of the Keys," the authority to keep notorious sinners from the sacraments and from absolution. Moreover, like his counterpart in England, the American priest was clearly a gentleman and bore "the post, charge, and countenance of a gentleman." While early in the reign of George III the gentlemen's fashion of wearing wigs began to wane, it held on among professional men and grew rapidly among American Anglican clergymen.[12]

The venerable Society for the Propagation of the Gospel in Foreign Parts furnished these ministers with subsidies that sometimes allowed them to assert their prerogatives against the claims of vestries and congregations. This was particularly important for the Anglican clergymen in New England and the Middle Colonies, but less so for those in the South, where the Church was closely controlled by the local vestries and the clergy seemed quiescent. Many of the Episcopal clergymen of the southern colonies were Europeans, unsure of their positions and therefore pliable, whereas the most eminent leaders of northern Anglicanism were natives, usually recent converts and much more confident and assertive. In the North, at least, the growth of Anglicanism was linked to a desire for order, elegance, ministerial authority, and honor—and the serene faithfulness that was thought to accompany those acquirements.[13]

The growth of Anglicanism furnished worthy exponents within American Protestantism of the sacramental and hierarchical conceptions of the ministry. From this standpoint, the Episcopalians joined issue with Congregationalists and Presbyterians in a recurrent series of disputes on the nature of the ministry during the last half of the eighteenth and the first half of the nineteenth century.[14]

What is striking about the debate is that the Congregationalists and Presbyterians did not avail themselves of the doctrine that all Christians were priests; rather they relied upon the argument that all priests were bishops. This in itself tells a great deal about the development of the Congregationalist and Presbyterian ministry in this era. They were well aware that the Anglican clergy looked down upon them as if they were unauthorized quacks, and they had fought successfully against the scheme of establishing a bishop in America. Such a prelate in England held political powers, and it was difficult to imagine a similar Church dignitary in America without them. Surely a bishop would exercise those powers for the preferment of the Anglican Church, its priesthood, and its growing congregations.

Yet if the dissenting clergy faced diverse threats from above, they also faced them from below, from their own laity as well as from the more radical religious groups which had less standing. The principle of the priesthood of all believers, in fact, was used against Congregationalists and Presbyterians by more radical religious groups. Congregationalist and Presbyterian clergy, however, insisted that their concept of the ministry was completely Scriptural. This was their first requirement, for they followed Calvin, who held that "the books of the New Testament contain divine directions in all the most important parts of worship and discipline." (Anglicans, by contrast, were often closer to Luther, who believed that while Scripture was authoritative in matters of doctrine, it need not be treated as binding in matters of worship.) The Reformers not only believed that Scripture was authoritative where it applied, but that its teaching would be clear to all redeemed Christians. The history of Christianity since the Reformation, however, describes a remarkable variety of Protestant groups, each believing themselves redeemed Christians, who read Scriptures differently.[15]

In the hands of the Congregationalists in America, the Scriptural doctrine of the ministry ran to contraries. This was apparent from their earliest formulation of principles of Church government in the Cambridge Platform of 1648. This code, a definitive statement of the New England Way, was to have considerable influence for long afterward. All believers were God's priests, yet God set aside the minister as his special instrument. "There may be the essence and being of the church without any officer," yet God had provided for officers, and therefore the Church would have them. The minister was called by God, but through the votes of Church members. He was needed for the performance of the sacraments, yet others might stand in "the watch and care" of the brethren. Only the minister might "preach with authority," but he had no dominion over the faith of the elect. The "power of the Keys," of correction and excommunication, was in the hands of the Church members, yet the minister had a veto on all acts of Church government.[16]

The resolution of these contraries was brought about largely in nondoctrinal ways. The minister was accorded the rank of a gentleman (he bore the insignia of the gentleman, a liberal arts education, and often adopted the fashion of wearing a wig). He would, therefore, usually be granted deference by those "goodmen" who made up the bulk of the Church members, and of course by the mobile mass of servants below them. In addition to class sanctions, the minister could draw upon psychological supports. New Englanders consciously and persistently pressed for the transference of some of the emotions and attitudes engendered within the family, and originally directed toward parents, to all figures of authority in society at large. In the Fifth Commandment, "Honor thy father and thy mother," father and mother were interpreted to refer to "all our superiors whether in family, school, church, or commonwealth." When Anne Hutchinson was brought to trial for defaming the New England ministry, she was charged with violating the Fifth Commandment. This transference was systematically inculcated through such Puritan texts as *The New England Primer* and the more advanced *Shorter Catechism* of the Westminster Assembly, the most ubiquitous and closely studied volumes of New England society.[17]

The minister also relied upon conscience. For he was both teacher and exhorter, and his sermons contained both doctrine and admonition. In admonishing, the minister spoke of the congregation's danger and of its duty. It was the Christian's conscience that enabled him to recognize his duty and that condemned him if he did not perform it. Conscience was the link between the law of God and the will of man. From Ames and Perkins to Thomas Shepard, the Mathers, the two Jonathan Edwardses, and Timothy Dwight, the ministers studied the conscience, its power, its fallibility, and its good uses. It was an internal lawgiver, monitor, witness, judge, and tormentor. Jonathan Edwards, Jr., explained that the conscience was "the principal in human nature by which the true preacher of the gospel may take the most advantageous hold of sinners." The minister was a director of conscience, and from that position could instill a sense of obligation to the ways of God, to the New England Fathers, and to the minister himself. The conscience was "the preacher in the bottom of every man," explained Cotton Mather. And so closely linked was the minister with conscience that the minister took on some of its force. This was why John Cotton called the authority of the minister a moral power, and Cotton Mather described the conscience as a bond between the people and their pastors. The minister found sanction for his authoritativeness within the psyches of the brethren.[18]

Yet, as John Cotton learned in his conflict with Roger Williams, conscience was not only an ally of the ministers, it could be their enemy. The criteria that conscience employed in its acceptances and rejections did not always wholly fit with the generally accepted standards and ideas received from society. Conscience could serve, therefore, not only for the introjection but also for the rejection of social norms. Protestantism not only gave authority to Scripture, it also gave enormous importance to the personal dimension of faith. While the Reformers saw this as religious truth coming *to* the person and his or her experience, it could easily be reversed and turned into a sense of religious truth coming *from* the person and his or her experience. Nevertheless, obedience to conscience usually meant acceptance of the social order, and the minister's power, allied with conscience, was often seen as a kind of moral power.[19]

These doctrinal, social, and psychological supports for the Congregational minister's authority, however, must be placed into the broader setting of the general religiosity of the community. During the first years of settlement in New England, the ministry was both more and less than a profession. It was more, because it embodied the leading purposes of the community, and because ministers were officers who, along with magistrates, gave direction to the society. Yet it was less, because the work of salvation was too important to be left exclusively to ministers, and therefore Church elders actively shared Church rule and even some of the minister's tasks. By the early eighteenth century, the leadership and purposes of the community had changed. The increased pressures of the British government were partly responsible for this; the Puritan Commonwealth fitted too awkwardly into the invigorated colonial system as envisioned in London. Moreover, by the early decades of the eighteenth century, many New England ministers began to take on the bearing of the English professions, adopting the style of the urbane British nonconformist ministers of the day. However, the religious upheaval at midcentury, the Great Awakening, interrupted this development and brought the ministry under attack. The different ways in which the ministers absorbed and deflected that attack gave rise to the diverging types of New England ministry that persisted into the early nineteenth century.[20]

The Reverend Benjamin Colman's election-day sermon of June 1708 is an advantageous starting point from which to trace that general development. When Colman stood before the General Court of Massachusetts to plead that the ministry should not be brought down to the rank of ordinary "Liberal Imployments," it was already apparent to many of those who heard him that just such leveling had been going on for quite some time. Colman addressed Governor Joseph Dudley in particular and dedicated the published version of the sermon to Dudley's wife. Yet the very fact that Joseph Dudley sat in the Governor's chair meant that much of Colman's plea would go unheard. For Dudley's government marked a distinct shift in the public purposes of the Massachusetts Commonwealth. Though he was the son of the Bay colony's second governor, the pious Thomas Dudley, the son was strikingly free from the father's religious engrossments. It was only with difficulty that Joseph restrained his contempt for his elders, their obsolete kinds of guilt, and their archaic religious standards. He aspired to the worldly sophistication and culture of the English ruling classes and looked upon Massachusetts from the perspective and attachments of Whitehall.[21]

Colman nevertheless boldly insisted that the ministry's "Rank and Place among men has always been next to the Civil Magistrate," for surely that had been true of the minister's position in New England during much of the seventeenth century. Yet in the eighteenth century a new class of royal officials and leading merchants had risen to power, and New England society had become more highly differentiated. While the minister was still undoubtedly considered a gentleman, that title had new claimants, many of whom ranked above him. This was reflected even at Harvard, the matrix of New England's learned ministry, where the order of the class lists came to represent social standing rather than scholarship. The sons of magistrates and wealthy merchants were placed as a matter of course near the top, but the sons of ministers were given no such preference. The ministers' gentlemanly standing, however, still counted for something. Colman assumed that superior social position when he addressed the "Inferior People" in his election-day sermon, telling them that they "must needs hold themselves obliged in their Places" and "ought conscientiously to Love *their Ministers,* to Pray for 'em, to assist and support 'em."[22]

Colman also expounded the minister's relationship more broadly to the commonwealth. Here his guide was the standard Reformation doctrine that state and church must work together for the glory of God. This meant, as Colman interpreted it, that the state must sustain and strengthen the powers of the Congregationalist ministry in relation to the parishes. The chief difficulty was that Governor Dudley sat as a vestryman in an Anglican church and was not particularly interested in buttressing the Congregationalist ministry. Colman, therefore, tried to argue in terms that would be pleasing to the Governor and not too displeasing to himself. It was the duty of civil rulers to support public worship and observance, and this required, Colman explained unabashed, that the central government pay out of the public treasury the salaries wrongly withheld from the ministers by their towns and tax the towns in proportion. Such procedures would assure the minister's proper honor and dignity. Was not the superior order of clergy in England "grac'd in the first *Rank of Nobles*?" asked Colman in an audacious comparison. As for the great noble houses in England, their counterparts in New England were the rich mercantile families, and it was the duty of these rich to devote "a Select Son to the Service of the Temple, leaving him an inheritance equal with his Brethren." That would raise the tone of the ministry, making it more respected and imposing.[23]

Moreover, the ministers themselves could do much to ensure their own standing. They could establish and support ministerial associations and councils. Colman had been a founding member of the Cambridge Ministerial Association, itself the progenitor of many Massachusetts associations that grew up and spread throughout the colony in the eighteenth century. He had spent a number of years in England, in the more polished nonconformist circles there, and had returned to Massachusetts with the lofty expectation of bringing their more dignified forms to the New England ministry. The ministerial association would further this. The associations usually took as their goal the restoration and promotion of New England's faithfulness, "to advance the interest of Christ." The means of effecting this, however, were quite specific: they would invigorate the ministry. Colleagueship would be fostered and divisiveness forestalled. "Whether we think the same things in small points of church order," wrote Colman, "yet ought we to appear one in faith, in charity, in zeal for practical holiness." Also, the ministers should provide some judgment on the qualifications of those admitted to the office. "The church has the liberty to choose its own ministers," explained the Cambridge Association, "nevertheless, this liberty may be abused in their election of an unqualified person, and therefore great advice is to be taken by them in the use of it."[24]

Three years earlier Colman had proposed the setting up of ecclesiastical councils, under the sway of ministers, to "consult, advise, and determine" on a broad range of religious issues that had traditionally belonged to the particular churches. He had won the support of many ministers, Cotton Mather among them, but Colman believed that state backing was essential, and Governor Dudley was unsympathetic. These proposals failed in Massachusetts, yet a similar scheme was adopted in Connecticut. This "Saybrook Platform" set up consociations of churches to enforce discipline and doctrine and also established associations of ministers to resolve religious questions and to examine candidates for the ministry. The Platform provided a general association of ministers, as well, to oversee Connecticut's church affairs. Massachusetts's ministerial associations, without such formal recognition and support, yet with Colman's active encouragement, pursued similar ends in less forceful and conspicuous ways.[25]

One of the chief improvements that Colman thought these associations might bring about was to strengthen the integrity of the ministerial office by insisting that it should be a full-time occupation. Many seventeenth-century Congregationalist ministers outside of Boston had been part-time farmers, finding the income from that work necessary to supplement their ministerial salary. But the secular cares and diversions of agriculture led to the neglect of the minister's appointed tasks and perhaps even to a confusion of vocation and avocation. Moreover, as the Reverend Samuel Deane observed, those with a "liberal or polite education" increasingly came to think it degrading to work at practical agriculture for their support. Colman fretted about this, and pressed for separating the minister "wholly from worldly things."[26]

The principal task that a full-time ministry made more practicable was pastoral care. Earlier, pastoral visiting was generally expected in times of sickness or special need, but by the beginning of the eighteenth century a systematic visiting of families came to be regarded as indispensable. On such visits the minister would rebuke and comfort in a fatherly way; he would catechize the children and speak to the particular vices and neglected duties of others. Colman looked to the Anglican Bishop Burnet's warm but lofty discussion of pastoral care for his model. By the beginning of the eighteenth century, public personal confessions before the brethren became less frequent, and the secrecy of disclosures to ministers was more generally respected. "Watch and care" was more exclusively the minister's work; the body of ruling elders that had once shared the responsibility for the preservation of congregational purity disappeared in most churches.[27]

Clearly, the diminished social prominence of the minister (in the increasingly diverse and divergent New England society) that Colman's sermon suggests was not accompanied by any decline of the minister's importance within the Church itself, as Colman's sermon also makes plain. In fact, the opposite was true. The ministers' increasing complaint of a lessening of religious intensity brought with it a heightening of ministerial assertiveness and occupational self-awareness. When the seeking of salvation was the chief business of New England, the separation between the saved and the damned was a sharp and living reality, and the distinction between the minister and the rest of God's elect was less significant. When the division between the elect and the unregenerate was blurred and less exigent, the disparity between the ministry and the laity became increasingly sharp, and religious responsibilities became more singularly the minister's. John Winthrop, in his famous lay sermon delivered on the deck of the Arabella, called the new settlement in America "a city upon a hill," an example for the entire world; a hundred years later, New England ministers adopted the same Biblical phrase to refer not to the New England Way but to the order of the ministry itself.[28]

This changing relation between the minister and his church clearly was linked to a changing relation between the church and the broader society. Scholars, however, differ in their understanding of these more general changes. Some, relying heavily upon the growing number of reproving sermons in which the ministers compared their own generation unfavorably with those of their fathers and grandfathers, have described these changes as a declension. Other scholars, pointing to statistical measures of church membership which suggest that affiliation was growing or at least was cyclical, deny any decline in Puritan piety. However, these two very different kinds of findings need not be set against each other. For the statistical studies do not usually consider the changing meaning of church membership. While in the early seventeenth century such membership was a primary and all-encompassing commitment, by the early eighteenth century it seems to have been increasingly a partial commitment, perhaps still fervent, but nonetheless one among others. Its significance for economic activity, politics and power, and even family life was no longer clear-cut and unmistakable. The growing prosperity and diversity of New England society worked in this direction, and paradoxically, Protestant belief did as well. The internalization of piety, though it originally provided impetus for protest, now also lent itself to accommodation. Spirituality, whatever its intensity, could become more concentrated within the church and more attenuated outside of it. Along with the growth of church membership in orthodox eighteenth-century Connecticut, there was also a growth in the number of dancing schools. For the minister himself, however, religious commitment remained primary and all-encompassing by virtue of his occupation. In that sense his profession became the "city upon a hill." The minister embodied the memory and legend of that overriding singleness of purpose of an earlier era, and he could use the community's sense of guilt, of having fallen from that blessed state, to good advantage. Yet such uses were now increasingly more limited. While previously ministers argued the religious uses of society, in time ministers would more often argue the social uses of religion.[29]

By the 1730s, Congregationalist ministers were unmistakably a distinct order of men with discrete religious functions—some emphasizing polished and eloquent sermons, others more formal and elaborate observance of sacraments, and almost all a fatherly concern for pastoral work for the "cure of souls." Ministers had begun to place a much greater importance upon their collegial bodies, and through them took up the work of mutual assistance and discipline in order to advance the ministry as a devoted religious vanguard. The bond between colleagues was becoming more tightly knit, and that between ministers and their congregations less so. Yet this broad movement toward the clearer definition and elevation of the clerical office soon came under furious attack, in a remarkable religious upheaval that broke out in the mid-eighteenth century.[30]

This tumultuous revival, which came to be known as the Great Awakening, ranged up and down the colonies, moving previously sober congregations to fits of extreme emotion and behavior. What had begun with exciting and overpowering sermons to bring worshippers back to a more fervent piety, quickly became a religious upheaval often breaking away beyond the control of those who started it. Itinerants and lay exhorters ("private persons of no education and but low attainments in knowledge") scoured the cities and countryside with convulsive preaching, denunciations of regular ministers, derision of constituted authority, declarations of private revelations, and exhibitions of "disorderly tumults and indecent behavior." At one point, the popular itinerant James Davenport pranced about half naked in torchlight stamping out the devil. It was enough to make a preacher swear and others in commanding positions respond even more furiously.[31]

At the heart of the Awakening was a renewed emphasis upon the significance of the experience of conversion and a new attention given to the emotional components of that momentous event. The innumerable conversions of the revival reawakened among the Congregationalists the old Puritan ideal of a church composed exclusively of the regenerate. Where such churches could be reestablished, they rediscovered the sharp distinction between the saved and the damned and obscured much of the distinction between the minister and the brotherhood of elect. Lay exhorters, some of them women and even children, seemed to preach with greater effectiveness than trained ministers. The

Anglican churches of the northern colonies were for the most part immune to these commotions, and they served to "open peoples' eyes," wrote Samuel Johnson, "and awaken their attention toward the [Anglican] Church as their only refuge." Some did flee to Johnson's Church (as others like them have done ever since) to escape what seemed to be the disorderly nature of Protestant nonconformist piety. A much larger group ultimately joined those denominations that accepted and even prized the turbulent aspects of religious life.[32]

Nevertheless, at the time, the Awakening broke New England Congregationalism into four conflicting factions. Among the leading issues that divided these Congregationalists were the emotionalism of the revival itself, the hope it inspired of setting up pure churches of regenerate Christians, and the expectations it raised for restructuring authority within those churches. At one extreme stood the Separates who enthusiastically supported the revival with all its excitements and aspirations; at the other stood those, later to be called liberals, who resolutely rejected the Awakening and all its works. Between them, with more qualified acceptances and rejections, ranged the Edwardsians and the Old Calvinists.[33]

The Separates, the extreme enthusiasts of the revival who left the Congregationalist churches of New England to set up pure fellowships of converted Christians, vociferously attacked the established ministry. The regular congregations were "spiritually dead," the Separates insisted, largely because "dead" men led them. This "unconverted, hireling ministry" was self-seeking, preaching merely for their salaries. The minister's salary, these enthusiasts argued, must come only from voluntary contributions, and many Separates refused to pay taxes for ministerial support. They soon broadened their attack and struck out against any form of religious establishment. Man must stand "naked before God," and no human authority can intermeddle; ecclesiastical bodies set above the "brotherhoods of saints" were a danger, for they were responsible for religious callousness.[34]

Within the Separates' churches some of the functions and authority of the ministry were dispersed among the "saints." The minister's ordination was by the hands of the church members and he was called "brother" like all the others. Separates also encouraged lay preaching and exhorting (they denounced the very term "laity"), and they considered "watch and care" the responsibility of all the brethren. Much like the general calling of all saints to Jesus, the minister's calling to his office was an inward command. This call and the nearly spontaneous agreement

of church members on a particular candidate—"a marvelous confluence of spiritual evidence"—was a sure sign of a truly regenerate ministry. Outward gifts, especially the "fleshy wisdom" of
classical learning, were put aside for the truly spiritual preaching
which the Separates believed to be a form of immediate divine
inspiration. Far from making any claim to be gentlemen, their
ministers often described themselves as humble brethren and
companions.[35]

By contrast, the Congregationalist ministers who were first to
condemn the Awakening were also those who especially prided
themselves on their gentlemanly status. This group of clergymen,
whom later scholars have come to call liberals, resided for the
most part in eastern Massachusetts. They had earlier come
under the influence of English Enlightenment ideas, but they
were driven by the excitements of the Awakening even farther
away from the austere mysteries of Calvinist doctrine and toward
a greater reliance upon the religion of reason and morality.
Charles Chauncy, minister of Boston's First Church, was their
champion. "In the face of heaven," he poured scorn upon the revivalists and their peremptory divinations as to anyone's regenerate state. There lay only confusion and disorder, for no one
could read another man's heart. That was Christ's power alone.
The abuse of learned ministers that issued from the Awakening
was a sure sign that the movement was not the work of God.
Ministerial associations must rely upon qualities such as education and morality that were outwardly discernible, Chauncy explained. The discernible qualities, however, usually resembled
those of polite gentlemen. One liberal minister suggested that if
a young man had the money for a college education, it was evidence of God's will that he had a call to the ministry.[36]

Chauncy and the Separates both preached to conscience, but
with a difference. The revivalists preached to that internal witness of inevitable sinfulness and to the internal judge whose certain judgment was damnation. The consequence of that damnation, consignment to Hell (a place of real physical torment), was
described vividly. In many of the revivalist sermons, conscience
therefore became an internal witness to the horror of death and
Hell; it was ineluctably joined to fear and became an instrument
for conversions. The liberals, however, under the influence of English theological discussion, had become uncomfortable with the
Calvinist notion of the predestined damnation of much of hu-
mankind. "We had better have no God," remarked the reverend
David Barnes, "than one who is partial, unjust, severe, and
cruel." Charles Chauncy's belief in the benevolence of the Deity

led him to reject the traditional notion that some were destined to Hell forever (Newton and Locke, the two sages of the Enlightenment, had come to similar conclusions); eventually all would be saved. If ultimately the distinction between the saved and the damned disappeared, or if only the willfully wicked would be damned, then the consequences of sin were somewhat less dreadful and one could turn to a preaching style that was less menacing.[37]

The liberals still preached strongly to conscience, but for them the lawgiver of conscience was more benevolent and rational, and the monitor more active. The result of this preaching was not a tempestuous conversion but moral behavior. Ministers were useful officers of the state, Zabdiel Adams explained, because they preached up the duties of morality and thereby contributed to order, peace, and the welfare of society. "Even supposing that there were no future state, one should no more object to provisions being made for ministers than for magistrates." For some liberal ministers this type of conscience took on importance as an end in itself, and their successors, who ultimately came to reject conversion, made the development of this conscience the purpose of the Christian life.[38]

One of the effects of the Awakening and its disruptions was to alter the understanding of the nature of the bond between the minister and his people. There was a growing disposition, particularly among liberal ministers, to see that bond as a civil contract; mention of the divine sanction in the call from the Church became more vague and infrequent. Cotton Mather had given a traditional account of the *vinculum pastorale* many years earlier. A young man's own inclinations and any other temptations must be put aside. "One consecrated into the ministry, is thus *pro termina vitae* (for the full time of his existence); nor may a man setting his hand to this plough, at his own pleasure look back." Mather would have been distressed to see Isaiah Dunster spending two years in negotiations with three different churches for settlement, with the question of pay the chief issue. It was not that Dunster thought one should enter the ministry merely for monetary reward. The minister was still Christ's ambassador, steward, and shepherd over his flock. But he did not seem to think that attachment to any ordinary flock was required of the shepherd. Especially since this particular shepherd turned out to be such a high-toned gentleman.[39]

Between the Separates and the liberals were two distinct groups of Congregationalist ministers: one openly and decisively supported the Awakening, and the other, more equivocal, often welcomed it at first and later opposed it. Yet the lessons both drew from the upheaval, insofar as the ministry was concerned, eventually were similar. Jonathan Edwards and his followers, who were among the principal instigators and promoters of the revival, like the Separates, were drawn to the ideal of a church of the regenerate. But Edwards placed more stringent tests upon the evidence of election than did the Separates. While he welcomed the emotional fervor of the conversion, he did not gauge its authenticity by its intensity but rather by its relation to all other experience. "Affection . . . must have some apprehension of understanding, some judgment of mind, for its foundation." And upon this principle the position of the learned clergy, trained in judgment of mind, was secured.[40]

Edwards accepted and endorsed the work of lay exhorters, yet he insisted that they must counsel in a brotherly way; only the minister can teach as a "father amongst a company of children." The ideal relationship of the minister to his church was one of authority and intimacy. Yet, except at the height of the Awakening, there was much that was theoretical about this intimacy. Edwardsians were a highly theoretical group, bound by an abstruse metaphysical system that set them off from those who were unmindful of it. Their predilection for doctrinal preaching and their austere requirements for Christian sainthood did not encourage warm attachments on the part of their churchgoers. But among themselves the Edwardsian ministers, united by a unique and self-renunciatory doctrine (as well as by marriage alliances and teacher-student ties), set up a strong, if informal, colleagueship that brought them closer to a Presbyterian footing than their statements about church order would suggest. When Edwardsians found themselves in the majority in the consociations set up in Connecticut under the Saybrook Platform, they effectively used these councils (which the Separates denounced as ungodly) against their opponents.[41]

Many of the Congregationalist ministers who had been moving more self-consciously toward Presbyterian forms in the early eighteenth century ultimately came out against the Awakening. Unlike the liberals, however, they still held to a modified Calvinist orthodoxy. In its early days, when the revival seemed to be simply a call to a more fervent piety, these ministers had usually welcomed it. Yet they were not won over to the vision of a church of exclusively regenerate membership, and they were appalled by the licentious disorders, and more particularly the attacks on the ministry. To these "Old Calvinists," the Separates, with their notions of "internal call" and their attack upon authority, civil and religious, seemed to be simply dangerous Antinomians. In response to such dangers, the Old Calvinists asserted ministerial authority more rigidly than they had done before.[42]

The Great Awakening was not as shattering for the Presbyterians as it was for the Congregationalists. Of the three major American denominations of the eighteenth century, the Presbyterians were growing and expanding the most rapidly. This advance was tied to the heavy Scotch-Irish immigration to America. When the Scotch-Irish Presbyterians began to pour into New England in the early eighteenth century, their reception was less cordial than one might expect. To some New Englanders it seemed that the morals of these new immigrants were too lax and the bearing of their ministers too arbitrary. While the creedal standards of the New Englanders were quite close to those of the Scotch-Irish, their folkways were quite distinct. The new immigrants had come from a land forcibly taken from the Irish, among whom they lived, but subject to the English, who ruled from afar. These Scotch-Irish had despised the Irish and resented the English. Their religion was a vivid expression of their isolation and vulnerability. It was a polemically orthodox Calvinism braced by the Westminster Confession, a code that served as a compendium of doctrine as well as a remembrance of Scottish political and religious power at its height. Their ministers, usually vigorous and overbearing, were religious and ethnic leaders in one.[43]

The institutional supports for the authority of the Presbyterian ministers were more substantial than those the Congregational ministers could rely on. The Presbyterians fixed primary ecclesiastical power not in the particular churches, as did the Congregationalists, but in the presbyteries, regional councils of ministers and ruling elders. The elders were laymen elected within each church and they could give voice to the layman's sentiments. Yet in all Presbyterian assemblies the ruling elders played a subordinate role. The ministers, who dominated the church, were licensed by the presbytery, then elected by the congregation, and finally ordained by the presbytery. This was the institutional resolution of conflicting doctrines—the priesthood of all believers and the divine appointment of the ministerial office. Many of the Scotch-Irish who came to New England found the region uncongenial, and they gradually drifted south into the Middle and Southern Colonies where most of this immigration settled.[44]

Congregationalist ministers had been moving toward Presbyterian forms for reasons of their own, but those who migrated from New England (where ecclesiastical rates were levied by town law and collected by local sheriffs) to the Middle Colonies (where the church was not established, leaving the minister more at the mercy of his congregation for his livelihood) turned even more strongly toward ministerial fellowship to rectify the uncertainties of their situation. Moreover, unlike the churches of New England, which originated in communities of "gathered saints" that elected their ministers, the churches of the Middle Colonies were often the work of energetic ministers who gathered a previously unconnected membership into new congregations. Such initiative and responsibility helped create vibrant bonds of colleagueship between those who shared such arduous duties. Yet that colleagueship also brought with it unanticipated encroachments of fraternal discipline for New England ministers who came to the Middle Colonies. Fraternal discipline was an important element in the two crises that shook the young Presbyterian church in the eighteenth century, first in the subscription controversy, and later and more vehemently in the Great Awakening. Both conflicts centered upon doctrine, but not upon the content of doctrine, rather upon the way in which doctrine should be held. Furthermore, the issue was not so much the way the doctrine should be held by the congregation but, more in keeping with the Presbyterian sense of the Church, by the ministers themselves.[45]

The effect of the Great Awakening upon the Presbyterians of the Middle Colonies was strongly influenced by the outcome of an earlier controversy. When in 1721 some of the foremost Scotch-Irish ministers proposed that all the clergy subscribe to the Westminster Confession and promise not to preach or teach anything contrary to it, Jonathan Dickinson, a leader of the New Englanders in the Presbyterian Church, opposed the scheme. Under the Saybrook Platform, Connecticut ministers accepted the Westminster Confession as a valid statement of doctrine, but they were not required to assent to it in every particular. The Bible alone, said Dickinson, was deserving of such high regard, and it alone was a sufficient bond of union and doctrine. To hold any man-made creed with such awe was an invasion of Christ's royal power; it was overstepping for "proud worms to make any addition to that perfect pattern, which He has given us." Enlargements and alterations, even in the name of tradition, antiquity, or order and decency, pointed the way to the mistaken path taken by the Church of Rome and the Church of England. Creeds were useful and necessary, for they helped the Church rid itself of heresy and scandal. Yet binding the ministers so closely to a creed was a grave error "when our consciences . . . tell us that God requires no such thing at our hands." With Dickinson, conscience provided not only a sense of obligation but also a particularly sharp sense of inner right, derived from a perception of divine mandate, that could strike out against external restraint.[46]

For John Thomson, who headed the subscriptionists, a pledge to uphold the Westminster Confession in all its particulars was not so much a restraint as a protection. Presbyterianism without this pledge, he said, taking up a metaphor of considerable resonance for his fellow Scotch-Irish, was "a city without walls." The defenseless condition of the Church made the need for fortifications urgent, otherwise the Church would be swallowed up: "Have we not reason to consult our own safety?" Thomson asked. Such an oath would keep out the promulgators of corrupt doctrine and help make the Church zealous in the spirit of unity that derived from a uniform creed. The Church would not easily lose sight of received truths and wander from them inadvertently. Subscription would make the present generation worthy of those ancestors who "sealed the . . . truth with their blood." Those who thought that subscription violated the dictates of conscience should separate, Thomson believed, allowing the Church to be a cohesive body, bound by doctrine. Schism was much to be preferred to allowing doctrine to be so vague that heterodox ministers might legitimately besmirch religious truth and enfeeble the Church itself.[47]

The pressures of the Scotch-Irish, who were a majority in the ministry, could not be withstood. The New Englanders yielded to a compromise measure, the Adopting Act of 1729, requiring subscription to the Confession by all ministers but permitting dissent from those portions the presbytery might allow as nonessential. At subsequent synods the allowance for any dissent was apparently eliminated. The Scotch-Irish style of ministry had won out. The ministry as a collective body was exalted; for the Westminster Confession, which now stood as a codification of faith, was the work of ministers. The individual minister was now more constrained, for he was obliged to declare his agreement with that codification as divine truth, as a condition for his admission into office. The clamor of these disagreements over subscription, however, should not obscure the fact that there was substantial agreement within the Church on the relationship between the minister and his congregation. The minister stood as an austere and authoritative figure. Dickinson saw the clergyman as "the ruler of Christ's household" who preached with authority and spoke to the consciences of his congregation. And Thomson, as might be expected, went further to insist that the authority Christ granted to the minister gave him the right to command "as a parent commands his child to obey even against his will."[48]

The upshot of the subscription controversy, consolidating church organization around the Calvinist stipulations of the Westminster Confession and subordinating clergymen to church bodies, had an important effect upon the Presbyterian response to the Great Awakening in the Middle Colonies. Factions resembling the liberals and the Separates were very small and insignificant. Almost all antirevivalists boasted of their Calvinist orthodoxy, and almost all revivalists condemned lay exhorters. When the revivalists broke away from the established synod, they did not condemn church structures but rather set up a church structure of their own. The Presbyterian supporters of the Great Awakening in the Middle Colonies came from both Scotch-Irish and New England origins. The Tennents, a remarkable ministerial family that led the Scotch-Irish group, had been among the subscriptionists, but they showed a particular interest in ardent piety that distinguished them from most of the others in that group. Gilbert Tennent, after what seemed to him too many ineffectual years in the ministry, turned to a fiery and extemporaneous style in preaching and quickly became a thunderous success. His achievements encouraged him and his family to denounce the regular ministry's stress upon formalism and outward proprieties, and to set up a school, with a somewhat restricted curriculum, for the training of clergymen with a warm faith and virtuous habits of conduct. Moreover, the Tennents encouraged such clergymen to enter parishes other than their own, and this inevitably led to clashes and finally schism. The Great Awakening in the Middle Colonies provided new incitements toward, and demands for, the experience of regeneration, but within the Presbyterian Church the resulting embroilments were more often exclusively over the spiritual qualifications and behavior of the ministry than they were over the qualifications and behavior of the church members.[49]

Jonathan Dickinson and his followers welcomed the news of the Edwardsian revivals in New England, and after some hesitation endorsed the revival work of the Tennents in the Middle Colonies. Like Edwards, Dickinson was intent upon distinguishing the conversions from their counterfeits, but like the Tennents he did not place any new requirements upon admission to baptism or communion. The New England party finally joined the Scotch-Irish revivalists to form a new synod that remained separated from the antirevivalist party for over a decade. Dickinson, like

Edwards, was uncomfortable with the accusation that the revivalists were lowering the educational standards for the ministry. The Tennents had denounced the attempt of the Philadelphia synod to examine the graduates of their "Log Cabin College" in "philosophy, divinity, and languages" and had sometimes even encouraged laymen to judge ministerial "sufficiency," stressing the inner call of the ministry rather than the outward call of church judicatures. In part to offset such proclivities, Dickinson set up a broader and more substantial school to replace the Tennents' "Log Cabin College." His school, the College of New Jersey (later Princeton), became for a while the foremost training center for Presbyterian ministers in the Middle Colonies, and Dickinson became its first president.[50]

John Thomson, Dickinson's opponent on the subscription issue, was also one of the leaders of the antirevivalist party. He saw the Awakening as the work of God, but claimed that it was God's punishment for the Church rather than His blessing. While Thomson favored a more diligent piety, the unbridled emotionalism of the revival and the divisions it produced were perplexing and disheartening to him. Ministers must not scare the people to Jesus, but "as by a schoolmaster, lead them to Him." Moreover, the attempt to build a church polity upon judgments of spiritual states, if only those of the ministers, would bring chaos. It led to attacks upon the rightful powers of Church judicatures and ultimately upon Christian subordination itself. Christians owed obedience to the rulings of Church courts, and it was only the enemies of Christian liberty and conscience who called upon those concepts in order to stand in opposition to just and lawful authority.[51]

Such assertions of authority could not suppress the Awakening, particularly among the Presbyterians who did not have the civil devices available to established churches. The revival was not quelled in the Middle Colonies (or anywhere else); it burned itself out. Gilbert Tennent had preached a sermon in 1735 entitled "The Necessity of Religious Violence," but less than a decade later he was explaining "The Necessity of Studying to be Quiet and Doing our Business." The revivalist synod, nevertheless, had grown more rapidly than the antirevivalists, and when the two were finally reunited the church was dominated by a sedate form of revivalism. Itinerancy was forbidden but an "evangelical and spiritual" preaching was endorsed. Church courts must be obeyed, but only on those issues "indispensable in doctrine and in Presbyterian government." The ministerial candidates would be tested for their learning and skill in divinity but also for their "experimental acquaintance with religion." More-over, the new college soon came under the moderating influence of John Witherspoon. While the slogan of the revivalists had been "new birth" and that of the antirevivalists "Christian subordina-tion," Witherspoon succeeded in hitching these together under his preachments of "Prudence."[52]

That Witherspoon had come straight from Scotland, brogue and all, won him favor from some antirevivalists, most of whom were of Scottish origins; that he had led the evangelical party in Scotland won him the approval of some revivalists who found his insistence that the minister must have "a lively sense of religion upon his own heart" to their liking. Yet the religion of the heart, for Witherspoon, needed to be balanced by a sense of conse-quences. He quickly drove from Princeton the rigoristic Edward-sian teachings which insisted that virtue was produced only by regenerate and therefore selfless motives, and replaced such ten-ets with a more common-sensical doctrine of morality that looked not only to motives but also to results. In so doing, he brought some of the impress of the eighteenth-century British discussion on morality to America. During his tenure as president of Prince-ton (which was longer than the terms of his five predecessors put together), the school prospered, turning out Presbyterian minis-ters who were trained to be polished gentlemen with a warm piety.[53]

Witherspoon himself was just such a gentleman, and he felt comfortable even with those more secular-minded, gentlemanly leaders of the struggle for the American Revolution, in which he took an active part. For many of the churches, the Revolutionary era initiated a period of distraction and disruption. Yet for the Presbyterians, who largely supported the Revolution, the impair-ments were comparatively slight. Never having tasted the benefits of support from civil authority in America, some leading Presby-terians, after the Revolution, looked forward to a system of mul-tiple establishment, "the protection and favor of government to all denominations of Christians." When this proved unfeasible, they quickly turned to the centralizing of ecclesiastical govern-ment in order to strengthen their Church.[54]

The Presbyterians met in Philadelphia shortly before the Con-stitutional Convention and in much the same spirit, to set up a General Assembly, above the various synods, that could deliber-ate upon the common issues of the Church and hear appeals from lower tribunals. The new church constitution fostered greater unity and more ministerial control. When the Second Great Awakening erupted, the Presbyterians were in a position to take advantage of it. They had a cohesive ministry friendly to the vivid outpourings of the revival, equipped with a preaching style to further it and a well-devised organization to control it. Of the three largest churches in the eighteenth century, only the Presbyterian maintained its relative position in the nineteenth.[55]

While for the Church of England in America, the Great Awakening had been of little consequence, the Revolution seemed disastrous. When the Revolution broke out, most of the Anglican priests in the colonies remained loyal to the King. This loyalism discredited the Church and was one impetus toward its disestablishment after the war. Cut off from English jurisdiction and deprived of civil support, the Church became accessible to republican notions of ecclesiastical government. Unexpectedly, however, this was counterbalanced by the very fact that it had become a voluntary organization. In such organizations the most zealous and esteemed can lay hold of disproportionate influence, and in the Episcopal Church at that time those were the ritualists.[56]

The American Church got its first bishop after the Revolution, in the person of Samuel Seabury. He was consecrated by nonjuring bishops, which is in itself suggestive of his traditionalism and his belief in a clergy untrammeled by lay controls. From the General Convention of 1789, where assertive laymen and accommodating clergymen were in the majority, Seabury wrested a constitution providing for a separate House of Bishops (with a negative on proceedings) and a Book of Common Prayer with many traditional formulae of nonjuring usage. He gave the powers and prerogatives of the clergy liturgical definitions. Even the radical doctrine of the priesthood of all believers could be made acceptable when translated into a sacramental setting. The Eucharist, Seabury explained, was a "true and proper sacrifice," and when partaking of that sacrament, the laity became priests. In this restricted, ritual sense, the whole body of Christians could still be called a holy and royal priesthood. While such sacramentalism might actually secure the position of the clergyman, it set the Episcopal Church against the prevailing drift of American piety. The Church did develop its own evangelical wing in the nineteenth century, yet the denomination lost its leading position and increasingly became a conservative form of upper-class religious and cultural dissent.[57]

The Congregationalists, like the Presbyterians, overwhelmingly supported the Revolution, and benefited from that allegiance. Such support and the approbation that derived from it help explain the easy reestablishment of the church in the new state constitutions of Massachusetts, Connecticut, and New Hampshire. Bolstered by these establishments, there was a less pressing need for the Congregationalists to enact a church constitution than there had been for the Presbyterians and Anglicans. Yet there was something strikingly new in these reestablishments. In Massachusetts, for example, where state support for the church was to last the longest, the state constitution justified it in purely secular terms. It would secure good order, government stability, and happiness.[58]

This suggests some of the broader shifts in thought and circumstances that occurred over the eighteenth century. Not only had growing numbers of Americans become preoccupied with matters of war, trade, government, and nation building, but the ideas they brought to these concerns were quite different from those held by Americans in the previous century. When the early Puritans used the word liberty, as they sometimes did, they meant primarily freedom from sin; when their descendants at the end of the eighteenth century used the word liberty, as they frequently did, they meant primarily freedom from unnecessary coercion. This shift was supported by the fundamental Enlightenment doctrine that rights preceded duties. While that doctrine clearly contradicts received Calvinist teachings, the contradiction was not apparent to orthodox preachers of the day. Not only were most American ministers supporters of the Revolution, they were also principal conveyers of Enlightenment ideas. Because Jedidiah Morse, though he considered himself an orthodox Calvinist minister, could speak of "the cause of LIBERTY which is the birthright of mankind," he was also able to heartily endorse the great founding documents of the republic which declared of rights and happiness, but made no mention of sin and salvation.[59]

That endorsement reflected a collaboration of some remarkably different kinds of Americans during the Revolutionary era. All manner of patriots holding varying and even antithetical combinations of Protestant and Enlightenment ideas joined the fight for independence, and they were to be found on both sides of the struggle over the Federal constitution. Such accord, however, fell apart in the last years of the eighteenth century. At that time, leading ministers opened a frenzied and largely successful assault upon radical forms of the Enlightenment. Significantly, many of the principles and structures of the moderate Enlightenment—especially in the public realm of politics and law, where they were already widely accepted constituents of the status quo—escaped the onslaught. But within religious life, the temper of the early nineteenth century was one of sharp repudiation of "infidelity," that is to say, the beliefs held by many of the standard-bearers of the Revolution and even some ministers along with them.[60]

It was against this background that American theological seminaries were established. Previously, American colleges provided what was considered adequate formal preparation for the ministry. But with Harvard in the hands of liberals and Princeton's urbane president suspected of heterodoxy and worldliness, orthodox Congregationalists and Presbyterians began looking for more reliable instruments for the training of faithful ministers. One anxious advocate thought it was particularly important to separate the theological scholars from "the follies and vices" of the worldly-minded students. Others were more concerned with establishing denominational distinctiveness, and all were looking for ways to greatly increase the number of ministers and yet still ensure that the ministers were learned. These seminaries turned against the "disorderliness" of the radical revivalists and the skepticism of the Enlightenment. Edwardsians and Old Calvinists joined together to set up Andover Theological Seminary in 1808, and Middle-States Presbyterians established their seminary at Princeton in 1812. The Reverend Timothy Dwight was a guiding influence for both, and his sermon preached at the opening of Andover tells us much about the expectations that clung to these seminaries. Just a hundred years after the Reverend Benjamin Colman had pleaded that the ministry should not be brought down to the rank of "Liberal Imployments," Dwight argued that the ministry should not be allowed to fall below them. After all, pastors were still a gift from God and His chief agent for the saving of men. One must demand, therefore, an education for ministers that was at least comparable to that required of physicians and lawyers. The minister must be a cultured professional who held an elevated social standing and whose person and office carried authority and honor within the community. For that, the minister must be pious, but he also stood in need of a liberal education and a "professional science." Such a science, like that of the other professions, involved a complex theoretical understanding, but the science of the minister, of course, rested uniquely upon the truths of Revelation. The seminary would stipulate a college education as an entrance requirement, and it would help foster righteousness and that professional science. The resulting elevated position of the minister, however, was not sought simply for his sake. "If Ministers are respectable, Religion will by mankind in general be respected. . . . If they are dignified; it will be believed to be noble. If they are pious; it will be acknowledged to be real. But if on the contrary Ministers are contemptible; Religion will be despised." Such was the awesome self-assumption and responsibility of ministers.[61]

This minister was perforce a well-educated, high-toned, and pious gentleman. He was "affectionate, paternal, and dignified; calculated to inspire respect and dependence, and to repel the approach of presumptuous familiarity." The loose, somewhat implausible general notions of gentlemanly stewardship became more exacting and more credible among ministers. For the minister was a gentleman by virtue of his occupation, and that occupation invoked its own peculiar mix of dignity and abnegation. All callings served God, yet the ministry, Increase Mather had once explained, was "of all Callings the most desirable." It was not "beneath the best or greatest men on Earth to be so imployed." A saying popular among ministers noted that "The God of Heaven had but one Son, and he made him a Minister." That exemplary divine minister, however, though he was preeminently exalted, also provided a model of renunciation and self-sacrifice. Unlike other gentlemen, the minister was urged to cultivate an indifference to much of the world's enjoyments. While Christ had demanded that all Christians renounce earthly distractions for him, the minister especially was expected to respond to that demand. He must live "honourably," that is with a moderate income befitting a gentleman, yet he should definitely not take up his calling "for filthy lucre's sake." Toward the end of the eighteenth century, as the foremost merchants, planters, and lawyers rose greatly in wealth and esteem, the sacrifice involved in choosing the ministry became more apparent. "To embrace the office of the ministry," remarked Princeton's president, "is in our country, to abandon the road to civil honors and employments. It is . . . to confine genius and talents to an humble sphere from which they can never hope to emerge." The Reverend John H. Rice's observation that the ministerial office is "greatly underrated by men of the world" was corroborated by the declining proportions of Harvard graduates entering the ministry.[62]

Yet few would deny the importance of these "Ambassadors of Christ." If they no longer stood near the helm of the ship of state (as they had in seventeenth-century New England), they still supplied moral ballast. The ministers' increasingly eager assertions that religion fostered happiness and good order were generally accepted. Undeniably, by the early nineteenth century, it was apparent that others advanced happiness and good order more directly, yet hardly anyone would gainsay the minister's contribution. The more Calvinistic clergy might still insist that there was no calculable way from moral effort to salvation, but all ministers agreed—and such agreement grew in importance—that God had commanded moral behavior, and obedience to those commands was obligatory. In a society whose fundamental political principles placed rights before duties, the benefits of a countervailing system of beliefs that taught the practice of the duties of life were evident. By the early nineteenth century, the ministry took on a heightened moral aspect. Among the liberals this resulted from doctrinal shifts, and among the orthodox it owed much to more unwitting and impulsive accommodations. The ministry had always been a special ally and even an embodiment of the conscience, but now in this new social setting, the ministerial career itself was a further link to renunciation. For someone choosing it knew that young men with comparable talents, but more mundane and overt self-interest, had found other opportunities with remarkably gratifying rewards. Moreover, as the venerable Protestant doctrine that all vocations serve God began to fade rapidly, and most occupations were seen more explicitly in terms of economic goals, the vocation of the ministry remained one with spiritual and moral purpose, now even more distinctly so by comparison. Though no longer foremost of the professions, the ministry still afforded work that was especially elevated by moral purpose, and in this regard it still set a standard for the others.[63]

At the beginning of the eighteenth century, particularly in the northern and middle sections of the country, it was generally assumed that a capable young man of intellectual bent who wished to rise in life would seek a career in the ministry rather than in medicine or law; at the beginning of the nineteenth century that was no longer true. By that time the ministers of the three leading American denominations counted for less outside their churches; however, they counted for more within them. They shouldered more of the burden for the spiritual well-being of the Church, and became more studied in their tasks. The ministers had also weathered the storms of the mid-eighteenth-century religious upheavals, moving nearer to colleagues though often growing more distant from the church brethren. The ministers had also come through the tumults of the Revolutionary era, absorbing some Enlightenment ideas, adjusting to others, and helping to subdue its most radical aims. At the beginning of the nineteenth century, the minister's social position was still assured. While he was not within the ruling groups of his society, he was still among the better sort. Most other occupations ranged along the social scale according to wealth, but the minister of these three denominations usually held his position as a polite gentleman almost regardless of his income. That his motives were not mercenary was presumed and respected in a society that was becoming increasingly mercenary. The ministry assured aspiring young men that there could still be a special eminence and authority in America without wealth, family, or political power.

2

The Doctors' Dilemmas

While the Enlightenment, with its great regard for the natural sciences and the powers of reason, presented both a threat and a stimulus to the profession of the ministry, this same intellectual movement seemed to provide unequivocal and advantageous support for the profession of medicine. At least that appeared to be the case initially. As it turned out, however, the very predilections of the Enlightenment led the most influential American doctors of the era to a kind of overreaching that proved to be ultimately disabling for the profession and disastrous for many of their patients. Yet, despite some unexpected bafflements and setbacks, what is striking about American doctors of this era is that they nonetheless managed to establish an eminent profession, if not a preeminent one.

Important to that achievement was the appropriation, in the eighteenth century, of the usages of the upper ranks of the British medical profession by practitioners in America who were originally of much lower standing. Earlier, American medicine was provincial medicine. It had been largely in the hands of surgeon-apothecaries, clergymen, midwives, and makeshift doctors of various sorts. Yet, by the end of the eighteenth century, many of those diverse American healers had been pushed aside by medical men assuming the style of the English physician, an imposing figure who dominated the metropolitan medical institutions of that day in the mother country.[1]

It was chiefly in London and its environs that the three ranks in medicine (physician, surgeon, and apothecary) kept to their proper places. In the provinces, the surgeon-apothecary, who took on all medical work, prevailed. He was "the physician to the poor in all cases and of the rich when distress or danger [was] not very great." When Americans in the eighteenth century went in search of proper decorum, however, it was to London and not to the provinces that they looked. The upgrading of American surgeon-apothecaries and their attempt to assume the bearing and authority of the English physician found expression in two burgeoning colonial medical institutions: the medical societies and, what in the long run became more consequential, the medical colleges. Within both of these, it was often the American-born physician with a European medical degree who led the way. He had the local patriotism that most of the immigrant physicians lacked and the self-assurance and aspiration often wanting in those native medical men trained exclusively through apprenticeship.[2]

The medical societies sprang up in the major seaboard cities of the colonies during the second half of the eighteenth century. The first order of business for some of these associations was to devise a fee bill, a table of recommended charges for specified tasks of doctoring. In New Jersey, the newborn medical society immediately urged such a fee bill, while in New York the medical association condemned the practice as "inconsistent with the dignity of the profession." In England, fee bills were customary among surgeons but scorned by most physicians. That some American medical societies resorted to such tables of charges was indicative of the hybrid origins of the American profession. Yet it would be a mistake to see fee bills simply as economic devices for, in that regard, they were usually ineffectual. The market for medical services was a traditional one where "connections" rather than competitive prices were the primary regulatory mechanisms. The doctor was usually chosen on the recommendation of family or friends rather than on the basis of a comparison of charges, and the physician himself, with or without a fee bill, customarily varied his rates according to the patient's ability to pay. Similarly, the licensing laws of this era, which ostensibly placed monopolistic restrictions on entry into the practice of medicine, were by modern standards not very effective. Enforcement was by fits and starts. Yet those laws did select out the most reputable doctors for recognition and give them improved access to an upper-class practice with the most profitable clientele. Whatever their economic benefits, however, licensing laws and fee bills, more importantly, identified and unified the more respectable segment of the profession and helped raise such doctors to elevated positions with respect to their patients. Those devices lent support to the medical associations' efforts to foster affability and good fellowship among their members, helping them to "avoid condemning and calumniating each other before the Plebeians," and often even creating a corporate sense of the profession.[3]

In their endeavors to advance their medical societies and more strikingly in their efforts to build their medical school, the doctors of Philadelphia were particularly enterprising and ambitious. Philadelphia became the medical capital of the American colonies—the center for the transfer, naturalization, and dissemination of British medical institutions in America. This is not at all surprising, for in the years just before the Revolution, Philadelphia was the most populous and prosperous city in the colonies. It had a wealthy upper class that looked to British metropolitan ways for models and might support a London-style physician. It also had a sizable lower class supplying charity patients to the Philadelphia hospitals where young doctors could develop their skills. (The English Samuel Johnson declared that such doctors "grew wise only by murder.") Moreover, Philadelphia also happened to have an adroit and strong-minded medical elite; preeminent within it were Dr. John Morgan and his pupil and friend, Dr. Benjamin Rush. Morgan and Rush, owing to their talents and also to their location, were to have an extraordinary influence upon American medicine.[4]

In John Morgan's early career, ontogeny recapitulates phylogeny; the elevation of the profession can be seen in the rise of this aspiring young man. Morgan, after a six-year apprenticeship, took up practice as an Army surgeon, but left that service to acquire a classical education at the College of Philadelphia. He then moved on to the University of Edinburgh for his M.D. degree, adding some study with the great London surgeon John Hunter and then the polish of a Grand Tour of the Continent. James Boswell, who accompanied Morgan on part of that tour, called him a "coxcomb," and the brittleness that Boswell's tag suggests would be Morgan's chief impediment in his efforts. Loaded with honors, medical learning, and a sense of good form, he returned to Philadelphia and set out to rectify American medical practice.[5]

Morgan's program for reform appeared in his celebrated *Discourse Upon the Institution of Medical Schools in America*. One of his chief aims was to set up the three traditional orders of the medical profession in America. He announced that he would not practice surgery or supply drugs, and he urged the separation and subordination of the surgeon and the apothecary as a matter of general policy. He suggested that such ranking was a point of good form, that it was in the nature of things, and that it was useful. In America, where a well-secured traditional hierarchy could not be taken for granted, the usefulness of rankings was to be an important justification for them.[6]

Morgan's argument rested chiefly upon the notion of division of labor. Before Locke, the benefits of such division were usually thought to derive from the fact that each man was exerting his natural and particular gifts. (Plato was only the most renowned advocate of this version.) Adam Smith, by contrast, thought that the proficiency of the men within each division came in large part from the repetition of their tasks. Morgan, writing before Smith and after Locke, argued both ways. A physician needed a particular "genius for deliberation, reasoning, and judgement," while the surgeon's success required dexterity and hardihood. Those were very disparate talents, rarely found in the same man. However, repeated practice also might make each man better at his work. The three branches of medicine were to be separate and the physician was to oversee the whole of medicine. This could readily be done by someone gifted with the physician's qualities for he could study the principles of all three branches. The physician was like a general of the army who "should be acquainted with every part of military science and understand the whole detail of military duty from that of a colonel down to a private sentinel." But there is no need, Morgan added, "that he should act as a pioneer and dig in a trench." The British army in the eighteenth century incorporated a hierarchical division of labor based upon a complacent joining of class position and military skill. That Morgan found such an analogy to his liking (Dr. James McClurg, professor of medicine at the College of William and Mary, also chose this comparison for the same purpose some time later) says something of the unexpressed connotations of his argument.[7]

The recommendation that physicians not mix or sell drugs was eventually accepted by many practitioners, particularly in Philadelphia; however, Morgan's attempt to separate the work of the physician from that of the surgeon had little effect. A group of the most eminent doctors, most of whom had studied abroad— John Redman, Morgan himself, Benjamin Rush, Samuel Bard, Benjamin Waterhouse, James McClurg, and Samuel Danforth among them—avoided surgery out of a sense of the dignity of physic. For all of them, this fastidiousness involved economic sacrifice. Rush complained that some families insisted upon going to one man for both physic and surgery, and when he told them he would not do the work of a surgeon, they turned to another practitioner. Dr. McClurg of Virginia deplored the fact that if he had no other source of income, he would not be able to support his family from his medical practice, owing to his refusal to practice surgery. Young doctors, who as yet had no reputations, found that daring operations drew popular applause and wealthy patients, making surgery particularly helpful to their careers. Rush therefore recommended that his son practice surgery, and McClurg with much distress urged the same course upon his nephew.[8]

Even more unavailing was Morgan's attempt to bring the English physicians' conventions of medical payment to America. He announced that he would not charge fees but would "leave the patients themselves to give what they please." He quickly added that those unfamiliar with the etiquette of professional payment, or who had no adequate notion of the true value of medical attendance, might ask him what would be appropriate and he would gladly tell them. Yet all this was "too refined for this papermonied country," as one critic wrote, and the honorarium did not take hold. Perhaps it might have survived if there had been more practitioners, "gentlemen of independent estate and fortune," who did not need to worry about how their patients' gratitude or lack of it would affect their livelihood. However, there were not many of such in the American colonies. Morgan's additional proposal, to elevate the local medical societies through a supervening Royal College of Physicians in America—a chartered society of leading physicians with special privileges and duties of self-regulation, much like the societies of London and Edinburgh—was also rebuffed. In this case it was the Proprietor's agent, claiming that such a Royal College was premature, who blocked the way.[9]

Despite these setbacks, Morgan was not disheartened. For his most important proposal, the setting up of a school of medicine in Philadelphia, was a quick and reassuring success. The apprenticeship training that had been the typical preparation of American medical men was clearly inadequate for the new model of the American physician that Morgan had in mind. The European medical education that he himself had received was too costly for most would-be American physicians; but the new medical school in Philadelphia, patterned after that in Edinburgh, could provide comprehensive and systematic medical instruction at a cost that made such education available to a much broader group of aspiring medical men. The medical school served as the repository and propagator of medical theory and as an instrument for the socialization of young doctors. Command of medical theory was one of the most important differentia of the physician. For medicine was not merely a miscellany of information about diseases and cures, derived in a hit-or-miss way; such empiricism was but half-learning, adequate perhaps for surgeons but not for physicians. The physician practiced medicine as a science—that is to say, in the light of knowledge discovered, formulated, and systemized with reference to general truths. It required, therefore, that "genius for deliberation, reasoning, and judgement" that Morgan thought were necessary attributes of a physician.[10]

Much of the medical theory of the eighteenth century was linked to the work of Herman Boerhaave, the celebrated Dutch physician, who occupied the Chair of Medicine at Leyden. With great energy, erudition, and acumen, Boerhaave had gathered a vast store of medical information and placed it into a somewhat coherent arrangement. Newton and Harvey were his intellectual masters; Boerhaave took as the frame of his medical teachings the general architecture of Newton's system and Harvey's singular discovery, the circulation of blood. Fundamentally the human body, like the solar system, was a machine, Boerhaave explained, and at its center was the pulsive heart. The body, in fact, resembled a hydraulic pump, and most disease was simply the obstructed and disturbed movement of its parts. Though such teaching might lead to materialist conclusions, Boerhaave (unlike his devoted pupil, La Mettrie) did not draw them. The underlying nature of reality, he argued with impressive diffidence, was hidden from us.[11]

Those two closely related issues—the theory of vitality and the theory of disease—that were important to Boerhaave's teaching were also prominent in eighteenth-century medical theory. Up until the seventeenth and eighteenth centuries, medical learning derived largely from the Greek and Roman heritage that had been absorbed into a Christian framework during the Middle Ages. Because Greco-Roman medicine had been so sharply divorced from Greek and Roman religion, it could readily be adapted to Christianity. However, the new discoveries in the seventeenth and eighteenth centuries—in anatomy and physiology, as well as in physics and chemistry—drew medical science away from classical teachings and strained its moorings to traditional religious doctrines. The outcome was the great eighteenth-century debate between mechanism and vitalism. While Boerhaave asserted that for medical purposes it was best to treat the body as a machine, his renowned scientific contemporary, George Ernst Stahl, argued to the contrary that neglecting the differences between organism and mechanism hampered the proper understanding of disease and health.[12]

Many of the leading European physicians took part in that debate (Hoffmann in Germany, Theophile de Bordeu and Bichat in France, Robert Whytt in Scotland), but only its echoes were heard in America. Nevertheless many of the most eminent American physicians occasionally felt called upon to declare themselves upon the issue. When Dr. Benjamin Rush, Morgan's successor at the Medical School in Philadelphia, discussed the nature of vitality, he followed closely the Scottish students of Boerhaave who had held sway at the medical school at Edinburgh when he studied there. "The human body is an automaton, or self-moving machine," wrote Rush, "but it is kept alive and in motion by constant action of stimuli upon it." For Rush, such a conception led to reassuring religious conclusions, for it seemed to underscore man's dependence upon God. "Self-existence belongs only to God." The real danger, Rush believed, was a naturalistic pantheism, and the belief in vitalism was but a step in that direction. "Admit a principle of life in the human body, and we open the door for the restoration of the old Epicurean and atheistical philosophy. . . . The doctrine I have taught cuts the sinews of that error. For by rendering the *continuance* of animal life, no less than its commencement, the effect of constant operation of Divine power and goodness, it leads us to believe that the whole of creation is supported in the same manner."[13]

This view that man was a machine had more practical results as well. It supported the drastic style of interventionist medicine that flourished in the eighteenth century. The earlier belief in the healing power of nature and the admonition to let nature take its course were widely discredited, and no one inveighed against those notions more sharply than did Rush. Machines do not fix themselves if you leave them alone. Rush and many of his fellow doctors demanded a bold and resolute therapy—a mode of healing that was called "heroic medicine," leaving it unclear whether the heroism was required of the doctor or the patient.[14]

Rush's theory of disease also had its origins in the teachings of Boerhaave and his followers, but here Rush became something of an innovator in his own right. Cullen, Rush's teacher at Edinburgh, had already modified Boerhaave's scheme, contending that it was not the circulatory system but rather the nervous system that was the source of life. Disease, Cullen explained, was due to the failure of the regulatory powers of the nervous system. Rush at first adopted Cullen's views and flaunted them before the old-fashioned doctors in Philadelphia who still looked to Boerhaave. However, Rush soon felt obliged to propose a system of his own, and it combined various features of both Boerhaave's and Cullen's teachings. Cullen was right in finding that too much or too little stimulation was important to disease, but he had not noticed the connection between these states and the irregular convulsive action of the blood vessels, which Rush claimed was the fundamental condition of disease. Since there was but one morbid state, there need be but one treatment—a therapy that would reduce the excitement of the blood vessels. Rush recommended a restricted diet, heavy purging with jalap and calomel, and bleeding to the limit of tolerance. This treatment seemed to have some of the simplicity and grandeur of Newton's great system. Moreover, Rush contended that it was more scientific and more indigenous than any theory and treatment American doctors had known before.[15]

Rush's teachings had a great and woeful effect upon American medical practice. Beginning with the terrifying Philadelphia yellow fever epidemic of 1793, when Rush first announced his new ideas on disease, his doctrine grew rapidly in prestige and remained influential well into the nineteenth century. This despite the strong lay and medical objections to it that never completely disappeared. The key to much of the success of Rush's teachings, devastating though their effects were, lay in a kind of *ad hominem* argument. Rush embodied some of the most admired qualities of his age. His obviously sincere humanity, his personal heroism, his fervent devotion to science and reason, his patriotism—all worked to lend credence to his ideas. In addition, Rush held a strategic position as professor in the Medical College of Philadelphia. That school produced more physicians than any other of its day, and Rush himself, who taught there for forty-four years, trained over two thousand doctors. "Your theory and practice of medicine gains ground rapidly," wrote one of his South Carolina students. "The terrible dread of bleeding has entirely disappeared . . . and to whom is the credit due, but to you my good sir, the author of such principles and practice as will stand the test of time." As late as 1840 a reputable Philadelphia-trained doctor treated what seems to have been a case of appendicitis by bloodletting and morphine, with deadly results.[16]

Medical theory was a matter of science and style, an intellectual system, and a lofty pursuit. It was an abstract and empirical construction after the manner of Newton, and it was also an enterprise especially available to gentlemen. Though few American physicians were as zealous about medical theory as Rush, and fewer still presented systems of their own, yet the fondness for such medical theory was widespread. Rush might have considered Dr. James McClurg too flippant, irresolute, and roguish when he recommended that doctors not be wedded to any system but "treat it as a mistress; embrace it with ardour at present and discard it whenever we are disgusted with its defects, or attracted with the superior qualities of another." McClurg was probably not denying the importance and usefulness of either mistresses or medical theory. We know that he was an ardent devotee of medical theory at least. "Every step of experience approaches toward system; since, by discovering the natural relation of things it prepares us for establishing principles; and theory, or the application of these principles in explaining the phenomena around us, [is necessary to] the natural progress of knowledge." If system were rejected, "impenetrable dullness should henceforth be as necessary an appendage to the profession, as inflexible gravity. Genius must quit, in despair, a walk so little accommodated to his exertions; and art, considered as a mere species of traffic, must fall into the hands of the stupid, and sordid part of mankind." Here, Rush and McClurg were in complete agreement. Medicine practiced in the light of "system" afforded great "pleasure to the understanding." Learning and discovery were part of the work of the physician and necessary for the improvement of medical science; if the doctor neglected these, "he practiced medicine as a trade, instead of a profession."[17]

The contrast between a trade and a profession in the eighteenth century was, in the first place, a means of social elevation. In England, that distinction was supported by the loosely correlating class distinction of commoner and gentleman. In America, where class differences were much more vague and unstable, some of the accouterments of rank were called upon more insistently to support social distinction in oblique ways. Theory was usually linked with leisure, which, in turn, was often linked with income, which was frequently linked to class. Again, in America such linkage was slack and separable owing to more widespread wealth, more general leisure, and more broadly accessible education, but it never was completely absent. Medical theory, along with the empirical lore that constituted a good part of the medical curriculum, made the physician a more proficient healer, it was believed, but it also gave him the bearing of a gentleman; and this was also much the bearing of a professional man. The belief that classical learning should be prerequisite to medical education or, for that matter, "for any employment above those of the mechanic arts," had a similar basis. Such learning was "a fine preparation for acting in society with complacence, propriety, and dignity."[18]

Coupled with the usual curricular instruction at the medical schools was the cultivation of what was considered the proper self-regard for young medical gentlemen. This was what Rush had in mind when he commended that "portion of knowledge which floats about schools of medicine which is imbibed by every student, without his being conscious of it and which contributes to give his mind a medical texture." Fundamental to the doctor's self-regard was his relation to his patient. It was a friend and correspondent of Rush, Dr. Thomas Percival, who presented the most influential eighteenth-century discussion of that relationship. Percival's code of medical ethics was written to resolve a jurisdictional dispute between hospital physicians and surgeons, but he soon expanded it to cover other significant questions. Percival was himself a provincial Manchester physician who greatly admired the eminent London doctors, and in his more unpolished and precarious setting he felt called upon to render explicit what those worthies could take for granted. In one of the salient passages of his code, Percival bid doctors "so to unite *tenderness* with *firmness*, and *condescension* with *authority*, as to inspire the minds of their patients with gratitude, respect and confidence." (Emphasis in the original.) This prescription was so appealing that it was included in the medical codes of local American medical societies and was later incorporated into the code of the American Medical Association (1847), where it remained for the rest of the nineteenth century.[19]

The formula deserves careful scrutiny. What is immediately apparent in the phrasing is that the ideal attributes of the doctor, in a characteristically eighteenth-century way, are set in balance. The doctor is to unite "tenderness" (i.e., sympathy with suffering, affection, even attachment to the sufferer) with "firmness" (i.e., attachment to what is necessary or right, to principle, or even to duty). Tenderness is emotional and is offset by firmness, which is more likely to have a rational aspect, so that neither would become excessive. Such a balance was much sought after and not easily achieved. Rush, for example, wrote during the yellow fever epidemic of 1793, "I even strive to subdue my sympathy for my patients, otherwise I should sink under the accumulated loads of misery I am obliged to contemplate. You can recollect how much the loss of a single patient once a month used to affect me. Judge then how I must feel in hearing every morning of the death of three or four!" The patients were persons whose joys and sorrows Rush had sometimes made his own, yet they were also machines that had broken down and should be repaired. The physician's firmness lent itself to a kind of self-abstraction that sometimes permitted Rush to see himself as "an instrument in the hands of Providence." This seems to have relieved much anxiety and strengthened Rush's attachment to duty. He was twice stricken by yellow fever himself during the epidemic, but he refused to leave Philadelphia. "I had resolved to perish with my fellow citizens rather than dishonor my profession or religion by abandoning the city." Some other doctors fled, but Rush remained, and his heroism was widely acclaimed.[20]

Percival's admonition that doctors should unite "*condescension* with *authority*" at first might not seem balanced at all. However, once we discover that the word "condescension" in the eighteenth century meant humility (Dr. Johnson calls it "voluntary humiliation: descent from superiority") rather than arrogance, then the symmetry becomes apparent. Condescension was a peculiar form of humility that was available to those of elevated mind and station. It was the humane act of a superior, who while he committed it remained superior still, for what he was doing was an act of grace toward those on whose level he was placing himself. Doctors were cautioned against becoming angry at anything a sick man said or did. The physician must be affable and receptive: he could be familiar "without losing a particle of respect." One should not be too familiar. Dr. Philip Turner thought it best that doctors not choose their friends from among their patients.[21]

Condescension must be balanced by "authority," the right to command. Despite their assumption of the ways of the English gentleman, with its accompanying habit of command, many eighteenth-century American doctors still felt the need for a more incontrovertible justification of their right to take charge. Their argument here was usually functional, that is to say, they claimed that their authority derived from the nature of the work itself. (This resembled Dr. Morgan's justification of ranks in medicine.) Medical science was not amenable to common sense, therefore doctors had often to think and act in ways that contradicted the notions of the general population. Clearly, patients should obey prescriptions and not oppose their own inclinations and judgments to those of their physicians. A doctor must command in order to cure. Here the emphasis was decidedly more upon science than upon style.[22]

Occasionally, some physicians contraposed science and style. That should not be surprising in that the science of American doctors, for the most part, came from Edinburgh—those Americans traveling to Britain for medical study were usually dissenters and were excluded from English universities—while the style came from London. At times these two renowned centers of medical influence were antipathetic. Imagine the exasperation of the learned Dr. John Gregory, a professor at Edinburgh, who sedulously kept abreast of the most advanced Continental medical science, when he came up against the policy of the more backward, yet more decorous and prestigious, Royal College of Physicians in London that excluded Scottish-trained licentiates from becoming Fellows. Gregory attacked the special dress, the solemn and stately demeanor, the "corporation spirit," and the affectation of mystery as fraudulent supports for the physician's authority. The true foundation of the physician's right to command was his science. Gregory had no doubts that scientific learning would readily gain proper deference. The populace was ready enough to trust physicians, if vanity did not make physicians greatly overshoot their mark. After all, "nature," Gregory believed, along with many leading European Enlightenment thinkers, "never intended the bulk of mankind to think or act for themselves."[23]

Rush, Gregory's loyal and admiring pupil, at one point in his career pushed the opposition between science and style even more radically. "We pity the errors of those," he wrote, "who think that there can be no government without kings, no religion without priests, and they err as egrigiously [sic] who suppose that the science of medicine cannot exist without physicians." Yet even this flaunting declaration was not as radical as it might seem at first. Though Rush was avowedly intent upon throwing off the shackles of kings, he was equally certain that rational and representative governments required strong executives with broad discretion; while he scorned priests, he favored scriptural Protestant ministers; and though medical science might exist without doctors, nonetheless, somehow, physicians would always be necessary, only fewer of them. By simplifying medical science and educating laymen (Rush advocated both), the inequality between doctor and patient could be lessened, but it would not be eliminated. Shorn of the rigmarole of the haughty London physician, medical science still needed its exponent and emissary. In a somewhat implausible anecdote about the yellow fever epidemic, Rush told of being sent for by a foreigner whose only son was very seriously ill. Rush prescribed his usual simple and baneful remedy, bloodletting. He may have accompanied that prescription with a capsule summary of his medical theory. Then, "after a short pause, with a look of anguish directed upwards, he [the father] cried out in the French language, 'I will follow Reason to the last moment of my life.'" That French language, the unmitigated trust in Reason, and the look upwards were still, in the summer of 1793, harmonious for many Americans and linked to various kinds of deliverance. But important also was the physician called to the foreigner's side, for he was the agent of Reason and even Providence.[24]

Yet such idyllic scenes did not occur frequently, and, in fact, probably occurred less often as the years passed. Rush increasingly complained of "the slow and feeble operations of reason," and his disappointments with the events in France also led to some skepticism about the possibilities of reason in the broad range of human affairs. Nonetheless, he became more insistent upon his medical theory and its prescription of drastic bleeding. This remedy clashed with strong popular sentiments on healing, and the gap between science and general understanding widened. While Dr. Gregory in Scotland could confidently assert that scientific learning—by which he meant in part his own system of "Gregorian Physick"—would readily gain proper deference, Dr. Rush in America could never arrive at that kind of untroubled confidence. Though Rush's system, no more disastrous than Gregory's, ultimately won great influence in this country, that result came only after a number of reverses and much discomfiture, even at the hands of laymen. One of his most humiliating embroilments was the clash with the bilious English journalist, William Cobbett, then resident in Philadelphia, who wrote a series of tirades against the French Revolution and against those Americans who gave it even the mildest support. Cobbett could not resist a smash at Rush and his "bleeding system." With a lively mixture of invective, ridicule, and some rudimentary statistical investigation, Cobbett tried to tell the world the fate of those innocent mortals who fell into the clutches and systems of a doctrinaire friend of humanity. Rush was furious and summoned up all the power and connections at his disposal to drive Cobbett out of the country. Nevertheless, for many, Cobbett appeared to have come out the better in that encounter.[25]

Moreover, Rush seemed to move toward more prescriptive notions and greater authority as he became interested in mental illness and psychosomatic ailments. To what extent could a lunatic agree to his or her own treatment? Locke himself had thought that the insane had reverted to the state of beasts. Rush pressed forward to the use of psychological techniques in order to help deal with ordinary illness. "The introduction of moderate fear into the sick room of a patient with highly inflammatory fever," he wrote, "cooperates with other sedative remedies, for it [fear] is a passion which induces silence, a disposition to body rest, and restrains the appetite." He went further than this to suggest that even when doctors advised remedies of doubtful efficacy, those remedies often had beneficial effects owing primarily to the patients' belief in the doctors' judgment. Toward the end of his career, Rush was arguing that the physician's scientific knowledge, his gentlemanly bearing, and even the establishment of medical societies help maintain the physician's authority. Medical societies helped beget confidence in the profession, thereby leading sick people to send for their doctors more generally and to reward them more liberally. "We should appear to them [the patients]," Rush explained to his students in one of his last lectures, "as deputies from heaven, commissioned to guard the health and lives of our fellow citizens."[26]

Another support for the physician's authority was the custom of family practice, generally considered to be the most expedient way of administering healing. "A patient should confine the care of himself and his family exclusively and constantly to one physician. He will thereby acquire a correct knowledge of their habits and tempers; of the sympathies and antipathies of their constitutions; and of their individual predispositions to disease: all of which will contribute to render his practice more successful." This made possible a close relationship between the doctor and the patient; the physician was not only concerned with the patient's health and sickness (and in extreme situations, his very life and death) but also with such problems as his debt, his love, and his guilt. "Domestic troubles, when concealed," explained Rush, "are all very powerful countercurrents to the efficacy of medicine." The doctor's traditional vow of secrecy made personal disclosures seem safe and acceptable. Moreover, the physician drew closer yet, for his work required that he actually touch his patient and sometimes undress him, as a parent might. The various indications of the transfer of emotions from the parent-child relationship to the doctor-patient relationship, therefore, are not at all surprising. Doctors often mention their patients' "almost idolatrous expressions of gratitude and attachment"; the patients' descriptions of their feelings are less easy to come by. Yet there is much scattered and circumstantial evidence. For example, what is one to make of the reports that some eighteenth-century families put on mourning clothes when the family doctor died, or that the female patients of Dr. John Moultrie wept bitterly at his death and that some wore black for almost a year after?[27]

What is unmistakable is that doctors wished to foster a spirit of deference in their patients. The ideal attributes of the doctor in Percival's code were set in balance; the ideal attitudes of the patients toward their doctors ("gratitude, respect and confidence") were not. There was no worry about excess there. Such deference was important to the professional relationship, for the doctor was not simply selling—he was, in some degree, commanding. That was the basis of much of the "professional ethic" developed during the nineteenth century. The doctor, in prescribing, was in some measure responsible for the outcome. *Caveat emptor* was inappropriate here because the buyer was of necessity acting on someone else's say-so. The doctors' authoritativeness and dignity could never be carelessly dispensed with. They must be brought to bear upon those who ranked above the physician socially as well as those who ranked below. Rush held the mild and forbearing Dr. Fothergill—who walked out on a "lady of high birth, and wife of a nobleman in one of the most ancient families in Great Britain," rather than be kept waiting—as a model. Though Fothergill had been widely denounced for "his supposed insolent conduct," her Ladyship soon came to wait upon him for his advice and prescriptions, Rush reported with evident gratification.[28]

The students at the Medical College in Philadelphia who came under the influence of Dr. John Morgan and, more particularly, Dr. Benjamin Rush, were therefore fitted not only for the work of the physician but also for the social position and outlook that their teachers thought were connected with medical work. This student body was a sizable group because the College in Philadelphia produced more physicians than any other school of the day, and those young doctors carried its teachings to the leading metropolises and the backwater villages of the country. Nevertheless, the gentlemanly medicine, as practiced in the various seaboard cities and coastal regions, quickly took on distinct, local characteristics that were important and required some attention.[29]

Rush's influence was particularly marked in the South, because that section received and accepted the prevailing modes of medical thought and practice but produced little medical science of its own. The South had no enduring medical school and no teaching hospital until the 1830s. The absence of major cities in Virginia helps explain much of the quiescence of this largest and most populous Southern state. The opportunity to see and compare many medical cases over a brief span of time provided an important stimulus to medical thinking and learning that was not easily available to Virginians. A good number of them went to Edinburgh to study and brought back the science and style of the British doctor, which they sustained in a region well stocked with home-grown surgeon-apothecaries. By the early nineteenth century, many of the better-trained Virginia doctors took their education in the North, principally in Philadelphia but sometimes in New York.[30]

Crevecoeur thought that Charleston was the most brilliant of American cities, and, clearly, it gave rise to the most lively medical center in the South. Yet its swift and luxuriant medical burgeoning did not strike deep roots in native soil. The numerous medical publications struck off by the Charleston presses were largely the work of physicians born and educated in Europe. Such men were usually without strong local attachments and did not give much of their energies to the setting up of medical institutions in Charleston. David Ramsay, an exception, was born in America and educated at the Medical School in Philadelphia. Writing to his teacher, Benjamin Rush, Ramsay explained: "I am a citizen of the world, & therefore despise national reflections; & hope I am not inconsistent, when I express my ardent wish that Law, Physic & Divinity may be administered to my country by its own sons. . . . British goods were not more necessary to these Southern states than British Doctors, Lawyers & etc. I want America to be *'totus in se ipso teres atque rotundus'* [thoroughly well developed, in all respects independent]."[31]

Ramsay rose to the leadership of the medical profession in Charleston, conducting his practice along the lines laid down by Dr. Rush; his success owed much to his own remarkable vigor as well as to the fact that some of the notables who had led the medical fraternity there were discredited by their Loyalism during the Revolution. Ramsay helped organize the Medical Society of South Carolina and soon became its president. This group immediately petitioned the legislature for licensing and censorial powers, to keep "improper persons, and those not duly qualified, from practicing the medical art." They also planned to inspect the apothecary shops in order to guarantee the quality of drugs. Significantly, the seal of the Medical Society featured a profile of Benjamin Franklin and its first honorary member was Benjamin Rush. Charleston, however, did not support the illustrious medical community that Ramsay had hoped to build. His journal, *The Charleston Medical Register*, survived for only one issue. Ramsay's own nephew, though properly trained in Philadelphia and active in the Medical Society of South Carolina, abandoned medical practice to become a cotton planter, finding that calling more honorable and profitable.[32]

That Charleston did not become a serious contender with Philadelphia for the leadership of American medicine might have been predicted; but that New York City did not is somewhat surprising. Up to the Revolution, Philadelphia was America's largest city, but after 1775 New York quickly overtook and surpassed Philadelphia in population and wealth. Medicine in New York was off to an auspicious start before the Revolution, and much of that promise can be seen in the careers of Drs. John and Samuel Bard, father and son. John Bard was born in Philadelphia but, after finishing his apprenticeship with an English surgeon living in the city, he moved on to New York, looking for more ample opportunities. In New York he prospered, doing the work of a physician, surgeon, and apothecary, and treading upon the heels of the newly established Anglican office-holding classes that came to dominate New York society. John Bard decided to give his son, Samuel, the education that would enable him to enter such fashionable society with ease. Samuel therefore attended King's College and upon graduation sailed for Europe to study medicine at Edinburgh. He completed his medical studies there two years after John Morgan, and he returned to New York to follow Morgan's lead and set up a medical college in New York City.[33]

Samuel Bard occupied the Chair of Theory and Practice of Medicine at the New York school as Morgan had in Philadelphia. The New York medical school thrived right up to the Revolution but, at that point, the parallels between the medical histories of New York and Philadelphia disappeared. Unlike Morgan and Rush, who were patriots (Rush was a signer of the Declaration of Independence), the Bards, father and son, were Loyalists. After the war they retired from public activity, and Samuel was replaced by Nicholas Romayne in the leadership of medical education in New York City. Romayne, a brilliant but tempestuous young man, had received an extraordinary medical education in Edinburgh, London, Paris, and Leyden. "His superior attainments in literature and medicine elevated him with high notions, and filled him with contemptuous notions of some who had been less fortunate in education than himself." This haughtiness was particularly disabling for leadership of that motley group of patriot doctors, most of whom had much less preparation for their profession than did Dr. Romayne. The outcome was the growth of various fissiparous coteries and factions, and Samuel Bard quickly returned to the fray.[34]

It is not easy to make sense of the divisions and bickerings among the rival professors, medical schools, and political authorities in New York. There were Patriots and Loyalists, Presbyterians and Anglicans, Democrats and Federalists—but such categories rapidly ceased to be in any way descriptive of the complicated factions engaged in the struggle. Amidst such strife, medical education in New York declined precipitously. In the twenty-five years after the reestablishment of medical teaching at Columbia College, the faculty graduated only thirty-five students.

Factionalism was New York's undoing. Not that there were no divisions in the medical community in Philadelphia; but there, one faction achieved dominance and moved ahead with vision and energy. That, conspicuously, was not the case in New York.[35]

Such dissension was not a serious issue in New England. Though New England was the major habitat for the forming of the American clergy as a profession, it remained on the periphery of the movement for the creation of the American medical profession. The turning aside from established ways in piety and worship that had been the impetus for the founding of New England society lent support to the turning aside from established ways in medicine and even law. Few British physicians came to New England, and there was no way to properly train physicians according to the standards of the day until Harvard Medical School was organized after the Revolutionary War. Before then, much of the work of physicians was done by ministers and surgeon-apothecaries.[36]

The ministers, the most highly educated group in colonial New England, through their knowledge of the classical languages, had access to the medical treatises that made up a large part of the education of a physician. These ministers, dedicated to the cure of souls, often attended to the bodies as well, and members of their congregations turned to them for instruction and treatment when beset with the menacing diseases that were endemic in colonial America. Even those ministers who did no healing often took an interest in medical matters, and the weight their views carried is indicated by Cotton Mather's successful introduction of small-pox inoculation into Boston against the opposition of most of the leading physicians of the town.[37]

Mather not only read widely in the classical and contemporary treatises in medicine, he added a work of his own. His *Angel of Bethesda* (1724) is a remarkable study that reveals some of the social and intellectual setting in which New England medicine developed. The book contains an assortment of religious and moral admonitions, medical theories, disease descriptions, drug recipes, and maxims for good health and long life. The underlying theme of Mather's book is the doctrine of Providence. The health and well-being of our bodies and our souls are in God's hands, and most sickness is punishment for sin and incitement to repentance. However, not all illness was providential punishment, and the resort to medicine was "obedience to God, who has commanded the use of means." Mather's discussion of syphilis, an extreme example, for it was an illness most closely connected with sinning, went like this: "The French pox . . . 'tis a new scourge, which the vengeance of a righteous God, has not until the later ages inflicted on the growing wickedness of the world." It was so foul that Mather did not linger on its symptoms. "Lett thy sin, be now repented of; and not only with the attrition of a sorrow for having injured thyself, but with contrition of a sorrow for having displeased the Great God." He did not want to recommend any remedies, yet "whoremongers and adulterers God shall judge." Therefore, he included one recipe—a quarter of an ounce of cologninesda infused in a quart of proper wine—and then commanded "gett ye gone to the Cheirurgeon"![38]

The honored physician got his comeuppance from this minister. Mather, with incomparable erudition, devoted an entire chapter to the listing of conflicting opinions of eminent doctors on ailments and remedies. He also ridiculed medical theory: "There was a physician so celebrated for his learned writing, reasoning, disputing, distinguishing, and making of conclusions, that his auditors expected, he would not only cure diseases, but even raise the dead. But after all, when he came to practice, hardly any of his patients escaped with their lives. They did by their death so generally expiate the empty knowledge of the professor, that with confusion he bid adieu to the world, and ended his days in a convent." Yet Mather's work was not without theory. In fact, he proposed a germ theory of disease a century and a half before American doctors came to accept it, and he entered into the debate between the animists and the mechanists, siding with the animists. Yet for Mather these theories were conjectural and had little effect upon the assortment of remedies he collected and presented.[39]

Even after the "Angelical conjunction of Divinity and Physic" had been sundered in the late eighteenth century, New England medicine maintained much of the earlier nonspeculative bias. When the Harvard Medical School opened in 1783, the most influential medical men did not take the Chair of Theory and Practice, as in New York and Philadelphia, but rather the Chairs of Anatomy and Materia Medica. Neither John Warren nor Aaron Dexter, who filed these two positions, had ever trained in a medical school, and neither had an M.D. degree. The Chair in Medical Theory was given to Benjamin Waterhouse, an outsider, whose checkered career at Harvard indicated, among other things, some of the hostility that the modes of the English physician could excite in New England. Waterhouse had studied medicine in Europe for six years and returned wearing the full costume of a London physician. In his theoretical work, he aligned himself with the animists, considering George Ernst Stahl the great medical thinker of the age. This was probably more acceptable than the mechanical notions (Waterhouse had been required to declare himself a Protestant Christian before he took his chair) but as Waterhouse himself observed, New Englanders characteristically downgraded the importance of medical theory altogether. "The systems of Physick are mostly compilations and differ from one another rather in neatness, order, and arrogance, than in anything material," the constitution of the Middlesex Medical Association stated. When Rhode Island opened its medical school in 1811, the trustees did not appoint a professor of Theory and Practice of Medicine at all.[40]

Waterhouse's unpopularity had many sources, for he was a Jeffersonian Republican and a Quaker, and he was given to loose and ambiguous discourse about those unenlightened days when "the priest, the conjurer, and the physician were united in the same person." From the beginning, his relations with the Harvard medical faculty and the leading Boston doctors was strained. By 1812 the tension had become too great and Waterhouse left Harvard in a cross-fire of affronts and accusations.[41]

From Philadelphia, the New England distrust of theoretical innovation in medicine seemed to be a matter of provincial conservatism. New Englanders, of course, saw it as a steadiness that protected them from sliding into the ways of improvidence and error. After some of the more elegant Tory doctors had gone, the leadership of New England medicine shifted to a group of bold and skillful surgeons resembling, somewhat, the English surgeon-apothecary in practice and culture, yet better educated than their English counterparts. In the seventeenth century, home-bred medical men in New England learned their skills through an apprenticeship, which they usually had entered after a primary school education. By the eighteenth century, the most prominent native-born medical men took their apprenticeship training after graduating Harvard. And by the late eighteenth century, some study and practice with an eminent London surgeon (but rarely formal study in a European medical school) was part of the training of the New England men of first rank. In a day when medical theory had such grievous consequences, the stolid practical-mindedness of New England doctors could be of great advantage. Nevertheless, their suspicion of what seemed to be metropolitan sophistication—exploratory, challenging, modern therapeutics—meant that New England could not truly contest Philadelphia's preeminence in American medicine. Some of the most prominent young men from Boston went to Philadelphia for their medical training.[42]

It was in Philadelphia, therefore, during the years 1750–1830, that the authoritative standards and goals of the American medical profession were defined. This cluster of ideas, which arose in the medical schools, blended with the more immediate professional accomplishments, which usually came from the medical societies. The Revolution brought together physicians from all parts of the continent, and the army formed them into a temporary society that made them "more sensible of the importance of unity in their endeavors." The active spirit of professional organization spread rapidly and was accompanied by the enactment of medical licensing laws aimed at raising the standards and perhaps the incomes of practitioners. By 1830 there were only three states without medical practice laws. The Medical Department at the University of Pennsylvania, at the urging of Rush and others, had set high educational requirements for the medical degree in the hope that the honor, authority, and income of doctors would be raised. The department also appealed to the legislature to drive irregular practitioners, those "not qualified by education or talents," out of business. Yet for Rush and his colleagues, the concern for the doctor's honor and authority took precedence over the concern for his income.[43]

The notion of the honor and authority of the doctor that emanated from Philadelphia derived originally from a British setting. What these leading men of American medicine were trying to do, with various degrees of awareness, was to transfer and adapt the knowledge and bearing of the uppermost rank of British medicine to American medical practice. This transfer was most obvious in the appropriation of the varied appurtenances of the British physician—his classical learning, his medical theory, and often even his costume. The leaders of the American profession also accepted some of the British gentleman's ostensible disdain for commercial means and ends. More fundamentally, they saw the axis of the relation between the doctor and the patient not in the sale of services but in the giving of directives. Adopting the mode of the British physician was helpful here, but clearly it was not enough. American doctors also felt called upon to explicitly develop a functional justification for their authority—they must command in order to cure. Moreover, the psychological conditions of the doctor's system of family practice helped foster the deference of the patient, and the restraints of the medical practice laws and medical school admissions discouraged alternative medical styles. It was this variegated assortment of striving and

accomplishment that was packed into the exuberantly annuncia-
tory slogan—that medicine should be practiced as a profession
and not a trade.[44]

Yet an awareness of the fragility of much that had been
achieved was also apparent. Complaints by physicians about
popular resistance to "the operations of reason" and its dictates
were common. While the medical theory of the gentleman-
physician strengthened his resolve to impose a "heroic" treatment, the lamentable outcome of those measures led many patients to call into question the physicians' pronouncements and
presumptions, and to look elsewhere for healing. Along with the
increasing number of medical practice acts adopted by the various state legislatures, signifying the arrival of the gentleman-
physician, there was unmistakable evidence of a concomitant
rapid and vigorous growth of "quackery," all manner of unorthodox and sectarian medicine. This augured a less propitious era
ahead.[45]

3

The Rise of the Lawyers

The extraordinary hold that law and lawyers have upon American society today owes much to a remarkable conjunction of events that occurred two hundred years ago. The rise and establishment of the American republic in the last decades of the eighteenth century went hand in hand with the rise of American lawyers to preeminence among the professions and to influential positions within the community at large. It was from those positions that American lawyers unselfconsciously imposed their particular occupational near- and farsightedness upon the very structure of the new nation, with lasting effects. The rise of the nation and of the bar aided and impelled each other, however both clearly drew upon broader sources. As for lawyers, their unusual importance might readily have been expected in the swiftly expanding and yet decentralized society of the late eighteenth century. For in such a society, public rules seemed precarious and indispensable. The law, moreover—that great body of public rules derived from England—adapted to local conditions, and practiced and promoted by lawyers, proved particularly congenial to many Americans. It comprised both ideals and restraints, justice and order; it protected rights and stimulated enterprise. Furthermore, the rise of the bar was also linked to the growing social inequalities of late eighteenth-century America. These lent a new attractiveness to the English society of ranks, making the eminent Westminster barrister and his usages, like those of the Anglican priest and the London physician, models for ambition and emulation.[1]

Even so, the American lawyer ultimately achieved an importance in his country that far surpassed that of his counterpart in Britain. The remarkable conjunction of the ascendant nation and bar goes far to help explain that fact. This was most evident in that grand and gravid event of the late eighteenth century, the making of the Constitution. The framers, most of whom happened to be lawyers, described that Constitution, in a phrase within the text itself that was to have far-reaching consequences, as the "supreme Law of the Land." Since then, innumerable politicians and scholars have argued over the significance of the adjective supreme. They, like the framers, have almost taken for granted the basal noun *law*. Yet, in construing the Constitution as law, the framers provided the momentous option of interpreting and enforcing the fundamental principles of our national government through routine judicial processes.[2]

This was simultaneously a narrowing and an expansion of the concept of constitution. Derived from the Latin *constitutionem*—meaning disposition, temper, and aggregate of powers—the term constitution, by the eighteenth century, denoted a body of fundamental principles through which a nation was formed and governed and by which its government might be criticized. Those fundamental principles could be imbedded in customs and institutions as well as in laws. When Jefferson, in 1776, accused the king of combining with others "to subject us to a jurisdiction foreign to our Constitution and unacknowledged by our laws," he was drawing upon this loose but awesome sense of the word. Still, in 1787, the framers created a constitution in which fundamental principles were translated into explicit rules set out in statutelike form that might be interpreted and given force by the courts.[3]

The legal profession, therefore, could become an *ex officio* interpreter of our national credo. This was something almost uniquely American. There had been some fitful and uncertain precedents for such a role within the British legal tradition, but by the eighteenth century, whatever else the British Constitution was, it was for the most part whatever Parliament said it was. Also, in the litigation of the Confederation period, some state courts occasionally drew upon what they considered primary truths of government in deciding particular cases. However, they could not depend upon their constitutions as warrant for such powers. The written state constitutions of that era (like those later adopted by other nations) frequently contained high-flown principles but usually made no provision for given such principles effect—except insofar as legislatures, executives, or public sentiment chose to do so. The Massachusetts Constitution of 1780, for example, perhaps the most doctrinally sophisticated constitution of that period, simply stated:

> A frequent recurrence to the fundamental principles of the constitution, and a constant adherence to those of piety, justice, moderation, temperance, industry, and frugality, are absolutely

necessary to preserve the advantages of liberty and to maintain a free government. The people ought, consequently, to have a particular attention to those principles, in the choice of their officers and representatives; and they have a right to require of their lawgivers and magistrates an exact and constant observance of them, in the formation and execution of the laws necessary for the good administration of the commonwealth.

There was as yet no hint that the courts might have a special role in interpreting and giving force to those principles.[4]

Nonetheless, such a view was gaining support in America, particularly among lawyers and judges. Even Jefferson, before he tangled with his Federalist judges, had cautiously taken up this idea. "In the arguments in favor of the declaration of rights," he wrote to Madison supporting the adoption of what became the first ten amendments, "you omit one which has great weight with me; the legal check which it puts into the hands of the judiciary. This is a body, which, if rendered independent and kept strictly to their own department, merits great confidence for their learning and integrity. In fact, what degree of confidence would be too much, for a body composed of such men as Wythe, Blair and Pendleton? On characters like these, '*civium ardor prava jubentium*' ('wayward zeal of fellow-citizens') would make no impression." The Constitution, in declaring itself law, gave sanction to such an elevated function for the courts and for the privileged access of the American legal profession to grand and consequential causes.[5]

The meaning of the Constitution and its underlying principles became much the speciality of the courts and their lawyers. That was not made inevitable, in and of itself, by the clause that described the Constitution as law and declared that "judges shall be bound thereby." That clause, however, did provide the basis for the far-reaching Judiciary Act of 1789, adopted by the first Federal Congress, and for the Marshall decisions that followed.[6]

How the bar achieved the position that enabled it to impose, in this way, its occupational partiality upon the nation as a whole deserves some examination. There was no professional bar for most of the seventeenth century in the American colonies, and a large part of law work of that era was in the hands of laymen and laywomen. Those "going to law" in the Mayor's Court of New York, for example, and who were unable to appear to conduct their own cases, would appoint their wives or friends to act for them. Gradually, a few names began to show up on the records of the court more and more often, identifying attorneys who represented many different litigants. These seventeenth-century attorneys usually had little formal education in the law, and the judges who presided at these courts often had even less. Nevertheless, together they managed to bring the rudiments of English law into the colonies, along with some intended and unintended modifications; it was a law closer to that of the local and provincial courts in England than to that of the King's Courts. One of the reasons there was little objection to mere attorneys pleading before all the tribunals in the colonies before the mid-eighteenth century was that these tribunals were originally considered comparable to the county courts and the Courts of Quarter Session in England, and attorneys had the right of audience at those. In the course of the eighteenth century, however, the superior courts in the colonies increasingly were likened to, and modeled after, the more exalted and methodical Westminster courts, and the upgrading of the American legal profession went hand in hand with that comparison.[7]

Not only were the social usages at the King's Courts more elaborate than those at local courts, but the legal practice itself was more intricate and consequential. The fundamental document of the legal practice at these principal common-law courts was the writ. This was a device whose object, in the eighteenth century, was the definition of the issue for decision. A major part of the counsel's pleading was a nice discrimination between rival writs. By the eighteenth century, the process of pleading had been overlaid with an accumulation of technicalities from which the interests of the litigants emerged only with difficulty. English lawyers had yielded to the fascination that subtlety sometimes exercises over intellect and learning, and they had invested the mysteries of writ and pleading with a prestige that the brightest American lawyers would find hard to resist. But a feature of the English legal system of much greater significance for American lawyers was its linking of law to broad public concerns. This was the legacy of the political struggles of the seventeenth century, and Sir Edward Coke, a lawyer skilled in the crabbed scholarship of feudal holdings and at the same time a man of affairs active in the great political contests of his day, was its illustrious exemplar. Coke, through his *Institutes,* enjoyed an extraordinary reputation among the learned and ambitious American lawyers of the eighteenth century; he seemed to identify the blessings of liberty with the services of the common law.[8]

The acceptance of English rules of practice was closely tied to the adoption of the English system of courts, and this adoption, irregular and incomplete as it was, provides one of the clearest indications of the rise of the legal profession in America. The making of the legal profession took place largely in the law courts. Lawyers did establish bar associations in the eighteenth century comparable to the contemporary medical societies and ministerial associations, and they did set up a variety of educational enterprises; the law school at Litchfield, Connecticut, almost matched the medical school in Philadelphia in national reputation during the early national period. However, as important as these associations and schools were, they were outweighed in influence by the courts themselves in the forming of the profession. Unlike the doctors and ministers, the lawyers' day-to-day work brought them together in a spectacular forum where they could contend, collaborate, fraternize with each other, and develop the cohesiveness of common customs of the law.[9]

American higher courts of the eighteenth century adopted some of the pageantry, technicality, and doctrine of the English Courts of Westminster. Chief Justice Hutchinson of Massachusetts introduced the distinction between barrister and attorney; only barristers were permitted to plead before the Superior Court. These Massachusetts barristers were not, for the most part, men who had studied at the Inns of Court, but simply the most learned and most respected lawyers in the province. Where ranking was adopted in the other colonies (New Jersey went further than most in setting up the grade of serjeants as well as barristers), the upper ranks were also usually home grown. Only in South Carolina did most of the barristers who prevailed at the higher courts actually attend the Inns of Court in England. Even where no distinguishing titles were officially adopted, as in Maryland and Pennsylvania, the gap between the lawyers who gained a hold upon the higher courts in the province and those who thrived amidst the simpler and unpolished justice of the country courts widened sharply in the eighteenth century. When Massachusetts's higher courts took up the wearing of legal gowns and wigs, the New York Supreme Court quickly adopted the costume, and a similar practice spread throughout the colonies. Even folksy and genial Patrick Henry, scorned by Jefferson for his triumphs before the amateur judges and rural juries of local courts, knew enough to discard his buckskin britches for dignified black dress and a freshly powdered wig when he came before the General Court of Virginia.[10]

The bench and bar of the American superior courts in the eighteenth century gradually set aside the more informal legal devices of the previous century and increasingly resorted to an assortment of ancient writs, some of which were already obsolete in the King's courts back in England. New York's leading lawyers, for example, discussed the use they could make of the antique writ of right, which dated back to Henry II in the twelfth century. The chief obstacle to its use was that the process appropriate to this writ required knights, and these were in short supply in New York. The lawyers, nonetheless, resolved this difficulty by deciding that "substantial freeholders" would do for this purpose. They also urged the more extensive use of special pleading. Soon the most eminent lawyers throughout the colonies came to pride themselves on their skill in such pleading, which they held to be the acme of the common law—along with Coke's Whiggish teachings. It is remarkable, but not surprising, that from among these "reactionary" lawyers came many of the revolutionary leaders in the colonial struggle with England.[11]

Part of the responsibility for the elevating of these superior courts and their bars lay with British policy. The attempt to assert control over the colonies and to bind them more closely to the mother country predisposed British officials toward measures of centralization—particularly those that gave more importance to officers appointed through the prerogative of the King, as were most superior judges. The creation of the Chancery Courts (which in the absence of Courts of Exchequer, dealt with quitrents) and Admiralty Courts (which enforced the Navigation Acts) promoted imperial regulation and also brought the colonial court system closer to the English model. British merchants urged the centralization of the judicial system and the giving of full play to the appellate process in the higher courts, in order to protect their business transactions from the vagaries of local custom. Colonial governors, uneasy with what they considered the backwardness and eccentricity of American justice, tried to bring the provincial legal order into line. "It would grieve a man," wrote Governor Bellomont, "to see our noble English laws so miserably mangled and prophaned." Such displeasure was often shared by the colonial upper classes of the eighteenth century and the foremost colonial lawyers, who were usually of them or served them.[12]

For the lawyers, the advance of legal science (which involved adoption of English ways) and the advance of the legal profession amounted to almost the same thing. They argued that the judges of the superior courts must be lawyers and not simply political favorites. This would make judgeships, honored and remunerative positions in the colonial era, more accessible to lawyers and would give more sophisticated legal forms and doctrines broader acceptance. In addition, many lawyers urged the restriction of entry into the profession. This would not only benefit those already in it but would improve the system of justice as well. The "unletter'd Blockheads" in particular must be kept out. Their ineptitude "profaned and dishonour'd the Law," and led them inevitably to "pettyfoggery," cheating clients through artifice and "chicane," for such lawyers could survive in no other way. The most acceptable method of limiting entry into the profession was the raising of educational qualifications. A college education as well as an extended apprenticeship with a recognized lawyer became prerequisites for practice in many jurisdictions.[13]

These requirements reveal the hybrid quality of the American profession. Though the leading practitioners would strive for the elevation of the English barrister and the Courts of Westminster, they could never completely expunge the traits of the more lowly English attorney and the Courts of Quarter Session. The broadening and polish of a liberal arts education was expected of the barrister but only the more mechanical and subservient apprenticeship training was required of the British attorney. William Livingston, one of the most influential lawyers of the Middle Colonies, complained that apprenticeship was "a servile Drudgery . . . fit only for a slave to submit to. . . . As if, in order to be fitted for a Profession, of all others the most genteel and venerable, and which requires a penetrative Genius and assidious [sic] Applications to reading, a Man must devote himself to the servitude of Scribbling eternally; a Way of spending time most irksome and intolerable to a young Gentleman of a thoughtful and studious Turn of Mind." Thomas Jefferson recommended that young law students devote themselves to private study and avoid legal apprenticeship; Alexander Hamilton escaped apprenticeship and simply "read law" under the guidance of Robert Troup. Nevertheless apprenticeship in a lawyer's office remained the prevailing form of legal training in America.[14]

The usages of payment that the American lawyers adopted also suggest the mixed origins of the profession. Like the English attorney, the American lawyer's payment was based upon a fee schedule usually set by the legislature or the courts. The lawyers insisted that both the legal system and the profession would benefit if those fees were high. For then, gentlemen of distinguished abilities would apply themselves to the work, and frivolous and immoral litigation might be discouraged. Yet these fees were often given an honorary character. In some early decisions of the courts; the American lawyer, like the English barrister, was not permitted to sue for his fee—that seemed too mercenary; and surely he should not sue for anything above the amount provided by the fee bill, however inadequate that might be.[15]

The setting up of the circuit courts in the eighteenth century was another extension of the more highly wrought English law and, at the same time, a boon to the better trained American lawyers. The circuits were formed in rough imitation of the English *nisi prius* system, through which judges and barristers of Westminster brought some of the King's justice to the provinces. In both England and America, the judges and lawyers of the superior courts on circuit usually traveled, ate, lodged, and caroused together, and the agreeable good-fellowship of this experience was acclaimed by lawyers on both sides of the Atlantic. The reverse aspect of this cohesiveness was exclusion. The superior court lawyers on circuit overawed the lawyers of the county courts and narrowed the jurisdiction of the local justices of peace,—those "poor, mean, ignorant and unworthy Persons." Among the favorite proposals of the eminent practitioners of the higher courts were blocking the county court attorneys from higher court pleading and lowering of the maximum that could be sued for before the justices of the peace. These proposals extended the range of a more rigorous legality and the market of litigation for the more learned lawyers.[16]

The varied and often short-lived lawyers' associations started up in many of the colonies during the eighteenth century also evinced the mixed beginnings of the American profession as well as its knack for linking public benefit and private advantage. Like the English attorneys' societies of that era, these American associations were usually informal clubs made up chiefly of the most eminent practitioners who met frequently in a local tavern to profitably mix business and pleasure. In Massachusetts, however, the associations may have included all who could professionally plead in the courts, much like the English barristers' Inns. In South Carolina, where most of the leading practitioners actually had been "called to the bar" by the various English inns of Court, lawyers did not form local associations, for many considered themselves already members of those English Inns. Where lawyers' associations did exist, they busied themselves with efforts to control entry into the profession and to influence the fee bills. Invariably they believed these endeavors would further the public good and at the same time "introduce more Regularity, Urbanity, Candor and Politeness as well as Honor, Equity and Humanity, among the regular Professors."[17]

The remarkable ease and constancy with which the lawyers could identify their own betterment with the well-being of society was not an indication of inordinate vanity, self-deception, or hypocrisy. They were no more predisposed to such shortcomings than anyone else. Rather it indicates that the lawyers were acting in an atmosphere of moral legitimacy that supported their increasing assertiveness and allowed them to apply their full strength in order to get what they wanted. Some suggestion of that atmosphere can be seen in the rapidly increasing numbers of young men in the colonies choosing the law as a career in the last half of the eighteenth century. Not only did the law overtake and surpass the ministry as the calling of the graduates of Harvard, Yale, and Princeton, but in the often expressed opinion of the day it was the brightest students who chose the law. Undoubtedly, this shift owed much to the growing profitability of legal practice in America, where increasing, wealth and lucrative suits probably went together, and also to the informing example of the mother country, where legal learning and ability could lead notoriously to sizable fortunes. Yet a closer look at the particular young men choosing the law reveals that such an explanation is incomplete. When Jefferson, for example, decided upon law in Virginia, the statutory restrictions on fees in that colony kept income from legal practice embarrassingly low. And while John Adams probably assumed that any of the learned professions would provide respectable earnings, nevertheless he seems to have given little consideration to income in his decision to become a lawyer rather than a minister. It was his doubts about Calvinist orthodoxy that turned him toward law, despite his feeling that his inclination was towards the ministry.[18]

Such doubts among some of the brighter and more fashionably minded young men in New England were part of a much broader shift in understanding that made mundane happiness and liberty—important notions to the lawyers of the day—watchwords of the eighteenth century. A new sense of God's benevolence, and His increasing remoteness from everyday life, filtered through much of the new writing in religion, science, politics, and literature. God wished man happy and, to this end, gave him conscious and reason and the liberty to exercise them. This implied a more favorable estimate of man than was characteristic of an earlier day. For happiness looked to man's desires, and liberty depended upon his conscience and reason—requiring that the desires, conscience, and reason of men be less impaired than previously would have been allowed. For the Puritans, perhaps too extreme an example of that earlier day, liberty usually referred to Christian liberty (freedom from Adam's sin and Jewish law) while happiness (more often called blessedness) was more directly dependent upon God's grace. James Wilson's declaration that happiness was man's end and the aim of his government, and Daniel Dulany's assertion that liberty was salvation in politics, would have discomfited the generation of their parents. In America in the eighteenth century, liberty, happiness, and rights, with all their built-in and ineradicable ambiguity, were characteristically translated into rules; and rules were the lawyer's business. The lawyers, therefore, became the embodiment of some of the commanding ideas and discriminations of the era—not a perfect embodiment, far from it, but a more perfect embodiment than any other compact group in America. This was one source of the honor and prominence of the eighteenth-century American legal profession.[19]

From such an elevation, the lawyer was prepared to deal with his client with authority. That authority was supported by the rules of the court in which the lawyer practiced. As an officer of the court, he was clothed in some measure with the court's power. His engagement in a case gave him the right to command the court's processes of summons and subpoena, and the court's lower officers were at his call to execute his will in behalf of his client. Again, the mixed traditions of the American profession provided a unique amalgam. The American lawyer, whatever his title, took an oath to the court, as did the English attorney. Such an oath might seem demeaning to an English barrister, whose conduct was governed by his Inn and by the unwritten code of the gentleman—a mixture of the class manners and morals of the English gentry. But for the American lawyer, the oath could be dignifying, precisely because he was not usually a member of an illustrious Inn and there was no comparable gentry class in America to provide protective coloration for a position of command. As an officer of the honorable court, the American lawyer pledged his fidelity, and he was expected to balance his obligation to the court against his obligation to his client. Some closeness to his client was encouraged by the common-law rule of privileged communication, which legally recognized the confidentiality of the information the client divulged to his lawyer. But it was the client who was prompted to confess to the lawyer and not the lawyer to the client. In the American setting, that particular kind of closeness served to give the lawyer an august magnanimity. He could sympathize with the client but must not identify with his cause. In a twofold relationship resembling that of the doctor and the patient as well as the minister and his flock, the lawyer owed fidelity to his client but also to the system of justice that supplied the lawyer's reason for being. The Delaware Oath of 1704 required that the lawyer not only be faithful to his client but that he "stand with the order of the law."[20]

In the actual process of pleading, the American lawyer took on some of the prerogatives of the English barrister. As long as the lawyer was retained, he had exclusive control of the litigation. The client had no right to interfere with the "due and orderly conduct of the suit." Whatever proceedings the lawyer chose were considered by the court to be approved by the client in advance. The lawyer could also bind the client in many matters related to the case. Such dominion, however, was relieved by its narrow scope and its transience. American lawyers rarely served as general agents for families and estates as did the English attorneys. The lawyer's relation to the client was much more short-lived and restricted than the doctors' and ministers' relations to their patients and parishioners, and therefore it lacked any similar emotional bond. Such aloofness was apparent in Theophilus Parsons's reply when he was asked if it were true that he had never lost a case. "It is Sir. . . . I assure you that it is literally and precisely true. I never lost a case in my life; and the reason I suppose is, I never had one. My clients have lost a great many; but their cases were not mine."[21]

Such remoteness and prominence meant that the lawyer could readily be cast as either hero or villain depending upon circumstance, and, in America, circumstances were varied enough so the lawyer would be given both roles. Antilawyer sentiment had a venerable history reaching back to the beginnings of the profession. The belief that a lawyer must be some sort of a scoundrel found expression intermittently among almost all classes in this country. To debtors, the lawyer seemed to be a despoiler who, as the agent of creditors, hardheartedly wrested away poor men's sustenance; to merchants, the lawyer often appeared as an obfuscator who delayed the straightforward resolution of conflicts through a self-serving adherence to outmoded forms; to ardent patriots after the Revolution, the lawyer presented himself as the ally of Tories trying to reclaim their holdings and undo the just punishments of revolutionary justice. The courts themselves with their adversary system could be perplexing. That the lawyer usually felt it his duty in those courts to defend even those whom he believed to be guilty was a moral position too sophisticated for many onlookers. "[W]e in the Country know no difference between a Lawyer and a Lyer," explained a popular almanac. Inattention to that difference owed something to an enduring Puritan tradition of enmity toward English legal proceedings. Imagine the dismay of those still deeply influenced by that tradition when the rise of American lawyers seemed to demonstrate that the wages of sin were now fame and fortune.[22]

Perhaps it was this complex and sporadic enmity of laymen

toward the bar as well as the weakness of the bond between individual lawyers and their clients that helped give a peculiar vitality to the bond between fellow lawyers. Enlarging upon the
time-honored and somewhat idealized camaraderie of the circuit,
lawyers frequently boasted of the affability within their profession. They addressed each other as "brother," and often shook
hands at the end of each trial to offset the sharpness of legal
combat. They admonished each other to put the good opinion of
professional brothers above their reputation with the public.
Sooner or later, it was said, the public would endorse their estimate of the bar. Still, the applause of the laymen could not be
completely ignored. A lawyer who won public acclaim in a sensational case (like the doctor in a sensational operation), and
who rose to wealth on increasingly large fees by moving up to yet
richer clients, was rarely snubbed by his brothers.[23]

The more traditional path of honor for a learned lawyer in
America, as in England, was, ostensibly, to a judgeship. But unlike the English, the American lawyers in large numbers would
rise out of the profession altogether to two pursuits close at
hand: politics and land speculation. In the England of the eighteenth century, the parliamentary lawyer was a recognizable species. However, in America, where there were no comparable well-
established aristocratic and gentry classes that were customarily
accorded and accustomed to the business of political rule, politics was a much more accessible field. In the era before the Revolution, lawyers quickly assumed political prominence through a
series of celebrated legal cases that aroused heated public debates and partisanship. From the Zenger trial through the Writs
of Assistance case, Parson's cause, and the Boston Massacre trial,
the bar raised issues that had important bearing upon the wid-
ening debate over the nature of the tie between the colonies and
the mother country. With the Stamp Act, many lawyers readily
moved from the law courts to the congresses, conventions, and
legislatures. It was not that most became revolutionaries; in fact
the majority of the New York and Philadelphia bar may have sided
with the King; nonetheless whichever side they chose, the lawyers often took a leading part in the debate and conflict. After the
Revolution, the lawyers did not abandon that prominence. On
the contrary, with the spread of republican forms, which produced many new elective offices, the lawyers who were adept at
swaying juries often seemed equally adept at swaying elector-
ates.[24]

Parenthetically, it might be worthwhile to glance at some of the
consequences of the fact that men of legal training have over-

whelmed American government throughout most of its history—
if only to underscore some familiar but important observations.
The American joining of law and politics has generally encouraged a less rigorously ideological politics and a more flexibly political law. Men trained in an adversary system—where the experience of winning and losing was hedged with formalities,
where broad issues were centered in particularities and set rules,
where attachment to causes was usually brief, adventitious, and
somewhat distant—such men were not promising material for
ideological zealotry. Also, lawyers and judges who moved in and
out of politics often brought to their legal judgment a strong political will that appeared as a vivid concern for the political consequences of legal designations and legal decisions. This interworking of law and politics has had a pervasive and lasting effect
upon American public life, and the hosannas and imprecations
that greeted it have a long history of their own.[25]

Proximity and know-how also prompted American lawyers to
venture into land speculation. A glance at Coke's *On Littleton*, an
early text for many colonial lawyers, or Blackstone's *Commentaries*, which usually superseded it, will reveal how much of
eighteenth-century English law was land law. In England it was
very difficult to buy land, owing to its relative scarcity as well as
to the practices of primogeniture and entail. Ownership, however, was only the most extensive right over land, and such rights
ranged downward, through a complex series of leaseholds and
easements, to the right of a man to cross over his neighbor's land
to get to his own. Real property law, therefore, was particularly
difficult, abounding in abstruse and recondite principles and distinctions, and providing an intricacy in substantive law comparable to that of special pleading in procedural law. Since a large
part of the American legal practice of the late eighteenth and
early nineteenth centuries dealt with real property law, real estate
titles, mortgages, and the construction of wills, American lawyers
picked up a familiarity with much of the technicality of English
land law.[26]

But with a difference. The availability of land in America with
few limitations or restrictions of sale, while it did not eliminate
the fine points of real estate law, did greatly simplify the law as it
was actually practiced. Also, the booming land market provided
an important alternate source of income for American lawyers.
Men with land to sell came to county courthouses during trial
days, and litigation over estates and inheritances brought mar-
ketable lands into the lawyers' hands at other times as well. The
papers of late eighteenth- and early nineteenth-century lawyers

will often hold as many documents relating to their real estate ventures as to their legal cases. When the *Delaware Reports,* for example, recorded that Judge Johns was absent from court "neither in sickness nor in trouble . . . but increasing his estate," it was simply using the idiom of the day to say that the venerable judge was speculating in western lands. Such speculation impelled some lawyers to leave legal work entirely, sometimes to great wealth, but surely as often to economic disaster.[27]

The link between law and economic enterprise was as intricate as the link between law and politics. In both cases, law was distinct—having its own purposes, principles, and standards—while at the same time it significantly influenced and was influenced by politics and economics. *In principle,* law was a free good. The Massachusetts Constitution was simply stating explicitly what was generally taken for granted when it affirmed that every member of the commonwealth "ought to obtain right and justice freely and without being obliged to purchase it." Blackstone traced this guarantee of access to law "freely and without sale" back to Coke, who in turn traced it back to the Magna Carta. Yet, upon this free good rested the entire system of market exchange of commodities. Law, which fixed the rules of ownership and exchange—what is mine, yours, ours, and the penalties for theft, fraud, and carelessness—gave that security of expectation that did so much to stimulate economic enterprise. Conversely, in a society of widespread property ownership and vaulting commercial ambition, the rule of law itself readily found broad support. Moreover, in law as in the economy, justice and general prosperity would somehow be wrought out of "our own self-love, that universal principle of action," as Blackstone described it. Still, for all such resemblances and interworkings, law remained a unique discipline and career. Lawyers might supplement their income with land speculation or might add to their honor with public office but these were clearly recognized as callings of another sort.[28]

Though politics and land speculation were to become two of America's important growth industries, the time-honored course that led an able lawyer to cap his career with a stately and respected judgeship continued to attract many. A judge was the guardian of the law. It was his responsibility to administer the adversary system of the courts so that the outcome of the partiality of opposing counsel, disputing often before a jury, might be close to impartial justice and well-regulated order. Justice and order were the aims of his office, yet each of these objects was beset with its particular dangers, and both taken together often brought conflicting claims. Justice customarily meant rendering to each his due, and such rendering was always vulnerable to the prejudices of politics and power. The "pestilential breath of faction may poison the fountains of justice," warned Hamilton, expressing a familiar complaint. Nonetheless, some were confident that such a threat might be offset. Owing to an awareness of the vicissitudes of power, the stronger "are prompted by the uncertainty of their condition, to submit to a government which may protect the weak as well as themselves." It was not so much the love of justice as the fear of suffering injustice that usually protected the courts, "as no man can be sure that he may not be tomorrow the victim of the spirit of injustice, by which he may be a gainer today."[29]

While order also might be endangered by external, self-aggrandizing passions, many of its more compelling difficulties came from within. For order required careful attention to rules, and such attentiveness brought with it a particular inflexibility and narrowness that often worked against any spirit of improvement and in some cases gave rise to obvious injustice. Even such widely accepted and approved rules as *stare decisis* and the Statue of Limitations, when resolutely applied, yielded a number of decisions that the judges themselves felt were inexpedient or iniquitous. In such instances, some judges evaded the straightforward application of the rules, but that course also had its dangers. For litigants stood in need of assured protection against judicial arbitrariness, and the legal system required safeguards against disabling uncertainty. Jurists, therefore, generally agreed that judicial discretion somehow must be sharply restrained by rules. The capacity of "weighing" and "balancing" diverse considerations, in the interplay of rules and discretion, was usually called judgment—a form of practical reason necessary, and much prized, for judicial office. Of all branches of government, the judiciary, as a function of office, gave reasons and appealed most explicitly to Reason, that "noble faculty . . . [which] exalts human creatures almost to the rank of superior beings." Behind the ostensible and politically necessary diminishment, Hamilton was unobtrusively exalting the judiciary when he assured the readers of the *Federalist* that this branch had neither force (vested principally in the executive) nor will (vested principally in the legislature), but "merely judgment."[30]

Judges were often older men who were expected to draw upon their long experience in the law and the life beyond it. They were honored, as a rule, not only from within the bar but more generally in society at large. It is not surprising, therefore, that when

American colleges, in imitation of the famous Blackstone Viner-ian lectures, set up their own series of law lectures addressed to future lawyers and gentlemen of liberal education, they invariably looked to the most distinguished American judges of the day to serve as instructors. Of these law courses, perhaps one of the most celebrated was that given by Supreme Court Justice James Wilson at the University of Pennsylvania, with President George Washington, Vice President John Adams, and leading members of Congress in his audience for the inaugural lecture.[31]

James Wilson's career might have been used as a cautionary tale on the snares of a rough-and-tumble America for the ambi-tious and unwary. He began his days here as a confident, aspiring young Scotsman slated for the ministry, and ended them a dis-traught fugitive in the Carolina back country, hiding to escape creditors. This ignominious death did much to obscure a bril-liant life. Wilson came to this country with a gentlemanly liberal arts education, studied in the office of the distinguished John Dickinson, and soon demonstrated the legal skill and learning that enabled him to become one of the most respected and pros-perous lawyers in the Middle Colonies. Almost as a matter of course, Wilson entered politics, plunging into the Revolutionary struggle against England, serving the Confederation govern-ment, taking part in the deliberations at the Constitutional Con-vention in Philadelphia (where his influence was second only to Madison), and finally accepting a position on the new Supreme Court. As a land speculator, his course seemed equally promis-ing, at first. But here the extraordinary ambition and optimism that served him so well as a lawyer and a politician led him on to an overrunning of resources that brought all three pursuits to a wretched *finis.* Yet, when Wilson stood addressing his renowned audience at the University of Pennsylvania with his lectures on law, he was at the height of his remarkable career.[32]

The lectures of William Blackstone at Oxford in 1753, later col-lected and published as his *Commentaries on the Laws of En-gland,* not only supplied the precedent for Wilson's lectures but provided much of the legal material he relied upon and that he took as his task to republicanize. Blackstone was the Boerhaave of the common law. He was a systemizer whose sharp focus upon the contours of eighteenth-century law enabled him to gather its particulars without losing them in a blur of detail. Starting with the famous definition of positive law as "a rule of civil conduct prescribed by the supreme power in the state, commanding what is right and prohibiting what is wrong," Blackstone erected a much-admired symmetrical structure with which he housed the miscellany of English law in four equiponderate volumes, comprising rights of persons, rights of things, private wrongs, and public wrongs. This confident overlapping of ethical and legal meaning in his use of right and wrong gave moral force to his scheme and at the same time permitted it the technicality that enabled it to handle complex tasks. For many contemporaries, that was all to their liking. Blackstone replaced Coke as the chief mentor of American lawyers on the principles and particulars of the common law. To Wilson, Coke's *Institutes* were still "a cabinet richly stored with jewels of the law," but somehow those jewels now seemed "strewed about in endless and bewildering confusion." Blackstone's "scientifical performance," by contrast, was particularly noteworthy in setting the law in a regular order, and, "in point of expression, the *Commentaries* are elegant and pure." Wilson, nevertheless, believed that it was his task to place Blackstone's structure of the law upon a new foundation, one more in keeping with the unique political order in America. He therefore felt called upon to devote far more time and attention to those "first principles" that Blackstone had grandly flaunted than did Blackstone himself.[33]

According to the *Commentaries*, the connection between man and his natural rights had been interrupted by the setting up of civil society. While the legitimacy of that civil society rested ultimately and ambiguously upon rights, its efficacy rested upon positive law, and that was Blackstone's principal concern. Moreover, for Blackstone, law "always supposes some superior who is to make it"; therefore it was inextricably tied to a graded society. Wilson began his republican revision of law by trying to undo that tie. It was not that he disparaged gradations in society but rather that, in an extended and pertinacious discussion, he tried to show that they were irrelevant to law. Men, Wilson believed, though differing in power, virtue, and talent, were equal in natural rights and duties which, Blackstone notwithstanding, they brought with them undiminished into civil society. This gave rights an individualistic inwardness very Protestant in spirit. "No exterior human authority can bind a free and independent man," Wilson claimed; therefore all human obligation must be self-obligation.[34]

Consent was the device of authority and self-obligation that Wilson tried to extend throughout the entire social order. However, this grand endeavor was doomed to failure. For there were important positions of authority that Wilson was willing to accept as legitimate and yet to which it was quite difficult to ascribe the agency of consent. The danger in his undertaking was that the term consent would become so vague that it could not be easily distinguished from compliance, conformity, or even submission; or that the maxim that authority rested upon consent might simply become the legal fiction of republicanism much as the maxim that all lands were originally granted by the king had been the legal fiction of feudalism. Yet Wilson persisted in his effort.[35]

Ascribing consent to the decisions of majority rule and the discretionary powers of officials was relatively easy. While a citizen might not agree with particular rulings, he had approved of these mechanisms of decision and their general purposes. As for the common law, "one of the noblest births of time" and "the most important part of our system of jurisprudence," the relevance of consent would be more difficult to prove. Still, Wilson characterized the common law as customary law, and "a custom long and generally observed carries with it intrinsic evidence of consent." Men declared their will, Wilson argued, not only by suffrage but also by conduct. Construing conduct as consent was particularly helpful for his attempt to extend consent throughout society, particularly in a society with limited suffrage. For Wilson, along with many of his contemporaries, felt that considerations of safety and order made it necessary to keep suffrage from those who were largely dependent upon the will of others.[36]

Even when self-obligation was so broadly interpreted, there was no assurance that a society could be held together by it. If laws were not commands but ultimately self-obligations, then promises became a much more important element of social cohesion. That might make for a serious weakening of the social bond, in that promises were easily withdrawn. Wilson came up against that problem when he set out to expound the law of treason. His interest in that subject went back to the days of revolutionary struggle in the Middle Colonies, where the number of Tories bulked so large as to give the conflict there the appearance of a civil war. Wilson served on the Committee of Spies in the Second Continental Congress, along with Jefferson, John Adams, and Robert R. Livingston. These last three were also on the Committee to Write the Declaration of Independence, and but four days before their Declaration was to announce that governments derived their just powers from the consent of the governed, the Committee on Spies requested treason legislation based upon the principle that protection prescribed obedience. Not only residents, but "all persons passing through, visiting, or making a temporary stay in any of the said colonies, being entitled to the protection of the laws during the time of such passage, visitation or temporary stay, owe, during the same time, allegiance thereto." A law of treason, written on the principles of consent, would have provided little effectiveness in fighting Tories. It is not clear what kind of effectual treason law could have been written on those principles. For the Tories dissented from the most fundamental tenet of the new governments; these "loyalists" refused to recognize the right of those new governments to exist. In fact, they declared that the setting up of such governments was in itself an act of treason. Was there any other basis for suppressing these Tories beside the appeal to naked force? Such justification would have been abhorrent to the lawyers on the Committee of Spies.[37]

Wilson, in his very first political writings, had described the relation of the prince and his subjects in terms of protection and obedience; that was good Blackstone. Subjects owed their prince a debt of gratitude for his protection of them that could never be fully repaid. Any payment of that debt took the form of allegiance and obedience. The Committee on Spies transferred this relation of the prince and his subjects to the relation of the state and its residents, transient as they might be. Clearly the bond of protection and obedience was closer to a feudal than to a republican principle, and intrinsic to Blackstone's notion of law. Nonetheless, when Wilson lectured on the law of treason in 1790, perhaps with the exigencies of the Revolutionary War still in mind, he drew upon the doctrine of the Committee on Spies.[38]

When he discussed the authority of the lawyer, Wilson again turned to the relation of protection and obedience. "Like a skilful pilot, he [the lawyer] has studied correctly the chart of law: he has marked the places which are dangerous, as well as those which are safe. Like a pilot, honest and benevolent as well as skilful, he cautiously avoids every danger, and through the channels of security steers the fortunes of those, who intrust them to his care." The metaphor already had a distinguished lineage when Plato had drawn upon it to justify the authority of his guardian class. For Wilson, it was still rich in implication. The lawsuit was a difficult and perilous course which left the client vulnerable and dependent upon the protection of his lawyer. The client might choose among lawyers as the shipper or passenger might, more indirectly, choose among pilots, yet once the action had begun the client was largely in this lawyer's hands, much as the passenger or shipper must rely upon the pilot. Though the lawyer, like the pilot, was not the chief officer, nonetheless, he was given a decisive responsibility requiring that he be "honest and benevolent as well as skilful." Those requirements resembled the idealized standards of the upper ranks of English professions.[39]

Along with Benjamin Rush, his friend, political ally, and personal physician, James Wilson drew a sharp distinction between those who practiced their calling as a profession and those who practiced it as a trade. The law was not a "mere instrument of private gain," though it should assure a competence; rather it was a career that provided opportunities for exercise of benevolence as well as skills. And its skills were not simply a matter of technique but of knowledge based in science. Science and benevolence were rarely claimed by English attorneys but American lawyers, reflecting the hybrid origins of their profession, did not hesitate to make such claims. Those who did not practice law as a profession, Wilson remarked disparagingly, but who engaged in "the retail business of law," were commonly the products of a patchy legal education and therefore had not been elevated above the money-grubbing appetites that led to chicanery and pettifoggery.[40]

Apprenticeship training alone was stunting, Wilson remarked, and it produced illiberal lawyers who busied themselves with the artificial rules formed for the convenience of the courts and who were bound to the incidental details of the legal form books. The lawyers who practiced law as a profession, by contrast, looked to the underlying principles of science, and secure in these, could range widely and boldly in their practice. They were able to distinguish the appearance of things from their reality, "to contemplate their beauty, to investigate their utility, and to admire the wonderful harmony, with which beauty and utility coincide." They also took as their responsibility the discovery of improvements in the law and the furtherance of such discovery.[41]

Such high-minded lawyers also took as their responsibility the broadest diffusion of legal knowledge as was possible. This was an act of beneficence, for it promoted an intelligent and capable citizenry. Blackstone, in aristocratic England, addressed the need of the ruling classes, "gentlemen of all ranks and degrees," to know the law; Wilson, in republican America, argued that the citizen must be made aware of those fundamental liberties and duties enshrined in the common law. Extensive as that knowledge might become, however, it would clearly never permit everyone to become his own lawyer. For the common law was not only the bearer of the liberties of the people, it was at the same time an inductive science that required special skill and training to elicit its truths. Unless the law was made "a peculiar study of some, it could never be an object of knowledge for all." What was attractive about such an argument was the ease with which it permitted the blending of the relationship of protection and obedience with notions of self-obligation. The American lawyers, Wilson believed, should be the advocates of the extensive application of the doctrine of consent, as vague as its application might become. For, certainly, if consent were to be effective, it must have its rules, and those rules, their science. Moreover, truths of that vital science could not be derived from consent. Or put differently: even in a republican society, law could not be only will, it must also be reason; and the dictates of reason were not derived by majority votes.[42]

By the late eighteenth and early nineteenth centuries, leading American lawyers had won positions of honor and authority, as well as a comfortable income. William Wirt, son of a tavern keeper who rose to the post of Attorney General of the United States, described the esteem of the profession through which he himself had been raised. "Men of talents in this country have been generally bred to the profession of law," he wrote in 1803, "and indeed throughout the United States, I have met with few persons of exalted intellect whose powers have been directed to any other pursuit. The bar in America is the road to honor." At that time, the elevated position that the lawyer had achieved was supported by a somewhat deferential society and still powerful English legal traditions. It is remarkable, however, that in the more egalitarian age to come, the lawyer sustained his preeminence. Foreign visitors who flocked to America in great numbers during that later era often commented with some amazement that the American lawyer seemed to be a peculiar kind of aristocrat particularly congenial to democracy.[43]

Part II

The Egalitarian
Interregnum of
the Professions
and the
Great Valley,
1830–1880

Daniel Webster addressing the Senate in full splendor, circa 1848–51. Webster
exemplified the conjunction of preeminence at the bar and preeminence in politics during the interregnum era, 1830–80. (Boston Art Commission, Faneuil
Hall)

Overview
of Part II

At the turn of the eighteenth century Americans pushed westward from the seaboard and piedmont and descended into the valley beyond the Allegheny mountains. What lay before them was the great Mississippi River network. It stretched from the head of the Ohio River to the foothills of the Rockies, from Lake Elk, Minnesota down past New Orleans to the Gulf of Mexico. With European claims quickly lifted and the Indians expeditiously dispossessed, the vast river basin of fertile lands was open to settlement. The aftermath of the American Revolution bore some resemblance to the aftermath of the French. Both ultimately resulted in widespread expropriation of land (in the American case, land not of church and nobility but of the American Indians) and in the distribution of a good part of that land to small landholders who became ardent supporters of the new regime. The irony that the American Revolution, which was fought in the name of life, liberty, and the pursuit of happiness, contributed to the decimation and dispossession of the Indians and indirectly even to the spread of Black slavery in the South, has not escaped the notice of historians. Adding to the moral complexity of these events, however, is the fact that they also provided the basis for the growth and prosperity of a vibrant and sometimes humane, if also limited, democracy. And nowhere did this species of democracy prosper more vigorously than in what was called "The Great Valley."[1]

By the 1830s, steamboats had penetrated the remote reaches of the Mississippi system, and the wharfs of bustling river ports like Memphis, St. Louis, and Louisville were loaded down with cotton bales, timber, and farm products from the hinterlands. Pittsburgh, where the confluence of the Monongahela and Allegheny rivers flowed into the Ohio, boasted its booming iron works, and Cincinnati, farther down the Ohio, was on its way to becoming the largest meatpacking center in the world. Most of the Mississippi River trade drained south through New Orleans, but by the fifties some railway lines joined the Valley with the seaboard, promising stronger east-west ties.[2]

The Mississippi basin not only offered a rich and productive terrain for agriculture and industry, it also provided the bases for many exuberant projections and fictions. Among the principal arguments of these works was the insistence upon the intrinsic unity of the region, its indigenous powers, and its glorious future. The river network, the reasoning went, so closely bound the area together that it would never be disjoined. The very vehemence with which this was put forward, however, often suggested that at least some of its proponents had their doubts. Jessup W. Scott, a Whig publicist from Ohio, brashly claimed that the Mississippi Valley guaranteed the continuance of the Union. Even an outsider like James H. Hammond, the famous South Carolina "fire-eater," declared that the Mississippi was a "bond of union made by nature herself. She will maintain it forever." For some, the force of geography was to be supplemented by human effort. Dr. Daniel Drake, the celebrated physician of the region, urged "the importance of promoting literary and social concert in the Valley of the Mississippi" and spent much of his career in that effort. Drake went further yet in his medical work to propose that the natural unity of the region had scientific significance. Owing to the broad interrelations and similarities of climatic conditions and soils, from whose miasmatic effusions Drake thought disease often arose, the great Mississippi territory became an advantageous unit for medical investigation and discovery. His acclaimed magnum opus, *A Systematic Treatise on the Principal Diseases of the Interior Valley of North America,* rested upon that supposition.[3]

In addition to this insistence upon the unity of the region, many of its boosters praised its peculiarly indigenous force and influence and its future greatness. The supposedly simple and fraternal terms upon which its inhabitants met were sure to wear away the prejudices that settlers brought with them into the new territory. This, perhaps, left them cruder than the residents of the seaboard states, yet it allegedly made the settlers of this new region more openhearted; perhaps inferior in refinement, nevertheless superior in energy, robustness, and love of country. Such fancies were in keeping with the broader shifts of the era. If in the past America had been culturally provincial—taking some of its most important standards from the great metropolitan centers of Britain—now the nation was becoming culturally more parochial—taking many of its standards more exclusively from local habitats. Spokesmen of the inland valley busied themselves in declaring a grandiloquent assortment of cultural Monroe Doctrines. After a seven-year stay in Cincinnati, the transplanted

Virginian, Moncure Conway, succumbed to that hopeful spirit and announced that "no forecast of what humanity is to accomplish in his next great home—the Mississippi Valley—can approximate the truth." Such cheerful forecasts of the accomplishments of the Valley were soon to be disappointed. Yet the reverberations of these pronouncements echoed late into the nineteenth century—in Twain's nostalgic tales of antebellum childhood along the River and later in Frederick Jackson Turner's notion that this Valley was somehow "the real America."[4]

It was the very fertility of the Valley that helped split it apart. In the southern portion the spread of cotton strengthened slavery, and in the northern section the expansion of corn and wheat gave rise to extensive commercial farming. Two distinct societies emerged. The one in the North was democratic, capitalistic, morally confident, and growing fast in people and political power; the other, in the South, was based upon slavery, with a planter aristocracy on the top that set the tone—seemingly self-assured, high-flown, violent, and proud. While some regional promoters continued to stress the undoubted economic interconnections of the Valley and tried to create an allegiance to the region itself, the cultural attachments of these diverging westerners came to resemble those of their neighbors to the east. When the Civil War came, the Great Valley divided north-south much like the rest of the country.[5]

Linked in a complex way to the rapid expansion into the Valley was the powerful egalitarian movement of this era that swept before it many of the landmarks of a society that had been run by finished gentlemen. This egalitarian impulse, joined with the spirit of expansion to inspire a widespread attack upon various forms of exclusiveness, restriction, and monopoly. Clearly it was an equivocal egalitarianism. It mixed a vague animus for leveling with a distinct eagerness for rising in the world. That volatile mixture was compounded in varying proportions in different sections and segments of society. The most popular spokesmen of the era pronounced against artificial distinctions but agreed that natural distinctions must be recognized and respected. What counted as natural and artificial had shifted sharply since Jefferson's day and allowed for a multitude of claims that he would not have recognized. "They hate distinctions," observed one skeptical politician, "unless shared or created by themselves."[6]

The principal sources of this egalitarianism were the expanding political democracy, market capitalism, and evangelical Protestantism. Each took on new force and momentum in this era. Clearly they did not originate in the Mississippi Valley, yet in this newly settled region where established modes and institutions were often attenuated and susceptible to novelty and innovation, those political, economic, and religious movements prospered mightily and the effects of their successes even flowed back to the older, more settled sections of the country. At some points these movements were at odds with each other, but more frequently in this era they worked together. Still, they pressed against different kinds of exclusiveness for the sake of dissimilar sorts of opportunity, and projected distinctive styles of leveling. Gentlemanly authority and honor, those qualities of the professions that distinguished them from ordinary occupations, were deeply affected.[7]

The leveling impulse in evangelical Protestantism was clearly equivocal. Protestantism embodied an attack on authority, but it could also provide a justification of existing conditions. Two principal and interrelated developments within evangelical Protestantism in this era were the gradual erosion of the Calvinist distinction between God's predestined elect and all others, and the emergence of the seasonal revival, with its unique spiritual technology, as a central institution of Protestant piety. Both were expressions of a new era of religion of the willing heart. This upheaval turned evangelical Protestants away from church establishments, hierarchies, ritual, elevated and learned clergy, creeds, and sometimes even separate denominations. It turned them toward such vagaries as perfectionism and millennialism, latent with social disruption. Yet strictly speaking, evangelical Protestant egalitarianism extended to the realm of salvation but not to the scheme of creation. That is, Protestantism could easily accept ranks in the social order, and historically it had looked upon secular rulers as God's instruments.[8]

However, in America in the mid-nineteenth century such categories as salvation and creation were not leakproof. Peter Cartwright, Methodist minister and sometime locofoco candidate for Congress, could not mask his delight in seeing "those proud young gentlemen and ladies dressed in silks, jewelry, and prunella" take "the jerks" and roll in the mud, humbled by the revival. And perhaps more significantly, the usually staid and strait-laced judge, Charles P. James of the Superior Court of Cincinnati, nonetheless insisted that the "process of christianity [*sic*] will not desist until we shall no more be able to distinguish the mechanic, after he has laid his working tools aside, the merchant, when he has left the counting room, the lawyer without his brief, nor the minister of religion, in the common intercourse of life." It was a lowercase christianity that Judge James relied upon to eliminate distinctions "in the common intercourse of life." This was not the Christianity of particular churches and well-defined creeds, but the general teaching common to them all. As Doddridge had explained, we all were descended from Adam and were made in God's image. Significantly, the world of work was exempt from the egalitarianism. The requirements of success within particular occupations placed limits upon the requirements of fairness. Yet even Judge James did not hold rigidly to this qualification, and he went on to bring what he saw as the equalizing tendencies of christianity into the courts, so as to diminish the professional distinctiveness of its lawyers and its legal proceedings.[9]

Moreover, the evangelists' frequent identification of piety with passion endangered the role of intellect and learning in spirituality, and beyond spirituality in the world at large. The very evanescence of emotion, impelling but giving little clear direction, led the revivalists to rely heavily upon the externals of morality to give order to their society. The terrible swift sword of moralism was also used to cut through great, knotted problems of theology. Whatever seemed to contradict the dictates of morality was obviously wrong, as were the ideas put forward by those who were themselves immoral. Paradoxically, however, some leading revivalists felt called upon to prove this through intellection. Who would have predicted that Charles Grandison Finney, the greatest revivalist of the age, would spend his last years as president of Oberlin College racking his brain over problems of metaphysics? Finney was well aware of the fact that while his preaching reached multitudes, his attempts at systematic theology would reach only a few. "I fear," he wrote, "that with all my painstaking, the book will not be understood even by many who desire to understand it, on account of my inability to simplify and explain so profound a subject. With this thought I have been much oppressed." Notwithstanding such uneasiness, Finney published his magnum opus, and it became proof for the fact that intellect could not be completely expunged from spirituality and that Christianity's placement of spirit above matter still raised learning to a position of some authority.[10]

Similarly, the effects of evangelical Protestantism upon the notions of honor were also mixed. Honor as a special warrior code of behavior had come under Christian criticism for a very long while. The principle of a code of honor, clergymen had argued, must be virtue. Those features of the traditional code like courtesy, that could be given moral purpose (although its original purposes were quite otherwise) were acceptable; but those like the duel, that chivalric display of physical courage much less amenable to Christian moralizing, were condemned. Pulpits resounded with denunciations of such "affairs of honor," and state legislatures, even in the South, responded with legislation outlawing the duel. Honor as a dispensation of social prestige brought less discord. In a society that was becoming increasingly Christian owing to evangelical efforts, in an orderly world ruled by a benevolent God, the righteous and the successful could not too often be too dissimilar and too disconnected. In the somewhat dreary intermissions between revivals, and often within the revivals themselves, those to whom society granted honor, if they were not flagrantly immoral, would be accorded honor by evangelical Christianity as well.[11]

The expansion of political democracy in this era, through suffrage extension and the new political devices that accompanied it, to all appearances made most white males, irrespective of social standing, religious belief, merit, and even virtue, members of the ruling class. In addition, increasing numbers of the common people actually came out to vote and to hold office. Government was no longer the exclusive domain of cultivated gentlemen. Political authority in the United States had always rested upon the consent of the people, but now that the people was defined more broadly than had previously been imagined, the meaning of consent became increasingly abstract. Government by gentlemen, which often was so vociferously attacked, gave way to government by political machine, which was so equably acquiesced in. The voter exercised his right to command in that peculiarly impersonal way, through the ballot box, and then only on widely separated occasions. It is not surprising, therefore, that some writers came to believe that the authority of the people in democratic politics was not accompanied by substantial consequent powers.[12]

The honor of office remained, though somewhat diminished from the time when the king was the fount of such honor. Legislatures gave the title "honorable" to numerous elected officials but also tried to place limits on their esteem. "Office holders," explained a Whig newspaper, "should not be raised by distinctive marks or unusual incomes above their fellow citizens," nor should "extraordinary dignity attach to their stations." However, the solemn and sometimes lavish inaugural ceremonies that persisted not only for national offices, but also for state and often local offices, suggest that the draining of honor from public office and public service was far from complete.[13]

Unmistakably, a hunger to be a somebody, amidst everybody,

repeatedly breaks through in diverse ways during this era: in the outlandish national boasting that many visitors from abroad described; in the frenzied attack upon that exclusive honor-making-machine, the Masonic Order; and in that organization's survival in fine fettle and subsequent expansion. The astonishing growth of various fraternal orders in this era owes something to the insurance work they did, but that cannot explain their eager appetite for hierarchies and festal regalia. One of the significant appeals of these orders was that they provided office and dignity to almost all. A member might rise in the fantastical hierarchy even if he could not give evidence of much economic success, political importance, or conventional religious piety—just so long as he displayed his loyalty to the organization by regularly attending meetings and indicated his general moral rectitude by avoiding scandal. Everyman could not be a king, but he might become an exotic princeling of some sort.[14]

Market capitalism, quickened by the rapid improvement of transportation and more generally invigorated by public support for the construction of social overhead capital, unwittingly furnished an extraordinary corrosive for the prescriptive and decorous ranks in society. Ambitious businessmen broke into markets that had been based upon local connections, traditional restraints, and various insular forms of monopoly. They supported their incursions with a program of halfway laissez faire, often urging public subvention for enterprise but little public regulation. More thoroughgoing laissez-faire arguments were taken up by more radical men, who saw their proposals as a broad attack upon the well established. However, "a fair field and no favor" became a common platform, variously interpreted.[15]

In the world of commerce and industry, authority and honor took on new connotations. At first sight, it appeared that the market had dissolved authority, for exchanges were not based upon command but rather upon seemingly uncoerced agreements. However, even such ideal markets rested upon the jurisprudence of property and trespass and upon the law of master-servant, giving owners power over nonowners and employers command over the employed. Most jurists and publicists argued that these relations were neither iniquitous nor oppressive, for both were based, ostensibly, upon consent and, more important, both were temporary. In free and bountiful America, it was claimed, property was readily available to anyone with gumption, and no white man need remain a servant for very long. Yet in the nascent factories of this era, the supposed equality of parties in the labor contract appeared increasingly doubtful, and the untoward consequences of selling labor seemed more apparent and irrevocable. Unlike marketing products, selling one's labor meant selling the right to be commanded, and those who earned their living in this way did not easily find other options.[16]

Among businessmen, the code of honor became indistinguishable from the prescriptions of Christian virtue except for a special emphasis upon trustworthiness in commercial dealings. Here, however, honesty could often be policy rather than duty. Honor, as the bestowal of esteem, was translated into giving special recognition to success in the marketplace as, in the past, success in politics, art, and war had been given distinctive approbation. This had less significance in the rural North where the bulk of the American population lived. In that region, dominated by commercial agriculture and small holdings, markets worked with the fewest restraints, and the distribution of wealth was probably brought closer to some sort of equality than at any other time or place in the nation's history. This was the equality of condition that Tocqueville sensed as he traveled across this part of America. In the major cities, however, the honor granted to commercial success helped justify the increasingly unequal distribution of wealth that characterized those urban areas. Tocqueville noted this as well and warned against an ignoble aristocracy of manufacturers, for he could not believe that the marketplace could fashion admirable character and talents.[17]

What is evident in this incongruous egalitarianism is that while evangelical Protestantism, political democracy, and market capitalism frequently discountenanced customary rankings in society, they did not often challenge rankings as such. In fact they occasionally acknowledged grades, honor, and authority of their own making. What made these grades seem acceptable was that those in inferior positions might often have a say about who stood as their superiors. Catherine Beecher argued arduously and conservatively for such rankings:

> [I]t is needful that certain relations be sustained, which involve the duties of subordination. There must be the magistrate and the subject, one of whom is the superior, and the other the inferior. There must be the relations of husband and wife, parent and child, teacher and pupil, employer and employed, each involving relative duties of subordination. The superior, in certain particulars, is to direct, and the inferior is to yield obedience. Society could never go forward . . . unless these superior and subordinate relations be instituted and sustained.

Beecher was quick to add that for many stations "in a truly democratic state, each individual is allowed to choose for himself, who shall take the position of his superior." Nonetheless, for many of her contemporaries this type of argument smacked too much of monarchy and aristocracy.[18]

The effect of this discordant environment upon the traditional standing of the gentleman is significant. There was no clamorous demand that the title gentleman be abolished and a less exalted designation, like citizen for example, be put in its place. Rather, the bulk of the white male population without much fuss simply took on and was granted such title. An English visitor attending an American political rally was therefore somewhat perplexed when he heard the speaker address the crowd as ladies and gentlemen, for when he looked about him he could find no ladies and no gentlemen present.[19]

As the term profession earlier had been narrowed and now most often referred to particularly esteemed occupations (while retaining the less frequently used, older, but now secondary meaning of any occupation), so the term gentleman now broadened and most often referred to almost any well-behaved white male, while retaining some of the older and now secondary meaning referring to particularly respected men. Of course even that more restricted secondary meaning had changed importantly since the eighteenth century. In America all trace of the distinction between gentleman and tradesman had disappeared, at least in the North, while the notion that the gentleman, nonetheless, held an elevated social standing was retained.[20]

One of the most renowned mid-nineteenth century depictions of the American gentleman was Francis Lieber's discourse *The Character of the Gentleman*, originally delivered to the students of Miami University, Ohio, in 1846. It quickly went through three American editions and a Scottish printing as well. Lieber, a learned and talented German liberal who fled persecution in Prussia, had risen to prominence in his adopted country as a respected professor and publicist. This outsider loved America and wished to be loved by it. The truths that most Americans might take for granted Lieber sought to make explicit and to set on more modern and informed foundations. This was evident in his various erudite works in political science as well as in his later remarkable military code that was to be adopted by the Union armies in the Civil War. His discourse on the gentleman was a parallel attempt with similar purpose except that in this work, Lieber, still resident in South Carolina but addressing a Northern audience, also tried to adjust the growing differences between Northern and Southern notions of the gentleman.[21]

Gentlemanhood in America, like an antique chair, was coming

unglued. Lieber proposed to refit and refurbish it by lopping off what seemed to be extravagant, bracing its frame with simpler, stronger materials, and trying to reserve it for limited use. He would make American gentlemanliness in different ways both accessible and exclusive. Lieber's discourse contrasted sharply the "monarchical gentleman" whose dignity rested upon ancestry with the "high-bred republican gentleman" whose standing depended somehow upon character. As Protestantism had internalized piety, so in a comparable way this Protestant culture internalized social structure as character. Emerson, the great expositor of "character," at one point announced with the intention to shock: "I find the caste in the man." Most others were less self-aware. Lieber, in emphasizing character rather than ancestry, felt that he was making gentlemanhood more accessible: first, because the distinctive character traits that he required derived from *both* nature and training (both the Antinomian and the Arminian possibilities), with the contribution of each unfixed and incalculable; and second, because some of those most prized traits were admittedly already widespread in the population. At one point, Lieber's logic and sentiment led him to grant gentlemanhood even to "an old, now departed, negro slave" whom he had known and who was "a gentleman in his lowly sphere." Sure enough, Lieber quickly recoiled from the dangerous possibilities of such a gentleman, explaining that "as a matter of course, this can take place by exception only." For the principal tenor of Lieber's discourse was to restrict the notion of gentleman both morally and socially. From a moral standpoint, he denounced the touchy duelist who was but an "arrant bully" and brushed aside those who thought the gentleman's bearing could be maintained "in spite of religion." It was only with the moral aid of Christianity that the character of the gentleman could be maintained. This argument brought Lieber's essay within the long literary tradition—stretching at least from Malory's *Morte D'Arthur* and of course including Doddridge's *Life of Col. James Gardiner*—which brought Christian standards to bear upon chivalric usage.[22]

Lieber's social restrictions upon American gentlemanhood were equally important. Particularly helpful for the fostering of gentlemanly character, Lieber believed, was "the freemasonry of liberal education"—that tacit fellowship and sympathy formed by classical training but available to very few. Even more restrictive was Lieber's linking of gentlemanly character to power. For "power, physical, moral, purely social or political," he insisted, "was one of the touchstones of genuine gentlemanliness." It was from such positions of power, variable and unsteady as they might be in this era, that gentlemanly character could be most fully displayed. Lieber turned to the professions as his principal exemplars of those positions of power and, somewhat oddly for his Northern audience, included military officers among them. However, that inclusion enabled him to call upon George Washington for the office of grand paragon of American gentlemanhood. The impressment of Washington for such service carried with it the suggestion of the earlier English exemplars of the gentleman— landed proprietors living principally off the rents of their estates. Nonetheless, the professions were the central focus of Lieber's essay. While in England the professions had borrowed much of their style of gentlemanhood from the landed gentry, in Lieber's America the professions themselves were now the models.[23]

Except for the South. There the great slaveholding planters, who more closely resembled the English landed gentry than almost any other segment of American society of that day, became the model. As early as 1775, John Adams had contrasted the New England gentlemen with those of the South, where they "have large plantations of slaves, and the common people among them are very ignorant and very poor. These gentlemen are accustomed, habituated to higher notions of themselves, and the distinction between them and the common people, than we are." In the South, owing in part to its peculiar institution, gentlemanly honor underwent a special and atavistic flowering, recapturing some of the swaggering and barbarous features of the warrior-gentleman of days of yore. Slavery, undermined a monopoly—the state's monopoly of violence. For it was bodily punishment that helped make slavery work. This decentralization of violence gave the South much of its extraordinary, hybrid, feudal-capitalistic cast.[24]

Lieber's rebuke of the duelist, the gambler, the ruffian, and the gallant ("treating ladies deferentially but not caring how many servant girls may be seduced") took on special resonance in the South. However his intent was to win that section over to a more elevated gentlemanhood. A Southern reviewer praised Lieber for setting "his standard as high as he has done" but noted sardonically that the essay had the fault of being "inapplicable to the commonplace realities of the world." Honor, that essential of the gentleman, was not a matter of morals or religion; rather it was a code by which "men of the world" govern their conduct. Moreover, it was "intimately associated with the practice of private war." John Randolph had earlier linked it to the command of slaves, and a writer for the *Southern Literary Messenger* to the avoidance of "base submission to another's will." The Southern reviewer of Lieber's essay thought that "exemption from labor, from the spade, the symbol of all labor, makes the great point of distinction" between the gentleman and the common man. Clearly, slavery gave a special flavor to Southern gentlemanhood and honor. In the South, however, the English landed proprietor remained a conspicuous model. "To hold a plantation, to command a certain number of labourers, white or black, to feed one's friends and their horses liberally, to discharge creditably the various duties of justice of the peace, and commissioner of the roads, and of good fellowship and neighborhood generally, make up with us the character of a country gentleman. . . . Landed property has great efficacy in making its possessor a gentleman."[25]

Though Daniel Drake, the distinguished Cincinnati doctor, was as intent as Lieber in trying to bridge the differences between the North and South in the tumultuous antebellum years, nonetheless, his version of the gentleman seemed even more decidedly sectional. Drake distinguished between "heroic ages" and "civilized ages." The ideal man of the heroic age was the "man of spirit." Brave, independent, even splendid, he was also savage and arrogant. In a simpler society such a man of spirit might well be celebrated. However as civilization advanced, Drake argued, "connections and relations" in society became more complex, and man's social duties became more serious and commanding. In contrast to the man of spirit of heroic ages stood the "man of honor" of civilized ages, and for him the path of social duty was the road to honor. His passion through conscience was transmuted into discipline. His duty could summon a constrained bravery that the heroic ages would not understand. Moreover the gentleman of social duty, Drake concluded, would obviously be a Christian gentleman, blending the responsibilities of social position with the obligations of Christian faith. In the despair of the bloody defeats and indecisive battles of the Civil War, some Northerners would later call upon notions of duty and honor much like those that Drake had proposed. "The Christian Faith, we believe," explained a wartime editorial in the *New York Times*, "teaches that it may be, and often is men's duty to fight, though they may never win: their duty to die, when they may die in vain—to lose all, though the sacrifice may seem utterly worthless. This is perhaps the noblest, and it certainly proved the most fruitful of Christian ideas. Any other theory of men's duty than this one leads by a straight road to the lowest depths of personal and national baseness." This was a gentlemanly duty and honor, alloyed with a peculiar stoical and Calvinistic Christianity. Yet one could still faintly hear the song of Roland.[26]

Though Northern and Southern notions of honor and gentlemanliness were developing along divergent lines, they still shared many circumstances and events. Both had to adjust to the widespread attack upon classical learning in this era as exclusive and useless. This campaign was not new in this country except for its new breadth and impetuousness. It persuaded many in both sections to diminish the importance of classical learning for gentlemanliness. Behind such concessions lay that shift of sentiments and judgments that has come to be called romantic. Emerson, for example, though strongly attracted to the ancient languages which in their "great beauty of structure contain wonderful remains of genius," still felt that they were now superfluous, "shells high and dry on the beach", even for the broadly educated. In the face of this widespread attack, the colleges, those propugnacula of classical education, raised their circumvallations yet higher. With the famous Yale Report of 1828 as their apologia, most American colleges rejected reform and maintained their classical regimen with only minor concessions. This, however, was at the expense of increasing isolation from the centers of intellectual life and achievement in this country. College graduates were undoubtedly gentlemen, but by this time they clearly held no monopoly upon that title.[27]

This was apparent in the professions themselves. Not only did leading publicists like Lieber turn to the professions for exemplars of gentlemanhood, but the professions themselves ardently laid claim to that exalted standing. Nonetheless, after 1830 a growing portion of young men bypassed the colleges on their way to the professions. In New England, the section of the country that most prized schooling and where those headed for the professions had created much of the demand for college education, college students now declined in number and in proportion to the population. Those professionals without a liberal arts education "took even ground at once with the oldest of the regular graduates, and in a few months the most conservative circles of Boston and New York had quite forgotten who of their gownsmen was college-bred, and who was not."[28]

This gave new importance to technical education for the professions. American professional men had never been as nonchalant about their technical education as the English. Even in the earlier era, Americans made their technical education systematic by setting up medical schools like that in Philadelphia, law schools like that in Litchfield, and theological seminaries like that in Andover. But after 1830, two seemingly opposite tendencies in connection with technical education for the professions came to light: first, a widespread downgrading of training for these occupations, in favor of giving free play to natural talents and aptitudes; and second, a booming market for technical instruction resulting from an onrush of young men into the professions. The outcome was the rapid growth and proliferation of proprietary schools for the awarding of professional degrees. These professional colleges were usually profit-making enterprises established by practitioners and supported by student fees. Competition was brisk and admission to these schools became easy, with graduation a matter of course.[29]

Between 1830 and 1845, the number of medical colleges doubled. Apprenticeship training, long considered preliminary to formal instruction, and affording some means of restriction through its prerequisite of personal connection, fell into disuse. The schools themselves were much more accessible. There were too many schools, medical men complained, therefore too many doctors, and these, it was said, were too poorly trained. The legal profession was rife with proprietary schools, as well, but these were of less consequence. For in law, many considered apprenticeship alone adequate for practice, and others simply resorted to do-it-yourself instruction, Blackstone in hand. The most reputable proprietary school, at Litchfield, which had catered to young men with bachelor's degrees, closed in 1833. The small number of college-connected law schools that survived could not maintain fixed entrance requirements. Most lawyers in this era did not get their training through formal education.[30]

This seems to have been true of the ministers as well. The growth of the Methodists and Baptists, traditionally suspicious of an educated clergy, meant that most ministers would have little formal instruction. Even among the customarily learned Congregationalists there was a sharp decline in the proportion of college graduates in the ministry. Nonetheless, a movement developed to offer systematic training in seminaries to replace irregular study with a minister. This movement took place chiefly among the older denominations but also as the work of a few zealous men in the Methodist and Baptist churches. In some ways the growth of theological seminaries resembled the rapid increase of proprietary schools in medicine. Commercial promptings were not wholly wanting. There were no hopes of direct profits for the theological seminaries themselves (they depended upon charity for survival), but their presumed benefits to land values turned such schools into manna in the wilderness for land speculators. Many seminary catalogues bravely listed a bachelor's degree as a prerequisite for entry, yet students more often seem to have come directly out of the revivals than out of the colleges.[31]

This burgeoning of proprietary schools was but the outcome of that momentous and far-reaching development of the era—the disestablishment of the professions. The egalitarianism of this period, though a mixture of ideas and impulses, nevertheless readily led to a partial discrediting of the professions and to the condemnation of their licensing laws as conspiracies against the laity. These middle years of the nineteenth century, from the standpoint of organizational power and effectiveness, were the nadir of the professions in America. In 1800 three-quarters of the states had set educational requirements for the practice of law; by 1860 only one-quarter had any such requirements; in 1800 almost all states had medical licensing laws; in 1860 almost none had them. With such restrictions lifted, the proprietary professional schools easily flourished. Licensing laws in themselves had rarely granted effective monopoly powers to the professions. Yet they had endorsed the professions' distinctions between rightful and wrongful practitioners and had provided public recognition to the professions' claims to authority and honor. Now popular leaders became more popular by denouncing such laws as aristocratic and monopolistic, as plots against the public interest, and as frauds perpetrated by trampling upon the people's natural right to take up any occupation they pleased. A number of professional associations, particularly among the lawyers, disbanded because they despaired of fostering esprit de corps if the professions were without clear boundaries. Some professionals and many laymen came to reject the distinction between profession and occupation as outright humbug.[32]

The disestablishment of the clergy had been a foreshadowing of that combination of external attacks and internal doubts so important to the disestablishment of all the professions. The predicament of the Protestant minister in asserting his authority over his congregation lay in the fact that some of the fundamental doctrines of the Reformation, though often carefully qualified, could be used against him. Of the three major eighteenth-century denominations in America, the Anglican clergy had the best muniments. However, the most commanding of these clergymen had preached submission to the English crown during the Revolution and suffered the consequences of having chosen the losing side.[33]

Though the Calvinist teachings on the ministry had created some difficulty for the Congregationalist and Presbyterian ministers, much more damaging in the long run was the decline of the Calvinist theological system itself. Its basic doctrines had seemed to deny that man could be active in his own salvation. Yet in times of declining religious fervor some ministers brushed dogma aside and appealed to all Christians to "make a new heart and a new spirit." The very successes of this religion of the heart in the long series of revivals stretching through the nineteenth century led some of the most renowned Calvinist theologians to becloud fundamental issues and some revivalists to downgrade doctrine altogether. What was the recourse of the ministry, the guardians of orthodox doctrine, when the lowly evangelicals joined the patrician statesmen of the American Enlightenment to decry "priestcraft" as a corruption of the pure and simple teachings of Jesus? That somewhat unearthly combination dis-established the already discredited Anglican churches after the Revolution as well as the Standing Order in Connecticut and Massachusetts some time later. By 1850, the three largest de-nominations in the United States were the Methodists, the Bap-tists, and the Presbyterians, the first two led by a ministry of largely rudimentary education, culturally on equal terms with their unpolished congregations, while the Presbyterians were left with a ministry of greatly varying attainments.[34]

The technical learning of the physician of the eighteenth and early nineteenth centuries had been fixed in a humoral type "sys-tem" explaining in comprehensive terms the cause and cure of disease. In complexity and contentiousness, the arguments over rival systems easily matched disputes over Calvinism. Yet adher-ents to these varying systems usually joined in recommending "heroic" treatment—bleeding, mercurials, and narcotics. The melancholy experiences of doctors along with the more woeful experiences of their patients and the offsetting findings of the school of mid-nineteenth-century French clinicians shook the belief of many physicians in their systems and led them to con-clude that medicine was an uncertain science. A leading physi-cian of the Massachusetts Medical Society announced that "the amount of death and disaster in the world would be less, if all disease were left to itself."[35]

Such qualms lessened the resolve of physicians in their endless battle against folk medicine and various medical sects. It was not unforeseeable, therefore, that the simple but patented "Botanic medicine" of Samuel Thomson and the more abstruse teachings of Hahnemann's homeopathy would find many takers—Botanic medicine by the commonalty and homeopathy by the upper classes. The licensed doctors tried to use governmental powers against the sects, but the "Botanics" struck back with Samuel Thomson in the lead and various evangelicals as allies. (Thomson praised John Wesley's medical writings and claimed the endorsement of Andrew Jackson.) When the dust had cleared most states had repealed their medical licensing laws. Amidst these confusions, many regular doctors banded together into newly formed societies to fight "quackery" or at least distinguish themselves from it.[36]

Dr. Nathan Smith Davis, who himself had been able to enter the profession because many of the traditional barriers had come down, was unwilling, however, to see his own achievement so quickly devalued. He gathered about him a band of zealous doctors whose common cause was the raising of the profession to its former standing. This group became the basis of the American Medical Association (AMA), one of whose chief concerns was the improvement of medical education. Improving medical education, it was thought, would at the same time end the glut of doctors. "Numbers should be restricted," wrote Davis, "by adding to the standard of requirements." This was precisely the kind of reform that doctors found appealing. Duty and interest would be the same: doctors would protect the public at large, they believed, and at the same time advance the profession. In this interim period, the AMA accomplished little. Nonetheless, it persisted and thereby became the saving remnant that carried the memory and ambition of an earlier day into a later, more favorable era. Similarly, state medical associations sprang up with purposes much like those of the national organization. These, however, were even weaker and often short-lived.[37]

The decline of humoral systems of medical orthodoxy opened the way for specialization. From the perspective of humoral pathology, the causes of disease were general, and studying the organs meant giving uncalled-for attention to symptoms. Only quacks who were ignorant of medical science or charlatans who pandered to popular superstition for the sake of profit would be specialists. Regular doctors stigmatized early ophthalmologists and laryngologists with both labels, and they were not altogether mistaken. Yet with the breakup of the humoral systems, the customary scorn for specialists was more difficult to maintain.[38]

In this regard, the checkered career of Dr. Horace Green was a turning point in American medicine. To offset his poor medical education and to move ahead in the highly competitive conditions of a New York City medical practice, Green decided to devote himself exclusively to laryngology. He also made exaggerated claims for his techniques. Amidst great uproar and bitterness, he was accepted, expelled, and then welcomed back by the New York Medical Society, to be remembered as America's first outstanding medical specialist. At the AMA convention in 1854, a motion recognizing specialties as legitimate fields of practice was tabled, and it was not passed until 15 years later. As late as 1863, Worcester's dictionary defined specialist as "a practical man."[39]

Specialization not only served to subdivide medical practice but led to the setting up of new healing professions as well. For this, the humbling of the three traditional professions was also an important condition. It not only brought the professions more broadly within the reach of men of lower social origins, but it seemed to bring professionalism within the reach of occupations that had previously been considered "mechanical" or merely trades. The downgrading of medicine encouraged those who had done its most menial work to aspire to equal standing with the doctors. Apothecaries, traditionally filling the lowest rank in medicine, laid the groundwork of the new profession of pharmacy in this era. And men who had combined the crudest procedures of minor surgery of the mouth with skillful cosmetic embellishments now began to call themselves dentists. In America, dental work had been done by surgeons, barbers, silversmiths, and tinkers; many of the early dentists were self-taught itinerants traveling long distances in order to support themselves on a market that was thin and dispersed.[40]

By the 1830s, however, there was a sizable group of resident dentists in the major cities, and a society of surgeon-dentists of the city and state of New York was formed. This association, the beginnings of organized dentistry in America, had as its chief goal the suppression of new technology—the use of silver-mercury amalgam for filling teeth. The technique was less costly, less painful, and required much less skill to apply than gold foil, which had been used up to then. Yet America's leading dentists announced that amalgam was good only for stealing patients and poisoning them, and that the use of "mineral paste" was malpractice. This controversy over amalgam troubled organized dentistry right up to the Civil War, however the use of mineral paste gradually spread, especially in work with lower-class patients. The early dental organizations soon developed broader interests, giving character and respectability to the occupation and more generally promoting the welfare of its practitioners. Soon it would "no longer be a disgrace to be called a dentist," promised the first president of the National Society of Dental Surgeons. One of the difficulties blocking this rise in status was that dentists for a long while could not decide whether their calling was a specialty

within medicine or a new profession with purposes and characteristics all its own. The foremost dentists of the day were usually
proud possessors of fictitious or honorary medical degrees; but
at the same time, the American Society of Dental Surgeons provided in its bylaws that "each and every acting member, or fellow
of the Society . . . shall be entitled to a diploma, or degree of Doctor of Dental Surgery."[41]

The founding of the Baltimore College of Dental Surgery in
1839 provided a somewhat more reputable form of credentialing
and the eventual answer to the perplexity of occupational identity. Though largely a mechanical craft, dentistry was to be a respectable subject of instruction dealing with disorders of the
teeth and placing special emphasis on particular skills that no
medical school bothered to teach. By the time of the Civil War
there were three dental schools going, and these had graduated
over five hundred students. While most American dentists still
trained only through apprenticeships, it was the graduates of the
dental schools who ultimately defined the new calling. Dentistry
was not to be a department of medicine; the medical learning
represented by the D.D.S. was much too scanty (and therefore
medical societies would not admit its holders as members). Its
kinship with medicine, however, was not to be neglected, for this
made its professional status more persuasive. Dentistry was to
be a new health profession with all the display of a profession
and a domain of learning and doing all its own. Because they
focused so exclusively and attentively upon disorders of the
teeth, dentists claimed that they could deal with them better
than anyone else. And in fact, American dentists did win a reputation for proficiency in both Europe and America. In contrast
to American doctors of this era, dentists, despite their troubles
and contentions, were often cheerful about the prospects of their
calling.[42]

Lawyers also maintained their good spirits. For however they
may have been endangered as an honored profession in this era,
they clearly prospered as an occupation. Law served democracy
and capitalism and had an affinity for both, though it was often
at odds with evangelical Protestantism. The American lawyer
combined the barrister's work of public argument with the country attorney's employments touching ownership and transfer of
ownership. Moreover, the sporadic and migratory nature of his
work as well as his forensic skills fitted him for the embroilments
of the legislature and stump-speaking politics. In addition his
conveyancing skills gave him entry into the world of business. He
was present at the birth, crisis, and death of most business en-

terprises, and he was on tap for their day-to-day operations. If this commercial work rarely led to fame, it sometimes led to fortune. The lawyer in this era, therefore, was often an accessory and even a principal in politics and business, and he could assume the democratic and capitalistic authority and honor of public office and wealth.[43]

Nonetheless, when compared to its earlier eminence, the legal profession may well have declined in its particular kind of renown. It had been the foremost profession since the era of transfer of professional institutions to America, from 1750 to 1830. In New England, the rise of the lawyers had been sharply outlined against the background of the decline of the ministry. In the nation as a whole, the rise of the lawyers in the eighteenth century had a significant effect upon American culture. Owing to their gentlemanly positions of honor and authority in that era, and to their occupational affinity for some of the central issues of the day—rights and liberties—what lawyers took for granted many other Americans would often take for granted as well. This became apparent in the framing of the Constitution and in deliberations of the law courts, which became forums for the discussion of the essential problems of the nature of government.[44]

Yet those courts were primarily institutions for the resolution of private disputes through litigation. Those less elevated proceedings had generated an elaborate body of erudition of their own. In its complexity, the technical learning of American lawyers of the late eighteenth and early nineteenth centuries had overshadowed that of the Calvinists or the medical philosophers. American law derived from a long and venerable accumulation of custom, judicial decision, and legislation, most of which, to the disgust of some patriots, was received from England. Between the law and the litigant stood a high barrier of procedure and formalities, which only time and money and a lawyer's know-how could hope to surmount. The substantive law was intricately entangled with procedure; the common law was still confined within the various forms of action, loosened somewhat by use of judicial fictions and a lax sense of precedent. Blackstone's *Commentaries*, intended as a lure to interest some of the better classes of England in legal careers, became in America a manual for aspiring young lawyers. Even more ironic was the fact that Blackstone's attempt to give a connected and rational account of the whole legal system led willy-nilly away from the forms and fictions he cherished. The very comprehensiveness and clarity of his work raised the hope that law might be freed from inherited modes to deal more directly with the problems of law in a more egalitarian and democratic society.[45]

In addition to such partly theoretical problems, there were some very practical embarrassments. To the extent to which Americans accepted the common-law rule of *stare decisis*, the many American courts, with their ever so many rulings, threatened to boggle the wits of even the most learned lawyers. Justice Story complained that the mass of law was accumulating with almost incredible rapidity, and that it was not possible to look at new volumes of printed cases coming from the presses without some discouragement. The legal profession, therefore, was divided by its doubts when faced by the resolute campaign for the reform of law led by the young Jacksonian lawyer David Dudley Field. The law, Field contended, could be so simplified and codified that its basic principles might be understood by ordinary folk, and their need for lawyers reduced. Field still held to America's inherited notions of natural law and natural rights, but these he believed, in his characteristically hardheaded and practical way, could be derived from experience and would become matters of plain fact rather than lofty theory. Some codifiers attacked the common law and its procedures because they seemed to give judges unseen and unexplained legislative power. The codes, these reformers argued, would place those powers where they democratically belonged, in popular assemblies, and would bring the law closer to commonly understood morality.[46]

Along with codification, the rapid spread of contingent fee practice also alarmed the more conservative segment of the bar. It was primarily the less well-established lawyers who seized upon this device that allowed them to take fees as a percentage of the award. These same attorneys then would find it to their interest to persuade unprosperous and previously excluded clients to go to law and win their rights. The abhorrence of the "old school" members of the bar toward the contingent fee, they said, lay in the fact that the contingent fee lawyer seemed to step down from his position as an officer of the court and place himself on the level of his client, as a partner in the litigation. Moreover, the contingent fee brazenly invited the spirit of avarice into the lawyer's office.[47]

The dangers of both codification and contingent fee practice, however, turned out to be of less consequence than conservative lawyers had imagined. Even where codes were adopted, it remained the task of the court judges to construe them, and the judges usually interpreted the codes in terms of the preexisting common-law usages. The codifiers did simplify the law, making it less technical and more routine, though not necessarily more just as some had hoped. Although those simplifications allowed lawyers with less training to practice with the codes, they certainly did not make Everyman his own lawyer as had been threatened and feared. Within the law office, the lawyer was still authoritative and imposing. Those attorneys who did resort to contingent fees usually put them to use with a clientele from the humblest levels in society. With such, the lawyer could easily be lordly; if a partner, then a dominant partner. Moreover, the common-law rule of privileged communications, ensuring that the lawyer could not easily be made to divulge the confidences of his client to the court, encouraged clients to confide in their advocates. If lawyers' memoirs are to be trusted, many of their clients often came to depend upon them in an unguarded, childlike way. The lawyer's authority was consensual and provisional, yet it remained in large measure gentlemanly and even paternal.[48]

Furthermore, despite the fact that law was increasingly practiced as a craft (by rule of thumb, form books, and routine) and as a trade (with commercial measures of success), it rose above either of these and was still honored as a lofty intellectual pursuit. The law necessitated and employed general standards of jurisprudence, a coherent body of legal principles based upon theoretical explanations. The most fundamental issues of government, constitutional questions, the very ends of dominion and sovereignty, as lawyers were wont to assert, were all within the practitioner's ken. To the extent that lawyers could extol the domain of the Law as a national holy of holies, in some such degree they themselves became honored Levites of that shrine. The lawyer's work could not only be exalted, it was also in other ways peculiarly gratifying. While the workday world of growing numbers of Americans was becoming increasingly subjected to discipline and restriction, the lawyer's employment remained a happy mixture of work and play, with ample scope for wit, whim, gaudy melodrama, and entertainments. It also afforded a rough-and-tumble camaraderie at the bar that many found so appealing, and which later would be commemorated in the histories of bench and bar of so many diverse cities, counties, and states.[49]

While the lawyers' authority and honor may have dimmed somewhat in this period, when compared to the previous era, the legal profession nonetheless retained much vigor and resiliency. Ministers and physicians could not as easily adapt themselves to the new deliverances and constraints of the era. Yet all three professions maintained gentlemanly authority and honor within their work setting, though they surrendered some of both in society at large. All adopted a strategy of attempting to strengthen what they took to be the centers of professional distinctiveness and coherence when they found the boundaries to be increasingly undefendable. Clearly, in the era 1830–1880 the American professions acquired a vernacular spirit and form. The very openness of the professions to new men and new ideas, unpolished and outlandish as both often were, allowed for distinctive accomplishments. While American Protestant theology often became either inflexible or flaccid, nevertheless the American ministers reached out and captured the common people just as European Protestant ministers seemed to be losing their hold on their lower classes. And if American medical theory was muddled, American surgeons (and dentists) were advancing in dexterity and effectiveness. It was precisely in this period of quackery that W. T. Morton, a dentist with a smattering of medical school training, introduced ether anesthesia, and American doctors quickly accepted it. Moreover, though an eminent legal scholar writing about the organized bar of this time described the period as an "Era of Decadence," when dealing with the law rather than legal organizations, he observed that "the creative legal achievements of this period will compare favorably with any period of growth and adjustment in legal history."[50]

The central fact of this era for the professions was that they were able to maintain the distinction between the specially honored and authoritative profession and the ordinary occupation. Relinquishing some of their more vulnerable features—such as the disdain for manual labor and trade, the insistence upon a classical education, the hankering for the differentia of licensing laws—left the professions more accessible and yet still distinguishing and alluring. That was a prodigious accomplishment and invites attention to the factors that made it possible.

First of all, as has been suggested, the leveling attack upon the professions was peculiarly equivocal. While some Americans wanted to bring all barriers down and looked upon the distinctiveness of the professions as pure humbug, others wanted to make entry less restrictive but somehow keep the special dominion and esteem of the professions intact. In this bewildering setting, the adroit efforts of many zealous leaders of the professions to stand up against the popular enmity that harassed their activities and associations had considerable effect.

Less obvious, yet still important to the survival of the professions, was the local sheltered market situation they enjoyed. The professional bestowed a service that was usually individualized, specific to the provider and recipient. The client usually chose a professional through personal connections, and that meant that the market for professional services was local, personal, and differentiated. Despite the breakdown of restrictions on entry into the professions, sellers when compared to buyers were few and relatively cohesive. Professionals, for the most part, could also avoid sharp rivalry and even price competition through fee bills, statutory assessments, and customary remuneration. Such restraints on consumer choice allowed the professional to maintain a bearing of authority, even if at some pecuniary loss. That loss rarely meant failure.[51]

Furthermore, the professions, despite the difficulties in their "science" in this era, remained significantly the work of intellect. That meant they would be a respected kind of work. This was, in part, because such work often seemed useful but, more important, because insofar as it was mental, such work became somehow spiritual. In this connection, we must remind ourselves of the obvious. The United States was a Christian society and placed spirit, variously defined, above matter. Spirit therefore was frequently granted some right in directing society—if not often through any collectivity, then commonly in a very Protestant way, through each person's psyche. Intellect still retained some of its association with elevated standing in the community.

Moreover, the three traditional professions dealt with men and women who were in peril or pain, leaving them dependent and sometimes even in a childlike position. The structure of the situation brought to light the circumstantial inequality between the bestower and the recipient of the service. The professional relation of authority and dependence echoed that reciprocal relation of protection and subordination that had pervaded the feudal era in Europe, when central governments had been greatly weakened, particularly in their protective powers. Vulnerability was intrinsic to both the feudal and the professional relationship. The vulnerability of the client was more circumscribed in time and amplitude; nonetheless when he or she sought professional help, limited and sporadic as that encounter might be, the professional and client together recreated in that situation a shadowy simulacrum of the feudal relationship. It is not surprising, therefore, that the professional found the various usages of the traditional gentlemanly class particularly congenial.

In order to discern more clearly how the professions resisted the peculiar egalitarian onslaught and gave new meaning to their honor and authority in this interregnum, the years 1830 to

1880, it is helpful to look at particular communities. Such a view enables us to see more comprehensively the professional's relationship to his community. Of course, this type of close-up has its obvious drawbacks. Magnification can bring clarity, but it also inevitably narrows the range of vision. Choosing the point of focus therefore becomes a critical decision.

To observe particularly the new characteristics of professional life in this era, it is advantageous to consider the region that contemporaries called the West. Though clearly integrated into the nation, and subject to its economic swings, religious enthusiasm, and political alignments, this West was, nonetheless, undoubtedly new. Moreover, what was new about it was on top, apparent, and often dominant; what was old usually obtruded incongruously, and was therefore conspicuous as well. Tocqueville caught some sense of this as he left Cincinnati en route to Memphis on his western tour in the winter of 1831: "All that there is good or bad in American society is found there [in the states of the West] in such strong relief, that one would be tempted to call it one of those books printed in large letters for teaching children to read; everything there is in violent contrast, exaggerated."[52]

For studying professionals in America, cities are especially revealing places. They were centers of professional leadership, innovation, and institution building, radiating their influence widely into the surrounding regions. The bulk of the practitioners lived and worked in cities; it was their natural habitat. There is much that is inevitably indirect in studying the professions in local settings, for we must give considerable attention to particular urban histories. However, the indirect influences of circumstance, so important to the professions, can best be seen in just this way. The cities that we study should be placed so as to disclose the two distinctive subcultures that had emerged in America of this era, that of the South and of the North.[53]

Memphis and Cincinnati, two cities that Tocqueville found so revealing on his western tour, are particularly instructive to us as well. Like the country as a whole, both cities were growing rapidly and exuberantly, as were their bustling coteries of professionals. They were situated along the great Mississippi River system that gave much to the events and ideas of the nation in this era, yet each city reflected some of the salient characteristics of its section. Memphis was booming on cotton and slavery, Cincinnati on diversified industry and the energetic labor of a remarkably varied population. Cincinnati was much larger than Memphis but in this they reflected their sections as well. Cities were generally larger in the North than in the South—and in 1860, Cincinnati was the sixth largest in the North while Memphis was the sixth largest in the South. Both were upstart cities, and their accompanying social discomposure and social cataclysms has much informing value. Both were deeply and extensively connected not only to their sections but to the country at large as well; therefore studying them closely suggests much that is beyond them. These two cities consequently are two unrandom samples—they are decidedly intended to be indicative rather than representative. Let us then turn to Memphis and Cincinnati.[54]

4

Memphis: A Southern Exposure on the Professions, 1830–1880

By the early months of 1847, the outcome of the Wolf River canal project had become evident, and that result was to decide the course of events in Memphis for many years to come. The project had been a source of immense enthusiasm. This plan to build a canal from the Wolf River to the Mississippi was bound up with the attempt to diversify the economy of the city. The canal would not only provide cheap water power and promote manufacturing, proponents claimed, it would help vary the agriculture of the region as well. Wheat could be grown and milled into flour; sheep could be raised and their fleece would provide for a local woolens industry. There was much that was appealing in this vision. Yet it was a matter of much cry and little wool. There was great excitement over the project: the mayor favored it, as did a unanimous council, and a majority of the voters whose approval had been registered in a proper election. However, the wealthiest and most influential taxpayers (many of them with heavy investments in cotton and the railroads that brought cotton into and out of town) announced that they "would not submit to being taxed for such purposes." Thereupon the project quickly fizzled.[1]

That such a peremptory declaration could so readily overturn an official decision of the city suggests that by 1847 any attempt at economic diversification was already too late. By then, Memphis was shackled to cotton. The most obvious consequence of this attachment was that it brought to Memphis a species of newly rich cotton merchants and factors, volatile and splendiferous, often with little feeling for the city itself but with a veto power over its affairs. If the city would be inhospitable, one of them warned, there might be another town nearby that was more welcoming. Memphis's strong ties to cotton also meant close connections to those great plantations, based upon slavery, that flourished on the fertile soil in the environs of the city and also to the social predispositions toward violence and gentility that emanated from plantation life.[2]

Southern gentility itself rested upon a code stemming initially from an admiration and imitation of the life of the English landed gentry but taking on vernacular qualities, in American setting, that the English would come to consider somewhat exotic. Nonetheless, the Southerners successfully transplanted two principal qualities of English gentry life—the preference for rural ways and for the gratifications of "the habits of command." The Southern gentleman of fact and fiction, embodying both those qualities, loomed large in the Southern imagination. This was apparent in the career patterns common among ambitious Southerners, even when plantation profits seemed to be declining. "No matter how [some] one might begin, as a lawyer, physician, clergyman, mechanic, or merchant, he ended, if prosperous, as a proprietor of a rice or cotton plantation." Around Memphis, where cotton was booming, such a shift to the ownership of plantations and slaves, and with it the shift to rural life, was especially alluring. For some of its most successful citizens, the city became a way station to a better life, undercutting the development of an extended sense of responsibility and allegiance. Memphis, ironically, owing to this very air of transience and makeshift, could be more singularly capitalist—it could become primarily a business proposition, and a shortsighted one, at that.[3]

For the professionals living in the city, this had far-reaching significance. It meant that some of them, particularly some of the leading lawyers, would be drawn away from their own standards and gratifications to those of the surrounding planter class. More frequently, it meant that urban professionals would try to maintain the ideals of both ways of life even when those ideals were in conflict. However, it also meant that those who held steadfast to the traditional values of their vocation, particularly some of the doctors, would occupy subordinate positions in making the decisions that affected the future of the city.

Cotton trading did not begin in Memphis until the 1830s, and when it did, it took on some of the spirit of earlier enterprise. Memphis's first asset had been its location. It was a convenient stopover for Mississippi riverboat traffic and became a rough-and-tumble town for the crews of those boats and for the merchants who catered to the boatmen's various appetites. When cotton became the principal crop of the hinterland, cotton factors, brokers, and buyers joined the local merchants and real estate speculators as the leading classes of the city. It is remarkable how many of these cotton men speculated openly and dangerously, considering their dependence upon liberal extensions of credit and the fact that such speculators were thought to be poor credit risks. Brooks, Neely and Co. was one of the largest of the speculators; W. B. Glisson, one of the smallest but respected; William L. Steward and Bros., one of the most long-lived; W. B. Galbraith, one of the most flamboyant. One of the most droll was the Dickensian firm of Dodge C. Trader and John A. Fleese. Mr. Trader, "rather visionary, trying to do more than his means will allow," was probably lost in one of those visions when Mr. Fleese, living up to his name, transferred the assets of the company to that of his brother.[4]

Plunging cotton merchants could be as profligate as rakehell-ish sailors. This waywardness was most conspicuous in the reluctance of leading Memphians to support the levying of taxes and even to pay those that were levied. One of the common ways of escaping the burden was to let the taxes go unpaid and settle accounts later at a much lower amount. A reputable tax collector, one of the eminent businessmen in town, was himself found to be a defaulter to the sum of $300,000. Selling city bonds and issuing scrip became a favorite method of raising revenue. Since a sinking fund maintained through taxes was rarely set up to pay off this indebtedness, bonds and scrip quickly depreciated, were brought up cheaply, and were returned to the city at face value in the payment of taxes. One bond issue was *initially* sold at one quarter its listed value.[5]

"We know of no city in the South-west—perhaps there is none in the Union—having as ample revenue means in proportion to its population as Memphis," wrote a local journalist. The citizens were rich but the city was poor. Municipal services were stunted and haphazard, the city growing rapidly any-which-way. The public school system set up in 1848 was starved, and a disheartening campaign for a public library brought no result until 1893, when the bequest of a New York merchant who had done business in Memphis provided the funds for its establishment. Street paving was rudimentary and there was no organized garbage collection. Sewage was dumped into the sluggish waters of Gayoso bayou which ran through the city. As a result, Memphis became a permanent sump for the breeding of diseases that were visited upon the population in periodic epidemics of increasing destructiveness until the terrifying paroxysm of yellow fever in 1878 that took five thousand lives.[6]

The prevailing temper of the city until the eighties—one of spasmodic hopefulness and self-indulgence—could be seen most easily at the top and the bottom of the social order. Roughneck sailors had their whorehouses and prosperous cotton merchants their ornate bordellos, the sailors their craps and the cotton merchants their elegant racetrack, the sailors their savage affrays and the cotton merchants their histrionic duels. Slavery contributed to the violence of the society. The need to preserve the power of the master over the slave set broad limits to the state's control over violence. So did the overwrought sense of personal independence that free white men clung to in this peculiarly egalitarian slave society. A certain amount of hot temper and bloodthirstiness was looked upon as something like a natural right reserved to all white males and not delegated to any government. The slave, by stark contrast, was "subject at all times to be restrained in his liberty, and chastised in his body, by the capricious will of another."[7]

The Civil War had less impact on Memphis than one might have expected. The city itself was captured by Union troops without a battle and quickly became a center for contraband trading in cotton. Real estate values in the city had actually increased during the War. Though the slaves had been freed, the Blacks of Shelby County remained a depressed caste and continued to supply the cheap labor that provided the basis for the widespread cotton cultivation of the region. Certainly the gentlemanly ideal had coarsened and faded, but it was still manifest and permeating. Local civil leadership after the War clearly became more raffish and rapacious. Antebellum leaders—Robertson Topp, Robert C. Brinkley, John T. Trezevant, and Seth Wheatly—had been well-educated men with elevated aspirations. Topp, Trezevant, and Wheatly were lawyers who invested successfully in real estate and railroads, as well as in cotton plantations to which they retired. Though they cultivated the dignified life of the plantation aristocracy, they never gave up their active interest in their real estate or railroads.[8]

The four city fathers of the 1870s and early 1880s—Napoleon Hill, D. P. "Pappy" Hadden, Henry Montgomery, and Archibald Wright—were something of a come down from the pre-War city leadership. Among them, none was conspicuously the leader. Hill was probably the richest man in town. He had made his money trading in cotton and then invested it in banking, insurance, railroads, city traction, and various other businesses. Hadden also got rich in cotton but, unlike Hill, he went in for local politics where his influence as a wirepuller and officeholder was considerable. Montgomery, in running his enormous press that packed the local staple tightly enough for direct shipment to the markets of the world, helped put Memphis on the map as a great distributing center of the middle South. Wright was their lawyer and friend, who had aided them in winning their place and fortune and assisted them in preserving those winnings. To the antebellum city fathers these men would have seemed culturally impoverished. Hill and Montgomery had just about a grade-school education, Hadden somewhat more, and Wright never read any books except on the law. They clearly did not fit the style of the traditional Southern gentleman. The three cotton men had all managed to be elsewhere when the great battles of the Civil War were fought. Montgomery was harsh with his Blacks. Hill talked mostly about cotton and money. Hadden was known for his wisecracks and tomfoolery. And Wright, though he had sat on the bench of the Tennessee Supreme Court, was not ashamed to sit on the curb of the Memphis streets, pull off his shoes, and stroke his aching bunions. Despite their wealth and successes they were conspicuously come-at-able. This reflected, in part, the influence of openness of the Memphis cotton market itself, where family ties, traditions, prejudices, and decorum came to count for less than they did in most places in the South.[9]

Mitigating such brazenness and the general loosening of social bonds that this kind of leadership gave rise to was a countervailing predisposition toward cohesiveness and restraint that was most apparent in the middle layers of society. If Memphis were *only* a business proposition, that would be too flattening and unsatisfying for many of its inhabitants. Few wished to quarrel with their bread and butter, yet a sympathetic reading of even the crudest Memphis boosterism often discloses the attempt to link warm personal and social attachments to the economic well-being of the city. Such sentiments were often tied to what might be called a civic folk mercantilism. This was an outlook on public economy that viewed the city as a particular and discrete entity in rivalry with other cities, and stressed the mutual interest of the local residents in the city's advancement. One of the supports for this outlook was the common experience of diverse and disparate urban real estate owners who almost all benefited when the city prospered. In addition, such civic folk mercantilism drew upon the interest of the small merchants in the proposal to "buy local." Ostensibly, such a policy would maintain a high level of demand for local goods. This logic often led to a proposal for the promotion of local manufactures and perpetual and ineffectual talk of ridding the city of her dependence upon cotton. "Commission and forwarding houses," one writer explained, "require but few hands. They do not invite population, they build up no manufacturers, and they enhance but little the value of real estate. They may exist without the accompaniment of a great city." [10]

Related to these notions of civic folk mercantilism was the practice, more rudimentary, resilient, and consequential, of maintaining "connections." This was not primarily an economic policy, although it had important economic results. What the people of Memphis meant by connections was an elaborate network of favors and obligations having its origins in family ties but extending to friends, acquaintances, and associates. The chief rewards and punishments of this system were varying degrees of amity and enmity, but they could include inheritance and disinheritance, custom, and boycott. The first case of a young lawyer coming to town quite likely would be the suit of rich relatives; the next perhaps the cause of their close friends, and then cases of other friends and acquaintances who were somehow obligated. [11]

Informal lines of connections were also the lifeblood of the growing immigrant communities of Memphis—the Irish, who were primarily poor laborers, and the Germans, who were largely craftsmen, merchants, and professionals. By 1860 such immigrants made up roughly a quarter of the population, but by the eighties that proportion had declined sharply. [12]

The system of connections surfaced and was formalized in a variety of social organizations, the two most important being the Old Folks Association and the Masons. The Old Folks Association, founded in 1856, restricted its membership to families that had lived in Shelby County for twenty years or more! Pride in Memphis's material advance was often expressed at its meetings, but with the insistence that the only sure and legitimate way to wealth was hard work and clearly not "pure Bull Luck." In fact, gambling, deception, and the "heartless selfishness [that] surrounds us on every side" were denounced. Duty, it was advised, must accompany power. In his "Ode to Memphis," James D. Davis, Esq., the official historian of the society (and the author of the first history of the city) praised the city's pioneers, "a band of brothers," as well as the subsequent "wise and moral population," and more particularly the "thrifty merchants, free from spoil / Their trade secure." [13]

The Masons, established in Memphis in 1848, were less attached to the city's past but no less public-spirited or selective in membership. The lodges seem to have been made up largely of respectable small businessmen, professionals, and skilled artisans. "Masonry is a temple for good, true, industrious, and well-to-do men to live in. The rich, as a general thing, are too cold and penurious to add to its strength; and the impoverished are but a dead weight taken upon the order to weaken the strength of the building." Character was the primary test for membership, yet somehow women, Blacks, and those who could not pay the ten dollars yearly dues were automatically excluded.[14]

The social teachings of Masonry fit closely with its notions of character and virtue. The effect of the "reverence to the Divine Being," it was thought, was a subdual of passions and the encouragement of temperance in habits. Masons condemned those "sordid money-seekers," speculators, duelists, gamblers, and tipplers who abounded in Memphis. However, even the Masons' own fraternal sociability was in danger of being put to venal use. For one Mason would legitimately prefer business dealings with another, or hiring a "brother" of whom it could be assumed that he would be sober and upstanding. The Order, therefore, was often admonished to guard against those joining simply for mercenary reasons. Such bogus members would detract from Masonic fellowship and might weaken the endeavors to moralize economic relations—the setting up of a "just and reliable comity of interests, whereby both [buyer and seller] are benefited." Some of the more ardent Masons also belonged to the Howard Association, a benevolent public health organization, many of whose members worked selflessly and heroically in aiding the victims of the various epidemics that struck Memphis periodically.[15]

The sociability of the Old Folks Association and the Masons, even when tied to the claims of patriotism and good works, met with some reproof because it was also associated with explicit exclusiveness. Similarly, the professions, which also often justified their exclusiveness by good works and by special merit, likewise ran into difficulties. Most overt exclusiveness was suspect in a society that was repeatedly and ambiguously declaring its allegiance to equality. Equality was a paradoxical standard. To those who had less, and to those who were excluded (and they were often the same), it could mean simply I want more and I want in. But in addition, despite all its common-sensical translations, equality also referred to a supersensible notion of intrinsic human worth in which there were no degrees. And this notion left its imprint upon those who were in, as well as those who were out. With its various meanings, equality provided a standpoint for the attack upon exclusiveness and even merit.[16]

Broadly speaking, the professions in Memphis were a force for cohesiveness and restraint within their own circles and, to varying degrees, beyond. The gambling spirit was antithetical to the notion of reward to merit, an ostensible standard of professional distinction. Also, the professions gave support to the slogan "buy local" and were quite adept at the system of connections. Their customary ban on advertising, going back to the era when one of their chief identifying characteristics was their distinction from trade, ineluctably tied the professions to connections. Advertising would also imply that clients could properly judge the merits of professionals, something most professionals were not willing to admit. A new doctor or lawyer in town might put his professional card in the newspaper for a while without giving offense, but any vaunting of abilities before the public was taboo.

Professionals' services were not sold on anything like an open competitive market; rather they were most often dispensed along a network of personal ties and relations. These conditions supported the professionals' efforts to join together and their efforts (each profession in different ways and differing degrees) to tame the heedless individualism of the entrepreneurial spirit that dominated the city. The professions therefore bore a strong resemblance to the other middle-range occupations in the city, yet they stood apart from those other occupations in asserting their own special kind of authority and honor.[17]

The most variegated of the professions in Memphis, most deeply enmeshed in a wide range of local affairs and most clearly reflecting the divergent tendencies of Memphis life, was the law. Lawyers became plantation aristocrats and advisors of plantation aristocrats, small businessmen and agents of small businessmen, cotton tycoons and handlers of cotton tycoons, politicians and go-betweens for politicians, officers of the courts and exponents of legal thought. The day-to-day work of the courts, and the inherited body of knowledge and theory, interacted and influenced each other. When Memphis lawyers talked about "the science of the law," they most often meant constitutionalism. The federal Constitution was "the supreme law of the land," and the ordinary processes of litigation and judicial decision making were the primary devices of interpretation and enforcement. American lawyers were ex officio constitutional theorists. They prided themselves upon these concerns, for these concerns lent special honor to their profession; constitutionalism was the most exalted and decorous portion of their legal science.[18]

"The Constitution," wrote Henry Craft, one of Memphis's leading lawyers, "is the sacred covenant by which personal independence is surrendered, and the sacred measure of the extent of that surrender." For Southern lawyers the stress lay on the second half of that formula. Among the many balances in the Constitution, one of the most important for these lawyers was the counterposing of Southern mores and the more generally held notions of justice and equality. Before the Civil War, the "three-fifths clause" was the fulcrum of that balance. Constitutional rights and Southern usage were sometimes fused and confused—as when the Tennessee Supreme Court decided that it was a constitutional right of a responsible citizen to carry a "rifle, shot gun, musket, and army or navy repeater . . . at pleasure in any manner, concealed or otherwise," free from interference from the legislature. Often the Constitution was considered the archetype of all law in weighing personal independence and Southern mores against what was sometimes claimed to be their socially necessary abridgement; Southern lawyers usually came down on the side of personal independence and Southern mores.[19]

"The science of law" also referred to the vast collection of miscellaneous information, both substantive and procedural, about the workings of the courts. The very miscellaneousness of the law was important. It was fed by the increasing volume of judicial decisions as well as the outpourings of the active Jacksonian legislatures. The masters of this type of law were of a special sort. The pleadings of Archibald Wright, one of the foremost lawyers in Memphis, were careful, laborious, painstaking, and shapeless. He argued all that could conceivably be argued on his side, "submitting every proposal that could possibly bear on the case." Few could match his erudition on the statutes of Tennessee or the state's leading cases. Most of the traditional forms of action of the common law had disappeared or had been combined and given general names in Tennessee through legislation or judicial decision. This seemingly brought the law closer to prevailing notions of fairness and common sense, but it made it more difficult to determine the point at issue in any particular case. Trials were more chaotic, and lawyers could usually be more spontaneous, orotund, and amusing.[20]

This was particularly true of criminal law practice in Memphis. The leading criminal lawyer of the fifties was Edwin M. Yerger. One of eight brothers scattered throughout Tennessee (seven of them attorneys), Yerger was clearly among the great "natural" lawyers of the state. He had little academic training and a strong aversion to the details of case preparation. Yet those were considered minor shortcomings, easily offset by his retentive mind, his keen powers of reasoning, his melodious voice, and his sparkling comic talents. When portly and affable Yerger was to address the jury, the courtroom quickly filled, and young ladies of the best families were often to be seen in the audience, Yerger rarely disappointed them. In one notable trial he addressed the jury for seven hours in order to fully develop his case; the opposing lawyer tried to match him with a seven-hour oration the next day. Entertainment was well served, but justice probably less so.[21]

This miscellaneous character of the workaday law encouraged the growth of the codification movement in Tennessee. The remarkably varied admixture of materials that went to make up the law placed burdens upon practitioners whose preparation had been skimpy, and often left the law itself uncertain. As with the New York codification movement of David Dudley Field (to which the Tennessee advocates owed some inspiration), this project to simplify the law was to be a purely inductive effort, avoiding all the heady issues of natural rights and the tangled questions of first principles. The reform occasionally got out of hand, and the attack upon legal technicality sometimes led to an attack upon the legal profession itself. Governor Andrew Johnson, an erstwhile lawyer with a hankering to somehow make law and morality the same, took up the cause of codification under the startling slogan, "Let all restraints and barriers be removed." The distinction between law and equity he thought should be abolished; cases at law were to be tried on their "naked merits"; the courts would always be open so that a litigant could enter "without a cent's cost and have his relief instantly." There would be little or no preparation of a case for hearing and the skillfulness of counsel would be much less necessary. The parties themselves could state their case, be examined, and have justice done at once.[22]

Such simplicity dismayed most lawyers, yet the practitioners never lost control of the movement. They pushed aside the standpatters who claimed that almost all existing legal distinctions were rooted in the nature of things and fended off the ultras who thought that most distinctions were conspiracies against the common man. The Tennessee Code of 1858, shepherded through the legislature by J. B. Heiskell (soon to become one of Memphis's leading lawyers) retained the distinction between law and equity and provided a loose analytical arrangement (apparently based upon Blackstone) of statutory materials, judicial findings, and common-law usages. It remained the basis of Tennessee practice for roughly three-quarters of a century.[23]

The code itself was revealing of the distinctive regional qualities of Tennessee law and lawyers, and the sections devoted to slavery made the distinctiveness unmistakable. Before the Civil War, the institution of slavery gave rise to a large volume of litigation, chiefly for breach of warranty on the bills of sale as to the "soundness" of the slave. Slavery, as one lawyer explained, was a vital necessity for the South, yet this necessity must be subject to law. The Constitution, the highest law, restrained the federal government from interfering with it, and the state code restrained the slave owner from exercising despotic cruelty over those he held in bondage. Undoubtedly the chief object of the slave code was to protect the institution of slavery and keep the Black man in his place within it; nevertheless the courts and the lawyers sometimes endeavored to protect the slaves through the use of the formal procedural devices of the law. The essential difficulty lay in the peculiar status of the slave; he was both human and property, and the legal rules for neither could fully apply.[24]

Slavery's link to violence was demonstrated in the endless brawls of Bolton, Dickens, and Co., "the most extensive slave traders in the World," who provided Memphis with a series of feuds, murders, and duels that kept local lawyers busy. Some lawyers themselves fought duels eagerly, if anxiously. Duels were a requirement of gentlemanly honor in the South, and lawyers saw themselves as gentlemen. Dueling, however, was illegal in Tennessee, and dueling lawyers who wished to accept the highest judicial offices had to bring themselves to swear that they had never exchanged shots on the field of honor. One lawyer justified such behavior with a unique interpretation of the old distinction between *lex scripta* and *lex non scripta*, in which these categories were made not only distinct but in this instance diametrically opposite. Dueling lawyers, therefore, remained in this sense law abiding. Some lawyers refused to duel, and others courageously refused to carry arms. Yet most were unwilling to see any conflict between professional and class values. Dueling in the Southwest, one of these attorneys wrote, "was the primal obligation of a class of chivalrous men who adorned the highest class of society."[25]

Rank and profession were often more in accord when lawyers assumed a position of authority with regard to their clients. The lawyer was an officer of the court, and the client was someone "who, unable to act for himself, seeks him [the lawyer] out and places himself in his hands, reposes in him confidence." Those going to law to protect life or property were usually well aware of the vagaries of legal contests and their dependence upon the lawyer for a favorable outcome. As we have seen, the relation of authority and dependence found expression in the common-law rule of privileged communications. Technically this was a privilege of the client which he might invoke in order to prevent his lawyer from being called upon to testify about information that had passed between them about the case. Actually, it had resonance far beyond the courtroom. Lawyers were ardent in its praise. "The minds of troubled men," wrote a Memphis lawyer, "must have some place where they can unbosom and lay bare the inward suffering of the heart, repose the details of their life with the laws' protection from exposure." As a drawer of wills and an intermediary in family disputes, a lawyer might become the repository of personal and ancestral secrets. Comparable to the relationship supported by the common-law doctrine of privileged communications was the connection fostered by the equity doctrine of trusts. Established lawyers often served as legal trustees, holding and administering property for those proverbial "widows and orphans" and protecting them from the designs of villains and wastrels. The lawyer stood as champion of the vulnerable in a fiduciary relationship from which he was to derive no immediate material benefit. Lawyers made much of that role.[26]

The relation of authority and dependence and the anxieties it bred may have had some bearing upon contradictory emotions that pervaded the local folklore about lawyers. While particular lawyers were praised, the profession in general often came up against the age-old disparagements that it was heartless, mercenary, and conniving. The clash between law and morality, always perplexing to laymen, also contributed to the disquieting image of the lawyer. Again, what was John Q. Public to make of the lawyer pleading the statute of limitations (which seemed to hold that a crime was not a crime if it was old enough) and the lawyer's practice of indiscriminate advocacy (that permitted him to take a fee in order to defend what he may have thought to be wrong)? The arcane and ostensibly obfuscating terminology of the law was particularly suspect. "Law is law," mocked one writer, "and is such and so forth and hereby and aforesaid, provided always, nevertheless notwithstanding." It was the lesser lawyers, with names left unmentioned, who were most often berated. Newcomers without connections in Memphis usually became the debt collectors, often for out-of-town creditors. These "cold-

blooded collecting attorneys" would resort to "all the harsher ex-
pedients known to law." The customary fee was ten percent of the
amount collected, and such payment provided ample income for
beginners. The established firms were more moderate in their
collecting and often gave up this work to the newer men.[27]

The first prodigious flow of legal talent into Memphis came in
the decade before the Civil War, when the city was booming.
"Memphis," wrote an established lawyer to a beginner, "although
the most disagreeable at present as a residence, offers the greatest inducement to the young." The city soon boasted the ablest
bar in the Southwest. Growth of the bar was interrupted by the
War but resumed in the decade that followed the peace. In the
fifties the most important legal connections were still linked to
families, but by the seventies (and this may be related to the
sheer growth of the city) various kinds of institutional amity took
on increasing significance. The fraternal orders, the Confederate
veterans organizations, political parties, churches, and the Bar
Association itself provided connections. Institutionalized amity
was more open to the outsider. The legal careers of Jews, men
without good family connections, may illustrate this. Jacob J.
Peres, though quite talented and energetic, could not make a go
of it in the fifties, while Leopold Lehman, capable not only in the
law but also in the ritual and associational skills of Masonry,
built a highly successful practice in the seventies. Lehman was
also admitted to the Bar Association which had been founded in
1867; ostensibly, any practicing or retired lawyer of the vicinity
could join. However, the membership fees were high, and that
kept the less prosperous lawyers out, gradually transforming the
association into an elite organization. Its declared objects were
the maintenance of "the honor and dignity of the profession of
law, the cultivation of the science of the law, the promotion of
social intercourse among its members . . . [the] aid and assistance of the administration of justice . . . [and] the formation and
establishment of a permanent law library." The library was an
important focal point of the association but almost equally important were the various social gatherings the association spon-
sored. The sharp rivalry of the adversary system within the courtroom ("Every time a lawyer loses a case he hurts his legal
standing," explained a Memphis lawyer) made some measure of
affability outside the courtroom almost obligatory if lawyers were
to maintain any cohesiveness at all. Memphis lawyers, unlike
doctors or ministers, were renowned for their storytelling, their
humor, and their practical jokes. The gala annual dinners of the
Bar Association were occasions for these, and even more so were

the roisterous meetings of "The Pastor's Aid Society"—gathering of Memphis lawyers for draw poker.[28]

Though requirements for entry into the profession in Tennessee had fallen greatly by the fifties when the Memphis Bar began to take shape, the education of its leading members was comparable to that of the seaboard lawyers of the earlier era. As for the rest of the Memphis Bar, their learning varied considerably. Those citizens who were nimble-witted and who could avail themselves of a year of intensive study of legal textbooks and forms might stand a chance of a successful practice in Memphis. Yet amidst the relatively widespread illiteracy in Tennessee such apparently minimal barriers were insuperable for most. The diminished requirements, nevertheless, encouraged horizontal mobility among professional men. There were eminent lawyers in Memphis who had earlier careers as ministers, engineers, military officers, and Botanic doctors.[29]

The law itself was a bridge to other careers. Memphis lawyers went on to careers in politics and business, and many successful lawyers deserted Blackstone for the plantation. This made preeminent positions in the Memphis Bar more accessible. Lehman left Cincinnati, a larger more vibrant city with a much larger Jewish community to support its professionals (where nevertheless he felt opportunities closed off), and came to Memphis where he rose rapidly to become one of the leading lawyers in the city. While many lawyers tried to combine politics, business, and legal work, most luminaries of the bar devoted themselves chiefly to the law and seem to have derived most of their income from it. Some rose to wealth and reputation through the law and entered into the whole range of Memphis life, representing almost all segments of society and advocating their various causes.[30]

Politics did not seem to divide lawyers in Memphis very deeply. The president of the Bar Association in the seventies was a Republican while the leading member of its board of directors was the Democratic ex-governor of Tennessee who led the state out of the Union during the Civil War. Some of the law firms were partnerships of Democrats and Republicans (Koterecht and Craft was the most eminent of these). Even during the secession crisis, the bench and bar showed a surprising cohesiveness. Most leaders of the bar, for example, supported the reelection of Judge McKinney, although his loyalty to the Confederacy was in doubt; and later, when Memphis was occupied by Union troops, loyal Judge Connelly F. Trigg admitted Confederate lawyers to practice almost indiscriminately. The fact that so many of the Memphis lawyers had been Whigs before the War may have contributed to the sense of cohesiveness in the bar. However, the widespread and staunchly held belief that courtroom proceedings should be free of political considerations was also important. Democratic and Whig politicians urged the election of Democratic and Whig judges, respectively, because only their party would not "carry party feeling into courts of justice."[31]

Popular election of judges did not bring them closer to the people but rather closer to the bar, from which judges usually came and to which, after short terms of elective office, they were likely to return. The candidates for judgeships were invariably lawyers, and the bar had an informal influence upon their selection. "No man with a proper sense of professional propriety," wrote one judicial candidate, "would offer for the position against the wishes of his brethren of the bar." If judges became somewhat less exalted, lawyers became somewhat more so. Leading lawyers entertained the notion that they might become distinguished lawgivers through their important briefs. Leopold Lehman and George Gantt, two Galahads of the Memphis Bar, squared off in chivalric combat, bringing their great learning and ingenuity to bear against each other for a notable case in which the legal issue at stake seemed to be of great consequence, but the money at stake was only seventy-five dollars.[32]

Victory in such forensic combat could advance the law and bring special honor to the winner. Memphis lawyers, of course, hoped that legal renown and wealth would go hand in hand, that wealth and intellect would be allied. Yet they were willing to acknowledge that this was often not the case. There was a different kind of respect given to Archibald Wright and Joseph B. Heiskell. Wright's forceful personality, extensive legal knowledge, and go-getting business exploits were recognized and approved. However, the bar gave its particular esteem to Heiskell, a lawyer with little eloquence and only moderate wealth, but with a precise technical knowledge of the law and the power to move with ease within its structure, handling its complexities with remarkable finesse.[33]

Heiskell also exemplified that segment of the bar that took its public responsibilities seriously. He had been a leader in the fight for the adoption of the Tennessee Code and later became a tax reformer in Memphis, lecturing its citizens on the tie between taxes and necessary regional improvements. Like many Southerners, he set himself against the dangers of "centralization," but he joined this argument to a program for making local government energetic and answerable to local needs. Like many in Memphis, but clearly not those who dominated civic affairs, he argued that dependence upon cotton was the great corrosive of the South, and the South would never escape from it and diversify its economy if economic matters were left simply to individual self-interest. Only an active government could "promote what the individual cannot." Heiskell went further still and earnestly admonished his fellow citizens to turn away from narrow self-seeking. "In proportion as we are actuated by some sense of justice, of duty to others, and regardlessness of self, we are worthy of the name civilized." Such preachment seemed excessive and unusual for local lawyers and clearly not what Memphians expected of them. Some of the foremost attorneys might be high-minded, yet in ways usually less discordant with the prevailing temper of the city. One writer suggested that most Memphis lawyers had "one eye on heaven, but the other on the main chance."[34]

The divided vision of the Memphis ministers was of a much different sort. The ministers looked to man's wrongdoing and to God's salvation. Yet their sense of man's wrongdoing remained so highly personalized as to make many of the social wrongs of their region almost indiscernible. While the lawyers became the profession most broadly and deeply involved in the day-to-day workings of Memphis society, the ministers became the most insular profession, often shut off from the most important doings of the city's life. This was particularly true in the revivalist churches of Memphis.

Revivalism was a mixture of cathartic preaching and high-pressure stratagems that stirred the deepest emotions and produced what seemed to be spiritual revolution of heart and soul within sinners. One of its chief drawbacks was that it could not easily be made to fit with the religious understanding derived from Calvinism that informed most American denominations. Even the eminently intellectual American churchmen of the nineteenth century, however, found it difficult to resist revivalism's ostensible successes. Technique swallowed understanding. The Calvinist vision of the overwhelming magnificence of God and his unlimited powers, that found expression in the doctrine of predestination, clashed with the revivalists' unmitigated insistence upon human agency, will, and responsibility—which seemed to be an essential part of the workings of nineteenth-century revivals. Some ministers of Calvinist tradition tried to preach and practice the ways that would respect both Calvinist doctrine and revivalist measures. This formula would keep doctrine pure but would leave it lifeless. More common was the answer given in this instance by a Baptist: "We must strike the golden mean between granite Calvinism on the one hand and the low marshes of Armenianism [*sic*] on the other." Such a golden mean was to be found in the specific and practical work of salvation. For most Americans the highest praise one could give someone's religion was to call it "practical and evangelical."[35]

In Memphis, the churches that had absorbed revivalism—chiefly the Baptists, Methodists, and Presbyterians—dominated the religious life of the city. The Catholics, Jews, and even some Episcopalians stood on the periphery. All evangelical churches usually considered each other as "members of the visible body of Christ," but ministers asked for special devotion to their own denomination, which they claimed to be the Church in its purest form. Much of the doctrinal preaching that poured from the Memphis pulpits centered upon those questions that justified denominational uniqueness. It was as if God's relation to man and the universe could be epitomized in the question whether *baptizo* meant sprinkling or immersion or whether *episkopos* meant bishop or elder. In place of the complex and unified religious vision for which the earlier Calvinists strove, these controversialists seemed to be chiefly concerned with product differentiation, much like the competing sellers of a commodity that is fundamentally the same. The *members* of these evangelical congregations were more ecumenical. Attending another church to hear a good preacher hold forth was common. A Methodist might take part in a Presbyterian communion service, a Baptist might ask a Methodist minister to perform a funeral service when his regular minister was out of town, and bury his wife in a nondenominational cemetery. Switching denominations, when reported, was not described as a climactic religious decision.[36]

What was fundamentally the same about these denominations was the importance they gave to the revival experience, which itself seemed to be fundamentally the same across the denominations in the South. Because of the extraordinary bodily and affectional gesticulations that accompanied the revivals, the evangelical churches gave close attention to the "manifest tokens" which seemed to be similar in all churches. A Presbyterian revival presented in a Baptist newspaper described the sinners:

> They fall with a deep groan, some with a wild cry of horror. . . . [They] intensely plead "Lord Jesus have mercy upon my soul." The whole frame trembles like an aspen leaf, an intolerable weight is felt upon the chest, a choking sensation is experienced, and relief from this found only in the loud urgent prayer of deliverance. Usually bodily distress and mental anguish continue till some degree of confidence is found. Then the aspect of

anguish and despair is exchanged for that of gratitude, and triumph and adoration.

Conversions could be seen, felt, and counted. Newspapers were replete with statistics on conversions; spirituality could be given a peculiar kind of materiality.[37]

The interest in manifest tokens fit with the special attention these evangelicals gave to the most discernible sins (Sabbath-breaking rather than pride, obscenity rather than avarice) and to the starkest of mysteries—death. Of course the warning to the sinner that eternal death hovered over him and that he was "rushing madly on the broad, bleak road to everlasting ruin" had a long history in Christian preaching. Also the deathbed scenes given extraordinary attention in sermons and obituaries had their counterparts in the polite verse and fashionable art of the day. Yet the evangelicals brought an unusual explicitness to these subjects. Compared to the vague melancholy of Bryant's *Thanatopsis*, a Baptist sermon on the deathbeds of infidels (not only Tom Paine, "who had scorned the Lord Jesus Christ," but also Dr. Johnson, "who knew nothing of spiritual religion") had the preternatural vividness of a waxworks museum.[38]

The downgrading of the importance of systematic theology in some of the revivalist churches diminished the teaching role of the minister and his need for much formal education. "In the gospel," wrote a Memphis Baptist minister, "there is a certain irresistible efficacy . . . no ignorance can misconceive, no darkness shut it out. . . . It can neither be overcome nor impeded. . . ." Such a ministry therefore required less preparation than did law or regular medicine; entry was easier and the work less remunerative. The Presbyterians, however, did preserve the ideal of an educated ministry, and the leading Presbyterian minister was usually one of the most learned men in Memphis. Methodists and Baptists also gradually raised the educational requirements for their ministers during the last half of the nineteenth century. The Methodists thought ministers "should, for the most part, be somewhat in advance of their hearers," and the educational levels of their congregations seemed to be rising. The Baptists, who were increasingly troubled by denominational infighting, came to look more favorably upon education that might help them to "wield the battle-ax of truth, by which to demolish the citadel of error."[39]

For most evangelical ministers, however, expressiveness, fluency, vehemence, and pathos counted for more than education. "If you have never shed tears," wrote a hard-as-nails Memphis lawyer, "you have never been near your God." It would be a mistake simply to smile at such lachrymal worship and ignore its power. Revivalists tried to carry their listeners into extreme emotional regions in order to create religious immediacy and to excite spiritual discovery; such piety placed its own particular requirements on the minister. "His natural endowments," wrote an admirer of one evangelist, "were of a high order. His person was commanding, his voice was clear and musical, his powers of endurance unsurpassed." Of course the requirements of the most successful revivalists were greater. These evangelists, while holding themselves instruments of the great powers of the Gospel, also drew upon their own feelings and personality. Such a minister must "bring to the surface from the depths of his own heart [the] most passionate longing of his own spiritual nature, . . . words that burn. He holds in himself the key that unlocks the feelings and impulses of others."[40]

This placed enormous responsibility upon the minister, for much could depend upon his own zeal and piety. Like artists and entertainers under similar pressures, some ministers would fluctuate between self-abnegation and self-assertion, self-denial and self-assertion. "The ministry," wrote Nicholas M. Long in his diary, "[is] the sublimest and most important station a mortal can fulfill. Yet how faintly I realize it. Thou who knowest the blackness of my wicked heart! I abhor myself—yet strange inconsistency! I idolize myself." The Reverend Mr. Long went on to become the greatest "prince of the pulpit" in Memphis, leaving the Presbyterian Church, which he felt too restrictive, to take over a declining Congregational Church and rebuilt it as a personal vehicle for his abundant talents.[41]

Being "commanding in person," an attribute often ascribed to the most successful revivalists, seemed to accompany these ministers' ability to evoke fear and guilt. "The soul [of the unregenerate] is felt to be guilty and lost. Horror unutterably overwhelms the heart. . . . it produces an intense fear, an awful agonizing horror of eternal condemnation." In addition, there was a deep and sorrowing sense of "great unworthiness, the basest ingratitude, of infatuated unfaithfulness to the wronged, patient, the precious Savior." Such sentiments were as old as revivalist preaching; however, in this era they seem to have been given a particular explicitness. "The sinner looking to Him on the Cross," wrote a devout Presbyterian layman in his diary, "must come to feel that *he himself* was one of His murderers—that his sins drove the nails and urged the spear—he must look upon Him whom he has pierced." However, in this era also, such fear and guilt was increasingly matched with a more effusive preachment of the love of Jesus for men and the comfort He offered. This was apparent in the poetry printed in the religious press, in the hymns, and in the sermons themselves. Again and again, Jesus was a refuge for the naked and destitute, a shepherd to the flock, food for the hungry, and drink for the thirsty. And the minister, as herald of the Cross, "hid himself behind the Cross."[42]

Preaching became, in effect, the central sacrament of the evangelical churches in and around Memphis. This emphasis diverted ministers from other tasks and other relations with their congregations. Pastoral care often languished among the evangelists and almost disappeared among the Baptists, most of whose ministers spent the week in secular occupations. Moreover, in the country Baptist churches around Memphis—aside from periodic revivals and extended meetings—the minister appeared but once a month. Brotherly "watch and care" was taken up by the church members and this, in part, was responsible for the notorious contentiousness of such churches. Class meetings, class leaders, and local preachers (also part-time ministers like most Baptist ministers) provided some "watch and care" among the Methodists. The circuit preachers, however, the elite of the church who spent a relatively short time with each congregation and were shifted to a new circuit every two years, were obliged to neglect "the more private means of grace." Even among the Presbyterians, a Memphis minister, who tried to visit each family of his congregation three times a year to read Scriptures and pray, found such diligence difficult to maintain and somewhat of a distraction.[43]

The insistence that the sermon was the paramount duty of the minister rendered him more public and somewhat aloof. Also, the rapid turnover of ministers (among Baptists around Memphis usually every year, Methodists every two years, and Presbyterians about every six years) served to diminish the intimacy between the minister and the congregation and prompted him to develop closer ties with the broader denomination. This was apparent even among the Baptists, who were congregationalist by doctrine and ostensibly gave ministers powers only with regard to a particular congregation. The separation of southern Baptists from the national organization in 1845 actually strengthened the importance of supervening organizations of the Church, because the new Southern Baptist Convention was a much more homogeneous body than the national body had been. State conventions and district associations also flourished from the midforties, and it became easier for Baptist ministers to speak of a

Church beyond the church and to look outside the bounds of their congregation for their legitimacy. Titles were indicative. Baptist ministers gradually dropped the term Elder, a rank derived from local church election, and adopted the title Reverend, signifying a more general conception of ministerial distinction. Increasingly, "D.D.'s were appended to the names of the leading ministers.[44]

Early Baptist ministers usually took whatever salary they got out of the collection plates: "If they can open the hearts of the people with the sword of the spirit, the people will open their purses." But ministers and associations pressed for fixed salaries, annual contracts, and an indefinite ministerial term based upon good behavior. Proper respect for the ministry, it was claimed, was tied to stable terms and salaries. However, Baptist ministers usually depended upon income from their secular occupations to supplement whatever salary they got. Most were farmers, some were merchants (even liquor merchants), and R. G. Graves, the leading Baptist controversialist in Tennessee, sold trusses. Those Baptist ministers who became rich in their secular occupations were looked upon more favorably as ministers. When the Civil War broke out, the Confederate States government adopted the Baptist customs with regard to their army chaplains. The chaplains had no rank, no uniform, low pay, and the ration of a private soldier. Since the chaplain had no duty but to preach on Sunday, he was expected to earn his living by acting as a sutler or doing similar tasks.[45]

The Black preacher was distinctive, yet in his customary demeanor and observances he strongly resembled the minister of the prevalent evangelical denominations. Most intellectually talented Blacks had few other outlets for their abilities aside from the ministry. Law, medicine, and business were much less accessible. Moreover, the Black church after the Civil War was an esteemed institution that was completely within Black control and that reached out to the entire population of the race. Even before the War there had been some exclusively Black worship in Memphis, but after Appomattox the Blacks poured out of the basements and balconies of the White churches, to which they had been confined, and set up their own congregations. Like lower-class Whites, the Black found the passionate religion of the Baptists and Methodists most appealing. Later in the twentieth century, a Black Baptist minister explained: "Now, they go to all churches. They go to Catholic or Episcopal Church in the day, but go to some Baptist or Methodist Church at night. They must have the real thing at least once a day." These ministers usually took their salaries out of the collection plate, but this did not prevent them from becoming vigorous and commanding leaders. While, as might be expected, the illiterate but highly successful Rev. Morris Henderson of the Beale Street Baptist Church attracted the most attention and even affection in the Memphis press, the well-educated Rev. R. N. Countee, W. A. Brinkley, and Dr. Sutten E. Gross also had large followings. Acceptance of Black ministers by the White community enabled them to become race leaders, and in that capacity they generally accommodated themselves to the mores of the region. However, it was in such accommodation that they resembled the White ministers of Memphis.[46]

Aside from revivalism, it was slavery that left the deepest imprint on the Memphis ministry. At the beginning of the nineteenth century, there had been active antislavery ministers in all the major denominations in the South. However, as slavery became more strongly entrenched in the area, most of the ministers found themselves unwilling or unable to array themselves against what quickly became one of the most formidable institutions of the Southern states. In this setting revivalism, in focusing its religiosity upon intense spasmodic episodes, proved inadvertently congenial to the churches' absorption of regional usages and attachments. The rapidly expanding American evangelical churches, despite their varying organizational structures, all became in some measure decentralized, and their ministers often became local patriots. To the Northern accusation that slavery was a sin, the Southern churches had a ready defense in the literalist interpretation of Scripture. The Bible, it was claimed, indicated that slavery was God-ordained and that the White race would care for the Black because they were kindred. (This defense, one scholar has suggested, helped fasten a straight-laced literalism upon Southern churches for a long while after.) Nevertheless, the moral teaching of the Golden Rule was not as easily reconciled with the "peculiar institution," and many ministers were rankled by the charge that Southern slavery was destructive of Black family life. There were scattered indications that some clergy were uneasy in the defense of slavery. One of Memphis's leading Presbyterian ministers, for example, after calmly trotting out the routine arguments that were generally believed to crush Northern objections, added unexpectedly with sudden bitterness "but if it is a sin, we must answer for it to our conscience and to God, and not to you [the North]; it is our concern not yours."[47]

In response to the movement of the Northern churches into antislavery politics, some Southern ministers came to emphasize more strongly the historic separation of church and state; however, that declaration easily translated into the separation of church and society. The church, it was urged, must address itself to men's souls and not become entangled in worldly and shifting issues about the social order. Most of the antebellum reform movements, from a Southern perspective, easily became tainted with abolitionism. Even temperance, which among the Methodists was almost a doctrinal principle, remained a teaching directed to "each man in his heart." The Methodists, in this era, usually stepped back from legislative efforts as "the friends of civil liberty refusing to take part in controversy which, however important in its results, would go to favor ecclesiastical interference in political matters." Ministers in Memphis concentrated upon preachments to men's hearts and upon the ultimate issues of life and death.[48]

The Civil War turned temporal matters into matters of life and death, and the citizens of Memphis flocked to the churches. Responding to the surge of religious feeling and exulting in their opportunity to show God's work in history, the ministers suddenly bridged the separation between church and state and found that the cause of the South was God's cause. Generally, the more evangelical the church the more passionate the ministers' support for the War. "The Manifest Hand of God in Our Revolution" and "The Present War, Its Origins, and Inevitable Results" were two notable Baptist efforts. One Methodist preacher formed a military company and marched to the front; a Presbyterian minister became a captain of "irregulars" and roamed the countryside around Memphis burning cotton to prevent it from falling into Union hands. The Bishop of the Episcopal Church wavered but finally came to accept secession and even withdrawal of his diocese from the National Church. Catholic and Jewish clergy maintained a cautious neutrality, praying for the powers that be.[49]

The Catholic priests ministered to a rapidly growing Irish working class, while the Jewish rabbis served a small but prosperous German-Jewish middle class. The priests turned much of their energy toward building distinctive religious institutions for their somewhat separated flock. The rabbis did some of this, but they also felt especially called upon to represent favorably their more conspicuous and perhaps precarious community to the surrounding society. The young rabbi Simon Tuska was particularly good at that. He also endeavored to bring the new ideas of Reform Judaism to his congregation, and that was not without its difficulties for rabbinical authority. Traditionally, a rabbi had been a layman whose special training enabled him to serve as a judge on religious law. In denying the commanding power of that law, Tuska seemed to deprive the rabbi of long-standing prerogatives. Yet as if by compensation, Tuska came to invest the rabbi with more sacral power, transforming him into something like a priest—even suggesting that the rabbi pronounce the ancient Priestly Benediction over his congregation. Whatever innovations he may have encouraged, Tuska did not feel impelled to break with any of his Northern colleagues, a fact to which he did not draw any attention, especially during the secession crisis.[50]

The career of Rev. Robert C. Grundy, perhaps one of the most brilliant and powerful antebellum ministers in Memphis, suggests some of the perplexities of Southern evangelical Protestantism and sectional allegiance in this era. A native of Kentucky and a graduate of Princeton, Grundy came to Memphis as the pastor of the Second Presbyterian Church and quickly gained a reputation for eloquence and intellect. He defended slavery but was also known for Unionist views. Swept up in the exhilaration of the first days of the war, Grundy delivered a sermon on "The Cause of Confederate Freedom," affirming that the war was a defensive one on the part of the South, and expressing confidence that the South would win because "right is might." However, disillusionment quickly set in. Memphis became a wartime boom town selling cotton to the North and munitions to the South and attracting adventurous plungers and "jayhawkers" who struck it rich on the exchange. Grundy, in observance of a Fast Day declared by Jefferson Davis, delivered a scorching sermon comparing Memphis to Nineveh. Sin, he declared, was rampant; Memphis was submerged in licentiousness, intemperance, gambling, Sabbath desecration, idolatrous pride, and luxury. Unless the city reformed, its fall was imminent. Three months later Memphis did fall to Union troops and Grundy stayed on, continuing his censorious sermons and expressing doubts about secession and even slavery (not wrong in itself but wrong when it destroyed Black family life). He gradually began to cooperate with Union troops and grew more explicit in his condemnation of secession. At the request of his congregation, staunchly Confederate in sympathy, the Memphis Presbytery dissolved Grundy's relation to the Second Presbyterian Church. He continued to preach for a while in Memphis "to a large and intelligent congregation" at the Odd Fellows Hall but soon found this unsatisfactory and moved to Cincinnati. There, installed in a principal church of the city, he condemned secession in more drastic terms. Even Union generals were upbraided for allegedly permitting Southern ministers to preach sedition in Memphis while the Confederates allow no ministers to teach loyalty to the Union behind their lines. By the end of the War, Grundy had become a Radical Republican, and he never returned to Memphis.[51]

The preacher who replaced Grundy in the front rank of Memphis ministers was the Reverend C. A. Davis of the Cumberland Presbyterian Church. During the excitement of the secession crisis and its immediate rush of religious emotion, Davis declared that God and Right were on the side of the South, as did most clergymen and laymen. But the South lost. Still tasting the bitterness of that defeat, the Reverend Mr. Davis now drew a different lesson. A church, he argued, must preserve its infallible truths by keeping them apart from fallible concerns: the Church must be kept "entirely distinct from matters which concerned the commonwealth." Preachers of the gospel "are the best and most useful men in the world, in their place; that is, when they mind their own business." Their business was to speak directly to the hearts of individual men "and make them good and holy." From this line of conduct ministers should never depart "however threatening the aspect of political affairs may be." Davis took up the favorite text of the revivalist and gave it more explicit meaning: "I resolve to know nothing among you save Jesus Christ and Him crucified."[52]

This was a return to the stance of the Memphis ministry of the antebellum period, now more rigidly held. Such a position might not cramp the style of the rural clergy dealing with a simple society; however, it was particularly disabling in turbulent Memphis. When in the seventies the Reverend George A. Lofton of the First Baptist Church made the cause of total abstinence from alcohol his own, preaching upon it repeatedly before large audiences in Memphis and its surroundings, he made no mention of licensing ordinances, local option laws, restrictions on the sale of small quantities, or prohibition. His remedy was a simple one: "Seek Jesus only," that was the only hope. The chief moral reform legislation pressed by the Memphis churches, and that only sporadically, was the Sabbath law closing places of business and entertainment on Sunday. This did not pass until 1879. During the period from 1830 to 1880 there was no concerted campaign on the part of the churches to close the numerous saloon and gambling houses, or even the thriving houses of prostitution (which in Memphis were duly registered and regulated by the city police) except, of course, on Sunday. The ministers did preach against drink, gambling, and fornication, but hoped to get rid of these by bringing about the time-honored change of heart rather than by passing city ordinances.[53]

If the lawyers were caught up in and reflected the diverse currents of Memphis civic life, and the ministers in their own manner stood somewhat detached, the doctors to a much greater degree than the other professions joined the party of "responsibility." Nineteenth-century medical science was conducive to this. Despite its dissensions on such central questions as the origin and spread of disease, it nevertheless provided some mandate for the restraint of individualism and the insistence upon social connectedness. This helped keep the doctors closer to the precapitalist gentry outlook and to the ambit of eighteenth-century professionalism. The honor and authority of the eighteenth-century gentleman had been linked to his rightful station involving a balance and correspondence between "self-love" and obligation. Such reciprocity seemed to be written into the workings of medicine. A man might choose to neglect his own soul or his own legal interests without his neighbor suffering much. But the various theories of disease suggested that just such a neglect of his own health or the sanitation of his own property might bring disaster to the entire community.[54]

Medical science, however, had fallen upon evil days in the era 1830–1880. The great eighteenth-century systems that had provided structures for setting in order the considerable accumulation of medical knowledge had collapsed. The common response was to turn toward practice, toward what was said to be the actual particularities of curing, while at the same time employing traditional remedies, some of whose theoretical justifications were no longer accepted. There was much talk of Baconism and induction among the more learned professionals, but most unmethodically strove to meet the exigencies of their occupations. Some of the leading American doctors came to rely largely upon the inherent curative powers of the human body. It was often said that medicine was an "uncertain science"; but uncertain as some doctors might believe it to be, nevertheless they were called upon somehow to prescribe.[55]

One of the fractious medical debates of the mid-nineteenth century concerned the spread of disease. The contagionists argued that many diseases were spread from person to person, and their opponents, the miasmatists, claimed that these ailments arose and spread through gasses given off by various soils under special conditions of heat and humidity. The contagionists asked for quarantines, the drastic limiting of the freedom of movement of men, animals, and goods that squeezed business—almost to the point of strangulation, some businessmen said. The miasmatists asked for the construction of sewerage systems, drainage, and the surfacing of streets. In Memphis both proposals were costly and both were usually ignored until some virulent disease actually struck. Then most doctors applied both kinds of remedies. An ardent miasmatist, for example, put in charge of quarantine regulations in Memphis, took up the work with great energy and did a praiseworthy job. Although competing theories might contradict each other and could be seen to be mutually exclusive, doctors often looked for a procedure that satisfied the requirements of both.[56]

Medical theories were still important distinguishing vestments of the medical profession; but if these were displayed vigorously, they were often worn tentatively. "Theoretical discussions should not be too freely indulged in during consultation," the Code of Ethics of the Tennessee Medical Association advised, "as they frequently give rise to much perplexity without any improvement in practice." Doctors placed great stress upon careful observation of somewhat indiscriminate instances, and this extended the range and kind of experience from which medical knowledge might be derived. "Although the possession of a diploma, honorably acquired, furnishes presumptive evidence of professional ability and entitles its possessor to preeminence in the profession," the Tennessee medical code explained, "yet want of it should not exclude practitioners of experience and sound judgment from the fellowship and respect of the regular graduate." The response of doctors to the decline of medical theory fit in with the growing practicalism and egalitarianism of American society.[57]

By the 1850s any sense of inferiority that earlier had been attached to the surgeon, as compared to the physician, had unquestionably disappeared. Howell W. Robards, the surgeon who performed the greatest number of major operations in Memphis, was one of the most respected and acclaimed medical men in the city. Surgery, which had not been closely tied to general medical theory, was not shaken by its demise. Moreover, the discovery and widespread use of anesthesia sharply increased the range of the surgeon's effectiveness and accomplishments. Even the most prominent physicians in Memphis practiced some surgery and obstetrics. The virtues of hard work, dexterity, and proficiency, that in the past had been associated with artisan occupations (and surgery among them), were now more broadly linked to medicine. In the eighteenth century, the professional was usually contrasted with a tradesman; in the nineteenth, he was more commonly contrasted with an amateur.[58]

This change favored growth of dentistry as a profession. The first dentists in Memphis were itinerants who originally considered themselves surgeons of a specialized sort. They assumed the honorific title of doctor, but they also supported their claims with testimonials from regular physicians. At the Memphis Dental Society, which had been formed in 1866, Dr. S. P. Cutler, a Botanic doctor who dabbled in the "science of microscopy of the teeth" and practiced as a dentist, argued for close association with medicine. Such association would lead dentists toward "nobler feelings" and "away from the hunt for the Almighty Dollar." It would also "inspire greater confidence toward our profession on the part of the public." W. T. Arrington, Cutler's chief opponent, was the first dental college graduate to practice in Memphis. Less impressed with microscopy, he stressed the importance of proficiency in the actual techniques of dental work, which dental colleges could impart. Arrington realized his insistence that dentistry was a new and unique profession, sharply separated from medicine, made the say-so of the dentist with his patient somewhat precarious. That realization was one of the considerations behind his strenuous and eventually successful campaign for passage of a professional practice law for dentists in Tennessee, after such laws had been off the statute books for over a generation.[59]

With the aid of egalitarian and antimonopolistic slogans, as well as disparaging attacks upon the efficacy of regular medical science, Botanic and Eclectic doctors had helped to overturn the medical practice acts in Tennessee. The science of these doctors was originally based upon the curative powers of the lobelia plant as discovered by Samuel Thomson. This self-made peripatetic herb doctor had set up a counterprofession of part-time doctors (often women caring chiefly for family and friends) using his patented manual and patented preparation. The Eclectic physicians looked to Thomson as their prophet, but they extended the range of botanical medicines beyond what Thomson would accept. They also discarded the notion of informal medical work and set up all the institutions and furnishings of the regular medical profession—journals, societies, colleges, degrees—presenting thereby a shadow image of it. Memphis had a flourishing Botanic medical college before the Civil War and a large corps of successful Botanic practitioners. These doctors, their patients, and their "connections" came from lower social strata than those of the regular doctors. Serving on the board of directors of the Botanic college were Democratic lawyers and Baptist and Methodist ministers. Serving on the board of directors of the regular medical college were Whig lawyers and Presbyterian and Episcopal ministers. College-trained Botanic and Eclectic doctors nonetheless scorned those irregular doctors who were simply self-taught.[60]

The regulars, in turn, disdained the Botanics and Eclectics and would not fraternize with them, serve with them on the board of health or in the city hospital, or meet with them in consultations. This policy excluded the irregular doctors from the prestigious civic medical institutions but did not seem to diminish their extensive practice in Memphis. Significantly, when the regular Memphis doctors wished to vilify the Botanics, they did not commonly reach for the traditional epithet—empiric. That term had been used to great effect in the eighteenth century, when the doctors had a comprehensive science and the quacks did not. But in the mid-nineteenth century even the regular doctors had no such science and were themselves becoming increasingly empirical. Therefore, when they denounced the Botanics, it was not for being empirical but for being *exclusive* (Botanics generally shunned mineral medicines). Regular doctors saw themselves as broad-minded, unprejudiced, and catholic, and they maintained their exclusiveness in the name of scientific anti-exclusiveness.[61]

The decline in respect for comprehensive medical systems, with their general formulas and clearly set standards, was accompanied not only by an increasing regard for practicalism and empiricism but also by a regard for the importance of personality. The parallels with law and divinity are striking. Among the Botanic doctors in Memphis, it was Lycurgus Gabbert who was noted for his bedside manner—his assured bearing, his solicitude, as well as his optimistic and affable ways. Among the regulars, it was Dr. Robert Fryerson Brown, the leading society doctor of Memphis, (with perhaps the best connections of any physician in the city) whose oracular aspect and confident demeanor won him a bevy of devoted patients, although "he was not a learned physician, as the phrase goes." When medicine was an "uncertain science," those doctors who were temperamentally self-assured often acquired an anomalous power within the profession. Generally it was agreed that physicians must "obtain an ascendancy over the minds of those labouring under disease." Dr. James Conquest Cross, a distinguished lecturer at the Memphis Medicine College, informed his students, "your first object should be to command, if possible, the confidence of your patients. Without it, you can never secure obedience or calculate upon strict compliance with your advice."[62]

Dr. Cross went so far as to recommend some petty deception in order to make the doctor seem all-knowing to the patient. This despite the fact that the doctor-patient relation seemed almost as a matter of course to be loaded in the doctor's favor. "There is something in sickness," explained a layman, "that breaks down the pride of manhood—that softens the heart, and brings it back to feelings of infancy." Women constituted a large part of the doctors' caseloads. This affected the relation between doctor and patient and even the description of that relation. The ideal doctor was "one who in the discharge of his duty exhibited the firmness of a man and the tenderness of a woman." This echoed Thomas Percival's famous eighteenth-century formula but omitted his praise for "condescension" with its class overtones and translated his explicit mention of authority into *masculine* firmness. It is significant that the doctor's authority, in the eighteenth century, was depicted in terms of the relationship between the classes and, in the nineteenth century, in terms of the relationship between the sexes.[63]

The Southern doctors were given a power of command over one category of patients, the slaves, that was unparalleled in the experience of their Northern colleagues. James Marion Sims's repeated operations on slave women to perfect his treatment of the vesico-vaginal fistula (succeeding with the slave Anarcha, after her thirtieth operation) suggest what liberties Southern doctors might take. However, slaves made up only a small portion of a doctor's caseload. Young doctors sometimes entered into plantation contracts and agreed to treat all the slaves at one location for a yearly fee, but established medical men in Memphis had only occasional slave patients. This did not diminish these doctors' sense of their unique capabilities to understand the Black race.

Blacks and yellow fever were two regional specialties in this era that set Southern doctors apart, and the two subjects were related. That Blacks were comparatively unsusceptible to yellow fever was one of the findings encouraging some doctors to argue that the Black race was not kindred to the White and, contrary to the Scriptural narrative, that the Black race had been created separately. Dr. Josiah Nott of Alabama, who openly contended this (he was also a leading expert on yellow fever and may have been the first doctor to suggest that insects or some lower form of animal life was somehow responsible for it), found disciples in

Memphis. The leading Memphis medical journal, however, refused to come out for or against this theory, a view particularly
troubling to "Bible-true" Protestants.[64]

The editor of the journal thought that the races were distinct
but that these differences had resulted from a gradual degenera-
tion of the Black race over the centuries. Blacks were not closer
to beasts than Whites, they were more like children. Slavery,
therefore, became a school. It was slavery and its disciplinary
contact between the races that raised the Blacks to an intellectual and cultural level that otherwise would not have been available to them. When the opportunity arose, therefore, this Memphis doctor considered it his duty to go before the American
Medical Association and justify slavery as a form of beneficence.[65]

That the doctors in Memphis, of all the professionals, argued
the most forcefully for slavery as a positive good was related to
the fact that they felt more generally responsible to the social
order than the other professionals. However, it was that sense of
responsibility that also made them critics, according to their own
lights. "A universal rage in the pursuit of wealth fills all hearts,"
lamented the committee to establish a medical school in Memphis.

> The character which this engrosing [sic] passion will in time
> form upon our people, unless modified and restrained, is pain-
> ful to contemplate. Selfishness and craft will obtain dominion,
> and money will be the end of ambition and standard of all merit.
> No better corrective for these tendencies is known than to create
> in our midst a class of persons devoted to the cultivation of sci-
> ence and literature, and spreading the beneficent influence of
> their pursuits over all the other classes of life.[66]

The doctors around the medical school looked upon themselves
as just such a corrective to the money-grubbing temper of Memphis life. Their school was their citadel; its standard of merit and
ambition would impart not only science but rectitude, benevolence, and culture. Two important offshoots of the school were its
scholarly journal, *The Medical Recorder,* and its coterie of cultivated and learned doctors, the Memphis Medical Society.
Founded in 1851 and designed to "contribute its part to the general diffusion of knowledge" as well as to offset the "evils arising
from selfish isolation" of Memphis doctors, their society nonetheless remained a select fraternity. Of course, the unbookish society doctor, Robert Fryerson Brown, was not a member, nor was
Dr. R. L. Laski, a Jew with European training, who remained
something of an outsider during most of his career in Memphis.

The medical society was dominated by the medical college faculty and provided a stepping stone to the Memphis Board of Health, through which it hoped to exert a broader influence in the city. Unhappily, that influence turned out to be quite limited. The city council, while lavishly supporting railroads, refused to support a dispensary and teaching hospital and ignored most of the board of health's sanitary recommendations.[67]

The foremost medical man in antebellum Memphis was Dr. Ayers Phillips Merrill. He was a professor at the medical school, editor of *The Medical Recorder*, president of the medical society, and member of the board of health. Merrill had demonstrated those powers of close observation and flexible intelligence so admired by his fellow doctors. Although a miasmatist on yellow fever, he carefully studied this disease among the urban population of Memphis and noted its similarity in pattern to that of the spread of boll weevil infestation in the local cotton crop. This, he thought, lent credence to a germ theory of disease, a general hypothesis discredited by most doctors of his day and even by most contagionists. On social matters, Merrill was a leading exponent of civic folk mercantilism. Memphis, he believed, must not only be a distributive center but must become a manufacturing center as well. Where the city would place its subsidies was the crucial issue; priority should not be given to investment in transportation but rather to the promotion of manufacturing. "Let us get all these things in operation and then the railroads and plank roads about which we now hear so much said, will follow as a matter of course."[68]

Dr. Merrill's omnibus reform was free public education. (For Whites only, of course; slavery was his recommended educational institution for most Blacks.) Free public education would help promote manufacturing by attracting to the city a large industrious population of mechanics and manufacturers. It would also qualify the children of the poor for their duties as citizens. (He did mention in an aside that the better-educated population would also choose regular doctors rather than quacks for medical care.) Most important, however, was that free public education would break down class barriers by placing the children of the poor alongside the children of the wealthy in "the arena of mental struggle for excellence." The school system like an ideal society would be built upon the principle that reward should go to intellectual merit alone. It was to be a "great community of thought and study . . . [that] improves the intellectual faculties, and moral sense and judgment." Of course, it must (like slavery?) have its appropriate constraints. The "quiet discipline of the school . . . will exert an influence over his [the student's] thoughts and actions, which he will not be able to resist." Even the taxpayers would be benefited by the inevitable rise in property values that would accompany the advance of public education. In sum, free public education would "build up a great city of happy and prosperous people abounding in intelligence and fraternal love."[69]

That these hopes were defeated in Memphis is less surprising than that they were asserted so strenuously there. Memphis, of course, stinted in its support for its public schools and did not provide anything like the education Merrill had envisioned. Quality private schools were quickly set up for the children of the rich. Merrill was also thwarted on his specific proposals for the board of health. There he argued that only with the construction of a proper sewer system and the draining of the Gayoso bayou would Memphis cease to be a sickly city. Yet the board of health itself was primarily an honorary and advisory body in this era, with "no money that it could control or no power to act in any manner." It became active during epidemics but usually disappeared when the sickness did, and its costly recommendations for sanitary improvements went unheeded. "Memphis must keep healthy as cheaply as possible," explained a newspaper editor just a year before the city's most disastrous epidemic.[70]

The doctors who flocked to Memphis after the Civil War usually brought with them the comradeship and the ardor of a common service in the medical corps of the Confederacy. Memphis was a gathering place for ex-Confederates second only to New Orleans. Some of these doctors (Robert Wood Mitchell, John H. Erskine, and Gustavus Brown Thornton in particular) carried forward Merrill's sense of public duty into the seventies. The civic-mindedness of these doctors, however, was often focused more specifically and narrowly on public health matters than Merrill's had been. Even in this restricted field they met with no more success than did Merrill. When yellow fever appeared in New Orleans during the summer of 1878, Dr. Mitchell, then head of the Memphis Board of Health, asked for quarantine measures. The city council, citing the division of medical opinion on the board, turned him down. The Memphis *Daily Appeal* did its part by trying to squelch rumors and maintain the proper spirit: "Go about your business as usual; be cheerful, and laugh as much as possible."[71]

When yellow fever struck, the population stampeded, displaying the bravery, the cowardice, and the terrifying stupor that such disasters often summon up. Much of reputable Memphis—25,000 people—fled, leaving 14,000 Blacks and 6,000 Whites, most of them the poorest Irish. City government collapsed and was replaced by a self-appointed directorate. Over 4,000 of the 6,000 Whites who remained in the city died, as did almost 1,000 Blacks. The wild scenes of turmoil, suffering, and wretchedness—carefully recorded and published almost immediately—seemed to bring the city to the edge of Hell. Some thought that Memphis would never survive as an urban center. But like an agonizing sinner rising exultant from the depths of hopelessness at a revival meeting, when the pestilence disappeared Memphis sought a new birth.[72]

The leading citizens who returned to Memphis and the notables who had stayed united in a new spirit of devotion to the service of the city as they saw it. The old city government was swept away, the charter surrendered, even the name Memphis given up (for a while). A commission government was established with "Dr." David Tinsley Porter as its head. He was a local wholesale grocer who had once apprenticed as a pharmacist (adopting the title of "doctor"), and one of his important qualifications for the job was that he had never held political office before. Dr. Porter, it was said, "squared all his conduct by the standard of Masonic integrity." He cleaned up the city. New pavement was laid, a sewerage system rapidly installed, systematic garbage collection finally organized, and unhealthy buildings destroyed (without compensation to their owners!). By December 1880, Dr. Thornton, president of the now powerful board of health, announced that the city's sanitation problems were solved. One of the chief lessons drawn from this sanitary reformation was that "the first duty of the State should be the preservation of public health." In order to do this, however, it must combat ignorance and selfishness. Unless the people "are forced by law . . . they will not, by sanitary operation do their part to prevent disease." At least in the realm of sanitation, the people must be compelled to act in their own best interest.[73]

The instrument of that compulsion was the new city government. This municipal regime was the outcome of older civic proclivities, tempered in the extremities of the epidemic. The new city government curbed universal manhood suffrage and reneged on full payment of its debts. Memphis surrendered its charter to the state and became a nondescript municipality known as the Taxing District of Shelby County, with a commission government selected through a complex system of state appointments and local election. The surrender of the charter, and direct taxing power that went with it, also freed the city from immediate payment on its debts.

After the depression of 1873, when cotton prices had fallen, some merchants—Robertson Topp and H. L. Brinkley, two of Memphis's wealthiest railroad promoters, among them—urged that the city declare bankruptcy, or better yet, commit something like corporate suicide by surrendering its charter. Some of the echoes of the Wolf River canal controversy could be heard in the debate over these proposals. Repudiating that debt was dishonorable, many argued, and it would make future municipal borrowing for needed civic improvements impossible. A man like Topp, who owned extensive real estate in Memphis, would surely want improvements that could increase the value of his holdings. But Topp was also a railroad promoter and cotton producer; he had broader and more pressing interests. Therefore, lightening his tax burden in Memphis, even if it meant a decided retrogression for the city itself, was something he found appealing.[74]

After the scourge of the yellow fever epidemic of 1878, the movement to repudiate civic indebtedness won increasing support from diverse segments of the community and on various grounds. It was said that the debt had been incurred by the Radical Republicans (actually much of the debt was antebellum and it had doubled *after* the Radicals were thrown out of office); it was said that the debt was held by "foreigners" (a large part of it had been bought up by New York and Baltimore capitalists); it was said that the measure would be economic justice (it would force bondholders to accept payment at less than the face value of the debentures, and closer to their purchase price); finally and most persuasively, it was said that only such a measure would allow the city to direct its funds toward the sanitary improvements necessary to avert future incursions of yellow fever. The proposal, which had been a sharply divisive one before the disaster, found sufficient support after it.[75]

The new government, in its early months, seemed to bring a vigor and enthusiasm to municipal affairs quite unlike anything that had been seen before. Yet this spirit quickly faded, and "manifest tokens" of backsliding soon began to appear. Judge James A. Anderson, distinguished member of the Memphis Bar and an important figure in the new regime, was found to have used the trust funds of yellow fever widows and orphans, which had been placed in his hands as public administrator, for land speculation in Texas and Mexico. "This crime staggered the public, and for a time completely undermined general confidence." Incredibly, Anderson escaped without punishment. From that point on, the city's unity of spirit went soggy. Dr. Porter resigned as president of the taxing district in July 1881, when his term had hardly started, and he was replaced by "Pappy" Hadden. The brief era of civic revival was at an end.[76]

By that time, however, the essential sanitary measures had been accomplished, and they were to be a lasting outcome of the brief period of civic activism that had followed the yellow fever catastrophe. An even more lasting outcome of the pestilence, little noticed at the time, was the sharp demographic shift within the city. The industrious German population that had fled to St. Louis during the devastation did not return in significant numbers, and the Irish inhabitants had been greatly reduced. Their place was taken by a large influx of rural Blacks. This shift eventually shook the hopes of many of those who had envisioned Memphis as a manufacturing center. For the Germans and even the Irish had been looked upon to supply the great force of skilled labor needed for the city's industrial growth. The increasing numbers of rural Blacks, however, for reasons of racial caste, would be relegated to unskilled labor and personal service. Moreover, in light of Memphis's dependence upon Northern credit, the effort to lighten and even abolish the city's indebtedness, as predicted in 1873, had a long-range dampening effect upon its economic growth. This may have reached even beyond the business of municipal bonds. "No city had ever descended quite so low in financial infamy," announced the *New York Times.* "The only course open," the editor insisted, was to "make the business classes feel individually the consequence of a measure destructive of all credit, and which could not have been enacted without their concurrence." Memphis continued to grow in population for the rest of the century, but its economic structure became somewhat fixed. Memphis maintained its role primarily as a distribution center for the mid-South, and it remains that today.[77]

The one segment of Memphis society to enter into the last decades of the nineteenth century with its reputation enhanced was the medical profession. During the yellow fever disaster, when most of those who could leave fled in panic (some Protestant ministers, conspicuously, and most lawyers inconspicuously), the doctors remained, and volunteer physicians came to the city to help out. Twenty-five resident physicians and sixty-eight volunteers died in the epidemic; Dr. Erskine, the city health officer, became a national hero. The doctors themselves came out of the experience with a different sense of their own requirements. While earlier, Merrill had thought that increasing popular education would inevitably ensure the proper respect and deference to regular physicians, now in a setting where it had been demonstrated that the people must be compelled to act in their own best interest, physicians once again turned to medical practice legislation to drive the "quacks" from the city and sustain the physician in his rightful place in society. This was evidently a narrower focus. With the sanitary measures completed and practice laws on the way, the leading Memphis doctors turned away from the kind of civic involvement that had been characteristic of their counterparts a generation earlier.[78]

5

Cincinnati: Not Porkopolis but Queen City, 1830–1880

Like Memphis, Cincinnati's first asset had been its location. It was situated on the north bank of the Ohio River, midway between the river's headwaters and its junction with the Mississippi. It also happened to be set at the base of Ohio's exceedingly fertile Miami Valley, facing across the entrance of the Licking River which reached out to large and productive areas of Kentucky. After the Indians had been driven away, land speculators were quick to see the site's promise as a center of trade. The Ohio Valley soon became one of the main channels of the westward rush of population, and through it moved a great tide of settlement and expansion. This migration brought rapid growth to Cincinnati.[1]

The city's Southern trade, down along the Ohio and Mississippi, quickly became one of the principal supports for Cincinnati's prosperity. Memphis and Cincinnati developed multifarious links: commercial, social, and even cultural. The idea of the Memphis Wolf River project owed much to the Miami Canal of Cincinnati which brought water power, manufacturing, and a diversified economy to the city. Cincinnati professionals drifted southward in search of opportunities, and a contingent of Cincinnati doctors rushed to the stricken city when yellow fever battered Memphis in 1878. The season of soul-searching and self-judgment in Cincinnati, resembling that in Memphis following the yellow fever scourge, arose not from an epidemic but rather from an undisguised social upheaval. The Cincinnati Courthouse Riot of 1884, however, can best be understood against the background of events in Cincinnati that preceded it.[2]

Tocqueville, arriving in Cincinnati in December 1831, was impressed by the immense variety of the place, in both its economy and its population, and this variety undoubtedly was one of the central facts of the city's life. Though by 1850 Cincinnati had become the greatest pork-packing center in the world, that industry did not dominate its economic life in the way that cotton held sway in Memphis. Along with meatpacking, Cincinnati had become a principal center for furniture making, steamboat building, foundry and engine shopwork, boot and shoe making, ready-made clothing manufacture, and book publishing. It also became a leading exporter of grain, flour, and whiskey. Moreover, the value of pork products was never more than a third of the value of Cincinnati's industrial output. Though some pork packers became the richest men in town, they did not form a ruling class; there was often something disparaging in popular descriptions of these men, and the sobriquet "Porkopolis" never lost its derisive resonance. Few of the most prominent Cincinnati families built their fortune wholly or even mostly on pork. "King Cotton" might evoke a sense of grandeur, but "King Porker," who lived high on the hog, was simply a comical vulgarian of local jokes.[3]

The broad mixture of population was usually noticed by even the most casual visitors. The first settlers of the town had been from New England, and they were soon joined by large numbers of migrants from New Jersey and Pennsylvania. (The grid of city streets was laid out in imitation of Philadelphia.) By 1825 a large group of Southerners had come, chiefly from Maryland and Virginia, and as the city expanded many settlers crossed the river to nearby Kentucky. However, the foreign immigrants were the most striking. By 1851 foreign-born and Blacks made up almost half of the population: Germans 28 percent, Irish 12 percent, English 4 percent, Blacks and others 2 percent. Cincinnati had once had a larger Black population, but race riots in 1828 and 1841 (instigated, it was said, by poor Whites recently arrived from Kentucky) made it an unattractive place for many Blacks. Irishmen came in large numbers during the great famines of the 1840s, and Germans in both the thirties and the forties.[4]

The Germans left the deepest imprint upon Cincinnati life and culture. Most of those who emigrated belonged to the landworking, handworking, and small shopkeeping classes. German craftsmen were particularly esteemed because they usually came with the training received in a long apprenticeship (increasingly rare in the United States), well-developed skills, and good work habits. Unlike the Irish, the Germans brought with them a group of intellectuals, small but highly vocal, and the immigrant community was sizable enough to support them. In Memphis, one German newspaper flickered on and off, briefly, and then went out. Cincinnati, by contrast, displayed a galaxy of German newspapers with differing religious and political persuasions, as well as literary weeklies, sports clubs, singing societies, and fraternal lodges. The Whigs, usually of New England background and with a strong sense of cultural stewardship, felt uneasy about German cultural aspirations and demands. For most Democrats, all that didn't amount to a hill of beans; they gladly gave these immigrants what they wanted on such matters. Up until the secession crisis, most Germans (upon the urging of such journals as *Der alte Hickory, Der Locofoco, Der Volksblatt,* and *Das Demokratisches Tageblatt*) voted Democrat. One result was that German and English were recognized equally as languages of instruction in many Cincinnati public schools until World War I.[5]

When Tocqueville and Beaumont visited Cincinnati, the Germans made up slightly more than five percent of the population and the Irish slightly less, yet these visitors were startled by the dissimilar elements found living together in the city and suggested that "their combination creates a moral being whose portrait it would be very hard to draw." Some of the agencies of coherence that were important to life in Memphis were less consequential in Cincinnati. The power of family "connections" was surely weakened. In the pioneer days of the city, family ties had been influential, and early and repeated intermarriages soon created a host of "kissing cousins." However family connections were quickly intercepted or bypassed by the conflicting interests that family members acquired. Even where family connections did seem to remain important, they were often broken by divorce, which apparently was more acceptable among upper-class families in Cincinnati than in Memphis.[6]

Some institutional connections were also weakened. The counterparts in Cincinnati to Memphis's Old Folks Association were the New England Society, the Pioneer's Association of Cincinnati, and the *Pionier Verein.* These were more narrow in their ancestral loyalties than the Memphis association, yet by force of circumstances they became weaker and even less restrictive. The New England Society, limited to those born in New England and their descendants, proposed to nourish Yankee ways in the unfamiliar environment of Porkopolis. A New England historical and genealogical library was established, meetings with social and cultural purposes were held, and an annual Founders Day procession commemorating the landing of the Pilgrims was perpetrated upon the city. One New England tradition that flourished heartily was divisiveness. When the Beechers insisted that the society abstain from the punch bowl at its meetings, the organization quickly languished and dissolved. The Cincinnati Pioneer Association suffered no similar embarrassments. While the New England Society marched to the Second Presbyterian Church for its ceremonies, the Pioneer Association marched to a luxurious hotel and refreshed itself there with a grand banquet and thirteen toasts of locally grown catawba wine. But the association seemed to live largely for its banquets and provided none of the social cohesiveness of the Memphis Old Folks Association.[7]

The *Pionier Verein,* from the start, was an appendage to its printing press. Carl Rümelin, first president of the association and editor of *Der Deutsche Pionier,* quickly discovered that it was necessary to draw upon the talents of very recent immigrants not qualified for membership in the association in order to make *Deutschtum* flourish in his journal. On the front pages of the *Pionier,* where the intellectuals presented their long and abstruse theoretical articles, the many meanings of *Deutschtum* remained somewhat mysterious; but on the back pages where the small shopkeepers serving German clientele placed their ads, one meaning of *Deutschtum* became clear—buy German. Of course aside from the *Verein,* German ethnic bonds were strong and found expression in a variety of religious and political organizations. Nonetheless, these were organizations of men and women who considered themselves outsiders and could not give direction to the entire community.[8]

The Freemasons, so important to the social life of the middle ranges of society in Memphis, had less comparable strength and penetration in Cincinnati. In fact, the lodges in the northern city found themselves in a surprisingly hostile environment. While in Memphis evangelical ministers had either ignored or sometimes even joined the Masons, in Cincinnati many preachers vehemently attacked the organization. The anti-Masonic crusade of the late twenties and early thirties, and Charles G. Finney's intermittent campaign against the Masons, lasting through most of his public career, had a decided impact. The accusations against Freemasonry were the usual ones: in its design "it is partial and selfish," in its ideas "it is a false religion," and in its practice "it is a virtual conspiracy against both Church and State." The local lodges tried to place particular emphasis upon the least controversial aspects of their work—the provision of sick benefits and the payments of funeral expenses for members. One spokesman tried his best to explain that the elaborate system of degrees within the order was not a gradation of honor and authority but simply a series of stations of moral achievement that allowed each member to measure more accurately his self-improvement. Nonetheless, Freemasonry in Cincinnati remained relatively weak and developed a reputation as "a house of discord and disunion." Cincinnati was a focal point for controversies in the seventies over the Christianizing of the Order and, even more troublesome, the debates over the recognition of the Black lodges. The obituaries of respectable and moderately prosperous merchants and professionals in Memphis usually announced Masonic funerals, but in Cincinnati that was rarely the case.[9]

However, if many of the accustomed forms of social connection so important to Memphis were quite weak in Cincinnati, the northern city created new forms that were barely known in the southern town. The most vital and far-reaching were the voluntary associations. It is difficult to read of the doings of any prominent Cincinnatian of the era 1830–80 without being struck by the incredible number of voluntary associations to which he belonged. One survey restricted to only the more formal associations extant in Cincinnati during the years 1840–41, found sixty-five such organizations. These associations contrasted sharply with the array of connections in Memphis. Each of these associations usually addressed a special purpose, allowing members to belong to many different societies and diminishing emotional attachments to each. In encouraging initiative and choice, these associations evoked an alternative style of behavior. The "self-made man," in the great catch phrase of the era, was someone who rose in life without access or resort to family connections; this was exactly the kind of ascent so often urged upon young professionals in Cincinnati.[10]

Cincinnatians not only rushed to form these associations, they also wondered at their doing so and came up with theories to account for this kind of sociability. Professionals, who easily became leading members of such associations, also supplied some of the most explicit justifications. Timothy Walker, a leading lawyer in Cincinnati, thought that the most remarkable advantage of these voluntary associations was their special kind of empowerment. "That large numbers of men are in the habit of combining together to effect those objects, which no individual could accomplish alone . . . [is] one of the greatest modern improvements. . . . We employ the mechanic lever to lift weights, which our unassisted strength could not lift. Why not employ the *social lever* in the same way?"[11]

For Dr. Daniel Drake it was more particularly the increased productivity that these associations seemed to afford that was most impressive. He thought that voluntary associations represented a broad social application of the notion of division and coordination of labor. Particularly in scientific societies, the special knowledge of each members "should have a point of concentration—a *sensorium commune* where all intelligence should be received, compared, digested and radiated to the profession and society at large to increase the powers of [the one] and the blessings of the other." This was more expansive and complex than Walker's simple mechanical analogy.[12]

Yet it was the Reverend James H. Perkins who saw this banding together of "men by acquaintance, common interests, and brotherly sympathy" in terms of the broadest purposes, purposes of which the voluntary associations themselves were largely unaware. These associations were expressions of that perilous historical interlude between the necessary dissolutions brought on by the Reformation and the future social and religious reintegrations that surely must come. Particularly in America, a country without a responsible nobility and a unifying Church:

> The whole course of things is toward the overthrow of authority, and the fullest reception of the doctrine of the Reformation. [By that he meant the right of private judgment and "simple, direct individualism."] Where, then, is our safety? . . . It must be upon the extension of intelligence and virtue and upon the influence of true and good men over the ignorant and low. . . . And who can do it? The Educated men; and they only by concert and union. . . . God has given birth to the associated efforts of the day; we look upon them as vital forms of organization, destined, in connection with the scattered fragments of the Church, and the labors of individual men, to supply for a season the place of that united and truly Catholic Church, which, in God's own time, may bring into one fold again the scattered sheep of our Savior.

Few association members would subscribe to such a lofty interpretation of their doings; however, Perkins' exegesis of events was not too far-fetched. A recent scholarly study of Cincinnati's voluntary associations in 1840 argues that these societies provided a network for a special kind of leadership (drawn from less than one-tenth of the city's householders) in which New Englanders and professionals were heavily overrepresented. That leadership acquired an influence in local affairs at first supplementary to the city's political institutions and then within them, striving to imbue the community with what it considered "enlightened public spirit."[13]

One unmistakable expression of that enlightened public spirit was Cincinnati's version of civic folk mercantilism, more sophisticated and more successful than the economic policies in Memphis. "Buy local" was a familiar slogan in Cincinnati, but city businessmen supplemented the slogan with more effective devices in order to keep the demand for local products high. Discriminatory tolls on Ohio canals, for example, were arranged so that "domestic" products would be charged less than competing out-of-state commodities. In addition, Cincinnati's municipal government took a more coherent and comprehensive public responsibility for the economic growth of the city. From its very beginnings until at least 1880, Cincinnati's public officials were deeply involved in lending, borrowing, building, and even regulating. Public officials, equipped with taxing powers, could command sufficient credit for the building of canals, plank roads, and railroads that enlightened public spirit thought essential for the growth and prosperity of the city.[14]

Civic folk mercantilism was based upon the belief that in developing towns the broader community often benefits, if only from the overflow effects, when some of its leading members prosper. In addition its Cincinnati proponents often argued that economic growth and cultural improvement must go hand in hand. An eminent lawyer who pushed for the development of the Whitewater Canal also organized the first law school west of the Alleghenies and helped establish the literary Semi-Colon Club, with its motto "The March of Intellect." A doctor who organized one of the city's first railroads and manufacturing companies also helped set up libraries, learned societies, and the local lyceum, which he thought would help "subdue avaricious appetites."[15]

In Cincinnati, the ardor of the countinghouse was often imbued with public spirit. The wealthiest man in Cincinnati, Nicholas Longworth, had been a lawyer and made his fortune in real estate. In that he resembled Robertson Topp of Memphis; but from there the resemblances receded and the differences grew. While Topp had built his large stately house upon his plantation far from town, Longworth's mansion was within the city. Topp exhibited the pride and punctiliousness of a high-flown gentleman; Longworth shunned all elegance and prided himself chiefly upon his raffish eccentricity. He dressed in a careless, even beggarly, fashion; he refused charity to the virtuous poor (others would relieve them) but gave generously to the unworthy, "the devil's poor," who were otherwise friendless. He supported an orphan asylum for Black children when others would not and donated the land for a municipal astronomical observatory, which Topp would certainly have considered foolishness. Of course, Longworth undoubtedly could not be typical of Cincinnati's mercantile class, but his wealth and preeminence gave him a far-reaching influence among them.[16]

In Cincinnati the "March of Intellect" and the progress of canal building were linked in an unusually explicit way. Micajah T. Williams, the city's proponent of government aid to canals, and Nathaniel Guilford, Cincinnati's leading advocate of public aid to education, organized a coalition in the state legislature between the friends of both causes so that, through some ambidextrous "log rolling," the legislation establishing the state's school system and canal system passed during the same session. Publicists praised the huge increase in water power made available to local manufacturing and the educated and virtuous citizenry that schools would train, almost in the same breath. Similarly, when in the spring of 1845 Cincinnati opened its astronomical observatory with the second largest refractor telescope in the world, this achievement was described as the joining of public education, scientific research,and practical benefits. Remarkably, the entire project had been financed through public subscriptions. Such an alliance between learning and enterprise, edification and economic power, was just the combination of qualities evoked by the name "Queen City of the West." The professions in Cincinnati, perhaps more than any other group, supplied much of the vision and energy to help forge the combination of mental and moral cultivation with economic well-being that served as a civic ideal in the era 1830–80.[17]

In Cincinnati the leaders of all the professions saw themselves as public men with a sense of social and civic responsibility; nonetheless those of the legal profession assumed a special eminence. That assumption, however, did not go unchallenged. Objections and misgivings with regard to the ascendant position of the lawyer came not only from outside the bar but also from within. The equivocal egalitarianism of the era is readily apparent in the curious and contradictory address that John Quincy Adams (surely no Jacksonian in any obvious sense) delivered to the bar in Cincinnati when he came to that city to lay the cornerstone for its new observatory. Adams bluntly told those advocates gathered to honor him that he did not consider lawyers more important than shoemakers, tailors, housewrights, or any mechanical occupations. "So deep is my impression of the natural equality of mankind, and of the fundamental rights that natural equality confers upon every human being, that I have been accustomed, and accustomed myself, to transfer that principle of equality to the professions of men, the honest professions adopted by men in the great varieties of human life." Clearly there was something forced in that attitude, for later in the same speech Adams could not refrain from saying something quite opposite: "The Liberty of the country depends more on the members of the profession of the Bar than on any other profession common to men." Such divided sentiments often appeared among the local lawyers themselves. "In the abstract," explained a distinguished Cincinnati attorney, the work of the mechanic and the lawyer were equally important and respectable, "yet everyone feels that they differ immeasurably in point of dignity." [18]

The dignity of the legal profession, as Adams suggested, lay in its vocation as protector of liberty, and that was usually said to derive from the work of expounding upon the Constitution. Constitutionalism, "the foremost element of our legal science," described a broad range of speculation and assertion in Cincinnati. In Memphis constitutionalism, for the most part, meant protection for local license; in Cincinnati it primarily meant restraints on various volitions and impulses. The sovereign will, "the highest earthly power," was not unlimited. It was restrained by rules it had itself prescribed, and by a body of rights of citizens that could never be completely surrendered to or appropriated by any government. All this was necessary and salutary, for liberty existed in proportion to wholesome restraint. A lawyer, returning from a visit to England, said the British had deceived themselves into believing that they had a constitution. As long as Parliament could do whatever it willed there was no constitutional government in that country. [19]

The noblest feature of the American Constitution was the provision that made the judiciary its final arbiter. "One cannot easily conceive of a more sublime exercise of power, than that by which a few men, through the mere force of reason, without soldiers, and without tumult, pomp, or parade, but calmly, noiselessly, and fearlessly, proceed to set aside the acts of government, because repugnant to the Constitution." The judiciary helped educate the people to restraint. [20]

From the mid-thirties, Cincinnati lawyers would rarely discourse on the Constitution without mention of the "dark omens abroad"—the threat of secession. "Oh, when the last throb of our matchless Constitution shall have ceased, and the dungeons and palaces of tyranny shall be ringing with shouts of fiendish triumph over the downfall of liberty, how unutterably bitter will be the consciousness of having inflicted the first parricidal stab!" Secession was seen as the unilateral renunciation of constitutional obligation; and if such obligation was rebuffed then others would dissolve, and liberty, dependent upon the keeping of pledges, with it. These fears were genuine, nevertheless it is apparent that the function of much of that great mass of constitutional discourse was also decorous and honorific. "Constitutional law employs in its theory the noblest faculty of mind," wrote one attorney, and Cincinnati lawyers were not shy about exhibiting that faculty. It was not until the crisis of the fifties that these lawyers' reading of the Constitution was tied to momentous personal and political decisions.[21]

Closer to the day-to-day work of Cincinnati lawyers was the hectic debate on Law Reform. What seemed to be the increasing complexities and uncertainties of pleading, of the construction and construing of conveyances, mortgages, and contracts, amidst the ever-growing corpus of judicial decision and legislation troubled many practitioners. The movement for codification was supported by widely held beliefs.

> Admitting that mankind are improving, from generation to generation, [explained Timothy Walker, a leading Cincinnati advocate of codification] how is it possible that rules and maxims, and usages, which grew out of, and were adapted to the condition of ages comparatively dark and barbarous, should be adapted to our present condition. . . . If hoary antiquity, and unbounded encomium had been permitted to preclude scrutiny, the philosophy of Aristotle, and the religion of Popery would still enslave the human mind.

Moreover, how could a citizen of the republic know what his rights and duties were if they were hidden in the unwritten common law and the bewilderingly numerous reported decisions of judges and statutes stretching back over the long lapse of years? The common law, in particular, "is the stupendous work of judicial legislation. Theorize as we may, it has been made from first to last by judges." Surely its acceptance violates the American doctrine of separation of powers, and often the principle that government must rest on consent. The law should be codified into one volume, explained a reformer, and placed upon every citizen's bookshelf alongside the Bible, so that he would easily understand his responsibilities toward man and God.[22]

The codification movement in Cincinnati was more widespread and effective than it was in Memphis. Yet, as in Memphis, leadership was assumed by essentially moderate men. Timothy Walker came from an unlettered Massachusetts farm family but, nonetheless, he succeeded in studying at Harvard College and at the Law School under Story. He brought to the movement erudition as well as an impatience with "the blind bigots of the law who are content with things as they are." Walker argued for codification in Cincinnati before David Dudley Field began his campaign in New York. The debate conducted in Walker's *Western Law Journal* was often more careful and sophisticated than the published New York discussions. Walker recognized the limits of his proposals: judicial discretion could never be completely eliminated, though he believed it was not strictly conformable to the American theory of government. Codification would set some bounds for judicial discretion that might not be easily transgressed. Both lawyer and client would benefit, he believed, for if judges were restrained, case preparation could be more effective.[23]

Walker hoped to simplify the law, but it was no part of his purpose to do away with lawyers or to accommodate those with poor training. As long as society was complex and sought to do justice, litigation must involve technicality and a set of men educated to deal with it. He was dismayed by the poor training of many Ohio lawyers and decided to establish a school where students could study law in a formal setting rather than by reading in lawyers' offices. The Cincinnati Law School was almost immediately successful, and Walker believed that its success was a vindication of his view that clients would recognize superior training even if the laws of the state did not.[24]

The register of the graduates of the Cincinnati Law School lists the names of a good number of prominent Cincinnati families, but it includes foreign-sounding names as well, as do the legal sections of the city directories. German lawyers, serving largely German clients, were prominent in Cincinnati even before the Civil War. John Bernard Stallo, who emigrated to Cincinnati from Germany in 1839, became one of the most remarkable members of the Cincinnati Bar. An active leader in politics, he was rewarded by the Democrats with a judgeship (most eminent Cincinnati lawyers were Whigs in the early fifties); but he, nevertheless, considered himself an independent, and he brought his loyal following—successively, and for principled reasons—into the Republican party in 1860, the Liberal Republicans in 1872, and then back to the Democrats in 1876. This political changeableness in no way diminished the respect with which he was held by the Cincinnati Bar. In the seventies, he was already publishing his extraordinary series of papers on the foundations of physics (later revised and incorporated into his book *The Concepts and Theories of Modern Physics* [1881]); nonetheless, it was his activity in local reform clubs that most often won him praise.[25]

Lawyers were prominent in the leadership of the great variety of reforms that appeared in Cincinnati. Timothy Walker argued for the abolition of capital punishment and gave his support to the burgeoning Women's Rights movement. Stallo spoke in defense of the Hungarian Revolution of 1848 abroad, and a merit system in civil service at home. A local civic reform club, a temperance society, a prison reform club, and a mechanics education society all met at the law library. The most popular of all the reform-minded lawyers was Bellamy Storer. Coming to Cincinnati from New England in the early days of the city's settlement, he brought with him a Unitarian optimism about human possibilities that found outlet in a scattering of good works. Characteristically, he praised individual initiative and responsibility and at the same time hailed the great moral revolution that demonstrated that "reciprocal dependence is closely connected with man's true value." Both the notions of individual responsibility and reciprocal dependence provided arguments for his wide-ranging civic mercantilism and for the great variety of reform organizations in which he played a prominent part.[26]

Of course many Cincinnati lawyers turned their backs on the reform enthusiasm of the era. Judge William S. Groesbeck was the most well known and respected of these. His skepticism about the benefits of human contrivance in social and governmental affairs and his belief that most existing arrangements were "quite good enough" helped sustain his conservative outlook. Responding to Walker and Storer, Groesbeck also turned his skepticism to the realm of law itself. The courts could not achieve justice, but rather "justice according to law." And law was "an artificial expedient system" that "could not make men good or happy" but could give them order and peace. That was an appreciable accomplishment.[27]

This well-mannered discussion about reform was but a lightsome prelude to the bitter and explosive controversy over slavery. While an abolition society had existed in Cincinnati since the early thirties, most reforming lawyers at that time shunned such radicals and preferred the vague proposals of the African Colonization Society. However, beginning in the late forties with a series of fugitive slave cases and rising rapidly in the next decade with increasingly more compelling events such as the Kansas-Nebraska Act, Dred Scott decision, and finally secession, the city's leading lawyers became deeply involved with the anguish of slavery, both within and beyond the courtroom.[28]

At the center of these events was Salmon P. Chase, serene, handsome, and as yet without the pompous verbosity that would characterize him later in life. Before Chase began to plead a series of fugitive slave cases in the Cincinnati courts, moderate antislavery lawyers thought those cases were legally hopeless. But Chase argued that the Constitution itself was an antislavery document. First, he read the Constitution as a statute, discussing the intent of the framers, who, in the majority, were opposed to slavery and looked forward to its extinction. To use that fundamental statute to perpetuate and strengthen slavery, he asserted, was therefore to misuse it. Then he claimed that slavery also violated natural rights, and only positive municipal law could create and sustain such an odious institution; it "can have no existence beyond the territorial limits of the state which sanctions it." Finally, and more radically, he urged that:

> Law cannot, speaking with strict accuracy, make men property, for man is not by Nature the subject of ownership. . . . No Legislature is omnipotent. No Legislature can make right, wrong; or wrong, right. Nor is any Legislature at liberty to disregard the fundamental principles of rectitude and justice. . . . No court is bound to enforce unjust law; but, on the contrary, every court is bound, by prior and superior obligations, to abstain from enforcing such law. . . . It is the duty of this court to rescue the Constitution from the undeserved opprobrium of lending its sanction to the idea that there may be property in men.

Chase lost most cases, but he repeated this argument each time and gathered an increasing number of lawyers to his side.[29]

When the Kansas-Nebraska Act was passed, a large meeting of lawyers was organized to declare against it. At the announcement of the Dred Scott decision "a select committee of the most distinguished Cincinnati jurists" declared it largely *obiter dicta*. Although some Democratic lawyers came to its defense, significantly, Judge William S. Groesbeck, now the most eminent Democratic lawyer in the city, found reason to condemn it. The law had always been a path to politics, but never before had "the working Bar" moved so directly into political affairs.[30]

After the War, though many leading members of "the working Bar" continued active political careers, most lawyers returned to their earlier pattern of dealing with community affairs through nonpartisan voluntary associations. Since the Democrats and Republicans were so evenly divided in the city after the War, voluntary associations had significant influence. As before the War, party politics entered the courthouse periodically through the election of judges, yet much as in Memphis, the most important effect of such elections seems to have been the shortening of judicial careers and the bringing of the bench and the bar closer together.[31]

The lawyer, in the adversarial situation of the courtroom, was usually expected to make the best case he could for his client without "attempting to mislead either the court or the jury by wilfully misrepresenting the law or the facts" and to leave matters of justice and the state of the law to that court and jury. However—as in Memphis, though much more frequently and conspicuously—the most renowned lawyers in Cincinnati struck judicial attitudes. There was much talk about the bar's responsibility for the state of the law and recurrent mention of prominent members of the bar who took influential but unremunerative cases. In the discussion of legal ethics, a favorite topic at commencement assemblies, memorial meetings, and bar association conventions, lawyers were admonished to remember their oaths as officers of the court.[32]

This attitude affected the lawyers' relations with their clients and that effect was most evident in Timothy Walker's various lectures at the law school. Walker opposed any recognition of the English class system in American law. For example, the traditional title *master and servant,* with its long history in English law and authoritative acceptance by Blackstone and Kent, Walker translated into *contract law* and *principal-agent law,* both dealing with relations between equals and therefore more in accord with a republican society. Yet when he discussed the lawyer-client relation, Walker refused to place it under the heading of *principal-agent law.* The lawyer was an officer of the court, and that made his relationship to his client unique. He must not simply serve his client, the lawyer must guide him as well. Walker, whose style was generally clear and even astringent, fell into a different kind of language when discussing the authority of the lawyers and the consequent confidentiality of the relationship between lawyers and their clients.

> [The law] exerts in its practice the cardinal virtues of the heart. . . . It is not given to man to see the human heart completely unveiled before him. But the lawyer perhaps comes more nearly to this, than any other; for there is no aspect in which the character does not present itself, in his secret consultations. All the passions, all the vices, and all the virtues, are by turns subjected to his scrutiny. He thus studies human nature, in its least disguised appearances. . . . His secrets must be buried with him. His honor is pledged never to violate professional confidence. Otherwise he could a tale unfold, compared with which all fictions would be stale and vapid.[33]

One of the justifications that lawyers relied upon to support their authoritative position with regard to their clients and their eminent position in society at large, was that such standing was the reward of talent and achievement. Salmon P. Chase told Tocqueville, somewhat hopefully, "It's still the influence of men of talent that rules us." There were at least two consequences that might follow from this way of looking at things: existing social distinctions would be loosely justified as the result of talent and achievement, or those standards might be used to criticize existing social distinctions. Timothy Walker seemed to assume both viewpoints when he claimed that some men of wealth were worthy of respect because their wealth was based upon achievement, but others must be scorned because they were simply scoundrels. While in Memphis the bearing of the planter was often taken up by lawyers with little talk about justifications, in Cincinnati there was nothing comparable. Actually, Nicholas Longworth, the richest man in Cincinnati, long retired from active legal practice, would wander down to the courthouse seeking to gain entry into the lively camaraderie of the Bar. Many Cincinnati lawyers clearly believed that the profession of law was "not a stepping stone to something higher. In fact there is nothing higher."[34]

Of course many Cincinnati clergy made similar claims for the profession of the ministry. To watch over the law was simply to stand guard over empty formulas, if there was not someone who would at the same time attend to the nation's piety and conscience. American society rested upon morality, which in turn was animated by Christian belief. That was a conception upon which most religious leaders in Cincinnati fully agreed, although they fully agreed upon little else. In fact it was the religious diversity of the city that was most apparent and worrying. For that diversity, it was thought, might lead to contentiousness and mutual enfeeblement or to a thoughtless tolerance and indifference. The three major religious bodies in Cincinnati in 1830, in order of size, were the Methodists, the Presbyterians, and the Catholics; in 1880 that order had shifted to Catholics, Methodists, Presbyterians. This shift gave a new force to worries about diversity, for many Protestants were uncertain as to whether Catholics were truly Christian, moral, and American. In Memphis the Catholic Church remained small enough to gratify anyone's propensity for forbearance. In Cincinnati Catholics might seem more threatening.[35]

One response to the religious diversity of the city was to rush to the defense of doctrinal purity. Joshua Lacey Wilson, Cincinnati's imposing Presbyterian minister, considered the care and protection of doctrine one of the minister's principal obligations. Fulfilling that obligation meant becoming embroiled in controversy, but controversy was the proper means by which to preserve truth. "These [religious disputations] are exercises of which a good man can never be sick—in which he is commanded never to be weary." Wilson rarely wearied. In fact, he confessed that neither eloquence, poetry, nor music was "as rejoicing to the heart as downright controversy." Of course, all his rejoicing was for a good cause—the defense of Calvinism as embodied in the Westminster Confession and the Shorter Catechism. His first opponents were the Methodists, and he left a bristling chronicle of that encounter in his extraordinary pamphlet *Episcopal Methodism: Or Dagonism Exhibited.* Wilson, however, saved his most vigorous efforts for his own church. At various times he took on at least four Presbyterian ministers resident in Cincinnati, but the most important of these battles was with the Reverend Mr. Lyman Beecher, whom he charged with heresy, hypocrisy, and slander.[36]

Beecher's heresy trial was but one of the early skirmishes in the larger struggle that split the Church nationwide into the Old and New School Presbyterians in 1837. In Cincinnati the Presbyterians were a divided church from 1838 to 1870. The most apparent aspects of the split were doctrinal and sectional. The Old School looked to Princeton, where close adherence to the Westminster Confession—denying man's direct role in his own salvation—was insisted upon; doctrine was kept pure but was not easily related to the revivals that were so important to the Church. The New School looked to Yale, where theologians modified traditional Calvinism to show that actual sin was in part voluntary, with the aim of providing an effective theological basis for their revivalistic efforts. In Cincinnati it also appears that the bulk of church members in the New School churches had come from New England and those in the Old School churches from the Middle States and the South.[37]

Beecher's performance at his trial is revealing. When called upon to present his theological views, he stated them in a form that was more strictly orthodox than the Yale theologians would have used, yet what he gave with one hand he took back with the other. He rejected the demand for uniformity in all religious thinking and language, and in so doing diminished the role of the minister as the protector of purity of doctrine. One of his requirements of doctrine was that it support a sense of Christian duty that would animate a Christian civilization. Although Wilson made occasional forays upon the "worldly" attractions in the city—he thought dancing and the theater were particularly sinful—he seemed less interested in the responsibility of religion in the forming of society than did Beecher. (Perhaps the fact that New School Presbyterianism arose from a setting in which the Church had once been established, and the Old School from a region where the Church never had such a position, was an important element of these differences.) Beecher wanted to preserve doctrine as best he could, but he did not want it (or the minister who maintained it) to lose broad influence in the rapidly changing culture of the nation.[38]

That was true not only of Beecher but also of the most notable leaders of the two other dominant religious groups, the Methodists and the Catholics. The most troublesome issues for the Methodists in Cincinnati during this era involved their church structure, which was both too equalitarian and too inequalitarian to suit many of its most prominent members. It is noteworthy that James B. Finley, Ohio's famous circuit rider, much revered in Church councils (whose position in Cincinnati Methodism was comparable to Beecher's in Presbyterianism) lent his support to some of the innovations that the Cincinnati laymen proposed. For the sake of decorum, the Union Chapel built family pews, although this violated Wesley's dictum that all seats be free, and that men and women sit separately. The leaders of the chapel also insisted that they had the right to refuse a minister sent by the Church hierarchy. This second issue would seem to be more important, although the comparative excitement of the discussions on the two subjects cannot be brought to support that judgment.[39]

Finley's response to these challenges was adroit. He recognized that the sexually separate and equal seating, while enshrined in Wesley's *Discipline* and appropriate for an earlier era when membership was made up almost entirely of the humbler classes, was inexpedient for an increasingly prosperous community. In 1852 the *Discipline* was revised, giving individual churches the right of choice in the type of seating used. But Finley resisted allowing the churches a choice in selecting their ministers. Instead he pressed for a more explicit definition of the bishop as a Church officer (rather than a member of a distinct priestly office) and for lay representation in Church councils. By 1872 both were accomplished. Finley was sure that his work had brought the strengthening of the Church and "the preservation of its unique message."[40]

Quite likely the most effective churchman in Cincinnati was

the Most Reverend John Baptist Purcell, appointed Catholic bishop of Cincinnati in 1833. He moved quickly to try to disarm Protestant suspicions of the rapidly growing Catholic church in Cincinnati. "He had the wide-awake mind of the typical American," one Protestant lawyer recalled, and that was a compliment that Purcell would have prized. He was a popular speaker and received invitations to address a great variety of audiences. He rarely refused.[41]

Purcell was an Irish bishop ruling a predominantly German archdiocese. He soon invited religious orders with a preponderance of German priests and began a German language newspaper (the first Catholic-German periodical in the United States), with proceeds of publication going to the German Orphan Home for Boys. When Protestants complained of the noise and distraction of the German beer gardens on Sundays, Purcell commended Catholics who avoided amusements on the Sabbath as a courtesy toward Protestant neighbors. At the height of the Know-Nothing agitation in Cincinnati, he replied to attacks with calmness, and he judged correctly that the disturbances were temporary and local and that they did not represent the more general attitudes of American citizens. He joined voluntary associations to boost Cincinnati's cultural life, and the cathedral he built (rejecting the traditional Gothic for the more modish Greek Revival) is still probably one of the most beautiful buildings in the city.[42]

Purcell wanted to see Catholicism as acceptably American but at the same time he insisted upon his loyalty to the Church and its priestly hierarchy and hoped that he could minimize whatever conflicts existed between sacred doctrine and American culture. He was an ardent promoter of parochial schools but was continually in search of some way of coming to terms with public school education. He believed that "no enlightened Catholic holds the Pope's infallibility to be an article of faith," and he fought vigorously against the infallibility declaration within the Ecumenical Council in Rome. At the public welcome accorded him in Mozart Hall, Cincinnati, a few days after his return, he read the infallibility decree and announced his acceptance of it.[43]

Conflict between Catholicism and American ways in religion presumably would arise from the nature of the piety itself, from the clash between ritualist and revivalist religiosity. However, revivalism in Cincinnati was quite varied. Among the Presbyterians and Methodists, it was kept under tight ecclesiastical control, while among the Lutherans and Episcopalians (both with evangelical wings in Cincinnati) it was suffused with liturgical and confessional standards. Baptist revivalism in Cincinnati was closest to the style prevalent in Memphis, and the Cincinnati Baptist Rev. Samuel W. Lynd's pamphlet on "manifest tokens" could as well have been published in that southern city. Yet the cardinal emotions upon which the conversions hinged (guilt and fear, then release and love) were similar, and revivalism in this era generally strengthened the authority of the minister rather than undermined it. Among the Presbyterians, even when an itinerant revivalist was used, he was welcomed in a formal manner to the pulpit and ceremoniously introduced to the congregation, signifying not only a transfer of authority but also where such authority customarily rested.[44]

The only group that seemed to threaten this disciplined revivalism, and then only sporadically, was the band of Finneyite itinerants, the "God's Revivalist Office" in Cincinnati, where the *Full Salvation Quarterly* was published. These itinerants in Cincinnati, who looked to Finney for guidance, came from various denominations and offered their services to all. They aimed at creating great religious anxiety among the coldhearted and halfhearted but controlling the response so that it took properly Christian and even denominational directions. The revivalist's own position of authority, even domination, was an important instrument. Finney himself wrote:

> No revival can be thorough until all sinners and backsliders are so searched and humbled that they can not hold up their heads. It is a settled point with me, that while backsliders and sinners can come to an anxious meeting and hold up their heads and look you and others in the face without blushing and confusion, the work of searching is by no means performed, and they are in no state to be thoroughly broken down and converted to God.

The Finneyites would supplement regular church services and conduct revivals only "at certain seasons of the year when the minds of both saints and sinners are less occupied with the necessary business of life." Despite all such restraint and caution, occasionally they directed onslaughts against unconverted ministers and denomination bodies rather than against the ordinary sinners and backsliders. But those attacks were scattered and irregular, rarely disturbing the regular ministers and church organizations.[45]

Even the Catholics pressed forward their counterpart to revivalism, the parish mission. This movement was a form of intensive preaching developed by those religious orders that were founded during the Catholic Counter-Reformation to strengthen religious feeling in communities where spiritual life had fallen into neglect. Parish missions were without much influence in American Catholicism until the 1830s, but then the movement developed rapidly, with Cincinnati as one of its centers. Its parallels to Protestant revivalism, particularly of the disciplined denominational style, are striking. Both focused upon an intense religious feeling and believed that such emotion would bring a change of heart and a new life of grace. Both relied heavily upon itinerants who developed new techniques of psychological pressure, usually drawing upon the feelings of guilt and fear for their effectiveness. Purcell was an ardent promoter of the parish mission movement. He brought Francis X. Weninger, the outstanding itinerant Jesuit preacher, to Cincinnati and provided the first official support for parish missions in America. These Catholic missions were embedded in an elaborately ritualistic and hierarchical church and therefore channeled the religious enthusiasm that they evoked into the work and ceremonies of the local church and parish.[46]

Unitarians and Jews were unaffected by the revivalist spirit. They made up a small segment of the religious community, but Unitarians, at least, owing to their social prominence, exerted an influence far out of proportion to their numbers. What the Unitarians and Jews of Cincinnati shared with many of the revivalists was their predilection to look beyond rituals as well as hard and fast rules. The First Congregational Church in Cincinnati had been Unitarian since its founding in 1830, and in the course of its history it had provided a pulpit for three high-toned, radical, and impassioned ministers: William Henry Channing, James Handasyd Perkins, and Moncure Conway. All three were deeply influenced by Emerson's Transcendentalism.[47]

It was during Conway's ministry, in the mid-nineteenth century, that the more orthodox members split away from the congregation to form a more conventional church. By that time, Conway no longer considered himself a Christian, although most of his loyal followers clung to that designation. Evidently they deferred more to his personality than to his shifting beliefs. "I fear we are more Conwayites than liberals," explained one of his admirers. It is not easy to understand the source of Conway's authority with his congregation. His predecessor, the Reverend Perkins, argued in a self-revealing and self-serving way that "the free man should be the leader of him who is less free." Conway himself was intent upon denying all authority. He preached Emersonian self-reliance—that the germ of all lies within oneself. Doubtlessly, for those who had difficulty in finding God elsewhere, that was a comforting gospel, and the example Conway set as a fearless seeker was awe-inspiring. In that sense, Conway, like the revivalist minister, spoke to the conscience of his flock, although the conscience of the Unitarians had been educated in a very special way.[48]

Rabbi Isaac Mayer Wise and Moncure Conway were good friends and shared many opinions, but Wise's hold on his congregation was quite different. Cincinnati was probably the second largest center of Jewish population in the country during the era 1830 to 1880. It was the headquarters of a vast midwestern trading network of Jewish peddlers, country stores, wholesalers, and even manufacturers, as Jewish entrepreneurs in Cincinnati increasingly found their way into the ready-made clothing industry. To this bustling community of Jewish merchants, Wise preached much of what they wanted to hear. Bringing some of the notions of the German-Jewish Reform movement to America, Wise set aside "casuistical rabbinism . . . ridiculous mysticism . . . and thoughtless observances." He presented a "Judaism independent of its forms" but true to its principles. Yet while the traditional forms were substantive, with a definite bearing on everyday life, Wise's principles were abstract and granted wide latitude in behavior.[49]

Particularly appealing was Wise's principle: "Whatever makes us ridiculous before the world as it now is, may safely be and should be abolished." Surely in a city where *The Merchant of Venice* was a particular favorite and where the leading Episcopal clergyman taught that the "soul is broadened by the disgust which the Venetian Jew excites," Jewish merchants did not wish to appear disgusting or ridiculous. Wise was an exemplar of a cultured, liberal, pleasing Hebrew gentleman, apparently well thought of; he frequently exchanged pulpits, at least with Unitarians. He was just the sort of respectable spokesman that anxious Jewish merchants, wishing to escape the ugliness that infects the life of the despised, would want. Ironically, when Wise's daughter ran off with a handsome young Gentile, one journal could not resist the Shylock parallel, mercifully without direct allusion to "O my ducats! O my daughter." Yet Wise was unquestionably the most presentable spokesman to be had. He was probably aware of this sort of support for his authority in the Jewish community, but he clearly wished for something more. Wise saw this Jewish Reform as a parallel to the Protestant Reformation—he linked the names of Luther and Moses Mendelssohn—and hoped for an upsurge of piety much like that which accompanied the earlier religious break with tradition. Of course breaking with customary religious usage, superstition, and unmeaning forms in order to promote "internal spirit" had decidedly different results in the nineteenth century than it did in the sixteenth.[50]

What these diverse clergymen—Beecher, Finley, Purcell, Finney, Perkins, Conway, and Wise—had in common was the desire to keep their religion relevant to the manner and character of their society and at the same time to preserve the authoritative position of ministers. Often these seemed to be the same thing. Among the Protestant ministers of Cincinnati particularly, owing to their greater acceptance and assurance within the broader community, there was a growing agreement that they should speak out on public issues, and a growing agreement on what they said when they did.

After 1854, many of the city's Protestant ministers found more agreement on slavery than on any other issue:

> We consider the voluntary enslaving of one part of the human race by another as a gross violation of the most precious and sacred rights of human nature; as utterly inconsistent with the law of God, which requires us to love our neighbour as ourselves; and as totally irreconcilable with the spirit and principles of the Gospel of Christ, which enjoin that "all things whatsoever ye would that men should do to you, do ye even so to them."

This one argument came from all antislavery pulpits. Some ministers added some oppressions of slavery that they considered particularly abhorrent. The breaking of slave families was often condemned. One minister linked slavery to Mormonism as a kindred barbarism, implying that both encouraged sexual irregularities. More generally, ministers held up the Golden Rule to "the peculiar institution" and found slavery sinful.[51]

When the war broke out, even those clergymen who had been silent before or had considered Lincoln's election a disaster (a sizable group, however, had openly endorsed the Republican party in 1860) announced their support. The Reverend John Purcell had an American flag hoisted to the top of the steeple of his cathedral and kept it there throughout the war. Emotions were at white heat during wartime, and the Cincinnati ministry, so experienced in moving the emotions of their congregations, transformed the war into a moral venture, a blending of Christian and national loyalty and a condemnation of the enemy and of his way of life as subversive of government, civilization, and religion. The unity of this diverse ministry in wartime was exhilarating. The local branches of the Sanitary Commission and the Christian Commission served as something akin to professional associations of clergy previously divided by denomination.[52]

By 1869 that unity was shattered and, in part, the damage was done by laymen wishing to achieve yet further unity. Soon after the war, while the exhilarating spirit of local solidarity still lingered, Catholic parents suggested a consolidation of the parochial and public schools in order to lighten their financial burdens. At first they received some encouragement—or at least no strenuous objection—from Archbishop Purcell. The board of education, with a large Catholic membership, then appointed a negotiating committee and also passed a resolution prohibiting all specifically religious instruction in the schools, including Bible reading, as a step toward this amalgamation. Purcell however, under pressure from alarmed conservative Catholics, came out against consolidation, and the negotiations were closed. The Bible resolution remained, however, and that gave rise to great uproar and divisions among the ministers as well as sweeping anti-Catholic denunciation. To one observer it seemed that the days of Know-Nothing agitation had returned.[53]

When a group of ministers sued the board of education to reinstate Bible reading, they put themselves into the hands of the leadership of the local bar, many of whom were less certain that the morality upon which American civilization rested was derived from Scripture and evangelical piety. Three of the most outstanding members of the Bar Association quickly took up the defense of the school board's action. They were Stanley Matthews (later U.S. Supreme Court Justice), George Hoadley (later Governor of Ohio), and J. B. Stallo. Though the majority of the Cincinnati court decided against the school board, Alphonso Taft (father of the future president William H. Taft) wrote a sharp dissent that won wide acclaim—including that of Rutherford B. Hayes, then governor of the state and soon to be president of the United States. On appeal to the State Supreme Court, Taft and the board's lawyers were upheld, and official Bible reading was stricken from Cincinnati's public schools. The Supreme Court summarized its decision with a quote from Madison: "Religion is essentially distinct from human government, and exempt from its cognizance. A connection between them is injurious to both." In Cincinnati, many ministers looked upon the decision as a second disestablishment. While some came to accept this setback in the schools, most refused to accept any sharp exclusion of religion, its ministers, and their assured benefits from human government and surely not from the broader society.[54]

Ministers, of course, remained active in the diverse voluntary associations of the city. However, by the 1870s when the baneful effects of Cincinnati's industrial development were becoming apparent, some ministers began to speak out from what they considered their own special vantage point. The Reverend Charles Boynton, who had earlier been active in antislavery agitation, now argued that the Church was the one agency set aside by Christ for the recovery of the world, and that God held the Church responsible for the removal of oppressive social evils. He was joined by the Reverend Dudley Ward Rhodes, whose impassioned book *Creed and Greed* (1879), unmistakably a precursor of the Social Gospel movement, called attention to the poverty, misery, and filth of the rapidly growing tenement districts. Such remonstrance from these eminent personages marked a turning point in the broader history of the city. For it called into question one of the fundamental assumptions of civic folk mercantilism— the belief in the inevitable harmony of interests in the local society, the assurance that the prospering of one segment of the community would ineluctably benefit everyone else in the city.[55]

The relationship between Protestant Christianity in America and the expanding capitalist economy had always been an ambiguous one. While ministers of most denominations extolled honest industry and accepted wealth as its reward, they also held that wealth could be debasing, even corrupting. "Ye cannot serve God and mammon" was the epigraph chosen by the Reverend Mr. Rhodes for his *Creed and Greed.* Moreover, the recommendation that men should primarily pursue self-interest, essential to the code of market relations, was overtly unacceptable. When Boynton called it "the doctrine of the pit" and claimed that it was "bringing hell to earth," he could avail himself of a good many Biblical citations. In even the most obvious sense, American Christianity drew upon much that was precapitalist and potentially anticapitalist. Undoubtedly, the placing of the spiritual above the material, the primordial support for the authority and honor of the minister, could also have such resonance. "The clergyman," a minister in Cincinnati proudly claimed, "is almost the only person, if not the only one, whose standing in the community is independent of wealth."[56]

Of course, Cincinnati doctors would also claim, with some justice, that their standing was independent of wealth. When Daniel Drake died—he was Cincinnati's most renowned physician—he left but a modest estate. His illustrious career stretched back to an earlier era, when the medical system of his great teacher Benjamin Rush was just beginning to fall apart. Already while studying at the University of Pennsylvania Medical School, Drake had heard Rush's young colleague, Casper Wistar, express misgivings about Rush's system; however, it seemed Wistar had nothing to put in its place but doubts. Later, when Drake returned briefly to Pennsylvania to secure his medical degree, he found that the most distinguished doctors in Philadelphia already had set aside Rush's systematic treatise on pathology and only Rush's students, scattered far from the centers of medical progress, were still attached to it and its most drastic remedies. Drake soon renounced Rush's theories and set himself the task of giving to medical science a comprehensive view of disease that would take their place.[57]

Drake's *Systematic Treatise on the Principal Diseases of the Interior Valley of North America*, vol. 1 (1850), might be seen as an expression of the medical achievements of his age. Many of his contemporaries judged it just that way. Therefore it is remarkable to find that Drake's *Systematic Treatise* was no systematic treatise at all. It did not develop a theory of the nature and transmission of disease. Rather, it was for the most part a record of forty years of observation of the natural history of the Mississippi Valley. Drake intended that Book I, which he published, would provide the background for the analysis that was to appear in Book II, which would demonstrate the relationship between the particular environment and various diseases of the "Interior Valley." But Drake never found that relationship for some of the most pervasive diseases, and he never published Book II. Still, the *Systematic Treatise*, Book I, a failed work of the highly talented, industrious, aspiring doctor, tells us as much about Daniel Drake's medical world as any great medical triumph of that era; perhaps it tells us more.[58]

It is helpful to compare Drake's work with that of his mentor, Rush. Benjamin Rush, like many medical men of the late eighteenth century, relied in part upon deductive reasoning to discover the organizing principles of his science. Dependence upon observation without far-reaching speculation would fail to produce any deep understanding. Rush talked about the need for "leaps of imagination" in order to capture a true knowledge of Nature's order. This was the kind of science that might be advanced primarily by men of genius. Drake by contrast proposed the substitution of "acute observation, accurate comparison, judicious arrangement, and logical induction" for metaphysical speculation. In a sense, science was being democratized. For those procedures, Drake explained to his students, were a matter of training, and discovery therefore became available to all who had the aspiration and the stamina.[59]

Drake's scientific study, moreover, not only contained a democratic message but also had an implied sectional meaning. It pointed toward the identification and fashioning of the "Interior Valley" as a region. Drake saw the Mississippi River basin as a natural geographic and economic unit and wished to make it a social and literary axis as well. This was not a regionalism to set against the Union and weaken it (Drake was a good nationalist Whig) but rather a regionalism to support the Union and strengthen it. When Drake began composing his *Systematic Treatise* in the 1840s, the acrimonious divisions between North and South were becoming each day more apparent and threatening. They foreshadowed the breakup of the nation and the splitting of that interior valley which Drake had come to know so well through his extensive travels and to which he had become strongly attached. Of course if attachments to that interior valley could hold, despite the divisive forces that had recently been set loose, then the Union itself might hold. Drake's scientific work endeavored to make the interior valley a coherent concept within medicine, a regional therapeutics, and a scientific bond between the doctors practicing over the length and breadth of the Mississippi basin.[60]

The greatest divisive force in that interior valley—slavery—was not discussed in Drake's *magnum opus,* though it surely was appropriate to his review of the "social etiology" of occupations and pursuits. Drake, like many Whigs, tried to wish slavery away and Blacks as well. While his scientific curiosity drew him to the problem of the comparative response of the various races to disease, Drake actually provided almost no discussion of the subject in his study. A year after giving the manuscript to the printer, he turned directly to a discussion of Blacks and slavery and argued, as had the Memphis doctors, that there was evidence to suggest the biological inferiority of the Black race. Yet there was a tentativeness in Drake's views that the Memphis doctors rarely shared. Earlier, he had printed in his *Western Journal of Medicine and Surgery* a report of a study on the brain weight and size of Blacks and Whites that found no perceptible difference. The study had concluded that "the apparent inferiority of the Negro is altogether the result of the demoralizing influence of slavery, and the long-continued oppression and cruelty which have been exercised towards this unhappy portion of mankind." But now when the political setting in America had become more threatening, Drake discounted the oppression and cruelty of slavery, accepted Black racial inferiority, but anxiously insisted, as if in recompense, that slavery was moving toward extinction. Race prejudice, nonetheless, would never be overcome, therefore, for everyone's good, Blacks must be sent back to Africa. It is remarkable that such an astute commentator as Drake should still contend for the program of African colonization of Blacks as a solution to the slavery question when leading adversaries on both sides of the issue had long given up that plan as unacceptable and unworkable.[61]

If by the 1850s Drake's program for the nation was clearly marked for defeat, a decade earlier his particular schemes for the advancement of medicine in Cincinnati had already foundered. Early in his career Drake had won a charter from the state for a medical school in Cincinnati and, shortly after, for a sizable public hospital. He had also helped to revive the Cincinnati Medical Society and had pushed for a city board of health run by doctors. All these measures were part of a grand plan to establish an important medical center in the Queen City and at the same time to lift its author to his appropriate renown. What followed, however, was a series of furious imbroglios involving a succession of medical schools and societies erratically breaking apart and reassembling, amidst vociferous exchanges of vituperation and even fisticuffs. Drake was challenged to a duel at least twice, but he disdainfully declined on both occasions. Gentlemanly honor in Cincinnati did not depend on such punctilios. Rather, for doctors, it rested upon achievements in the science and art of medicine. Both, however, were in disarray in Drake's time, and that contributed to the turbulence in the medical life of that day.[62]

It was through its science that medicine lay claim to professional standing. Most occupations had their particular skills and rules, but the proficiency and standards of professions were ostensibly based upon a body of connected truths brought under general laws and properly understood only through study. Doctors frequently spoke in elevated and overwrought terms of the dignity of the intellectual activity that their profession required and fostered. Science, explained Dr. John P. Harrison, Professor of Theory and Practice of Medicine at the Medical College of Ohio, will "call away the immortal mind from the gratifications of sense, and send it in quest of the joys of communion with the invisible Spirit"; it also will distinguish the "refined and the civilized" from those "abandoned to ignorance and sensuality." Oddly, though one might come to learn those general laws in various ways, they could be discovered only through scrupulous observation and logical induction. Some doctors, like Samuel G. Armor, were wont to state this in extreme ways: "Our science is not made up of doctrines—speculations—theories. . . . It is only a mass of facts." Quackery was slavery to "creeds"; it made "facts depend upon faith" while scientific medicine made "faith depend upon facts." To cultivate their profession, Armor admonished his students, they must "multiply its facts."[63]

But which facts? "Do not cram your brains with a heterogeneous jumble of odds and ends, such as one finds in an old curiosity shop," warned Dr. Samuel Hanbury Smith. He was soon to take on the assignment of trying to put into some order the three thousand manuscript pages for Book II of the *Systematic Treatise* that Drake had left at his death and trying to link them with Drake's notions of general etiology—a formidable task. Like most other doctors, Smith stressed the "just observation, that base upon which the superstructure of experience is reared," but unlike most other doctors he also appealed for "principles" without which "experience is a useless and blind guide." Exactly what those principles were Smith did not specify, nor did anyone else in a manner that was persuasive to most American doctors. The optimistic faith in pristine and unmediated experience was endemic to America of the mid-nineteenth century. Like the evangelist who thought the revival would point to a purer Christianity or the legal codifier who believed that judicial decisions and statutes would fall into intrinsic divisions and reflect natural justice, the medical thinker supposed that the facts would speak for themselves. Yet for most doctors, who like Drake, were trying to build a medical science without theories, the facts were either mute or, more commonly, cacophonous.[64]

The art of medicine, what we would now call medical practice, was in no better shape than its science. While it was generally agreed that the science of medicine should preside over its art, now that the science itself turned out to be more uncertain, its dictates became increasingly unintelligible. Even in the eighteenth century, when the various medical systems commanded greater confidence, their therapeutics always allowed for some tacit knowledge, for the solvent power of a strong and experienced judgment. In the mid-nineteenth century that judgment took on a more extended dominion, with all the indefiniteness such extension entailed. In this situation, many doctors held on to traditional medicines and procedures although they had rejected the theories upon which they were based. Those familiar remedies—calomel, tartar emetic, and bleeding, to counteract "sthenic," exciting diseases; and quinine and whiskey to counteract "asthenic," debilitating diseases—a regimen derived from the system of the eighteenth-century Scottish physician John Brown, remained standard treatments throughout the middle years of the nineteenth century.[65]

Medical practice remained conservative in this era, but it did shift in response to scathing criticism from within the profession and from without. The work of Pierre Louis in the Paris Hospital, the most prestigious medical center of the era, cast doubt on the widespread practice of venesection. But the most damaging aspersions came from sectarian practitioners—the Thomsonians, Eclectics, and Homeopaths—who added the insult of disparagement to the injury of winning away patients. One recent study suggests that some Cincinnati doctors in response to these hostile conditions actually returned to more drastic procedures to reassert their professional identity, which they associated with aggressive medical intervention. However, there is also evidence that others tried to maintain their authoritativeness and to deflect criticism by adopting somewhat less "heroic" therapeutics. Medical practice was the resultant of a varied assortment of conflicting influences and dispositions.[66]

Amidst the bewilderments of medical science and the confusions in medical treatment in this era, surgery—which had often been a lower branch of medicine in the great metropolitan centers of the eighteenth century—now in the nineteenth century advanced steadily in proficiency and rose to a new prominence. Surgery was not a formal specialty at this time; most physicians in America did some surgery. However, a relatively small group who had won a reputation for success in the more difficult operations gained special recognition as exemplary leaders in medical progress. Usually these illustrious surgeons taught in the medical schools, as did Reuben Dimond Mussey, Cincinnati's celebrated surgeon and professor at the Medical College of Ohio.[67]

He had "the courage of the lion, the nerve of the ox, and the delicacy of a woman's touch," wrote an admirer of Mussey; those were attributes long admired among surgeons. Surgeons' peculiarly tacit knowledge was also important, for accurate diagnosis and the ability to estimate the risks of different types of operations were essential to any successful outcome. That kind of surgical judgment was gained through long clinical experience together with the ability to learn from inevitable failures. After the increased use of anesthesia in the mid-nineteenth century encouraged the surgeons to undertake even more daring operations, the incidence of shock still set limits to any surgery, and judgments about those limits still came principally from the surgeons' melancholy experience. Mussey was especially praised for his judgment on such matters. His respect and standing in the profession became apparent when the American Medical Association came to Cincinnati in 1850 and chose Mussey instead of Drake as its president.[68]

Despite the many conflicts among themselves, most doctors enjoined cooperation and discovered an inescapable interdependence in the community at large. "We must remember," admonished a doctor, "that the prince and the pauper breathe one common air, and that the foul pestilential emanation of the hovel penetrates to the palace and produces its effects there." It was through the board of health that the medical profession would bring its understanding and expertise to Cincinnati. Yet the divisions among themselves and their conflicts with the various unorthodox forms of medicine that flourished in the city diminished the regular doctors' authority in public affairs. One layman argued that medicine, like theology, should be divorced from the state, and, as with the different religious sects, the various medical systems should be treated alike. "We go for free trade in doctoring," he wrote. This made for rapidly shifting membership on the board of health. At one point the Eclectic doctors were in control; at another, laymen cleared all doctors from the board and ran it themselves. In 1858 the regulars recaptured control, but when cholera returned they were irremediably divided on what advice to give the city. At another time, when they did join to recommend that prostitution be legalized and regulated, and that prostitutes be examined (as in Memphis) in order to prevent the spread of venereal disease, the ministers in town rose up in fiery wrath to defeat the measure.[69]

Remarkably, while the public authority of doctors was much diminished, their sway over patients seems not to have lessened to any comparable extent. Though Drake was stern with his patients (Harriet Beecher Stowe quipped that his bedside manner was that of a Calvinist minister delivering a discourse on Divine election), their testimonials were generally warm and grateful. Many of Mussey's patients were adoring. Undoubtedly the papers of physicians are biased sources, and they are less likely to preserve abusive letters than thankful and compliant ones; nonetheless the generally deferential tone is striking. The doctors, for their part, usually saw the patient's relation to them as a "defenceless and dependent relation [that] produces obligations which can scarcely be higher in any human relation. Every man in the practice of medicine should, therefore, feel himself bound by the most sacred obligation to faithfulness in the discharge of the high trust reposed in him."[70]

At the outset, some of the founders of dissenting groups in medicine hoped to destroy that relationship of authority and dependence. The Thomsonian school of Botanic medicine promised that everyone would be his or her own doctor, and Wooster Beach, founder of the Eclectic school, denounced "King-craft, Priest-craft, Lawyer-craft, and Doctor-craft." However, the animus behind those hopes quickly dissipated, and the dissident forms of medicine soon took to mimicking the orthodox practitioners, particularly in their social ambitions. It would not be easy, in mid-nineteenth-century America, to find someone more theatrically highfalutin than an irregular physician, particularly if he had begun to worry about the efficacy of his special brand of science and therapy.[71]

Cincinnati was one of the prodigious centers of unorthodox medicine in America. At one point it embraced two Eclectic Medical Institutes, two Physiomedical Institutes (Thomsonians), a Homeopathic Medical College, and a College of Vitapathic Practice. These found a considerable following among important laymen in the city and seriously challenged the regulars for control of the board of health and the municipal hospital. What these irregular practitioners held in common was a forceful condemnation of the heavy drugging and bleeding still practiced by many of the regulars; in this criticism they were largely right. But then each sect forged ahead to contrive an elaborate science and therapeutics of its own; in these contrivings they were largely wrong.[72]

One of the most successful groups of irregular practitioners in Cincinnati was the Eclectics. During the early and exciting years of their remarkable Eclectic Institute, all varieties and shadings of medical theory and practice were represented; but then, almost ineluctably, a particularly forceful teacher, immensely popular with the students, rose to the leadership of the institute with the program of regularizing Eclectic medicine as a "distinct and positive therapeutic system." Once in power, he expelled his opponents (as "quacks") and the women students, who earlier had been admitted on equal terms (as unqualified) and set the institute upon a more implacably "scientific" course.[73]

The other dissenting forms of medicine followed similar patterns of accommodation. The Thomsonians gradually shed their radical and egalitarian spirit and set up a counterprofession with much of the commanding manner and means of the regulars. The Homeopaths had always maintained the social usages of the orthodox, but now a group of them began to take up with more conventional drugs and with more appreciable dosages. It was in their resort to fervent controversy and angry schism among themselves, as well as to assaults upon rival medical sciences and therapies, however, that these irregulars came to resemble the regulars most closely.[74]

Open emulation of the regular medical profession was also unmistakable among the aspiring pharmacists and dentists in Cincinnati. One of the most energetic of those desirous of elevating pharmacy was William B. Chapman. He had graduated the Medical College of Ohio but chose to remain a pharmacist and worked to establish the Cincinnati College of Pharmacy where he taught and helped turn out a cadre of scientifically trained pharmacists. His election to the presidency of the American Pharmaceutical Association in 1854, it was said, marked the recognition of Cincinnati as an important center of professional pharmacy. Chapman's counterpart among the dentists was James Taylor who likewise acquired a medical degree but found the opportunities in dentistry attractive enough to continue his dental practice. Taylor promised to help elevate dentistry from a craft to a profession. The instrument of that elevation was to be the Ohio College of Dental Surgery, which Taylor and a group of doctors founded in 1845. He became its first dean. He also edited and wrote extensively in the *Dental Register of the West,* gaining a reputation for extensive erudition and assiduous observation. Few were surprised when Taylor was elected president of the American Dental Convention in 1856.[75]

It was not until after the Civil War, however, that the Ohio College of Dental Surgery attained the stability and rapid growth its founders had expected. The War was important for the professional ambitions of Northern dentists. The Union Army not only brought together practitioners from all over the North but ranked them as surgeons and gave them officers' pay. After that, it would clearly be less difficult for many to affect a medical demeanor. The most distinguished Cincinnati dentist of the post–Civil War era was Jonathan Taft, who held a chair at the College of Dental Surgery. The introductory chapter for his text is particularly illustrative of the arduousness of the rise from a craft to a profession. Taft insisted that dentistry was "an independent health profession," thereby ruling out any possible subordination to medicine. At the same time he provided a suitable discussion of etiquette, dress, and decoration of the waiting room, all laden with mimicry of medicine. Such emulation was fraught with anxiety and motive power. It was not surprising that the dentists in Ohio, like

those in Tennessee, were among the first to press for a professional practice act in this era and were among the first to succeed
in getting one.[76]

The growth of the professions in Cincinnati had accompanied
the rapid growth of the city itself. In fact, the leading professionals were important agents of that growth. Aside from Drake, the
lawyers were the most outspoken champions of the Queen City's
development, for their work readily brought them to commerce
and politics and to civic folk mercantilism. Among those lawyers,
Alphonso Taft was one of the most influential. Arriving in Cincinnati a young, well-educated New England lawyer, he soon prospered through quick wit and enterprise. Yet Taft did not busy
himself exclusively with his legal practice; that would have been
unacceptable to him. Rather he plunged into civic affairs with
great energy and won a reputation for public-spirited good works.
He served on the board of directors of the Astronomical Observatory and the House of Refuge; he headed the board of health
when it was in the hands of laymen, and he was later to lead in
the establishment of City University. Therefore, when Taft addressed a body of the city's most prominent citizens in January
1850, warning them that Cincinnati was in danger of losing its
place as the preeminent city of the northern Mississippi Valley,
he roused sharp concern.[77]

Taft's message was simple. Canals and river traffic had built
cities in the past; they had built Cincinnati. But now "it is the
rail-way which builds cities." The locomotive "has taken to the
land, and now raises, and depresses, towns and cities, at its pleasure." Undoubtedly, "the largest part of the national wealth and
population of the United States will soon be found, between the
Alleghenies and the Rocky Mountains"; unless Cincinnati
reached out to this region and beyond with railway lines, its ascendancy would be lost. Private enterprise alone was inadequate
for the task. Only the city, with its great taxing power, through
liberal and comprehensive subsidies, could accomplish this
work. Of course, timid and shortsighted businessmen might
worry about the sizable public debt this program involved, but if
they looked to the enormous growth it would bring, they might
understand that the greatly expanded tax base could make a
seemingly perilous public debt really quite insignificant. This
was a favorite doctrine of civic folk mercantilism. Despite the immediate enthusiasm Taft's speech evoked, he did not gather
enough support to carry through his program. Still he proved to
be an accurate prophet. During the decade of the fifties, for the

first time in Cincinnati's history, her rate of growth dropped sharply.[78]

It is not clear whether Taft's program or any other could have averted Cincinnati's relative decline, which continued through the nineteenth century. The westward expansion of farming and changes in Ohio's agriculture gave Chicago and St. Louis great advantages. Significantly, Cincinnati meatpackers shifted toward a better quality and more expensive product, thereby entering a more limited but less competitive market. This was actually closer to the practice, if not the preachment, of many of the city's professionals. In addition, the Civil War soon cut off Cincinnati's important southern market, and the postwar devastation in that region precluded any prospering connection with the South thereafter.[79]

This was an outcome that Cincinnati patriots could not easily accept. In 1868 yet another civic-minded lawyer, Edward Ferguson, urged that Cincinnati build a railroad southward to capture the southern trade and return the city to its earlier rapid economic growth. Ferguson's railroad would have to be city owned and built entirely out of city funds. Nevertheless, the distress at Cincinnati's economic decline had so roused the "civic-minded," who in turn roused the city, that the electorate voted ten to one to build their railroad. This was an unequivocal victory for Cincinnati civic folk mercantilism such that Memphis boosters could only envy. Yet this victory was to no avail. Long before the railroad was completed, it had become apparent that the real cost of construction would be three times what had been estimated and that the southern trade would fall much below all predictions.[80]

While the chamber of commerce continued to present optimistic reports on the progress of the railroad and what it was accomplishing for the city, many early supporters soon gave way to disconsolateness. Not only did the disappointments of the railroad dampen spirits, but the sharper social divisions in the city, to which some ministers were insistently calling attention, could not fit the booster vision of a progressive and harmonious society so important to civic folk mercantilism. When the violent railroad strikes of 1877 swept the nation, the apprehensiveness of Cincinnati's "respectable classes" was evident. The local railroad workers joined the strike but, remarkably, there was little violence in Cincinnati. The workers marched peacefully through Fountain Square and newspapers complimented them on their orderly behavior. When bitter social conflict broke out in Cincinnati almost a decade later, it caught many by surprise.[81]

The law and its lawyers were the focal point upon which much of the attention, distress, accusation, passion, and destruction converged in the riots of 1884. Lawyers had been of great importance in giving direction to Cincinnati's affairs, yet none of the more eminent lawyers of civic patriotism—Timothy Walker, Alphonso Taft, or Edward Ferguson—stood at the center of this upheaval. Rather, an unrenowned but influential attorney, Thomas C. Campbell, touched off the excitement. Campbell, a political lawyer who had risen through the police courts and a successful criminal law practice, by the eighties was generally considered to be the local Republican boss. Along with his Democratic counterpart, John R. McLean, he reputedly manipulated elections for city and county offices and provided protection for liquor and prostitution interests in the city. This was a new turn in city affairs, Campbell had little regard for the "respectable classes" and effectively shut out the civic improvers and their voluntary associations from local politics. Campbell also maintained his criminal law practice and liked to see himself as a defender of the poor, the oppressed, and the unpopular through his skillful use of all the devices of the law. He was clearly not the sort of man invited to join the Cincinnati Bar Association.[82]

When a distraught German immigrant asked Campbell to take the case of his son, a confessed murderer, Campbell readily agreed. His fee was $2,500—which was considered exorbitant for such a case in that day. Though the son had confessed to the callous and mercenary murder, the case, apparently, was not hopeless. Campbell had saved others similarly incriminated from the gallows. As the newspapers reported the brutal details, however, popular excitement mounted ominously. Campbell's defense was scintillating and resourceful, yet the evidence of premeditated murder was so strong that when the jury somehow decided that the young man was guilty only of manslaughter, even the judge denounced the verdict as outrageous. A group of leading citizens called an "indignation meeting" and drew an overflow crowd whose temper turned out to be unexpectedly angry and impetuous. Many believed that the jury had been bribed. The confused and unsubstantial resolutions passed at the meeting did little to assuage the excitement of the audience. As the crowd poured out of the meeting, a cry for a march on the jail set the riot in motion. Shots were fired, a rioter was killed, and the protest turned into an insurrection, besieging the center of the city for three nights. Before it was over, fifty-six people had been killed and over two hundred wounded.[83]

It would be exceedingly difficult to discover the diverse, anonymous motives that impelled the fury of the crowd. However, some of the acknowledged intentions are less obscure, and all observers agreed on many of the facts. There was no looting of private property, except for shops with guns and ammunition from which the rioters armed themselves. Most of the rioters were workers of German origin, as was the prisoner; therefore ethnic motives were probably not important. The most spectacular act of the rioters was setting fire to the grand and imposing courthouse, burning it to the ground, and destroying the legal records of the community. As the courthouse burned, a newsboy held a mock auction, calling for bids on the burning "Temple of Justice." This dramatized one of the compelling grievances of the rioters—that justice was for sale, that a guilty man with money could buy an easy sentence, but a man without money would hang. Law as restraint was accepted as long as law was justice. When it was not, both law and restraint could be attacked.[84]

The news of the riots spread throughout the country and Europe, giving Cincinnati a notoriety that dismayed its most distinguished citizens. Many of them despised Campbell and wanted to see him driven from the city. However the violence, death, and suffering, the overthrow of order, obligation, and constraint, as symbolized in the burning of the courthouse, shocked and frightened them. Class divisions in society, which they had often previously tried to deny, now seemed undeniable. Rabbi Wise compared the riots to the French Commune; the Reverend Charles Theodore Greve said they equaled "the worst days of the French Revolution."[85]

The most earnest attempt to understand the riots appeared in a book by Joseph Salathiel Tunison, a scholarly young journalist who had worked with Cincinnati newspapers for almost a decade before the riots. He decided that his study would provide more than a narrative of events; it would attempt to discover the underlying causes of the events and their broader significance. He intended to be radical and startling. The riots had confirmed his belief that traditional notions of democracy were no longer authoritative or even safe. The spontaneous loyalty of citizens to their government could not be depended upon. A dangerous class had appeared at the lower ranges of society whose way of life was alien to America's original principles. Its members were made even more dangerous by the exigencies of city life. Cincinnati in particular was "at the mercy of her proletariat." If one can no longer depend on inner assent and accord, then external devices for compliance must be strengthened. Tunison suggested various means: immigration restriction, suffrage restrictions, and the strengthening of militias. Let us have "well-settled orders of nobility," he conceded gloomily, "if the only other alternatives are the plutocrat, mobocrat, and the aristocracy of the whiskey shop and the houses of prostitution."[86]

Predictably, Tunison recommended the professions in place of those orders of nobility. In a sense, this was a return to the pre-Campbell days when those groups were influential. But Tunison insisted that the professions must become more exclusive. They must improve the caliber of their practitioners by raising admission standards, by requiring college degrees, and by raising the standards of the professional schools. Significantly, these were measures that the professions themselves were soon to demand.[87]

Tunison's tone was both melancholy and strident. It seems that he did not have unclouded faith in his own prescriptions. And, in fact, not only did Boss Crump succeed "Pappy" Hadden in Memphis, but Boss Cox was soon to succeed Tom Campbell in Cincinnati. Even the renovated professions were not to have the influence in Cincinnati that the professions had known earlier in the city's history. While Tunison genuinely cared for Cincinnati and found much in it that he esteemed, he was nonetheless an ambitious young journalist, and he decided to leave the city for New York. That is where opportunities could be found in the eighties. In the 1850s, Cincinnati drew aspiring talent from the East, but by the eighties the direction had been reversed. In the fifties, many bright young men could still believe that Cincinnati might become America's great metropolis, but in the eighties that was clearly unimaginable. The appellation, Queen City, now had something quaint and nostalgic about it. It had once suggested the joining of culture, refinement, and power. But by the eighties, New York City held much more promise of just such a coupling.[88]

Part III

The Reestablishment of the Professions in a New Social Order, 1880–1900

Overview
of Part III

"If I knew that the world was coming to an end tomorrow, I'd immediately go to Cincinnati," Mark Twain is reported to have said, slyly adding, "it's always twenty years behind the times." That joke cut many ways. When in March 1880 the Cincinnati Southern Railway finally opened for through traffic, it reached out for a South and its markets, so inviting just twenty years earlier, but now no longer there. Twain himself, however, as that railroad was being built, was also reaching out for a region no longer there. Both Edward Ferguson's enterprising rail line and Samuel Clemens's adventurous stories, books, and travel pieces, produced from the midseventies through the mideighties, were fraught with nostalgia. Clemens's nostalgia, however, paid off more handsomely.[1]

Written between *Tom Sawyer* and *Huckleberry Finn*, and incorporating magazine sketches he had published earlier, *Life on the Mississippi* was Twain's most wide-ranging commemoration of a world that was rapidly coming to an end. In 1882 he rushed not to Cincinnati but to St. Louis, and there, with purposeful change of pace, boarded a steamboat traveling unhurriedly downriver to New Orleans, with a number of stopovers along the way. He spent a week in New Orleans and then headed north by steamboat, again stopping at various points (including Hannibal, Missouri, to visit friends and haunts of his youth) and completing his river travel in St. Paul. There he boarded a swift train that carried him back to the East Coast. After this easygoing, five-week journey, Twain set down his observations and recollections in a long, unruly, omnium-gatherum of a book reflecting the long, unruly, omnium-gatherum river that was at the heart of his work. *Life on the Mississippi* was not only a celebration of the interior valley, it was also a eulogy for a preindustrial era whose traces were rapidly disappearing.[2]

Some of the most memorable sections of Twain's complex work are given over to a portrayal of those homespun varieties of authority and honor produced in the Mississippi Valley in the middle years of the nineteenth century. The steamboat river pilot was one of the remarkable figures of the day. Twain had been one himself and could describe this rough-and-tumble celebrity with a vibrancy and richness of understanding that make him come alive on pages of the book. The river pilot embodied those strong and conflicting impulses of the era—the resentment of formal rankings and the hankering for distinction; the insistence upon accessibility and the avidity for the setting up of restrictions, most of which turned out to be too makeshift and brittle to be long lasting.

The river pilot, much like a craftsman, picked up his skill through an apprenticeship, and that seemed broadly available when river traffic was booming. The skill itself was based upon tacit knowledge gained through experience. Only those with the right aptitudes, however—good memory, judgment, and also a dash of heroism—could acquire such skill. While Twain sometimes talked of the "science of piloting," he let it be understood that this was an unconscious science that could not be reduced to reason. The pilot would come to know it "naturally" and would never be able to explain it. Nonetheless it was an indispensable skill. The lives and property of all those who needed to use Mississippi River steamboats were entrusted to the skill of the pilot in reading the tricky currents and recognizing the concealed and treacherous sandbars of the river. The special vulnerability of those aboard ship and their dependence upon their helmsmen were parts of a traditional metaphor drawn upon by a long line of writers—that included James Wilson and reached back at least to Plato—in discussing the nature of authority. Twain and his fellow pilots lived that metaphor, plainly unaware of the ancient arguments they were reenacting.[3]

"A pilot in those days," wrote Twain with enthusiasm and exaggeration, "was the only unfettered and entirely independent human being that lived in the earth. . . . he received commands from nobody, he promptly resented even the merest suggestion. . . . By long habit, pilots came to put all their wishes in the form of commands." Twain clearly delighted in such exercise of authority. Formally, the pilot ranked below the captain, but in fact he could not interfere with the pilot's work. The pilot "was treated with marked courtesy by the captain and with marked deference by all the officers and servants; and their deferential spirit was quickly communicated to the passengers. . . . his pride in his occupation surpassed the pride of kings."[4]

Still the income that went along with such employment, and the employment itself, could be menaced by the workings of the market. When the number of apprentices and new pilots increased more rapidly than the river traffic, pilots' wages dropped. They then formed an association that restricted entry and raised wages to impressive heights. For all that, however, the expanding railway network soon lured away passenger traffic, and for freight alone "a vulgar little tug" with a tow of barges could easily underbid the grand and imposing steamboat. "In the twinkling of an eye, as it were, the association and the noble science of piloting were things of the dead and pathetic past." Unlike the craftsmen that became professionals, the pilots could not find or fashion a sheltered market. Twain was of at least two minds about all this. He welcomed progress and the civilizing powers of capitalism, but even when he stops to praise, often other voices can be heard.[5]

Twain ended his river journey in St. Paul, at the head of Mississippi navigation. By the 1880s St. Paul had become a great railway center with comparatively insignificant river traffic; unlike Hannibal it represented the future, not the past.

> St. Paul, giant young chief of the North, marching with seven-league stride in the van of progress, banner-bearer of the highest and newest civilization, carving his beneficent way with the tomahawk of commercial enterprise, sounding the warwhoop of Christian culture, tearing off the reeking scalp of sloth and superstition to plant there the steam-plow and the school house— ever in his front stretch arid lawlessness, ignorance, crime, despair; ever in his wake bloom the jail, the gallows, and the pulpit.

This paradoxical linkage of savagery and repression with progress was one of those jokes that much of Twain's audience managed to ignore, or at most, respond to with nervous laughter.[6]

For many Americans of the eighties the belief in progress lacked such ominous overtones. One of the seemingly obvious signs of such progress was the rapid advance in technology and the industrial uses to which that technology was put. The railroads were conspicuous examples and agents of such uses, indicating also the many social transformations such uses encouraged. The railroads became the prototypes of centralization, hierarchy, rapid expansion, and—oddly enough—new types of restriction. No other business enterprise governed such a large number of employees scattered over such a large area, and no other matched the railroad in the use of a hierarchical and centralized bureaucracy as an instrument of such governance. In the 1880s, railway expansion astonished even some of its most sanguine promoters, adding at least a hundred thousand miles of track, a greater amount than the total previously in use. This increase was accompanied by the growth of cartel arrangements and then nationwide railroad systems ultimately controlled by New York investment bankers. Such developments sharply restricted entry into railroading; the days of local initiative (as with the building of the Cincinnati Southern) were at an end.[7]

Although railroads spread out in all directions, the most heavily used trunk lines moved east-west, extending markets and binding the country economically along those lines. The linking of an inland city or town with a coastal metropolis transferred decisions in important economic affairs to the metropolis. While an astute observer like Alphonso Taft might forecast extraordinary economic powers for Cincinnati and the inland valley in 1850, by the end of the eighties such predictions no longer seemed plausible.

New York City became the economic capital of America. As the country had looked across the Atlantic toward Britain in the era between 1750 and 1830 and had turned much of its attention toward the West during the interregnum of 1830 to 1880, now, with the growth of national markets and the nationalizing of big business, the reflux of national economic energies poured into this great metropolis. New York bankers financed the expansion and consolidation of the railroad, telegraph, and telephone industries, and most of the diverse national corporations that grew up in this era established headquarters in the city. The gravitational pull of such developments was prodigious. William Dean Howells moved down from Boston to New York to become the Dean of American Letters, and William Randolph Hearst crossed the country from San Francisco to New York to become the Grand Sachem of the American popular press. The drive to sell culture in the smaller markets of the interregnum period had helped make that culture general, promiscuous, and in a sense democratic. The expanding markets for culture in the eighties and nineties helped make that culture more specialized, discriminating, and hierarchical. New York City increasingly became the capital of both high and popular culture.[8]

The railroads and the new communications industries contributed to such changes and also epitomized some of the broader shifts of which they themselves were part. More generally, America in the eighties continued to expand, as it had in the past, but now in more structured ways—a growth usually accompanied by consolidations and constrictions. New, more overriding hierarchies appeared more generally, as did a more general acceptance of them. Behind rising tariff walls, a diverse assortment of large corporations appeared, whose size allowed for efficiencies of scale. These corporations also required such substantial capital outlays as to sharply limit entry into the new booming industries in which those large firms were dominant. The size of the industrial labor force also grew rapidly and the workers were more frequently led by men who accepted the circumstance of being workers as a permanent condition, trying to use the advantages of that position to improve their economic well-being. The American social order, so it seemed, was becoming increasingly polarized and segmented. This was evident in the growing and tumultuous cities, segregated by ethnic group and income level, but in which squalid tenements occasionally stood within spitting distance of exquisite mansions. The most influential utopian novel of the era, Bellamy's *Looking Backward,* invented a unified and harmonious society, but bound it together with a disciplined, hierarchical industrial army, compulsively projecting into the glorious future much of the most inglorious present.[9]

Political democracy, evangelical Protestantism, and market capitalism all reflected these developments. They all expanded but also became more restricted and rigid. The number of voters casting ballots grew; however, a greater proportion of Blacks and aliens were deprived of the vote in each succeeding election. In addition, the two great national representative assemblies, the Senate and the House, grew in size, becoming more elaborately and tightly structured, with power concentrated in a small inner circle. Similar developments appeared on a state and local level, provoking an eruption of talk about political "rings," "machines," and "lobbies." As for the churches that considered themselves evangelical, their membership grew substantially in the last decades of the nineteenth century, though revivalists of the era brought few new effective techniques. Revivals increasingly became religious exercises for members of rural and socially less prominent churches. Market competition between firms with high overhead costs, a situation typical of large-scale manufacturing, often gave rise to a kind of destructive rivalry that sent the most ardent competitors in search of "pools," "trusts," and various styles of combination. While in the mid-nineteenth century political democracy, evangelical Protestantism, and market capitalism seemed to work together, in this era they often diverged and clashed. Furthermore, each was assailed from several and different quarters as ineffective and even immoral. Whatever leveling force they had mustered in the earlier era was now largely dissipated.[10]

Open and self-confident attacks on "the dogma of equality" became more acceptable, and those who defended equality in the middle-class journals justified it in its more unsubstantial and unintelligible forms—as the equality in moral freedom or the equality in good manners. "Inequality appears to be the divine order," wrote one prominent journalist, and he was joined by the leading Darwinians, who unhesitatingly found it to be the natural order. Social exclusiveness no longer seemed as un-American as it once had; in fact the "epidemic of Sons, Daughters [of the American Revolution], and [Colonial] Dames" which broke out in the 1890s combined a devotion to social exclusiveness, "genealogical superiority," and ardent patriotism. The drive for immigration restriction often drew upon similar sentiments. When Henry George, a principled egalitarian, argued for the Chinese Exclusion Act, however, he implicated the unrestrained market economy. It was the new, technologically advanced, low-priced transportation that brought the "non-assimilable" Chinese to this country as cheap labor. These Chinese could easily undersell the American laborer and inevitably supplant the White race. A free market economy meant the "Mongolization" of America. George asked for restraints on that market economy in the name of patriotism and morality.[11]

The mingling and confounding of the moral and the prudential critique of competition gave such judgments much power. The liberating notion that the unhampered pursuit of self-interest would bring social beneficence, so important to the earlier era, now seemed increasingly suspect. An up-and-coming, young, conservative college professor, Woodrow Wilson, raised his voice against "the competition that kills" and called attention to the "antagonisms between self-development and social development" where competition reigns freely. Perhaps the clearest and most influential criticism of unrestrained competition came from the various books, pamphlets, and speeches of the political economist and educator, Arthur Twining Hadley. Hadley never confused the moral and prudential criticism of unrestrained competition but advanced both with great vigor. He argued that combination was inevitable for a large part of modern industry and that trade unions were necessary as well. He urged a "true collectivism of spirit" that would supersede both socialism and individualism, and he accepted a limited role for government regulation of the economy. Hadley was not an obscure commentator. Rather, he was the president of Yale and had served as professor of political economy alongside William Graham Sumner. Hadley's preachments were not as mordant and startling as Sumner's, and for that reason, in part, Hadley was probably more influential. Diverse arguments for some regulation, restriction, and the acceptance of hierarchies were frequently proposed in this era, with claims that each of these provided important social benefits. Such arguments gave reasonability and encouragement to those who wished to move in those directions.[12]

In the setting of the social and intellectual shifts of the eighties and nineties, the invigoration of the professions is not surprising. Now they more readily found endorsement for their claims to authority and honor and to that comfortable income that would go hand in hand with the satisfaction of those claims. Even the policy of restriction of entry into their ranks appeared less sinister. In the eighties, the American Medical Association, which had earlier lapsed into an asthenic condition, now found new vitality. The American Bar Association, which had recently been formed, quickly gained strength and extended its influence. With the cooling of revivalist ardor and the narrowing of its range, churches with liturgical and sacramental emphasis gained new recognition and force, and as a consequence their clergy, upholding more priestly and gentlemanly notions of the ministry, also took on greater importance. Along with these traditional callings, the newer professions were also quickened and strengthened. Three recently formed national engineering societies, each devoted to a newly established speciality, allied themselves with the American Society of Civil Engineers to confirm what had previously been uncertain—their status as a recognized profession. The national organizations of dentists and pharmacists, heretofore somewhat erratic and unsettled, stabilized and grew. Even college professors now appeared as a separate occupational interest and increasingly were seen and saw themselves as a distinct profession.[13]

These were the most conspicuous of the professions in the late nineteenth century, either because of sheer numbers or because of traditional prominence accorded them in America. They made up that family of occupations that, when taken together, provided the principal referents that gave meaning to the idea of profession. These professions will be considered in the chapters that follow. Yet along with them were the architects and the military, professions that were less conspicuous—architects because of their comparatively small numbers and the military because of its special cultural anomalousness. Both reflected and utilized the conditions of the late nineteenth century that were favorable to all professions; however, for both, this was more an era of professional programs and principles than of substantial achievements.

The rapid growth of cities and the rise of a class of newly rich who had a zest for lavish spending created a boom market for civic, commercial, and residential building in the last decades of the nineteenth century. The leading American architects responded to these propitious circumstances by striving to remold their occupation into an esteemed and circumscribed profession. For much of the nineteenth century, most of the designing of buildings was done by carpenter-builders using various architectural handbooks, and most of the men who called themselves architects had little formal architectural education. The American Institute of Architects had been founded in 1857, and though its requirements for membership were unexacting, its membership remained small until the eighties. The most important impetus for elevating the standing of the profession came from the Society of Beaux Arts Architects, founded in 1894. This was truly the elite of the profession, made up of Americans who had studied at that famous Parisian school. Until the 1880s, England with its craft tradition in architecture was the chief influence in American practice, but in the last decades of the century, the French tradition, which held that architecture was both a fine art and a rational science, became dominant. That shift brought with it the ideal image of the French architect. He combined the temperament of the artist with the authoritativeness of the scientist. That ideal image did much for the educational reforms, the licensing laws, and the professional codes of ethics in the years that followed.[14]

A shift in European models was also important to the American military in the last decades of the nineteenth century. Prior to the Franco-Prussian War, the American army had borrowed many of the patterns and practices of the French, but by the eighties German organization was gradually replacing them as the model. The military attitudes, standards, and manners of American officers, however, went back to yet an earlier model, that of the English gentleman-officer. This was an eighteenth-century version of the ancient ideal of the gentleman-warrior, whose virtues were courage and courtesy, and whose honor was appropriate to his rank. Sequestered at West Point, this tradition withstood the powerful leveling assaults of the Jackson era. West Point itself was attacked as aristocratic and "wholly inconsistent with the spirit of our liberal institutions," but still it survived. The setting of the eighties provided conditions both adverse and hopeful. In that bustling and enterprising era, the twenty-five thousand soldiers living off the taxpayers' earnings seemed like an unproductive encumbrance. Other professional gentlemen might insist upon a commanding bearing, but at least they were usually working gentlemen. In the popular slang of the day, to "soldier" meant to avoid work. However, as if by compensation, the rising hierarchies that spread through American society of the eighties now made the military organization and authority less anomalous. The once popular accusation that the army officer was aristocratic gradually faded. In any event, in the eighties, the junior officers took on a new spirit and entered upon a wide-ranging discussion about their professional standing and how to improve it. This discussion resembled that of many of the professional associations of the day. Raising the educational standards for officers and barring entry to the incompetent were recurrent themes. In addition, the junior officers who took part in this discussion offered a broad restatement of the professional ideals of the military, which they frequently placed in contrast to the commercial character of civilian life. The officer's code rejected moneymaking, selfish gain, and luxurious living. Oddly, the gentleman-officer could easily slip into a disdainful attitude toward the society he had vowed to protect.[15]

If, for the architects and the military, the last decades of the nineteenth century were largely a period of self-definition and the setting of goals, for the more prominent professions it was a time of more substantial accomplishments. Many of the national associations set up restrictions on entry into their organizations, and some raised the qualifications for practice of their profession through state licensing laws based upon new and more stringent educational requirements. These professionals argued that the disciplines upon which their work was based were becoming increasingly scientific and that scientific understanding could be best inculcated through formal education. Academic training, it was generally believed, brought dignity and social standing. "It may be laid down as a general rule," wrote Thomas Davidson, philosopher and educator of the era, "that whatever is taught in school will soon become respectable and gentlemanly, while that which is picked up in the home or workshop will always be regarded as menial." The professionals undoubtedly looked to the increased educational requirements to enhance their honor and generally increase their income as well. Nonetheless it seemed obvious that the better educated the practitioner the more likely that he would be competent, and therefore society also benefited. This last point was requisite to the wholeheartedness with which the professionals pressed their argument.[16]

The most influential public acceptance of that argument came through the Supreme Court in the leading case of *Dent v. West*

Virginia (1888). Mr. Justice Stephen Field, long known for his championship of the inviolability of individual rights against state interference, now found, along with a unanimous court, that no one had the right to practice a profession without the necessary qualifications determined by "an authority competent to judge." That authority turned out to be the profession itself. This important decision not only upheld the professions' restriction of competition, it also set off the professions as unique occupations with distinctive and appropriate powers. Furthermore it endorsed a large body of state legislation which, employing the doctrines of police power, had already given the professions similar recognition. What is striking about this reestablishment of the professions in the eighties is how readily it was accepted by much of the public, with only a few orthodox Spencerians and some unorthodox professional practitioners and their friends protesting.[17]

Along with the reestablishment of the professions in the 1880s, medicine became the preeminent profession. In part, this can be ascribed to the fact that medicine most fully embodied the justifications of that reestablishment and could lead in the reassertion of professional claims to authority and honor on a new basis and with the new social supports that American society of that era provided. Law was still much esteemed, but medicine clearly overshadowed it and became the model for other would-be professions to emulate. The advance of the medical profession was most directly impelled by the remarkable accomplishments of medical science in the late nineteenth century. The cumulative progress of physiology, the spread of anesthesiology, and the sudden revolutionary burst of success sparked by germ theory provided new supports for the doctors' aggressive therapies. The additional self-confidence of the doctors was matched by an increased confidence that patients placed in them.[18]

Moreover, the intellectual basis for the doctors' ascent to preeminence among the professions was new and unique. When the lawyer spoke of his legal science, as he frequently did, he meant an orderly and coherent body of knowledge such as Blackstone had outlined, which, once mastered, conferred the power to move with ease in the field and pronounce lucid and authoritative judgments. When the physician of the late nineteenth century spoke of medical science, as he frequently did, he meant a body of knowledge based upon experimental investigation and the methodical acquisition of new knowledge through research. This science was not simply knowledge but rather seemed to be the most rigorous form of truth. The national professional societies reflected this. The central event in the history of the American Medical Association in this era was the displacement from its leadership of those who derived their science form the bedside, as most doctors did at midcentury, by those who derived their science from the laboratory, as did the most advanced doctors at the end of the century. The American Bar Association, by contrast, remained a gentleman's club throughout the period. Its leading figures were courtroom lawyers, skilled in the adversary system, as had been the main body of the most eminent lawyers at midcentury. By the end of the century, however, sharp-witted and prosperous corporation lawyers of great influence, whose work was much like legal engineering and who rarely appeared in court, practiced in all the major American cities. Yet these corporation lawyers stood at the periphery of the American Bar Association.[19]

The new preeminence of medicine was also part of a broader intellectual shift, a new understanding of human nature and the requisites of human happiness. As I have suggested earlier, over the broad span of years encompassed by this study there was a conspicuous shift in attention and understanding on the part of some of the makers and movers of American cultural life. This was a shift from an anxious concern with sin to an eager reward for rights, and then to a sharpened awareness of the constraints of human needs. Of course this schematic outline may be helpful only in suggesting the direction of a gradual change. In 1900 Calvin was alive in Princeton Seminary at least, and Locke impended in many important Supreme Court decisions. Surely the sense of sin and the demand for rights were powerful moving forces in the late nineteenth century; yet now they were mitigated by the insistence of the rapidly advancing biological sciences that man must also be seen as a complex organism and that much of his conduct could best be understood in those terms. While some doctors and physiological psychologists in the late nineteenth century worked to formulate a perspective for human understanding based on needs, what is even more impressive is the way such notions filtered intermittently into the popular journals of the day.[20]

When the poet laureate of Topeka, Kansas rhymed, "Human hopes and human creeds/Have their root in human needs," his verse evoked a remarkably cordial response. About the same time, to a more select audience, William James audaciously recommended, "Believe what is in line with your needs." Of course, James placed restrictions on such belief and he also tried to specify the meaning of needs. There was a "front door" and a "back door" of human experience. The front door was consciousness and constructed habit; the back door was the mental and bodily inheritance of evolution that arose out of the struggle for survival. James was anxious to assert the value of the front door but he recognized the importance of the back. Needs were also often linked to instincts, an equally ambiguous notion but one with even more primordial and incursive connotations. "The law," remarked Justice Holmes, relying upon this perspective for caustic purposes "can have no better justification than the deepest instincts of men." The doctors themselves were less intentionally provocative. Instincts usually "express the needs of the system" explained Dr. Austin Flint, and he was referring to the concept of physiological equilibrium that was becoming more influential in medical thought. But this medical notion of need, more restricted though it was, helped bring doctors' concerns to a central place in American thought of the era.[21]

The preeminence of medicine among the professions gave doctors a predominant role in defining the meaning of profession in this era, not only by their affirmations but also by their example. Characteristically, most doctors declared that a profession was the calling of a gentleman, by which they meant an occupation endowed with rightful powers and esteem. Some looked back to the "golden age" of the late eighteenth century and called for a return to the "ancient standard" of classical education as prerequisite for entry into the profession. Yet the leading physicians brushed this appeal aside. While they would carry forward many of the attachments and prepossessions of the bygone gentlemanly class into the modern era, the supports of such a bearing would be largely new ones. The doctor's authority and honor now rested upon his recent and more rigorous science, the esprit de corps that it fostered, the licensing laws that it justified, and even to some extent the comfortable incomes those licensing laws made possible.[22]

Moreover, gentlemanly honor and authority took on new definition from the polarized social setting in which the doctor found himself. Confronting such a world, this professional asserted that he was neither a capitalist nor a worker, rather that he stood in some third position with an outlook arising from that standing. He was not a capitalist because his authority and honor were not derived from wealth and the dollar was not the best indication of his achievement. He was not a worker, though he was employed, because he worked from a position of command, guided in part by his science, and was therefore never wholly at the bidding of those who employed him. Furthermore, in that his work seemed to be largely intellectual, it brought with it a proper respect and afforded special gratifications. Worker and capitalist were guided by self-interest and expected the resultant to be social benefit; interest and obligation for them were almost the same. The professional by contrast maintained precapitalist presumptions. He was not self-denying, but his self-interest was directed and constrained by the requirements of his vocation. For him, duty guided self-interest; and duty arose out of an abiding relationship between persons and entailed action that one's position or station required. The authority and honor of the professional was an elaborate social construct, and from his third position the professional usually supported neither economic laissez faire nor collectivism.[23]

More broadly, the very terms honor, duty, and gentleman often took on not only anticommercial but antipolitical connotations as well. The workings of the political parties and their patronage system had pushed "the class of educated men" to the sidelines. The traditional link between public office and honor seemed to have been broken. Many of the advocates of the "merit system" in civil service were intent upon reestablishing that link. Dorman B. Eaton who led the campaign for the merit system also led in the effort to set up the Bar Association of the City of New York. He would reestablish honor and duty within American politics and in the profession. Some lawyers despaired of such a dual campaign. "It is a sad and ominous thing for a country" wrote Edward Deering Mansfield, a prominent Cincinnati lawyer and publicist, "when it can be truly said: 'the post of honor is a private station.'" For those like Mansfield, the honor and authority of the class of educated men lay within the professions alone.[24]

6

The Lawyers: A Stratified Profession

Much of the honor and authority of American lawyers in the nineteenth century rested upon the link between law and justice. Americans usually looked to the courts to resolve conflicts in a controlled and orderly way, and they expected that the decisions of those tribunals would give each party its due. In the courthouse itself, there was a moral division of labor. The judge, his powers often shared in different ways with juries in various courts, determined what the rules were, decided whether they had been broken, and fixed a punishment or compensation to be paid. The court was responsible for law and justice and most Americans assumed that these were the same. The lawyer was an officer of the court, but his primary responsibility was to see that his client received the full benefits of the law. He was neither judge nor jury, nor was he accountable for the ultimate outcomes. This permitted a one-sided and combative acting out, for the sake of law and justice. The echoes of trial by combat, not formally abolished in Great Britain until 1818, still resounded in American courtrooms throughout the nineteenth century.[1]

James Bradley Thayer, himself "not enough of a partisan ever to take the highest rank as a lawyer," gave mixed praise to the advocacy of his former partner, George Shattuck:

> Never did client have more devoted counsel. His associates wondered to see him so warm in the cause, disturbed so much at the capacity of the adversary to hold out against the truth, and settling into such dark suspicions against the opposite client. But this warmth of feeling and deep interest in the cause which he had espoused was a great source of power.

Yet there must be limits to such partisanship and its power. Could the lawyer destroy evidence, suborn juries or witnesses, knowingly resort to bribed judges? After all, the latitude and license given to his aggressiveness was in the interest of seeing justice done.[2]

Yet as the restrictions upon the entrepreneur's self-interested activity in the American marketplace diminished, so the limits on lawyers' audacious efforts in nineteenth-century courtrooms became blurred. Behind the increased freedom in both realms was a broadly optimistic sense that things would somehow work out for the best and therefore the weight of personal social responsibility might be lightened. Writers discussing the duties of lawyers often quoted, with fascination and cautious mitigation, Lord Henry Brougham's speech before the House of Lords in defense of Queen Caroline. It was a page out of Walter Scott. Brougham, a daring champion, impetuously defending a queen's reputation against the obloquy of scheming politicians!

> An advocate, by the sacred duty which he owes his client, knows, in discharge of that office, but one person in the world, that client and none other. To save that client by all expedient means—to protect that client at all hazards and costs to all others, and among others to himself—is the highest and most unquestioned of his duties; and he must not regard the alarm, the suffering, the torment, the destruction, which he may bring on any other. Nay, he must be reckless even if it should unhappily involve his country in confusion for his client's protection.

Most commentators softened the extravagance of this declaration, but few rejected it outright.[3]

The other troublesome pronouncement, often quoted in discussing the lawyer's responsibility, was barrister Charles Phillips's justification of his conduct in the defense of Courvoisier. In the course of the trial Courvoisier had confessed to Phillips that he had killed Lord William Russell. Yet Phillips, to shield his client, cast suspicion upon others whom he knew to be blameless and made a solemn appeal to God before the jury of Courvoisier's innocence, the barrister's critics claimed. Phillips, denying particular allegations, nevertheless asserted that "the counsel for a prisoner has no option. The moment he accepts his brief, every faculty he possesses becomes his client's property. It is an implied contract between him and the man who trusts him." In the English setting, despite the overcharged eloquence of Brougham and Phillips, it was understood that an advocate was exalted in a vehement defense of a wronged queen, and that when a polished and imposing barrister said that his faculties were the property of a foreign servant, an ax-murderer, it was a gesture of noble condescension. In the American setting these pronouncements were much more ambiguous, inviting, and dangerous. Judge Thomas M. Cooley, one of the most respected jurists of the era, granted some weight to Brougham's and Phillips's assertions and yet cautioned that the lawyer must not pervert law or facts, nor abuse an opponent for his client. Despite the lawyer's necessary partisanship, he remained an officer of the court and must somehow assist in seeing justice done.[4]

Legal writers placed their chief reliance on the impartial judge and jury in the courtroom, much like the beneficial "hidden hand" in the marketplace, to transform the lawyers' ardent partiality into an instrument for achieving justice. In addition, the informal restraints of courtroom camaraderie contributed to that result. Ties to clients were usually short-lived, while the recurrent encounters of lawyers in the courts often created rough but durable bonds of fellowship. Regard for the acceptance and approval of colleagues set limits to the unconscienced devices to which these friendly rivals would usually resort.[5]

The moral division of labor, however, was not always self-regulating. If judges or juries were corrupted, or if lawyers used their skills to thwart the regular legal processes, then the outcome would be iniquity and possibly even disorder. It was amidst such disorder that the beginnings of the bar association movement of the last decades of the nineteenth century took shape. In the Erie Wars between Vanderbilt and Drew, Gould, and Fisk, both sides enlisted the foremost lawyers of New York, as might have been expected. Less expected, however, was that Gould and Fisk, with the help of their friend Boss Tweed, would enlist some judges to their side. As a result, the New York judiciary was caught in the crossfire of a legal barrage ostensibly of its own making, issuing injunctions and receiverships enjoining and commanding diverse and opposite actions. The upshot was a private war between armed gangs that was stopped only by calling in the state militia. In response to this alarming spectacle and the opprobrium it cast upon the New York bench and bar, some of the most prominent members of that bar gathered in January 1870 to form a new professional organization, the Bar Association of the City of New York, to "maintain the honor and dignity of the profession of law," and "to increase its usefulness in promoting the due administration of justice."[6]

The new organization turned its energies against the Tweed judges (and later the Tweed machine itself), against one of the lawyers who had used these judges to get favorable rulings for his clients, and more broadly against the Jacksonian egalitarian outlook that many of the founders of the association saw as the source of the scandal and corruption. Ultimately two Tweed judges were impeached and a third resigned. Yet the corruption of judges was not only the fault of particular men, argued Dorman B. Eaton, a leader of the association; it was more the fated outcome of the elective judiciary that had been set up by New York's reform constitution of 1846. An elective judiciary was the institutional expression of a ruinous confusion of justice and politics. Justice rested upon moral and legal principles that could be discerned only by a striving after impartiality, Eaton explained, while politics was based upon interests and power in which success demanded the most ardent partisanship. The association took a strong stand against the elective judiciary and campaigned to remove it from the constitution.[7]

The lawyer who bore the brunt of the association's reformatory zeal was David Dudley Field. It was not so much his defense of Fisk and Tweed in the courts that angered association members, but rather their belief that he had knowingly made use of corrupt judges to get advantageous rulings. William M. Evarts, first president of the association, alluding to Field in the organization meeting, declared:

> Why, Mr. Chairman, you and I can remember well (and we are not very old men), when for a lawyer to come out of the chambers of a judge with an *ex parte* writ that he could not defend before the public, before the profession and before the Court, would have occasioned the same sentiment toward him as if he came out with a stolen pocketbook.[8]

Field denied that he had done anything unprofessional, maintained that his accusers had done much the same, and endorsed Brougham's dicta as to the proper attitude of counsel to client. Some of the animosity toward Field undoubtedly stemmed from the fact that he was an able and contentious defender of some of the ideals of Jacksonian democracy in an era when they had come to seem almost pernicious. Field had taken up the cause of codification in the 1830s and had never relinquished it. He also persisted in urging upon all who would listen that peculiar mix of Jacksonian ideas—equality, brotherhood, individualism, and laissez faire—underpinned, for him, by a cosmic optimism which he said he imbibed from the texts of William Paley and Joseph Butler. Even his link with Tweed is not completely surprising, for many looked somewhat favorably upon that genial plunderer as a Robin Hood who readjusted the distribution of property, with some benefits for the poor. Admittedly, in the setting of the late nineteenth century, Field put some of his Jacksonian notions to surprising uses. When he denounced Benjamin Harrison it was for his "paternalism"; and he joined the conservative Earl of Wemyss in his Liberty and Property Defence League to protest the encroachments of meddling governments and to argue that the state should best "leave each to the pursuit of happiness as most desired."[9]

Yet it was as a champion of the New York state constitution, a landmark of Jacksonian democracy, that Field seemed particularly obnoxious to many lawyers in the association. Field esteemed that constitution especially because it had given him the go-ahead in his grand reform project of codification. It also had set up an elected judiciary, abolished ranks in the legal profession, and made entry into it much easier. Even Boss Tweed and his cronies, with little or no legal training, became lawyers (so that the charges of $100,000 that they placed against the Erie they labeled "legal fees"). All the spokesmen for the new association agreed that such openness was disastrous. The bar had become so large that the informal regulating power of courtroom camaraderie no longer worked. The only way to protect the sound body of the Bar was to sever the "plague spot" of corruption. Shutting out unworthy men would create once more a spirit of professional brotherhood. This was brotherhood through exclusion. At this point, these eminent New York lawyers did not expect to sway the entire Bar of the city; rather they wished to establish well-recognized distinctions within it. "Outside of political rights and relations," explained one of the founders, "distinctions must exist everywhere—they are necessary for the very welfare of society." This declaration and the confidence with which it was expressed represented a clear reversal of some of the characteristic proclivities of Jacksonian culture. Its echo would be heard again at the founding of the various bar associations that followed close upon the New York meetings and at the meetings of the numerous and diverse professional associations established in the eighties.[10]

The association's "first business is to control itself," advised a speaker at the organization meeting. One of the most important elements in this control would be restriction of membership. The high initial fee of $50 and the annual dues of $40 immediately limited membership to the more successful lawyers, and the admissions committee would select from among them only the "gentlemen." That designation seems to have excluded the growing ethnic bar. (A horrendous mistake had been made, protested one lawyer who had been rejected—he was not Jewish but German! But to no avail.) The association set up a grievance committee to investigate misconduct of members, and in 1884 extended its jurisdiction to nonmembers. The work of this committee underscored the moral harmony that these lawyers believed to be inherent in a professional calling: duty and interest might be made the same. Dorman B. Eaton said: "We will contribute to our personal consideration and to our usefulness in the administration of justice in our capacities as officers of the Court. It is one of the felicities on which we may congratulate each other, that by a duty to ourselves will be in great measure the discharge of our duty to judicial tribunals, to the state, and to our clients." It was the association's duty to protect the public from negligent and dishonest lawyers and in doing so it upheld the honor and authority of the profession, and more particularly of its leading members. In controlling itself in this way, the profession both maintained "distinction" and precluded control by others.[11]

Yet the association and its activities betokened the fact that the moral division of labor of the courts was not self-sustaining. In the courtroom, with its enlarged and diverse Bar, the partisanship of the advocate on behalf of his client seems to have overshadowed his position as an officer of the court. Within the association, the lawyer's duty to promote the administration of justice was given an important place. The work of the lawyer in the association gave support to his work in the courts and served to ensure that the link between law and justice was not broken.[12]

Following the lead of the New York City lawyers, attorneys in eight cities and states set up bar associations resembling the New York organization in structure and purpose. These were capped by the American Bar Association, organized in August 1878 at Saratoga Springs, New York. Simeon Eben Baldwin, a Yankee born and bred, who could trace his descent from Edwardsian ministers, a signer of the Declaration of Independence, and an active antislavery family, was the prime mover and guide in the founding of the American Bar Association. Baldwin later went on to become an ardent mugwump and to busy himself throughout his long life with a remarkable variety of reforms whose unvaried element was reliance upon well-educated gentlemen for leadership. A number of leading members of the Association of the Bar of the City of New York joined Baldwin in his early efforts on behalf of his national organization. William M. Evarts, a founder and president of the New York association, signed the call to form the new national organization, and three of its presidents in the late nineteenth century were also presidents of the New York City society. Other prominent members of the New York organization took positions on key committees of the American Bar Association.[13]

The choice of Saratoga Springs for the first meeting and for the yearly meetings during the next decade was significant. Saratoga was a nationally known watering place for the well-bred and well-to-do. It was the place where Judge George G. Bernard, the most notorious of Tweed's judicial sidekicks, was impeached. It was also the place where, just a year before, the very proper Jewish financier Joseph Seligman was turned away from the Grand Union Hotel as socially undesirable. Saratoga exemplified some of the diverse and growing exclusions and distinctions of the era. Of course wealthy Southern lawyers were usually welcome, and they came in large numbers to escape their sweltering summers. Just when the yellow fever epidemic in Memphis reached its most dismal and murderous days, two of the city's eminent lawyers were in Saratoga to attend the first meeting of the American Bar Association and to loll about in the cool summer air.[14]

The seventy-five men who gathered to form the American Bar Association could not consider themselves representative of the profession. They were more prosperous than most lawyers. The cost of travel to Saratoga and the expense of its posh hotels made participation in the conventions a luxury beyond the reach of the majority of the profession. The association was also inaccessible to particular minorities. Jews did not appear at the meetings until the executive committee decided to move the sessions out of Saratoga, eleven years later. Women were not admitted until the First World War, and Blacks not until after the Second. Also significant was the fact that the lawyers of the new large "factory firms," still few but growing in number more rapidly than the profession as a whole, and the "corporation lawyers," serving the largest industrial firms, did not usually appear in the leadership of the American Bar Association. Such "factory firm" lawyers who did (Rufus King, George Hoadley, Joseph Choate) were primarily courtroom advocates whose professional outlook was much like that of the lawyers of small firms. The most renowned corporation lawyers of the day, who worked with the largest industrial firms, such as James B. Dill and Francis Lynde Stetson, never entered into the leadership of the association.[15]

This is significant because the American Bar Association stood at the head of the profession in the important work of creating the lawyers' professional self-understanding. The experience articulated by the association helped fix the meaning of what it was to be a lawyer. Less well-articulated experience, either of ethnic minority and female lawyers or of the factory firm lawyer, was more shadowy by comparison and not as easily owned and responded to. While some scholars have suggested that the counselor replaced the advocate in the leadership of the profession in this era, the evidence for such a shift is quite weak. American lawyers, unlike their British counterparts, always handled both legal advising and advocacy. This legal ambidextrousness reflected the eighteenth-century experience of the American profession, when many of it practitioners rose from the position of attorney to the rank of counselor without abandoning the work to which they had previously become accustomed. In the early decades of the nineteenth century, legal advising had already taken on great importance in the marine insurance practice of New York and Philadelphia. By the late nineteenth century the lawyer's work as business advisor increased greatly with the growth of large corporations, themselves largely a legal invention. Nevertheless, the advocate was still the focal point of attention and admiration within the profession and beyond it. This was both the cause and the effect of the fact that courtroom lawyers held positions of leadership in the rapidly forming bar associations of the last decades of the nineteenth century.[16]

We must begin, at least, with the lawyers in the leadership of those associations, examining their intentions and the assumptions that underlay them. There were four principal aims that the founders of the American Bar Association proposed in forming their organization. These were pompously stated in article 1 of the ABA constitution:

> Its object shall be to advance the science of jurisprudence, promote the administration of justice and the uniformity of legislation throughout the Union, uphold the honor of the profession of Law, and encourage cordial intercourse among the members of the American Bar.

These aims can serve as an entry device with which to discover what these renowned lawyers were about. Clearly they aimed both to improve and to preserve—to advance, promote, encourage, and also uphold. They would meet new opportunities and challenges, but also sustain traditions that were still alive or that could be revived.[17]

The science of jurisprudence that the association would advance was ambiguous enough to reach backward to Blackstone's "absolute rights and duties" and forward to point toward Holmes's contingent "prophecies of what the courts will do." In its traditional sense, science was simply a body of systematized knowledge organized through general principles. However, as the natural and experimental sciences of the nineteenth century grew more productive and impressive, the requirements of the term became more rigorous for those who would own it. Blackstone thought that one of the great advantages of law's being a science was that it became "proper for a gentleman to learn." This advantage was never completely absent in the nineteenth century. It was the science of law, for Blackstone, "which employs in its theory the noblest faculties of the soul, and exerts in its practice the cardinal virtues of the heart." Blackstone was continually and respectfully cited throughout the nineteenth century, and new and extensive editions of his *Commentaries* continued to appear at least until 1915. As late as 1900, entering students at Harvard were expected to have read and absorbed it.[18]

Yet while the *Commentaries* might serve as a useful student handbook as late as the end of the century, Blackstone's notion of the science of law had been modified in important ways even by those who relied upon it. The most significant change was the new importance given to change itself. What had been fixed and immutable principles were now usually seen as principles arising out of flux and describing its path. One of the foremost exponents of an evolutionary science of law among the American lawyers of the era was James C. Carter, president of the ABA and first-term president of the Bar Association of the City of New York. "There is no part of the universe which is not forever under the dominion of change," he explained; fixedness or even social equilibrium was a vain illusion. Legal science was not like Newtonian physics but rather like the discipline of the naturalist or the evolutionary biologist. "Law reveals itself as an Inductive Science engaged in the observation and classification of facts." Judge and jurist "observe the transactions of men and arrange them in orders, families, genera and species according to proper description from the jural point of view." The chief propelling force of legal change was evolving custom. Society in its progress and development outgrows its old usages, and forms new ones. Yet custom is also an "imperishable record of the wisdom of the illimitable past reaching back to the infancy of the race, revised, corrected, enlarged." Most of that change arose in response to particular issues, and the general direction it took was not consciously determined, yet it was somehow beneficial.[19]

This view of law and legal science meant turning away from Blackstone's notion of a fixed, universal, natural law, which stood behind positive law and provided standards with which to measure particular laws or from which to construct rules of decision not covered by positive law. That kind of natural law, serving as a source of legitimacy for the legal structure, gradually disappeared. Changing custom opened the way for an exciting and dangerous breath of relativism. "Polygamy may be wrong in New York," wrote Carter, "but it is right among the Turks." This view also gave recognition and importance to the unintentional, unpurposed, habitual, and instinctive in human affairs. Blackstone's definition of law as a rule prescribed by the supreme power in a state commanding what is right and prohibiting what is wrong, and Austin's more restricted definition, asserting that law was a command proceeding from a superior to an inferior and enforced by a sanction, were both inadequate. How could they account for the fact that the sovereign is subject to law? It was not the law of nature that made the sovereign a subject, Carter explained, rather it was the law that evolved from custom.[20]

Carter's legal science resembled the science of laissez-faire economics in that unwitting general benefits arose from the decisions of those preoccupied chiefly with the particular results. Alongside the hints of relativism was the strong belief that immanent within the judicial process was the growth of justice, whose principles are "wrapped up with the transactions they regulate, and are discovered by subjecting those transactions to examination." Yet justice, a "subtle essence," was written into the workings of the universe. It "animated a multitude of formulas, but was grasped and held by none." We approach "by slow and almost imperceptible stages, toward that knowledge of abstract and absolute justice which human reason will never reach, but after which it forever aspires."[21]

The courts, like markets, were instruments of human progress; however, the courts, unlike markets, had indispensable positions of authority within them. One of the important tasks of Carter's science was the justification of the authority of judges and lawyers within the courts. In this American democracy where law purported to be the expression of the people's will, the most powerful judges of its courts of law, who seemed to decide what the law was, were not elected nor were those subordinate but influential officers of the courts, the lawyers. Carter's science explained away such difficulties by arguing that though the judges declared the law, they did not make it. Rather they found the law in "the rules springing from the social standard of justice, or from the habits and custom from which that standard has itself been derived." The judge was an expert in the vast system of rules. The function of applying the social standard of justice was delegated to the courts. They were not masters, but only agents of society. Not only must the judges be learned, in order to do the work entrusted to them, so must the lawyers, in order to do their part. "There is no short road to the science which we profess; but a real knowledge of the law—that alone which makes a lawyer—is knowledge of its purpose, its reasons, its philosophy, its methods, its limitations, its spirit." The members of the legal profession alone were able to apply the methods by which the administration of justice could best be secured. "Sciences can be advanced only by the labor of experts, and we are the experts in the science of law. The work must be done by us or not done at all." This was "the part which the legal profession ought to fill in a democratic state . . . [for] in the realm of law the people at large are wholly incompetent to the task."[22]

Carter brought his science to bear, and also worked out its implications, in the turbulent controversy that erupted in the eighties over David Dudley Field's renewed campaign for codification. During the hopeful reform campaigns of the Jackson era, Field, with the backing of the Van Buren machine, had pushed his code of civil procedure through the New York State Legislature in 1848. It was but the first step in his grand campaign to disencumber the law of what he considered its unnecessary and iniquitous intricacy, and reduce it all to statute form. This complex endeavor to simplify and codify the law drew from many sources, the most obvious of which was the basic democratic principle that law should be the expression of the people's will. Lawmaking was the work of legislatures, closely tied to popular sentiment, rather than the judicial chambers, secluded from and aloof to the concerns of the common people. Moreover, the law should be simplified and codified, Field argued, so that the man in the street might readily understand his rights and duties, the arbitrary discretion of judges might be restrained, and the number of lawyers might be reduced. In his first campaign, Field had greater success in winning the adoption of his various codes beyond New York State than within it. Ever energetic and determined, however, he returned to the battle in the 1880s and succeeded in steering most of his codes through the New York Legislature. With his final and culminating code, most ambitious and controversial of them all, Field failed ignominiously. No man was more responsible for that outcome than James C. Carter.[23]

Carter was easily a match for Field in vigor and resoluteness but, more important, Carter found support in the shift in America's prevailing sentiments and conditions. By the eighties, the egalitarian zeal of the antebellum reform movement was, for most Americans, but a sour memory. In addition, the ascendant evolutionary theories of the day seemed to lend support to Carter's

interest in Germanic historical jurisprudence and its conservative implications—pointing out the limits of reason and endors-
ing tradition. Carter based his opposition to Field's Civil Code on
the venerable distinction between written and unwritten law. He
linked that distinction to the equally venerable demarcation between public law and private law, which in turn went back at
least as far as Ulpian's *Digest* 1.1.4. Although never satisfactory
from a strictly logical point of view, this latter distinction had
served to guarantee a legal order that kept the private relations
of the citizens themselves free from the interference of state
power. These types of law, Carter maintained, had their own appropriate province. Public matters, "the performance of corporate
acts," might expediently be put into statutory form and codified,
while "the private transactions of men with each other," the substance of the Field Civil code, were best left free to develop
through judicial decisions, which Carter termed "unwritten jurisprudence." The "inherent flexibility and capacity for gradual
change and growth" of such unwritten jurisprudence "naturally
accommodates itself, by insensible gradations to the correspond-
ing insensible gradations in the progress and changes in human
affairs." Codification was too rigid for private law, and once "codified it would quickly diverge from the developing moral quality
of justice" and would be unable to "meet new problems unceas-
ingly raised by the activity and progress of the race."[24]

Confidently armed with such arguments, shaky though some
of them may appear to us today, Carter entered into the controversy, turning back the advocates of Field's Civil Code in New
York, then in Virginia, and, finally, at the meetings of the American Bar Association. The notion that the law, even in its fundamentals, was progressively evolving was shared by many in the
late nineteenth century who wished to emphasize its scientific
foundation. C. C. Langdell, dean of the burgeoning Harvard Law
School, was one of those who took such a point of view very seriously. His own arguments and aspirations did not have an immediate effect upon the ABA comparable to Carter's, yet ultimately Langdell's was a broader and deeper influence. Like
Carter, Langdell argued that legal doctrines could best be understood when their growth by slow changes over the centuries was
studied.[25]

Langdell's science, like Carter's, resembled that of the evolutionary biologist, with legal categories as species and genera, and
cases as specimens. Like evolutionary science, Langdell's jurisprudence also seemed to dispense with the *a priori*. There were
no didactic lectures or tight definitions; investigation began with

cases. His classes were laboratories, and the materials studied were an assemblage of such cases. From a study of the long historical development of legal decisions, Langdell and his followers derived principles and rules upon which to build a conceptual structure that eventually replaced Blackstone's compendium of law.[26]

Yet the differences between the two men and their outlooks were also significant. Carter had sharpened his wits in the give and take of courtroom disputation, and he had even known the usages of legislative lobbies; both of these Langdell studiously shunned. Langdell's realm was the law school. For him, law must be a science, for only then would it merit being taught at a university and only then could it be taught there advantageously. This science would provide standards of competence independent of success in the popularly esteemed skill of swaying juries and judges. For Langdell, the experts were the academic jurists (along with the elite of scholarly judges and lawyers) rather than the great mass of the profession. The materials from which Langdell's experts derived their science were more narrow and more precise than those included under Carter's notion of custom. Abstractly Langdell's formal structure rested upon considerations of justice, but these were rarely made explicit; rather they were thought to inhere in the fundamental principles that arose out of decided cases.[27]

Standing aside from the explicit moralism of some of the pre–Civil War legal writers and the many post–Civil War practitioners who held fast to such views, as well as from the implicit moralisms of the late nineteenth-century jurists and their followers, Oliver Wendell Holmes, Jr., bluntly propounded a law without justice. This was such a radical departure that its meaning did not register upon even some of his most fervent admirers. The *ultima ratio regnum* was force, Holmes observed, and a sound body of law should correspond with the demands of the community "whether right or wrong." A legal right was the same whether "founded in righteousness or iniquity." Of course "working beliefs," some of them moral, were forces that helped to determine the demands of the community. Yet Holmes maintained that man's moral life was ultimately based upon his instincts, the foremost of which was self-preference. (Here was a whiff of Thrasymacus's argument that the only sensible use of the term justice was that which connected it to the advantage of the strong).

Holmes was also skeptical about Langdell's attempt to educe logical sequence from temporal sequence. Legal history might disclose broad trends in legal development, but these did not follow an intrinsically rational path. The most inviting uses of legal history were therapeutic. Legal history could highlight the speciousness of the reasoning employed to explain and justify the many primitive survivals in the legal system. It could bring into awareness what had previously been largely unrecognized—the legislative function of the courts—so that judges might appreciate the part that social policy plays in their decisions.[28]

Holmes's audacious, provocative, and forthright views were anomalous. Many lawyers respected him as a learned judge, but those in this era who came to understand his legal philosophy usually rejected it. Depicting courts as legislative agents upset traditional notions of separation of powers and invited political interference in the legal order. Most lawyers argued that the rules the judges applied were ultimately based upon principles of justice subsisting in the nature of things and not in majority votes that arose out of popularly elected legislatures. Some of the leading members of the American Bar Association even found Carter's emphasis on flux disturbing. Though natural law doctrines disintegrated slowly throughout the nineteenth century, many of the foremost lawyers at the end of the century still spoke of fixed canons of justice accessible through reason and conscience by which the rules of law were themselves assessed. "Certain fundamental points are clear and unchangeable," maintained Edward J. Phelps. "We are not indebted to custom or any period for our conception of justice, or of any rule of law that stands upon or declares a natural right." He proposed a distinction between "the principles that underlie law, and the rules that result from it; between that which is law because it is right, and that which is right because it is law." The rules were subject to the changes and chances of this mortal life but the principles were enduring. "Those who are groping in history for the origin of justice, or for the source of our law that is irrespective of justice," therefore were clearly mistaken. Yet whichever theory of jurisprudence they found most persuasive, the spokesmen for the American Bar Association usually concluded that legal science and justice were intertwined; both helped the Bar to keep its place and power in society.[29]

It was not enough, however, for justice, legal science, and law to be blended in theory; it was necessary that they be given effect in the courts. This, in part, was what the second aim of the American Bar Association alluded to in the phrase "promote the administration of justice and the uniformity of legislation throughout the Union." In the midst of litigation, the client's interest loomed large, but at Bar Association meetings, lawyers might look to the general interest of court justice and its machinery. At such deliberative occasions, prominent lawyers bemoaned the law's delay and the barriers it placed before access to the courts. When the backlog of litigation before the Supreme Court grew beyond its ability to cope with the accumulation of cases, the American Bar Association discussed the crisis and examined various proposals for alleviating the problem. After much controversy, the association supported the scheme that Congress eventually adopted.[30]

Some of the most spirited discussions that enlivened the meetings of the association during the last decades of the nineteenth century were those that debated the value of the jury system. The broad direction in court procedure after the Civil War shifted toward the restriction of juries. During the first half of the nineteenth century, juries at criminal trials were judges of law as well as of fact in most American states. By the end of the century, juries were usually limited to questions of fact and increasingly controlled by directions from the judges. Nevertheless, many lawyers favored imposing further restrictions upon juries or even getting rid of them completely. This "relic of barbarism," the jury, increased the delay and cost of trials and helped lower the level of forensic advocacy. For those concerned with the law as a coherent scientific system, the jury trial was an inconvenience. Its vagaries were to be controlled by restricting it to fact finding under the supervision of a judge. In 1891, the association came out in support of a proposal to change the requirements for a verdict in civil cases to three-fourths of the jury. Some speakers hopefully predicted that the jury system was on its way out. Yet leading conservative lawyers, like John F. Dillon and Joseph H. Choate—who had been so remarkably successful with juries— could not believe that they were all bad. Such men defended trial by jury in the name of hallowed tradition. "On such a question better fifty years of experience than a whole cycle of theories. The jury was a means of admitting the people to a share in maintaining their wholesome interest in the administration of justice." It had proved itself "an indispensable factor in educating them in their personal and civil rights." In fact, the ancient rule of unanimity permitting the cooler sense and judgment of a minority to prevail, was invaluable in an era when the rights of property had come up against direct challenge. Trial by jury was, therefore, for Americans, "the best safeguard of their lives, their liberties and their property," an ancient landmark that should not be removed.[31]

In its constitution, the association had not only pledged itself to further the administration of justice but it had agreed to promote "uniformity of legislation throughout the Union." This aim reflected the association's interest in fostering national bonds, first among its members but also in the nation at large. The Civil War had been over but a little more than a decade when Simeon Baldwin sent out his call for the forming of the national lawyers' association. Among the signers of his call was Edward J. Phelps, who became the third president and took an active interest in promoting uniformity of legislation. "A system of law that obtains mastery over an enlightened people, and commands that reverence and support without which it would speedily fall to the ground, must reflect the national spirit," he asserted before a South Carolina audience. Moreover, members of the association were just those lawyers whose practice might take them across state boundaries, and uniform commercial laws in particular would readily increase these attorneys' proficiency. The association set up a national conference on uniform state legislation that met each year just before the entire association convened and proposed uniform state laws for its endorsement. After association approval these various uniform laws went out to the state legislatures where they met with varying degrees of success. The association's achievement in helping shape the National Bankruptcy Act was quite impressive, but it was much less effective in its attempt to bring uniform procedures to the federal courts. The future Senator Thomas J. Walsh, vigorous and politically ambitious, championed the interests of local lawyers at ABA meetings and helped block the way. Yet those technical reforms in the interest of legal uniformity which the association managed to push through attested to professional highmindedness, members believed, and provided a source of considerable pride and self-respect.[32]

Almost all the work of the organization was construed at various times as serving to "uphold the honor of the profession of Law," which was the third aim of the association. Surely advancing the science of jurisprudence and promoting the administration of justice and uniformity of legislation throughout the Union redounded to the honor of the profession. Yet it was the efforts to raise the level of education of practitioners that association spokesmen frequently pointed to when they laid claim to upholding the honor of the profession. Law should be truly a learned profession, for with that learning came competence and character, and honor would surely follow. Actually, the foremost members of the association themselves had little law school training. They had usually graduated college but had acquired their legal skills through an apprenticeship in a law office. But the growth of the bar association had paralleled a shift in legal training from apprenticeship to law schools, and the association generally supported that change. Some of the most influential members of the association were teachers in those law schools. Few at association meetings dissented from the usual argument that a thorough knowledge of legal principles was essential to both higher professional worthiness and success, and that systematic instruction at law schools was the best way to acquire such thorough knowledge. While Langdell's case method received a respectful hearing, it did not get the association's endorsement. Many of the law teachers in the association were strongly attached to pre-Langdellian techniques and philosophy. There was more agreement on the need for a wide-ranging preliminary education to provide the breadth of vision necessary for professional standing. But here again there were some differences as to exactly what kind of preliminary education could accomplish that. Some insisted upon classical learning, the traditional education of a gentleman, while others were willing to settle for whatever edification the new and growing American high schools afforded.[33]

As early as 1881 the association clearly indicated a preference for law school training over apprenticeship and requested that state and local bar associations support lengthening the period of study so that legal science might be properly inculcated. The association set up a section on legal education in 1893, and two years later it proposed extending the period of legal study to three years, a recommendation the association accepted. This section also organized the Association of American Law Schools, limiting membership to the "reputable schools" that complied with rising standards on student admission and length of study. In addition, the section called a conference of state bar examiners in 1898, which met every year thereafter in conjunction with the ABA convention, and took up the task of fostering more demanding examinations.[34]

The proponents of such measures, which they clearly saw would limit entry into the profession, often argued that such restrictions would meet the vexing problems of "overcrowding." For the prosperous lawyers of the association, this overcrowding did not hold much of an economic threat. Rather for them it seemed to bring the wrong kind of people into law and led to the sort of scoundrelism at the lower ranks of the profession that they believed brought disgrace to the entire fraternity. The rising standards of education at the reputable schools, however, never cut the growing number of students entering the law schools. In part, the appearance and flourishing of part-time and nighttime law schools accounts for this. Moreover, while more stringent examinations that some state boards were beginning to introduce in the late nineteenth century may have contributed to the slower growth in the number of practicing lawyers in the early years of the twentieth century, yet by the twenties those numbers were steeply rising once more despite the increased rigor of the tests. Many of these new entrants were sons of immigrants, who might have been kept out of the profession if it had still trained its new lawyers in apprenticeships. For the sons of immigrants typically lacked "connections." But the school with its impersonal standards so well adapted to systematic instruction and to the inculcation of the science of law was also just what the immigrants' sons (particularly those of Jewish origin) needed to break into the profession. Yet once these lawyers, arising out of the immigrant community, entered the profession, they usually remained in its lowest ranks and pointed up the growing stratification of the profession.[35]

While overcrowding seemed to afford a threat to professional honor, coming largely from below, the menace of "commercialism" did not emerge from any one part of the social scale. At the same time that the contingent fee, the bread and butter of the upstart lawyer without connections, loomed as a danger to professional bearing in the late nineteenth century, so did the astonishing earnings of the elite lawyers who acted as counsel to the great corporations. The dangers that such commercialism seemed to hold were to both the motives and the position of the lawyer.[36]

The contingent fee, critics argued, turned the lawyer into a hustler, an "ambulance chaser," who drummed up business with an eye to "mere pelf." Moreover, there was also a disposition of those lawyers serving the biggest firms, a prominent member of the ABA thought, "to seek after a large income rather than to pursue law as a science." Though pursuing law "as a science" was a somewhat vague activity, it clearly suggested elevated motives. "Our whole moral atmosphere is corrupted by a passion for sudden wealth," wrote an eminent attorney. "Can the lawyer escape the moral influence which has proved so fatal to tradesmen, to bankers, to all indeed in whom this passion is roused? His occupation brings him into daily contact with them. . . . how few are superior to the passion for mere wealth without the terrible sacrifice its gain may demand." Had the legal profession become simply a business? Such worries were part of an outpouring of anxiety that broke into the legal periodicals and popular journals of the day.[37]

Concern with the motives of lawyers, salient though they were, actually was subsidiary to uneasiness about the lawyers' honor and authority. The rise of the illustrious "kings of fortune" in late nineteenth-century America seemed to cast the acclaimed democratic aristocracy of the Bar into the shadow. In the past, one observer remarked, the "law was called a learned profession. Its members enjoyed a prestige in the community by reason of their general culture. The uneducated man [was] accustomed to give weight to learning." But now the "possession of money is sufficient proof to the popular mind" that its possessor "is the oracle they seek." Yet more disheartening than the presumed loss of preeminence was the prospective loss of authority—and even independence. The image of the "lawyer as a hired man" obeying "the command of his employer, without regard to the demands of justice," was a loathsome one. It was not surprising that leading lawyers grew indignant at the indecorous remark attributed to Jay Gould that "brains were the cheapest meat in the market." Moreover the expectation that the growth of "law factories" employing attorneys as subordinates, "mere pieces of machinery," was in the offing, dismayed many. The contingent fee lawyers, so it seemed, faced some similar fate. As far back as 1854, George Sharswood in his *Essay on Professional Ethics* claimed that the contingent fee deposed the lawyer from his position as an officer of the court and reduced him to a litigant, a partner, thereby losing any right to control his client.[38]

Defenders of the contingent fee answered that such practice demonstrated professional responsibility toward the indigent and ignorant who otherwise might not find access to courts of justice. Moreover, these clients came from a disadvantaged segment of the community who in fact inevitably looked to the lawyer for guidance, therefore fee arrangement did not in any way threaten the attorney's authority with regard to his client. Similarly, some corporation lawyers argued for the social usefulness of their work—it helped promote America's wondrous and beneficial economic advance. Nor would such work and such clients necessarily impinge upon the lawyer's authority. When Judge Edward Patterson, prominent member of the ABA, read the handwriting on the wall at a lavish Belshazzar's feast of gladsome lawyers to the effect that the legal profession was degenerating sadly, that it was no longer a profession but a mere trade, he was simply echoing what had by then become a familiar plaint. Nonetheless, he was quickly answered by Elihu Root, also a member and soon to be a prominent leader in the ABA, who claimed that the handwriting on the wall was but the graffiti of scaremongers. Young

Daniels, he thought, could beard the Wall Street lions in their dens and come out unscathed. Had not Root done just that himself? He enjoyed a reputation for technical proficiency and ingenuity in corporate law, he had won financial success through that practice, and yet he was sure that he maintained his professional independence. He did not see himself as a corporation lawyer, but rather as a lawyer who had corporations as clients. The rise of those large corporations, he believed, brought both great benefits and dangers to the country, yet in the complex and equivocal world that they had engendered, Root was confident that the lawyer could maintain his professional bearing. "About half the practice of a decent lawyer," he explained, "consists in telling would-be clients that they are damned fools and should stop."[39]

Doubtlessly, many lawyers could not maintain their difficult traditional position of both authority and advocacy with regard to their clients when such clients were rich and powerful businessmen or corporations. Clearly the range of the lawyer's authority was often constrained. Vanderbilt did not want to be told what not to do, but rather how he could do what he wanted. Yet most lawyers, even under such pressures, insisted that law was not a business—that one did not just give the customer what he wanted, but what was needed.[40]

In addition to advancing the science of jurisprudence, promoting the administration of justice, and upholding the honor of the profession, the Association wished to "encourage cordial intercourse among the members of the American Bar." Cordiality among lawyers was one of the time-honored features of the profession. Perhaps to compensate for the often scathing clashes within the courtroom, lawyers went out of their way to foster a free and easy camaraderie among themselves as soon as litigation was put aside. During trials, occasional sarcasm and raillery were good form; after trials, the wit was more lighthearted, though it sometimes retained its sharp edge. Ministers, by contrast, were rarely thought to be blessed with jocularity, and any sense of humor among doctors seemed to be readily benumbed by the grave and foreboding tasks that were their lot. For the lawyer, along with his lawbooks, briefs, and oratory, his banter was one of the important tools of the trade. The volumes that poured from the presses in the 1880s commemorating the bench and bar of ever so many counties and states are replete with such humor, and clearly it was something of a binding force for the motley group of practitioners down at the Old Courthouse. By the eighties that group had become much larger and much more diverse; the Old Courthouse typically was gone, and the local bar was more scattered, pleading before a number of more specialized tribunals. The informal sociability of the earlier era could not survive such a change in conditions, yet it was an affecting memory.[41]

The attempt to recreate the conviviality of the earlier, smaller, and more homogeneous groups of lawyers that had gathered around the Old Courthouses was one of the impulses that led to the formation of various kinds of lawyers' organizations in the late nineteenth century. However, in order to achieve this in the setting of a rapidly growing and diversifying bar, these associations often were more restrictive and deliberately even more homogeneous in membership than the earlier informal assemblages of lawyers had been. This was more conspicuous in the early years of the ABA than in many other lawyers' organizations, although the ABA had few ostensible restrictions. For those who came to the meetings it was clearly an occasion for good fellowship and amusement. The social highlight was the gala banquet, closed to the public and press, with its staggering number of courses, a long series of toasts, and an inspirational or humorous postprandial address, all set amidst the splendors of the Grand Union Hotel. Here some of the most eminent men of the state and local legal societies, by their very eminence in increasingly stratified local bars, could carouse and take their pleasure with their counterparts from all over the country. This was "cordial intercourse among the members of the American Bar," but a very small part of it. Less than ten percent of American lawyers were affiliated, even as late as 1920. Nevertheless this "gentleman's club," by its cohesiveness, its self-assurance, and its preeminence as a center of attention and awareness, exerted a remarkable influence upon the very definition of what it was to be a lawyer. "The standards of conduct in all occupations," wrote a distinguished lawyer, "are necessarily conserved by a limited number of able and high-minded men. . . . Their influence is based upon the recognition of their contemporaries . . . [and the] esteem by which they are held in the public redounds to the whole profession."[42]

While the notables of the ABA, who usually held prominent positions in state and local associations, commanded the respect of a broad range of less conspicuous practitioners, it is nonetheless necessary to look beyond the national association to consider how various were these less renowned practitioners who made up the bulk of the profession. The bar as a whole was growing rapidly at opposite ends of the professional spectrum—among the bustling ethnic lawyers and the sedate corporate counsel.

The demand for both expanded rapidly along with the rise of tort law and corporation law. Both of these were juridical creations and both were linked to the enormous growth of industrial manufactures in the late nineteenth century. The increasing number of accidents, along with the gradual shift in popular sentiment away from the notion that injury was a matter of bad luck or a shortcoming of character to the view that most injured people were entitled to compensation, provided the setting for rapid enlargement of the number of tort cases and the development of tort law. The interest in mobilizing capital in ever-increasing amounts, enabling businessmen to move to large-scale production, provided an incentive for the extension and amplification of corporation law and the development of various intricate juridical devices. There was nothing inexorable, however, about the rise of the American corporate bar or the increase in the number of personal injury lawyers. On the European continent, much of the work that would have been done in the United States by corporate lawyers was accomplished by state bureaucrats, and the extensive social insurance there greatly diminished the importance and extent of personal injury law. Nevertheless, in American circumstances, the rapid expansion of the personal injury and corporate bar was not at all surprising.[43]

The personal injury case, often taken on a contingent fee basis, replaced debt collecting as the bread and butter of the unprosperous but hustling lawyer. While tort doctrine of the late nineteenth century served to restrict the compensation awards of the courts, nevertheless injury cases were so emotional and unpredictable that the sentiments of judges and juries of the lower courts often offset doctrinal constraints. In Boston at the end of the century, as many injury cases were decided in favor of the plaintiff as were decided in favor of the defendant, with a good number settled before coming to trial. In the traction industry, for example, damage payments were second only to wages as operating expenses, and many businesses turned to liability insurance as a recourse. There was a whiff of class struggle surrounding the discussion of these injury cases, and lawyers who lived off such litigation were quickly cast as disreputable fomenters, ambulance chasers, and shysters.[44]

A conspicuous part of this seemingly debased segment of the bar was the growing array of ethnic lawyers in the great metropolitan centers. The American promise of an opportunity to rise out of a humble condition to prosperity and renown whetted the ambitions of a good number of immigrants and their children; and for some, the special honor of the learned profession made such occupations particularly attractive. This was noticeably true of the Jews, and the shift from the Law to the law for them came almost as a reflex action. The market in this era was an invisible but powerful benefactor of these ethnic lawyers. Entry became easier for them to the extent to which market relations rather than traditional or bureaucratic requirements influenced access to the field. Such imponderables as respectability, moral strength, and personality were often discounted in the market. Where such imponderables were considered essential, young men of recent immigrant background often lost out. The contrast between law and academia is suggestive, for while law was becoming increasingly a profession of the children of immigrants, college teaching was becoming increasingly a profession of the children of the native-born.[45]

The competing proprietary law schools that grew and flourished at the turn of the century, and particularly those offering part-time and nighttime instruction, put legal training within the reach of almost anyone who could pay the comparatively modest fees and absorb what was taught. That included many aspiring lawyers from America's ethnic communities. These lawyers usually found the resources to set up shop in their immigrant neighborhoods, where their ancestry at last became an advantage. Little, dingy law offices abounded in the thick of the clutter of stores and pushcarts, peddlers and pilferers; there the lawyer pursued his helter-skelter law practice, along with other things.[46]

The alarm over "overcrowding" (it must have seemed like infestation to the old-fashioned lawyers) did not become truly strident until the first decade of the twentieth century, when the growth of the profession as a whole slowed, but the inrush of ethnic lawyers did not. Yet already in the late nineteenth century, a good number of well-placed spokesmen gave warning. On the whole, it seems that the market for lawyers at the end of the nineteenth century was expanding, in that their number was growing rapidly without any discernible, general impoverishment. Yet if material interests were not sharply threatened at this time, ideal interests were. The perennial complaint about overcrowding in this era was as much as response to the type of men who were becoming lawyers as to their number. "A growing multitude is crowding in who are not fit to be lawyers," complained Supreme Court Justice David Brewer in 1895, "who disgrace the profession after they are in it, who in a scramble after livelihood are debasing the noblest of professions into the meanest of avocations, who instead of being leaders and looked up to for advice and guidance, are despised hangers-on of police courts. . . ." The rapid influx of lawyers whose attachment to traditional principles and assumptions seemed uncertain and whose social position was inferior threatened the dignity and influence of the profession.[47]

Some ethnic groups were not very successful in finding their way into the legal profession. The Blacks were clearly among these. They were certainly one of the most downtrodden and abused of all American ethnic groups, and their resiliency in the face of such adversity was truly remarkable. Yet the efforts of their professionals to achieve stability and respectability, much less authority and honor, were usually thwarted. With the end of Reconstruction, the gap between law and justice for Blacks in the South widened ominously. The legal insecurity of the Blacks was such that a Black lawyer had but little chance in court to protect a fellow member of his race; a "respectable" white dignitary was a much more effective protector, and by the end of the nineteenth century, even the local patricians were losing much of that power. Over a thousand Black men were lynched in the South between 1880 and 1900.[48]

Among Black members of the three traditional professions, lawyers understandably made up the smallest group. Most of these lawyers had but the rudimentary training that a correspondence course or a desultory apprenticeship could provide. Of those who could get to law school, the greatest number attended Howard, which graduated only 328 law students between 1871 and 1900. By then there were but 728 practicing Black lawyers in the United States. Significantly, almost all of these lawyers were in the North, where most could find a bit more dignity but little more prosperity. Even in Boston, Blacks rarely used the civil courts. In the North, most Blacks were completely shut out of the economic and political opportunities that the liberal capitalist society was creating in the latter half of the nineteenth century. The result, in Philadelphia for example, was the creation of a Black urban underclass with an elaborate criminal subculture based upon petty theft, political payoffs, gambling, and prostitution. The small and vulnerable Black urban middle class was caught between the aggressions of that criminal underclass and the prejudiced white society that used Black crime to justify discrimination against all Blacks. Under these circumstances, the opportunities for Black professionals, and more particularly for Black lawyers, were not plentiful even in the North. While there were a few successful Black lawyers, the severely restricted market would not support many, and a considerable number gave up active practice for other work.[49]

Washington, D.C. was something of an exception to this dismal picture. Black federal employees, more than ten percent of the government work force there, provided a base for a more secure middle-class life and supported a bar of some twenty-five Black lawyers. Nevertheless, even here, a brilliant young lawyer, Charlotte E. Ray, could not make a go of it, and she eventually left her law practice to take up public school teaching. Of course attorney Ray had the double disadvantage of being both Black and a woman.[50]

For most women who wished to be lawyers the prospects were in some measure more favorable. Many of the "pioneer" women lawyers of this era came from privileged backgrounds. They were often daughters or wives of judges and their families were generally well to do. "She belonged to a well-known family" went one account, "and clients came at once." In addition, these first women lawyers found support in the burgeoning women's movement of the last quarter of the nineteenth century and its contention that the right freely to enter all occupations in order to develop one's "God-given talents" should be extended to women. Moreover, the women lawyers would purify the courts of "the coarse joke and cruel laugh," of invectives against opposing counsel, and a female lawyer would extend protection "to her sister in trouble."[51]

The gatekeepers, judges in the various courts, generally tried to shut out the women who wished to gain entry into the bar. However, those solemn magistrates did not reckon with the zeal and ingenuity of these bustling gate-crashers. Rejected by the courts, they turned to the legislatures and carried them by storm. Belva A. Lockwood, who had been excluded by the Supreme Court, drafted the bill to admit women attorneys to that tribunal and successfully lobbied it through Congress. By 1900 thirty-four states admitted women to practice in their various courts.[52]

Yet the results were much less impressive than had been expected. Though the judicial and statutory gates to the profession were thrown open, very few women ventured into a legal career, and many of those who did left soon after. As late as 1910, women made up only one percent of American lawyers. This disappointing outcome owed much to the informal prejudice against women lawyers that undoubtedly persisted after the formal barriers were gone and to the peculiar self-doubts that accompanied women entering the field. Most of those women lawyers did office work— probate, real estate, writing briefs, filling out forms—and were not called upon to deal directly with clients or to take up unaccustomed positions of authority with regard to men. Nevertheless there were some women lawyers, the most spectacular, who were clearly at ease in such a situation and were even drawn to the embroilments of the courtroom. These were a minority. Most women lawyers could not ignore the dissonance between the American idea of womanhood (with its gentle graces, its purity, its delicacy, its sympathetic feeling) and the expectations of a successful forensic battler.[53]

More particularly, many women lawyers worried that pursuing a career in law meant sacrificing marriage and family for vocation. For most Americans, marriage and family was itself a vocation for women, and a sacred one at that. Some women lawyers, especially those in partnership with their lawyer husbands, managed to hold on to both vocations, but others found that too difficult. These "became entrapped by domestic duties" (as one modern-day scholar sees it) and left legal practice. Moreover, among those who stayed, there was an evident uneasiness. Women lawyers were "rather individualistic, or I had almost said abnormal," wrote one of them, attesting to popular judgment and to its absorption by women lawyers themselves. The broad dissonance between the expectations of a lawyer and a woman, as indicated in popular prejudice and women lawyers' self-doubts, helps explain why so few women entered the profession and fewer still remained.[54]

If the ethnic, Black, and women lawyers stood at the bottom rungs of the profession, the new and expanding group of corporation lawyers clearly stood near the top. In actual numbers, those lawyers who devoted themselves primarily to corporation work constituted a small segment of the profession, yet they attracted an enormous interest because of the notoriety of their clients and what seemed like the egregious fees that came their way through work with those clients. Along with the increased wealth of such lawyers came repute and regard. Yet with a few exceptions (Root was one of these) the foremost corporation lawyers did not become the leaders of the profession. This is one of the central facts of the history of the legal profession in the later nineteenth century, and its effects persisted for a long while after. The contrast with doctors of the same era is striking. For among the doctors, it was those who were responding to the newest developments in medical life who took over the leadership and transformed the profession in accordance with their ideals and their new conception of the discipline. The corporation lawyers, however, never developed distinct ideals or a new conception of the discipline upon which their profession was based.[55]

The necessary conditions for the appearance of the corporation lawyer were the development of corporation law in the late nineteenth century and the growing demand for the services of those skilled in that law. Of course these conditions derived from the growth of the corporation itself. As American firms expanded to take advantage of the enlarged markets, the advantages of accumulating large sums of capital and escaping the restrictions of the legal partnership greatly favored the corporation as a device of business enterprise. But the corporation was a legal contraption of intriguing complexity, and lawyers rose to the occasion. They quickly took on the work of drafting the documents to create, consolidate, and reorganize corporations and to enable them to issue a diverse assortment of securities with their various rights and privileges. The work was an expansion of the American lawyer's traditional solicitor work in conveyancing, trusts, title search, and debt collection. Much of the lawyer's work had always been done in his offices rather than in the courts. But now with the growth of corporation law, that office work became so consequential and rewarding as to almost overshadow the traditionally esteemed work of advocacy. Almost, but not quite. In the late nineteenth century the most honored lawyers were still the leading advocates, and even much later, after the growth of large legal firms dealing with corporation work, the member of the firm who took the case to court always retained a particular preeminence, because the decisions of the courts controlled the work of the corporation lawyers, and their most ingenious devices could not dispense with the required validation there.[56]

The apparition of the "law factory" already appeared ominously in the legal periodicals at the turn of the century, particularly in the writings of those given to Spencerian "inexorable laws of social compact." Much of this discussion amounted to a tendentious transfer of the most obvious characteristics of the factory to the law office: enormous size, rigid specialization, harsh discipline, and intricate subordination. (Such depictions were often laced with the mixed emotions of the tellers and hearers of horror tales, a peculiar distress and excitement. The large number of subordinate lawyers "become mere pieces of machinery," perhaps; nevertheless they "must go forward with the tireless march of progress.") The factory, however, was a loose metaphor. In order to come up with such factories for the turn of the century, a modern scholar defined them as firms of seven partners or a combination of ten partners and associates. Even today when many law firms have become much larger, they remain oddly unlike factories in the relations of the lawyers within them. A sociologist describes them as "underbureaucratized," with loose supervision and few written rules and procedures.[57]

Nevertheless such "larger" firms as did appear at the turn of the century often did corporation work, and a large number of these gathered in New York City. It was there in such a firm that Paul D. Cravath developed the plan, now adopted by most of the large firms, of hiring the top students from the best law schools and advancing to partnerships a select group who proved themselves capable. This created a regularized connection and conduit between the leading law schools and the ascendant law firms, and fostered a greater uniformity among the most eminent corporate lawyers of the Northeast. However, in the late nineteenth century many large firms were engaged in general practice, and much of the most important corporation work still went to small partnerships. Significantly, for both large and small firms, personal connections gave rise to some of the most important accounts.[58]

The corporation lawyers never developed a coherent, self-conscious point of view from which to review and revise the traditional standards and aims of the profession. That was one of the decisive facts in the history of the legal profession in the late nineteenth century. These corporation lawyers were among the most prosperous members of the bar, and in America's commercial setting, that brought with it a prestige of its own. Their work experience, a sort of legal engineering—the design and construction of efficient and economical corporate structures—was worlds apart from the adversarial courtroom litigation that had shaped the heroes and heroics of the established profession. Yet the corporation lawyers did not distill from their own work experience any new principles or ideals. Perhaps that was too much to expect from practitioners.

Langdell's Harvard Law School was the Johns Hopkins of the legal profession. Its methods did not win out in legal education until after 1910; however, the leading schools from which the most important corporation law firms recruited had already accepted Langdell's ideas by the turn of the century. The irrelevance of Langdell's teachings to the later corporate practices of its most successful pupils has not escaped notice. Responding to this anomaly, one scholar has brushed aside the actual content of Langdell's curriculum and emphasized the importance of the work discipline and the semantic code imbibed at the Harvard Law School. This bold and subtle argument, however, ignores the possible influence of what was actually taught, irrelevant and untoward as it might have been. Langdell's curriculum emphasized private-law and common-law subjects, endeavoring to extract from a historical examination of select cases some general principles to guide lawyers and even judges. The trajectory of these principles often took direction from early English cases and prepared the law student for an appellate advocacy much like the work of English barristers before the courts at Westminster. This training reinforced "the brotherhood that subsists, and we trust ever shall, between all the followers of the Common Law, here and on your side of the water," Frederick Pollock wrote in 1887.[59]

Yet barristers were primarily courtroom advocates and did very little of the corporation work that became the bread and butter of the elite of the American bar. Corporation practice was closer to the work of the solicitor or attorney than to that of the barrister. It was less a Langdellian science than a craft, having few general principles and calling for close adherence to accepted forms whose rationale was not often apparent. Much of it was learned on the job. The more corporation lawyers looked to their common-law brotherhood with English barristers or to Langdell's science, the more they would be disconnected from their day-to-day work. Yet it is remarkable how much Paul D. Cravath, the principal architect of American law factories, was enamored of Old English ways in the law. He became a bencher at Grays Inn, a rare achievement for an American, and wrote lovingly about the "many fine old customs of the Tudors and Stuarts" preserved there.[60]

As striking was Francis Lynde Stetson's equivocacy when he held forth upon the profession. Stetson was one of the great corporation lawyers of the late nineteenth century, often dubbed J. P. Morgan's attorney-general. Yet he worked out of a small law office in order to avoid what he felt to be the encumbrances of a large firm. When he descanted on "the lawyer's livelihood," he took up all the traditional themes. He scorned "the mere money-seeking lawyers" and paid his respect to the science of law, which elevated the lawyer and furthered his independence from clients. He acknowledged the lawyer's role as a public officer, bound to advise as to "the clear requirements of every valid law" and to promote justice, "the protection of every right." Yet the qualifications and digressions in this address suggest an orator at odds with himself. Lawyers should not be money-seeking, yet somehow even the most magnanimous and disinterested lawyers sometimes accumulated great fortunes. Protection of every right also meant those of the client, even when the client was a powerful corporation, though that entailed some danger. Stetson was of two minds, and in this oration he spoke both of them.[61]

James B. Dill, by contrast, gave up most of the traditional aspirations of the profession without much equivocation. For him, the corporation lawyer was "a businessman, specializing along the lines of legal principles." Neither a polished scientist nor a littérateur was required by the business of the day; "not more polish on the blade, but more temper in the steel." However, while this straightforward lopping off of professional scruples may have allowed Dill to rise more easily in the business world, it cut him off from a good part of the legal profession. Despite his celebrity and financial success, he was never elected to a position of honor or authority in a professional association.[62]

The prosperous corporation lawyers, Black and women lawyers, and the members of the American Bar Association, together constituted a minority of the bar. The bulk of the profession was made up of lawyers of moderate means practicing alone or in small partnerships and scattered throughout the country in small towns as well as in principal cities. That was an essential factor in the dynamics of the profession at the end of the nineteenth century, and it remains so today. Though these middling lawyers did not provide the leadership of the profession in this era, they did provide an increasingly active and vocal membership; if they did not set the direction for the activities of the bar, they did place limits upon the range of those activities. One of the indications of growing professional awareness among these lawyers was the rapid increase in bar organizations. By 1900 such lawyers had formed about three hundred state, county, and city associations. New York, Illinois, Ohio, Missouri, Alabama, and Oregon had the most active and effective state societies, and these set the pace.[63]

While many of the motives and aims of these organizations resembled those of the more select associations, like the ABA and the Association of the Bar of the City of New York, that had formed earlier, these state and local societies with more miscellaneous membership added a concern for economic well-being that seemed to be absent among the well-fixed lawyers who formed the first associations of the era. When Baldwin, founder of the ABA, urged the raising of educational requirements for entry into law practice, he explained that "we want our profession to rank as high as the profession anywhere," and he clearly had England in mind. By contrast, when local association spokesmen argued for boosting educational requirements, many of them had fresh competitors in mind and wanted to keep their numbers down. This greater emphasis on education meant a turning away from the prevailing sentiment of the interregnum years that native aptitudes rather than training made the lawyer. Yet even this shift was only partial. Who would want to shut out a Lincoln from the law? The successes of the profession in the earlier era and under previous conditions worked against innovation.[64]

Nevertheless, state and local societies, even with some hesitation and wavering, did push for increased educational requirements and stiffer bar examinations. The usual tactic with regard to bar examinations was to get them out of the hands of the local courts and under the control of appellate tribunals, which set up statewide committees to supervise the examinations and, of course, to make them more exacting. Yet the numbers were not kept down, and the legion of lawyers kept growing.[65]

It is very difficult to determine just what the economic condition of the bulk of American lawyers was. The ratio of lawyers to population does not tell enough about the demand for legal services. There is much to suggest that that demand was growing steadily throughout the nineteenth century—as standards of living rose, allowing an increased proportion of the population to resort to the courts to settle disputes, and as the courts themselves widened the market for their services by making a broader spectrum of actions litigable. Trust work, real estate, and debt collection were passing out of the lawyers' hands into those of specialized agencies, but the vast field of torts from personal injury was just opening up and coming within their grasp.[66]

It is equally difficult to determine what the bulk of American lawyers thought their economic situation was. By 1888, eleven of sixty-eight responding bar associations had established fee bills, a device particularly appealing to small-town professionals. Yet reports of "ratting" were common, and the widespread use of contingent fees left such fee bills precarious and usually ineffectual. The perennial cry of overcrowding, familiar in all the professions, was heard from time to time in the last decades of the nineteenth century, and there were occasional articles saying that the lawyers' standard of living had dropped; but there were as many reporting sunny opportunities ahead. Certainly lawyers did not set about in a concerted effort to proclaim economic grievances in a way comparable to what farmers of the day were attempting. The most widespread and recurrent declaration of dismay among lawyers of the day was the lament that law was falling from its honored position in society as a profession and had become an ordinary trade.[67]

The various bar associations responded to this particular plaint with some fervor. Many adopted codes of ethics to persuade themselves and others that law was more than a business.

They announced that the relation between colleagues was not primarily that of competition, and the relation between lawyers and clients could not simply be subsumed under contract. This was remarkable. For the law of contract was the social bond on which the profession had risen to great influence in American society. While the contract may have been a significant relation between litigants, it was not the primary tie between lawyers, nor the idealized bond between lawyers and their clients. That was the message of the code.[68]

This, of course, was an outlook shared by the ABA as well (though it would not adopt its code of ethics until the first decade of the twentieth century). The ABA, however, was too remote and exclusive for most lawyers. In the eighties, various local bar associations banded together to form a national association of their own. The National Bar Association was formed on federal principles and proposed to give national expression to the widespread and burgeoning state and local associations. Like the Bar Association of the City of New York and the American Bar Association, it turned against the indiscriminate access to the profession that had characterized the interregnum era. The leadership of the ABA was startled out of its complacency by this new rival. In response they decided to hold association meetings on alternate years at some location other than Saratoga, New York, so as to be more accessible to worthy lawyers across the country. They also began to accept delegates from state bar associations, but on an irregular basis. Nevertheless, with this shift in policy, membership in the ABA began to climb rapidly, while that of the National Bar Association began to sink. Its leaders lacked the renown and organizational effectiveness of those of the ABA, and it never found a distinctive purpose inspiring and impelling enough to justify its efforts. When the National Bar Association fell apart in the nineties, the ABA was left unchallenged as the preeminent promulgator of the ideology of the American legal profession.[69]

One of the essential features of that ideology was the supposition that lawyers were neither capitalists nor laborers, but something between the two and independent of both. Their authority, honor, and competence derived from the unique roles and abilities. In general, the spokesmen for the bar at association meetings were not unquestioning proponents of laissez faire. They usually did believe that, in a competitive market economy, both efficiency and social justice were natural outcomes, despite the short-sighted and self-regarding motives of most of the market's participants. There was a significant parallel between the court-

room and the market: the combination of partisanship and conflict in both could yield justice. However, both could be thwarted
and disrupted, and then the results would be disastrous.
"Trusts," wrote Thomas M. Cooley, president and respected worthy of the ABA, "are things utterly to be feared." They disrupt the
economy and corrupt democratic legislatures. "We cannot help
asking ourselves whether the trust as we see it is not a public
enemy." Such antipathy to the great new business combinations,
as well as to their owners' "arrogant wealth," was characteristic
of many of the leaders of the association in the late nineteenth
century.[70]

However, this aversion toward the mammoth corporations was
not matched by any special cordiality toward organized labor.
While the organization of labor was usually seen as a defensive
measure, nevertheless labor militancy held its own dangers and
could also create a "predatory class." If organized labor behaved
"with reasonable discretion," it might even accomplish some
good. But when Debs led his railway workers in what seemed to
be an illegal boycott, the upshot of which was the widespread
violence of the Pullman strike, Cooley, with the support of most
of the association, denounced the strike and its leaders. After the
strike was successfully crushed, however, a number of prominent
members of the association stepped forward to criticize the government's unrestrained use of the injunction, and a more sympathetic approach to the working classes surfaced again. The association proposed a formal system of arbitration as a means to
bring capital and labor together peacefully within a semijudicial,
lawful setting. Actually, this was also the purported program of
the Knights of Labor.[71]

This proposal of court-supervised arbitration was a reflection
of a broader and more vague predisposition that might be called
constitutionalism—a belief that power could be dissolved into legal relationships and that the result would be increased liberty
and justice. This was the projection of the courtroom situation
upon society as a whole. The courts, most lawyers believed, were
governed by rules and roles that allowed for the dispensing of
justice in a conflict between the socially powerful and the powerless. Though this might be possible in few other places, nevertheless it was possible in the courtroom. To the extent that legal
norms permeated society, liberty and justice would be available
to most citizens.[72] This legal near-sightedness (it also had an important influence upon American diplomacy, much to George
Kennan's dismay) was identical to the legal far-sightedness that
led to the construing of the Constitution as *law*, and that allowed

for the interpretation and application of fundamental principles of American government through routine judicial processes.

Another manifestation of this outlook, of course, was the association's exaltation of the Supreme Court and its prophet John Marshall. Both had done much to bring this constitutionalism into American society. On 4 February 1890, at the centennial anniversary of the organization of the Supreme Court, before a distinguished audience gathered at the New York Metropolitan Opera House, and before all the justices of the court, four presidents of the ABA led an elaborate and reverential commemoration of the court and its accomplishments. Of course in elevating the court and constitutionalism, the bar also honored itself, the agents of constitutional justice.[73]

7

The Clergy:
A Profession
in Adversity

The ministry in this era tenaciously maintained its standing as an honored profession. As earlier, it drew authority from the promises and claims of a world of spirit lying beyond and within the material world; but in these years the ministry also derived support from more modern auspices that were linked to the new social conditions of the material world itself. Despite its eminence, the ministry was the most widely dispersed and disunited of all professions. To its divisions by denomination were added the disparities that arose from living and working in the diverse settings of the nation's cities, villages, and hinterlands. Those disparities widened ominously in the last decades of the century. The increasing class, ethnic, and occupational differences that accompanied the rapid growth of industry, immigration, and cities left their mark upon American religion and the ministry that served it. Of course, ministers were not only objects but also agents of these developments. They provided divine unction for the wheels of progress, essential moral steadiness in the face of dizzying changes, and also a basis for reproof of the corrosive inequities of the newly evolving social order. Remarkably, amidst this welter of diversity, within and without, the ministry preserved its coherence and affirmed its identity as a leading profession.

The increasing social stratification of this era went hand in hand with the fractional distillation of Protestant denominations. By the end of the century, well-to-do Americans congregated disproportionately in the Episcopal and Unitarian churches; the middle classes in the Congregationalist, Presbyterian, and Northern Methodist churches; and the lower classes in the churches of the Baptists, Disciples, Lutherans, Southern Methodists, and Holiness and Pentecostal groups. This distillation, aided by the voluntary form of Protestant church membership, however, remained very imperfect. For while some families rising in social position left the denominations into which they had been born, others tried to make their old-time religion more respectable. John D. Rockefeller remained a Baptist; his son founded a splendorous nondenominational church, and his nephew became an Episcopalian. Stratification, therefore, appeared both within and among the denominations.[1]

Such disparities were a matter not only of membership but also of manner. Though the various American Protestant denominations shared a common body of doctrine, the characteristic stress they placed upon particular teachings and the distinctive way in which each held its system of belief were linked to their social composition. Among upper-class Protestant churches, inherited doctrine was mitigated by reason or ritual; among middle-class churches, doctrine was blurred for the purposes of cheerfulness and comfort; among the lower-class churches, doctrine was simplified, rigidified, and pointed toward various kinds of deliverance. As some churches became more genteel, those members wanting a more drastic and passionate worship split off to form their own religious groups. The break of the Holiness and Pentecostal sects from the Methodists in the eighties and the bitter dissensions within the Disciples in the nineties registered such shifts. By the end of the century, a rough indication of the social level of a Protestant congregation was its noise level.[2]

Ethnic divisions, arising from large-scale immigration and the hardening of racial prejudice, also gave increased diversity to American religious life. Owing largely to this immigration, Lutherans supplanted Presbyterians as America's third largest Protestant denomination, and the Catholics became the largest church in America. Neither Lutherans nor Catholics, however, exerted the influence upon American Christianity that might have been expected from their growing numbers. Most American Protestants found both these churches alien, unaccommodating, and therefore extraneous. Moreover, the Lutherans subdivided ethnically and clashed among themselves, while the Catholics were singled out as the carriers of a radically defective form of Christianity. One of the odd effects of the upsurge of the Catholic Church was the growth of Protestant interdenominational amity fostered to offset the growing "encroachments of Popery." The most rapidly growing religious groups of this era, however, were the Black denominations. The energetic evangelization among the freedmen and the gradual exclusion of Black members from White churches gave impetus to this growth. Yet the members of these Black denominations were among the most depressed,

powerless, and unrepresented part of the nation. The rapidly expanding Black and immigrant churches, therefore, while they
added a new complexity to religious life, did not set the direction
that American Christianity took in this era.[3]

To discover what that direction was we must not only look to
American religion but also consider its changing place within the
nation. "The great modern law of subdivision of labor," the Rt.
Rev. A. N. Littlejohn, Episcopal Bishop of Long Island, observed,
had narrowed the work of the Christian church. Earlier, the
church had provided for many of society's needs, but now "the
versatile genius of modern civilization" had allowed the church
to revert more nearly to "its original Apostolic simplicity" and become more "definite and concentrated in its aims." In the less
differentiated society of the early nineteenth century, the church,
in addition to its spiritual benefits, had furnished education,
charity, sociability, and even entertainment. But by the end of
the nineteenth century, those social services were more effectively
supplied by specialized agencies and industries. Some, like
Bishop Littlejohn, appeared to welcome this shift—"The religious
impulse of the race was never so deep and strong as now," he
assured his listeners—but even he seemed to have misgivings.
For prior to this "subdivision of labor," the church had been the
focal point for much of the layman's life, and its present curtail-
ment and displacement could easily be seen as a lessening.[4]

In order to recapture their central position in community life,
some Protestant congregations set up "institutional churches" to
reabsorb various social services back into the work of the church.
These endeavors were largely futile. Their arduous efforts to com-
pete with urban institutions and gratifications often diverted
these institutional churches from their particular religious aims.
The more rural Protestant congregations responded to their
sense of displacement by striking out against distracting and
subversive amusements. These churches not only declared that
the theater, the ballroom and the saloon were sinful but legislated
against them in church councils and state governments. The
outpouring of Sunday blue laws in the last decades of the nineteenth century derived from similar impulses.[5]

This constriction of church life was sometimes called secularization or secularism. Occasionally it was linked to the growth of
skepticism and unbelief. But this secularization was more clearly
tied to Protestantism itself. The Protestant redefinition of religion
gave extraordinary emphasis to man's spiritual inwardness and
God's ultimate providence, thereby often blurring sharp distinctions between sacred and profane. Some acts and objects, though

greatly reduced in number and significance, were still imbued with sanctity or sinfulness; yet the overwhelming importance of intent, both God's and man's—inaccessible as this quality often was—placed a great strain on the relationship between spirituality and manifestation. "Our nation is Christian," announced one writer somewhat mysteriously, "not so much in external form, as in its inner meaning and purpose or tendency." Precisely what religious and secular meant often remained uncertain, and that helped to stimulate and direct immense human energies toward previously neglected pursuits.[6]

The interplay between Protestant inwardness and economic enterprise has often been described; the connection between that inwardness and the American separation of church and state has also been recognized; yet the complex interworking of all of these and the growth of that enormously influential cultural institution of the late nineteenth century, the secular public school, deserves attention.

In general, it is easy to see how the opportunities of an expanding economy encouraged practicalism and how the imperatives of the separation of church and state restrained sectarianism in public education. It is apparent, nevertheless, that most American educators wanted the schools somehow to be Christian. They were thwarted not by irreligion but by the fervor and diversity of the churches themselves and their common commitment to "the rights of conscience." Working at cross purposes, the denominations entered into a long series of baffling disputes over what could be taught in the public schools. The outcome of these conflicts was the gradual evaporation of the religious content of curriculum. By the end of the century, public school education meant the inculcation of skills, moralism, and patriotism, plus some brief Bible readings at appropriate occasions. Most Protestant churches, nonetheless, strongly supported such public school education, because it claimed to develop the conscience and to honor the Bible—and because Catholics opposed it. Traditionally, schooling had been closely tied to the church but, by the end of the nineteenth century, the church had largely retired from the field.[7]

If not a potent force for secularization, unbelief, nevertheless, seemed to be growing in the late nineteenth century. What is striking about the party of unbelief is that it was undoubtedly quite small in comparison to the community of believers and that it also revealed the distinctive imprint of social position. At the upper ranges of society, with Henry Adams, Oliver Wendell Holmes, Jr., and William Graham Sumner, unbelief meant astringent skepticism and "the spirit of science." Among the middle classes—here Robert G. Ingersoll was the leading preacher—rejection of Christianity was often joined to a cheerful gospel of good living, domestic tenderness, hopefulness, and effusive moralism. It was from the "ignorant fear of the cruel fires of hell" that Ingersoll wished to free mankind, while he strangely held out some hopes for another life where "we know and love again the ones who love us here." Moreover, he would burn smut as vigorously as Anthony Comstock. At the lower ranges of society, among backsliding Baptists and Methodists, there was little evidence of skepticism but rather indications of indifference. Ministers, however, often interpreted a surrender to the two-step, the music hall, and the saloon as a sure sign of infidelity and the resistance of church-going Catholic immigrants to Protestant appeals as the "irreligion of the urban masses."[8]

The most painstaking census of religious affiliation in America in this era showed that church membership rose more sharply than the increase in population. One favorite explanation of this growth was that the American separation of church and state had awakened the denominations to a self-reliance and to an inner spiritual energy that gave impulse to their impressive conquests. This separation, the nation's primal act of secularization, was interpreted as the enshrinement of the doctrine of the right of private judgment and "the nearest approach to the spirit and purpose of the ideal church ever given the world." However, the incalculable Protestant inwardness could lead to other appraisals of this growth in church membership. "The Church is conquering the world," explained a Baptist writer, "because the world is really conquering the Church; numerical, financial, intellectual, social gains [are] at the expense of spiritual vitality and regenerative power; external victory and internal defeat." Even some of those who congratulated the churches on their growth noticed that an increased "formalism" accompanied the gain in numbers. The Methodist class meetings, those intimate gatherings of saints to relate religious experiences and to confess sins, gradually fell into disuse. The Baptist and Presbyterian prayer meetings became better regulated, with the minister assuming a more authoritative role; but attendance at such sessions also began to decline. American Protestantism was changing significantly. As the churches narrowed their functions and increased in membership, lay participation in church life declined.[9]

It is not surprising, therefore, that the churches of the day gave conflicting appraisals of the condition of religious life in America. Some said that the nation was becoming more religious; others claimed that it was becoming less so. Undoubtedly part of this disagreement lay in the terms of the discussion itself. Nevertheless, granting the intrinsic ambiguity of those terms and the deficiencies of the evidence, it is still possible to say that organized Protestantism and secularization were both growing in late nineteenth-century America. This was so because the nation as a whole was growing, but also because organized Protestantism and secularization often provoked and nourished each other in this era.[10]

The response of the ministry to the increasing stratification, segmentation, and secularization of American society was as intricate and varied as that of the churches they served. With regard to stratification, the abiding ministerial propensity to view the economic world as a moral testing ground and to link economic success to virtue lent itself to the fulsome acclaim of the new men of wealth. Drawing upon this hallowed tradition, ministers like F. W. Gunsaulus, the eminent Chicago preacher, justified the "righteous accumulation of wealth in the name of civilization." Drawing upon an even more ancient tradition, other ministers like Sam Jones, the raucous traveling evangelist, found that "generally speaking, God's people are poor people." Many zig-zagged. The Reverend T. DeWitt Talmadge extolled the "great hearts throbbing under rags" in one sermon, but in another announced that "the whole tendency of sin is toward poverty, and the whole tendency of righteousness is toward wealth. Godliness is profitable for the life that now is, as well as for that which is to come." In such sermons the successful Christian businessman had the best of both worlds. A few social gospel ministers denounced the selfishness they felt was linked to the accumulation of great fortunes and drew attention to the widespread suffering that accompanied America's industrial growth. But they commonly accepted social stratification and preached a brotherly love that would bind the social classes to each other. However, the predominant ministerial response to the new social conditions of the era was to refuse to divide society horizontally at all but to insist upon dividing it vertically between the spiritually lost and saved. Piety and character rather than social institutions were to be considered the crucial issues.[11]

Despite this, ministers increasingly came to see the divisions among the denominations themselves as something more than a matter of creed. "The denominations," explained a Methodist preacher, "in their variety and their methods of work and worship meet various needs of men, reaching all classes, conditions, peculiarities. . . . Each one which is successful now is actually needed by those who heartily adhere to it." Ministers rarely recognized such divergence as a matter of class, for they insisted that the crass standard of money was the worst gauge for ranking people. When they looked beyond creed, they preferred to describe denominational divisions in terms of education, taste, and temperament. "The Episcopal Church may be said to minister to culture, the Methodist and Baptist Churches to emotion, the Presbyterian Church to conservative intellect and the Congregational Church to progressive intellect," observed Lyman Abbott. From this standpoint, even Catholicism became somewhat acceptable, for without it "there would be large masses of population where conscience and reverence would be wholly unadministered to." [12]

Stratification within the denominations was most apparent in the cities, for the movement of congregations uptown to more prosperous and socially homogeneous neighborhoods became a subject for anxious inquiry and misgivings. While some ministers protested that converting a church into a "social club" was unscriptural, most of those who bemoaned the desertion of the downtown were mollified when the moving church agreed to support a missionary tabernacle ("a great Soup-kitchen, with a chapel attached") in the old neighborhood. Ministers quickly adjusted their own expectations and ambitions to the new situation. In the Presbyterian church in the early nineteenth century, those ministers most intent on maintaining a learned pulpit had insisted upon uniform requirements for the ministry, even at the cost of schism. By the end of the nineteenth century, the leading advocates of high standards of education for the ministry assumed that there would be various levels of learning among ministers suitable to the different congregations they served. A handbook written by a Methodist preacher explained that most young ministers would start with small, poor, rural churches but, if these beginners were diligent and improved themselves, they might move up to larger, richer, urban churches. Most clergymen accepted stratification among and within the denominations as an accomplished fact; yet a few (who held to more inclusive notions of the church, particularly among the Lutherans, Episcopalians, and Catholics) would occasionally argue that denominational lines themselves were sinful, and some others (particularly among the ministers who were downgrading the importance of creed) would claim that such divisions were inefficient. [13]

Ministers also expressed a similar diversity of judgments upon ethnic and racial segregation within society and in Christianity. By the nineties, many recognized that America was becoming an increasingly polyglot country. "These fatal Poles, these deadly Hungarians, these murderous and low-lived Italians," as a Baptist minister described them, seemed to resist purer Christianity. The nationality conflicts within the Catholic church and among the Lutherans often drew unsympathetic comment, and many Protestant ministers became fervent supporters of immigration restriction. As for those nationality groups that were already here, most ministers voiced the hope that they would eventually assimilate. Although some felt easy with the prospect of a long interregnum during which ethnic divisions would persist, many less accepting of such otherness did their best to discountenance and disregard it. Such varied sentiments found oblique expression at the Chicago World's Fair of 1893. The Rev. John Henry Barrows's Parliament of Religions exhibited the variousness of the world's nationalities and races almost as much as it displayed the diversity of the world's religions. Barrows affirmed that "all religions are broken echoes of the true," but clearly assumed that American Protestantism was the most true. At the same time, Dwight L. Moody staged a soul-stirring revival in Chicago, much more parochial in intent than the Parliament, and drawing much larger crowds that were also more parochial in membership and spirit. Yet even Moody provided preachers for the Germans, Swedes, and Bohemians in order to reach "all these different nations by the preaching of the Gospel."[14]

While the ministers' recognition of the national distinctions sometimes brought with it a lifting of the newcomer's status, the profession's growing acquiescence in racial distinctions in society and in Christianity was usually accompanied by a general lowering of the Black man's standing. In the old centers of abolitionism, a few ministers denounced the advancing segregation of the races. Perhaps more unexpectedly, conservative Calvinist theologian Benjamin B. Warfield, a man of Southern origins, spoke out against it in the name of "the fundamental law as the Church of the Living God, that in Christ Jesus there cannot be Greek and Jew, circumcised and uncircumcised, barbarian, Scythian, bondman, freeman." His liberal opponent, Charles A. Briggs, however, remained silent, deferring to the new revelations of science which alleged the racial inferiority of the Blacks. Most ministers, as far as one can tell, simply shrugged their shoulders.[15]

Ministerial judgments regarding secularization were not much more uniform than their sentiments regarding social stratification and segmentation. Some objected to any narrowing of the church's concerns and worried that such concentration would encourage laymen to shift attention more fully to worldly ambitions. Worldly things in themselves need not be contaminating as long as they could be given spiritual purpose; yet such purpose was often difficult to discern. "It is the intention behind the act which determines whether an actor should have praise or blame," explained a ministerial writer in the *Methodist Review*. "Two men, for example, are making money; the one a Christian and the other a worldling. It is perfectly plain that in most of the steps they take for the enlargement of their trade and increase of their profits they must do precisely the same things." The liberal ministers who were enamored with notions of God's immanence were most confident that secular pursuits led to God and that spiritual elevation inevitably provided social benefits. "Christianity," the Rev. William Jewett Tucker discovered, "was good for all the possible needs of humanity." [16]

When the social beneficence of religion was stressed, the kinship of the ministry and the other professions became more apparent. The professions had a special affinity for each other, one minister suggested, because they were "rooted in the necessities of man," and therefore they "constituted in a special sense the organs of society." Perhaps one of the most subtle forms of secularization in this era was the ministry's increased interest in its own professional attributes, the special importance it gave to those qualities that it shared with the other professions. [17]

Few would go so far as the Unitarian minister who was willing "to put aside all cant about divine call, and obeying the Lord's voice and following the way which Providence marked out—as if God were any more with ministers than he is with lawyers and doctors, or as if they were not influenced by the same considerations as other men." Luther had tried to raise secular occupations to the level of sacred callings, but the Rev. Charles H. Brigham would reverse that procedure and place the sacred calling of his ministry on the level of secular occupations. This was clearly a relinquishment of sanctity, because the Rev. Brigham, like most of his contemporaries, thought that occupations simply served social purposes. Most ministers, however, insisted that their work was a sacred calling as well as a profession; that the ministry was God-made as well as man-made; that it directly served God's purposes as well as men's needs; and that its authority derived from the summons to be God's ambassador as well as from the ascriptions of professional standing. However, in the late nineteenth century, ministers gave fresh consideration to the professional characteristics of their work. [18]

One of the odd things about being God's ambassador in America was that the pay came from the powers that received him rather than from the Power that sent him. There were many complaints that this pay was too low, but such grumbling was often answered with the assertion that the income of ministers was comparable to that of the other professions. Those who claimed that ministers were impoverished usually found the cause, as other professions did, in the oversupply of practitioners. "The issue is primarily economic," one writer argued. "We must restore the balance of demand and supply. It has been the fatal error of the Church that it has rendered the clergymen's labor one of the cheapest of all known commodities." He recommended that the denominations raise their requirement for admission to the ministry in order to cut down the supply.[19]

This was precisely the method of upgrading that most professions of the late nineteenth century adopted, always assuming that betterment for the profession meant beneficence for society. Though observers found ministers without churches, they also reported churches without ministers. Preachers often refused to take positions in country churches where, they thought, the salaries were so low as to preclude professional standing and make it impossible for them to educate their children so that they might enter the professions. In 1900, the Presbyterians, who had some of the best paying pulpits of the evangelical churches, disclosed that twenty percent of their ministers had transferred from other denominations.[20]

Whatever the differences in opinion regarding the adequacy of ministerial salaries, most ministers agreed that the payment must not be considered a *quid pro quo*. "His salary is not intended to pay him for preaching," one writer suggested, "but to enable him to preach." This was a precapitalist notion of payment, and it was linked to the ministers' predemocratic presumptions of authority. Most ministers still believed they had a unique source of authority in their divine call. But the success of the other professions in the late nineteenth century encouraged many ministers to take on the protective coloration of their fellow professionals and ascribe some of their own authority to their expertise. It was particularly in those Protestant churches whose members came from the upper ranges of society that the correlative professional attributes of the ministry gave rise to great excitement and endeavor in the late nineteenth century. However, the renewed interest in professional standing was also evident in lower-class congregations and even in those churches that were peripheral to America's religious life. Those ministers who in some way were unacceptable to the broader society were impelled by the very uncertainty of their position to adopt over-charged representations of professional standards, though they usually fell short of achieving those standards. Consideration of Catholic, Jewish, Black, and women clergy, therefore, serves to highlight the professional ideals as well as the great variety of professionals in the ministry of this era.[21]

The "Americanizers" in the Catholic church of this country provided much of the force behind the effort to remodel priests on the patterns of the professions. At first thought that might seem uncalled for in that, historically, the medieval clergy were the source and perhaps the prototype of the professions. However, whatever their remote origins, the most conspicuous traits of the professions were imprinted in the eighteenth century when those occupations had been considered proper work for English gentle-men. Accordingly, instead of the merits of poverty, chastity, and obedience, the professions leaned more favorably toward the vir-tues of equanimity, liberality, and independence. The American-izers, who found the position and temper of the professions at-tractive, were intent upon breaking the isolation of the Catholic church in America—and therefore the isolation of its priests as well. Part of that intent was a matter of diplomacy, strategy, and tactics: the success of the church was in some measure depen-dent upon its adaptation to American conditions. The extent of that adaptation, however, became a dangerous issue for Catho-lics. While some accepted the American separation of church and state as a limiting circumstance, others found it a positive virtue, and, like Lyman Beecher half a century earlier, explained the vig-orous growth of the church partly in terms of that separation. Yet for Catholics, it involved doctrinal difficulties. For under con-ditions of American separation, religion became a matter of pri-vate judgment and individual choice, and, for Catholics, any faith not explicitly linked to tradition and authority had to be deficient and perhaps vicious.[22]

Americanizers, however, avoided discussion of doctrine and emphasized methods and style. That, perhaps, was the chief im-press of their own Americanization. Formally, the American church was a missionary church; actually it was an activist church with a host of activist priests. In America, the adminis-tration of the sacraments and the routine of parish activity were but a small part of the work to be done. The priest was a fund-raiser, accountant, administrator, and booster who established churches, schools, orphan asylums, and charities and worked to attract and absorb the congeries of immigrants who in this coun-try were free of some of the social compulsions that had brought them to the church in their homelands. The American priest needed flexibility and gumption. One leading Americanizer looked admiringly to "the average businessmen of the day, [who] have no theories, no prepossessions, no prejudices, no routine. . . . They are on the ground among the people whose trade they look for, discussing, arguing, studying; plan after plan is tried and dropped until the right one is found." Even the devices of the Protestant evangelists were not scorned. Many American Catholic churches turned to parish mission techniques using itinerant religious clergy, adopting as many revivalist measures as a sacramental church could absorb.[23]

Proud of the immense achievements of the American church, some of the Americanizing priests thought they could provide a model for the rejuvenation of the church in Europe. For the church in the United States prospered in a country that clearly reflected "the new age" and might guide the Universal Church in its adaptation to that new age. Yet there were limits to such Americanizing. Only American Protestants could unabashedly believe that this was God's country. Catholics, despite their championship of American methods and style for the world, offset such enthusiasms with a recognition that the spiritual center of that world was Rome. When Pope Leo XIII condemned the heresy of Americanism in January 1899, though his censure was directed primarily at Frenchmen who wished to develop doctrinal implications from American methods, it also dashed the hopes of the Americanizers in the United States. Moreover, in the eyes of the Protestant majority of the late nineteenth century, subservience to Rome was seen as an inveterate element in the degeneracy of the Catholic form of Christianity, an element from which it must be cleansed or, by reason of which, these Protestants believed, Catholicism would disappear in this country. Americanism of that era, therefore, had a relatively limited career.[24]

Nevertheless, during the heyday of Americanism, some clergy pushed for the upgrading of the priesthood by improving their education and securing their "rights" with regard to the bishops, and in these ways bringing the Catholic clerical order closer to generally accepted professional patterns. "The priesthood is preeminently one of the learned professions," declared Cardinal James Gibbons, one of the most influential advocates of the strengthening of priestly education. "Piety in a priest, though indispensable, can never be an adequate substitute for learning. . . . 'Knowledge is power' not only in the scientific and mechanical, but also in the social and religious world. Knowledge is a recognized Leader. Men admire it, pay homage to it, and are swayed by it." Bacon's aphorism was exceedingly popular among professionals asserting the authority of expertise in the late nineteenth century, but few supplied such a straightforward explication as this. However, the habits of intellectual life inculcated in the seminaries, one educational reformer complained, dwarfed rather than enlarged the priest. Seminary graduates were not prepared to meet the great issues of the day. The reformers urged that scientific studies be set into the seminary curriculum, strict diocesan examinations be introduced to raise intellectual standards, and a Catholic University be established as a graduate school of theology for priests.[25]

The Catholic University was soon organized in Washington, D.C., with the young and energetic Rev. Dr. Edward A. Pace as one of its moving forces. Pace had studied with Wilhelm Wundt at Leipzig and with the foremost neo-Thomist thinkers at the American College and the Propaganda University in Rome. He envisioned the new Catholic University as a research center in both science and Thomistic theology that would train "pioneer professors" for the theological seminaries and open careers of scientific investigation to the younger clergy. Pace himself headed the Psychology Department and served as the dean of the School of Philosophy. Rather than furnish a center for educational innovation, however, the new university quickly became the scene of bitter ethnic-religious struggles, from which it did not recover until well into the twentieth century. The scholarly German clergy, who might have been expected to go along with this program for upgrading education standards, instead seemed to block the way. For they often linked Catholic belief to German culture—"Language saves Faith" was one of their slogans—and they attacked the predominantly Irish-American reformers as "Americanizers," "liberals," and "minimists." The energy behind this new educational program quickly dissipated. Moreover most of the clergy remained untouched by those efforts, for the largest group of American priests in this era were still recruited from Europe.[26]

Ethnic division also appeared in the campaign for "priests' rights," but with less effect. The aim of this movement was to limit the power of the bishops over the priest and to give priests some voice in episcopal elections. The American priest had little worry about his authority with regard to his parishioners, for they often looked upon him as "their father, their magistrate, their judge, their king, their 'papa,' their idol." However, he needed protection from high-handed bishops because "too many priests," one of them complained, "are uncanonically dismissed from the dioceses and thrown helplessly on the world." It was "the priests themselves," argued the Rev. Patrick Corrigan, that "have built up the Church and made her the wonder of Christendom." They were entitled to a more protected and privileged position. Manifestly, they should be given a voice in the election of bishops, for they knew the candidates best and were close to the problems that the bishop would confront. Moreover, this reform would bring a democratic spirit into the church, even though laymen would continue to be shut out of all positions of power. "In this country," wrote the Rev. Corrigan, "where the interests of the Priests and the people have been so identical, the people are willing to leave their choice to the judgment of the Priests. In giving the Priests the power asked, you give the people all they desire in the United States."[27]

The most outspoken advocates of the priests' rights movement were Irish or of Irish descent, and their campaign was often linked to the broader program of Americanizing the church. To their dismay, the first priests' society in America was formed by German clergymen, and that organization seemed more intent upon preserving German national culture than asserting the interests of the priesthood. As might have been expected, the Rev. Corrigan, a leading champion of the prerogatives of priests and an ardent Americanist, felt called upon to attack that society. If the language of the priests' rights movement at times seemed radical, its specific proposals were ostensibly quite conservative. The spokesmen usually appealed for the establishment of full canon law in America, claiming that all their demands were already granted in that traditional ecclesiastical code. It was only the unbefitting missionary status of the American church that gave such disproportionate powers to bishops, and that situation could be easily remedied by "regularizing the position of the church in this country."[28]

Though these priests did not win full canon law status in the late nineteenth century, they made surprising headway toward attaining some of their goals. The high point of their campaign was the Third Plenary Council at Baltimore in 1884, which provided for the appointment of irremovable pastors and gave priests some influence in proposing candidates for the episcopacy. Ironically, it was Rome's support for the priests' demands, in the complicated church politics of that era, that was largely responsible for those gains. The bishops resisted as best they could, Americanizing bishops as well as their more conservative colleagues, claiming that the peculiarities of the American setting made the application of what might be considered the general rules of the church inappropriate at that time. Moreover, the bishops diminished the force of these enactments through interpretation, selective enforcement, and rustication of the leaders of the priests' rights movement. Most of the gains made by American priests in the late nineteenth century were lost early in the twentieth.[29]

With the defeat of the priests' rights movement and, more broadly, the defeat of Americanism, the anomalous aspects of the Catholic priesthood became more conspicuous. One of the chief peculiarities of the Catholic priest in the American setting was that his ministry required celibacy, and that requirement shaped much of his life. These priests, of necessity, were to be educated to their distinctive piety from their very early years, "before bad habits have gained a hold on them" and before they lost their innocence. They passed from the hands of their mothers, who had been instructed to recognize and strengthen the divine call perchance made to one of their children ("a silent attraction to the things of the altar and a reverent longing to take part in the service of the Church"), to the hands of those who guided their education in the parochial school and seminary. The relationship between a childless priest and a young novice whom he instructed was often a warm and a close one. "To educate a child to the ways of one's own profession," wrote one priest, "soon becomes the keenest of pleasures. . . . [It] makes us look with a sort of pride toward the fruits with which the young seedling will one day bear, and of which we are sure to reap our share."[30]

In addition to the distinguishing affects of this celibacy, there were other special characteristics of the Catholic priest's life that set him apart from the surrounding society: his ministry was directed to predominantly alien populations, his piety raised the altar above the pulpit, and his office in the Church hierarchy allowed him to command with confident vigor and required that he obey with categorical obedience. Isolation was painfully evident in the situation of the rural priest, for he was often lonely in his estrangement from polite Protestant society which, in accordance with its standards of culture and taste, should have welcomed him and from his parishioners, who, owing to their limited education, offered him little companionship. The priest was both conspicuous and invisible. He rarely appeared in middle-class journals of opinion or works of fiction or even the mass circulation newspapers which helped define the American sense of reality. Yet the occasional novel that proffered a priest as a major character often depicted him as cunning, or at least esoteric, in his religion. The favorable portrayals were the most telling. When a liberal Baptist minister, Melanchthon Lockwood, turned novelist, he wanted to show that his heart was in the right place by describing the warm friendship of a forward-looking young Protestant minister and a worldly-wise Catholic priest. The priest's most forceful arguments in their confidential meetings, however, were for a multilayered religious reality, whose lowest levels only could be accessible to the masses. Similarly, Father Forbes of Harold Frederick's best-selling novel, *The Damnation of Theron Ware*, was a cleric given to much talk about "The Christ-Myth," a Christianity (like the pagan cults that molded it) serving the needs of the humbler classes, and to declarations that "truth is always relative." Such sophisticated and skeptical priests most probably were more numerous in the Protestant imagination than in the actual world in the late nineteenth-century American Catholicism.[31]

A more likely place to search for religious radicalism would have been among the first generation of Reform rabbis that appeared in America in the last quarter of the nineteenth century. This rabbinate moved resolutely toward the professional forms that resembled most closely those of the liberal Protestant clergy. Reform rabbis established a theological seminary in Cincinnati, set up a national ministerial program, and adopted a progressive credal platform. This Pittsburgh Platform made much of the subjective in religion, attesting to "the God idea" and "the indwelling God in man." It downgraded all religious externals except an extroverted moralism and a bland universalism. "He [the American rabbi] must not necessarily be a scholar, but he must be a teacher of morality. He need not be a philosopher, but he should be a physician of the soul." Such a drastic shift away from the traditional attitudes and practices made the reform rabbi seem remote and repugnant to the great mass of Eastern European Jews who came to America at the turn of the century. These new immigrants brought with them an older concept of the rabbi. He was a scholar devoted to the study of classic texts, who was granted the authority to decide matters of Jewish law, to teach, and to direct the religious life of the community. Though they agreed on this notion of rabbinical office, these new Jewish immigrants disagreed among themselves on various matters of ritual importance. They had come from diverse lands, often bringing with them attachments to particular practices and spirit. In order to remedy the ensuing confusions and embroilments and to bring harmony to the traditional religious community, a group of orthodox laymen sent to Vilna, Lithuania—the great center of Talmudic Judaism—for the esteemed scholar, Rabbi Joseph Jacobs, and tried to establish him as the chief rabbi of New York. This project turned out to be a rancorous and mortifying failure. The assimilative powers of the American environment, however, soon diminished such divisions and prompted new divergences, now arising from the manner and extent to which traditional Jews would come to terms with their New World setting. "No one can be a rabbi in America," the foremost leader of Conservative Judaism remarked, perhaps in dismay, "who does not know how to play baseball as well as study Talmud."[32]

The Black preacher served an even more severely depressed and excluded people than did the newly arrived Eastern European rabbi. Yet the ministry was one of the few careers with any social respectability available to ambitious and intelligent young Blacks, and it was an occupation in which there was a measure of charitable support for his higher education. Most Black ministers had very little schooling, yet for those who had some college training, it was a great source of pride. Such education was not only the basis for their higher professional standing but also the underpinning for their sense of manliness in the most liberal sense. The racial slurs of the streetcorner Gobineaus placed the Blacks among the lower animals, and anxious, if ostentatious, demonstration of intellectual culture could somewhat mitigate such outrageous abuse. "The Preacher is the most unique personality developed by the Negro on American soil," wrote W. E. Burghardt Du Bois. "A leader, a politician, an orator, a 'boss,' an intriguer, an idealist. . . . The combination of a certain adroitness with deep-seated earnestness, of tact with consummate ability, gave him his preeminence, and helps him maintain it." The overbearing demeanor of the educated Black minister before his congregation was complained of and usually interpreted as one of the legacies of his "schooling under a slave system." However, the ideal of the clerical profession itself as an occupation vested with authority clearly had much influence. Booker T. Washington scolded this educated Black ministry for believing that manual labor was inconsistent with its professional standing and for leaving the countryside, where they were most needed, to take more comfortable positions in the cities. In this, of course, they closely resembled the White ministers of the day. And in fact the resemblance was often not as close as the Black clergy wished. The Rev. George Marston, who had been educated at Oberlin, and who ministered to the African Methodist Episcopal (AME) Church in Lincoln, Nebraska, found that he could not support his small family on the salary that his congregation provided and, despite his longing for professional dignity, was led to take work in a local barbershop to supplement his earnings. His situation was probably not unusual.[33]

The doctrine preached by the greater part of the Black clergy, Black Methodists and Baptists, was remarkable similar to that preached by White ministers of those churches. The vertical division of society, so widespread in the social vision of White preachers, appears in the sermons of Black ministers as well. Yet it soon became apparent that the upper reaches of the American social order were "For Whites Only" and that somehow the misdeeds of the most lowly Blacks were usually placed upon the entire race. In the decades immediately following the Civil War, it was possible for Black ministers to believe that race prejudice would soon disappear. But with the hardening of racial lines in the nineties, such expectations were more difficult to maintain. Black ministers responded in various ways. The Rev. Francis J. Grimké spoke out with great courage against the color line and the brutal atrocities that accompanied its extension and maintenance in the nineties. He castigated the White ministers for their silence, the Black ministers for their obsequiousness (noting honorable exceptions in each case), and urged even armed resistance when possible. By contrast, the Rev. Matthew Anderson looked upon Black suffering as God's purification of His people and predicted that they would emerge from their torment and humiliation with "the highest conception of the religion of Christ" to become the spiritual teachers of the world. The Rev. T. G. Steward transposed this vision into apocalyptic terms. The fall of perverse Saxon civilization was at hand, and "the really righteous" shall finally "come forth to lead Africa's millions" to welcome the universal Christ. Some Black ministers placed a new emphasis on the missionary role of Black Christians in Africa and among other colored populations. Others adopted the condemnations of Black conduct that were used to justify racial discrimination in order to rebuke their congregations and urge them to better behavior, in the hope that this would lead to greater acceptance of them by Whites.[34]

Religious rapture and morality were more distinct in Black religiosity (and among White Holiness and Pentecostal groups, according to the opponents of those churches) than they were in White middle-class piety. One Black minister stressed the difference between spiritual and fleshly sins, admitting that even saints sometimes succumbed to the latter. But generally, immoral conduct was considered the great shortcoming of Black Christianity, a deformity inflicted by slavery. Bishop D. A. Payne charged that two-thirds of the Black ministers were wayward.

Some suggested that, for the Black masses, it was not only the slave past but also the discouraging present (making rewards for virtue more completely spiritual for Blacks than for others) that should be considered. Nevertheless, Black ministers, particularly those with better educations and professional aspirations, took it upon themselves to preach vehemently against drink, fornication, and stealing. Perhaps it occurred to some that, in the depressed and iniquitous conditions in which the Blacks found themselves, moral conduct and keeping in one's place were somehow linked. In a relaxed moment, the Rev. George A. Marston, an ardent prohibitionist who was noted for his sermons demanding moral purity, put this little joke into his commonplace book:

> A. Hear dat Rastus wuz put t'jail fer horse stealin'.
> B. Serves 'im right!—shoulda stuck t'chickens.[35]

If the problems of moral purity bedeviled Black preachers, those same issues helped propel women into the ministry. To the extent that the winds of doctrine were becalmed and morality was found to be the essence of Christianity, women—who in this era were often considered to be the essence of morality—discovered that the ministry was somewhat more accessible than it had been previously. Yet women were rarely given position of command in society, except over children; therefore, they were often led to downgrade the sense of authoritativeness in their work in the ministry and instead, to stress its self-denying beneficence and service. "Since the office of minister," as the Rev. Anna Howard Shaw saw it, "is no longer that of a schoolmaster, and he is not so much a propounder of theological dogma as a persuader of mankind toward a life of purity and righteousness, woman seems particularly adapted to the ministry." Nevertheless, women were excluded from the ministry in all the major denominations. For the orthodox churches, Scriptural passages were relied upon (usually 1 Cor. 14:34) but, more generally, churchgoers found the ordination of women disconcerting if that gave them the right to rise above men and direct them. Even when women were sent as missionaries (but not as ministers) to foreign lands or sent to care for immigrants in American cities, they were usually restricted to bringing the good news to other women and children. Women did gain the right to preach in churches that were peripheral socially, economically, or theologically—the churches of the Pentecostals, Free Will Baptists, Methodist Protestants, Salvation Army, and Christian Scientists, and the smaller and poorer Unitarian and Congregationalist churches. But even those churches that did avail themselves of the ministerial services of women did not accept women on the same basis as men.[36]

This was unmistakable among Catholics, where women had traditional orders of their own. Yet if priests were publicly invisible, nuns (who outnumbered them four to one in the late nineteenth century) were even less often noticed. Except, of course, for the world of subversive fantasy, where Maria Monk's *Awful Disclosures* was still available and augmented by the tales of Edith O'Gorman's *Convent Life Exposed* as well as Hudson Tuttle's *Secrets of the Convent* (which explained that "all novices are the brides of Jesus Christ, and as all priests are one with Jesus, it follows by unanswerable logic that all novices are brides of all priests"). Nursing sisters flocked to the aid of the stricken, as panicky citizens fled in the great Memphis yellow fever epidemic of 1878, and gave their lives heroically to fight the epidemic. Yet instead of commemorating the nuns' services, the city set up a memorial to a lone Protestant woman whose nursing services were effusively praised but remained somewhat uncertain. For many Americans, the nun was unnatural and exotic; she was either stunted or immoral. As William Dean Howells explained, she had "given up the most precious part of her woman's nature, and all the tenderness that clings about the thought of wife and mother."[37]

The general exclusion of women from the clergy (and the subordination of those who were admitted) suggests some of the limits of "the feminization of American culture." In this era, the ministry was predominantly masculine. When the Southern Baptists, in 1885, formally denied women the right to sit at their conventions simply as delegates, the action went almost unnoticed. There was some hint of nervousness in the late nineteenth-century enthusiasm for "muscular Christianity" and in the frequent and advertent praise of the manliness of the preacher, yet the unguarded metaphors describing the minister's work were also redolent with masculinity—"wielding the sword of faith," "penetrating the barriers of indifference," "piercing the sinful heart," "stripping the worldling of vanity." Henry Ward Beecher, whose phrases were usually much more tender, muted, and bisexual than those of the other preachers of the gospel of love, nevertheless extolled the ministers who "could overflow and pour down this style of motive and representation [i.e. love] upon the congregation from week to week, meeting the already nascent feeling in those that listen to them, unfolding it and educating it." That was just the sort of thing that got him into trouble.[38]

Women always had easier entry into the corps of lay evangelists who brought so much energy to the evanescent revivals that shook American Protestantism in the nineteenth century. Yet these evangelists themselves had become more peripheral to the religious life of the country by the end of the century. Among the Holiness and Pentecostal groups, the lay evangelist remained an important figure, but among the Baptists, Methodists, and Northern Disciples, the work of the evangelist (lay and clerical) became clearly subordinate to the work of the pastor. The revival itself changed in purpose. Earlier it had reached out to the unconverted and helped to bring a great host of new brothers and sisters into the fold. From a Protestant perspective, there could hardly be a more momentous event than a new convert's standing up for Jesus. But the audiences of the late nineteenth-century revivals were made up largely of those already converted, and the revivals served largely to reinvigorate their piety. This was surely a serious task, but less crucial than had been the work of earlier evangelists. Even Dwight L. Moody, the greatest lay evangelist of the late nineteenth century, began to lay stress upon the importance of Christian education in the last years of his career.[39]

In this emphasis he was easily outdone by a rapidly growing section of the regular ministry in the major denominations, who not only acclaimed the advantages of a general Christian education but also insisted upon the necessity of an enhanced training for the clergy. "The time has come," wrote a student at the Southern Baptist Theological Seminary, "when the Baptist denomination demands an educated ministry. . . . The demand of the people is seconded by a strong desire on the part of young men just entering the work of the ministry." Even the Methodists, who were "slow to admit the professional idea because they claim a converted and called ministry and the Holy Spirit as teacher," conceded that God also works through secondary causes and that neglecting the means He provided for increasing ministerial power would be an error. They accepted the need for a ministry with different levels of education to meet the requirements of diverse congregations. The usefulness and prestige of the largely self-taught itinerant circuit rider declined as the nation's population grew and concentrated in the increasingly well-settled countryside. The church gradually permitted longer pastorates for its preachers, and wealthy city congregations entered into "extra-disciplinary contracts" in order to hire better-educated ministers. By the end of the century the Methodists prided themselves upon an outstanding theological seminary in Boston complete with German-trained scholars expounding the most recent discoveries in theological science. This reflected the broader movement toward an educated clergy within the American denominations that became particularly apparent in the churches higher up on the American social scale. In the nation as a whole, the number of theological seminaries and enrolled students grew prodigiously.[40]

Many of the students came from rural settings and even from ministerial positions with rural congregations. They expected to acquire the knowledge and polish that would enable them to find jobs in sophisticated, urban churches. Most students, however, found different kinds of gratifications and vexations than they expected. The usual three-year course of study often initiated them into an invigorating fellowship with "a select body of godly companions" who established bonds of brotherly attachment that would hold them for many years afterward. It also initiated them to hard and painful truths that would transform their religion. Professor Benjamin B. Warfield, who dominated the Princeton Seminary in this era, described his curriculum as "just the hammer needed to beat men into ministers of power." In the leading conservative seminaries, like Princeton and Louisville, this meant a type of ministerial Calvinism, a theological science that "the common mind does not perceive," which would set off the minister's grim doctrines from the more comfortable and optimistic beliefs of his congregation. It took great courage, a Baptist minister explained to seminary students, to preach the unpopular truth of elective grace, which left many seemingly religious people out of God's plan of salvation. In the leading liberal seminaries, like Union, Boston, and Andover, the hard and painful truths were usually the heterodox teachings of the great German theological scholars of the era, which shook many traditional religious beliefs and even left Scripture, the foundation of Protestant faith, somewhat unsteady.[41]

"Believing as I do that you are thoroughly corrupt," wrote one student to Dr. Hinckley G. Mitchell, a Boston University Professor of Theology and an advocate of Higher Criticism, "I cannot be satisfied that I have done my duty 'till you are outside the Methodist fold." It was just this sort of animus that gave impetus to the series of heresy trials erupting within the American theological seminaries in the last decades of the nineteenth century. The young scholars, who had gone to Germany to upgrade their theological training, came back to teaching positions in the seminaries not only with unorthodox doctrine but with what was clearly linked to such doctrine, the example of professors of theology who were neither responsible nor subject to the churches and their standards. The Rev. Paul Van Dyke, a fledgling instructor just returned from Germany, insisted that his beliefs were sound, yet he resigned his position at Princeton Seminary rather than give a pledge of orthodoxy which he thought was demeaning. Professor Crawford H. Toy and President William H. Whitsitt, both with German training, left the Southern Baptist Seminary in Louisville—Toy, owing to this "looseness" on the doctrine of inspiration of scripture; Whitsitt, because he insisted that he would teach "Baptist history free from fable." Rev. Henry Preserved Smith, American disciple of Wellhausen, was forced out of Lane Theological Seminary, and Mitchell out of Boston University Theological School. The five professors who were accused of heterodoxy at Andover were ultimately victorious, but at the expense of clear and clarifying argument.[42]

Clear, if not clarifying, argument was a virtue that the Presbyterians prized highly, therefore their seminary controversies serve to highlight some of the issues that were disturbing even those schools that preferred to muffle conflict for the sake of institutional tranquility. Two conspicuous Presbyterian disputants were Benjamin B. Warfield, who helped preserve orthodoxy at Princeton, and Charles A. Briggs, who led Union Theological Seminary into heterodoxy. Both had studied in Germany (Warfield briefly at Leipzig and Briggs for four years at Berlin), but Warfield returned unshaken in his belief that Calvinism, as set forth in the Westminster Confession, was "the final crystallization of he very essence of evangelical religion," while Briggs, who had thoroughly imbibed the German historical vision, became one of the leaders in the movement to revise the doctrinal standards of the church. Both acclaimed theology as an exalted science. Yet for Warfield it was a fixed science, because Christian truth was perfect and unchanging. His ideal form was Systematic Theology, which was comprehensive, symmetrical, and also forensic. In Warfield's hands, theology came to resemble the American legal science of the era just passed, which had been based upon natural and unchanging rights. His theological polemics resembled lawyers' briefs, with extravagant stratagems of intellect, where the conclusion was assumed and the chief task was to summon the best possible arguments for the cause. It was a theology that enabled Presbyterian conservatives to believe ingeniously in the religion to which they had ingenuously subscribed.[43]

For Briggs, theology was scientific insofar as it was historical. While God's truth might be unchanging, man's understanding was not. The best way for man to study God's truth was to study its unfolding in human history: the "divine revelation and communication of redemption in the successive covenants of grace extending through many centuries and penetrating through many minds." Revelation was not a sudden stroke but a continuous process. Historical study would clear away the mists of scholasticism and mysticism; it was an avenue "to the presence of the Living God and Divine Savior." Briggs fashioned his theology to resemble the natural sciences on which the newly confident physicians of this era had rebuilt their profession. This theology downgraded the *a priori* and the partisan tendencies in the discipline and hoped for an objective presentation of issues. In the past, Briggs asserted, "the creeds have lorded it over scripture, and the dogmaticians have lorded it over the creeds," but now historical study would sweep aside such obstructions. For Warfield, theology would preserve denominational standards; for Briggs, it would open the way to Christian union.[44]

As they differed in their understanding of the science of theology, so Warfield and Briggs differed in their expectations of the seminary that would teach it. For Warfield, the seminary was primarily a practical training school that would provide a clear view of religious doctrine "in its nature and relations, an appropriate feeling with regard to it, and a power to communicate it in a manner congruous with itself and the mind which is to receive it." For Briggs, the seminary would be a center of research, brought closer to the universities and sharing their vigor and power. The regular ministers could receive their training there but, more important, there the most capable candidates would be fitted to assume the leading positions in the church and in the intellectual and cultural life of the nation.[45]

When the Presbyterian General Assembly, with Warfield's ardent support, suspended Briggs from the ministry, he helped transform Union Theological Seminary into a nondenominational school, establish ties with Columbia University, and thereby bring the school closer to German conditions. Through his followers, Briggs continued to have influence within Presbyterianism, but now he had additional influence in other denominations as well. When Union introduced "clinical training" for its students in the settlements and city missions, Yale Divinity School, Chicago, Boston University School of Theology, and Andover quickly did likewise. As for the "New Theology," the loosely gathered set of doctrines that found such favor in the liberal seminaries, Briggs' Biblical scholarship and his arguments for the notion of "development" (connoting some acceptance of biological evolutionary theory as well as Higher Criticism) carried much weight. He was decidedly less friendly to that other component of the New Theology, the doctrine of immanentism, which subordinated spirituality above and beyond to the spiritual power within and about. But he endorsed the widespread attempt of this New Theology to make moral law central to religious thinking.[46]

The usual effect of a seminary education was to bind its graduates more closely together and to set them off more sharply from their congregations in fellowship and belief. The late nineteenth-century growth of ministers' clubs, often called Monday Morning Clubs, provided something like a renewal of the seminary milieu—a place where ministers could meet, speak freely, and trust that what they said would be held in confidence. If their sophisticated beliefs often separated them from their congregations, the ministers' religious uncertainties, frequently linked to that sophistication, detached them even more fully. Most laymen came to church in order to have their faith confirmed, not shaken. Ministers, therefore, were sometimes cautioned not to vent unbelief before their congregations. "If you have doubts," warned one ministerial guidebook, "keep them to yourself. Do not inoculate others with your views. . . . Tempt no lowly mind to skepticism by suggesting your own." Another adviser urged that "doubts should not be flaunted by the man in the pulpit" because he had been called upon to preach belief and not doubt. Yet some ministers found such counsel difficult to follow, for it seemed starkly to suggest that they maintain one religion for their study and Monday Morning Club and another for the pulpit. "Shall it be counted his [the minister's] duty," asked one writer, "to maintain a policy of altruistic deception?" Notions of esoteric understanding did not come easily to American Protestantism in the late nineteenth century.[47]

The heightened sense of collegiality among ministers in the last quarter of the nineteenth century was apparent in almost all denominations. When the preacher called someone "brother" at mid-century, he was usually referring to a member of his congregation; by the end of the century, he was more likely to be addressing a fellow minister. A leading conservative preacher of the era proposed that "ministers should be linked closely together as a profession, loving one another, helping one another, sympathizing with one another." Furthermore, "the mean competition of ministerial life and labor should be spurned," as it was in the other professions. One ministerial handbook spelled out the etiquette for the relations of ministers within one's denomination, and another guide extended the dictates of good form to ministers of other denominations as well. If ministers wished the people to respect and reverence their calling, one of them wrote, then "we must set them the example by honoring and highly esteeming those who occupy like positions as ourselves in sister churches."[48]

Ministers drew their respect and reverence from more substantial sources as well. The unique significance of the minister's work, his office within the organization that maintained him, and the customary techniques and tasks of that office (which had been shaped by the social prominence and habit of command of those who had held such positions in the past) all enhanced his authority. The minister, through his work, presented the hopes and demands of the Kingdom of God. To the extent that this realm of spirit was given dominion in the workaday world, as was often said, the position of the minister would be given importance as well. For the minister was an ambassador of a Power that not only negotiated with men but also commanded them; this emissary therefore took on some authoritativeness in his own right. The religion he presented was not the religion men wanted (for they were sinful and would desire to persist in their sinfulness), but the religion they needed. Liberal ministers who deemphasized men's waywardness stressed their backwardness instead, and this served as a basis for the authoritative position of such ministers. For the educated clergyman was almost sure to be in advance of his people. The recent reconstruction in theology, explained the Rev. Frank H. Foster, created "the necessity of expert dealing with great themes." Here only the educated minister could lead. Both the conservative and the liberal minister insisted, therefore, upon their freedom from the dictates of laymen—in fact, as one minister boldly suggested, their "freedom from everything but the yoke of Christ." The very nature of his work, therefore, seemed to support the minister's authority and autonomy.[49]

The minister's office within the organization that maintained him became more important and imposing in the late nineteenth century. This was the obverse side of the decline in the layman's share in the generation, nurture, and spread of piety that characterized late nineteenth-century religious developments. It was also linked to the declining importance of the revival. For with the spread of the belief that conversions were less likely to be instantaneous and easily recognized, but rather that they might be gradual and imperceptible, the role of day-to-day church functions and regular duties of the minister took on greater significance. At midcentury, American Protestant denominations usually defined themselves in terms of the rejection of the clericalism of the more churchly groups to the "right" on the spectrum of denominations. By the end of the century this particular predilection was greatly weakened (except among Holiness and Pentecostal groups). The denominations in the nineties often looked more favorably to the canonical dignity of their churchly neighbors on the right, and the most churchly of them, the American Episcopalians, looked abroad with obvious admiration and envy to the episcopacy of the Church of England.[50]

Among the Baptists, who had prided themselves on their independent congregational structure, with each individual church exuberantly wielding the powers to hire and fire preachers, those powers were now hedged, at least in the North, by the setting up of permanent councils to advise local churches on their selection of ministers. The Baptist preachers also established ministerial employment bureaus to widen their choice of churches and give themselves some leverage against the dictates of any particular congregation. Moreover, they fell to acquiring DDs, thereby calling attention to recognition and even legitimation that came from beyond the dominion of the congregation. With the decline of itinerancy among the Methodists, the unordained local preachers (previously they had carried important ministerial duties) were pushed aside by the former circuit-riders, who now increased their powers in church councils at the expense of the bishops and laymen. When John A. Wright, an eminent layman, protested that the ministry as a "class or party" were separating themselves from the laymen and molding the church to suit their ambitions, he found to his dismay that he could summon little support in his attempt to turn back such encroachments. Among the Presbyterians, where the educated minister had long held sway in church councils, a number of the leading clergymen began to stress the liturgical and sacramental role of the ministry and the divine component of the act of ordination where some claimed that "a special grace" was conveyed. Presbyterian ministers began to wear robes once more, as they had a century earlier. The growing Lutheran churches added their weight to the increased interest in the liturgical and sacramental aspects of the ministry. For the Lutherans as well as the Episcopalians, the ministry retained some sacerdotal powers to offer a Eucharist sacrifice that was at once mysterious and saving.[51]

Even those denominations that shunned elaborate liturgy and denied any sacrificial notions of the Lord's Supper, gave increased attention to the minister's work of pastoral care and regular, well-ordered preaching. The pastoral visit, in its traditional techniques and situation, clearly underscored the minister's authority. "It is the minister's vocation," asserted the Rev. Dwight Pratt, "to gain access to the hidden inner life" of his congregation. He comes to counsel the perplexed and afflicted within the privacy of their homes, and they "will unbosom themselves to him sooner than to any other." The minister, of course, would never violate their confidence and trust. The "cure of souls" was part of the minister's noblest work; "his is to understand, to help, to comfort—for these people are his children, his pupils, his patients; they are the sheep Christ has given him, for whom Christ died." It was particularly in the visitation of the sick, whose hearts were softened and whose "natural opposition to the truth is gone," that the minister could effectively bring God's word to his people. for the infirmity of the sick heightened the traditional and situational ascendancy that the minister usually brought to the pastoral visit. "If you want to lift men up," explained one ministerial manual, "you must stand higher than their level and have a grip on God's hand."[52]

Whatever the increased yet varied interest among the denominations in liturgy, sacramental piety, and pastoral care, most Protestants agreed that the chief work of the minister was preaching. The setting and technique of preaching brought with it a unique kind of primacy. The preacher commanded attention through his very place in the pulpit, elevated and apart from the pews. He stood alone and addressed "men in the mass, yet each individual hearer fccls himself to be addressed." In contrast to the pastoral visit, the minister from the pulpit could "enter impersonally into the intimate life of the audience, speaking generally, for which they supplied the particular." This allowed for an unusual and distant attachment. "You knew him, I suppose," someone asked a mourner at the funeral of a minister. "Knew him . . . no," the layman said—at least according to this somewhat soppy ministerial account—"I never spoke to him, but I owe to him my soul."[53]

Of course the minister's right to enter the pulpit, as with his right to take up his other stipulated tasks, derived in part from the overt claim that the came as Christ's ambassador: "it is because he is plenipotentiary of His kingdom that he is to speak with authority, and not as other men." Yet it is more apparent in the numerous treatises on preaching than in the discussions of the minister's other work that some of the authority of his office derived form the psyche of his congregation. For the minister, according to a maxim of the day, preached to "the head, the conscience, and the heart" (designations, oddly, not too dissimilar from the Freudian categories of ego, superego, and libido). While most commentators who turned to this formula recognized that intellect, morality, and emotion were not impervious to each other, yet these writers suggested that each element could be distinctly addressed and could provide distinctive advantages. From a present-day perspective, it seems that the minister in speaking to the head, the conscience, and the heart took on some of the right to command from each.[54]

In addressing the intellect, the minister warded off dangers from within and without: he "schooled the heart" and he repelled those external adversaries, misbelief and skepticism. It was particularly in the upper-class churches, whose congregations were clearly turning away from revivalism and at the same time finding it difficult to avoid the scientific and scholarly challenges to traditional belief, that preaching to the intellect took on special importance. No one denied the value of religious feeling. "It is like the fire in the engine which supplies the motive energy for the whole machine," explained a minister in a revealing metaphor. "But like fire, it is an exceedingly dangerous thing unless it is properly guarded and used. In the hands of a skillful engineer fire may furnish the motive power for a very large establishment, while in the hands of an incendiary it becomes a demon to destroy a city." This engineer was intellect, but he was also the minister who addressed intellect. Moreover, both not only directed religious feelings but, more significantly, gave such feelings meaning. "Regeneration is not a fact of experience," explained the Rev. Benjamin Warfield, "but an inference from experience." Intellect drew—and the minister guided—those inferences, to assure that any evangelism would be safe and sound.[55]

For many, the external dangers to religious truth had become especially fearful in the late nineteenth century. "There are ages which have been saved from sin by evangelism; this is an age which must be saved from skepticism by knowledge," announced the Rev. John Watson. the minister of a fashionable congregation was expected to be able to somehow reconcile the discoveries of science with religion and to absorb or fend off the findings of Higher Criticism. While he must become aware of the existing state of knowledge in science and Biblical criticism, he need not render himself a savant. "We must accept the distinction between a professed scholar and a working minister, as we do between a consulting physician and a general practitioner," wrote Arthur T. Pierson. "We are the general practitioners, who owe a debt of gratitude to the experts, and can best discharge it by using their work. Our sphere is that of theological middlemen, who will distribute among the public the selected and assorted produce of the schools." Washington Gladden devoted his Sunday morning service to "practical" preaching and the evening service to such apologetics. The acceptance of Higher Criticism, however, an evangelical preacher complained, removed the word of God from the common people by assuming that only scholars can interpret it. "While Rome puts a priest between a man and the Word, criticism puts an educated expositor between the believer and his Bible." Even in the more orthodox churches, the minister was expected to preach occasional doctrinal and exegetical sermons in which he demonstrated his special competence in explaining the dictates of reason, fact, and faith as embodied in Scripture, and he himself derived some warrant from that competence and those dictates.[56]

If he preached to a socially prominent, "high-minded" church, the minister also stood in need of some literary culture, and he was obliged to draw upon the inspired but not sacred writings of the great authors of the ages in order to amplify his sermons. He must show that piety could accept not only the findings of science but also the emanations of sweetness and light. "For poetry and Christianity live and move and have their being in the same region," enthused one minister, and "religion includes culture as the greater includes the less," insisted another. The minister generally used literature to exalt spirituality and of course the spiritual-minded as well. In addition, he resorted to literature in order to teach morality by example. Yet he had a more potent instrument of moral betterment at his disposal, and that was the direct appeal to conscience.[57]

As with the address to the intellect, the minister's address to conscience was a traditional avenue to the soul, which in this era took on some notable improvements. The minister drew authority from the appeal to intellect because he stood as an ally of the right of intellect to direct, advise, and ascribe meaning; in a similar manner he drew authority from the appeal to conscience because he stood as an ally of the rightful commands of the superego. Even Phillips Brooks, who self-confidently cast aside many of the traditional supports of ministerial authority, held fast to the minister's office as "the director of the human conscience." Conscience was "the voice of God in the soul of man," and the minister's job was to make man listen to that voice and obey it. In fallen man, the conscience became defective; therefore the minister must enlighten it and sometimes "even step in and do for a while the work which conscience failed to do." For the evangelical preacher, the appeal to conscience would help bring conversion, in that the conscience bore witness to evil thoughts and deeds and suggested the terrible retribution that awaited. The evangelical minister used the conscience to break down pride, produce the conviction of sin, and lead the sinner to Christ. For the liberal preacher, the appeal to conscience would help bring moral conduct. The conscience was that moral law within that created a sense of obligation to do right and a restraint from doing wrong, shaping a life of duty and righteousness.[58]

Some liberal ministers, owing in part to their favorable estimates of men's goodness, wished to use the conscience to evoke rather than to discipline. If one could set a lofty ideal before men, it would be so attractive to the sense of right within them that they would seek to be moral. Moreover, that ideal could be embodied in human exemplars, ministers among them. The principal authority of the minister, Charles W. Eliot argued, was "derived from the purity and strength of his character." And character, that greatly celebrated nineteenth-century composite of morality and will, inherited and educated and organically fused, displaced the earlier notion of discrete mental and moral faculties and became a prime requisite of ministers. "To character and the influence that grows out of it, more than to anything else," one minister maintained, "our Lord committed His cause."[59]

Some ministers would rather exemplify than demand. This was often true of the "Princes of the Pulpit" who absorbed the vainglory of American transcendentalism, with its pumping up, spiritualizing, and moralizing of personality as a way of relocating a pervasive and indistinguishable God. Preachers like Phillips Brooks, Henry Ward Beecher, and Frank Wakely Gunsaulus, combined in varying degrees the resort to moralized and spiritualized personality, overblown sentiment, and pure theatricality. The saintly Phillips Brooks, one of his admirers reported, did not speak to his people, "he rather speaks before them, in their presence. He soliloquizes." Most ministers, however, both exemplified and demanded. They also absorbed into the dictates of conscience the local mores of society and often dangerously lumped together Christianity and the demand to quit the saloon, the ballroom, and the theatre.[60]

The last of those three avenues to the soul—intellect, conscience, heart—clearly became the favorite of the preachers in the nineteenth century. The address to the heart usually meant the rousing of fear and love; and by the end of the century, as has been often shown, the emphasis in much of American religion had shifted from fear to love. Yet fear was not to be completely pushed aside, particularly in lower-class congregations, for "he is ready to be taught," explained a Baptist, "who has first been awakened to a sense of danger." Even Henry Ward Beecher, the most famous pathfinder on the way from fear to love, cautioned that "to destroy fear without finding an equivalent motive is both unwise and mischievous." However, Beecher and many others thought they could forswear the ancient warning to the sinner that he must flee from the wrath to come. The effect of this shift could be seen even in a preacher like John A. Broadus, the leading preceptor at the Southern Baptist Theological Seminary, who advised his students against elaborate description of the agonies of Perdition. In the 1850s, the admonition to "Preach Jesus" meant urging ministers to dwell upon Jesus' death as a sacrifice for sin; in the 1890s, it meant advising them to graphically describe Jesus' life as the supreme type of love.[61]

There was no intention, in this gospel of love, to loosen the bonds of morality. Quite the contrary, these ministers preached a "constraining love," often turning to the verse: "Hereby ye may know that ye love me because ye keep my commandments." Dwight L. Moody, the greatest revivalist of the era, employed the image of God's arm and hand to describe a love that supports, enraptures, and yet restrains. "Let his loving arm be beneath you, let His loving hand be about you; and He will hold you with mighty power. He will keep you, and fill that heart of yours with tenderness and love." Other preachers often alloyed this love with guilt in order to securely affix obligation to it. As a lesser minister described it, perhaps too vividly, "He [Jesus] stretches out that grasping hand, with a nailhole in it, to lay hold upon you, and you slip from His clasp, and oppose to His love a negligent and unaffected heart. . . . Is there any sin like the sin of ingratitude?" God's love was a love that binds.[62]

Yet the gospel of love always had its dangers. While it was clearly not intended to be a fleshly love, it was difficult to completely extract the sensual from it. The heart was the source of all desires, and though God might purify it, the more Calvinistic ministers believed that, even among the regenerate, this purification was rarely complete. Long before Freud, the Rev. Benjamin B. Warfield found in men's dreams the revelation of the "inordinate desires" of the heart. Those dreams disclosed that "beneath the calm exterior of one's outward conduct, beneath the habituated purity of our innermost thoughts, beneath the very reach of our waking consciousness, there ebbs and flows a great black sea of evil that threatens to overwhelm, at any unguarded moment, the whole fabric of our moral lives." When such ministers addressed the heart with preachments of love, these appeals were carefully qualified by the restraints of intellect and conscience.[63]

It was specifically the *souls* of his people that the minister was usually told he must love, even when it was allowed that this love could be "burning of red heat." Along with that specification went the practical maxims to ensure strict soulfulness. "Do not receive a lady visitor in your study," instructed one handbook. "The gravest and greatest peril which confronts ministers," explained another, is that they "forget themselves, as to be overcome by beastly sensuality, make debauchers of themselves and bring their brethren into ill repute. . . . David's sin," this guide conceded, "is not extinct in David's priestly line." Perhaps owing to these troublesome effects of the "irresistible and conquering power of love," ministerial guides often shifted to the less heated emotion of sympathy in describing the ideal bond between a preacher and his people. Occasionally these advisors would recommend the classical aristocratic virtue of condescension, which had originally meant to descend to the level of one's fellow man— a form of humility. But that virtue had passed through the egalitarianism of the middle years of the century and had emerged as its opposite, the vice of arrogance. Sympathy, by contrast, was the great goodness of the Romantic era. It was more strictly a matter of feeling, but it also implied an acknowledgment of an underlying humanity beneath varying conditions—"the common feeling of the Body of Christ," as one minister defined it. Sympathy meant the power of imaginative fellow feeling, it suggested a magnetic attraction between men, and it never lost its alchemical possibilities of manipulation and control. Though based upon a sense of likeness, in the late nineteenth century it often underscored differences. "Sympathy" explained a lecturer to divinity students, "measures the respect we feel for those who are in circumstances and conditions below us." It enables the minister to draw such people to him, and "to the degree he is receptive he thereby becomes influential." It gives the minister "the power to read the souls of men"; and "to the magic touch of frank and genial sympathy these men will yield—even with the trust of children." While the essential purpose of the address to the heart (like those to the intellect and conscience) was to help bring the sinner to Jesus, it ineluctably also braced the rightful powers of the minister.[64]

The minister drew his authority from a variety of sources. To the extent that Americans gave credence to a spiritual dimension of reality, they gave importance to the minister who stood as its representative. Where spirituality commanded, the ministers took on some of its authoritativeness. Where spirituality became complex and difficult, the minister assumed the role of an expert. In addition, the minister's office within the institution of the church, its particular commissions and usages, brought with it a traditional elevation and influence. Moreover, in the late nineteenth century, when the layman's role within the church became more passive, the minister's charge became more forceful and encompassing. It was not only from within the domain of faith but from the broader society that the minister found support for his authority. The social importance of his work was generally acclaimed. "We cannot be unmindful of the fact, wrote a newspaper editorialist, "that the pulpit is of immense importance to the peace, happiness, and progress of society. Even where it does not convert, it cultivates; it imparts a thoughtful and comparatively elevated tone to the popular mind." In a society whose watchwords were freedom and order, it seemed that both could be maintained only if the ministry inculcated "the duty of unswerving obedience to all rightly constituted authority and especially to moral law." In a society where fluctuating commercial values were given such unfettered sway, even the entrepreneurs looked to religion and ministers to counter possible excesses.[65]

But beyond moral guidance, the minister and the religion he preached provided general purposes and ends that helped explain the incidence of things and changes in a person's life. Charles S. Peirce thought that these all-important "teleological considerations" must be left to religion. It furnished a story within which men and women could understand their own particular doings and undoings. Ministers, in the late nineteenth century, supplied three conspicuous stories—Calvinist, revivalist, and liberal. The first was a mystery, the second a melodrama, and the third a temperate, optimistic romance. Different as they were, they shared a subplot, varying in importance in each, which told that men and women were called to some task, and nothing could really profit those who neglected to discover and follow that calling. This subplot, of course, was particularly important to the professionals. Within these stories, the minister's right to guide and advise, and sometimes even to command, received widespread acceptance.[66]

8

The Professors: A Profession in an Academic Bureaucracy

Professors and engineers had already appeared as distinct occupational groupings in pre–Civil War America. In that antebellum era, however, their numbers were small, their qualifications were not yet explicitly defined, and their career patterns were unsettled and shifting. It was not until the eighties, when both occupations grew rapidly and took on more stringent and unyielding demarcations, that they were accorded full recognition as professions and placed among the professions when these were listed. In contrast to dentistry, which gained such recognition in an earlier era when ranks in medicine and the community were collapsing, college teaching and engineering won general acceptance as professions amidst the rising of hierarchies in business, education, and society at large. Two momentous and related developments of the eighties—the spread of large scale organization with its reordering of social bonds, and the growth of science and its much acclaimed application to industry—had important consequences for professors and engineers. Both occupations became largely professions of subordinates in organizations; both drew upon the prestige of various kinds of science to claim for themselves, within the somewhat uncongenial environment of organizations, the authority and independence that had customarily been granted to the traditional professions.[1]

Previously, the independence of the professions had almost been taken for granted. Authority commonly meant the right to command, and independence, the exemption from command. Doctors and lawyers, usually self-employed enterprisers offering their services upon a market, were clearly exempt from direct command in their workaday world. Protestant ministers, though not as unconstrained as doctors and lawyers, often held positions remarkably free of external control. Doctrine and circumstance contributed to this. Most Protestants believed that the ministerial office had been granted fixed powers by Scripture, and while the particular minister might be removed, his powers in office could not be diminished. Moreover, though ministers usually were employees of congregations and seemingly could be hired and fired almost at will, nevertheless that will often emanated from a diverse and divided body. A minister with fair diplomatic skills, therefore, would find much free scope in his work. Even those Protestant ministers locked into denominational hierarchies soon discovered that in the American egalitarian setting such hierarchies were much weakened and could be counterbalanced by the ostensibly increased powers of congregations.[2]

As compared to the Protestant churches and denominations, the organizations in which both professors and engineers found themselves were definitely more cohesive and coercive. There were significant differences, however, in the organizational settings of each of these two new professions. Engineers had to answer to business organizations that were subject to the demands of a market economy and that were set up with the clear and overriding purpose of making profits. Professors, by contrast, dealt with college and university organizations that were in great measure subsidized and, therefore, somewhat sheltered from the imperatives and uncertainties of markets. The purposes of higher education, moreover, were obligingly unclear, and the professors could take part in shaping them. Colleges and universities could not be completely indifferent to their own special markets, however. Two-fifths of their income came from tuition (as compared to one-tenth of the income of the even more insulated English universities) and much of the rest, particularly in private academic institutions, from nonspeculative investments. Yet such revenues were relatively stable and were designed to encourage noncommercial standards of achievement. By contrast, although the large business organizations into which engineers entered were assiduously trying to mitigate the rigors and uncertainties of their markets, nevertheless the primary purpose of these businesses was making money, and this placed sharp limits on all other purposes.[3]

Despite such important differences, both business organizations and universities shared the exigent perplexities of bigness. Executives within both organizations, therefore, tried to centralize authority and the supervision of work while, at the same time, decentralizing the performing of the work itself. They also endeavored to wrest from those with formal authority—trustees and stockholders—the initiative and command within the organizations and place much of it in their own hands. Professors and engineers, therefore, as employees in such organizations, often happened upon similar difficulties and advantages.[4]

The emergence of the university was one of the major cultural events of late nineteenth-century American history. In contrast to the pre–Civil War colleges, those strongholds of Protestant scholasticism and genteel cultivation situated physically and culturally at the quiet backwaters of the American republic, the new universities of the eighties and nineties moved almost directly into the midst of the booming and bustling society of the day, and aspired to giving it informed and public-spirited guidance. They absorbed the popular enthusiasm for science and for those practical arts made more effective and honorable through the application of science, yet they maintained an attachment to broad notions of gentlemanly culture. Paradoxically, it was the acceptance of German ideas about higher education that helped American universities become more open to American life. The spirit of the German university of the nineteenth century was *Wissenschaft*. That translated loosely into science, but more accurately, it denoted a disciplined study of all subjects for the purpose of discovery. Behind this venerated concept lay the Romantic notion of flux—that truth in all its complexity continuously developes and must be revealed progressively through new experience and research. The rise of Darwinian science in the late nineteenth century seemed to confirm such a view. Within the German University, *Wissenschaft* meant a faculty devoted to research, specialization, and graduate education, with students granted the liberties of an elective course of studies. The bringing of these institutional effects to America helped make universities and colleges more receptive to the scientific and the utilitarian, whereas earlier, such schools had been much less accommodating.[5]

These changes also diminished the importance of classical studies and, more strikingly, the incidence of overt Christian teaching. The most renowned university presidents were all religious men. They, like the ministers of the era, responded to the dazzling growth of worldly knowledge and power in the nineteenth century with the rhetoric of division and inclusion. Harper of Chicago argued that religion was "something in itself and for itself, fulfilling a separate role," and that it could be set apart from other forms of inquiry and left to individual initiative. Charles W. Eliot of Harvard thought that ultimately the sacred and the secular were inseparable but, less than ultimately, one might devote oneself to the sacred privately and to the secular publicly. A. T. Hadley, the first lay president of Yale, was satisfied with the formula that "faith in man, truth, and God are but different names for the same thing." But that dictum, like the deliverances of Harper and Eliot, served chiefly to diminish qualms as the energies of the university were directed increasingly toward mundane ends. The universities and colleges, through the inclusion of science and practical studies, took on a more up-to-date, serviceable aspect. Gradually, the college degree once again became a prerequisite to placement in and promotion to the upper ranks of the professions, and soon even to joining the management level in the new corporations. As in the late eighteenth century, when they trained the class of gentlemen who ran the society, so in the late nineteenth century, when they trained an increasing part of that more open, diverse, and democratic elite that came to occupy positions of command, the colleges and universities were important places. "No institution," observed a leading engineer, as the nineteenth century drew to a close, "has greater responsibilities at this time of change, than those which rest upon the university."[6]

As the university and college grew in importance, so did the professor. In the early nineteenth-century college, the professor had often been a clergyman and, sometimes, a failed clergyman. He was usually assisted in his work by young tutors who looked upon their positions as way stations to a more rewarding career beyond the college. A few professors gained reputations for saintliness and erudition, and even won some independence and power, but most were hardly illustrious and stood diffidently if not obsequiously before the board of trustees and the college presidents. The stereotype of the professor as a milksop, as the embodiment of ineptitude and fecklessness in the world of men, stems from the early nineteenth century. That image was never wholly dispelled, but added to it in the late nineteenth century was the portrayal of the professor as a man of affairs, who was sometimes a meddler and possibly a dangerous one.[7]

The number of professors shot upwards, increasing by more than four times between 1870 and 1900, yet significantly, these academics seem not to have been recruited from a broader segment of society than earlier, but most likely from a more narrow one. At Michigan, for example, one of the most ambitious and prestigious land grant schools, the faculty became socially more homogenous in this era, drawing more exclusively from professional families of Congregational and Presbyterian backgrounds.

The gradual adoption of the doctorate as a requirement for college teaching may also have had a narrowing effect. It defined the path to the profession more clearly, and limited entry to those who were willing and able to take that path. Although in its original Germanic setting the Ph.D. signified a career of research, the large mass of Americans with Ph.D.s did very little of it. Social origins had some bearing upon this. The German Ph.D.s usually came from families wealthy enough to support their young scholars during their stay in postdoctoral limbo as *privatdocents*— when they did little teaching and brought in little income, but could direct their energies toward research and winning a reputation for scholarly achievement. The American Ph.D.s were usually obliged to go about earning a living immediately after gaining the degree, and they took jobs with as little delay as possible in the numerous small colleges scattered throughout the countryside. These colleges, alive as they were to the honorific value of the Ph.D., were not as appreciative of the research efforts which had been the basis of its esteem, and they imposed heavy teaching responsibilities upon the young professors. In those circumstances, scholarly ambition and vigor easily evaporated.[8]

The research scholar, however, became the beau ideal of the universities, and of those aspiring colleges that followed the universities' lead. The researcher's discovery of new truths, sometimes very practical and even profitable truths, gave promise of the expanding benefits that higher education could provide and helped justify the increasing expenditures that were furnished for it. Yet such scholars were comparatively few and were surrounded by a much larger assemblage of academics who had given up their ambition for notable scholarly research. These professors were usually content to follow an academic career that afforded a respectable, modest, and comfortable way of life. Barring incapacitating illness or flagrant violations of propriety, they were assured a place in the company of gentlemen, the gratifications of influence over the young, and long vacations.[9]

Such a world of safe second prizes was even more commonly found among the women faculty who taught in the state universities and more often in the women's colleges. Since they carried the chief responsibility for educating women students, these teachers suffered from the diffuse uncertainty of purpose always associated with women's education in this era. It was usually said that female education must prepare women for their duties, and that these must center, by and large, in the home; yet the consequences of this requirement for the curriculum were not always apparent. Because they seemed most appropriate, morally elevated cultural subjects and something like home economics did win out in women's education. The exalting spirit of research, however, could not easily enter into such realms. Women's colleges, therefore, retained much of the secluded atmosphere of the pre–Civil War college, and working in such a habitat in this new era could not but bring with it some self-deprecation. Women's colleges were the setting for inspirational teaching, intense friendships, extravagant emotions, and worries about "hysterical excess."[10]

Despite the clamor about research, the teaching experience remained the chief preoccupation of most professors; and of course the students' learning experience had some bearing upon that. Intrinsic to the students' learning was their loosening (not breaking) of intellectual and emotional ties with their homes, with their immediate localities, and occasionally with their social class. Though they had adult bodies and minds, the students were granted a delay in assuming most adult responsibilities. In this respite, they had the opportunity to develop special skills, new attachments, and perhaps the unusual ability to conceptualize, that is, to consider abstract and remote possibilities. Such skills and such emotional and intellectual resiliency would be particularly useful to those who would later find their way into positions of leadership in society. In the late nineteenth century, it was hoped that most college graduates would find their way to those positions.[11]

The bonds of allegiance and friendship established at college often lasted long afterwards. As the colleges and universities grew rapidly and became less cohesive (the elective system aggravated this), the locus of most vivid attachment shifted from the school, to the school class, and finally to the fraternity or social club. The school life of ardent sociability was part of the "social machine," and stood apart from, and often against, the curriculum. The curriculum stressed individual skills and achievements; the social machine countered with good fellowship and gregarious loyalty. The curriculum created intellectual standards and expectations; the social machine countered with athletics and its physical heroism and skills. The social machine dominated student life because of its very cohesiveness and its often upper-class provenance. Many students, however, were excluded from the adventures and engagements of the social machine, and this was particularly true of the "grinds," "digs," and "polers" who adhered most closely to the curriculum and its requirements.

Only William James, inveterate champion of the underdog and enemy of smug social conformity, could call these "almost always lonely creatures," the True Harvard. Few took him seriously.[12]

The primary task of most professors was teaching, therefore it is important to view them from the vantage point of that pressing duty. Three principal styles prevalent among the professors can be distinguished, and for the sake of clarity they might be labeled the scholarly-edifiers, the old-school-ties, and the iconoclast-priests. The scholarly-edifier brandished the most venerated and generally approved academic style. He inherited the hortatory tradition of the old-time college president as well as the task of justifying the ways of God and the social order to young men. The edifiers hoped to build a bridge between the young men and the world, taking into account the special liberties of student life but preparing the students to take up their responsibilities in the world and perhaps the leadership of it. The scholarly-edifiers were often found in the departments of philosophy, which had replaced those senior courses in mental and moral philosophy that had served as a culmination of the students' entire college career and had formerly been taught by the college presidents. George Herbert Palmer of Harvard and George Holmes Howison of Berkeley were two outstanding exemplars of the scholarly-edifier. Palmer, "one of the great teachers of Harvard College of his generation," saw as one of his chief purposes the cultivation in the student of a "responsive respect for the institutions which surround him," for they were things which "sweetly and friendily answer to his desires." The student was encouraged to gratefully accept the social order, while being "ever ready to offer subordinate criticism or readjustments as will tend to make the whole more harmonious." The professors, in turn, must "surround those committed to their charge with the unnoticed pressure of the moral world" and shape those "sentiments about what constitutes good form."[13]

Howison, having to grapple with the wilder and more irascible West, made his edification more vigorous and authoritarian. Students under him often felt "as though the mind itself had been laid hold of by him and twisted on its stubborness." He taught a philosophy that would be "a pilot of life"; it helped young men and women "toward character." His three principles were "authority, allegiance, and liberty." But this liberty, which echoed the liberties of student life, exhilarating as it might be, ultimately turned into duty and self-denying patriotism. Such transformations were not accomplished by argument alone. Howison drew upon some of the histrionics that teaching affords. He set up, for his exclusive use, a lecture room with tinted walls, carpets, heavy oak chairs, book cases, and an open fireplace. This room exuded the aura of a gentleman's study and made palpable the dignity and taste that befitted his message. Unlike the gentleman's study, however, Howison's lecture room was fitted out with a railed-off dais that elevated the professor above his students.[14]

Such elevation, actual and symbolic, was less apparent in the relation of the old-school-ties and their pupils. While the scholarly-edifiers took cognizance of the freedoms of student life and pointed the students toward adult responsibilities, the old-school-ties often championed the exuberance of student life, itself, against its later demise and against the demands of the curriculum. The American college and university of this era produced a strange anomaly, the anti-intellectual professor. Usually not astonishing scholars themselves, they argued that scholastic work tends to remove a man from humanity and that a mere scholar was always musty and dry, knowing little of "real life." The old-school-tie was, frequently, an alumnus, and like the other alumni to whom he provided an important link, he often displayed a nostalgic envy of college boys' virile bodies and carefree minds. He embraced the athletics and the fraternities of the school as his vehement and glowing cause.[15]

The old-school-ties were not often well known beyond their local habitat, and recollection of their good deeds must usually be exhumed from the back issues of alumni magazines or deciphered from the faded plaques near the college gymnasium doors. Eugene Lamb Richards of Yale had a wider reputation than most. He taught freshman math, but was obviously "more interested in boys and games than teaching or faculty meetings." He raised huge sums for the building of a new, splendidly equipped gymnasium and then served as its director for many years after. He worked assiduously to diminish faculty control of athletics and was known for his "whole-souled sympathy" for Yale teams. He was not ashamed to yell himself hoarse for the Elis and to exult when they won. Eugene Lamb Richards became the very embodiment of "Yale pluck."[16]

The iconoclast-priests instilled a different sort of spiritedness. They were priests of science (or occasionally, but infrequently, of aristocratic high culture) and iconoclasts of the idols of the tribe. Their lectures were often crowded and controversial. They had both despisers and disciples and were often the teachers later remembered most vividly by students, not usually for exactly what they said, but for the irreverent way in which they said it. During the peculiar interregnum of college life, the appeal of irreverence to students was to be expected. The professor, himself, justified that irreverence in terms of some higher truth; but those truths could be quite various. Such otherwise dissimilar professors as William Graham Sumner, E. A. Ross, Barrett Wendell, Thorstein Veblen, and William James all took on the style of iconoclast-priests.[17]

The contrast between these teachers and the scholarly-edifiers is readily apparent. Instead of justifying prevailing forms of social solidarity, as Palmer usually did, James urged that education give impetus to "making the conventional fluid again, or imagining foreign states of mind." Sumner fascinated many of his students, one of them explained, because "we were looking for a teacher who could free himself from old ways of thought, and whom we could rely upon to speak boldly, honestly, and clearly from a new point of view." That this point of view contradicted what the student had been provided with at home and was out of harmony with what the officials and supporters of the college maintained, made it all the more exciting. Barrett Wendell, one of his admirers suggested, was "absurd, cynical, caustic . . . , [flaunting] a profound detestation of philistinism. He would rather shock than soothe, because in this way he could at least be free from the suspicion of buying favor by vulgar conformity." Given the intellectual and emotional shifts that often accompanied undergraduate life, high-minded irreverence usually went over big, and therefore it became an enduring professorial style. Of course, iconoclast-priests need not be of the caliber of James, Sumner, or Wendell, otherwise this style would not have survived at all. Smashing lares and penates was not very difficult. Secondhand warmed-over hocum could easily serve as dazzling flashes of insight for most college students.[18]

The authority that the teacher held over his students was deeply affected by his professorial style. The scholarly-edifiers, like the pre–Civil War college presidents whom they succeeded, were expected to be kindly but resolute and unflinching; they must have an ample heart, but "never lose the whip-hand." Actual flogging had long disappeared from the colleges, as a form of discipline unbecoming the education of a gentleman, but an elaborate series of graded punishments for misbehavior, culminating in expulsion, remained an important feature of college life. The traditional theory was that the professor stood *in loco parentis;* that he must act as a parent and bear the responsibility of forming the character of his students. Palmer was drawn to this theory and expounded upon it forcefully. The teacher like the parent should be "directive," Palmer explained, but his discipline was justified primarily because it served to make the student strong. The professor commanded what the student himself would wish, had he sufficient experience and knowledge. (In this sense, the teacher ruled by consent.) The student's obedience, therefore, "enlightens, steadies, invigorates his independent will." The more often the student obeyed, Palmer claimed, the less subservient he became.[19]

For Palmer, not only was the end of education increased independence but the preferred means should be overtly uncoercive. The teachers were not only parents—and here Palmer shifted to a surprising metaphor—they also acted as hypnotists. They should address the student's intellect, but in addition "approach the subject while he is unconscious and while the will is dormant." What is taught the pupil unaware, "penetrates and becomes the pupil's own." For many modern psychologists, this shift in metaphor would not be discordant or surprising. They claim that hypnotism is a "transference phenomenon," in which the hypnotist acquires the authority of the parent (sometimes an imposing father, a Svengali, and sometimes a stroking, soothing, nurturing mother) and the hypnotized surrender part of their egos and adopt childlike responses. Palmer may have had some inkling of a connection between these metaphors, because he seemed to bring them together when he added that in order for suggestion to be effective, the teacher "must submit to be admired." Teachers must allow their pupils to idealize them and even furnish grounds for admiration. Palmer esteemed scholarship, erudition, and explicit instruction, but he concluded boldly, "it is better to be loved than understood."[20]

The old-school-tie was on the shakiest ground in asserting authority or even eliciting respect. For these professors were invariably doing homage to those virtues in which the students themselves excelled. If the message of manhood was in the physical contest or in the rough and easy camaraderie of the club house, then the middle-aged professors could at best enlist as cheerleaders for such pursuits. Perhaps these old-school-ties might have served as spokesmen for ancient and distant chivalric values—the heroism of warriors, the claim that none but the brave deserve the fair, that the *ultima ratio regum* was physical prowess and physical beauty—all congenial to student codes of behavior. But there is little evidence that any professors did that Rather, a few drew more comfortably upon hazy notions of muscular Christianity, linking athleticism to spiritual virtues. While men like Palmer and Howison were sometimes sympathetic to such efforts, they usually considered muscular Christianity a stunted form of devotion. Some students took the preachments of Christianity and athleticism seriously, but more seem to have ignored them. To students, Eugene Lamb Richards, who sometimes maintained that athletics served to make a Christian gentlemanly, was known with affection and some condescension as "Dicky-Bird" Richards.[21]

The authority of the iconoclast-priest with regard to the students, while ostensibly scientific (or in rare instances aesthetic), was also, in large part, moral. These priests served a type of truth that they saw to be one of the higher forms of good. "To avoid looking into the support of any belief from fear that it may turn out to be rotten"—rotten, not just mistaken, wrote the sometime professor Charles S. Peirce, "is quite as immoral as it is disadvantageous." A clear "logical conscience" did cost something, "just as any virtue" did, but such an exaction was purifying and uplifting. Those conscientious and upright German professors, who were "sacrificing wealth, political distinction, church preferment, popularity, or anything else for the truth of science," wrote Sumner, were truly exemplary men. The discipline that the iconoclast-priest usually preferred was somehow to be derived from the inspiration of such an ideal and not from the customary policing of student conduct that had made up so much of faculty activity in the past. In addition, the iconoclast-priest often distinguished more sharply than did the scholarly-edifier between the intellectual and moral authority that the teacher held over his pupils. That intellectual authority, the right to command attention and to expect intellectual deference, derived from the professors' superior knowledge. Under the exigencies of the elective system, moreover, many professors seem to have felt uneasy with the full responsibility for shaping the character of their pupils, and they provided strong support for the setting up of specialized officers, deans and the like, even student councils, to handle at least the minutia of day-to-day regulation of student conduct.[22]

Though the iconoclast-priest need not be a research scholar and a research scholar need not teach in the style of the iconoclast-priest, there was a definite affinity between the two. At the least, the image of the research scholar could serve as the model of virtues and the source of justifications for the iconoclast-priest. The research scholar, it was thought, in his discovery of new truths would inevitably come up against conventional belief, and the assumed rightfulness and beneficence of his position in that conflict provided warrant for irreverent and unconventional postures. Moreover, according to popular impression, the research scholar seemed to live a life of self-denial,

forsaking discernible comforts and social graces in order to follow his calling. That image already appeared in the fiction of the
nineties, and it did so quite clearly in Robert Herrick's somewhat
eerie figure of Professor Stralpero, the unkempt recluse who lived
a life of ardent research amidst the surroundings of academic
repose.[23]

The inner workings of the researcher's life were suggested in
idealized terms in the accounts of Granville Stanley Hall, which
served as publicity in the campaign to foster academic research
in America. Scholarly investigation, he explained, afforded professors "the priceless experience of self-abandonment to some
happily chosen point" but, at the same time, it wondrously empowered them to "come face to face with the genius of their own
personality." It was such experience that impelled the researcher
yet further into the intense, absorbing, and devoted labor of
scholarship. That labor, however, in and of itself, could not yield
discovery. Discovery, like revelation and justification, was somewhat mysterious and subject to a scheme much like that of faith
and works. Devoted efforts might enable the scholar to find truth,
but truth did not give him the full control over its discovery.
"Where the spirit of research breaks out," Hall wrote, "there is
life; the Holy Ghost speaks in modern accents." Another writer,
shifting Testaments, explained: "these wonderful men do not create the laws of nature, as they almost seem to, but they go up the
trembling mountain and the thick darkness, and bring down the
tables on which they are written."[24]

Those coming down from such a mountain, undoubtedly also
brought with them a new personal radiance and sense of authority. Though among the professors, these research scholars were
a small minority, nevertheless, the benefits derived from their
merits, accomplishments, and requirements were broadly dif-
fused. The recognition granted to their scholarship not only provided college teachers with reinforcement of their authority in
the eyes of their students, it also afforded professors support for
authority and independence within the academic organization of
which they were part.[25]

Yet, the most striking feature in the development of governance in higher education in the late nineteenth century was not
the increased authority of professors, although there is evidence
for that, but rather the growing influence of the presidents. Lord
Bryce, with the contrast of European conditions in mind, was
strongly impressed by the prominence of those college and university presidents in society and their almost monarchical positions in their schools. Though in America the legal powers of

boards of trustees were complete, most boards lacked the time and energy to actually govern. With the growth in size and complexity of the colleges and universities in the late nineteenth century, the trustees' control became even more remote. It was the university and college presidents of the late nineteenth century who initiated the celebrated academic "revolution" of the era, from above. They led in the adoption of research as a preeminent university function and in the granting to practical subjects a respected place in the curriculum. The undoubted success of this academic revolution allowed the presidents to bask in the acclaim of that achievement. While trustees retained veto powers and the right of intervention in issues of broad policy and budget, initiative in academic leadership shifted more decidedly out of their hands.[26]

Presidents, in addition, balanced the powers of the faculty and the boards against each other in order to broaden their own range of control. Often, it was the presidents who encouraged the growth of the collective powers of the professors. These academic executives were, after all, ex-professors, and the claim that some faculty authority was indispensable to their work flowed easily from presidential pens. Yet, the various academic senates that grew in influence in this era, particularly in the larger universities, also owed something to a new and increasingly spirited faculty assertiveness. The academic revolution not only empowered the presidents, it gave professors a new self-confidence. For now they believed that they included within their ranks illustrious discoverers and notable social benefactors and that this must redound to their standing. The eminence of the German professor within his university, moreover, was not lost upon the up-and-coming young American professors with the Germanic Ph.D.s. Daniel Coit Gilman, who had argued for the notion of faculty powers in academic governance, nevertheless bemoaned the fact that college controversies and skulduggery had become endemic in the last decades of the century.[27]

As size was on the side of the president in his conflicts with the trustees, so it was in some measure also on the side of the professors in their attempt to extend their authority within the universities and colleges. Before the growth of large, salaried staffs, faculty were called upon to perform many administrative tasks and were granted a broad range of decision in that work. Some of these tasks were handed over to the faculty senates and others to the academic departments.[28]

The presidents had created the academic departments to embody the new spirit of specialized research and to answer to the new requirements of specialized teaching under the elective system. But the academic departments could also become centers of professorial authority. In part, to offset this, presidents resorted to those reliable instruments of executive control—routine and hierarchy—which, whatever their other benefits, allowed for increased separation of decision and performance, for the centralization of authority and the decentralization of work. William Rainey Harper of Chicago set up a dystopia of departments with twelve ranks of instructors in each and a chairman at the head. This would create a world of rewards and punishments for professors as they rose in the ranks, and it would also favor centralized supervision and control. Though such devices placed limits on departmental powers, their growth in this era was not decisively blocked. The very important increase of departmental influence in the hiring of new faculty was an indication of this.[29]

Specialization, here and elsewhere, worked to the advantage of the professors. It was feared that the dissolution of the bond of common intellectual discipline owing to specialization would weaken professorial solidarity, yet any such weakening seems to have been offset by the professors' growing sense of common privileges within the academic organization. Specialization helped professors resist the oppressions of hierarchy with heightened self-confidence and with augmented market power. The growth of specialty associations in the physical and social sciences, although these never developed the strong allegiances of the German *Fachgenossen*, gave the professors a sense of the dignity of their work as well as an awareness of job opportunities outside of their particular institutions. Specialized skills were not easily replaceable in the expanding market for university and college teachers of the eighties and nineties, and specialists could use market demand to lighten the weight of bureaucratic subordination. This was most apparent in such relatively simple and forthright matters as salaries. "It is an open secret" one commentator observed, "that the professor finds and frequently claims his opportunity to secure an increase in salary in the offer of association with another institution."[30]

However, assertiveness regarding salary did not provoke the degree of excitement that the professor's claim of freedom from any control in what he taught set off. Professors supported this bold demand for independence in teaching upon the prerogatives of specialization as well as upon a more vaulting claim derived from the very nature of scientific truth itself. In the past, fundamental truths may have seemed simple, fixed, and self-evident, but now they appeared more obviously complex, changing, and esoteric.

Only the untrammeled and free-spirited scholar could find his way to such truth and make it available to his students in the classroom and to others beyond. Josiah Royce was the most eloquent champion of this expansive argument for academic freedom in the heated controversies that erupted in the last decade of the nineteenth century. In those disputes, he was joined by other various and differing professors, (some with divergent notions of science, and others with attachments to the old classical curriculum), by eminent spokesmen for the trustees, and, of course, by leading university and college presidents. Almost every sector of the academic community took part in these contentions; therefore, it is helpful to look at them somewhat closely.[31]

Both Josiah Royce and John Dewey based their arguments for the professor's freedom from interference in teaching upon what they considered the very nature of science. Yet Royce's science was antinomian and Dewey's Arminian. Science, for Royce, was never a closed system, but an ever growing body of knowledge; therefore, in both its fundamental concepts and new particular acquisitions it must always be in dispute. The investigator, whose office and spirit were essential to the university, as Royce saw it, always dealt with doubtful questions. His freedom to doubt, believe, and declare his doubts and beliefs was not a personal privilege but a function of his office. "The very air of investigation is freedom" wrote Royce, it was essential to the discovery of truth. The professor, therefore, must be "wholly free to do what he can," and the only demand that should be placed upon him is that he do his work and do it well.[32]

There were two important elements in this argument. One was the new emphasis upon changing truth and the resulting necessity and value of doubt and dispute. The other was the much older notion (going back at least to Plato) that certain tasks had intrinsic requirements for effective performance, and the expert practitioners must be granted exemption from the dictates of others in the carrying out of those delimited tasks. One might choose a doctor, but one could not tell him what medicine to use; one might choose a ship to travel upon but not expect to tell the captain how to navigate. In both those examples, which Royce draws upon (as did Plato before him), independence—exemption from command—shades off into authority—the right to command—as it does to a different extent in different social situations. However, in the university, independence and authority were often separable and could draw upon separate supports. Royce's principal claim was for freedom from command.[33]

Dewey's notion of science was more unqualified than was

Royce's, but oddly enough Dewey's notions ultimately led him to a more equivocal defense of academic freedom. Dewey's ambitions for science were probably linked to his disappointments with religion and to the expectation that science might do much of what religion once did. If science eventually was to be given broad social uses, one could not make as much fuss about its doubtfulness as Royce had made. For Dewey, science was the most rigorous form of truth. It had accurate and accepted techniques and well-defined domains in which those techniques were supreme. Moreover, it had produced an authentic body of truth through its exacting instrumentalities of inquiry and verification. For Dewey, the practitioner of such a science had not only the prerogative of intellectual independence but, more unmistakably than with Royce, was entitled as well to intellectual authority, the "right to determine belief" even in conflict with received opinion. This was assuredly warranted in a university, for "the university function was the truth function" and the only thing that was inherent and essential to it was the idea of truth.[34]

However, if judged by Dewey's demanding requirements, many disciplines that called themselves sciences had not yet achieved "a scientific status." They were sciences only in a tentative and somewhat aspiring sense. It just so happened that those tentative sciences were also some of the most vital and controversial subjects of the day—economics, sociology, psychology. In such fields, "an expression of opinion of a university instructor remains, after all, nothing but an expression of opinion" with no right to determine belief. If such opinions were granted unlimited freedom in German universities, that was simply an indication of the detachment of German universities from German life—a situation that Dewey deplored. In America, where universities should take a hand in the shaping of social institutions and social conduct, the professor of these tentative sciences had a special responsiblity. He needed tact as well as scholarship; he must avoid dogmatism and partisanship and cultivate an objective, historic, constructive bearing. Assuredly, he must not inflame the passions. From Dewey's standpoint, academic freedom in all those controversial subjects—where it was principally at issue—"becomes to a very large extent a personal matter." The professor needed the mental and moral poise to counterbalance his scholarly inquiries with a sympathy for human interests, with a "reverence for things that mean so much to humanity."[35]

Dewey's equivocations on academic freedoms, however, differed from those of some defenders of the old classical curriculum and those of the leading spokesmen for the rights of trustees. Dewey spoke for the rising power of science in higher education, while they spoke for the declining power of classics and lay boards. Professor Martin Kellogg, who taught Latin at Berkeley, had known Royce in his California days and had resented his loftiness. The flux of scientific findings that Royce had held up to view must be placed in the setting of those fixed and eternal verities so powerfully expressed by the "voices of the past," Kellogg argued. These set the bounds for the freedom of teaching. One could not ignore the authority of "all those presumptions, rules, customs, influences and antecedents." Specialized scientific truths, when certified by a consensus of scientific men, were of course inviolable; however, on broader and more fundamental issues, and clearly that included political matters, traditional views and maxims of propriety and conduct should get first and full hearing as well as strong presumption. This was not a matter of crushing academic freedom but rather the finding of a golden mean, Kellogg thought.[36]

The honorable Alton B. Parker did not balance academic freedom against the eternal verities but rather against the rights of property. Parker had been an eminent lawyer, judge, active college trustee, and he was soon to be the Democratic Party nominee for the presidency. Legally, he maintained, professors were employees of the boards of trustees. The professors, therefore, "who argued that their freedom was unconditional," were clearly mistaken. Founders and donors also had rights; the "freedom to insist upon it that the doctrines they believed to be true" shall be propagated in the institutions they founded and supported was one of them. Royce, however, had already answered that argument, by claiming that the assertion of such a trustee right was self-defeating. It would foster only irresponsible and ineffective teachers. "If you force me to teach such and such dogmas," Royce had argued, "then you must be responsible for them not I, I am your mouthpiece." The students could easily tell the difference between a man and a mouthpiece and would withdraw respect from such a pathetic surrogate. Parker backed away from the assertion of the full legal authority of ownership and construed the situation as one of a conflict of rights that could be adjusted. Outside the classroom the professor might be granted freedom of expression; that was his right as a citizen. Within the classroom, the professor might express his opinions, but somehow he must not subvert the purpose of the founder.[37]

Perhaps the most sophisticated and audacious reply to Royce, was that of Arthur T. Hadley, president of Yale. Yale had a strong tradition of professorial rights and powers, and Hadley, who had been one of its leading professors before he assumed the presidency, was appreciative of that tradition. As president, however, he felt the need for some counterpoise to faculty assertiveness. Hadley not only accepted Royce's view of scientific truth in flux, but he placed it in the context of the discipline of human flux itself, history. The study of history, Hadley suggested, revealed an ever-changing interaction of freedom and order. Freedom brought progress, and order absorbed the benefits of that progress and provided the condition that made freedom possible. The explicit legal restraints, so important to Parker, had been necessary to preserve social cohesion in the past, but as society evolved, its increasing orderliness made possible an enlargement of freedom and a lessening of external restraints.[38]

One-sided assertions of freedom, however, were dangerous and irresponsible. Hadley boldly chose the *locus classicus* of the defense of academic freedom, the trial of Socrates, to argue his point. Socrates, Hadley claimed, was both a great benefactor of the human race and a corrupter of youth. He taught students not only to despise sham but also to disdain piety. The Socratic defense before the Athenian assembly, that a teacher cannot corrupt because "the worse cannot harm the better," was obviously mistaken and quickly disproved by experience. For it was Alcibiades, Socrates' favorite pupil, who, after a long tutelage with his mentor, coldly betrayed Athens to Sparta over a matter of personal pique. If anything, the case of Socrates indicated that a teacher had obligations to social cohesion as well as to truth.[39]

Conflicts between these obligations moreover would be resolved by a resource to history and not to grand abstractions. Fortunately, in progressive communities, improvements in standards and habits had lightened anxieties about social cohesion and had allowed for increasing freedom in investigation and teaching. It was still necessary, nevertheless, Hadley conveniently decided, for the university president to stand between the professor and the community in order to protect both.[40]

The conflict between the professorial ideal of unfettered teaching and the anxiety of important sections of the community over the discord and disruption that might follow was resolved in diverse ways on campuses across the nation. At Harvard, when Royce refused to deliver the Lowell lectures because of the requirement that he sign a brief statement of belief, he endangered his tenure and diminished his income but he nonetheless stayed on and fashioned a career for himself as a distinguished scholar and professor. At Wisconsin, Richard T. Ely also prevailed and managed to teach his Yankee version of the Germanic "Socialism of the Chair." E. A. Ross lost to Mrs. Stanford, but won the support of his *Fachgenossen*, the American Economic Association (in which scholars of divergent political beliefs united to support his academic freedom) and a good position at another campus. Moreover, the furor provoked by the disputes at Brown and Chicago (where Andrews won and Bemis lost, respectively) served notice upon trustees that encroachments upon the professors' freedom of expression was increasingly fraught with the danger of unwelcome commotions and perhaps longlasting damage to the school.[41]

Even the presidents of the smaller schools were sometimes given to lofty declarations "that the principle of academic freedom is of supreme importance" and to affirmations of support for "free discussion without fear or favor." Yet, these presidents usually expected that professors would not be rash in discomforting any interests important to the school. Particularly at the smaller colleges, self-imposed restraint, much as Dewey had described it, was expected as part of gentlemanly conduct. That is what President Thwing of Western Reserve meant when he said of the professor: "Let him be a gentleman, and then let him have full freedom. If a teacher be not a gentleman, he is not worthy of his college position." On the whole, freedom in teaching was enhanced in this era, with the most prestigious universities at the forefront of this advance and the various smaller schools trailing somewhere behind. This development, as we have seen, occured amidst notable shifts in the character of the professor's authority and independence. For many professors, authority with regard to students still rested upon the understanding that they stood *in loco parentis* and imparted eternal verities broadly derived from Protestant Christianity and the classical curriculum. However, as the elective system—as well as the new ideas of higher education that found expression in that system—spread rapidly through American universities and colleges, the traditional view of college instructors was supplemented by a new image of the professor, who now assumed a position much closer to that of an expert. When many important truths could no longer be persuasively described as fixed, clear, or in any way self-evident but rather appeared to be increasingly impermanent, complex, and even obscure, then the professor, who was the investigator of changing truth (or was at least fully informed of the results of such investigations) acquired an exclusive or even a monopoly position in a field of knowledge from which he could command attention and intellectual deference.[42]

The professor's authority in university governance in this era grew significantly yet remained quite limited. In part those limitations reflected the fact that the domains in which the professor exercised authority—research and teaching—were not granted undisputed preeminence in higher education. The president, the trustees, the student body, and also the alumni (whose influence was growing at the end of the century) all had their stake and their say. The claim that education should be imminently useful, that it provide fun and games, that it not be too disruptive of society, and that it needed specially skillful economic management afforded justifications for circumscribing the professor's dominion. Moreover, the professor's appetite for authority was itself limited and delicate. Dewey complained that the ponderous machinery of university organization absorbed too much time and energy and distracted the professor from his primary tasks of research and teaching. Independence in these tasks was paramount, and authority in university governance took on importance principally as it protected or impinged upon that independence. Moreover, the leading professors of this era seem to have been a quirky lot who did not take easily to being drilled to even a common agreed-upon end. Put together on any sort of parade ground, they often went marching off in all directions, while their democratically elected sergeant bellowed helplessly.[43]

As a result, the professor transformed independence to autonomy. This set him apart, somewhat, from the self-employed professionals, for the professor's independence was exercised from a position of subordination. His independence did not mean complete freedom from external control but rather that the most essential commands that he obeyed he himself should give. The justification for giving those commands would not come from his own will or from the organization of which he was a part, but from exalted values beyond the reach of both. He would be largely self-directed and, at the same time, responsible. He would be sovereign and, at the same time, subject. This was the source of the dignity that was associated with the burgeoning profession of the professoriate.[44]

9

The Engineers:
A Profession in a
Business
Bureaucracy

In a staid magazine like *The American Engineer,* humor was something unexpected. The jocular article "Suggestive Seals" in the November 17, 1882 issue was therefore a surprising lapse in the general tenor of this usually technical, matter-of-fact, sober-minded journal. The drawings for this article were also odd. Most of the illustrations in *The American Engineer* were depictions of intricate machinery with sleek, metallic surfaces that afforded a pleasing sense of power and composure. The hasty pen sketches that illustrated "Suggestive Seals" were impetuous and fidgety, giving some inkling of the furtive tension beneath its jollying.[1]

"Suggestive Seals" reported that the Western Society of Engineers, newly incorporated in Chicago, had invited its members to submit designs for a society insignia. Among the proposed emblems were three humorous ones, all probably from the same artist, and *The American Engineer* decided to publish them with a few words of explanation. All three seals depicted the engineer bound in one way or another. In the first, the engineer, "ye modern martyr," was tied to a stake by various cords identified as corporations, ignorant directors, lack of appreciation, cheap work, "economy," and "would be C.E.'s" [Civil Engineers]. In the second seal, the engineer was skewered to the boot of "ye corporation" (clearly shown to be soleless) by a lance with a banner reading "small pay, cheap work, lack of appreciation." The third seal was a coat of arms showing a bloated "ye director," champagne bottle at his feet, facing a weazened "ye engineer," his feet entangled in measuring tape. Between these cartoon figures on this third seal was a divided shield with moneybags on the director's side and busy bees on the engineer's side. "Not a fair divide" read the banner beneath. Of course, it was a joke.[2]

Yet this joke gave voice to sentiments from the largest, most rapidly growing, and yet least audible segment of the engineering profession—the engineers who were lesser employees of large organizations. In a seemingly lighthearted way, the cartoons complained that the corporation subjugated these engineers, impaired their professional standing and esteem, and deprived them of just rewards. To understand such ranklings and to evaluate their significance properly, it would be helpful first to place them in the broader setting of the developments of engineering in the last decades of the nineteenth century. For in that era American engineering was transformed. Along with and linked to the growth in scientific knowledge and the expansion of business enterprise, engineering activity served to bring great changes into American life, and engineering itself was greatly changed in the process. It became more specialized and hierarchical, and it absorbed more thoroughly the traits and persuasions that had characterized the gentlemanly professions of the pre–Civil War era. Most striking was the fact that membership in the profession expanded rapidly and, at the same time, access to it became more restricted.[3]

The expansion in membership was linked directly to the growth of the economy, and the restriction of entry was tied to the growth of science and its application to engineering. The cluster of pre–Civil War engineers was, like that of college professors of that era, a mixed multitude. Men of differing social origins and disparate preparation could take up the work and shift easily in and out of the profession. Among those who built the pre–Civil War canals, bridges, mine shafts and stopes, power mills and steam engines were the graduates of West Point and Rensselaer Polytechnic Institute, and gentlemen amateurs with an interest in technology. However, greatly outnumbering these prominent practitioners were those who had entered the field through apprenticeships—men with little science and often with little formal education. Nomenclature reflected this fluidity. Before the 1880s, the distinction between engineer and mechanic was often vague, and the term engineer, itself, referred to machine tenders as well as to machine designers.[4]

The widespread application of science to technology in the last half of the nineteenth century drastically changed much of this. Those engineers who had a scientific and mathematical training seemed to have such a decided advantage over those without it that apprenticeship, which did not provide this training, could no longer readily serve as a path into the profession. The best places went to the graduates of the engineering schools. Of course, owing largely to the Morrill Act, the engineering schools and their graduates were multiplying. Yet success at those schools was limited to those students who had the required preliminary education as well as the income and cultural impetus to devote four years to such training. Entry into engineering was now much more likely to come from the middle rather than from the lower ranges of the social order. The accompanying technical changes in engineering practices were even more unmistakable and were often described as a shift from "rule of thumb" to rule of science. By the end of the century, a leading civil engineer could find no fact more curious than the fact that "up to fifty years ago, bridge building stood upon a purely empiric basis." Empiricism now meant incompetence. The engineer was still a practical man, but now he must be a practical theorist. Only in exceptional cases could personal experience or native genius take the place of systematic scientific training.[5]

Understandably, there were many who berated this change. Opposition to the increased emphasis upon school training came from mechanics, from those engineers who had successfully risen through the ranks to positions of authority without school training, from the gentlemen engineers who had learned their skills in even more informal ways, and even from college-trained engineers who found that new graduates were insisting upon more science and mathematics than the older college men had been taught. They found the new graduates "cheeky and lippy" and claimed that these graduates did not readily subordinate themselves. "Because they know some things better than their superiors," wrote one seasoned engineer, "they too often think they know all things better; or because they think they know all those things better which are taught in school, they belittle the knowledge of other things." In part, what was at stake was the clash between the usages and appraisals of the school and those of the shop, field, and mine where the graduate would make his life's work.[6]

A related but somewhat different clash, also linked to the growing importance of science in engineering, was the conflict between material and commercial efficiencies. Efficiency was one of the central concepts of engineering in the late nineteenth century, and the engineer dealt with two kinds. Material efficiency was the output/input ratio of matter or energy, while commercial efficiency was the relation of price to cost. Occasionally these efficiencies came into conflict. Because most engineers endeavored to produce goods and services that sold on a market, it was assumed that the requirements of the market would prevail. With the increased application of science to technology, however, questions of material efficiency took on a fascination of their own and provided scope for a type of ingenuity and intellection that did not always provide commercial benefit and reward.[7]

"There is such a genuine pleasure in pursuing and executing the exact, for its own sake, and striving to incorporate it into practice," wrote one of the editors of *The American Engineer*, "that there is a steady tendency of men not engaged in practice to forget that engineering implies dollars and cents." The engineer "engaged in practice," however, was expected to give up some of his enthusiasm for the alluring problems of material efficiency when they seemed to have no discernible economic payoff. He was admonished to accept the dictum that "the money test is a just and equitable one." This meant, implicitly, that the engineer was obliged to accept the belief that a capitalist system of ostensibly self-regulating markets was in general a productive one and that its results were, for the most part, moral. Yet, when a precise money test seemed not to be available, the productiveness of the market system seemed doubtful, or its outcomes not clearly moral, then engineers sometimes fell back upon notions of material efficiency, which after all were their own special areas of competence and excitement, for guidance.[8]

The engineer who designed long lasting public works, for example, could estimate present costs for structures of varying durability, but he could not easily judge the future demand for the services of those works. The coming generations of users, nevertheless, would be compelled to pay, in part, for those structures. In such instances, commercial efficiency became a murky notion. The engineers, in that situation, leaned toward notions of material efficiency, and that frequently meant choosing the most durable alternatives that were available. "These works," an eminent engineer wrote, should be "permanent in character." They should be designed, he explained somewhat cryptically, "for all time to come . . . insuring the greatest good for the greatest number in the present and succeeding generations of men."[9]

Since productiveness seemed to advance general well-being, and as material efficiency was one of the measurements and guides to productivity, material efficiency itself often turned out to be a good thing. This attitude had broad support in American culture. Of course, productivity was also tied to commercial efficiency. For the standard of commercial efficiency helped focus upon costs and profits, and increased productivity was one of the ways of lowering costs and raising profits. Yet, when profits seemed to be divorced from productiveness, as in speculation, then considerations of commercial efficiency became morally doubtful and perhaps even corrupting. This sentiment was evident not only among the critics of American society but among its staunchest defenders as well. The editors of *Bankers Magazine,* for example, argued that "speculation does not add to the nation's wealth" and, therefore, should be condemned as a form of gambling. In speculation, as in gambling, one man's gain was simply another's loss, and this stood in contrast to productive business enterprise which brought benefits to almost all. Andrew Carnegie, the illustrious business hero of the era, often expressed a similar view. Furthermore, when considerations of commercial efficiency actually blocked productivity, as in the case of some monopolies, then even the conservative *Commercial and Financial Chronicle* objected. A monopoly device like the patent system, which promoted technological development, won widespread approval, particularly among engineers. Yet when it appeared that some corporations were buying up patents and burying them in order to maintain profits, or that others drew upon chicanery to make up for their lack of technical knowledge and to cheat poor inventors, then these corporations roused the wrath and despair of many engineers. At such times, "the weight of moneybags" seemed to be destructive of both industrial advance and justice.[10]

Most engineers saw no necessary conflict between material and commercial efficiency, yet they looked to technological improvements as the primary source of economic progress. "The profits of the new epoch" announced the president of the American Society of Civil Engineers, "must be made, not by buying cheap and selling dear, but by reducing the cost of production. . . . permanent success will depend not on commercial drummers, but on the civil engineer. . . . The sharp mercantile spirit must gradually go down." One prominent engineer predicted that the day was coming when the leading economists would erect a monument to honor "the man who above all others contributed the means for obtaining the wealth of nations," James Watt; and then they would burn their treatises and disquisitions.[11]

The chief significance of the occasional divergence between commercial and material efficiency for the engineer was that it provided an entry point for a leavening of precapitalist, anticommercial sentiments that had been attached to the gentlemanly professions. It encouraged a detachment from commercial goals. "The engineer does not work only for pelf" explained Robert H. Thurston, first president of the American Society of Mechanical Engineers (ASME). Of course, one of the key words in that assertion was *only*. For Thurston, like many engineers, often had a deep respect for the achievements of honest and productive business enterprise and usually considered such firms a resource rather than a threat. Nonetheless, he had imbibed a sense of high purpose that seemed to flow from scientific endeavors, and such purpose separated him even from those businessmen whom he esteemed. Pecuniary gain should not be the only motive for engineering work, rather the love of the work, in part for its own sake and in part for the sake of the great social beneficence it bestowed, must also be a motive. Work, therefore, was restored with moral purpose. One of Thurston's favorite quotes was Louis Agassiz's pronouncement "I cannot affort to give my time to making money." Such a rising above cupidity was important for Thurston, and men like him who were among the founders of the engineering societies in the late nineteenth century, but it could be accomplished only by those who already stood at an appropriate elevation. Men who could not afford to give their time to making money were those who were somehow assured of having enough money to give their time to other purposes and things. Moral purpose and the various restrictions upon entry into engineering that enabled a professional to look forward to a competence, sufficent income for comfortable living, were therefore inextricably entwined.[12]

When engineers in the late nineteenth century remarked that science had transformed engineering from a trade into a profession, they probably had in mind many things—the setting aside of traditional ways in the workplace; the recognition of technical ingenuity; the regard for material productivity and its precedence when the requirements of the market seemed to be unclear, wasteful, or iniquitous; and the replenishment of the moral purpose of work. But they most often used this phrase to expressly refer to the fact that engineering now rested upon a growing and yet restrictive body of knowledge that only fellow practitioners could properly appraise and advance. The professional society, with its technical meetings, discussions, and publications, was the institutional recognition of that fact. The number of such engineering societies multiplied rapidly in the 1880s and 1900s, and by the end of the century, the four national "founder societies" of civil, mining, mechanical, and electrical engineers had emerged and had come to look upon themselves as spokesmen for the profession as a whole.[13]

The constitutions of these societies disclosed those elements of traditional professionalism that took on importance for engineers. The profession was defined by its exclusive knowledge, its positions of authority, and its social beneficence. Though each of the national associations evolved its own series of ranks of membership, all set up a special professional rank that prescribed technical competence for admittance. Membership in the professional rank also required that the engineer hold a post of command. The Civil Engineering Society, for example, stipulated that a professional member should be "in charge of some work in the capacity or rank of Superintending Engineer, as the term is now understood." The preambles of these constitutions usually described the social beneficence of the profession, often in vague terms, and that beneficence was set forth more fully, if not less vaguely, in the ceremonial presidential addresses and the other exhortative orations that frequently appeared in the proceedings of the societies.[14]

It would be a mistake to consider those addresses as *merely* ceremonial, although ceremonial they surely were. For these addresses provided a necessary persuasion such as never follows simply from social position. They preached the moral purpose of work in a social order that increasingly appraised work chiefly in terms of its exchange value. They preached a professional self-respect that stirred the associations to a spirited assertiveness and left its mark upon the diverse endeavors of the societies in this era. In present-day lingo, these ceremonies were "consciousness-raising," giving rise to an invigorating pride and, on occasion, like modern consciousness-raising, to an overweening pride. Commodore Benjamin F. Isherwood (ex-Engineer-in-Chief of the U.S. Navy), speaking before the Association of Mechanical Engineers assembled, insisted that "of all professions, the most important is engineering. It is the only productive profession. In comparison with what the engineers have done for the race, the achievements of poets, artists, priests, lawyers, soldiers, doctors, writers and statesmen seem insignificant. . . . the labors of modern engineering are responsible for bringing man out of 'the dark ages'." While some of his listeners surely thought that the commodore had gone a bit overboard, they probably felt that there was more than a sprinkling of truth in what he said.[15]

Such preachments, moreover, were often joined to appeals for collegiality and esprit de corps. Self-esteem was intricately linked with mutual esteem, particularly in the increasingly selective engineering societies. "Every honorable professional associate should receive the highest degree of respect and courtesy at the hands of every other . . . [for] the good opinion of professional brethren is more important than that of the public. Sooner or later the public endorses professional opinion." The man who worked alone, without measuring himself by others, never did his best, yet the upshot of emulation was not wasting rivalry but rather professional brotherhood. The body of scientific knowledge that engineers shared provided an assured basis for such professional brotherhood. "The best work is never done by separate men," wrote the president of the American Society of Civil Engineers, "it is only accomplished when professional knowledge so permeates all the members of the profession that the work of one is virtually the work of all."[16]

If professional knowledge, as many believed, also divided engineers, then those divisions based upon specialized knowledge were clearly acceptable. Market forces, moreover, seem to have been as important for that specialization as the growth of engineering science. The actual historical development of engineering divisions paralleled more closely the growth of new markets than the growth of new knowledge. In fact, the evolution of engineering specialities affords its own particular account of the development of the American economy.

The civil engineers—when still a loose grouping of practitioners differentiated from the military engineers principally by the condition of being civilians—were the builders of the roads, canals, and railroads that formed the basis of America's "transportation revolution" of the nineteenth century. The mining engineers, the first to break from the body of civil engineers, were not impelled primarily by new knowledge but rather by the opportunity to do mining work exclusively. The prosperity of the booming mining industry had been made possible by the transportation revolution. For access to cheap transportation in the handling of bulky shipments often meant the difference between a profitable and an unprofitable mine. The expanding mine industry, in turn, supplied the inexpensive fuel and metals for the growing manufacturing industry, where the mechanical engineers, the next secession, found their employment. Perhaps new scientific advances were more important to the electrical engineers, the last major division within nineteenth century engineering, than to earlier specialities; however, much of that science had been available for quite a while, and the demand for more convenient forms of power and illumination by the manufacturing industries and the cities that grew up around them provided an impetus for the development of that knowledge.[17]

Expanding new markets for engineering work, therefore, created enlarged opportunities for practitioners and for specialization, just as Adam Smith had taught. The expanded markets also brought with them a new precariousness and the insecurity of unregulated competition, leading to specialization in ways that Adam Smith overlooked. "The adoption of specialties in any particular profession" explained an engineering editor "decreases the evils of competition for it tends to establish a real fellowship and a healthy Free Masonry in the profession. . . . Competition is narrowed down to the same class of specialists in any given profession, and the number of these will be limited to the demand for their service." This specialization encouraged a cohesiveness and a cooperativeness among sellers, in contrast to the buyers, who usually remained separated, divergent, and therefore comparatively ineffectual in creating favorable market conditions. Specialization might allow for some control of entry into the field, and more generally it could promote the development of oblique monopoly powers.[18]

By the end of the century, most engineers identified themselves within one of the four principal specialties and with their standing in the gradations that developed rapidly within these specialties. It would be worthwhile to examine these specialties somewhat closely—and particularly to examine the national organizations that gave them leadership, coherence, and self-awareness—and then to give attention to those divisions that cut across all the specialties. Civil engineering was unique and paradoxical in that some of its leading spokesmen denied that it was a specialty at all. They insisted instead that civil engineering was all engineering done by those who were not soldiers. This was an afterimage of the pre–Civil War era in American engineering. One of the most distinguished presidents of the American Society of Civil Engineers (ASCE) claimed that his organization was simply "the leading engineering society of America" and that all specialties should belong to it. It differed from other engineering societies, he argued, primarily in that its membership standards were higher. Such pretensions were evident in two hotly contested decisions that the society took in this era. It rejected Carnegie's gift of a free headquarters building to house the four "founder societies" in luxurious surroundings, and it turned back an attempt to incorporate local societies into the national organization. The first proposal would have recognized the parity of all the national engineering societies, and the second would have given more influence to the less distinguished and less prosperous engineers who were readily accepted in local organizations.[19]

By the 1890s, however, the turning of various engineers to their separate and distinctive associations had clearly transformed civil engineering organizations into societies largely for those engineers who constructed public works, railroads, and commercial buildings. Nevertheless, civil engineering organizations remained unusual and unique owing to the high proportion of consultants in their ranks. This gave these societies a closer resemblance to the associations of the traditional self-employed professionals than organizations of other engineering specialties and prompted the civil engineers to try to adapt themselves more closely to the honorific professional notions and practices. In no other branch of engineering were the preeminence of science, the importance of professional authority, and the social beneficence of engineering work preached more ardently than among the civil engineers.[20]

If among all the branches of engineering, the civil engineers lauded professional ideals the most, then clearly the mining engineers esteemed such notions the least. Many mining engineers were part-time businessmen who speculated in mining stocks or who tried to build their fortunes from the sale of mining property or the promotion of mining companies. Even the young mining engineers were quickly educated to the enterprising spirit by the unusually high fees that often came their way. In an industry where profits could be very chancy, scrimping on engineering fees was not worth the effort and could be self-defeating. High fees and venturous spirit brought American mining engineers to distant places—south of the Rio Grande, north to the Yukon, to the Transvaal, and even to Australia. Such exciting and glamorous activity did not lend itself readily to a restraint upon cupidity or to a sense of social responsibility.[21]

The mining industry of the era comprised two quite different types of enterprise—first, the coal and iron mines that were usually exploited in a methodical fashion and were frequently controlled by well-established business interests, often in vertically integrated organizations; and second, the nonferrous metal mines (gold, silver, copper, zinc) that were highly speculative and still open to all sorts of men-on-the-make with risk capital. One historian claims that the nonferrous mining business of this era can best be understood as a type of lottery. The American Institute of Mining Engineers (AIME) exhibited the tight central control characteristic of the leading iron and coal companies and yet allowed for an ease of access much like the rough-and-tumble enterprise in the Western nonferrous mining. In the AIME, these traits reinforced each other. The close management of the institute permitted its leaders to be easygoing about the qualifications for membership. Rossiter W. Raymond, who served as secretary for over a generation, preserved all the governmental forms of nomination and election of presidents, vice-presidents, and councils; nevertheless, he had an unusual influence upon all outcomes. The constitution, which Raymond wrote, accepted mine owners and operators as associate members, granting them many of the privileges of practicing engineers. Raymond, himself both a distinguished engineer and a coal company executive, saw to it that Abram S. Hewit, a prominent iron manufacturer, twice served as president of the institute. Although a formal distinction between engineers and others remained, one of the principal goals of the organization was to bring into harmonious and mutually helpful relation the various interests in the mining and metallurgy industry.[22]

Labor was excluded from that accord. It is remarkable that in such a hazardous industry as mining—with a history punctuated by so many terrible disasters (well-informed observers protested that sending the workers into the mines was sending them into the jaws of death)—that Raymond, the foremost spokesman of mining engineers in this era, could insist that no regulation was necessary and that the enlightened self-interest of owners would provide all the necessary protections. Of course, some notable mining engineers, like Robert P. Rothwell, did raise such issues as labor welfare, conservation, and even free silver. But Raymond usually kept subjects of that sort out of Institute meetings. The Institute, under his direction, seemed to reduce the meaning of a profession to that of a scientific business and the notion of a professional society to that of a technical trade association.[23]

The mechanical engineers were spared the blandishments and dangers of close ties to any one particular industry or group of industries. The power-driven machines that provided the demand for the skills of the mechanical engineers spread rapidly to all American manufacturing in the late nineteenth century. Between 1880 and 1900, mechanical power used in manufacturing more than tripled. The steam engine was the principal source of this power, and the application of science to those heat engines gave impetus to the increase of industrial productivity and to the high spirits of the mechanical engineers as well. "Man as a prime mover" commented Robert H. Thurston, one of the founders of the American Society of Mechanical Engineers, "is feeble and helpless before the great powers of nature; man as the master and guide of nature's power is only less than omnipotent."[24]

The growth of power-driven machines brought with it the rapid expansion of the factory system. Within the factory of this era, most of the machines could be run from one source of power and the burdensome transportation of materials at various stages of production could be diminished. That meant great gains in efficiency and productivity. Gathering machines to one place also meant gathering workers, and the factory system, therefore, afforded yet another source of productivity: labor discipline. This was the irony behind Thurston's grandiloquence. Scientific industrialism undoubtedly did bestow new power and scope upon Man the producer; however upon most of the men who were the producers it conferred new restraints and limitations. The factory was the setting for the work of the mechanical engineer, and he undertook to introduce greater efficiency through mechanical improvements, coordination of operations, and labor discipline.[25]

The most celebrated mechanical engineer of this era who entered upon all those tasks was Frederick W. Taylor. He was unsparing and innovative in each of them. Taylor helped develop high speed steel in order to increase the output of the machine shop, he devised numerous techniques of routing and accounting in order to integrate the flow of work in the factory, and he originated time and motion studies in order to permit greater control of the worker's exertion and workmanship. Taylor envisioned the factory and all its employees as one complex machine that could be made to perform with increased efficiency. Underlying his vision were two important principles: that all work could be transformed through the application of science, and that the men who did the work could not understand its science and must be guided by the engineer who did. This was a new legitimation of the engineer's position of being "in responsible charge of the work." The engineer held his authority not simply as a representative of ownership but rather as a scientific organizer of productivity. Such authority had serious implications not only for the worker but for employees on the other levels of the organizational hierarchy as well. The most radical disciples of Taylor would later turn their authority against ownership itself.[26]

The very coherence and aspiration of Taylor's vision made it quite unlike that of the other mechanical engineers who took up similar tasks. Taylor willy-nilly begot something that none of the others would produce, that is, an *ism*. Nevertheless, in their less resolute and systematic way, many other mechanical engineers moved from the efficiency of machines, to factory coordination and labor discipline. Holbrook Fitz-John Porter, for example, who had been at Bethlehem Steel when Taylor was working out his system there, developed a type of industrial management that diverged significantly from Taylor's. His technical innovations— new methods for making steel forgings and nickle steels—as well as his cost accounting system to coordinate factory performance, paralleled Taylor's work. However, his device for labor discipline— the setting up of shop committees with employee representation in order to enlist the workers' intelligence, enthusiasm, and co- operation—denied some of Taylor's essential principles and helped provide a countervailing style to Taylor's in industrial en- gineering. With a more restricted sense of science, a broader sense of the worker's resources, and beneath it all a more ingen- uous sense of paternalism, Porter's industrial management was a more typical specimen of what mechanical engineers would come up with. This unique sort of productivity, the making of industrial management systems, was in keeping with the large number of the elite of mechanical engineers who held executive and superintendent positions in industry during this era.[27]

The American Institute of Electrical Engineers (AIEE) was the last of the four founder societies to be established, and it seemed to recapitulate some of the varying characteristics of the engi- neering societies that had preceded it. Like all of them, the elec- trical engineers developed a professional awareness in part to dis- tinguish themselves from an indiscriminate body of mechanics, in this case the "electricians," who, with little formal training, did much of the operative work that kept the electrical machinery running. Such a separation was easiest for the electrical engi- neers, for, of all the branches of engineering, electrical engineer- ing had a scientific basis that was the most esoteric and baffling to the unschooled mechanic. Even among the knowledgable en- gineers, "The electrical engineer" wrote Robert H. Thurston, "finds application for mathematics, for the sciences, for refined and elaborate construction, in a greater degree than perhaps any other member of the profession of engineering." The electrical en- gineering curricula originated in departments of physics rather than in the schools of engineering, and the president of the In- stitute of Electrical Engineers in 1895, Louis Duncan, bran- dished a Ph.D., the first such president of any of the national societies.[28]

Paradoxically, though the proportion of college-bred engineers in this branch was much higher than that of all the other spe- cialties, the most widely known and celebrated practitioner in electrical engineering of the era had come to his fame and for- tune with less than three months of formal schooling. This was Thomas Alva Edison. Beginning as a telegraph operator, with little theory and much ingenuity, Edison bounded ahead from invention to invention, to growing popular adulation. The telegraph and telephone benefited from his improvements, but he truly demonstrated his knack of making science pay off in his work with the phonograph and the incandescent lamp. During the eighties and early nineties he turned to the generating and distributing of electric power, heat, and light. To the scientific engineer, Edison was a prodigy and something of an embarrassment. Edison himself was sometimes bewildered by his success. "If you want to know anything about electricity," he told his secretary, "go out to the galvanometer room and ask Kennelly [his physicist]. He knows far more about it than I do. In fact, I've come to the conclusion that I never did know anything about it."[29]

There were many electrical engineers who heartily agreed with that. For much of their self-esteem and satisfaction came from their proficiency in an increasingly abstrust discipline of electrotechnology. Some of the aloofness seen in the national civil engineers association was discernible in the newly formed national association of electrical engineers. However, the electrical engineers trusted to the exacting scientific requirements of their field, rather than to stiff membership requirements, to preserve their distinctiveness. In fact, their organizational structure resembled that of the mining engineers, in that the AIEE accepted as associates a large number of auxiliary members who were commercially interested in the field. They clearly intended to keep the professional engineer on top, however, and depended upon the esoteric nature of their work to accomplish that. The AIEE also escaped many of the tendencies of a trade association, because one such association already existed, the National Electric Light Association, consisting largely of public utility executives and engineers.[30]

Electrical engineering also had an affinity for large-scale enterprise in a manner somewhat comparable to that of mechanical engineering. Within the factory itself, electricity actually lessened the technological requirements of centralization. The divisibility of electricity allowed the manager to place power directly into the tool that the operative used, much to Taylor's regret, for Taylor thought that this impaired the influence of central direction. Yet for the industry as a whole, technological considerations of electrical engineering encouraged consolidation. Those holding patents on part of the rapidly growing and yet interconnected electrical technology could block the manufacture of a wide range of products, and their competitors, who often held equally strategic patents, could check them in return. In addition, where entry of new firms was easy, low prices and "chaotic conditions" generated a desire to "stabilize" the industry. In 1880 the electrical industry was populated by an assortment of bustling scientific inventor-entrepreuners, but by 1900 the industry was dominated by two major companies, Westinghouse and General Electric. This shift was reflected in the membership of the American Institution of Electrical Engineers, where inventors and entrepreneurs in its leadership gave way to administrators and executives of large corporations. More elaborate rankings also appeared.[31]

That shift highlighted changes affecting all branches of engineering in varying degrees. Divisions appeared within each of the branches, and engineers increasingly identified themselves not only by specialty but also by their position within it. The membership of the national association made up only a small minority of all engineers—the more successful part of the profession—yet, even within these associations, the leadership set about to establish more distinct rankings during this era. Such gradations were thought to be based upon competence, and formal recognition of competence was seen as purification. "Purification of the professional atmosphere," wrote one engineering editor, "the recognition of the status of several grades of engineers among themselves and before the public," would give engineers a new self-respect and more respect from the public, and would therefore elevate the profession as a whole. Moreover, ranks based upon competence were broadly acceptable because it was assumed that the capable and the qualified, wherever they might start from, would inevitably rise to the top, and that this was efficacious and just.[32]

Ranks in the engineering societies, however, also paralleled ranks in the world of work. Full membership in the societies was reserved for those "in positions of responsible change." There were four paths to positions of authority for engineers. They could rise to ownership of industrial firms, to executive positions in the bureaucracies of the great corporations, to professorships in the faculties of the engineering colleges, and finally to that special eminence as independent consulting engineers whose claim to authority rested exclusively upon their engineering expertise. For some engineers, these paths were not mutually exclusive. William Kent, a mechanical engineer of the era, shifted from management, to ownership, to education, to consulting, and then back again. But clearly, Kent was exceptional, and such shifts became even more unusual as the nineteenth century drew to a close.[33]

Rising to positions of ownership also became unusual by the late nineteenth century. The production of standardized machinery came to be the work of the large corporations; this required considerable investments of capital and often resulted in a shift of ownership and control to the major suppliers of the capital. Even in venturous Western mining, controlling ownership by engineers became increasingly infrequent. A study of the membership of the American Institute of Mining Engineering (AIME) in the nineties, claimed that less than six percent could be considered owners of businesses. As opportunities for ownership in technical industries declined for engineers, however, their chances for management positions seemed to increase. The same study listed almost a quarter of the ASME membership as executives and superintendents, and the percentage in the AIEE was even higher.[34]

By the end of the nineteenth century, some engineers in managerial positions were in search of an outlook that would distinguish the responsibilities of management from those of ownership. Because he believed that the relations between owners and managers of the corporations "have not been settled," engineer George S. Morison, after serving over a decade as a railroad manager, took it upon himself to sketch out what he thought those relations should be. The managers were a third category, he argued, not to be completely identified with either owners or workers, but rather to be empowered to act as a trustee for both. Management did have primary responsibilities to owners, but like trustees, the managers must not always bend to the will of ownership. If they invariably acquiesced to complete distributions of profits, for example, the managers would not be fulfilling their responsibilities. Moreover they had duties toward the workers as well. Management must see to it that the workmen were competent, that they were cared for, and that they shared in the benefits of increased productivity to which they contributed. Robert H. Thurston, who also had served as a manager at one point in his career, thought that labor unions might serve a legitimate purpose in compelling fair treatment and restraining tyrannizing employers. More commonly, however, it was the manager who was expected to preserve fairness by bringing something like a professional perspective to industry, by giving ownership and labor not what they wanted but what they needed.[35]

The pull of professional ideals was also evident among the teachers of engineering in the various colleges and universities. As entry into engineering became largely restricted to those with a technical education, the engineering professors, though few in number, took on a new importance. They could not only wield some control over entry into the field but they could have a decided influence upon the varying ingredients of engineering training. Yet teachers of engineering, as well as their students, were something of an anomaly in the late nineteenth century colleges and universities. While other professors were increasingly assuming the attitudes of professionals and acquiring Ph.D.s as honorific designation of that status, the professor of engineering was usually a man without a Ph.D. or any graduate education, who came to his post from industry or directly from undergraduate studies. Similarly, while many college students looked upon their undergraduate work as instruction in a broad, gentlemanly culture preliminary to professional training, the engineering student was a collegian who was given over to the inculcation of technical skills, and who was provided with little opportunity for liberal cultivation. The unsuccessful attempt on the part of some of the leading engineering professors to raise engineering studies to the level of a graduate program calls attention both to the influence of professional aspirations and to some of the difficulties that impeded them.[36]

One of those difficulties was the fact that the engineering societies took little interest in raising educational standards or in any deliberate effort to restrict entry into the profession at this time. The market for engineers was booming, and the increase in numbers did not seem to be troublesome, at least in the upper reaches of the profession, from which the leadership of the national societies was recruited. The engineering executives were buyers of engineering labor and had no interest in restricting its supply. The engineering students, themselves, wanted to keep their education as inexpensive as possible yet serviceable enough to allow them to get ahead in the engineering world. Even some of the professors of engineering expressed concern about "dry[ing] up their business" with overly severe requirements. The curriculum would be rigorous enough, but it would be completely useful. A number of engineers complained that the sense of the useful had become too narrow, that particulars that could be learned on the job were taught—making the transition from school to work easier—but that fundamentals were neglected. Yet, in general, there was little conflict of interest between educators and the rest of the profession, and the scope and development of engineering education was left largely to the professors themselves.[37]

If engineering education was not to be a graduate study, nevertheless some of the most prominent professors hoped that the engineering school would become a center for original investigations. This was in keeping with the professional ideal of their academic colleagues. Much exhortation was expended in this direction, but the results were not impressive. Here again the insistence upon usefulness encouraged the most narrow sense of usefulness. During the last half of the nineteenth century most of the fundamental engineering innovations and original contributions were the work of Europeans. The American professors did, however, keep up with the latest discoveries and help disseminate them to industry and government; for many professors supplemented their salaries through an extensive consulting practice, and keeping up with the latest innovations was an important part of that job. As for the advance of professional interests within engineering, perhaps the most important work of the professors took the form of preachments to their students. Instruction upon the ideals of the engineering profession readily found its way into the curriculum. If such teaching was often somewhat vague and inflated, nevertheless it reiterated significant themes: that science had transformed engineering from a craft into a profession; that the new effectiveness of engineering brought with it a new authority and responsibility; and that the unique and prepossessing quality of the work made it elevated, beneficent, and work that could be loved for its own sake.[38]

It was the full-time consultants, nevertheless, who were the principal advocates of professional ideals among the engineers. While, as has been mentioned, the civil engineers were preeminent in arguing for professionalism, this was linked to the fact that there was a high proportion of consultants among them. The champions of professionalism in the other branches of engineering were usually consultants as well. Again, the resemblance in economic circumstances of the consultant to the self-employed professional encouraged the consultants to propose the adoption of professional usages which also served as market control devices—codes of ethics, higher membership standards, and even minimum fee bills. These engineers stood outside of bureaucracies and dealt with clients rather than employers. The relative independence of that position was important. The consultant claimed that he provided his client with disinterested advice and assistance. When the demands of the client conflicted with the engineer's expertise or his sense of right and wrong, he was urged to disregard those demands. "The engineer cannot sell his independence," one consultant explained, for it was intrinsic to his professional status. Some consultants questioned whether engineers who were subordinates could truly be professionals, and one proposed that the only way to raise the professional standing of engineers was to increase the proportion of consultants among them.[39]

While his market position within his specialty, as a member of a rather cohesive group of sellers confronting often a relatively scattered and disparate group of buyers, lent support to the independent position of the consultant, his scientific knowledge provided yet another basis for such standing. Here independence shaded into authority—exemption from command into the right to command. The authority of the engineer who rose to a top position in a large corporation owed something to the rights of ownership; the authority of a consulting engineer rested more conspicuously upon his scientific knowledge. That knowledge gave him access to the great forces of nature, those "physical laws of power and strength [that] are mathematically exact and admit no trifling." When a consulting engineer gave directions, it was not with regard to his own will, ostensibly, but in obedience to "the corrective touch of physical nature." Such obedience provided the measure of his rightful powers and the basis of deference to his judgment.[40]

It also enlarged the extent of his benefactions. The notion that the application of science to industry gave rise to an immense increase in material productivity and that progress in higher culture rested upon that productivity was almost a commonplace in late nineteenth century America. However the most exaggerated forms of this belief were to be found among the consultants, and, of course, they stressed the role of the engineer in the unfolding of this great drama of human ascendence. It was to the engineering profession "that the world must look for nearly all future advances in civilization." The engineer was "the best corrector of human depravity . . . because he must deal with conditions, while others may deal with symptoms." He will bring about a new epoch that will gather all the races of the globe together, free them from delusions which held back men in the past, break down national divisions, and make humanity a single, great whole, "working intelligently in ways and for ends which we cannot yet understand." The engineer would be the priest of this new epoch, "a priest without superstitions."[41]

Making independence, authority, and social beneficence of such importance to professional status created difficulties for the largest and most rapidly growing segment in the engineering profession—those employed in subordinate positions in large organizations. Their independence and authority could hardly measure up to that of the consultants (nor to that of the engineers in executive positions, nor even to that of the professors of engineering) and whatever public beneficence could be ascribed to their work was closely linked to the particular product of their firm (and therefore often much like the social benefits generally attributed to commercial enterprise). Salaried engineers in subordinate positions shared the title and some of the technical knowledge of the other strata of the profession and also absorbed some of the aspirations of those more elevated strata. Yet the conditions of work of the engineers in subordinate positions were likely to disappoint such aspirations.[42]

Some of that disappointment was evident in the article "Suggestive Seals" printed in *The American Engineer* for 17 November 1882. If we return to that article and view it in the light of what we know about the circumstances and aspirations of the profession as a whole, the meaning of the emblems becomes clearer, and "Suggestive Seals," therefore, more suggestive. Some of the details of the three cartoons indicate that the artist was most likely a low-ranking civil engineer employed by a railroad. Railroads were the first of America's large-scale corporations and among the first to develop the techniques and observances of bureaucratic business enterprise that later spread to much of American industry. The expansion of the railroad system in an earlier day had allowed engineers to rise rapidly into executive positions, but in the era of consolidation at the end of the century, fewer such positions were available. The engineering departments of this era typically consisted of one chief engineer, a few assistants, and thirty to forty draftsmen who need not be trained engineers at all. Promotion in those departments was increasingly difficult. If a young engineer wished to rise to a top position in the railroads, one writer suggested, his best bet was to get out of the technical departments as soon as possible and to move into supervisory work; he must shift from "staff," where he utilized his technical training and where his authority rested upon his scientific knowledge, to "line," where nontechnical talents were uppermost and authority was delegated from ownership.[43]

Such daunting considerations, along with counteractive professional aspirations (acquired from engineers who worked in much more favorable conditions) were reflected in "Suggestive Seals." The artist depicted the engineer as a somewhat emaciated Prometheus, bound, skewered, and entangled by a series of restraints that were illustrated in sharp, finicky, discursive detail. The foremost restraint was the corporation itself, with its concentration of powers and operations and its impersonality. The

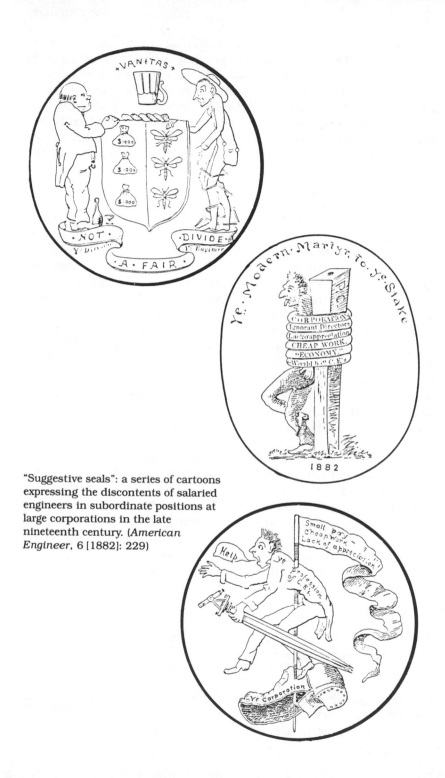

"Suggestive seals": a series of cartoons expressing the discontents of salaried engineers in subordinate positions at large corporations in the late nineteenth century. (*American Engineer*, 6 [1882]: 229)

directors who presided over the corporations and over the engineer's work were also portrayed as encumbrances. The artist labeled them "ignorant" directors, who, despite their lack of understanding, held the right to command, and who took for themselves an unfair share of the rewards—or at least so one of the cartoons alleged. More important, however, was the fact that these directors imposed the standard of discipline in the corporation, which the cartoons pictured as yet another separate and distinct constricting cord holding the engineer captive. This was economy, or rather "economy." The cartoonist placed quotation marks about the word to argue that it was a specious economy that the director often required; and perhaps also that it was shortsighted and complicated by an occasional conflict between commercial and material efficiency. Nonetheless, economy, as the directors interpreted it, was the almighty standard of discipline. The overriding purpose of the firm was the making of profits, and to that end (singular, distinct, and calculable), everything and everyone was required to submit.[44]

The engineer depicted in the cartoons felt vexations not only from above but also from below. For the sake of "economy," the directors often hired "would-be" engineers, whom the artist pictured as yet another fetter. The would-bes were apprentices or self-styled engineers, without college training, who took up the simpler tasks or rote work that might be split off from the engineer's job. To the college-bred engineers of this era these would-bes were incompetents or vain pretenders, and in order to drive such "quacks" from the field some of those college-bred engineers entered upon a campaign for the licensing of engineering practitioners that in later years would meet with substantial success.[45]

However, much more harmful than these cheap engineers was the cheap work (represented in the cartoons as yet another impediment) that the legitimate engineer himself was called upon to do. This cheap work was not work that paid little; small pay was portrayed separately. Cheap work, rather, was inferior work that afforded little pride or satisfaction, and as such was too much like the tasks given to the apprentices or even the ordinary laborers. The complaint against cheap work can be best understood in the context of those orations on the greatness, importance, distinction, renown, nobility, beneficence, and so on, of the profession of engineering that were heard at the meetings and appeared in the journals of the professional societies. For recurrent in such orations was distinction between designing and performing. Designing, clearly part of the engineer's job, was mental work that required a breadth of knowledge and vision in order to be most successful. It was often linked to high position, and the designer himself could not be closely supervised and directed. The work of design, therefore, reified social relations of nonconstraint, and was work to which the engineer felt he was entitled because of his science and proficiency. Cheap work, by contrast, was almost devoid of intellectual scope and was subject to close and degrading supervision.[46]

Significantly, the most often repeated complaint of these cartoons was also the most immaterial. This was the complaint over the "lack of appreciation." There was much to suggest that this lament was deeply felt. Behind it one can again hear the echoes of the professional society ceremonial oratory and more particularly those declamations that admonished the engineer to preserve his self-regard. Yet how could the engineer who was an employee of the corporation maintain his proper self-regard if the corporation and its directors did not recognize his due worth. If they did not grant authority, at least let them allow for honor. Of course, there was a gesture of deference in this complaint, for it recognized the corporation and its directors as appropriate sources for the bestowal of honor—and a much diminished honor at that. There was only the slightest hint of honor as an autonomous code of behavior in these cartoons. What remained was honor as esteem (or prestige, that increasingly fashionable term just losing its etymological connotation of something illusory). In actuality, by the early years of the twentieth century, when growing numbers of large firms began to rationalize their organizational structures, prestige would be the easiest thing to grant young engineers. However, in the 1880s, "lack of appreciation" was a vehement issue.[47]

For all the disappointment and resentment that these cartoons disclose, they do not indicate that the salaried engineers set themselves at defiance. Their tone certainly suggests something else. There is nothing truculent or implacable about the cartoons. They are complaints and not protests; they try to affect a lighthearted humor that half accedes to what it opposes. They do reveal the vexations of engineers in the lower ranks of corporate organizations who tried to assume the bearings of engineers more favorably placed. However, they also suggest that under improving circumstances these engineers might readily swallow some of their discontent and make the best of their situation.

There were several improving circumstances, some peculiar to the era and others of more lasting importance, that encouraged the low-ranking salaried engineer to come to terms with the corporation and its directors. Foremost was the ringing promise that the engineer who knew his stuff and was no slouch would rise out of the lower ranks to more commanding and rewarding positions as an executive, consultant, or perhaps even an owner. Those not moving up, moreover, could often move out, or at least threaten to do so. Engineers, like professors, used the invisible hand of the growing market demand for their skills to lighten the weight of the visible hand of bureaucratic management upon them. The fragmentary evidence that we have regarding the careers of engineers in this era shows many of them on the move from organization to organization.[48]

One of the immediate circumstances of the last quarter of the nineteenth century that allowed those low-ranking, salaried engineers who seemed to be immobile to more readily accept that condition was the promise of the patent system. Today it is not easy to appreciate the excitement and imaginings that patents stirred among engineers of that era. The astonishing outpouring of inventions in metallurgy, mechanics, and electricity fed hopes of fame and fortune or, at least, of independence within the organization in which the engineer was employed. The patent system also fostered such hopes, for it seemed to be on the side of the little man. According to the patent law rules of that day, if an engineer made or perfected a discovery while an employee, his employer could use it in his own business but had no further rights in it. The invention, so the law stipulated, was the property of its inventor. By the early twentieth century, however, employers easily circumvented such rules by making the signing over of patent rights a condition of employment.[49]

Of more long-range importance in making a subordinate position agreeable was the fact that the engineer was eventually granted greater esteem, independence, and security than the mass of the employed who made up the surrounding work force. Although his independence could not measure up to that of an executive or a consultant, yet the supervision of his work was frequently loose and indirect in comparison to that of the workmen who ranked below him. The pressures of professional ideals within the bureaucracy often granted to the engineer some control over his own work, "which nothing but intelligent knowledge gives." Like the independence of the professor, this condition is more accurately described as autonomy, for it involved obedience to rules beyond the sway of one's immediate superiors. The salaried engineer of the late nineteenth century helped develop those conventions of the workplace that became associated with "white collar" status and provided at least the bearing of self-possession and prestige despite his actual subordinate position. The etiquette of payment reflected this. The engineer received a monthly salary instead of the weekly (sometimes daily) wage of the laborer. This monthly salary not only indicated the more comfortable situation that its amount made possible, and a greater security of employment, but also a disjoining of payment from closely supervised performance. This modicum of autonomy and prestige were the significant indications of the professional status of the low-ranking engineer within the bureaucracy. His position was subordinate, but he did not consider it subservient.[50]

Both engineers and professors could trace the origins of their callings far back into the past, yet, as cohesive and effective professions, both occupations came of age in the late nineteenth century, an era of large-scale organization. Many of the practitioners of these two professions worked within such organizations and endeavored to maintain the authority and independence of the traditional professions in these new settings. For the engineers, an important aid in their efforts was the presence within their professional organizations of a unique group of practitioners, the consultants, whose economic situation closely resembled that of the traditional, self-employed professionals and who provided the ferment of a professional ideology of independence, authority, honor, and social beneficence. For the professors, their unusual advantage (contrasting sharply with the situation of the engineers) was that as academics they worked in an organization whose overriding purpose was suitably unclear, and which they helped to define. Often, they helped define it in a way that gave them importance, esteem, autonomy, and authoritativeness. Such outcomes tell us a great deal about the professions, but also something about bureaucracies. Life and work in bureaucracies owed much not only to the structures of those organizations but also to their purposes, their market settings, and the aspirations of their members.

10

The Doctors: A New Model Profession and Its Emulators

Got very enthusiastic all by myself over the Utopian idea of making the Surgeon-General head center of the medical profession," scribbled young Captain John Shaw Billings in the Spring of 1866. Dr. Billings, however, was not all by himself in such enthusiasm. He was just one of the many Northern veterans who descended upon Washington after the Civil War, intent upon carrying the spirit of wartime achievements into peacetime America. Perhaps Billings was a bit unusual in viewing both himself and his hopes with a light sense of skepticism. For it was only in retrospect that another man about Washington at that time, Henry Adams, adopted a mildly scoffing tone in describing those young veterans: "Full of faith, greedy for work, eager for reform, energetic, confident, capable, quick of study, charmed with a fight, equally ready to defend or attack, they were unselfish and even—as young men went—honest." Yet despite such winning ways, most of those men were disappointed in their various hopes. The Surgeon General's office, to which Billings attached himself, for example, did not become head or center of the medical profession. For Billings, however, this setback was not completely dispiriting. He somehow found his way to the very center of the many important medical events and developments of post–Civil War America—the founding of the Johns Hopkins Medical School, the spectacular advance of medical sciences in this country, the growth and spread of the public health movement, the progress of medical organization and licensure, the renovation of the AMA, the rise of the specialists, as well as the heightening of professional awareness, authority and honor of American doctors—and played an influential part in most of them. It is not easy at first sight to account for Billings's remarkable career. Undoubtedly his Civil War experience was important. The War brought a mingling of civilian doctors, reputedly more skilled, with army doctors, who had been sequestered from the life of the broader society and had preserved a "high and unwavering sense of the dignity of their calling" from the acids of "egalitarian sentiment." Both were invigorated by the interchange. Moreover, the scale of action that the War demanded led the doctors to problems of macromedicine that they had not come up against previously.[1]

Soon after the firing on Sumter, young doctor Billings enlisted, and he quickly developed an admiration for the corps of Army physicians and surgeons. He not only acquired a taste for the honor that went with rank but also for the esteem awarded to deeds of courage. Billings volunteered to go right into the thick of the fighting, and he served as a surgeon just behind the lines at Chancellorsville and Gettysburg. Amidst the tumult and outcry of battle, he demonstrated, to himself and those about him, a coolheadedness and skill that won considerable respect. Perhaps it was in response to such bloodshed that he developed his odd insistence upon calling attention to the serious costs of the reforms he would advocate. He also came out of the war talking about "the sweets of command."[2]

Warfare, moreover, broadened Billings's notions of what mattered in medicine. He shifted his attention from the direct encounters of doctors and patients to those conditions that preceded and followed such encounters and greatly affected them. Billings took up the work of military sanitation as well as the tasks of building, organizing, and managing military hospitals, and to his surprise, he found such work to his liking. It gave him the chance to introduce the newest medical ideas and instruments into traditional military medical practice. The discovery of such opportunities and gratifications helped him decide to stay with the Surgeon General's office after the War. From that post, he thought he could exert influence upon post-War American medicine overall.[3]

At the Surgeon General's office, Billings developed the immense and invaluable medical library, with its printed catalogue and supplements of current medical literature. He also turned to collecting vital and medical statistics, some of which he published in the expansive census of 1880 and in various other reports. Billings saw this work as part of a program to make the experience and findings of doctors available to other doctors, and to enable them to study disease in the aggregate and over the long run. When the public health movement began to make rapid progress, Billings quickly joined and soon assumed a leading position. He was named to the short-lived National Health Board, but the need to chase after the grudging and uncertain support of Congress dimmed his hopes for far-ranging reforms through his government work. Therefore, when the trustees of the munificently endowed Johns Hopkins Hospital and Medical School approached Billings about their still somewhat vague plans, he leapt at the opportunity to show what he could do. Hopkins could truly be the head center of the medical profession. The hospital and the medical school were both central institutions from which the profession might be set in new directions. Billings became closely associated with Hopkins and, for the next quarter century, helped establish and extend its extraordinary influence.[4]

When the trustees selected Billings as an adviser and agent, they knew that he could draw upon his considerable military and government experience for guidance. However, almost as important in shaping his agenda at Hopkins was his less well-known experience in those bustling cities of mid-America, Cincinnati and Memphis. The lesson he drew from his work in those cities was straightforward and forceful—the laissez faire of market capitalism was an inadequate policy for medical education and public health. There was no hidden hand in those realms that turned private interest into public benefit, therefore individual initiative, though invaluable and constructive, was not enough. In America, Billings thought, the notion of personal rights was overblown, much to the detriment of the welfare of the community. Some agency of social cooperation must be called upon in matters of medical education and public health to restrain and guide self-interest so that society would be served.[5]

It was to Cincinnati that Billings had gone to get his medical education. The Medical College of Ohio, where he studied, was reputable enough; it claimed to be one of the best in the country. Yet the college was a proprietary school largely dependent upon student fees for survival, and scholarly requirements could not be so stringent as to unduly restrict enrollment. Moreover, the faculty was given to internecine quarreling as well as to clamorous vendettas with the faculties of the two competing regular schools of medicine. Under such conditions it is not surprising that Billings came to regard the formal medical education that he received at the school shoddy and nugatory. In due time, Billings became a first-rate doctor, but he thought that was accomplished largely by studying on his own and by taking up voluntary hospital work during his student days. The most valuable thing he learned at medical school, Billings grimly remarked, was a placebo cough mixture prescription for tuberculosis.[6]

It was in Memphis that Billings worked out many of his ideas on the requirements of public health and hygiene. The city fathers' eagerness to keep taxes low led them to the obviously shortsighted and disastrous policy of neglecting sanitation. "It is hard to persuade a city that it is ill, or in danger of being ill," he explained, "so long as the trade pulse beats strongly and clearly, and it is still harder to induce it to submit to any treatment which may slacken the pulse even temporarily." But nature, he insisted, exacted the severest retribution upon those who would violate its laws. Dispatched to Memphis to combat the yellow fever epidemic, Billings prevailed upon the city to submit to the most drastic treatment. He set up a *cordon sanitaire* and then systematically cleansed the city, destroying all materials and even buildings that he believed to be repositories of infection. For Southerners, Billings's position as a somewhat remote military officer strengthened his authority as a doctor. He was "received by the most diverse and conflicting interests with an unquestioning acceptance which would have been denied him were he one of our citizens or even a civilian from abroad, no matter what his eminence or reputation." He tried to teach Memphis the basic lessons of public hygiene. The salubrity of a city was communal, for the health of the well-to-do depended upon the health of the impoverished who could not support their own medical care. Furthermore, the city must look beyond customary business considerations even if it wished only to prosper.[7]

What made Hopkins especially attractive to Billings was the fact that it was generously endowed, therefore not closely bound by market restraints, and that it was in the hands of a small band of educable trustees, therefore free from the vagaries of democratically elected legislatures. Moreover, it was new. Billings recognized the efforts of Charles W. Eliot at Harvard and William Pepper at Pennsylvania to raise the quality of American medicine. But Eliot, for all his organizational savvy, and Pepper, for all his earnest ambition, had to contend with powerful medical faculties and associations that were set in their accustomed ways. Hopkins would start from scratch, and Billings could bring the impress of his military, government, and municipal experience to bear upon that new undertaking and meet with little opposition. In addition, he could freely draw upon the achievements of European medicine.[8]

Billings greatly admired the medical attainments of both Germany and England—Germany for its science, England for its style. Early in his career, Billings had taken up research in microoganisms, and when the great German advances in physiology and bacteriology came to light, he quickly became medically verdeutsched. Yet he also was deeply respectful of English medical ways. They were the venerable provenance and counterpart of the demeanor that he had so much admired in the American physicians and military surgeons. Billings prided himself on his friendships with Sir Henry Acland, Regius Professor of Medicine at Oxford and Sir Lauder Brunton, the leading consultant in London's medical circles. With the broad powers that he was given by the trustees, Billings hoped to bring Brunton to Hopkins. But cornering an English baronet was beyond even Billings's negotiating powers, and therefore he settled for an up-and-coming Canadian doctor to head the department of clinical medicine. Little did Billings realize, at the time, what a stroke of good fortune it was to get William Osler. Gentlemanliness in Canada was a more factitious, self-conscious, and studied achievement than in an English setting, and therefore something more readily taught.[9]

Osler was an gracious, handsome man who combined a broad, classical education with a good scientific training. He was at ease in the laboratory and did some respectable work there, but his natural habitat was the hospital ward. "Stick to the wards always," he urged his students; the laboratories were secondary. Osler's morning "rounds" were remarkable events. He strolled through the hospital dressed immaculately in his grey Prince Albert coat, with a flock of students at his side, examining patients, making perspicuous diagnoses, and finding the occasion for pronouncements on culture, morality, medical history, and ethics. His motto was equanimity—or rather, "aequanimitas"—and this, the physician's bearing, along with medical knowledge and techniques, was what Osler so assiduously taught. At a distance it was easy to be put off by his decorous culture, his lofty posture, and his implacable wholesomeness. Nevertheless, in the setting of Johns Hopkins, which was to become the matrix of scientific medicine in America, it was Osler, more than anyone else, who sustained an awareness that a disease was not only a disturbance in the function or structure of a body, but it was also something that happened to a person.[10]

Billings was equally fortunate in his selection of William H. Welch to head the pathological laboratories at Hopkins. Welch was a brainy and ambitious Yankee who had gone over to Germany after graduating medical school at home in order to find out about the extraordinary achievements of German medical science and to bring them back to his native land. The contrasts between Osler and Welch were striking. Osler was the champion of the ethos of the profession—its purpose, its ideal excellence, its entitlements—as embodied in British gentlemanly medicine. Welch was the apostle of the science of the profession—its generative principle of research, its discoveries, and the institutions that made it possible—as exemplified in German medical science. Osler loved the day-to-day practice of medicine; Welch shunned it. Osler was affable, with self-assured good form; Welch was standoffish and somewhat abrupt. Osler and his charming wife opened their home to students, faculty, and visiting dignitaries; Welch was secretive about his personal life. Students quickly became enamored of Osler and idolized him; they usually found Welch awesome. Yet Osler and Welch deeply respected each other's abilities and purposes, and they worked brilliantly together.[11]

Welch, the first medical appointment that Billings made, promptly took a preeminent position among the Hopkins staff in shaping the institution. The sway of Germanic science was unmistakable from the first. Welch, with Billings's enthusiastic support, set up the pathological laboratories to provide guidance for the different hospital departments and to put a scientific stamp on them at once. The hospital was an educational institution, linked to the medical school and university and, as in Germany, under the control of the medical faculty. Full-time, salaried professors ultimately stood at the head of each department and enjoyed access to all the resources that would help evoke the spirit of research. (This contrasted sharply with most proprietary medical schools where the faculty of moonlighting practitioners was too busy scrambling for student fees and for the consultation fees that came by way of former students to undertake much scientific research.) Moreover the fixed salaries of the professors was an additional support for the professors' authority, making them "entirely independent of students"; professors could "therefore afford to consult their students' welfare instead of their wishes." The Hopkins faculty put those students through a four-year, graded curriculum that trained them thoroughly in the latest medical techniques and knowledge. These students, moreover, were a preferred group, selected from those who could pass the unusually stiff entrance requirements. A Hopkins medical graduate immediately stood apart from the graduates of other schools as a new physician of the first rank.[12]

The justifications for these various innovations in medical education rested upon the unprecedented advance of nineteenth-century biological science. That progress was marked by the rapid growth of physiology in the first part of the century, the upsurge of Darwinian evolution in the middle years, and the startling burst of discovery and excitement in bacteriology as the century drew to a close. The work of Magendi, Muller, and Bernard in physiology in the second quarter of the century gave new meaning to the traditional view that had defined health as balance. Bernard showed that organisms were dependent upon a stable internal environment and set about to discover and explain the diverse mechanisms that regulated this *milieu intérieur*. American doctors learned about much of this work through textbook writers like Adolphe Gublier, whose famous maxim "l'organisme se guérit lui-même" (the organism heals itself) gave support for their turn away from the early nineteenth-century interventionist, "heroic" medicine. In addition, Bernard's studies on "nutrition" (metabolism) led some scientific authors to characterize well-being in terms of "needs," and others to claim that the new physiology provided, for the first time, "a foundation for rational therapeutics."[13]

The Darwinians who took up the notion of *milieu interieur*, ostensibly a static concept, described it as an evolutionary product which enabled the organism to thrive in diverse environments. Darwinism, unlike physiology and later bacteriology, had not come out of the laboratories, but from the descriptive and collecting sciences like botany and geology, and this theory placed the biological world in historical perspective. Because of its breadth of implication it divided doctors, much as it had scientists and laymen. Yet by reason of that very breadth of implication, those doctors who accepted it argued that it "forcibly and permanently affected every department of medical thought." The general effects were most important. The Darwinian theory had shown what science, "The Great Explainer," could do, and therefore it inspired "fresh hopes along every highway and byway of scientific endeavor." Darwinism, Welch thought, had strengthened the belief that "mechanical" explanations were sufficient for the interpretation of biological phenomena and had encouraged the search for such explanations.[14]

More particularly, Darwinism also portrayed organic life as the scene of perpetual warfare, and this view had a decided effect upon the new science of bacteriology. The astonishing eruption of bacteriological discovery at the end of the nineteenth century was initially the work of medical outsiders. Pasteur was a chemist, Koch was a provincial military doctor working on veterinary problems, and Ferdinand Cohn was a botanist and a Jew. At first the reputable physiologists and medical scientists stood aloof. But Koch's meticulous technique of systematically eliminating other explanations persuasively linked bacteria and disease in a way that few scientists trained in the rigors of the experimental laboratory could resist. The physiologists soon responded to the challenge of new explanations of infection and immunity (Metchnikoff's work on bacteriophage introduced notions of Darwinian struggle directly into the world of microorganisms) and soon produced the "serum therapy" of antitoxins. [15]

The diphtheria antitoxin was the clincher. Diphtheria was a horrible and frightening disease that could choke a helpless child to death before one's eyes. There had been no effective treatment before 1892 when Behring announced the discovery of his antitoxin. Though the doctors were divided in their response, the general public greeted the news with anxious hopefulness. The results seemed to justify that hope, for deaths from diphtheria were soon drastically reduced, and the leading medical scientists promptly proclaimed the victory of germ theory. Actually such proclamations were somewhat misleading, for although germ theory greatly improved medical men's ability to make diagnoses, direct and effective therapies for the most widespread bacterial diseases came much later. Yet Welch, looking back upon the late nineteenth century found those years perhaps the most wonderful in the history of medicine, for he believed that they had brought a revolution in medical thought. "Those living today," wrote Welch some decades later, "can hardly realize the enthusiasm and youthful spirit which stirred not only among medical men, but in the general public." Osler, reviewing the advances of medical science in the nineteenth century, described them as "the Promethean gift of the century to man"; while Billings declared that the medical progress made in that era was greater "than had been made during the previous two thousand years." Such immense pride and assurance impelled this triumverate not only to make Hopkins a great center of scientific medicine, but to turn it into a base for the spread of the new truths and glad tidings throughout American medicine. This work was carried forward not only through formal organizations (the Association of American Medical Colleges, the American Hospital Association) and publications (*The Johns Hopkins Bulletin* and *The Johns Hopkins Hospital Reports*) but also through those extraordinary Hopkins graduates, many of whom went on to leadership positions in medical schools and hospitals all over the country. [16]

Such quickening of spirit was also felt in the American Public Health Association, which was founded in 1872 under the leadership of doctors appreciative of the new advances in physiology. Yet their theoretical notions about disease and its prevention were usually quite diverse and disconnected. Dr. Stephen Smith, in his inaugural address before the association, acclaimed the "new science now dawned upon the physical destiny of man," but he praised equally an early advocate of germ theory, a physiologist who fixed particularly upon fungi as the agents of most disease, and another who blamed the noxious emanations from the soil. This clash of theories was not troublesome to public health advocates, however, because such views could somehow support their practical programs based upon the apparent link between disease and dirt and upon their favorite remedy of urban cleanup. In the shapeless, scrambling, and boisterous American cities it seemed obvious that dirt brought illness and that it also offended against order.[17]

More troublesome was the new science of evolution. Dr. Henry M. Lyman, stolid disciple of Herbert Spencer, cooly advised his listeners at the American Public Health Association to recognize the substantial work of contagion in singling out "the low-spirited, the intemperate, and the debilitated," leaving a stronger humanity more capable of resisting disease, and ultimately promoting the evolution of a vigorous and immune race. The would-be humanitarian health reformers, he argued, promoted race deterioration and in the long run greater suffering. Such argument undermined the entire public health program. The reformers struck back with many counter-arguments, the most elemental of which was a faith that the wonderful progress of scientific discovery could uplift all. "We cannot tell what may come to light, even tomorrow, which will put a new weapon in our hands to make us laugh at infection," wrote Dr. Charles V. Chapin. "Surely we must have enough hope in the future to warrant not only the continuance, but the re-enforcement of our efforts to preserve life." Billings, characteristically, discounted the millenial expectations of both Spencerians and reformers. The great improvements in medicine and sanitation were clearly advantageous, he thought, but they did not do away with "nature's methods" of decimating "the unfit". Our duty remained what it had always been, to do what we could to lessen suffering.[18]

Like many leading doctors in the public health movement, Billings did not see the full implications of germ theory until the eighties. The heavy asphalt floors that he required for the Johns Hopkins Hospital are still there today protecting patients from those mysterious emanations from the soil that the eminent Dr. Pettenkoffer, the leading miasmal hygienist, had warned against. The drastic fumigation policy and the inordinate property destruction that Billings imposed upon Memphis demonstrated his respect for time-honored, but soon to be outmoded, sanitary maxims. Not all empirical sanitation, however, was as excessive and inappropriate. The water filtration that Billings prescribed, intended originally to get rid of dirt and odors in drinking water, also inadvertantly but effictively eliminated dangerous bacteria. But by the eighties, Billings had switched from Pettenkoffer to Koch, and he was giving special emphasis to the establishment of public health laboratories for diagnostic service and bacteriological research.[19]

During his stint on the National Health Board, Billings was hopeful that it could become an effective command post for the campaign against epidemic disease. This board, set up in response to the disastrous yellow fever epidemic that swept up the Mississippi Valley in 1878, was given broad advisory and quarantine powers. There had been widespread suspicion that the New Orleans authorities had concealed the early cases of yellow fever for commercial reasons, to the great misfortune of the entire Valley. This provoked the demand for action on a national level. Billings, who played a leading role in persuading Congress to establish the board, was one of the first presidential appointments to its directorate, and he moved quickly to use its powers in full. He also tried to make the board a center of education to combat the "selfishness, ignorance, or terror" that heightened the danger of pestilence; it was disastrous for Americans to continue to rely upon the awesome "lessons which epidemics themselves give." After four troubled years, the National Health Board, much to Billings's disgust, succumbed to Congressional parsimony, bureaucratic infighting, and states' rights bombast.[20]

Billings continued his work in the public health movement, rising to the presidency of the American Public Health Association in 1880 and working to assure that it would be the physicians who gave this diversified organization its direction. From this platform he again expounded the lesson that "individual efforts are not sufficient to secure the best possible protection to life and health but that compulsory legislation and skilled supervision are necessary." In a country so long given to proclaiming that essential truths were self-evident, Billings's stress on the skilled supervision necessary for the protection of life and health was somewhat unusual; and in a society so accustomed to whooping it up for the individual and the sacredness of his consent, Billings's emphasis upon the ineluctably collective and coercive aspects of a responsible commonwealth was disconcerting to some. Yet Billings went on to argue, perhaps too simply, that "if the object aimed at be good, if the compulsion employed be such as will attain it, and if the good obtained fully over-balance the inconvenience of the compulsion, then the compulsion is right and proper." Many doctors were uneasy about such compulsion and strongly opposed it when it threatened to come between themselves and their patients, for that might undermine their authority. Yet when governmental power was used to strengthen the doctors' authority and elevate their honor, the support of most doctors could be depended upon.[21]

Medical licensing proved to be one of those uses of government power that appeared as a public health reform in this era and won the enthusiastic backing of most regular physicians. At one of the earliest meetings of the American Public Health Association, Dr. Stephen Smith, one of the founders of the organization, argued that the low educational qualifications of the medical profession created a health hazard. Billings, of course, strongly endorsed that view and argued further that government powers might be drawn upon in raising the educational qualifications of the profession. State licensing laws, by adding stringent requirements in medical education, could do the job. Already in the 1870s, doctors on various boards of health and from the medical societies successfully pushed licensing laws through the state legislatures. In the eighties, the number of states with such laws had more than doubled, and by the end of the century all states had medical licensure.[22]

There were many considerations behind the medical profession's campaign for licensing laws. Certainly economic concerns were among them, particularly for the less prosperous doctors. The claim that the profession was overcrowded had become almost a commonplace in the nineteenth century, and it required but little reflection to understand that raising the educational requirements for entry might not only improve the caliber of physicians but might also limit the supply and raise the income of those who were and those who would become doctors. Yet it is striking how infrequently the doctors, even in their own proceedings, presented straightforward economic arguments, as did contemporary capitalists or workers when they gathered to promote their well-being. This was not a matter of deception or self-deception among the doctors but rather a reflection of partially ordered priorities in which the profession's noneconomic ambitions and rewards limited the ways of economic gain and sometimes their effectiveness. In turn, those priorities stemmed from a resolutely sought-after relationship with patients—old, changing, but persistent, that of protector and dependent—and from the fondness for the authority and honor that went with that relationship. From this standpoint, the moral fervor of those medical men who were shocked by the human suffering brought on by poorly educated doctors and the desire of medical men for the honorific recognition that licensing might provide were understandable and could sustain the drive for licensing even when its powers to limit the supply of doctors were slight.[23]

Nevertheless, it is still surprising how unrestrictive most of the licensing laws passed before the end of the century actually were. Homeopaths and Eclectics were usually granted licenses alongside regular physicians, and the ratio of doctors to the general population continued to grow. The level of education of medical men rose, however, with the increasingly stringent requirements for licensing. Many doctors, therefore, believed that the public health benefits that came from the elimination of some of the most ignorant practitioners, the commendations that derived from official recognition in licensure, and the added dignity that accompanied the increased learning of physicians were important steps in the right direction. "Let the medical practitioner be a homeopath, allopath, or no path at all," wrote a leading advocate of licensing laws, "only see to it that he is an educated man."[24]

Yet a good number of doctors were distressed by the fact that most licensing laws seemed to give Homeopaths and Eclectics a dignity comparable to regulars. After West Virginia set up its State Board of Public Health empowered to restrict medical practice to graduates of reputable schools, the regular doctors controlling the board moved quickly to shut out irregulars. Their principal case in point was the grandiloquent Dr. Marmaduke Dent, graduate of the American Medical Eclectic College of Cincinnati, perhaps the most reputable Eclectic medical school in the country. Outraged when his diploma was rejected, Dent sued and carried his case to the Supreme Court. Justice Stephen Field, long known for his championship of the inviolability of individual rights against state interference, ruled along with a unanimous court against Dent. Field was persuaded that medical licensing was a public health measure and that the states might use their general police powers to protect the lives of their citizens. No one, therefore, had the right to practice medicine without the necessary qualifications determined by "an authority competent to judge." That authority in this instance turned out to be the regular profession itself. This was an ideological victory for medical licensing and for the authority of the regular doctors who, with the backing of the state, might "secure people against the consequences of ignorance and incapacity." The practical effects of the decision in West Virginia were less exclusionary than the regular doctors had hoped, for the irregulars having failed in the courts, turned to the legislature and got separate boards to license Homeopaths and Eclectics.[25]

Nonetheless, the Dent case encouraged the state medical societies to push for yet more demanding licensing laws. Most of these state societies traced their origins back to before the Civil War, but many of them had languished by midcentury and some had even disbanded. Now in the more favorable setting of the late nineteenth century, state medical societies took on new life, ardor, and activity. In the discussions of medical licensing at state society meetings, arguments about improved social standing and economic well-being were linked to public health. The revivified Illinois State Medical Society and its leading activist John Henry Rauch had set the pace early on. Rauch was one of the founders and first presidents of the American Public Health Association and the driving force on the Illinois Board of Health, which the Illinois State Medical Society had helped call into being. Rauch's blunt and persistent message was that individualism and laissez faire were inadequate for the requirements of public health. The licensing of doctors and the raising of educational qualifications for those licenses, he urged, were essential public health measures. The control of entry into the profession, therefore, must be taken from the propriety medical schools and placed in the new state boards of health and their licensing boards. Rauch, with his pertinacity and prodigious energy, was surprisingly successful in raising the educational requirement for physicians in Illinois—and even more startling, he drove some of the more aberrant practitioners from the state. His work was an encouragement and incitement for other boards of health and state medical associations.[26]

The reinvigoration of the state medical societies was paralleled by similar stirrings within the American Medical Association. Since its founding, the AMA and its national conventions had served as rallying points for regular physicians scattered throughout the country who were trying to maintain what they considered authentic scientific medicine, which they felt was engulfed in a sea of quackery. Between conventions, the AMA was, for the most part, a local organization centered in Chicago and in the person of Nathan Smith Davis. Even the most superficial appearances—Davis's ruff of neck whiskers, his daily costume of the old-fashioned swallow-tailed coat and top hat, and his abrupt and unbending manner—suggested that under his leadership the organization would not be open to many of the new developments in medicine. By the eighties, the AMA had come in for some harsh criticism for the meagerness of its scientific work and the ineffectiveness of its reform efforts. Nevertheless, even in its most listless days, the AMA, through its perennial lambasting of horrific quackery, helped perpetrate a respectable sense of identity for the regular physician. Through this work of vehement contradistinction, the AMA worked in some measure as an honor making machine, at least.[27]

The requirements of such repute demanded some internal vigilance as well, and it is not surprising that among the first to suffer the effects of the doctor's appetite for esteem and self-respect were those who, in the general judgment of society, were rarely granted honor or authority—women and Blacks. In the nineteenth century, a woman's honor was simply her chastity, and her authority usually extended only over other women and children. Blacks as well were excluded from White man's honor and authority. Therefore, accepting Blacks as equals into the AMA promised to weaken the association's power to reflect honor upon, and strengthen the authority of, its members. Such forebodings reflected not only the common presuppositions and prejudices of the era but also found support in the newest findings of science. Those who wished to argue that women and Blacks could not make worthy doctors might draw upon the latest physiological science and the teachings of the leading Darwinians.[28]

As the incapacities of women and Blacks were often linked together in the scientific literature, their exclusion from the AMA was linked as well. Not only were women barred from membership, but men who held positions in medical colleges in which women taught and were taught, or who served in hospitals alongside women doctors, could also be barred. The White professors of Howard University medical school, who led the fight to gain the admission of their Black colleagues into the AMA conventions, therefore lost out, ostensibly because it was discovered that a woman served on their faculty. Some of the irregulars, with less claim to gentlemanly honor and authority and with less ardor for the new sciences, more readily accepted women and occasionally even Blacks.[29]

Though excluded from the AMA, both Black and women physicians made important advances in the late nineteenth century. Despite great obstacles and discouragements, Black doctors grew in numbers and gained better opportunities for training and practice, segregated though these usually were. At the 1895 Cotton States Exposition in Atlanta, where Booker T. Washington publicly announced his acquiescence in the social separation of

Blacks, Black doctors gathered and formed their own National Medical Association, relinquishing their struggle to gain admittance into the AMA. Among the founders of the new association were Drs. Daniel Hale Williams and Myles Vandahurst Lynk, both active in the improvement of medicine among Blacks. Williams was clearly exceptional, and because of that he could play a leading role in the general advancement of Black doctors; Lynk was more typical, and therefore his career suggests more distinctly what most Black doctors were up against.[30]

Daniel Hale Williams was born into a free Black family, raised in Wisconsin, apprenticed to a leading doctor (a former Union surgeon who had served with Grant), and then went on to study at Chicago Medical School where he graduated near the top of his class. Williams became an extraordinary and much honored surgeon. He served alongside Rauch on the Illinois Board of Health in the effort to upgrade the requirements for medical practice, but at the same time, he worked arduously to improve Black medical education at Howard University, Shaw College, and Meharry Medical Collage in order to qualify their graduates to meet such rising standards. In addition, Williams organized hospitals where Blacks would be accepted as patients and where Black doctors and nurses could get their training.[31]

Myles Vandahurst Lynk's education was rudimentary when compared to Williams's. After a brief apprenticeship with a local Black doctor in Tennessee, Lynk scraped together the wherewithal for study at Meharry, a school that had been set up in Nashville by the Freedman's Aid Society of the Methodist Church. In those early days of Meharry's history, the medical training it offered was clearly inadequate. Sensing this, Lynk returned some years after his graduation for yet further instruction. The expectations and excitement awakened by this education emboldened Lynk to launch a medical journal that would provide a forum for Black doctors and would urge them on to scientific work.

Yet the outcome of all this effort was not encouraging. The medical journal failed after a few issues, and his own medical practice did not prosper. The market for medical care among Southern Blacks was a constricted one. Most Blacks were poor, and many resorted to self-medication as well as to folk medicine. Lynk therefore supplemented his medical work with a law practice and even established a proprietary "university" to train Black nurses, dentists, pharmacists, and yet other doctors. While many White doctors were moving toward specialization in this era, most Black doctors, like Lynk, pursued the nonspecialized professional careers that had been characteristic of an earlier era.

Notwithstanding such straitened conditions, Black doctors and medicine won some limited successes in the last three decades of the nineteenth century: By 1900 there were some 12 hospitals that accepted Black doctors, nurses, and patients, and the number of Black physicians had doubled.[32]

Women doctors, as well, often entered upon segregated careers, but their special kind of separation at first sight seemed to be in step with the latest development in American scientific medicine, specialization. Most women doctors devoted themselves exclusively to the treatment of women and children; they took up the newly developing specialties of gynecology, obstetrics, and pediatrics. Even the leading woman dentist of the era confined her work for the most part to women and children. Clearly, this specialization is more indicative of the constraints than the opportunities that women doctors faced. In contrast to Blacks, however, many women doctors had the advantage of being reared in well-to-do families, with the important economic and educational support, as well as the social connections, that such families could provide. Those women doctors also took encouragement from the burgeoning women's movement of the era. The advocates of women's rights frequently advanced seemingly divergent reasons for urging women into medical careers. Such careers would broaden women's worldliness and at the same time they would protect feminine innocence. The occupational choices available to women were too narrow and stultifying, and it was argued that women needed a wider range of experience in order to give expression to their powers. A medical career could be particularly elevating and broadening, yet at the same time, it would help preserve womanly virtue. The horror of vaginal examinations by male doctors (an accepted procedure in France, when the most eminent midcentury American doctors had studied) brought frightful shudders and evoked righteous wrath from many of the masculine and feminine protectors of womankind. If women needed any such examination in the interest of their health, then those procedures should be performed by women doctors. The Blackwell sisters, who pioneered in opening the medical profession to women, were also leaders in the social purity movement. "As long as mankind marries in order to indulge in licensed sexual intercourse," announced another woman doctor—who advocated women's entry into medicine as well as the principle of social purity—"it will seek happiness in vain." Women's advance, health, and prudery were frequently linked in the late nineteenth century.[33]

The careers of women doctors not only often separated them

from other doctors but also, in more subtle ways, from other women. Young Mary Putnam described that estrangement as "the curious feeling that often comes over me, when with a lot of women, of being a sort of wild animal escaped from the cage in which my fellows were confined and to which they had grown accustomed." There was both exhilaration and anxiety in that feeling. The anxiety stemmed in part from the widespread belief that a woman taking up a medical career must relinquish the "holiest relations" available to her, those of wife and mother. "I have chosen, Howard farewell!" rings out the last line of a melo-dramatic story written by a young woman doctor describing such a relinquishment. Yet most American women of the day would more likely have chosen Howard. That, as well as the important remaining overt barriers, helps explain the disappointingly small number of women who entered medicine after the first vanguard of women physicians had broken into it.[34]

The extraordinary Mary Putnam, however, did marry and pur-sue a noteworthy career in medicine. Her husband, Dr. Abraham Jacobi, a socialist who had fought alongside Marx and Engels in the revolutions of 1848 and had become an enthusiastic propo-nent of the advancement of scientific medicine, was not dis-suaded but rather pleased by her medical career. Moreover, she had the support of her eminent and well-to-do family in becom-ing a doctor. She graduated from the Women's Medical College in Philadelphia and capped her training with five years of study in Paris. Yet, the special sense of liberation that her medical work gave her was accompanied by a special requirement of discipline that she thought it demanded. For Mary Putnam Jacobi accepted the scientific teachings of that day about the weak physiological and emotional makeup of women. Females, she explained "had a less quantum of force . . . vitality than males over the needs of nutrition." A woman doctor, therefore, must compensate with a more rigorous discipline and make herself "an instrument of pre-cision." She must also turn severely away from the subjectivity to which she was prone and cultivate a strict disinterestedness. Mary Putnam Jacobi's last scientific work was an instance of that; it was a case study of her own fatal illness. "Happiness," she once wrote, "is the expenditure of force in successful effort." Few women, and few men, would warm to such an exacting and ob-jectified happiness.[35]

Though she developed much of Jacobi's intensity and vigor, Dr. Bethenia Adair was favored by few of the advantages of her more illustrious contemporary. Neither Jacobi nor Adair was a typical woman physician—it would be difficult to know what a typical woman physician was—nonetheless their very different careers can be broadly informative about the situation of many women doctors of the era. Adair was born on the Missouri farming frontier and was married, at fourteen, to a backwoods ne'er-do-well whom she divorced shortly after the birth of their first child. She then began her long stint at schooling, which led ultimately to the study of medicine, supporting herself through a succession of poorly paid teaching jobs. Adair took her M.D. at the Eclectic Medical College in Philadelphia, after one year's study there, and quickly set up a practice specializing in women's and children's ailments—favoring "medicated vapor baths combined with electricity" as a treatment. She prospered. When compared to Black doctors, many women doctors, though they faced harsh discouragements, found barriers permeable and their markets extensive. Yet Adair became dissatisfied with her accomplishments and uneasy under the affronts of the regular physicians, who derisively dubbed her "the bath doctor." She enrolled at the University of Michigan Medical School and took up orthodox practice after graduation. The diseases of the eyes and ears became her specialty, though her patients were still largely women and children. Along with her successful practice, Adair found time and energy to champion temperance, women's suffrage, and her chief reform cause, the eugenical sterilization. Now scientific with a vengeance, and caught up in hereditarian notions, Adair worked arduously for legislation to sterilize "criminals, epileptics, insane, and all feeble-minded persons committed to State institutions," with some success. Yet along with Jacobi, Adair also found the occasion to urge the advance of women within the profession of medicine.[36]

Many distinguished members of the AMA objected to the policy of excluding Blacks and women, but the issue did not bring widespread dissension or disruption to the association. The restrictive policy toward "irregulars," by contrast, threatened to break the organization apart. This clash reflected some of the broad changes within the organization and in the profession beyond it. It gave singular expression to the rapid advance of the medical sciences in the second half of the nineteenth century and the new confidence that progress in those sciences gave to the physicians who had mastered them. It was also linked to the growth of the great urban markets for medical care and the specialization that those markets made possible. On one side of this conflict over the irregulars stood the growing number of medical specialists of the large metropolitan centers, especially on the East

Coast, and more particularly in New York City. Broadly sympathetic to this group were many of the younger men in the profession who had been fortunate enough to gain a first-class medical education either abroad or at the best schools at home. On the opposite side of the controversy, and at that time in control of the AMA, were the "family doctors," general practitioners often with less impressive medical educations and scientific attainments. These were frequently older men, commonly from small Midwestern towns; their headquarters was in Chicago and Nathan Smith Davis was their chief. This controversy was a struggle over authority and honor within the AMA, and it mirrored the medical profession's struggle for authority and honor in society at large.[37]

One of the essential tasks of the AMA since its founding, as has been suggested, was its self-assumed charge to distinguish and derogate. It was established just as the supports for the imposing edifice of the eighteenth-century healing art and science were crashing to the ground, and under those circumstances it was impossible to turn back the onrush of irregular medicine. Yet the gentlemanly physician and surgeon could set himself apart from the engulfing mixty-maxty assortment of healers by allegiance to an association that claimed to hold steadfast to the science and traditions of medicine. Doctors drew a heightened sense of identity and affective strength from such membership.[38]

Towards the end of the nineteenth century, however, an important segment of the profession, highly educated and well trained in the advancing medical sciences of the era, came to see itself as being almost as distant from the less learned and distinguished doctors within the AMA as from the heterodox practitioners outside of it. In addition, many Homeopathic and Botanic doctors had broken away from the restraints of their received teachings and adopted a practice much like that of the regular physicians. In this light, some of the elite doctors, confident in their acquirements and eminence, suggested that it would be best for the profession not to turn its back upon the irregulars but rather to welcome them and crush their sectarianism in the embrace of vigorous scientific educational requirements. However, for less self-assured and presuming doctors, the growing indistinctness of the irregulars seemed to make them even more dangerous. One defender of the old discriminations argued that the need to draw a sharp line between regular and irregular doctors was much like the need to maintain the color line. "Experience has shown," he wrote, "that, when inferior races become closely intermingled with superior races, neither one is improved, but in the unnatural embrace both go down together." A free and easy policy was irresponsible and an unconscionable deviation from rectitude.[39]

Nonetheless, in February 1882, some of the most celebrated New York specialists announced that they would disregard what they considered the outmoded prohibiting stipulations of the AMA code, in the interest of patients, and enter into consultations with Homeopaths when called upon. This announcement touched off a storm of righteous indignation within the association. The interest of bank accounts, not of patients, Davis hissed, was what the specialists had in mind. On the contrary, the specialists answered, they maintained the gentlemanly bearing of the profession while the standpatters had long ago descended into catchpenny commercialism, as their encouragement of setting minimum fee bills indicated. Both sides were partly right. Economic well-being was of importance to both, but of primary importance to neither, in these practices. Consulting fees undoubtedly enhanced the incomes of specialists, yet more importantly the consultations enhanced reputations and prerogatives and helped establish a standing as full-time specialists. Fee bills certainly helped establish a minimum income for some general practitioners, yet equally as important, those fee bills fostered a cordiality and solidarity among doctors that reinforced their authority with patients. Significantly, both sides argued in terms of the various aspects of professional honor and authority. The specialists claimed that they were upholding the gentlemanly "autonomy" and magnanimity of professionals who wore "no man's livery." Their opponents claimed that they were upholding the professional solidarity of worthy and principled practitioners against self-seekers allied with quacks and misguided laymen.[40]

Owing to their imposing reputations and deft maneuvers, the specialists brought the New York State Medical Society and the New York Academy of Medicine behind them. Nathan Smith Davis then moved quickly to expel the New York State Medical Society and to help set up a rival New York state medical society in its place. However, the New York doctors were among the most illustrious medical men of their day. They had brought honor to the AMA and had enabled the less distinguished members to take honor from it. The expulsion of such doctors clearly weakened the association.[41]

Some indication of the outcome of this conflict became immediately apparent in the response of John S. Billings. Billings despised the Homeopaths. When a hospital in the District of Columbia called upon him to direct its work, he immediately took steps to ensure that no Homeopaths would be admitted to the staff. Billings was no medical specialist, although he sometimes looked upon his own work, which he took to be the coordination and direction of medicine, as a new and indispensable specialty made necessary by specialization. Clearly, he felt a greater affinity for the New York eminences than for their opponents. When Billings returned from the 8th International Medical Congress that was held in Copenhagen in 1884, where he had been sent as head of the AMA delegation, he announced with much satisfaction that he had persuaded that renowned international medical organization to hold its next meeting in Washington, D.C. This was a major triumph, for it seemed to mark the world recognition of American medicine's coming of age. Billings promptly set up a committee to plan the international meeting and lead the scientific sections. Most of those whom he chose were distinguished Eastern physicians, some of them New Yorkers who had rejected the code provisions on consultations. Davis and his friends were outraged. At the next AMA convention, they repudiated Billings's committee and set up another one more representative and avowedly more democratic, with members from each state and with the requirements that only those who accepted the AMA code in full could serve.[42]

This immediately broadened the code fight, and many who had been somewhat indifferent to that issue now found themselves alongside the New York doctors. Osler was sufficiently aroused to try to organize the leading physicians in Boston, Philadelphia, and Baltimore in support of Billings's committee. Many of those named to the Davis committee declared that they would not serve without the New Yorkers. Science, Billings wryly observed, was not advanced by regional representation or by counting heads. For a while it seemed that the plans for the congress would collapse, but that was to underestimate the zeal and organizational skills of Nathan Smith Davis. Bereft of the most renowned American doctors (many eminent Europeans also stayed away) the Washington congress was nonetheless held, and Davis himself served as president. Much to the embarrassment of the new-style, scientific, American doctors, Davis addressed the meeting with a rambling and crotchety attack on germ theory, the watchword of the coming era in medicine.[43]

Amidst this commotion, a group of specialists and research-minded doctors gathered in 1886 to form the Congress of American Physicians and Surgeons, which some believed might serve as a rostrum for medical leadership outside the AMA. Though composed of specialty societies with limited membership and rigorous scientific requirements, it described its members as "the representative men of the profession in America." Billings became its first president. The founders disclaimed "any intention of offering any obstacle of opposition to any other association in America," nonetheless Davis suspected that they intended to displace and supplant the AMA. He denounced the snobbery of these "exclusionists" who wished to "work and dine without personal contact with the sunburned and weathered-beaten general practitioners of the healing art." Perhaps some of the founders of the congress had intended it to supersede the AMA, yet most members of the new organization apparently believed that the AMA could still be reformed from within.[44]

One of these was Solomon Solis Cohen, member of both the congress and the AMA, distinguished professor at the Jefferson Medical School in Philadelphia. He took the lead in a campaign to move to AMA headquarters from Chicago to Washington, D.C., hoping to take the association out of the clutches of Davis and his friends. Cohen also worked to raise the scientific level of the articles printed in the *Journal* of the AMA, just as some doctors of the hinterland were complaining that the journal was already too advanced. Yet his most troublous campaign was his endeavor to get the *Journal* to refuse advertisements of proprietary medicines, particularly those nostrums that did not list their contents. For such efforts Cohen was attacked in a pseudonymous letter, which the editor of the *Journal* chose to print, as a Hebrew who was promoting the interests of European drug manufacturers at the expense of native American producers. Some were outraged at such scurrilous abuse but would not give up on the AMA.[45]

When the AMA Convention came to Baltimore in 1895, Osler pushed through a resolution to replace the permanent secretary, a member of the Old Guard, with an annually elected officer. But it was not until four years later that a turning point was reached, with the appointment of George H. Simmons as general manager of the association and editor of the *Journal*. Simmons personified the elite doctors' stand on irregular medicine. A graduate of a homeopathic medical school, Simmons became convinced of the inadequacy of his training and went abroad to study, returning to take a second medical degree at a regular medical college in Chicago. Under the auspices of two reforming presidents, Charles Reed (a scholarly and accomplished Cincinnati gynecologist) and young Frank Billings (a research-minded Chicago physician, friend but not a relative of John Shaw Billings), Simmons helped revamp the AMA, through a special organizational com-

mittee that wrote a new constitution for the organization. Welch
was appointed to help revise the AMA code, which he did almost
single-handedly, eliminating the restriction on consultation with
Homeopaths. The two New York state medical societies were
united, and after many years of absence, John Shaw Billings finally returned to the AMA meeting, vindicated. The spirit of this
new era of the AMA was described by P. Maxwell Forshay, a member of the special committee that had brought about reorganization of the association. "Conflict of opinion ends," Forshay explained, "in the supremacy of the views promulgated by the
leaders of scientific medicine."[46]

The ascendancy of these leaders of scientific medicine within
the AMA should not be overstated. For the new energy and enthusiasm that the reorganization of the AMA generated rapidly
swelled the ranks of the organization and extended the membership more broadly and deeply through the state and county medical societies. The influx of general practitioners and small-town
doctors was extraordinary, and they remained a predominant
force in the House of Delegates where many political and economic matters were decided. However, the prominent specialists
and other medical dignitaries directed the work of the scientific
sections and took over the executive offices where they received
the deference appropriate to their renown. Preeminent honor and
authority shifted from those whose medical science had derived
largely from the sickroom and battlefield to those whose medical
science came increasingly from the findings of the medical laboratories. The AMA was now more clearly differentiated; it was
both more aristocratic and more democratic. With the inclusion
of many less-prosperous doctors, the impetus for improving the
economic well-being of the profession sharpened. With the placement of the most learned scientific doctors into leadership positions, the association became a more respectable forum for the
new advances in medicine. Under this apportionment of honor
and authority, the AMA could move forward with a cohesiveness
and power that few had previously imagined.[47]

The new importance of medical specialists in the AMA marked
a drastic shift in nineteenth-century American medicine. At the
beginning of the century, specialization was considered a form of
quackery, but by the end of the century, specialism betokened
the highest science. The growth of large urban markets for medical care was a necessary condition for medical specialization, yet
it was clearly not a sufficient condition. For such markets existed
in the early nineteenth century long before specialization took
hold. Lacking at that time was a set of beliefs that would justify

specialization. For the widely accepted doctrines of Rush in America and Broussais in Europe taught that, despite the apparent diversity of causes and symptoms, patients succumbed to a disease condition rather than to different diseases; that "symptom worship," localized treatment, and specialization were irrational and unscientific. Under these conditions, most educated and principled physicians scorned specialties. Yet even during the height of Rush's influence, customary remedies that had arisen from a long tradition of trial and error were not completely abandoned, even by Rush himself. Common ailments of the eye, nose, and throat were usually dealt with by local treatments. Nonetheless, it was not until the collapse of the monist medical systems and the growing popularity of "Baconian" notions of medical science—enjoining close observations, meticulous collection of "the facts," and careful surmise therefrom—that new intellectual support was given to localized investigation and treatment. With such support, those physicians with the incentives to take advantage of the extended urban market could do so.

By the mid-nineteenth century, a somewhat coherent body of ideas on specialization was available, and it diverged markedly from the contemporary notions about division of labor in industry. Physicians rarely mentioned markets (more appropriate for a trade) or increased manual dexterity (more appropriate for a craft). Instead, they usually stressed the need to come to terms with the "unparalleled accumulation of human knowledge." Such rapid accumulation was a glorious sign of human progress, yet in order to assimilate this knowledge, physicians must focus upon a limited field. In that way they could avoid "shallow diffuseness" and lay hold of that "clearness and definiteness" necessary for effective treatment and medical discovery. Support for this view also came from the increasingly specialized academic medical disciplines of the prestigious German universities where medical discovery was flourishing. Because doctors usually believed that the distinctive feature of a profession was its theoretical understanding, an explanation of specialization in medicine based upon expanding knowledge had intrinsic appeal. Moreover, it made specialization seem inevitable. There were few arguments that more readily turned aside objections or discouraged alternatives than those of inevitability.[48]

Yet while Baconian notions helped promote specialization, they did not explain it; they had too many logical and empirical shortcomings for that. The sheer accumulation of knowledge was not an essential consideration for the growth of specialties. In effect, the amount of information was always infinite. What mattered was the information relevant to important inquiries, and even here quantity was not often significant. The Baconian explanation obscured the variety of conditions and incentives that fostered specialization. It also concealed the parallels between specialization and division of labor in industry. In important ways these were dissimilar, but even the differences can be seen most clearly when placed alongside resemblances.

The contrasting development of surgeons and cordwainers, for example, is instructive. In the nineteenth century the diverse skills of the cordwainers became resources for the managers of shoe factories, and those skills were divided, mechanized, and redistributed among numerous, less-skilled, low-priced workers. In competition with the shoe factory and its cheaper products, those who practiced the craft of cordwainer—combining all the skills required in the making of shoes—lost out and eventually disappeared. The extended market for shoes was a necessary condition for this development; the increased dexterity arising from narrowed tasks was the means; the greater profits were the primary incentive.[49]

For much of the nineteenth century there was no sharp division between physicians and surgeons in America. Most physicians practiced some surgery, sending the most hazardous cases to practitioners with reputations for skill in such work. When, in 1880, many eminent surgeons gathered to form a national association, even the most renowned among them still maintained a general practice in addition to his surgical work. It was not until the last decade of the century that the exclusive practice of surgery became widespread. The incentives leading a surgeon to choose full specialization were usually mixed. The specialty gave him greater control of his work (it was now more orderly and its conditions more predictable), it raised his esteem (he was now seemingly more accomplished, scientific, and recondite), and it often provided a larger income (his work was an increasingly differentiated service with few providers and a growing demand). By the turn of the century, surgery was a recognized and estimable specialty. What in the eighteenth century had been the most humble branch of medicine was now one of the most imposing.[50]

It is remarkable how loosely the rise of surgery as a specialty fit with the prevailing notions of specialization. For while the discoveries of anaesthesia, antisepsis, and asepsis were essential for the progress of surgery, it was not so much the increased knowledge that these discoveries put before the practitioner as the new opportunities they provided for developing increased manipulative skill. The importance of increased dexterity for specialization in surgery invites comparison with the division of labor among cordwainers, in that the focusing on a limited set of tasks in order to achieve an increased dexterity was important to both. Yet what becomes immediately apparent is that specialization for surgeons meant the creation of a skilled occupation, while division of labor for cordwainers meant the destruction of a skilled and venerable occupation.[51]

This was related to their different institutional settings. As the factory was the habitat in which industrial division of labor was fully developed, so the hospital was the place that fostered the growth and advancement of surgery. The best techniques of anaesthesia and antisepsis could be practiced in hospitals, enabling surgeons to perform operations with greater audacity and safety. The hospital also extended the market for surgery, yet the surgeon's skills were not divided and redistributed. There were three principal reasons for this: first, the particular characteristics of hospitals as institutions; second, the standing and beliefs of surgeons who worked in the hospitals; and ultimately, the connection of that work to the broader beliefs of society at large.[52]

Hospitals were subsidized and charitable institutions, somewhat protected from the demands of the market and generally free of the drive for profit—both of which gave special impetus to the division of labor in factories. Moreover, physicians and surgeons had access to, and sometimes even sat on, the boards of trustees that set hospital policy. Those boards increasingly deferred to the views of the medical staff on medical matters. Not only did the doctors insist upon a direct and unconstrained relationship with patients, they also claimed that medical work was often in part indeterminate, so that the discretion of the doctor doing the work could never be ignored. Rigidly formalized procedures necessary for a division and redistribution of tasks, though a hospital administrator might have been interested in them, presented unmistakable disadvantages in surgery. For under such procedures, disregard for the singularity of any particular case was quite likely. In shoes, poor fit or indifferent workmanship simply meant lower price or quick replacement; the human body was once and for all. In the hospital, ordinary markets and prices did not readily reflect society's sense of imperatives. From a strictly economic and managerial perspective, making shoes and fixing human bodies had much in common. However, from the cultural perspective of American society, a shoe was an expendable commodity while a human life was a sacred entity and event; one was dispensable and the other in important ways indispensable; one easily exchangeable and the other in intrinsic ways not.[53]

Hospitals became a new and formative habitat not only for surgeons, but for most specialists and many general practitioners as well. Earlier, they had served the poor primarily, and people of other classes who had come down with certain contagious diseases. But in the last decades of the nineteenth century, even well-to-do Americans came to hospitals to get a quality of medical care that antisepsis, asepsis, and anaesthesia made possible there, and which patients could not easily receive at home. Hospitals soon became the primary center of American health care. The first inkling of the influence that this would have upon the medical profession came in the 1870s when Harvard, and shortly afterward other leading medical schools, gave up the admissions requirement of an apprenticeship with a private practitioner and recommended a postgraduate hospital internship. By the nineties, Johns Hopkins Medical School had added the German system of residency for yet further training. The hospital came to supplement the medical school as a place where young doctors would gain technical training as well as the tacit knowledge of the authority, honor, and conventions of medical practice. "Indeed, to a large extent," reported the *Journal* of the AMA in 1900, "the hospital with its wards, outpatient department, its operating rooms, its dead-house, and its laboratories, is the medical school." Even practicing physicians maintained their ties to the hospitals, and, through the hospitals, with each other. For American hospitals, unlike those in England and much of the Continent, did not set up closed staffs: rather they extended their privileges to most regular physicians, allowing them to bring their private patients for treatment.[54]

Within the hospital it was the laboratory that incorporated and exemplified some of the important changes that had taken place within medicine in the nineteenth century. The laboratory was the lodgment of the new medical science. Throughout the nineteenth century all the professions had boasted of their science, for a profession was often characterized as an occupation based upon science. Yet, by science, professionals in the first half of the nineteenth century century had usually meant a systematic arrangement of knowledge resting upon broad and coherent principles. This notion reflected the preeminence of the collecting and classificatory sciences like geology and botany. By the end of the century, the term science had come to mean a body of knowledge with very rigorous requirements for proof, and at the same time it suggested an increased possibility for practical usefulness. This reflected the new preeminence of the laboratory sciences such as chemistry and physics. There was now, therefore, something archaic about the lawyers' talk of the science of jurisprudence and the ministers' talk of the science of theology, for those were sciences in the old sense. However, there was nothing stilted about the doctors' talk of the science of medicine, for thanks to its absorption of physiology and bacteriology, medicine was a science in the new sense. This was but one aspect of the rise of the reputation of medicine in the late nineteenth century. All professions were still occupations ostensibly based on science, but now professionalization increasingly came to mean the process of becoming more like medicine.

Mimicry of the medical profession was most conspicuous in the kindred, emulous, and still insecure professions of dentistry, pharmacy, optometry, and veterinary medicine. Pharmacy and dentistry had staked their claims to professional status in the pre–Civil War era when many ranks and distinctions in American society were falling. Both of these new professions were responding to affronts from medicine—the dentists to their exclusion from medical societies and the pharmacists to the doctors' attempt to supervise apothecary shops and warehouses. Both new professions gave vent to those seemingly contradictory impulses so often displayed in that era, the penchant for egalitarian leveling and for ambitious social climbing. By the last decades of the nineteenth century, when optometrists and veterinarians had joined the pharmacists and dentists in their climb toward professional status, the egalitarian language had disappeared from professional preambles and manifestoes. "Civilized society the world over is stratified," wrote a leading dentist of the era. "In this country wealth, education, and politics draw dividing lines. In spite of all doctrines of equality proclaimed by the constitution, political platforms, creeds, sermons, and humanitarian schools, *higher* and *lower* are meaning terms" (emphasis in original).[55]

The hankering for somebodiness, apparent in both eras, was most flagrant among the founders of the new professions, who typically appeared out of the shadows of uncertain backgrounds. The quadumvirate of New England dentists who founded the profession of dentistry in the Jackson era—Eleazer Parmly, Solyman Brown, H. H. Hayden, and Chapin Harris—were exemplary in their nondescript origins and flamboyant careers. Parmly, a rural Vermont teacher and newspaper reporter, then an itinerant dentist, spent his early years floating down the Ohio and Mississippi rivers on his dental "ark," practicing as he went. He eventually landed a prominent New York heiress, after having failed to tie the nuptial knot with the offspring of yet another millionaire, the daughter of John Jacob Aster. Some ascribed his various escapades to an all-absorbing cupidity; yet in all fairness it could not be called all-absorbing. For amidst his new-found wealth, Parmly decided to continue practicing dentistry, but now upon a select clientele of wealthy New Yorkers. His most notable apprentice was Solyman Brown, a defrocked Congregationalist minister turned Swedenborgian, Fourierist, poet, and dentist. Brown combined some of his various talents in a splendiferous ode, *Dentalogia, A Poem on the Diseases of the Teeth*, which explains that "plain vulgar prose my subject seems to claim/Did not ambition prompt the higher aim/The nobler pride." H. H. Hayden, for the most part a self-taught dentist, and Chapin Harris, a medical school flunk out, both assumed M.D. degrees (as did Parmly and Brown) without the benefit of having graduated any medical college; they helped establish a professional association that granted the degree of Doctor of Dental Surgery as a reward to all who joined.[56]

Similarly mercurial and ambitious worthies stand out among the founders of veterinary medicine and optometry. The ardent Robert Jennings announced that it was his goal to lift veterinary medicine from its "low and degraded position, confined mainly to the hands of a very illiterate and intemperate class of men," known chiefly as sellers of horse tonics. The aspiring Charles Prentice, complained that just fitting glasses was beneath his dignity, "as the public did not seem sufficiently impressed with its scientific importance." He insisted upon prescribing as well as fitting glasses. This brought him up against the medical profession, and in the heated and noisy altercation that followed, the optometrical profession was born.[57]

While these kindred medical occupations were intent upon declaring their independence of the medical profession, at the same time they abjectly aped the physicians' ways and means. All these would-be professions pressed for licensing laws to limit entry into their pursuits to those with some semblance of scientific training. Rather than depend upon broad, public recognition for such enactments, some leaders of these up-and-coming professions became adept at lobbying in state legislatures. "So-called public opinion" in this regard, argued Prentice, "is more or less a myth." The licensing laws were often poorly enforced. Nonetheless if they did not yield anything like monopoly powers, explained a pharmacist, "these laws did impress upon the public mind a deeper sense of the responsibility of the calling . . . and incidentally a better appreciation of the pharmacist." All the kindred medical occupations urged more extensive and rigorous professional education to increase scientific claims and justify the restriction of entry. Colleges of pharmacy introduced a three-year course "to keep pace with medicine," and the American Dental Association recommended a similar move, because "the hedges are too low." Veterinarians succeeded in setting up a department at Harvard in 1882 and soon after established a school at the University of Pennsylvania. Optometry, however, was still taught in proprietary schools and did not gain university affiliation until the early twentieth century.[58]

This mimicry was most telling where these kindred professions tried to assert the kind of prerogatives and honorific status that doctors assumed in relation to their patients. The dentist, according to his code of ethics, "should be firm, yet kind and sympathetic." Dress, deportment, and even office layout should be so arranged, the dental journals recommended, as to reinforce professional bearing. For optometrists, the location of the office was important. Such offices should be set up on the second story where doctors usually placed their offices, and not on the street level where merchants usually put their shops. And the display of the customary street sign of large wooden spectacles, traditional with opticians, should be avoided by optometrists. Though the actual patients of the veterinarians were beasts and birds, the professional journals make much of the veterinarians' relation to the owners of these creatures. The veterinarian must teach them a humane sympathy for animals and also an awareness of those diseases that could spread from animals to humans. American veterinary journals endorsed germ theory before many medical journals, and they were the first to publish Pasteur's work on anthrax, a disease which could spread from animals to humans. Veterinarians were disposed to emphasize their "close brotherhood with practitioners of human medicine."[59]

The ostensible aloofness of medical professionalism from the crass, mercantile aspects of earning one's livelihood troubled the pharmacist more than others. For most pharmacists were part-time compounders of medicine and part-time general store keepers—Dr. Jeckle, pharmacist, and Mr. Hyde, tradesman. In the eighties, the strain of this dividedness was aggravated with the expansion of the American pharmaceutical industry and the resulting increase in retail competition. In addition, this was the era of the rapid growth of large downtown department stores and specialty shops. The pharmacists, as local small tradesmen, bucked the commercial logic and power of these trends by extending the range of sundries that they sold, and despite straitened circumstances, they grew in numbers. Owing to their commercial difficulties, perhaps, many pharmacists insisted emphatically that they were not simply shopkeepers. Typically, they not only maintained membership in the National Association of Retail Druggists, to preserve their small businesses, but also in the American Pharmaceutical Association, dedicated to the advancement of the science and dignity of their profession.[60]

It is not easy to determine exactly when these kindred medical occupations came to be considered professions. That condition involved not only self-regard but also public appraisal. By the turn of the century, general discussions of the professions in the popular press and periodicals often made mention of dentists and pharmacists; optometrists and veterinarians also begin to appear, but less frequently. What is clear is that such professional status was achieved only with such devising, dedication, and even daring. The dentists, for example, showed unexpected resoluteness in their clash with the Census Bureau over the all-important question of nomenclature. Robert Porter, the superintendant of the census, decided in an offhand way to group dentists with manufacturers on his lists because many dentists manufactured dentures. To his surprise, organized dentistry rose up in protest and refused to supply information to the Government unless dentistry were classified as a profession. Dire warnings of imprisonment and fines were of no avail against these mild-mannered, yet punctilious insurrectionists. Just when this conflict threatened to turn into a seriocomic calamity, to the relief of all, Porter backed down, and professional identity and dignity won the day.[61]

Keeping up with the doctors in the late nineteenth century became increasingly an uphill struggle, because the medical profession itself was gaining so rapidly in vigor, self-regard, and public estimation. The number of doctors grew more rapidly than the population, but in the advancing economy of this era, explained an editorial in the *Journal* of the AMA, the market for doctors grew more rapidly still. The old complaint about the overcrowding of the profession was pure bugbear. "Our prospects as a profession," the editor concluded cheerfully, "were never brighter and more hopeful than they are today."[62]

Nonetheless, the medical profession of this era insisted that it was not simply an economic or political interest group intent upon maximizing income or influence. Clearly, other ambitions limited and directed the acquisitiveness and outlook of these physicians and surgeons. As has been suggested, the doctors sought a relation with their patients unlike that between seller and buyer or between politician and voter; rather, they aspired to the traditional relation of protector and dependent, and to the authority and honor that often went with it. That relation, unlike the commercial exchange, was based upon an intrinsic inequality; unlike democratic politics, it looked back to a society of ranks. The protector/dependent relation was succinctly depicted in that hallowed formulary and guide for nineteenth-century American doctors, the AMA code of ethics. Again, this code called upon the doctor "so to unite tenderness with firmness, and condescension with authority, as to inspire the minds of their patients with gratitude, respect, and confidence." Within the sickroom, that innmost realm of the relation, the doctor was to command and the patient to obey. In return for such obedience, the doctor gave not only his skill and attention, but also his fidelity. The physician's benefactions "were of such a character," explained the code, "that no mere pecuniary acknowledgement can repay or cancel them." This, in effect, was a stand (perhaps a reactionary one) against the depersonalization of mass markets and the egalitarianism of democratic politics.[63]

The doctor's professional outlook, therefore, had this duality within it. It was a third way, influenced by contemporary social developments and dangers, but it was at the same time retrospective, with points of attachment and complex allegiances to earlier acceptations and ambitions. Moreover, these old ways found reinforcement in the new medical sciences. Those sciences had for a while brought conflict to the profession, yet durably and significantly, they provided new supports for the doctor's traditional relation with his patients. Billings believed that progress in medical science, in fact progress in civilization, meant "increasing the power of the strong to protect and care for the weak."[64]

By the turn of the century, patients as well as doctors had come to believe that the physicians's power to cure had increased markedly, and along with such presumed power had come more apparent rewards for obedience and punishments for disobedience to his instructions. The gap in knowledge between the doctor and patient had widened, and the physician's new knowledge gave him the confidence to adopt an aggressive interventionist medicine reminiscent of eighteenth-century-style treatment. Not only the patient's knowledge but even his bodily instincts now seemed less reliable. There were "conditions of disease, in which the instincts fail to express the needs of the system," warned the renowned Dr. Austin Flint, Jr. "Under these circumstances, the knowledge and judgment of the practitioner must as far as possible take the place of nature's indications; science must assume control." The physician must prevail in order to heal.[65]

This seemed to be appropriate not only because the patient had physical needs that he could not understand but also because he had emotional needs that were inherent in his ailing condition. "Men and women," wrote Flint, "often become on the sick bed, in a mental and moral point of view, children, and are to be managed as such." American doctors did not have any explicit theory of transference, yet they did notice that patients commonly extended to them an unusual filial respect and affection, "a deference altogether extraordinary." Osler, therefore, apprised his students that "often the best part of your work will have nothing to do with potions and powders, but with the exercise of influence of the strong upon the weak, the righteous upon the wicked, the wise upon the foolish. To you as a trusted family counselor the father will come with his anxieties, the mother with her hidden grief, the daughter with her trials, and the son with his follies." The exercise of such salutary influence was the physician's right and duty. At times, even deception in the form of a "*placebo* remedy" might be necessary, nevertheless if it were resorted to in the ultimate interest of the patient, such a stratagem was acceptable.[66]

The doctor's emotional bond with his patient also had its own unique perplexities. The "excess of sensibility" that some physicians felt for the suffering of their patients, Dr. S. Weir Mitchell thought, endangered the effectiveness of medical treatment; yet the opposite, too little sensibility, he believed was worse. Osler's recommendation of "equanimity" was not easily maintained. In order to act as a protector, the doctor often diminished his awareness of his own vulnerability. He could not honorably avoid treating the many infectious diseases of that era, and many doctors succumbed. Yet this lowering of awareness made it more difficult to understand the feelings, thoughts, and motives of patients. Instead of empathy, many doctors more readily linked their own sense of worth to their success in curing their patients; but that had its own drawbacks. "'Don't you hate it, sir,'" Mitchell reported the famous Dr. Samuel Gross to have blurted out after a consultation. "'Hate it; What?' I said, 'hate what?' 'Oh to spend a life like yours and mine, and be beaten-puzzled-licked, sir—by a miserable lump in a woman's breast.'" Mitchell, after a long career in medicine, confessed that he never saw a death or a serious failure to cure that did not hurt him personally.[67]

The doctor's traditional authority not only found its supports

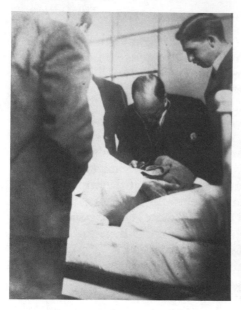

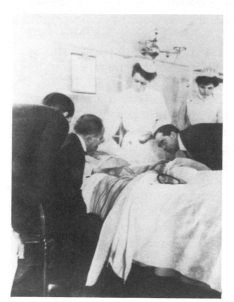

Dr. William Osler and his students making rounds at the Johns Hopkins Hospital in the late nineteenth century. Osler, one of the most renowned medical teachers of the era, urged the enhancement of the prerogatives and dignity of physicians. (*International Medical Museums Bulletin*, 9 [1926]: 105)

in the new sciences and in the situation at the bedside, but it was also sustained by influential institutions: the medical societies, the state legislatures, and the hospitals. Some doctors claimed that the principal achievements of the medical societies were the lessening of distrustful antagonism among medical men and the resulting enhancement of the doctor's authoritativeness with laymen. "To exert our legitimate influence over society," an association president advised, "we must work and act together." Whatever contributed to such solidarity would be advantageous. Mitchell thought that the gratuitous medical care that doctors bestowed upon fellow doctors was important to fraternal bonds. In addition, he claimed that the societies not only reinforced the physician's authority, they also strengthened his autonomy. "We have no public to which we bend with abject submission, no judge or jury to listen to us; no press or public to look on to applaud or condemn. What we do neither the patient nor his friends can fully understand." Only fellow doctors could fully understand and judge. As some medical societies adopted more stringent requirements for membership in the late nineteenth century, that membership itself became an attestation to the public of a doctor's competence.[68]

State legislatures provided direct acknowledgement and support to the special medical relation through laws placing broad restrictions on legal access to the confidential interchange between doctors and patients. By 1900, most states had such laws. By that date, all states also had enacted the medical licensing laws that gave doctors public recognition of their training and fitness for their distinctive powers. Hospitals also gave conspicuous recognition to the doctor's authority. The dictates of hospital etiquette, dress and address, appurtenances and perquisites, all reflected the doctor's commanding position. In the influential teaching hospitals, such conventions augmented the explicit precepts of exemplary demeanor imparted by the distinguished professors to generations of students, interns, and residents during the many and varied ceremonial and casual occasions at which it seemed appropriate to descant upon the prerogatives of medicine.[69]

Honor and authority were closely intertwined for doctors. Like his authority, the doctor's honor was not derived from election to high office, nor was it derived from accumulation of great wealth; like his authority, the doctor's honor had something quite traditional and yet much that was very modern about it. It was latent in the conditions of protectorship and personal dependence that had been common to many past times, places, and persons, and that reappeared at the bedside and operating table. "Humanity never failed to offer homage" to medical men, Dr. Loomis, president of the Congress of American Physicians and Surgeons pointed out, for "those who (have been) in 'the valley of the shadow of death' have learned to know what manner of men we are." Personal heroism, much like that which had won honor for protectors in the past, helped bring honor to nineteenth-century American doctors. For sometimes in their day-to-day work, but more dramatically in the disastrous epidemics that periodically struck towns and cities in nineteenth-century America, doctors rushed into the center of the danger to help the stricken, while many inhabitants fled in panic. In such circumstances doctors at times were called upon "to give up their lives for others," and they did. Those doctors were widely acclaimed, and the profession as a whole came to share in the treasury of merit garnered by way of their bravery.[70]

The new medical sciences enhanced the doctor's honor, for they seemed to impose new and exalted discipline and duties. "Science," wrote Dr. Charles V. Chapin, "is an ideal by which to live, work, and think." Acquiring that science, moreover, was an arduous task. For what is worthwhile needs be difficult, a leading physician remarked, yet the greater the difficulty, he observed, the greater the distinction and glory. Even more important: as medical science seemed to become increasingly efficacious, doctors claimed that it joined a more vigorous form of truth and a more effective form of good—the impersonal requirements of truth with the beneficence and humanity of healing. The doctor declared his unwavering allegiance to what his era considered true and good and was thereby elevated by it. Yet the honor of doctors not only involved the esteem and respect that they won from the lay world but also the differential regard which they bestowed upon each other. The most honored within the profession were not the most prosperous (those were often quacks) but those who had done most in the "support of professional character" or for "the enrichment of medical science." For much of the nineteenth century, the most honored doctors within the profession were the leading professors at the well-known medical schools, who had not only gained an extensive practice but had contributed to medical knowledge through scientific publications and had trained a congery of students who later called upon their learned professors for consultations. Frequently these revered medical professors assumed a patriarchal stance with regard to their students, former students, and even the broader medical profession, somewhat like that assumed by many doctors with regard to their patients. By the end of the century, this elite had been broadened to include specialists, research scientists, and then the full-time professors of medicine.[71]

Perhaps the most remarkable depiction of the honor accorded to eminent doctors of the late nineteenth century can be seen in the two great paintings by Thomas Eakins, *The Gross Clinic* and the *Agnew Clinic*. It would be exceedingly difficult to come up with portraits of eminent political leaders, businessmen, lawyers, or clergymen of the era treated with such unabashed awe and reverence. The scene of both pictures is set in a somber medical amphitheater, with Drs. Gross and Agnew each in full light, paused in the course of the operation, scapel in hand, explaining the surgery to tier after tier of students dimly portrayed. While the explicit portrayal of bloody hands and instruments as well as exposed body parts shocked genteel critics, the heroic characterization of Gross and Agnew drew praise.[72]

There is something fierce and harrowing about these scenes, yet their entire aspect is somehow the figure of the doctor "who can look on disease and pain and record them truthfully," as one critic wrote. The medical men are glorified as rarely before, valiantly defending mankind against the forces of darkness and disease. They exude the imperturability and disinterestedness of medical science, but also its humanity.[73]

While close attention to the workings of authority and honor is particularly helpful for an understanding of the medical profession, it would be a serious mistake to ignore the importance of economic interest. The medical profession was not self-abnegating with regard to its authority or its honor, and it was unlikely to be self-abnegating with regard to its economic welfare. Some of the doctors who took up specialties, as we have seen, found the increased earnings a considerable incentive, and many of the physicians who urged more stringent licensing laws were well aware of their economic benefits. Moreover, the fee bills (setting recommended minimum charges for various medical services) adopted by a variety of local medical associations during the nineteenth century were overt attempts to ensure comfortable incomes for all practitioners. Yet, as suggested earlier, these measures were impelled by mixed motives and accompanied by exalted justifications. It is significant that doctors did not make straightforward economic claims or rely upon direct economic inducements.[74]

Those who wished to restrict the supply of doctors, for example, could only resort to the raising of educational requirements, which though moderately successful as educational reform, proved ineffectual in this era in stemming the growing proportion of doctors to population. Even the fee bills were not justified in terms of maximizing income but rather as providing a "competence," sufficient means for the comfortable existence that would allow the doctor to carry on his work. This was closer to the precapitalist notions of just price than to capitalist notions of market price. As indicated, fee bill charges often became customary charges unresponsive to market conditions, and most physicians never relinquished their traditional practice of varying fees with the ostensible income of the patient—and treating the poor gratis. Fee bills were probably more important in fostering a general collaborative spirit and collegial solidarity than in raising doctors' incomes.[75]

In addition, some professional observances actually reduced doctors' earnings. The ban on patenting medical discoveries was serious enough during the nineteenth century to force Ohio doctors out of the AMA, and they were received back only after accepting the restriction. The code provision prohibiting advertising was a contentious issue for a long while. It undoubtedly brought hardship to young doctors who were without connections, yet most medical societies were unbending in enforcing it. For advertising, the standard-bearers of the profession argued, was directed inappropriately to the uniformed and unguided judgment of laymen, and it also heightened rivalry among doctors. Yet what the doctors themselves, with some warrant, pointed to most often as illustrative of their placing the general good above personal economic advantage was their advocacy of public health. Through their efforts toward compulsory vaccination, purification of water, drainage of malarial swamps, and scientific quarantine of contagious disease, they claimed, physicians were actually "devising and disseminating means for reducing the volume of business and its attendant profits." One doctor proudly contrasted the gathering of politicians and capitalists on one end of Pennsylvania Avenue, contriving to raise the tariffs and to take for themselves hard-won earnings from the pockets of the people, with the concurrent meeting of the Congress of American Physicians and Surgeons at the other end of the avenue, endeavoring to introduce new measures of disease prevention, all to the great benefit of the people and to the possible diminishment of professional incomes.[76]

At least from the 1880s onward, as state and local medical societies grew in strength and self-confidence, their spokesmen gave increasing attention to what they usually called "State Medicine and Public Hygiene." The AMA also showed a growing interest, and from its membership came virtually all the early presidents and officers of the American Public Health Association. Most likely, the average practitioner contributed little to the public health movement, yet he deferred to a leadership that played an important role. The advocacy of public health, the foremost doctors insisted, exemplified the placing of professional duties over narrow self-interest.[77]

The scanty information that we have about doctors' incomes at the turn of the century suggests that their average earnings were surprisingly small—about the same as ministers' and less than civil servants'. Yet many young men rushed into the profession, and a large contingent among them was made up of the sons of doctors. Families of doctors, spanning many generations, were not unusual. Perhaps the most notable were the six generations of the enduring Drs. Flint—the last three were all Drs. Austin Flint, all connected with Belleview Medical Center (if the final Dr. Flint had not been childless, we might still be availing ourselves of that persistent line of healers today). Such steadfastness of attachment in this able and advantaged family, amidst an ever-changing national life with its increasingly diverse and bountiful opportunities, suggests something of the persistent and peculiar attractiveness and gratifications that the medical profession afforded. The profession did not demand self-abnegation nor encourage unrestrained self-assertion, but it allowed for a sober and restricted pursuit of self-interest—a self-interest not defined in narrowly economic terms.[78]

Though the medical profession as a whole may not have prospered in the late nineteenth century, clearly it gained increasing respect and influence. This was most apparent in personal health care and on the public health boards and commissions. One of the principal lessons that the doctors on these boards taught was that contagion brought interdependence and that interdependence of this sort justified increased measures of compulsion. (This paralleled the shift in medical therapy from a broad reliance upon the natural recuperative powers of the body to an increased insistence upon active, interventionist practice.) A few eminent doctors went further yet in their public health addresses, arguing that nonmedical conditions—poverty, ignorance, social derangement—could bring disease, and that a medical standpoint might provide some remedial prescriptions for society. One brash young physician, in an address before the AMA, seemed to place government in the role of doctor, and society in the position of patient. "It is the duty of every government to study the needs of the people. . . . all governments must be parental, whatever their constitutional form may be." That doctor went on to become president of the AMA and played a decisive part in the reorganization of the association at the turn of the century. If his ideas were unusual, they were also not considered absurd. For they found some corroboration in the daily experience of doctors and in a broader cultural setting in America.[79]

Yet most doctors were much too taken up with their day-to-day duties and prerogatives to work out any comprehensive notions about the relation between their vocation and their society. Particular external threats to their authority, honor, or income of course they denounced, yet doctors provided appreciative audiences for a remarkable variety of contradictory proposals for the mutual betterment of medicine and the commonwealth. One medical spokesman recommended a more equal distribution of wealth, another talked about the natural elimination of the "idle, vicious, and unfit," while a third looked to a concerted social improvement under the leadership of the "more intelligent and better favored classes." Even later in the Progressive Era, though one could find many doctors as well as other professionals in the ranks of the progressive reformers, if one looked at the doctors and professionals themselves, they would appear scattered among diverse political affiliations.[80]

Though the American medical profession did not fashion a coherent political program at the turn of the century—politics for doctors was usually contingent and secondary—it did form distinctive work techniques, usages, and institutions, as well as a general occupational perspective. This was the perspective of the Third Way—a claim to a unique social position—as well as the assumption of a standpoint that derived much of its vision and many of its principles from an earlier society of stable social ranks. Such past attachments did not make medical men an anachronism; on the contrary, it gave them great relevance and vitality. For while the capitalism of the late nineteenth century enhanced material wealth, and democracy legitimized the social order, neither the capitalism nor the democracy of that era provided a high sense of purpose or a vigorous and durable sense of community. The medical profession, for its own members at least, did both.

Epilogue:
Since 1900

When I first began to take an interest in the professions, back in the late sixties and early seventies, it seemed that the traditional notions about them were nearing collapse. Young physicians were setting up hospital meetings with nurses, social workers, occupational therapists, physical therapists, and even orderlies, to discuss the patients' progress. Young lawyers were giving up practice to write books showing how almost anyone could do his or her legal work without lawyers. Young priests were shedding their distinctive dress and rushing out to social confrontations without attempting to say anything distinctive about their spiritual significance. Having been taught so persuasively that the Owl of Minerva took flight at dusk—that one could best understand an era when it was drawing to a close—I thought that it would be a good time to study the professions, for if they were not going to disappear, then surely an era in their history must be coming to a close. For all that, even before I had advanced very far in my research, it became apparent that the darkening I had thought was dusk was simply a passing cloud. What had to be explained was not decline but persistence.[1]

Initially, I had thought I might start in 1900 and bring the story down to the present. The year 1900 seemed to be a good point at which to begin, because at that date one could find a comprehensive definition of the professions that would be readily acceptable today. Be that as it may, a historian interested in continuity often willy-nilly falls backward in time, and I did. The result is this book, which spans a hundred and fifty years and ends in 1900. Yet present-day concerns could not be absent. Most historical work involves an interplay between past and present. If it is good historical work, the past will have something to teach; at the least, a richer sense of the past might safeguard us against an oversimple depiction of the present. Yet it is the present that proposes the questions we ask, and the present-day contentions and excitements over the nature of the professions and their importance furnished the impetus for this study.

From at least the nineteenth century until today, the professions have stood out as a model and guide to a special kind of accomplishment. For much of that time, an increasing proportion of Americans have come to earn their livelihood by selling their labor. Unlike marketing products, selling one's labor usually involves selling the right to be commanded. The extreme case is factory work, with its tightened discipline and intensified division of labor, but it is true of many other kinds of work as well. Already in Adam Smith's day, many were worried that factory labor would be oppressive and even damaging, but along with Smith, they felt that the ill effects could be lessened by various measures taken outside of the work itself. Later some reformers argued that increased productivity might permit shorter hours and higher wages, so that an enriched leisure might compensate for an impoverished work experience. The professions, and particularly the traditional professions, appeared in stark contrast to this, for they exemplified gratifying work.

The foremost professionals sold their labor but not the right to be commanded. The presence of the past, in their outlook and ambition, was important for this outcome. The traditional professions had once been occupations of a class accustomed to positions of authority, and this provided much of the impulse and aspiration to maintain such authority in the work setting long after customary ranks had disappeared in America. The sheltered markets these professionals came upon and fashioned were important to this achievement, but the significant factor was that they put the markets to such use. In addition, the esteem of the professions, drawn from diverse sources in the broader culture, augmented their attractiveness.

That attractiveness continued to exert its influence into the twentieth century. The history of the professions since 1900 is complex and challenging. Valuable studies have been written about particular professions, and the scholar who brings that material together will have much to teach us. Some of the broad outlines of the story are already discernible. The rapid growth and expansion of engineering among the professions excited notice almost immediately, but the sheer number of engineers did not give them preeminence. Most of them were employed within the industrial bureaucracies, and such engineers were among the most constrained of all professionals and among the most uncertain of their status. Medicine, though no longer having the largest membership, remained preeminent and the common model for imitation and emulation. However, the very existence of a large body of professionals with a clearly limited range of authority and autonomy gave members of occupations working in even more limiting circumstances encouragement to strive for professional recognition.[2]

The rise of the service sector in the American economy, after 1900, generated many such occupations. That development reflected a shift in the labor force from agriculture, mining, and manufacturing to leisure industries, civil service, and education; within manufacturing itself, from direct production to planning, allocation, and distribution. This shift produced new jobs, some better and some worse than those they replaced in the smokestack industries. Most of the new jobs were less susceptible to the rigorous work discipline characteristic of the industrial factory. It is not surprising that many of the workers in such jobs reached toward professionalism. The conspicuous appetite for professional status in the service sector is one of the unmistakable elements in the growth of this important part of the American economy.[3]

Historically, the market economy in America has provided an impressive growth of industrial productivity as well as a notable rise in living standards. Yet this was not achieved without cost. Intrinsic to that achievement was the development of less gratifying work and the gradual loss of a larger and more elevated purpose for economic endeavor. The leading professions, in bringing to the modern world ideals and predispositions of an earlier era, strove to retain just what the market economy relinquished. Professions are occupations and, therefore, can be understood in part as economic interest groups. Yet they offer much more than economic betterment—they offer a way of life. This is the power of their attraction.

Notes

Preface

1. For extensive recent historiographical discussion of the study of the professions, see: Gerald Geison, ed., "Introduction," in *Professions and Professional Ideologies in America* (1983), 3–11. See also Andrew Abbott, *The System of Professions* (1988), 1–34, for a discussion of the sociological literature. Abbott's ostensible analysis is almost the opposite of mine, yet I have gained much from his book. Historiographical disputations aside, scholars can learn a great deal from from works whose methodological presuppositions and general outlook differ greatly from their own. Abbott makes jurisdictional disputes the basis for his analysis, although they are surely not peculiar to the professions nor characteristic of many of them. Nonetheless, his book is astute, informative, and very valuable. See especially his exhaustive bibliography. For a study whose approach parallels mine, see Burton J. Bledstein, *The Culture of Professionalism* (1976).

2. The principal neo-Marxist study is Margali S. Larson, *The Rise of Professionalism* (1977), while one of the most self-consciously Weberian studies is Jeffrey Berlant, *Professions and Monopoly* (1975). The neo-Weberians stress modernization arguments, emphasizing the importance of expertise and monopolization. The neo-Marxists pay greater attention to class perspectives. However, there is much overlap. Both favor "systematic" analysis and insist upon the primacy of the current-day setting for an understanding of the real importance of the professions. One might also distinguish between right-wing Weberians who grant some legitimacy to the professions by virtue of their ostensible expertise and the left-wing Weberians who dispute the legitimacy of the professions by virtue of their effort at monopolization. Geison's essay (see n. 1) reflects this conflict. For my own historiographical discussion, see Samuel Haber, "The History of the Professions," *Encyclopedia of American Social History*, ed. Mary Kupiec Cayton (forthcoming).

3. A full discussion of the methodological supports of this standpoint would lead too far afield. In the recent historiographical debate on the primacy of text or context, see David Harlen, "Intellectual History and the Return of Literature," and David A. Hollinger, "The Return of the Prodigal," *American Historical Review* 94 (June 1989):581–626. Obviously, I find the latter view more convincing. Here the writings of Donald Davidson—*Essays on Actions and Events* (1980) and *Inquiries into*

Truth and Interpretation (1989)—have been the principal influence. See also Graham MacDonald and Philip Pettit, *Semantics and Social Science* (1982), chap. 1, for their illuminating discussion of the role that practical social activity plays in giving determinativeness to the meaning of words in our language, written and spoken.

4. Such a perspective also helps guard against procrustean and protean definitions of the professions. Seen in the setting of the rich historical record, the professions cannot be readily construed simply as economic interest gropus who were bent upon monopolizing the services they supplied in order to maximize income. Many such interest groups did not claim and were not given the designation of professions, and those occupations given such designation characteristically settled for economic second prizes rather than endanger their social perquisites. Similarly, the definition of professionals as experts, historically considered, is too inclusive and not inclusive enough.

5. Max Weber's discussion of the origin of the word profession, in *The Protestant Ethic and the Spirit of Capitalism* (1958), 265, is persuasive. Samuel Johnson, *A Dictionary of the English Language* ([1755], 1973). J. R. Western, "Professionalism in Armies, Navies and Diplomacy," in *The Eighteenth Century*, ed. Alfred Cobban (1969), 210–11. In America the military did not figure prominently among the professions; See the overview of part III in this book.

6. Daniel Defoe, *The Compleat English Gentleman*, ed. Karl D. Bühlbring, 257–58; Joseph Addison, *The Sir Roger De Coverly Papers*, ed. O. M. Myers ([21 July 1711] 1938), 75–80; Thomas Gisborne, *An Enquiry into the Duties of Men in the Higher and Middle Classes of Society in Great Britain* (1795), 218, 332; Viscesimus Knox, *Essays, Moral and Literary* (1815), 3:250–53.

7. Gisborne, *An Enquiry into the Duties of Men*, 494; Isaac Barrow, "The Industry of a Gentleman" [1689], *Half-Hours with the Best Authors*, ed. Charles Knight (1845), 244; David Erskine Dun, *Lord Dun's Friendly and Familiar Advice to the Country Noblemen and Gentlemen of Landed Estates* (1754), 88; William Blackstone, *Commentaries on the Laws of England*, 10th ed. (1787), 1:406.

8. Dorothy Marshall, *English People in the Eighteenth Century* (1956), 52, 119; Knox, *Essays*, 1:4, 14; Karl D. Bühlbring, "Introduction," in *The Compleat English Gentleman* ([1729] 1890) by Daniel Defoe, xl–xlii; Geoffrey Holmes, *Augustan England* (1982), chap. 1; David Matthew, *Social Structure of Caroline England* (1944), chap. 5.

9. John M. Murrin, "Review Essay," *History and Theory* 9 (1972): 226–75; Murrin, "Anglicizing an American Colony: The Transformation of Provincial Massachusetts" (Ph.D. diss., Yale, 1966); Gary M. Walton and James F. Shepherd, *The Economic Rise of Early America* (1969), 143–51. The discussion of the trade-off between interest and duty was usually found in the particular professional codes that appeared in various forms in the late eighteenth and early nineteenth centuries. However, for a wide-ranging treatise, see Gisborne, *An Enquiry into the Duties of Men*, chaps. 1, 9, 11, and 12. Duty was often distinguished from

obligation in that duty (literally, what is due) arose out of a permanent relation or station rather than particular cases.

10. See chapters 4 and 5. For an earlier discussion see Samuel Haber, "The Professions and Higher Education in America: A Historical View," *Higher Education and the Labor Market,* ed. Margaret S. Gordon (1974), 246–57.

11. See chapters 6 through 10 in this volume, and Haber, "The Professions," 257–62.

12. Perhaps the connecting of ideas to institutions can serve as a response, in some measure, to those who find fault with intellectual historians for not dealing with the problem of self-deception. Of course historians have no access to true consciousness. if we can show how ideas affect behavior we have accomplished a good deal. For example, we may find the gentlemanly poses of the rough-and-tumble Jacksonian doctors in the fledgling AMA seemingly spurious, yet when such notions led those physicians to expel a powerful phalanx of Ohio doctors who insisted on patenting their inventions (and "reducing our profession to a trade") then the historian must take such poses and notions seriously. In such a setting, the imputation of false consciousness becomes both tenuous and tendentious. Those Ohio doctors later repented, swore off patenting inventions, and were admitted back into the AMA. See Ohio State Medical Society, *Transactions* (1855): 24–56, and American Medical Association, *Transactions* 17 (1866): 521–28.

Overview of Part I

1. Jacob M. Price, "The Transatlantic Economy," in *Colonial British America* (1984), ed. Jack P. Greene and J. R. Pole, 18–40; Gary M. Walton and James M. Shepherd, *The Economic Rise of Early America,* chaps. 4 and 7; John J. McCusker and Russell R. Menard, *The Economy of British America, 1667–1789* (1985), chaps. 4 and 13; John M. Murrin, "Review Essay," *History and Theory* 9 (1972): 226–75. The most comprehensive discussion of the eastward turn of eighteenth-century American culture is still Thomas J. Wertenbaker, *The Golden Age of Colonial Culture* (1942).

2. James A. Henretta, "Wealth and Social Structure," in *Colonial British America,* 262–85; John M. Murrin, "Political Development," in *Colonial British America,* 432–47. Gary B. Nash, *The Urban Crucible* (1979), has influenced this discussion. See also Richard Hofstadter *America at 1750: A Social Portrait* (1972), chap. 5; Jackson Turner Main, *The Social Structure of Revolutionary America* (1965), chap. 9; Ethel E. Rasmusson, "Democratic Environment—Aristocratic Aspiration," *Pennsylvania Magazine of History and Biography* 90 (1966):155; Arthur M. Schlesinger, "Aristocracy in Colonial America," Massachusetts Historical Society, *Proceedings* 74 (1962):3.

3. For a suggestive discussion of eighteenth-century provincialism, see John Clive and Bernard Baily, "England's Cultural Provinces: Scotland and America," *William and Mary Quarterly,* 3d ser., 11 (1954):200. William L. Sachse's *The Colonial American in Britain* (1956) is also

helpful, as is Agnes M. Sibley's *Alexander Pope's Prestige in America, 1725–1835* (1949). Daniel Boorstin, *The Americans: The Colonial Experience* (1958), 189–239, presents a contrasting view.

4. Bernice Hamilton, "The Medical Procession in the Eighteenth Century," *The Economic History Review,* 2d ser., 4 (1951):141–69; Lester King, *The Medieval World of the Eighteenth Century* (1958), 232–33; Arnold Chaplin, *Medicine in England During the Reign of George III* (1919), 8; Charles Newman, *The Evolution of Medical Education in the Nineteenth Century* (1957) chap. 1. See also Edward Hughes "The Professions in the Eighteenth Century," *Durham University Journal,* n.s., 13, ii (1952):46–55.

5. Alan Harding, *A Social History of English Law* (1966), 285–91; W. S. Holdsworth, *A History of English Law* (1927) 6:chap. 8, and (1938) 12:chap. 3. For the seventeenth-century antecedents, see Wilfred R. Prest, *The Rise of the Barristers* (1986).

6. Vicesimus Knox, *Essays, Moral and Literary* (1815), 1:58–63, 102–3; Dorothy Marshall, *English People in the Eighteenth Century,* (1956), 162; Norman Sykes, *Church and State in England in the Eighteenth Century* (1934), 147, 156–81.

7. Thomas Gisborne, *An Enquiry into the Duties of Men in the Higher and Middle Classes of Society in Great Britain* (1795), chaps. 9, 11, and 12; Knox, *Essays,* 1:4, 14; Marshall, *English People,* 52, 119; Preserved Smith, *A History of Modern Culture* (1930), 318; James Westfall Thompson, *Literacy of the Laity in the Middle Ages* (1939), chap. 7; Andriano Tilger, *Work, What It Has Meant Through the Ages,* (1930), chaps. 1–4; William Harrison Woodward, *Studies in Education* (1924), chap. 13; Lawrence Stone, *Crisis of the Aristocracy* (1965), chap. 12.

8. Holdsworth, *History of English Law* 6:493–99, and (1938) 12: 71–101; William Holdon Hutton, *The English Church from the Accession of Charles I to the Death of Anne* (1903), 276–77; Newman, *Evolution of Medical Education,* 122–23, 127–28.

9. See the discussion of "the Cardinal sciences" of Theology, Physick, and Law, and "their great necessity and noble use" in John Guillim, *A Display of Heraldry,* 6th ed., (1724) 291; Ernest Gordon Rupp, *Religion in England, 1688–1791* (1986), 56–64, 493–517; John Gregory, *Lectures on the Duties and Qualifications of a Physician* (1772), 141; Paul Lucas, "Blackstone and the Reform of the Legal Profession," *English Historical Review* 77 (1962): 477–80; Brian Abel-Smith and Robert Stevens, *Lawyer and the Courts* (1967), 25–27.

10. Sir William Blackstone, *Commentaries on the Laws of England,* 10th ed. (1787), 1:171–72.

11. The connection of the professions with upward mobility in America is discussed by Main, *Social Structure,* 112–13, 219, 275. See also Alice Hanson Jones, *Wealth of a Nation to Be* (1986), 322. For England, see Robert Robson, *The Attorney in Eighteenth-Century England* (1959), app. B.

12. One of the most illuminating discussions of the eighteenth-century gentlemanly class is H. J. Habakkuk, "England," in *The Euro-*

pean Nobility in the Eighteenth Century (1953), ed. A. Goodwin. An informative contemporary description is in Gisborne, *An Enquiry into the Duties of Men,* chap. 14. For some interesting descriptions of plantation owners and merchants taking on English gentlemanly ways see Rhys Isaac, *The Transformation of Virginia* (1982), 124–31, as well as the older and still valuable Thomas J. Wertenbaker, *The Founding of American Civilization: The Old South* (1942); Carl Bridenbaugh, *Rebels and Gentleman* (1942), 179–83; and Bridenbaugh, *Cities in Revolt* (1955), chap. 6. See also James A. Henretta, "Economic Development and Social Structure in Colonial Boston," *William and Mary Quarterly,* 3d ser., 22 (1965): 79–92.

13. Alexander Hamilton, "The Federalist no. 35," in *The Federalist,* ed. Jacob E. Cooke (1961), 219–20, 220–21; James Madison, "The Federalist no. 54," *Federalist,* 370.

14. Hamilton, "The Federalist no. 31," *Federalist,* 193–95; Henry F. May, *The Enlightenment in America* (1976), chaps. 1, 2, and 3; Ernest Cassirer, *The Philosophy of the Enlightenment,* (1951), chaps. 1, 2, and pp. 234–53; Peter Gay, *The Enlightenment* (1969), 2:187–92, 596–97. Still valuable is Carl L. Becker, *The Heavenly City of the Eighteenth Century Philosophers* (1932).

15. Adam Smith, *An Inquiry into the Nature and Causes of the Wealth of Nations,* ed. R. H. Campbell and A. S. Skinner (1976), 1:123; "Competence," *The Oxford English Dictionary* (1933), 2:718–19.

16. For a preliminary description see James J. Walsh, *The History of Medicine in New York* (1919), 43–48; Milton M. Klein, "The Rise of the New York Bar," *William and Mary Quarterly,* 3d ser. 15 (1958): 334–58; Carl Bridenbaugh, *Mitre and Sceptre: Transatlantic Faiths, Ideas, Personalities, and Politics, 1689–1775* (1962), 247–48, 266. John Allen Krout, *Completion of Independence* (1944), 292. A more detailed analysis can be found in chaps. 1, 2, and 3 of this book.

17. Arthur W. H. Adkins, *Merit and Responsibility: A Study in Greek Values* (1960), chap. 3; Maurice Keen, *Chivalry* (1989), chap. 9; Eugene Vinaver *Malory,* (1929), 70–84; Helmuth Kittel, *Die Heerlichkeit Gottes* (1934); Robert Ashley, *Of Honour* ([1603] 1947), chap. 4; William Beveridge, *Sermons* (1729), 1:408; Dr. James Fordyce, "On Honour as a Principle," in *Addresses to Young Men* (1777), 1:216.

18. Mervyn James, *English Politics and the Concept of Honour, 1485–1642* (1978); W. T. MacCaffery, "England: The Crown and the New Aristocracy, 1540–1600," *Past and Present* 30 (1965): 52–64; Jerrily Green Marston, "Gentry Honor and Royalism in Early Stuart England," *Journal of British Studies* 13 (1973): 21; John Phillips Cooper, "Ideas of Gentility in Early Modern England," *Land, Men, and Beliefs* (1983), 43–77; Blackstone, *Commentaries,* 1:271; John Brown [1715–1766], *Honour: A Poem* (1743); David Erskine Dun, *Lord Dun's Friendly and Familiar Advice to the Country Noblemen and Gentlemen of Landed Estates* (1754) 25 ff.

19. John Guillim, *A Display of Heraldry . . . To which is added a treatise of Honour Military and Civil by capt. John Logan,* 6th ed.

(1724), 67, 269; Guillim is quoting, without attribution, Sir Thomas Smith writing in 1583. But this seems to have been a familiar quote in the eighteenth century. See Blackstone, *Commentaries,* 1:406; John Hildrop, D.D. [1725–1756], *An Essay on Honour in Nine Letters,* Evans 23446 ([1741] 1791), 11, 13, 14, 62.

20. Phillip Doddridge, *Some Remarkable Passages in the Life of Col. James Gardiner* (1747). The title varies. This work went through nine American editions and three printings. The variations among these editions are interesting but not pertinent to my purposes. My citations are from the American Sunday School Union edition of 1828. For an appreciative discussion of Doddridge's life and thought, see Rupp, *Religion in England,* 162–71.

21. Doddridge, *Life of Col. James Gardiner,* 3, 7, 13, 14, 25, 31, 40, 41, 163.

22. The most accessible edition of this essay, with a discussion of its origins and authenticity, is William E. Curtis, "An Unpublished Essay on 'Honor' by Aaron Burr," in *Cosmopolitan* 21 (1896): 557–60. Evarts B. Greene provides some interesting background discussion in "The Code of Honor in Colonial and Revolutionary Times, With Special Reference to New England," *The Colonial Society of Massachusetts Transactions,* 26 (1927): 367–88.

23. Burr, "Honor," 558–59. Of course the most well known discussion of natural aristocracy is in the correspondence between Jefferson and John Adams. See *The Adams-Jefferson Letters,* ed. Lester J. Cappon (1959), 2:387–90, 397–402.

24. Burr, "Honor," 559.

25. Frank Ezra Adcock, *Roman Political Ideas and Practice* (1959), chap. 3; P. A. Brunt, *Social Conflicts in the Roman Republic* (1978), 47–51; Doddridge, *Life of Col. James Gardiner,* 163. For a learned and sinuous discussion of the history of the idea of authority, see Leonard Krieger, "Authority," in *Dictionary of the History of Ideas,* ed. Philip P. Wiener (1973), 1:141–62.

26. Doddridge, *Life of Col. James Gardiner,* 87, 96, 100, 102, 105, 116, 175.

27. For a succinct discussion of Boudinot's political and religious ideas see Ralph Henry Gabriel, *Elias Boudinot* (1941).

28. Elias Boudinot, "Oration," in *The Life, Public Services and Addresses of Elias Boudinot,* ed. Jane J. Boudinot (1896), 2:356–78. This address, first printed in 1793, was often reprinted and found its way into anthologies. See Mayo W. Hazeltine, ed., *Orations from Homer to William McKinley* (1902), 7:2662–63. Boudinot ultimately became an ardent Federalist. For remarkably similar sentiments among his Democratic-Republican contemporaries, see Robert R. Livingston, *Oration Delivered Before the Society of Cincinnati,* (Evans 20464, ([1787] 1987); Duncan MacLeod, "The Political Economy of John Taylor of Caroline," *Journal of American Studies* 14 (1980):400–404. See also Gordon S. Wood, *The Creation of the American Republic* (1972), 70–75, 479–96.

Chapter 1

1. This story was long popular in the New England bar. For interesting variations, see Samuel L. Knapp, *Biographical Sketches of Eminent Lawyers* (1821), 201–3; James D. Hopkins, *Address to the Members of the Cumberland Bar* (1833), 28; William D. Northend, "Address before the Essex Bar Association," *Essex Institute Historical Collection* (1886), 23:17–18; Clifford K. Shipton, *Biographical Sketches of Those Who Attended Harvard College in the Classes 1722–1725* (1945), 7:518–30. Gridley himself had studied for the ministry before he switched to law. For Solomon Lombard, see Shipton, *Biographical Sketches,* 7:200–206.

2. For the comparative standing of lawyers and ministers in eighteenth-century Connecticut, see John T. Farrell, ed., *The Supreme Court Diary of William Samuel Johnson, 1772–1773* (1942), li–lii. John Adams seems to be referring to Benjamin Prat in his *Diary and Autobiography,* ed. Lyman H. Butterfield and others (1961), 1:73.

3. For helpful discussions of the eighteenth-century ministry, see John William Theodore Youngs, Jr., *God's Messengers: Religious Leadership in Colonial New England, 1700–1750* (1976); James Schmotter, "Provincial Professionalism: The New England Ministry, 1692–1745" (Ph.D. diss., Northwestern University, 1973); James Schmotter, "Ministerial Careers in Eighteenth-Century New England: The Social Context, 1700–1760," *The Journal of Social History* 9 (1975): 249–67; Daniel Calhoun, *Professional Lives in America* (1965), chap. 1; Donald M. Scott, *From Office to Profession: The New England Ministry, 1750–1850* (1978), chap. 1.

4. For good general treatments of the Church of England in America during this era, see William W. Manross, *History of the American Episcopal Church* (1950) and E. Clowes Chorley, *Men and Movements in the American Episcopal Church* (1948). John Frederick Woolverton, *Colonial Anglicanism in North America* (1984).

5. For a strangely partisan, modern study of the struggle of the American episcopacy, see Carl Bridenbaugh, *Mitre and Sceptre: Transatlantic Faiths, Ideas, Personalities, and Politics, 1689–1775* (1962). A comprehensive bibliography of the pamphlet war is provided by Rev. Edmund F. Slafter, *John Checkley, or The Evolution of Religious Tolerance in Massachusetts Bay* (1897), 2:235–98. The older study by arthur Lyon Cross, *The American Episcopate and the American Colonies* (1902), is more balanced. It is instructive to hear the Anglicans discuss the issue among themselves. See, for example, Samuel Seabury, Sr., to Thomas Sherlock, Bishop of London, 23 October 1753, Samuel Seabury Papers, St. Marks Library of the General Theological Seminary, Chelsea Square, New York; Cross, *American Episcopate,* 94, 239, 261; "William Harrison Letter," *Historical Collections Relating to the American Colonial Church,* ed. William S. Perry (Pennsylvania: 1870–1878), 2:127–28.

6. Thomas Bradbury Chandler, *An Appeal to the Public,* Evans 10578, 1767, 3, 31–34. For Chandler's broader social vision, see his *The Appeal Defended,* Evans 11203 (1769), 18–19, 59, 79, 179; *The Appeal Farther*

Defended, Evans 12007, (1771), 14, 59, 79, 111, 179, 212–13, 230; *Sermon Preached before The Corporation,* Evans 12008 (1771), 18; and *An Address to the Clergy of New York,* Evans 12021, (1771), 19. One of the best discussions of "the Old English Order" is in David Little's *Religion, Order, and Law: A Study in Pre-Revolutionary England* (1969), chap. 5. For the changes in religious and social thought within the Church of England after 1660, see Gerald R. Cragg, *From Puritanism to the Age of Reason* (1950). Blackstone's discussion of law is in Sir William Blackstone, *Commentaries on the Laws of England* (1765), 43.

7. A standard work on the Church of England in this era is Norman Sykes, *Church and State in England* (1934); a recent study is Ernest Gordon Rupp, *Religion in England, 1688–1791* (1986). More helpful for the intellectual history of the Church and the Bangorian controversy is Gerald R. Cragg, *Reason and Authority in the Eighteenth Century* (1964). S. C. Carpenter, *Eighteenth-Century Church and People* (London, 1959), 130–36. See also Benjamin Hoadly, *The Nature of the Kingdom, or Church of Christ* (London, 1715), 11, 31.

8. Chandler, *Appeal Defended, 22, 38, 49, 53; Thomas Bradbury Chandler, An Appendix to the American Edition of the Life of Archbishop Seeker,* Evans 13192 (1774), 12; Chandler, *Sermon,* 18; Chandler, *Appeal Farther Defended,* 177.

9. Samuel Johnson, *Samuel Johnson: His Career and Writings,* ed. Herbert Schneider (1929), 1:16; John Potter, *A Discourse on Church Government,* 3d ed., (1724), 259.

10. Johnson, *Career and Writings,* 1:6, 7, 11, 12, 13.

11. W. K. Lowther Clark, *Eighteenth-Century Piety* (1944), 1–29 and chap. 9; Sykes, *Church and State in England,* 284–90; Carpenter, *Eighteenth-Century Church,* chap. 4; Johnson, *Career and Writings,* 1:83, 93, 113, 357, 359, 483, and 2:17, 339.

12. Johnson, *Career and Writings,* 1:23, 20–24, 31; 2:19–20, 339, 438; 3:501–14; Clifford K. Shipton, *New England in the Eighteenth Century* (1963), 94; G. J. Cuming, *A History of Anglican Liturgy* (1969), 183–90.

13. Chandler, *Sermon,* 27; Charles Inglis, *A Vindication of the Bishop of Landoff's Sermon,* Evans 10934 (1768), 62; John Clement, "Anglican Clergymen Licensed to the American Colonies, 1710–1744," *Historical Magazine of the Protestant Episcopalian Church* 17 (1948): 207–50; William Seiler, "The Anglican Parish in Virginia," in *Seventeenth-Century America,* ed. James M. Smith (1959), 119–43; George M. Brydon, "Virginia Clergy: Governor Gooch's Letters to the Bishop of London, 1727–49," *Virginia Magazine History and Biography* 32 (1924): 209, and 33 (1925): 51; Thomas C. Reeves, "John Checkley and the Episcopal Church in New England," *Historical Magazine of the Protestant Episcopalian Church* 34 (1965): 349–60; S. Charles Bolton, *Southern Anglicanism: The Church of England in Colonial South Carolina* (1982), chap. 5.

14. Samuel Seabury, *An Address to the Ministers and Congregations of Presbyterian and Independent Persuasion in the United States,* Ev-

ans 22880 (1790), 3–9, 10–15. The argument was later taken up by Rev. John H. Hobart; see his *A Collection of Essays on Episcopacy* (1806) and *Apology for Apostolic Order* (1807, republished 1844 and 1856); Clara Loveland, *The Critical Years: The Reconstruction of the Anglican Church in the United States of America, 1780–1789* (1959), chaps. 7, 8, and 9. Robert Bruce Mullin, *Evangelical Vision/American Reality: High Church Theology and Social Thought in Evangelical America* (1986), chaps. 2 and 3, presents a good discussion of Hobart's thought.

15. For the Reformation doctrine of the ministry, I have generally relied upon James L. Ainslie, *The Doctrines of Ministerial Order in the Reformed Churches of the Sixteenth and Seventeenth Centuries* (1904); Sidney Mead, "The Rise of the Evangelical Conception of the Ministry in America (1607–1850)," in *The Ministry in Historical Perspective*, ed. H. Richard Niebuhr (1956).

16. The most succinct discussion of the Puritan doctrine of the ministry can be found in the Cambridge Platform of 1648. See Williston Walker, *Creeds and Platforms of Congregationalism* (1960), 210, 209–17. See also John Norton, *The Answer*, trans. Douglas Horton (1958), chaps. 4–9; Cotton Mather, *Ratio Disciplinae Fratrum Nova-Anglorum*, Evans 2775, (1726), 14–42, 103–20. See also Winthrop Still Hudson, "The Ministry in the Puritan Age," in *The Ministry in Historical Perspective*, ed. H. Richard Niebuhr (1956).

17. John Cotton, *Spiritual Milk for Babes*, Evans 42 (1656), 4; The Westminster Assembly of Divines, *The Shorter Catechism*, Evans 579 (1691), 19–20; The New England Primer Improved, Evans 8941 (1761), 41; Paul Leicester Ford, *The New England Primer* (1897), 1–53; Leonard T. Grant, "Puritan Catechizing," *Journal of Presbyterian History* 46 (1968): 107; David D. Hall, ed., *The Antinomian Controversy, 1636–38* (1968), 313–14; David D. Hall, *The Faithful Shepherd* (1973).

18. Jonathan Edwards, Jr., *The Works of Jonathan Edwards, Jr.* (1850), 2:60; Cotton Mather, *Love Triumphant*, Evans 2356 (1722), 10; Hall, *Antinomian Controversy*, 312–13, 323; John T. McNeill, "Casuistry in the Puritan Age," *Religion in Life* 12 (1943): 85; John Cotton, *The Keyes of the Kingdom* (London, 1644), 100.

19. Roger Williams, *Queries of Highest Considerations* (London, 1644), in Narragansett Club Publications, 1st ser., 2 (1867): 20; Roger Williams, "The Bloody Tenet Yet More Bloody," in *Puritan Political Ideas*, ed. Edmund S. Morgan (1965), 217.

20. For a discussion of the social transformation of New England, see Norman H. Dawes, "Titles as Symbols of Prestige in Seventeenth-Century New England," *William and Mary Quarterly*, 3d ser., 6 (1949): 69–83; James A. Henretta, "Economic Development and Social Structure in Colonial Boston," *William and Mary Quarterly*, 3d ser., 22 (1965): 75–92; Kenneth A. Lockridge, "Land, Population and the Evolution of New England Society, 1630–1790," *Past and Present* 39 (1968): 62–80; William B. Weeden, *Economic and Social History of New England, 1620–1789* (1890), 1:293–303, and 2:528–50; John J. McCusker and Russell R. Menard, *The Economy of British America, 1607–*

1789 (1985), chap. 5. For the loss of the charter and the new political order, see Herbert L. Osgood, *The American Colonies in the Eighteenth Century* (1924), 2:126–58; Wesley Frank Craven, *The Colonies in Transition, 1660–1713* (1968), 209–10, 241–46, 284. A good description of the urbane London Presbyterian ministers can be found in Michael Watts, *The Dissenters* (1978), 1:chap. 4. See also John W. Wilkes, "The Transformation of Dissent: A Review of Changes from the Seventeenth to the Eighteenth Centuries," in *The Dissenting Tradition*, ed. C. Robert Cole (1975), 108–22.

21. Benjamin Colman, *The Piety and Duty of Rulers*, Evans 1346 (1708), 13; Everett Kimball, *The Public Life of Joseph Dudley* (1911), 14, 17, 207, 209. See also "Joseph Dudley," in John Langdon Sibley, *Biographical Sketches of Graduates of Harvard University* 1–3 (1873–1885): 166–88.

22. Colman, *Piety and Duty of Rulers*, 13, 22, 26, 29. On Harvard class lists, see Clifford K. Shipton, "Ye Mystery of Ye Ages Solved, or How Placing Worked at Colonial Harvard and Yale" *Harvard Alumni Bulletin* 57 (December 11, 1954): 258–59, 262–63.

23. Colman, *Piety and Duty of Rulers*, 10–12.

24. Clayton H. Chapman, "Life and Influence of Benjamin Colman, D.D., 1673–1747" (Ph.D. diss., Boston University School of Theology, 1948), 6, 36, 191; "Records of the Cambridge Association," *Massachusetts Historical Society Proceedings* 17 (1879–80), 277; Walker, *Creeds and Platforms*, 467–71; Joseph Allen, *The Worcester Association and Its Antecedents* (1868), 9, 17; Ebenezer Turell, *The Life and Character of the Reverend Benjamin Colman*, Evans 6434 (1749).

25. Walker, *Creeds and Platforms*, 467–68, 493–94; Henry Martyn Dexter, *The Congregationalism of the Last Three Hundred Years* (1880), 511–12; Robert Middlekauff, *The Mathers: Three Generations of Puritan Intellectuals, 1596–1728* (1971), 225–26; Chapman, "Colman," 73–83; Mary Latimer Gambrell, *Ministerial Training in Eighteenth-Century New England* (1937), 53–55; Youngs, *God's Messengers* (see n.3), 69–78; David Harlan, *The Clergy and the Great Awakening in New England* (1986). Harlan provides the fullest discussion of the ministerial associations, but his work is unnecessarily polemical, exaggerating his differences with Youngs and Schmotter.

26. Colman, *Piety and Duty of Rulers*, 10–12; John Hancock, *A Sermon Preached at the Ordination of Mr. John Hancock*, Evans 2748 (1726), 29; John Tufts, *Anti-Ministerial Objections Considered*, Evans 2713 (1725), 21, 27; Samuel Deane, *The New England Farmer*, Evans 22450 (1790), 1; Frank Samuel Child, *The Colonial Parson of New England* (1896), chap. 3.

27. Cotton Mather, *Magnalia Christi Americana* ([1702], 1967), 2:240, 250, 256–58; C. Mather, *Ratio Disciplinae*, 105; Cotton Mather, *A Brief Memorial for Pastorial Visits*, Evans 2449 (1723), 1–3; Samuel Willard, "Circular Letter" (1704), *Massachusetts Historical Society Proceedings* 17 (1879–80), 280–81; Arthur Goodenough, *The Clergy of Litchfield County* (1909), 23. George Selement, *Keepers of the Vine-*

yard: The Puritan Ministry and Collective Culture in New England (1984) emphasizes pastoral care.

28. Youngs's *God's Messengers*, 90, discusses the shift in the use of the phrase. The writings of the Mathers reflect the broader shift in the relation between the ministry and the church. See, for example, "The Work of the Ministry Described," in Increase Mather, *Practical Truths, Plainly Delivered*, Evans 322 (1682), 104; Cotton Mather, *Bonifacus* (1710), ed. David Levin (1966), 69; C. Mather, *Magnalia*, 2:240, 256; C. Mather, *Ratio Disciplinae*, 192–93. See also Perry Miller, *The New England Mind: From Colony to Province* (1953), 53–67, 134–35; Edmund S. Morgan, *Visible Saints: The History of a Puritan Idea* (1963), 64–112.

29. Harry Stout, *The New England Soul* (1986), provides the most recent and extensive argument against "declension" and argues that New England piety moved in cyclical patterns. He does not discuss the extensive evidence that points to the differentiation in society and that suggests an accompanying sequestering of piety. See Selement, *Keepers of the Vineyard*, 85–87, for some indications of such development. Of course piety must be distinguished from moralism. The Puritan doctrine of "the moral government of God," which held that men were judged not only individually but also as members of nations which were collectively blessed or cursed on the basis of keeping God's moral law, remained a potent force throughout the nineteenth century in New England. See Joseph Haroutunian's classic work, *Piety versus Moralism: Passing of the New England Theology* (1932).

Among the important works describing the differentiation within Puritan society are Richard L. Bushman, *From Puritan to Yankee: Character and Social Order in Connecticut, 1690–1765* (1967), and Richard S. Dunn, *Puritans and Yankee: The Winthrop Dynasty of New England, 1639–1717* (1962). One colorful and oblique instance of such development is the rise of dancing schools in eighteenth-century Massachusetts and Connecticut. See Barbara Loomis, "Piety and Play: Young Women's Leisure in an Era of Evangelical Religion" (Ph.D. diss., University of California, Berkeley, 1988), chap. 5. J. Earl Thompson, Jr., "Perilous Experiment: The New England Clergymen and American Destiny, 1796–1826" (Ph.D. diss., Princeton University, 1966), describes the increasing ministerial use of arguments based upon the social uses of religion.

30. Youngs, *God's Messengers*, chap. 4, and Schmotter, "Provincial Professionalism" (see n. 3), chap. 6.

31. "Testimony of the Pastors of the Churches in the Province of Massachusetts Bay," *Source Book and Bibliographical Guide for American Church History*, ed. Peter G. Mode (1921), 222–26. For a brief overview, see Osgood, *American Colonies in the Eighteenth Century* 3:pt. 3, chap. 1. For more recent discussions, see Patricia U. Bonomi, *Under The Cope of Heaven* (1986), chap. 5 and David S. Lovejoy, *Religious Enthusiasm in the New World* (1985), chaps. 9, 10.

32. The quote is from Johnson, *Writings*, 3:230. The Reverend Dr.

James MacSparren, *The Sacred Dignity of the Christian Priesthood,* Evans 6871 (1751). Some of the standard studies are Edwin S. Gaustad, *The Great Awakening in New England* (1957); Leonard J. Trinterud, *The Forming of an American Tradition: Colonial Presbyterianism* (1949); W. M. Gewehr, *The Great Awakening in Virginia, 1740–90* (1930). Alan Heimert's *Religion and the American Mind: From the Great Awakening to the Revolution* (1966) presents a sharp, partisan view, but his anthology, *The Great Awakening: Documents Illustrating the Crisis and Its Consequences,* ed. Alan Heimert and Perry Miller (1967), is more balanced and useful.

33. Bonomi, *Under the Cope of Heaven,* 149–54, 156–60, 162–66; C. C. Goen, *Revivalism and Separatism in New England, 1740–1800* (1962), chap. 3.

34. Ebenezer Frothingham, "The Articles of the Separate Churches," 441–64; Solomon Paine, "A Short View of the Church of Christ," 411–22; and "A Letter from the Ministers of Windham," 399–410, in *Great Awakening,* ed. Heimert and Miller.

35. Goen, *Revivalism and Separatism,* 77, 126, 145–46, 166, 174–76; William C. McLoughlin, *Isaac Backus and the American Pietistic Tradition* (1967), 32–33, 41, 51.

36. Conrad Wright, *The Beginnings of Unitarianism in America* (1955), 28–58; Charles Chauncy, *Ministers Exhorted,* Evans 5358 (1744), 6, 7, 19, 21–22; Charles Chauncy; "Enthusiasm Described and Caution'd Against," in *Great Awakening,* ed. Heimert and Miller, 236–37; Charles Chauncy, *Ministers Cautioned,* Evans 5357 (1744), 15; Charles Chauncy, *Duty of Ministers,* Evans 10256 (1766), 18; Shipton, "Thomas Prentiss" in *Biographical Sketches,* 16:417.

37. Shipton, "David Barnes," in *Biographical Sketches,* 13:189–94; Shipton, "Charles Chauncy," in *Biographical Sketches,* 6:439–67; "John Elliot to Jeremy Belknap, July 31, 1779," *Massachusetts Historical Society Collections,* 6th ser., 4 (1891), 145; "Ebenezer Hazard to Jeremy Belknap, January 17, 1782," *Massachusetts Historical Society Collections,* 5th ser., 2 (1882), 179–84. For the European background to this excitement, see Daniel Pickering Walker, *The Decline of Hell: Seventeenth-Century Discussions of Eternal Torment* (1964).

38. Zabdiel Adams, *The Duty of Ministers,* Evans 24023 (1792), 20. For the successors to these liberal ministers, see Daniel Walker Howe, *The Unitarian Conscience* (1976).

39. C. Mather, *Magnalia,* 2:256–57; C. Mather, *Ratio Disciplinae,* 16, 19–22; Shipton, "Isaiah Dunster," in *Biographical Sketches,* 11:25–27; Daniel Calhoun, *Professional Lives in America* (1965), chap. 4; Isaiah Dunster, *Ministerial Authority,* Evans 9382 (1763), 8–10.

40. Jonathan Edwards, *The Works of Jonathan Edwards* (1832), 4:36; Jonathan Edwards, "The Distinguishing Marks of a Work of the Spirit," 204–13, "Thoughts on the Revival of Religion," 263–90, and "Qualifications for Communion," 423–40, in *Great Awakening in New England,* ed. Heimert and Miller; Gaustad, *Great Awakening,* 80–101.

41. Edwards, *Works of Jonathan Edwards,* 4:242–43: Jonathan Ed-

wards, *The Works of President Edwards* (1830), 1:644, and 4:365–66;
Jonathan Edwards, *The Works of President Edwards* (1844), 3:563,
566, 571, 597–99; Samuel Hopkins, *Life and Character of the Late Rev-
erend Mr. Jonathan Edwards*, Evans 10008 (1765), 43; Sereno Dwight,
Life of Reverend Jonathan Edwards (1830), 113–15; Williston Walker,
Ten New England Leaders (1901), 325; Edmund S. Morgan, *The Gentle
Puritan* (1962), 182. Nathaniel Emmons, one of the leading Edward-
sians, led so confidently that he is described with great admiration by
Simeon Baldwin (who adopted Emmons's method in the American Bar
Association) as writing out the resolutions of the ministerial conven-
tions *before* they met.

42. Isaac Stiles, "A Looking-Glass for Changelings," 320, and Solomon
Williams, "The True State of the Question," 435–40, in *Great Awakening*, ed. Heimert and Miller.

43. Chapman, "Colman (see n. 24), 202; James G. Leyburn, *The
Scotch-Irish; A Social History* (1962), pt. 2, 140–53. J. M. Bumsted,
"Presbyterianism in Eighteenth-Century Massachusetts: The Formation
of a Church at Easton, 1752," *Journal of Presbyterian History* 46
(1968), 243–53.

44. George Gillespie, *A Sermon Against Divisions in Christ's Church*,
Evans 4521 (1740), 23–30; Trinterud, *An American Tradition*, 131,
210; Ainslie, *Doctrines of Minesterial Order* (see n. 15), 5–6.

45. Chapman, "Colman," 198–204; Jonathan Dickinson, *The Danger
of Schisms*, Evans 4358 (1739), 38–40. Jon Butler, *Power, Authority,
and the Origins of American Denominational Order: The English
Churches in the Delaware Valley, 1680–1730* (1978), chap. 5, 76–77.

46. Jonathan Dickinson, *A Sermon Preached at the Opening of the
Synod at Philadelphia, September 19, 1722*, Evans 2428 (1723), 11,
18–19, 21–23.

47. John Thomson, *An Overture Presented to the Reverend Synod*,
Evans 3228 (1729), 15, 26; Maurice W. Armstrong, *The Presbyterian
Enterprise: Sources of American Presbyterian History* (1956), 30. For a
discussion of the subscription controversy in Europe and America, see
Marilyn J. Westerkamp, *Triumph of the Laity: Scots-Irish Piety and the
Great Awakening, 1626–1760* (1988), chap. 3.

48. Richard Webster, *A History of the Presbyterian Church in America*
(1857), 102–10; Bryan F. LeBeau, "The Subscription Controversy and
Jonathan Dickinson," *Journal of Presbyterian History* 54 (1976): 325;
Dickinson, *Sermon*, 5–6; Jonathan Dickinson, *Familiar Letters to a
Gentleman upon a Variety of Seasonable and Important Subjects in
Religion*, Evans 5572 (1745), 377–78; Thomson, *Overture*, 12; Thom-
son, *Government of the Church*, 63, 75.

49. Trinterud, *An American Tradition*, 181–82 and chap. 4; Webster,
Presbyterian Church, 387–97; Gilbert Tennent, "The Danger of an Unconverted Ministry," 71–99, and "Remarks upon a Protestation," 168–
75, in *Great Awakening*, ed. Heimert and Miller.

50. Dickinson, *Danger of Schisms*; Jonathan Dickinson, "The Witness of Spirit," 108, and "A Display of God's Special Grace," 178, in *Great

Awakening, ed. Heimert and Miller; John Maclean, *History of the College of New Jersey* (1877), 1:117–23.

51. Thomson, *Government of the Church*, v, 19, 57–66, 115, 121–28; John Thomson, *An Explication of the Shorter Catechism*, Evans 6429 (1741), 14; John Thomson, *An Essay upon Faith of Assurance*, Evans 40214 (1740), 64; Webster, *Presbyterian Church*, 355–57.

52. Gilbert Tennent, *The Necessity of Religious Violence*, Evans 3966 (1735); Gilbert Tennent, *The Necessity of Studying to Be Quiet and Doing Our Own Business*, Evans 5498 (1744); Gilbert Tennent, "Irenicum Ecclesiasticum," in *Great Awakening*, ed. Heimert and Miller, 367–75; C. A. Briggs, "The Plan of Union, 1758," in *American Presbyterianism* (1885), cviii-cxii; Trinterud, *An American Tradition*, chap. 9; John Witherspoon, *The Works of John Witherspoon, D.D.* (1805), 6:20 ff., 179–80, and 9:267–68.

53. Douglas Sloan, *The Scottish Enlightenment and the American College Ideal* (1971), 119–29; James McAllister, "John Witherspoon," *A Miscellany of American Christianity*, ed. Stuart Henry (1963), 183–224.

54. Elwyn Allen Smith, *The Presbyterian Ministry in American Culture* (1962), 92–94; Charles Grier Sellers, Jr., "John Blair Smith," *Journal of the Presbyterian Historical Society* 34 (December 1956): 211–14.

55. Samuel Miller, *Memoirs of Rev. John Rodgers* (1813), 251–61; Charles Hodge, *The Constitutional History of the Presbyterian Church in the United States of America* (1851), pt. 2, 408–19; Edward Frank Humphrey, *Nationalism and Religion in America, 1774–1781* (1924), 260–82; Trinterud, *An American Tradition*, 280–94, 295–306.

56. David L. Holmes, "The Episcopal Church and the American Revolution," *Historical Magazine of the Protestant Episcopal Church* 47 (1971): 261–91; E. E. Beardsley, *Life and Correspondence of the Right Reverend Seabury, D.D.* (1881), chap. 14; Bruce Steiner, *Samuel Seabury, 1729–1796* (1971), chap. 8; Horacy Weymes Smith, *Life and Correspondence of Rev. William Smith, D.D.* (1880), 2:51–52; Clara O. Loveland, *The Critical Years: The Reconstruction of the Anglican Church in the United States of America, 1780–1789* (1959), chap. 7, 8, 9. Frederick V. Mill, *Bishops by Ballots* (1978), chap. 2, 9.

57. Mill, *Bishops by Ballots*, chaps. 11, 12; Steiner, *Samuel Seabury*, chap. 8; Charles C. Tiffany, *History of the Protestant Episcopal Church in the United States of America* (1899), 7:312–84; Chorley, *Men and Movement* (see n. 4), 175–81; William W. Manross, *History of the American Episcopal Church* (1950), 197–201; Samuel Seabury, *Discourse on Several Subjects*, Evans 26148 (1793), 177–78.

58. For the Congregationalist support of the Revolution, see Alice M. Baldwin, *The New England Clergy and the American Revolution* (1958). On the church establishments in New England, see James Truslow Adams, *New England in the Republic, 1776–1850* (1927), 91, 220–23; Richard J. Purcell, *Connecticut in Transition, 1775–1818* (1918), chap. 2; Massachusetts Constitution [1780], Article III, in Francis Newton Thorpe, *Federal and State Constitutions* (1909), 3:1889–90.

59. The major work on the American Enlightenment is Henry May, *The Enlightenment in America* (1976), to which I am broadly indebted. See also Sidney Mead, *The Lively Experiment* (1963), chap. 3; Jedidiah Morse, *The Present Situation of Other Nations of the World, Contrasted with Our Own . . .* , Evans 29113, (1795), 10–11. See Joseph Phillips, *Jedidiah Morse and New England Congregationalism* (1983), 181 ff., for Morse's later patriotism.

60. May, *Enlightenment in America,* 252–77, 319–36.

61. Benjamin Rush to Ashbel Green, *Letters of Benjamin Rush,* ed. L. H. Butterfield (1951), 2:946, and 1:294; Lefferts A. Loetscher, *Facing the Enlightenment and Pietism: Archibald Alexander and the Founding of Princeton Theological Seminary* (1983), 122 and chap. 8; Dwight, *A Sermon Preached at the opening of the Theological Institution at Andover,* Shaw and Shoemaker, 14904 (1808), 3–4, 7–8, 10–11; Timothy Dwight, *Sermons,* (1829) 1:291–92 and 2;526–29. Harvard responded with a seminary of its own in 1818 and Yale in 1822; See Conrad Wright, "The Early Period," in *Harvard Divinity School,* ed. George H. Williams (1954), 27 ff.; Roland H. Bainton, *Yale and the Ministry* (1957), 79–95.

62. Edwin D. Griffin, *A Sermon at the Funeral of Alexander MacWhorter,* 22 July 1807, Shaw 126957, 33–34; I. Mather, *A Discourse Concerning Maintenance,* Evans 1269 (1706), 28; Ebenezer Parkman, *The Love of Christ Constraining Us* Evans 8965, (1761), 7, 13, 35; Samuel Stanhope Smith, *Discourse on the 22nd of February,* Evans 3281, (1797), 30; John H. Rice, *The Importance of the Gospel Ministry* (1817), 4. See Bailey B. Buritt, *Professional Distribution of College and University Graduates* (1912), 13–21, for Harvard. The trend was much the same at Yale, the University of Pennsylvania, Columbia University, Brown, and Dartmouth; see 21–46.

63. Compare Richard Salter Storrs, *Minister of the Gospel Characterized,* Shaw 1365 (1801), and Samuel Stearns, *Ministerial Fidelity,* Shaw 13639 (1807), with Donald M. Scott, *From Office to Profession* (1978), 7–17.

Chapter 2

1. For the preprofessional medicine of the seventeenth and early eighteenth centuries in America, see Henry R. Viets, *A Brief History of Medicine in Massachusetts* (1930), chap. 1; James J. Walsh, *History of Medicine in New York* (1919), 1:chaps. 2, 3; Joseph Carson, *A History of the Medical Department of the University of Pennsylvania* (1869), chap. 2; Wyndham B. Blanton, *Medicine in Virginia in the Seventeenth Century* (1930), chap. 3; Wyndham B. Blanton, *Medicine in Virginia in the Eighteenth Century* (1931), chaps. 5, 10; Malcolm Sydney Beinfield, "The Early New England Doctor: An Adaptation to a Provincial Environment," *Yale Journal of Biology and Medicine* 15 (1942): 99–132, 271–88; Robert T. Joy, "The Natural Bonesetters," *Bulletin of the History of Medicine* 28 (1954): 416–41; Whitefield J. Bell, Jr., "Medical Practice in Colonial America," *Bulletin of the History of Medicine* 31 (1957): 442–53; J. J.

Keevil, "The Seventeenth Century English Medical Background," *Bulletin of the History of Medicine* 31 (1957): 408–24.

2. Adam Smith, *An Inquiry into the Nature and Causes of the Wealth of Nations* (1937), 112; Joseph F. Kett, "Provincial Medical Practice in England, 1730–1815," *Journal of the History of Medicine and Allied Sciences* 19 (1964): 17–29. For a contemporary and enthusiastic appraisal of these medical schools and societies, see James Thacher, *The American Medical Biography* ([1828] 1967), 1:14–85. Most of them were modeled after the medical school at Edinburgh; see Samuel Lewis, "List of the American Graduates in Medicine in the University of Edinburgh," *New England Historical and Genealogical Register* 42 (1888): 159–65.

3. George Rosen, *Fees and Fee Bills: Some Economic Aspects of Medical Practice in Nineteenth-Century America* (1946), 2–5; Richard H. Shryock, *Medical Licensing in America, 1650–1965* (1967), 13–14, 17–18; Walter L. Burrage, *History of the Massachusetts Medical Society: With Brief Biographies of the Founders and Chief Officers* (1923), 1–23, chap. 2.

4. Richard H. Shryock, "The College of Physicians of Philadelphia in Historical Perspective," *Transactions and Studies of the College of Physicians of Philadelphia*, 4th ser., 27 (1960): 152; W. S. W. Ruschenberger, *An Account of the Institution and Progress of the College of Physicians of Philadelphia* (1887), 1–26; Samuel X. Radbill, "The Philadelphia Medical Society, 1789–1868," *Transactions and Studies of the College of Physicians of Philadelphia*, 4th ser. 20 (1953): 104; George W. Norris, *The Early History of Medicine in Philadelphia* (1886), 46, 125; Whitfield J. Bell, Jr., "Philadelphia Medical Students in Europe, 1750–1800," in *The Colonial Physician and Other Essays* (1975), 41–69. For a general description of Philadelphia in this era, see Carl Bridenbaugh, *Rebels and Gentlemen: Philadelphia in the Age of Franklin* (1942).

5. Whitfield J. Bell, Jr., *John Morgan, Continental Doctor* (1965), chaps. 1–4; Frederich A. Pottle, ed. *Boswell in Holland, 1763–1764* (1952), 10–11.

6. John Morgan, *Discourse on the Institution of Medical Schools in America* ([1756] 1937), 5, 44.

7. For Adam Smith, see his *Wealth of Nations*, 15. See also Morgan, *Discourse*, xvi, xvii, 14, 40, 44. John Morgan, *Apology for Attempting to Introduce the Regular Practice of Physic in Philadelphia*, Evans 41569 (1765), 15–17; James B. McCaw, "A Memoir of James McClurg," *Virginia Medical and Surgical Journal* 2 (1854): 474–75.

8. Benjamin Rush, *Sixteen Introductory Lectures*, Shaw and Shoemaker 23846 (1811), 236; "Benjamin Rush to James Rush, February 7, 1810," in Benjamin Rush, *Letters of Benjamin Rush*, ed. L. H. Butterfield (1951), 2:1036; McCaw, "James McClurg," 468.

9. Morgan, *Discourse*, vi–vii; Morgan, *Apology*, 6–9; Bell, *John Morgan*, 130–32; Norris, *Early History of Medicine*, 47.

10. Morgan, *Discourse*, xv–xxvi, 8, 14–15; George W. Corner, *Two Cen-*

turies of Medicine: A History of the School of Medicine of the University of Pennsylvania (1965), chap. 2.

11. Herman Boerhaave, "Commentariolus," trans. G. A. Lindeboom in *Herman Boerhaave* (1968), ed. G. A. Lindeboom, 261–63 and Herman Boerhaave, *Aphorisms: Concerning the Knowledge and Cure of Diseases,* trans. J. Delacoste (1715), 12, 40, 58, and chaps. 6, 8; Samuel Miller, *A Brief Retrospect of the Eighteenth Century,* Shaw and Shoemaker 4654 (1803), 1:255; King, *Medical World,* chaps. 3, 4.

12. Max Neuburger, *History of Medicine,* trans. Ernest Playfair (1925), 2:pt. 2, 46–116; Arturo Castiglioni, *A History of medicine* (1947), chaps. 14, 15; Miller, *Brief Retrospect,* 1:253–61; Michael Foster, *Lectures on the History of Physiology during the Sixteenth, Seventeenth, and Eighteenth Centuries* (1924), 168–73, 200–204; Tenney L. Davis, "Boerhaave's Account of Paracelsus and Van Helmont," *Journal of Chemical Education* 5 (1928): 671–81; H. E. Sigerist, "Boerhaave's Influence upon American Medicine," *Nederlands Tijdschrift voor Geneeskunde Jaargang* 82, no. 40 (1938): 4822–28.

13. Lester S. King, "Rationalism in Early Eighteenth-Century Medicine," *Journal of History of Medicine* 18 (1963): 259–62; Lester S. King, "Stahl and Hoffmann: A Study of Eighteenth-Century Animism," *Journal of History of Medicine* 19 (1964): 118–30; C. G. Cumston, *Introduction to the History of Medicine* (1927), 351–56; Daniel Adams, *An Inaugural Dissertation on the Principles of Animation . . . July 18, 1799,* Evans 35074, (1799), 1–27; Joseph Young, *A New Physical System of Astronomy,* Evans 39158 (1800), lxvi, 71–76. Quotes are from Benjamin Rush, *Medical Inquiries and Observations,* 4th ed. (1815), 2:7, 52.

14. Benjamin Rush, Introduction to *The Works of Thomas Sydenham, M.D.,* by Thomas Sydenham (1809), iv; Benjamin Rush, *Six Introductory Lectures,* Shaw and Shoemaker 1274 (1801), 47; Alex Berman, "The Heroic Approach in Nineteenth-Century Therapeutics," *Bulletin of the American Society of Hospital Pharmacists* 11 (1954): 322.

15. Benjamin Rush, *Medical Inquiries and Observations,* 3:10; Nathan G. Goodman, *Benjamin Rush: Physician and Citizen, 1746–1813* (1934), 230–33; George W. Corner, "Rush's Medical Theories," in *Travels Through Life, The Autobiography of Benjamin Rush,* ed. George W. Corner (1948), app. 1, 362–66.

16. Goodman, *Benjamin Rush,* 250–51; Richard H. Shryock, ed., "Letters of Richard D. Arnold," *Bulletin of the Johns Hopkins Hospital* 42 (1928):156.

17. McCaw, "James McClurg," 472–74; James McClurg, "Reasoning in Medicine," *Philadelphia Journal of Medical and Physical Sciences* 1 (1820): 1 ff.; Benjamin Rush, "Benjamin Rush to John K. Read, September 15, 1800," in *Letters,* 2:823; Rush, *Sixteen Lectures,* 229.

18. Samuel Bard, "A Discourse on Medical Education," in *Two Discourses* (1921), 9, 13; McCaw, "James McClurg," 474; Letter from Samuel Bard to John Bard, 29 December 1762, and 4 September 1764, Bard MS, New York Academy of Medicine; Morgan, *Apology for Attempting,* 12–14; Peter Middleton, *Medical Discourse,* Evans 11338 (1769), 52–

55, 63–65, 68; John Andrews, *An Address to the Graduates in Medicine*, Evans 31736 (1797), 14; John Redman Coxe, *Short View of the Importance and Respectability of Medicine*, Evans 37264 (1800), 15–16.

19. Rush, *Sixteen Lectures*, 319–20; Chauncy D. Leake, ed, *Percival's Medical Ethics* (1927), 27, 219, 240; David E. Konold, *A History of American Medical Ethics, 1847–1912* (1926), 9–10.

20. Rush, *Letters*, 2:641, 734; Rush, *Sixteen Lectures*, 217–18, 220, 226, 230, 233, 333–34; Andrews, *Address to the Graduates*, 15; Coxe, *Short View*, 18–19; Samuel Bard, *Discourse upon the Duties of a Physician*, Evans 11168 (1769), 5, 10, 14–15; Miller, *Brief Retrospect*, 2:292; Amasa Dingley, *An Oration on the Improvement of Medicine*, Evans 26892 (1794), 30.

21. See Percival's own discussion of the meaning of "condescension" in Thomas Percival, *A Father's Instructions*, Evans 21382 (1788), 320–22; Benjamin Rush, *The Selected Writings of Benjamin Rush*, ed. Dagobert D. Runes (1947), 314–15; Rush, *Letters*, 1:284–85; Rev. John McVickar, *A Domestic Narrative of the Life of Samuel Bard* (1822), 158–59; Middleton, *Medical Discourse*, 65–66; James Potter, *An Oration on the Rise and Progress of Physic in America*, Evans 17315 (1781), 9; Coxe, *Short View*, 24.

22. Benjamin Rush, *Essays, Literary, Moral and Philosophical*, 2d ed. (1806), 253–55; Rush, *Sixteen Lectures*, 265–71, 324–26, 328–29.

23. Clark, *History of the Royal College of Physicians*, 2:chap. 2; "John Gregory," *Dictionary of National Biography*, 8:545; John Gregory, *Lectures on the Duties and Qualifications of a Physician* (1772), 141, 153.

24. Benjamin Rush, "Introductory Lecture on Imposture in Medicine," November 1796, Historical Society of Pennsylvania MS, 26; Rush, *Sixteen Lectures*, 154; Benjamin Rush, "On the Application of Metaphysics to Medicine," 3 November 1794, "Introductory Lectures to a Course of Lectures on the Institutes of Medicine and Clinical Practice," Historical Society of Pennsylvania, MS, 45.

25. Goodman, *Rush*, 216–22; *A Report of an Action for Libel Brought by Dr. Benjamin Rush against William Cobbett* [1800], Evans 37103, William Cobbett, *Rush-Light* 15 February 1800, Shaw 32, 221–23, 267–75.

26. Benjamin Rush, "On the Application of Metaphysics" (1794), 16, and "Duties of Physicians Toward Each Other" (2 November 1812), 37, Historical Society of Pennsylvania, MSS.

27. Rush, *Sixteen Lectures*, 226, 320–23; Coxe, *Short View*, 19; Thacher, *American Medical Biography*, 1:409–10; *South Carolina and American General Gazette* (Charleston), 10 December 1771.

28. For a sample of doctors' views of the ideal patient, see Rush, *Sixteen Lectures*, 318–39; letter from Samuel Bard to Francis U. Johnston (Bard's grandson), ca. July 1820, Bard MS, Columbia University Library; Middleton, *Medical Discourse*, 65–66; Andrews, *Address to the Grad-*

uates, 15–16; Coxe, *Short View,* 24–25; Rush, *Sixteen Lectures,* 328–29.

29. Corner, *Two Centuries of Medicine,* chaps. 3, 4; William Frederick Norwood, *Medical Education in the United States before the Civil War* (1944), 74, 84–85; Goodman, *Rush,* 128–33.

30. Samuel Latham Mitchell, *The Present State of Medical Learning in the City of New York,* Evans 32488 (1797), 4; Carl Bridenbaugh, *Myths and Realities: Societies of the Colonial South* (1963), 4 ff.; Blanton, *Medicine in Virginia,* 83–92; Norwood, *Medical Education,* 259.

31. J. Hector St. John Crevecoeur, *Letters from an American Farmer* (1912), 158; Joseph I. Waring, *A History of Medicine in South Carolina* (1964), 65–71; Robert L. Brunhouse, "David Ramsay, 1749–1815: Selections from His Writings," *Transactions of the American Philosophical Society,* n.s., 55, pt. 4 (1965): 54–55, 213.

32. Waring, *History of Medicine in South Carolina,* 345; "David Ramsay to James Patterson, August 21, 1805," *Transactions of the American Philosophical Society,* n.s., 55, pt. 4 (1965): 157–58. See also, Robert Y. Hayne, "Biographical Memoir of David Ramsay, M.D.," *Analectic Magazine* 6 (1815): 204–24, and David Ramsay, *History of South Carolina: From Its First Settlement in 1670 to the Year 1808* (1809), 2:chap. 2.

33. Thacher, "Dr. John Bard," in *American Medical Biography,* 1:96–103; McVickar, *Samuel Bard,* 10; John Brett Langstaff, *Doctor Bard of Hyde Park: The Famous Physician of Revolutionary Times, the Man Who Saved Washington's Life* (1942), chaps. 3–10; Byron Stookey, *A History of Colonial Medical Education: In the Province of New York, with Its Subsequent Development (1767–1830)* (1962), 30–76.

34. Thacher, *American Medical Biography,* 2:27; Fred B. Rogers, "Nicholas Romayne, 1756–1817; Stormy Petrel of American Medical Education," *Journal of Medical Education* 35 (1960): 258–63; Mitchell, *Medical Learning,* 4.

35. David Hosack, "Sketch of the Origin and Progress of the Medical Schools of New York and Philadelphia," *American Medical and Philosophical Register* 2 (1812): 225–36; David Hosack, *An Inaugural Discourse, Delivered at the Opening of Rutgers Medical College* (1826), 20–83; Samuel Bard and Benjamin De Witt, *Memorial of the College of Physicians and Surgeons in the City of New York to the Hon. the Legislature of the State of New York* (1816), 6–8; Samuel Bard, "Address Delivered before the Dutchess Medical Society, 1809," *New York Evening Post,* 13 January 1810; Walsh, *History of Medicine in New York,* 2:363–74; Stookey, *Colonial Medical Education,* 83 ff.

36. Cotton Mather, *Magnalia Christi Americana* ([1702] 1967), 1:493–94; Samuel A. Green, *A History of Medicine in Massachusetts* (1881), pt. 1; Viets, *A Brief History of Medicine in Massachusetts,* 28–52.

37. Maurice Bear Gordon, *Aesculapius Comes to the Colonies* (1949), 73–88; Otho T. Beall, Jr. and Richard H. Shryock, *Cotton Mather, First*

Significant Figure in American Medicine (1954), 93–123; John B. Black, "The Inoculation Controversy in Boston, 1721–1722," *New England Quarterly* 25 (1952): 489–506.

38. Cotton Mather, *The Angel of Bethesda*, ed. Gordon W. Jones (1972), 7, 116, 118, 120, 188.

39. C. Mather, *Angel*, 189, chaps. 5, 7, 40.

40. Norwood, *Medical Education*, 170–72; Benjamin Waterhouse, *A Synopsis of a Course of Lectures*, Evans 20123 (1786), iv, 15–16; Benjamin Waterhouse, *The Botanist; and the Principle of Vitality* (1811), 240, 245–46, 251–52; Benjamin Waterhouse, "The Constitution of the Middlesex Medical Association," in *The Rise, Progress, and Present State of Medicine*, Evans 24987, (1792), preface, x; Gordon, *Aesculapius*, 272.

41. Waterhouse, *State of Medicine*, 5–6; Gordon, *Aesculapius*, 274–79; Joseph Charles Trent, "Benjamin Waterhouse," *Journal of the History of Medicine* 1 (1946): 357–64; Thomas Francis Harrington, *The Harvard Medical School* (1905), 1:1–35.

42. Viets, *Medicine in Massachusetts*, 95–97; Henry R. Viets, "The Medical Education of James Lloyd in Colonial America," *Yale Journal of Biology and Medicine* 31 (1958): 1–13; Leonard K. Eaton, "Medicine in Philadelphia and Boston, 1805–1830," *Pennsylvania Magazine of History and Biography* 75 (1951): 66–70.

43. Norwood, *Medical Education*, 84–85; Shryock, "College of Physicians of Philadelphia," (see n. 6), 152; New Haven County Medical Association, *Cases and Observations*, Evans 21296 (1788), iii-iv; New Hampshire Medical Society, *The Charter of the New Hampshire Medical Society*, Evans 24588 (1792), 1; Shryock, *Medical Licensing*, (see n. 4), 19, 23–24; Rush, *Letters*, 2:1179–84; Rush, *Six Introductory Lectures* (see n. 14),56, 60; Carson, *Medical Department of the University of Pennsylvania* (see n. 1), 105.

44. Rush, *Sixteen Lectures*, 229–31; Middleton, *Medical Discourse*, 63–64, 69.

45. Louis G. Caldwell, "Early Legislation Regulating the Practice of Medicine," *Illinois Law Review* 18 (1923): 225–44; Joseph F. Kett, *The Formation of the American Medical Profession* (1968), 22, 181–84; Shryock, *Medical Licensing*, chap. 1; William G. Rothstein, *American Physicians in the Nineteenth Century* (1972), chaps. 7, 8.

Chapter 3

1. For other discussions of the hold of law and lawyers upon American society, see James Willard Hurst, "The Law in United States History," *Proceedings of the American Philosophical Society* 104 (1960): 518–26, as well as his *The Growth of American Law: The Law Makers* (1950). Philip Selznick, "The Ethos of American Law," in *Americans: 1776*, ed. Irving Kristol (1976), 2:211–36, is a thoughtful essay.

2. Conyers Read, ed., *The Constitution Reconsidered* (1938), 159–258, still provides some of the most illuminating discussion of the influence of the Constitution upon American thought and behavior. For a

recent comment, see Michael Lienesch, "The Constitutional Tradition," *Journal of Politics* 42 (1980): 2–30.

3. Gordon S. Wood, *The Creation of the American Republic, 1776–1787* (1969), 260–82, provides a helpful discussion of the development of eighteenth-century Anglo-American constitutionalism.

4. James Otis, in the famous Writs of Assistance case, had argued that "An act against the Constitution is void." Of course he was referring to the unwritten British Constitution. Otis lost his case. For litigation in the Confederation period, see Edwin S. Corwin, "The Progress of Constitutional Theory, 1776–1787," *American Historical Review* 30 (1925): 521–27; Francis Newton Thorpe, ed, *The Federal and State Constitutions* (1909), 3:1892. After World War II, West Germany and India adopted written constitutions giving courts the powers of interpretation of fundamental rights. Israel, without a written constitution, seems to grant its Supreme Court such powers.

5. Jefferson to Madison, 15 March 1789, in *The Life and Selected Writings of Thomas Jefferson*, ed. Adrienne Koch and William Peden (1944), 462. Jefferson is quoting Horace, *Odes* 3.3.2, and the full section is significant: "A man who is just and holds to his resolve will not be shaken from his firm purpose by the wayward zeal of fellow-citizens who order wicked deeds, or by the countenance of a tyrant pressing upon him" (translation, Prof. Raphael Sealey).

6. A richly detailed analysis of the adoption of the Judiciary Art of 1789 can be found in Charles Warren, "New Light on the History of the Federal Judiciary Act of 1789," *Harvard Law Review* 37 (1923), reprinted in *Selected Essays on Constitutional Law*, ed. Association of American Law Schools (1938), 3:1246–54.

7. Richard B. Morris, ed., *Select Cases of the Mayor's Court of New York City* (1935), 52–57. A scattered discussion of seventeenth-century American legal practice can be found in Anton-Hermann Chroust, *The Rise of the Legal Profession in America* (1965), 1:27, ff., 81–84, 117 ff., 197, 220 ff., 234 ff., 249 ff., 277 ff., 297 ff., 322. See also Julius Goebel, Jr., "King's Law and Local Custom in Seventeenth-Century New England," *Columbia Law Review* 31 (1931); 416 ff., David H. Flaherty, ed., *Essays in the History of Early American Law* (1969); Francis R. Aumann, *The Changing American Legal System* (1940), chap. 2; Zechariah Chafee, Jr., "Colonial Courts and the Common Law," *Proceedings of the Massachusetts Historical Society*, 68:132–59; George Lee Haskins, *Law and Authority in Early Massachusetts* (1960). For the attorney's right of audience at Quarter Sessions, see Wallace Notestein, *The English People on the Eve of Colonization* (1954), 95, and Michael Birks, *Gentlemen of the Law* (1960), 102, 139, 197.

The eighteenth-century colonial superior courts' imitation of the Westminster courts is described in Julius Goebel, Jr., and T. Raymond Naughton, *Law Enforcement in Colonial New York* (1944) xxv-xxix, 73–91; John T. Farrell, ed., *The Supreme Court Diary of William Samuel Johnson* (1942), xi-liv; Paul M. Hamlin and Charles E. Baker, *Supreme Court of Judicature of the Province of New York, 1691–1704* (1952),

1:ix-xi, 40, 56–57, 66, 68 ff., 80, and 3:140; Carroll T. Bond, ed., *Proceedings of the Maryland Court of Appeals* (1933), xiv-xxxv; William H. Loyd, *The Early Courts of Pennsylvania* (1910), chap. 2; Oliver P. Chitwood, *Justice in Colonial Virginia* (1904), chap. 2; A. K. Gregorie and J. N. Frierson, eds., *Records of the Court of Chancery of South Carolina, 1671–1779* (1950), 54; John Murrin, "The Legal Transformation: The Bench and Bar of Eighteenth-Century Massachusetts," in *Colonial America: Essays in Politics and Social Development,* ed. Stanley Katz (1971), 438 ff.

8. On special pleading, see T. F. T. Plucknett, *Concise History of the Common Law,* 5th ed. (1956), 353–77; Alan Harding, *A Social History of English Law* (1966), 123–26; C. H. S. Fifoot, *Lord Mansfield* (1936), 35; Blackstone, *Commentaries on the laws of England* (1765), 3:chap. 20; Richard Wooddeson, *Elements of Jurisprudence* (1792), 185–87; *Boston Review* (March 1808), 162–64. On Coke, see J. W. Gough, *Fundamental Law in English Constitutional History* (1955), chap. 3; William E. Holdsworth, *Some Makers of English Law* (1938), 111–32; Samuel E. Thorne, *Sir Edward Coke* (1957), 17–18. See also, Julius Goebel, Jr., "The Courts and the Law in Colonial New York," in *History of the State of New York,* ed. Alexander C. Flick (1933), 3:32–33.

9. The courts, once established, set their own rules; yet the courts were set up through legislation, and legislatures from time to time might interfere with their workings. On the adaption of the English system of courts, see Erwin L. Surrency, "The Courts in the American Colonies," *American Journal of Legal History* 11 (1967): 253–76, 347–76. A convenient summary of the work of early bar associations and law schools can be found in Chroust, *Rise of the Legal Profession,* 1:90–108, 180–93, 204–6, 256–62; and 2:chaps. 3, 4. For the Litchfield School, see also Samuel H. Fisher, *Litchfield Law School, 1774–1833* (1933).

10. For ranking in the colonial profession, see Chroust, *Rise of the Legal Profession,* 1:xvii-xviii, 106, 200, 274, 282; Frederick Bowes, *The Culture of Early Charleston* (1942), 51–53; Alan F. Day, "Lawyers in Colonial Maryland," *American Journal of Legal History* 17 (1973), 163; Loyd, *Early Courts of Pennsylvania,* 106–8; John Murrin, "The Legal Transformation," 438–42; Hamlin and Baker, *Supreme Court of New York,* 2:385–86. Elizabeth McClellan *History of American Costume* (1942), 239–42; Clement Eaton, "A Mirror of the Southern Colonial Lawyer," *William and Mary Quarterly* 8 (1951), 533; A. G. Roeber, *Faithful Magistrates and Republican Lawyers, Creators of Virginia's Legal Culture, 1680–1810* (1981), chap. 3.

11. Richard Morris, "Legalism versus Revolutionary Doctrine in New England," *New England Quarterly* (1931): 201–15; Amasa A. Redfield, "English Colonial Polity and Judicial Adminstration, 1664–1776," in *History of the Bench and Bar of New York,* ed. David McAdam (1897), 1:60–88; F. W. Maitland, *The Forms of Action at Common Law* (1968), 16–21, 67.

12. Joseph H. Smith, "Administrative Control of the Courts of the American Plantations," *Columbia Law Review* 61 (1961): 1213, 1217,

1225, 1226, 1234–36; George A. Washburne, *Imperial Control of the Administration of Justice in the Thirteen American Colonies, 1684–1776* (1923), 82, 126–27, chap. 5; Erwin C. Surrency, "The Courts in the American Colonies," *American Journal of Legal History* 11 (1967): 254–57, 271–76, 353–62, 364–67, 369–73. Governor Bellomont's comment is from his letter to the Lords of Trade, found in *Documents Relative to the Colonial History of the State of New York*, ed. E. B. O'Callaghan and B. Fernow (1858), 4:441–42. The increasing social differentiation in the American colonies of the eighteenth century and the place of the leading lawyers in the social order are described by Jackson T. Main, *Social Structure in Revolutionary America* (1965), 101–3, 113, 147, 275, 285–87; Gary B. Nash, *Class and Society in Early America* (1970), 130–31, 133–88.

13. The ancient ideal of learned and impartial judges had been given political substance in England by the Revolution of 1688. The security of judges' tenure provided by the Act of Settlement, coming as it did after the destruction of prerogative courts in 1641, and strengthened as it was by the Statute of 1760, left the office and salary of judges largely independent of the crown. See Blackstone's discussion in *Commentaries*, 1:268. In the colonies, however, the situation was quite different. Both the King and the colonial legislatures upheld the ideal of learned and impartial judges, while they struggled to wrest control of these important officials from each other. See William S. Carpenter, *Judicial Tenure in the United States* (1918), chap. 1; Carl Ubbelohde, *The Vice-Admiralty Courts and the American Revolution* (1960), 203–11; Stanley N. Katz, "The Politics of Law in Colonial America: Controversies over Chancery Courts and Equity Law in the Eighteenth Century," in *Perspectives in American History*, ed. Donald Fleming (1971), 5:282–84; John Adams, *Diary and Autobiography*, ed. L. H. Butterfield (1961), 167–68; William Livingston, "Of Abuses in the Practice of the Law," in *Independent Reflector*, ed. Milton Klein (1963), 254; W. Raymond Blackard, "Requirements for Admission to the Bar in Revolutionary America," *Tennessee Law Review* 15 (1938): 116–27.

14. [William Livingston] in *The New York Weekly Post Boy*, 19 August 1745, 1; [William Smith], *The Art of Pleading*, Evans 6785 (1751) iv, 6; Livingston, "Of Abuses in the Practice of the Law," 301–2; Adams, *Diary and Autobiography*, 236, 316, 320; Thomas Jefferson to Thomas Turpin, 5 February 1769, in *Papers of Thomas Jefferson*, ed. julian Boyd (1950) 1:23–24; Julius Goebel, Jr., ed., *The Law Practice of Alexander Hamilton* (1964), 1:45–59; Auman, *Changing American Legal System*, 94–95, 118–19.

15. James Duane, "Ordinance of Fees for Courts, with Observations and Remarks about these Fees [at the Request of his majesty's Council]" (undated), in James Duane Papers, New York Historical Society; Livingston, "Of Abuses in the Practice of the Law," 255; Mooney v. Lloyd, 5 *Serge and Rawle* ([Pa.] 1819), 412.

16. Erwin C. Surrency, "The Courts in the American Colonies," in *American Journal of Legal History* 11 (1967): 168–69; Bond *Proceed-*

ings of the Maryland Court of Appeals, xiv-xv; Hamlin and Baker, *Supreme Court of New York,* 1:109–47, 3:228–30; James Derriman, *Pageantry of the Law* (1955), chaps. 9, 12; Charles Page Smith, *James Wilson: Founding Father, 1742–1798* (1956), 46–47; Thomas Jefferson to George Wythe, 1 March 1779, *Papers of Thomas Jefferson,* 2:235; Thomas Jefferson, "Bill for Licensing Counsel, Attorneys-at-Law, and Proctors," *Papers of Thomas Jefferson,* 2:587–88; Dorothy R. Dillon, *The New York Triumvirate: A Study of the Legal and Political Careers of William Livingston, John Morin Scott, and William Smith, Jr.* (1949), 55–56; "Draft of Protest against the Act to Continue the £5 Act" (n.d.), no. 197, William Smith Papers, New York Public Library.

17. Roscoe Pound, *The Lawyer from Antiquity to Modern Times* (1953), chaps. 6, 7; Chroust, *Rise of the Legal Profession,* 2:chap. 3; Robson, *Attorney in Eighteenth-Century England* chaps. 3, 4; Paul Hamlin, *Legal Education in Colonial New York* (1939), 162; James Hovey, Esquire, to Robert Treat Paine, Esquire, 22 October 1764, Robert Treat Paine Papers, Massachusetts Historical Society; Gerald Wilfred Gawalt, "Massachusetts Lawyers, 1760–1840" (Ph.D. diss., Clark University, 1969), chap. 2; Adams, *Diary and Autobiography,* 3:316.

18. For Harvard graduates, see John Murrin, "The Legal Transformation," in Stanley Katz, *Colonial America: Essays in Politics and Social Development* (1976), 430–31. For Yale graduates, see Gawalt, "Massachusetts Lawyers," 141, table 1. For Princeton, see Bailey B. Burritt, "Professional Distribution of College and University Graduates," *United States Bureau of Education Bulletin* 19 (1912), 105. For Kings College, see Hamlin, *Legal Education in Colonial New York,* 133, app. 1. On Jefferson's choice of the law, see Dumas Malone, *Jefferson and His Time* (1948), 1:chap. 5; Adams's choice of law is discussed by Charles Page Smith, *John Adams* (1962), 1:33–34, but see also his own recollection in his *Diary and Autobiography,* 3:262–64, and his contemporary letter, John Adams to Charles Cushing, 1 April 1756, in *Proceedings of the Massachusetts Historical Society* 46 (1913): 410–12.

19. The broad intellectual background of these shifts might be seen by juxtaposing Perry Miller's *The New England Mind: The Seventeenth-Century* (1939) and Henry Farnham May's *The Enlightenment in America* (1976). See also Perry Miller, *From Colony to Province* (1953), 278–384. For some discussion of liberty, happiness, and rights by American lawyers, see John J. Pringle, *Oration,* Evans 38326 (1800), 6–7, 32–34; John Faucherand Grimke, *Charge,* Evans 33824 (1798), 14; [John Faucherand Grimke], *The South Carolina Justice of the Peace,* Evans 21472 (1788), vii; Charles Pinkney, *Speeches,* Evans 38270 (1800), 6, 13; St. George Tucker, *Liberty, A Poem,* Evans 21508 (1788); Edmund Pendleton, "Address to the Virginia Ratification Convention, June 12, 1788," in *The Letters and Papers of Edmund Pendleton, 1734–1803,* ed. David John Mays (1967), 2:520–22; Samuel Chew, *Speech . . . ,* Evans 1387 (1741), 2–3; Jacob Rush, *Charges and Extracts of Charges . . . ,* Shaw 5005 (1803), 24, 40; William Livingston, *Observations on Government,* Evans 20465 (1787), 7, 10; James Kent, *An Introductory*

Lecture, Evans 27183 (1794), 4; Egbert Benson, Jr., "Liberty" (10 November 1804) 1, Egbert Benson Papers, New York Historical Society; John Adams, "Thoughts on Government," in *The Political Writings of John Adams,* ed. George A. Peek, Jr. (1954), 85–86; Thomas Jefferson to William Short, 31 October 1819, in *The Writings of Thomas Jefferson,* ed. Andrew A. Lipscomb and Albert Ellery Bergh (1903), 15:222–24.; James Wilson, *The Works of James Wilson,* ed. Robert Green McCloskey (1967), 723–24; Aubrey C. Land, *The Dulanys of Maryland* (1955), 82. Some of the values the lawyers championed contrasted sharply with those upheld by the eighteenth-century revivalists and their followers, who constituted the other and more numerous America. "As for the Business of an Attorney," wrote George Whitefield, "I think it is unlawful for a Christian, at least exceedingly dangerous: Avoid it therefore, and glorify God in some othe station" (Alan Heimert, *Religion and the American Mind* (1966), 180). Benjamin Rush, who had initially decided to study law, was directed away from it by Dr. Finley, his mentor and one of the leading evangelical ministers in the Middle Colonies. See Benjamin Rush, *Travels through Life, The Autobiography of Benjamin Rush,* ed. George W. Corner (1948), 37. See also *The Lawyer's Pedigree* (1755). Some of the nineteenth-century anti-lawyer sentiment also came from evangelical religious sources. See Jessie Higgens, *Samson against the Philistines,* 2d ed., Shaw 8348 (1805), 70–72.

20. For the oaths of English attorneys, see James Derriman, *Pageantry of the Law* (1955), 75–76, and for the explanation of the barristers not being officers of the court, James Robert Vernam Marchant, *Barrister-at-Law* (1905), 30. James Wilson's discussion of the balanced obligations to court and client are in *The Works of James Wilson,* 566–67, and William Livingston's can be found in *Independent Reflector,* 299–303. Chief Justice Gibson's are in Austin's Case, 5 *Rawle* (Pennsylvania, 1835), 203 and Rush v. Cavenaugh, 2 *Bar* (Pennsylvania, 1845), 189. The Delaware oath is in Josiah Henry Benton, *The Lawyer's Oath and Office* (1909), 45, where other eighteenth-century oaths can be found as well. See also Leonard S. Goodman, "The Historic Role of the Oath of Admission," *American Journal of Legal History* 11 (1967): 404–11. For an early discussion of privileged communications, see Heister v. Davis, 3 *Yeates* (1800), 4, and Scott v. Van Alstyne, 9 *Johnston* (1812), 216.

21. The broad authority of the attorney in the process of pleading can be seen in early reports. For example, in Pennsylvania see Somers v. Balabreyd, 1 *Dallas* (1786), 164; Coxe and Fraser v. Nicholls, 2 *Yeates* (1800), 546; McCullough v. Guetner, 1 *Binney* (1807), 214; Reinhold v. Alberts, 1 *Binney* (1808), 469. For New York, see Jackson v. Stewart, 6 *Johnson* (1810), 34, and Denton v. Noyes, 6 *Johnson* (1810), 297, with elaborate discussion by Chancellor Kent. Theophilus Parsons, *Memoirs of Theophilus Parsons* (1859), 155.

22. For the lawyer's relationship to the mercentile community see Morton J. Horwitz, *The Transformation of American Law, 1780–1860* (1977), 145ff. Quotation from Roeber, *Faithful Magistrates,* 126. See

also discussion in Wilson, *Works,* 2:565–66; Hugh Henry Brackenridge, *Law Miscellanies* (1814), x-xi; Richard B. Morris, *Studies in the History of American Law* (1930), 45–46.

23. Local studies best illustrate the good fellowship of the bar. See Alan McKinley Smith, "Virginia Lawyer, 1680–1776: The Birth of an American Profession" (Ph.D. diss., Johns Hopkins University, 1967), 300–306, chap. 10. Dillon, *New York Triumvirate,* 25–27; Herbert Allen Johnson, "John Jay: Colonial Lawyer" (Ph.D. diss., Columbia University, 1965), 37–41, 92–95; Gerald Wilfred Gawalt, *The Promise of Power: The Emergence of the Legal Profession in Massachusetts, 1760–1840* (1979), 21, 116–17. See also Charles Robert McKirdy, "Lawyers in Crisis: The Massachusetts Legal profession, 1760–1790" (Ph.D. diss., Northwestern University, 1969), chap. 6; Davis Paul Brown, *The Forum or Forty Years Full Practice at the Philadelphia Bar* (1856), 2:chap. 12.

24. For the English parliamentary lawyer, see Alan Harding, *A Social History of English Law* (1966), 211–15, 290–91; John Dykstra Eusden, *Puritans, Lawyers, and Politics in Early Seventeenth-Century England* (1958), chap. 2. A good place to begin to study the movement of American lawyers into politics in this era is with the career of John Adams, in *Legal Papers of John Adams,* ed. L. Kinvin Wroth and Hiller B. Zobel (1965), 1:lxxxiv–xciv. A broader discussion of Massachusetts lawyers is in Gawalt, *The Promise of Power,* chap. 2. For New York, see Johnson, "John Jay: Colonial Lawyer," 237–44, and Dillon, *New York Triumvirate,* 27–30. For Philadelphia, see Gary B. Nash, "The Philadelphia Bench and Bar, 1800–1860," *Comparative Studies in Society and History* 7 (1965): 204. Jefferson's belief that the legal profession would be the "nursery of Congress" reflected his Virginia experince in law and politics. See Dumas Malone, *Jefferson the Virginian* (1948), chaps. 5, 9, and Marie Kimball, *Jefferson, The Road to Glory, 1743–1776* (1943), chap. 5. See also, Jack P. Greene, "Foundations of Political Power in the Virginia house of Burgesses, 1720–1776," *William and Mary Quarterly,* 3d ser., 16 (1959): 488 ff., and E. Lee Shepard, "Lawyers Look at Themselves: Professional Consciousness and the Virginia Bar, 1770–1850," *American Journal of Legal History* 25 (1981): 1 ff. The movement of the lawyer into politics in Maryland is discussed by Dennis K. Nolan, "The Effect of the Revolution on the Bar: The Maryland Experience," *Virginia Law Review* 62 (1976): 992–93; Roeber, *Faithful Magistrates,* chap. 5. "The object of a Southern man's life is politics," wrote a Southern lawyer, "and subsidiary to this we all practice law." Quoted in Drew Gilpin Faust, *James Henry Hammond* (1982), 31.

25. For a recent imprecation, see Allan G. Bogue et al., "Members of the House of Representatives and the Process of Modernization, 1789–1960," *Journal of American History* 63 (1976), especially pages 300–302. James Willard Hurst, *The Growth of American Law; The Law makers* (1950), 352–55 presents a more favorable evaluation. A good discussion of the literature can be found in Heinz Eulau and John D. Sprague, *Lawyers in Politics: A Study of Professional Convergence* (1964), chap. 1. The great exemplar of the infusion of political will into

legal doctrine was Chief Justice Marshall. See Robert K. Faulkner, *Jurisprudence of John Marshall* (1968), chap. 3. For later periods, see John R. Schmidhauser, "Judicial Behavior and the Sectional Crisis of 1837–1860," *Journal of Politics* 23 (1961): 615; Charles G. Haines, *Role of the Supreme Court in Government and Politics, 1835–1864* (1957); Stanley Kutler, *Judicial Power and Reconstruction Politics* (1968); Martin M. Shapiro, *Law and Politics in the Supreme Court* (1964).

26. For English land law, see A. W. B. Simpson, *History of the Land Law*, 2d ed. (1986); on American land law, see James Sullivan, Introduction in *History of Land Titles in Massachusetts* (1801); Richard B. Morris, *Studies in the History of American Law*, 2d ed. (1959), chap. 2; also Wilson, *Works*, 2:82, 92; Lawrence M. Friedman, *A History of American Law* (1973), 51–57.

27. A good discussion of the simplification of American land law can be found in Friedman, *History of American Law*, 202–15. There is no systematic study of American lawyers as land speculators, but most biographies and manuscript collections of eighteenth- and early nineteenth-century lawyers abound with materials and information on the subject. At the New York Historical Society the papers of James and William Alexander, Joshua Delaplaine, James Duane, John Tabor Kempe, Alexander McDougall, John McKesson, and John Morth Scott are particularly rich in such materials. Aubrey C. Land, *The Dulanys of Maryland*, presents valuable information throughout this remarkable study, but see particularly 11–12, 98–102; Dillon, *New York Triumvirate*, chap. 9; Smith, *James Wilson* (see n. 19), chaps. 11, 25. Judge Johns' absence is recorded in Waller v. Dunnaho, 1 *Delaware Cases* (1797) 165.

28. Thorpe, *Federal and State Constitutions* (see n. 4), 3:1891. Law was *ideally* a free good. In actual practice going to law meant payment of lawyers' and various court fees. The major court costs, however, were rarely covered by fees paid by the litigants. The salaries of judges, court officials, and police, and the expense of courthouses and prisons were provided through general taxation, which was not levied in accordance with use. Still, in this era, the expense of lawyers' fees and court fees might have kept some of the poorer segments of society out of the courts in civil disputes. With the spread of the contingent fee practice in the later era, lawyers' fees became less of a barrier to the courts. Blackstone, *Commentaries*, 1:141, 40–41.

29. The three quotes are found in *The Federalist*, ed. Jacob E. Cooke (1961), no. 81, 544 [Hamilton]; no. 51, 352 [Madison]; no. 78, 528 [Hamilton].

30. Hugh Henry Brackenridge, *Law Miscellanies*, 54–64; Blackstone, *Commentaries*, 1:68–71; Wilson, *Works*, 1:208–9, 212, 229–30; 2:481–99, 502; *Federalist*, no. 78, 523 [Hamilton].

31. James Wilson's description of the ideal judge is illuminating. See *Works*, 1:296–99, 324–26, 500–502. See also Charles Pinckney, *Speeches*, Evans 38270 (1800), 20–22; Johnston, "John Jay," 229–33. For salaries and prestige of judges, see Jackson Turner Main, *The Social*

Structure of Revolutionary America (1965), 103–4, 205–6. For the American imitations of the Vinerian lectures, see Alfred Z. Reed, *Training for the Public Profession of the Law* (1921), chap. 1.

32. Smith, *James Wilson.*

33. Blackstone, *Commentaries,* 1:44. The best introductory study of Blackstone is Ernest Barker, "Blackstone on the British Constitution," in his *Essays on Government,* 2d ed. (1945). I found Daniel J. Boorstin, *The Mysterious Science of Law: An Essay on Blackstone's Commentaries* (1941) provocative, and Harold G. Hanbury's *The Vinerian Chair and Legal Education* (1953), chap. 3, too apologetic. H. L. A. Hart's "Blackstone's Use of the Law of Nature," *Butterworth's South African Law Review* 3 (1956): 164–74, is particularly sharp and illuminating. Wilson comments on Coke and Blackstone in *Works,* 2:563–64. On the American reception of Blackstone, see Charles Warren, *History of the American Bar* (1911), 177–79; see also Robert M. Cover's extensive review article on St. George Tucker's 1803 edition of Blackstone in *Columbia Law Review* 70 (1970): 1475–94.

34. Blackstone, *Commentaries,* 1:43, 127–28, 396–406; Wilson, *Works,* 2:588–89, 592–98.

35. Wilson, *Works,* 1:187–89, 241; Blackstone, *Commentaries,* 2:53.

36. Wilson, *Works,* 1:102, 122–23, 180–85, 192–93, 242–43; 2:502, 516, 730, chap. 12.

37. *Journal of the Continental Congress,* ed. Worthington Chauncy Ford, vol. 5 (24 June 1776), 475–76; Smith, *James Wilson,* 116–23. For Wilson's earlier discussion of the relationship of protection and obedience, see *Works,* 2:743–45, 285. His later discussion of treason is in *Works,* 2:663–69. For a helpful treatment of the early American law of treason, see Willard B. Hurst, "Treason in the United States," *Harvard Law Review* 58 (1944–45): 226–72, 395–444, 806–57, as well as Bradley Chapin, *The American Law of Treason: Revolutionary and Early National Origins* (1964), chaps. 1–6. Compare with Blackstone, *Commentaries,* 1:366–69; 4:74ff.

38. Wilson, *Works,* 2:663–69.

39. Wilson, *Works,* 2:565; *The Republic,* Book IV, sections 488–90.

40. Wilson, *Works,* 1:90, 237–38, 397–98.

41. Wilson, *Works,* 2:564–65.

42. Blackstone, *Commentaries,* 1:14; Wilson, *Works,* 2:561.

43. Wirt is quoted in Robert A. Ferguson, *Law and Letters in American Culture* (1984), 12. Tocqueville's famous comments can be found in *Democracy in America,* ed. Phillips Bradley (1956), 1:272–80. "Law is the only road to honor . . . if not riches," wrote Elisha Hammond to James Henry Hammond, 15 February 1828. Quoted in Faust, *Hammond,* 31.

Overview of Part II

1. The standard work on the westward migration of this era is Ray Allen Billington, *Westward Expansion,* 2d ed. (1960), chaps. 12 and 14. However, Edward Channing, *History of the United States* (1921),

5:chap. 2 is still very helpful, as is Frederick Jackson Turner, *The United States, 1830–1850* (1935) for a survey of shifting populations. C. O. Paullin and J. K. Wright, *Atlas of Historical Geography of the United States* (1932), plate 80A, indicates the movement of the statistical center of population. Among the historians who have emphasized the connection between the American Revolution and the later disastrous history of the American Indians, see S. F. Wise, "The American Revolution and Indian History," *Character and Circumstance; Essays in Honour of Donald Grant Creighton*, ed. John S. Moir (1970), 182–200; Dorothy V. Jones, *License for Empire* (1982), chaps. 6, 7; Reginald Horsman, *Expansion and American Indian Policy, 1783–1812* (1967), chap. 1. For a depressing demographic study, see Russell Thornton, *American Indian Holocaust and Survival* (1987); however, the author's inaccurate use of language casts some doubt upon the accuracy of his use of numbers. On the link between the Revolution and the spread of Southern slavery, see Eugene D. Genovese, *The World The Slaveholders Made* (1969), 99–100; Staunton Lynd, "Slavery and the Founding Fathers," in *Black History: A Reappraisal*, ed. Melvin Drimmer (1968), 117–31; Howard A. Ohlins, "Slavery, Economics, and Congressional Politics, 1790," *Journal of Southern History*, 46 (1980):335–60; and more generally, Donald 1. Robinson, *Slavery in the Structure of American Politics, 1768–1820* (1971). For a complex view, see David Brion Davis, *The Problem of Slavery in the Age of Revolution* (1975), chap. 7.

2. One of the more helpful scholarly discussions of the Great Valley system can be found in Henry Clyde Hubbart, *The Older Middle West, 1840–1880* (1936), chap. 4. See also Richard Wade, *The Urban Frontiers: The Rise of Western Cities* (1959). For a contemporary discussion, see James Hall, *The West: Its Commerce and Navigation* (1848). George Rogers Taylor, *The Transportation Revolution, 1815–1860* (1951), 102 ff. describes the shift from water transportation to railroads in the fifties.

3. Henry Nash Smith, *Virgin Land* (1956), 161 ff. Hammond's speech is available in *The Congressional Globe*, 35th Cong., 1st sess., Appendix, 70. Henry D. Shapiro and Zane Miller, *Physician to the West: Selected Writings of Daniel Drake on Science and Society* (1970), 229–30.

4. Moncure Conway, "The Queen of the West," *Fraser's Magazine* 73 (January 1866), 64; Frederick Jackson Turner, "The significance of the Mississippi Valley in American History," in *The Frontier in American History* (1920), 153, 177, 345–47.

5. Arthur C. Cole, *The Irrepressible Conflict* (1934), chap. 4; Francis P. Weisenburger, *History of the State of Ohio: The Passing of the Frontier, 1825–1850* (1942), 455–79.

6. On the dissonant strains in the egalitarianism of the era, see the writings collected in Joseph L. Blau, ed., *Social Theories of Jacksonian Democracy* (1947); Carl Russell Fish, *Rise of the Common Man* (1937), chap. 1. See also Lee Benson, *The Concept of Jacksonian Democracy* (1964), chaps. 1, 15. Some of the more interesting instances of popular

spokesmen distinguishing between "artificial" and "natural" distinctions are Andrew Jackson [Bank Veto Message] in Merle Curti and others, *American Issues: The Social Record* (1946), 245; Ely Moore, "Address . . .," in *Social Theories of Jacksonian Democracy*, ed. Joseph L. Blau (1947), 299–300; Robert Rantoul, Jr., *Memoirs, Speeches, and Writing*, ed. Luther Hamilton (1854), 248–50. The skeptical politician was David Dewey Bernard, *An Address Delivered before the Philoclean and Pei-thessophian Societies of Rutgers College, July 18, 1837* (1837), 26.

7. For a discussion of the susceptibility of newly settled regions to innovation and novelty, see Stanley M. Elkins and Eric McKitrick, "A Meaning for Turner's Frontier," *Political Science Quarterly*, 69 (1954):321.

8. The standard work on evangelical Protestantism of this era is Sidney E. Ahlstrom, *A Religious History of the American People* (1975), chaps. 26 and 27. Yet some of the older studies are still essential; see Sidney E. Mead, *The Lively Experiment: The Shaping of Christianity in America* (1963), chap. 7, and especially his "The Rise of the Evangelical Conception of the Ministry in America (1607–1850)," in *The Ministry in Historical Perspective*, ed. H. Richard Niebuhr (1956), 207–49. Winthrop Hudson, *The Great Tradition of the American Churches* (1963), chap. 5, 146–48 is also helpful. For the Protestant acceptance of rank in the social order, see Francis Wayland, *The Elements of Political Economy* (1852), 315 ff. See also Charles C. Cole, *The Social Ideas of Northern Evangelists, 1826–1860* (1954), chap. 5, and John R. Bodo, *The Protestant Clergy and Public Issues* (1954), vii; and Anne C. Loveland, *Southern Evangelicals and the Social Order 1800–1860* (1980), 32–33. For many Northern Protestants, antislavery ultimately became a momentous exception to this, but note the widespread Protestant acceptance of slavery. Larry E. Tise, *Proslavery: A HIstory of the Defense of Slavery in America, 1701–1840* (1987).

9. Peter Cartwright's comment is in his *Autobiography of Peter Cartwright, Backwoods Preacher*, ed. W. P. Strickland (1856), 48–49. Judge James's remarks are in Charles P. James, "Lawyers and their Traits," *Western Law Journal*, 9 (1852):65, 66–67.

10. For a stimulating but partial account of the anti-intellectualism of evangelical Protestantism, see Richard Hofstadter, *Anti-Intellectualism in America* (1963). For Finney's metaphysical struggles aimed at "studious and pious minds" see his *Lectures on Systematic Theology* (1846), viii–xii. For other leading evangelical Protestant leaders resorting to the sword of moralism to cut thoroughly theological problems, see Archibald Alexander, "Hindrances to Piety in Young Men Preparing For the Ministry," *The Quarterly Register and Journal*, 2 (1829):7–8; and Lyman Beecher, "The Faith Once Delivered to the Saints," *Sermons Delivered on Various Occasions* (1828), 77.

11. For the campaign against dueling, see Lyman Beecher, *The Remedy for Duelling* (1809); Nathaniel Bowen, *Duelling, Under Any Circumstances, The Extreme of Folly* (1807); Stephen Jewett, *Duelling Incompatible with True Honor* (1820). An antidueling society was formed

and pressed successfully for laws prohibiting dueling in many states. See Jack K. Williams, *Dueling in the Old South* (1980), chap. 5. The respect for the successful did not mean lack of compassion for the unsuccessful. See Timothy L. Smith, *Revivalism and Social Reform* (1957), chap. 11.

12. Chilton Williamson, *American Suffrage from Property to Democracy, 1760–1860* (1960); Edward Pessen, *Jacksonian America: Society, Personality and Politics* (1979), 150–56; James Stanton Chase, "Jacksonian Democracy and the Rise of the Nominating Convention," *Mid-America* 45 (October 1963):229–49. For a discussion of the increased voter participation, see Richard P. McCormick. "New Perspectives on Jacksonian Politics," reprinted in Felice A. Bonadio, *Political Parties in American History*, 2 (1974), 539 ff. For suggestive case studies, see Peter Levine, "The Rise of Mass Parties and the Problem of Organization: New Jersey, 1829–1844," *New Jersey History* 91 (Summer 1973):91–107; Ronald P. Formisano, *The Birth of Mass Political Parties, Michigan, 1827–1861* (1971); and *The Transformation of Political Culture: Massachusetts Parties 1790s–1840* (1983). For complaints about the powerlessness of the individual voter, coming from opposite sides of the political spectrum, see Bellamy Storer, *The Value of Man: An Address Before the Frankfort Atheneum, January 12, 1848* (1848), 7, and Orestes Brownson, "Politics and Political Parties" [1852], *The Works of Orestes Augustus Brownson*, ed. Henry F. Brownson (1882–1887), 16:359–60.

13. The Whig nespaper is quoted in Lynn L. Marshall, "The Strange Stillbirth of the Whig Party," *American Historical Review* 72 (January 1967):467. For a discussion of the inaugural festivities of this era, see Joseph Bucklin Bishop, *Our Political Drama* (1904), 203–19.

14. A suggestive state study of Masonry and its motives is Wayne A. Huss, *Master Builders: A History of The Masons of Pennsylvania 1731–1873* (1986), 1:164, 229. See also Dorothy Ann Lipson, *Free Masonry in Federalist Connecticut, 1789–1832* (1977), 90–91; Don H. Doyle, *Social Order of a Frontier Community: Jacksonville, Illinois, 1825–1870* (1978), 180–84, 190; Kathleen Smith Kutolowski, "Free Masonry and Community in the Early Republic," *American Quarterly*, 34 (Winter 1982):543–61. For the survival and later history of the Masons, see Lynn Dumenil, *Free Masonry and American Culture* (1984), 5–9, and chap. 3. A very helpful insider's view can be found in Walter B. Hill, "The Great American Safety Valve," *Century Magazine*, 44 (1822):383–84. Hill was a prominent Mason as well as a leader in the state bar association movement.

15. This description of market capitalism has been influenced by Schumpeter's notion of "creative destruction." See Joseph Schumpeter, *Capitalism, Socialism and Democracy* (1943), chap. 7. Stanley I. Kuther reflects a similar influence in *Privilege and Creative Destruction: The Charles River Bridge Case* (1971). For creative destruction in banking of this era see Bray Hammond, "Banking in the Early West: Monopoly, Prohibition and Laissez-Faire," *The Journal of Economic His-*

tory 8 (May 1948):1–25; he handles this topic more broadly in his *Banks and Politics in America from the Revolution to the Civil War* (1957). For creative destruction in the iron industry, see Paul Paskoff, *Industrial Evolution: Organization and Growth of the Pennsylvania Iron Industry, 1750–1860* (1983), 89 ff., 106. For coal, see C. K. Yearly, Jr., *Enterprise and Anthracite: Economics and Democracy in Schykill County, 1820–1875* (1961). Harvey J. Wexler, "How to Succeed in Business, 1840–1860," *Explorations in Entrepreneurial History,* 1 (1949):26 ff., describes the spirit of the entrepreneur. See also Roger L. Ransom, "Interregional Canals and Economic Specialization in the Antebellum United States," *Explorations in Entrepreneurial History,* 2d ser., 5 (Fall 1967): 12–35. Louis B. Schmidt's early study, "Internal Commerce and the Development of the National Economy before 1860," *Journal of Political Economy,* 47 (1939):798–822 is still useful. The role of the wholesaler in undermining monopolies in local markets is described by Glenn Porter and Robert Livesay, *Merchants and Manufacturers: Studies in the Changing Structure of 19th-Century Marketing* (1971). State and federal aid to economic growth is well summarized in Stuart Bruchey, *The Roots of American Economic Growth, 1607–1861* (1965), 95–138. The laissez-faire notions of political radicals in this era were first discussed by Arthur M. Schlesinger Jr., *The Age of Jackson* (1945), 314–17; then by Joseph Dorfman, *The Economic Mind in American Civilization* (1946), 2:653–59.

16. See Dorfman, *The Economic Mind* 2:684–86, 736–38, 759, 826–33. For a characteristic contemporary discussion of the jurisprudence of property, master-servant relations, and contract, see Timothy Walker, *Introduction to American Law,* 3d ed. (1855); Lawrence M. Friedman, *A History of American Law* (1973), pt. 2, chap. 5, 6, offers a present day perspective. See also Morton Horwitz's discussion of these subjects in *The Transformataion of American Law, 1780–1860* (1977), chaps. 2–4, 6. For the perplexities of the authority in the factory see Jonathan Prude, *The Coming of Industrial Order: Town and Factory, 1810–1860* (1983) 36–37, 45–46, 130, 155–57, 233; and Robert Doherty, *Society and Power: Five New England Towns, 1800–1860* (1977), 76–81.

17. For the expression of the spirit of commercial honor and authority, see P. Hone, "Commerce and Commercial Character," *Hunt's Merchants Magazine,* 4 (1841):129; F. Hunt, "The Advantages of Commerce," *Hunt's Merchants Magazine,* 1 (1839):200; William Howard Van Doran, *Mercantile Morals* (1852); J. H. Lanman, "The Commercial System of the United States," *Hunt's Merchants Magazine,* 11 (1844): 47; G. P. Marsh, "Principles and Tendencies of Modern Commerce," *Hunt's Merchants Magazine,* 33 (1850):147. Alexis de Tocqueville, *Democracy in America,* ed. Phillips Broadley (1956), 1:3 ff., 2:158–661. See also Tocqueville's discussion of honor, 2:230–42. Jeremy Attack and Fred Bateman, *To Their Own Soil: Agriculture in the Antebellum North* (1987), chap. 6. Edward Pessen, by magnifying the importance of Eastern urban cities, launched a single-minded attack upon a simplified version of Tocqueville's analysis; see Edward Pessen, *Riches, Class and*

Power before the Civil War (1973). Pessen's work has been sharply criticized, and he has replied somewhat vituperatively. See: Robert E. Gallman, "Professor Pessen on the 'Egalitarian Myth'," *Social Science History,* 2 (1978):194–207; Edward Pessen, "On A Recent Cliometric Attempt to Resurrect the Myth of Antebellum Egalitarianism," *Social Science History,* 3 (1979):208–27; Robert E. Gallman, "The 'Egalitarian Myth' Once Again," *Social Science History,* 5 (1981):223–34; Edward Pessen, "The Beleaguered Myth of Antebellum Egalitarianism," *Social Science History,* 6 (1982):111–25. See also Gloria Main's incisive review of Pessen's book in *Business History Review* 48 (1974), 251–53. All this casts doubt upon Pessen's interpretation of his findings and suggests that his seemingly "hard" statistics are quite impressionistic.

18. Catherine Beecher, *A Treatise on Domestic Economy* (1846), 25.

19. S. A. Ferral, *A Ramble of Six Thousand Miles Through the United State of America* (1832), 230.

20. This was apparent in the popular handbooks for would-be gentlemen and epitomized in what was perhaps the most popular of the lot, Charles Butler, *The American Gentleman* (1836), 24–36.

21. I have read all editions. Their changes are interesting but not relevant here. I cite Francis Lieber, *The Character of the Gentlemen* (1864), 3d and much enlarged edition, because it is the most widely available.

22. Ralph Waldo Emerson, "Aristocracy," ed. Perry Miller, *The American Transcendentalists* (1981), 228; Ralph Waldo Emerson, "Manners," *The Complete Works of Ralph Waldo Emerson,* ed. Edward Waldo Emerson (1903), 3:130. Of course, Emerson, being Emerson, could also say the opposite and he did. Lieber, *The Character of the Gentleman,* 20–21, 45.

23. Lieber, *The Character of the Gentleman,* 24, 46, 105. Even Emerson, whose arguments often seemed to be so etherial, linked gentlemanhood to power. Ralph Waldo Emerson, *Essays, First and Second Series,* ed. Ernest Rhys (1906), 271. For a similar use of Washington, see Butler, *The American Gentleman,* vi–vii.

24. John Adams to Joseph Hawley, 25 November 1775, *Letters of Members of the Continental Congress,* ed. Edmund C. Burnett (1921), 1:260. Clement Eaton, *The Growth of Southern Civilization, 1790–1860* (1961), 1–8; Rolin G. Osterweis, *Romanticism and Nationalism in the Old South* (1949), 8–21, 213–16; Daniel R. Hundley, *Social Relations in Our Southern States* ([1860] 1979), chap. 1. For violence and slavery, see Kenneth Stampp, *The Peculiar Institution* (1956), 171–91; Paul A. David and others. *Reckoning With Slavery* (1976), 57–93; James Oakes, *The Ruling Race* (1982), 24–28; 161–68, 188. The discussion of Southern violence is extensive. For some helpful studies, see Sheldon Hackney, "Southern Violence," *American Historical Review,* 84 (February 1969):906–21; John Hope Franklin, *The Militant South* (1970); Dickson D. Brice, Jr., *Violence and Culture in the Antebellum South* (1979).

25. W. J. G. [William J. Grayson], "The Character of the Gentleman,"

Southern Quarterly Review, n.s. 8 (January 1853):66, 80. Richard B. Davis, *Intellectual Life in Jefferson's Virginia* (1958), 415; *Southern Literary Messenger,* 1 (1834):6; W. J. G., "The Character," 73–74; Hundley, *Social Relations in Our Southern States,* chap. 1. Bertram Wyatt-Brown, *Southern Honor* (1982), chap. 4, provides a brilliant discussion of the Southern gentleman as well as the peculiar Southern notions of honor. Wyatt-Brown's approach is anthropological rather than historical.

26. Daniel Drake, "The Gentleman," 15 September 1830, 12–16, MS, Health Sciences Library, University of Cincinnati, "Discourse on the Philosophy of Discipline" [1834], Henry D. Shapiro and Zane Miller, *Physician to the West: Selected Writings of Daniel Drake* (1970), 260–84. For a more strident attack upon Southern notions of the gentleman and his honor, see Charles Sumner, "The True Grandeur of Nations . . . July 4, 1845," in *The Complete Works of Charles Sumner* (1969), 1:60–67. Editorial, *New York Times,* 30 August 1864.

27. Ralph Waldo Emerson, "New England Reformers" [1844], *Essays,* 342–43; John S. Brubacher and Willis Rudy, *Higher Education in Transition* (1958), 102–10.

28. Frederick Rudolph, *The American College and University—A History* (1962), 130–35, 218–20; Emerson, "New England Reformers," 343.

29. Albert J. Harno, *Legal Education in the United States* (1953), chap. 1; Maxwell Bloomfield, *American Lawyers in a Changing Society, 1776–1876* (1976), chap. 5; William Frederick Norwood, *Medical Education in the United States Before the Civil War* (1944), chap. 7.

30. Nathan Smith Davis, *History of Medical Education and Institutions in the United States* (1851), 115–17, 207; Nathan Smith Davis, *History of the American Medical Association from the Organization up to January, 1855* (1855), 19; Daniel Drake, *Practical Essays on Medical Education* ([1832] 1952), 12–13, 45–59, 99; George H. White, "Medical Education and Legislation," *Transactions of the Medical Society of the State of New York* (1846), 6:44, 138–43; Worthington Hooker, *Present Mental Attitude and Tendencies of the Medical Profession* (1852), 27. William G. Rothstein, *American Medical Schools and the Practice of Medicine: A History* (1987), presents a more favorable view of medical schools in this era. Undoubtedly, in view of the wide range of practitioners who had previously supplied various kinds of medical care, the increased number of mediocre physicians was probably a public health benefit. Richard H. Shryock, *Medicine and Society in America* (1960), 137–51; Joseph F. Kett *The Formation of the American Medical Profession* (1968), 35–64, 171–72.

31. Mark A. May and Frank K. Shuttleworth, *The Education of American Ministers* (1934), 2:20–22; Colin Brumitte Goodykoontz, *Home Missions on the American Frontier* (1939), 364–66, 385; William Warren Sweet, *The Story of Religion in America* (1950), 252; Sylvanus M. Duvall, *The Methodist Episcopal Church and Education up to 1869* (1928), 59–61; Robert G. Torbet, *The Baptists Ministry Then and Now* (1953), 32–38; Donald G. Tewksbury, *The Founding of American Colleges and Universities Before the Civil War* (1932), 7, 25–26; William

Adams Brown, *The Education of American Ministers* (1934), 1:80–81;
Archibald Alexander, "Hindrances to Piety in Young Men Preparing for
the Ministry," *Quarterly Register and Journal*, 2 (1829):2.

32. Walter Hugins, *Jacksonian Democracy and the Working Class*
(1960), 166–71; State Senator Scott, "Address," *Transactions of the
Medical Society of the State of New York*, (1846); app. 55–69; Roscoe
Pound, *The Lawyer From Antiquity to Modern Times* (1953), 223–28;
A. Z. Reed, *Training for the Public Profession of Law*, (1921), 85–89,
183; W. Raymond Blackard, "The Demoralization of the Legal Profession
in the 19th Century," *Tennessee Law Review* 16 (1946):314–18; Gary
B. Nash, "Philadelphia Bench and Bar, 1800–1861," *Comparative Stud-
ies in Society and History*, 8 (January 1965):220; Richard H. Shryock,
Medical Licensing in America (1967), 30. For lawyers rejecting the dis-
tinction between profession and occupation, see S.A.G. Carter, *The Old
Court House, Reminiscences and Anecdotes* (1880), 313–16.

33. J. L. Ainslie, *The Doctrines of Ministerial Order in the Reformed
Churches of Sixteenth and Seventeenth Centuries* (1940), 1–95; E.
Clowes Chorley, *Men and Movements in the American Episcopal
Church* (1948), 133–40.

34. Sidney E. Mead, "The Rise of the Evangelical Conception of the
Ministry in America," in *The Ministry in Historical Perspective*, ed. H.
Richard Niebuhr (1956), 207–49; Sidney E. Mead, *The Lively Experi-
ment* (1963), 103–33.

35. Kett, *The Formation of the American Medical Profession*, chaps.
4,5; Jacob Bigelow, *Modern Inquiries* (1867), 230.

36. Charles Rosenberg, "The American Medical Profession: Mid-19th
Century," *Mid-America* 44 (1962): 163; Alex Berman, "The Thomsonian
Movement and its Relation to American Pharmacy and Medicine," *Bul-
letin of the History of Medicine*, 25 (1951):421; Alex Berman, "Social
Roots of the 19th Century Botanics," *Actes du VIII Congress Interna-
tional d'Histoire des Sciences* (1956), 561–65; Samuel Thomson, *The
New Guide to Health* (1831), 4, 36. Some physicians responded to these
challenges with a more stringent application of traditional therapies.
See John Harley Warner, *The Therapeutic Perspective* (1968), chap. 3.

37. Isaac Newton Danforth, *The Life of Nathan Smith Davis* (1907),
chaps. 1–6; Davis, *History of Medical Education*, 227; American Medical Association, *Transactions* 18 (1867):362. William G. Rothstein,
American Physicians in the 19th Century (1972) interprets this era as
one of organizational vigor, at least on the local level. However, a reading
of the histories and proceedings of those state and local association discloses their weakness and fluctuating energies. See for example: Ronald
L. Numbers and Judith Walter Leavitt, eds., *Wisconsin Medicine: Historical Perspectives* (1981), 76–78; Fred B. Rogers, *The Healing Art: A
History of the Medical Society of New Jersey* (1966), 92–93, 116, 186;
Howard Kistler Petry, ed., *A Century of Medicine, 1848–1948: The History of the Medical Society of the State of Pennsylvania* (1952), 3, 33,
37, 59, 62, 79, 99. G.W.H. Kemper, *A Medical History of the State of
Indiana* (1911), 165–71. Kett, The Formation of the American Medical

Profession, 171–72; Henry B. Shafer, *The American Medical Profession, 1783–1850* (1937), 221–22.

38. George Rosen, *The Specialization of Medicine* (1944), 16; George Rosen, "Special Medical Societies in the United States after 1860," *Ciba Symposium,* 9 (1947):1132; Hooker, *Present Mental Attitude,* 24–26.

39. Daniel H. Calhoun, *Professional Lives in America* (1965), 184; Francis Randolph Packard, *The History of Medicine in America* (1931), 2:1153; Jacob Bigelow, *Modern Inquiries* (1867), 16; *Worcester's Dictionary* (1863), "specialist."

40. William J. Gies, *Dental Education in the United States and Canada* (1926), 7; Edward Kremers and George Urdang, *History of Pharmacy* (1951), 229–51.

41. "The Amalgam Controversy in New York," *Dental Intelligencer,* 3 (1847):161–76; An Expert, "Artificial Teeth," *Old and New,* 10 (1874):45; Charles R. E. Koch, *History of Dental Surgery* (1909), 1:173–76; *American Journal of Dental Science,* 1 (1839):164.

42. Dorothy Fahs Beck, "The Development of the Dental Profession in the United States" (Master's thesis, University of Chicago, 1932), 87–103, Gies, *Dental Education,* 39–44; Chapin Harris, "Observations," *American Journal of Dental Science,* 1 (1839):52–56.

43. For the lawyers' involvement in national politics, see Donald R. Matthews's, "United States Senators and the Class Structure," *Public Opinion Quarterly,* 18 (October 1954):5–22, where he finds that senators with legal education won 55, 95, and 77 percent of the seats in the Senate in 1789, 1845, and 1895, respectively. For the lawyers' involvement in business enterprise, see Horwitz, *The Transformation of American Law,* chap. 5; Alfred Konefsky, ed., *The Papers of Daniel Webster: Legal Papers* (1982)1:61 ff.

44. See chap. 3 in this book. My argument as to the relative decline of the legal profession in authority and honor in this era runs counter to the work of Maxwell Bloomfield, *American Lawyers in a Changing Society, 1776–1876* (1976), particularly chap. 5, which deals with this era. Bloomfield modestly calls his view "a working hypothesis," and I found it unpersuasive (see p. 137). Much of his information could be used against his argument and in support of the older view summarized by Pound, *The Lawyer from Antiquity to Modern Times,* 253.

45. Paul Lucas, "Blackstone and the Reform of the Legal Profession," *English Historical Review,* 77 (1962); James Wilson, *The Works of James Wilson* (1804), 1:77–80, chap. 5; Roscoe Pound, *The Formative Era of American Law* (1938), chap. 1.

46. Joseph Story, "Address Before the Suffolk Bar," *American Jurist,* 1 (1829):31; David Dudley Field, *Speeches, Arguments and Miscellaneous Papers of David Dudley Field,* ed. A. P. Sprague (1884), 1:229, 311, 337–38, 510; Charles M. Cook, *The American Codification Movement* (1981).

47. Francis R. Auman, "Some Problems in Growth and Development in the Formative Period of the American Legal System," *University of Cincinnati Law Review,* 5 (1931):408–29; New York State Bar Associa-

tion, "Report of the Committee on Contingent Fees," *Proceedings of the New York State Bar Association*, 31 (1908):101–4. The New York State Code of Civil Procedure of 1841 removed the restrictions on contingent fee agreements which previously had been held invalid as champertous.

48. Cook, *American Codification Movement*, 211. These judgments rest on examination of diaries and memoirs of lawyers in Cincinnati and Memphis in the era 1830–1880. Among them were: Carter, *The Old Court House;* John Hallum, *The Diary of an Old Lawyer* (1895); Timothy Walker Papers, King Family Papers, and Lawler Family Papers, Cincinnati Historical Society; William T. Avery Papers, John P. Caruthers Papers, Estes Family Papers, Memphis Room, Memphis Public Library; Howell E. Jackson Papers, Tennessee Historical Society; Robertson Topp Papers in the Burrow Library, Southwestern College at Memphis.

49. Timothy Walker, "The Dignity of Law as a Profession," delivered at the Cincinnati College, 4 November 1837, and "Ways and Means of Professional Success," *Western Law Journal*, 1 (September 1844):25; Rufus Choate, *The Position and Functions of the American Bar* (1845); Daniel Webster, "Speech at the Charleston Bar Dinner, May 10, 1847," *Charleston Courier*, 12 May, 1847. Daniel H. Calhoun, *Professional Lives in America, 1750–1850* (1965), 62 ff. For the more respected standing of law over medicine, see A. Z. Reed, "Restrictions upon the Professions Prior to the Civil War," *The Bar Examiner*, 2 (1933):31 ff.

50. "Human Occupations: Comparative Privileges and Effects of the Different Occupations in Life," *The Knickerbocker Magazine*, 12 (November 1838):437–42. For the difficulties and strategies of ministers, see "Authority of Ministers," *Congregational Magazine*, 20 (1837):1; E. Holt, "Ministers Degrading Their Office," *American Quarterly Register*, 12 (1837):333; H. Bently, "Ministers' Intimacy with Their People," *Congregational Magazine*, 21 (1838):478; "Dangers and Difficulties of the Ministry," *Theological and Literary Journal*, 2(1857):106; Paul F. Eve, "To What Cause Are We to Attribute the Diminished Respectability of the Profession in the Estimation of the American Public?" *Medical and Surgical Reporter*, n.s. 1 (1858):141, 143; Massachusetts Medical Society, "Medical Communications: The Medical Profession and Society," *Proceedings*, 10 (1866):400; Nathaniel Chapman, "Presidential Address," *Transactions of the American Medical Association*, 1 (1848):7; Steven Smith, *Doctor in Medicine* ([1872] 1972), 216–20. For the achievements in law, religion, and medicine, see, Pound, *The Formative Era*, 223 ff.; Reinhold Niebuhr, "The Impact of Protestantism Today," *Atlantic Monthly*, 181 (February 1948):57–62; Richard H. Shryock, *Medicine in America: Historical Essays* (1967), 172.

51. Fee bills, a traditional method of restraining competition among surgeons, had their origins in guild practices. Some medical societies in America early adopted such devices for setting minimum charges. Their effect upon esprit de corps, however, was more substantial than upon the doctors' income. Doctors customarily treated the poor without charge and adjusted the fees charged other patients according to their income. George Rosen, "Fees and Fee Bills," *Bulletin of the History of*

Medicine: Supplement (1945), 5–36; Henry B. Shafer, *The American Medical Profession*, (1936), 156; Philip Van Ingen, *The New York Academy of Medicine* (1949), 64; Donald E. Konold, *A History of American Medical Ethics, 1847–1912* (1962), 7.

52. George Wilson Pierson, *Tocqueville and Beaumont in America* (1938), 566.

53. The ministers were the least urban-centered of all the professions. More than with the others, therefore, it is necessary in studying the ministers to vary the scrutiny of the city with sidelong glances at the surrounding rural setting. This is made easy by the fact that the religious newspapers and publishing houses, run by ministers and located in the major cities, registered the significant and insignificant happenings of the day and reflected back to the ministry and the denominations a sense of themselves. In this era in particular, the religious newspapers flourished inordinately, and they provide an extraordinary source of information on the ministry and more generally on American religious life. See Wesley Norton's general discussion in his preface to *Religious Newspapers in the Old Northwest* (1977).

54. U.S. Census Office, Eighth Census, 1860, *Statistics of the United States* (1866), XVIII. The absolute disparity in numbers between Memphis and Cincinnati makes for some important differences; that most of the differences were not simply a matter of numbers is made evident by the heuristic exercise of matching Memphis in 1860 with two Northern cities approximately the same size at that time. I scanned the directory and newspapers of Dayton, Ohio, and Utica, N.Y., for 1860 and also dropped back to the year 1829 in Cincinnati when its population was roughly that of Memphis in 1860. The sharp contrast in the social order and culture of these northern cities and Memphis is unmistakable almost at first glance. Nonetheless, the difference in sheer size and its possible influence was kept in mind when Memphis and Cincinnati were compared.

Chapter 4

1. "Our Local Interests," Memphis *Daily Appeal*, 11 April 1845; "Local Improvements and Interests," *Appeal*, 31 July 1846; "Election Results," *Appeal*, 4 Sept. 1846; "Wolf River Canal," *Appeal*, 29 Jan. 1847; "Protest against Construction of the Wolf River Canal," *Appeal*, 5 Feb. 1847; Memphis *Daily Eagle*, 26 May 1848; John McLeod Keating, *History of the City of Memphis and Shelby County Tennessee* (1888), 1:241. See later comment in "Memphis and Its Manufacturing Advantages," *De Bow's Review* (May 1851), 527.

2. To identify the powerful group that quashed the campaign for the canal, I matched the signatories of the protest listed in the *Appeal*, Feb. 5, 1847, with the occupational and business listings in *Twynman's Memphis Directory and General Business Advertiser for 1850* (1849). *Daily Eagle*, 31 May 1848; Gerald M. Capers, Jr., *The Biography of a River Town, Memphis: Its Heroic Age* (1939), chaps. 3, 4; "Speculation

in Cotton," *Meriwether Free Trader*, 3 Dec. 1881. For more general discussion of cotton marketing in this region, see Harold D. Woodman,
King Cotton and His Retainers (1968), 17, 27–29, 68–70, 87–97, 220–
22, 229–34.

3. Daniel R. Hundley, *Social Relations in Our Southern States* [1860],
ed. William J. Cooper, Jr. (1979), 59; William J. Grayson, *James Louis
Petigru* (1866), 136–37. For the fictional Southern gentleman, see William R. Taylor, *Cavalier and Yankee* (1969), 219–20, 247–48; Bertram
Wyatt-Brown, *Southern Honor* (1982), chap. 4, tries to depict the Southern gentleman as he was. The movement from civic prominence to rural
splendor around Memphis was particularly noticeable among the leading lawyers in town.

4. Capers, *Memphis*, chaps. 3, 4; R. G. Dunn, *Credit Ledgers, Tennessee, Shelby County*, Baker Library, Harvard: Brooks, Neely & Co.,
1:337; W. B. Glisson, 1:273; William L. Stewart, 2:82; W. B. Galbraith,
3:168; Trader and Fleese, 2:359. See also Lewis E. Atherton, *The Southern Country Store, 1800–1860* (1949), 106–8; Memphis *Public Ledger*,
27 May 1872; "The Bucket Shop," *Meriwether Free Trader*, 11 Feb.
1882, 4.

5. One of the best discussions of Memphis debt practices can be found
in David Moss Hilliard, *The Development of Public Education in Memphis, Tennessee* (Ph.D. diss., University of Chicago, 1946), 68–69, Keating, *History of Memphis*, 1:440–41, 610–11, 616, 652, 692.

6. *Appeal*, 9 March 1847; Hilliard, *Development of Public Education*,
182; Keating, *History of Memphis*, 1:441, 651.

7. Prostitution was legal in Memphis during this era (1830–1880). It
was regulated by the police and was a source of revenue. Madams evidently paid their taxes. See Anon., *History of the Memphis Police* (1954),
44; Thomas Harrison Baker, *The Memphis Commercial Appeal: The
History of a Southern Newspaper* (1971), 64–65; *Public Ledger*, 9
March 1870; Memphis *Daily Avalanche*, 12 Sept. 1877; Keating, *History of Memphis*, 1:416. On Memphis gambling, see *Appeal*, 18 Sept.
1846; *Avalanche*, 18 March 1866; *Public Ledger*, 3 March 1870 and 21
Feb. 1872; J. P. Young, *Standard History of Memphis* (1912), 231–34.
On dueling, see Jerome G. Taylor, Jr., "Upper-Class Violence in 19th
Century Tennessee," *West Tennessee Historical Society Papers* 34
(1980): 33 ff., and Keating, *History of Memphis, passim*, who records
the more sensational duels and affrays year by year. A run of any Memphis newspaper will serve equally well. For a perceptive contemporary
account, see H. V. Redfield, *Homicide North and South* (1880), 232 ff.
The link between slavery and the fostering of violence within Southern
culture was suggested by Thomas Jefferson in *Notes on the State of
Virginia*, ed. William Peden (1955), 162. I find all the various explanations proposed to counter Jefferson's less persuasive. For a discussion
of these theories, see Edward L. Ayers, *Vengeance and Justice* (1984),
9–16.

8. Robert A. Sigafoos, *Cotton Row to Beale Street* (1979), 28, 45. The

Robertson Topp Papers in the Burrow Library, Southwestern at Memphis, is an invaluable repository not only for Topp's career but for economic discussion in Memphis.

9. For Hill, see Dunn, *Credit Ledgers*, 1:100; Keating, *History of Memphis*, 2:146–47; and Shields McIlwaine, *Memphis, Down in Dixie* (1948), 220–28 for valuable anecdotes. For Hadden, see Dunn, *Credit Ledgers*, 2:243, 311; *Meriwether Free Trader*, 6 May 1882, in the Meriwether Papers, Mississippi Valley Collection, Memphis State University Library; Keating, *History of Memphis*, 2:33–34; McIlwaine, *Memphis, Down in Dixie*, 230–33; for Montgomery, see Dunn, *Credit Ledgers*, 3:259; *Meriwether Free Trader*, August 1884; Meriwether Papers, Mississippi Valley Collection; Keating, *History of Memphis*, 2:158–59. The Montgomery Papers in the Memphis/Shelby County Public Library are chiefly pre–Civil War. For Wright, see Dunn, *Credit Ledgers*, A:546; L. B. McFarland, *Memoirs and Addresses* (1922), 75–78; Young, *Standard History*, 535; Memphis Bar Association, *Memorial Book*, 128, Memphis Bar Association Library, Memphis Court House; Forrest Orren Lax, "The Memphis Cotton Exchange" (Master's thesis, Memphis State University Library), 1–35.

10. The Memphis Room of the Memphis/Shelby County Public Library has a broad selection of antebellum booster pamphlets written principally by local journalists. See especially Henry Van Pelt, *The Future of Memphis* (1844); Dr. Solon Borland, *Science and Literature in Memphis* (1840); W. N. Stanton, *"Bluff City" and Its Growth* (1847); Leonardis Trousdale, *The Southern Metropolis* (1859). Some of the most vehement discussions of this civic folk mercantilism can be found in the newspaper editorials. See *Appeal*, 15 Jan. 1851, 22 Oct. 1851; *Public Ledger*, 19 Mar. 1873. This appeal for ridding the city of her dependence upon cotton comes from the Memphis *Baptist Messenger*, 24 Sept. 1859. For post–Civil War disucssion, see *Appeal*, 3 July 1870; "The Great Want of Memphis Home Manufactures," *Appeal*, 1 Sept. 1873; "Manufactures in Memphis," *Old Folks Historical Record* (1874), 1:125–26.

11. For a forthright discussion of the system of "Connections" in Memphis, see Walter A. Montgomery Papers, History of the South Collection, University of North Carolina, Chapel Hill, Box 1, Memphis Folder, 1872–1875; also "Autobiography" (Typescript), p. 7 ff. See also Henry Craft Diary (Typescript), Craft-Thorne Papers, History of the South Collection, University of North Carolina, Chapel Hill, 1:151 ff. See also Young, *Standard History*, 587; John Hallum, *The Diary of an Old Lawyer* (1895), xxii–xxiv.

12. R. G. Dunn, *Reports, Shelby County*, 2:116, 3:10, 87, 203; Joseph H. Shepherd, *Letterbooks*, vols. 1, 2 (1857–1863), Memphis Room, Memphis/Shelby County Public Library. The great yellow fever epidemic of 1878 struck heavily in the Irish slums, decimating that population. Many of the Germans, usually more well-to-do than the Irish, fled to St. Louis and did not return. "The Residential Distribution of Immigrants in Memphis, Tennessee" (M.A. thesis, Memphis State University, 1970), *passim;* Robert Rauchle, "Biographical Sketches of Prominent Germans

in Memphis, Tennessee, in the Nineteenth Century," *West Tennessee Historical Society Papers* 22 (1966): 78–85.

13. *Old Folks Historical Record* 1 (1874): 12, 55, 56, 58, 72, 86; 2 (1875): 522.

14. For a rough estimate of the social composition of the Masonic lodges, the officer lists were checked with the occupation listings in the city directories. The leadership may have come from a more prosperous segment of the membership, but the discussion of leadership problems in the *Masonic Jewel* suggests that this was not the case. The yearly dues of ten dollars probably kept poorer workers out. See Memphis *Masonic Jewel* 15 April 1872 and 15 Feb. 1875.

15. *Masonic Jewel*, 15 Feb. 1872, 15 Aug. 1872, 15 March 1873, 15 Aug. 1874, 15 Feb. 1875, 15 Sept. 1877; Anne Marie McMahon Falsone, "The Memphis Howard Association: A Study in the Growth of Social Awareness" (M.A. thesis, Memphis State University, 1968), 208–19.

16. For attacks upon exclusiveness, see *Daily Avalanche*, 14 July 1858, 8 July 1877; *Public Ledger*, 6 Jan. 1872, 9 Oct. 1872; *Baptist Messenger*, 30 Sept. 1859. For discussions of equality, see Memphis *Enquirer*, 8 June 1836, 9 July 1837; *Memphis Whig*, 3 May 1855, 25 Oct. 1856; *Appeal*, 23 May 1845, 16 Jan. 1846, 13 Mar. 1846, 25 Nov. 1848, 14 Feb. 1851, 23 Nov. 1851; *Public Ledger*, 6 July 1870.

17. For a good description of the changing responses of doctors to the question of professional advertising, see Susan Crawford, ed., *Digest of official Actions: American Medical Association, 1846–1958* (1959), 21 ff.

18. A clear description of the careers and involvements of Memphis lawyers can be drawn from the R. G. Dunn, *Reports, Tennessee, Shelby County*, 546–52, devoted primarily to lawyers. See also David J. Bodenhammer, "Regionalism and the Legal History of the South," *Ambivalent Legacy: A Legal History of the South*, eds. David J. Bodenhammer and James Ely, Jr. (1948), 3–29.

19. Henry Craft, "The Judiciary—What It Is, and What It Should Be," *Memphis Law Journal* 1 (1879): 18; Henry Craft Diary, Craft-Thorne Papers, 1:227–29; Henry S. Foote, *Bench and Bar of the South and Southwest* (1876), 16; Hon. A. J. Fletcher, *Speech on the Bill to Reorganize the Judicial System of Tennessee and to Reform the Code of Practice, Delivered in the Senate, December 13, 1855* (1856), 8.

20. *Public Ledger*, 6 March 1871; Hallum, *Diary of an Old Lawyer*, 54–57, 70; Keating, *History of Memphis*, 2:89; Foote, *Bench and Bar*, 79, 159, 213; *Old Folks Historical Record*, 1:56.

21. Louis Burchette McFarland, *Memoirs and Addresses* (1922), 76–78; J. J. Rawlings, *Miscellaneous Writings and Reminiscences* (1895), 43; Hallum, *Diary of an Old Lawyer*, 97–105.

22. Fletcher, *Speech*, 3–5; Return J. Meigs and William F. Cooper, eds., *The Code of Tennessee* (1858), 713–15.

23. Fletcher, *Speech*, 4; Samuel Cole Williams, *History of Codification in Tennessee* (1932), 17–26, 44–45.

24. Hallum, *Diary of an Old Lawyer*, 76; Arthur F. Howington, "'Ac-

cording to Law': The Trial and Punishment of Black Defendants in Antebellum Tennessee" (paper delivered at the Seventy-First Annual Meeting of the Organization of American Historians, 13 April 1878), 14–15; Henry Craft Diary, 8 August 1863; Andrew Allison, "Report of the Committee on Legal Education," *Proceedings,* Bar Association of Tennessee (1882), 53; James B. Caldwell, *Recollections of a Lifetime* (1923), 41–42. See also James W. Patton, "Progress of Emancipation in Tennessee, 1796–1860," *Journal of Negro History* 17 (1932): 67–102; A. E. K. Nash, "Reason of Slavery: Understanding the Judicial Role in the Peculiar Institution," *Vanderbilt Law Review* 32 (1979): 7 ff.; Arthur F. Howington, *What Sayeth the Law: The Treatment of Slaves and Free Blacks in the State and Local Courts in Tennessee* (1986); and more generally, Mark Tushnet, *The American Law of Slavery, 1810–1860: Considerations of Humanity and Interest* (1981).

25. Hallum, *Diary of an Old Lawyer,* 27–28, 76–86, 113–17; *Enquirer,* 16 Sept. 1837; *Appeal,* 26 Jan. 1846; Foote, *Bench and Bar,* 146–51.

26. Hallum, *Diary of an Old Lawyer,* 71, 167–68, 256–69; E. L. Beecher deposition in J. M. McKnight v. America C. Dill, Shelby County Chancery Docket no. 1399 Meriwether Papers, Mississippi Valley Collection, 100; Foote, *Bench and Bar,* 14. For important court decisions on the lawyer's authority, see Jones v. Williamson, 45 Tennessee Reports (1868), 380–81; Planters' Bank of Tennessee v. T. J. Massey, 49 Tennessee Reports (1870), 364–65. On privileged communications, see Lockhard v. Brodie, 1 Tennessee Chancery Reports (1873), 390–91. Henry Craft, "Reverence for Law," *Memphis Whig,* 5 July 1855; Henry G. Smith, "Lawyer and Client," *Daily Avalanche,* 13 Feb. 1872.

27. "The Bar in Memphis," Memphis *Bulletin,* 26 Mar. 1865; *Appeal,* 21 May, 1848; *Daily Avalanche,* 21 Mar. 1861, 11 July 1866, and 15 July 1866; *Baptist Messenger,* 23 Feb. 1860; *Public Ledger,* 11 Nov. 1874. Lawyers were sometimes denounced as accessories to the crime after it was committed. One Memphis lawyer admitted without shame that he had destroyed incriminating evidence in his zealousness to win a case. Hallum, *Diary of an Old Lawyer,* 38–42.

28. Foote, *Bench and Bar,* 55–56; Hallum, *Diary of an Old Lawyer,* 79; deposition of A. Wright, Shelby County Chancery Docket no. 7399, Meriwether Papers, Mississippi Valley Collection, 144; "The Bar in Memphis," *Bulletin,* 26 Mar. 1865; Memphis Bar Association, "Memoirs," Memphis Bar Association Library, Shelby County Court House, 60; Walter A. Montgomery, "Memoirs," Walter A. Montgomery Papers, History of the South Collection, University of North Carolina, Chapel Hill, 36–42; *Third Annual Report of the Board of Directors and Officers of Memphis Bar and Law Library Association* (1879), 83; Keating, *History of Memphis,* 2:72.

29. Henry Craft Diary, 118–19; Allison, "Report on Legal Education," 52–54.

30. Hallum, *Diary of an Old Lawyer,* 65, 69, 91, 220, 243; "Lehman

and Lehman," in "Memoirs", Memphis Bar Association; R. G. Dunn Reports, *Tennessee*, vol. A, Shelby County, *passim*; Asa Inglehart, "Is the Bar Unpopular?", *Memphis Law Journal* 1 (1878): 257–65.

31. *Daily Avalanche*, 21 May 1862; Henry Craft Diary, 1:151–52; "Memorial to Connelly F. Trigg" [1862], in Craft-Thorne Papers.

32. Foote, *Bench and Bar*, 60; Keating, *History of Memphis*, 1:332; *Memphis Whig*, 24 September 1855; *Public Ledger*, 2 April and 2 May 1870. For a broader discussion of the rise of the elective judiciary in this era, see Kermit C. Hall, "The Judiciary on Trial," *Historian* 45 (1983): 337–54.

33. 37 Tennessee Reports (1850), 423; Henry Craft, "The Judiciary," 22–26; Memphis Bar Association, "Memoirs," 104. John W. Green, "Judges Robert Caruthers and Archibald Wright," *Tennessee Law Review* 18 (1941): 637–41.

34. "Joseph Brown Heiskell," in *Biographical Directory of the Tennessee General Assembly*, comp. William S. Speer (1888); John W. Green, *Law and Lawyers; Sketches of the Federal Judges of Tennessee* (1950), 128–31; Joseph B. Heiskell, *The Relation and Duty of the Citizen to the State* (1876), 8, 12–15, 23; Joseph B. Heiskell, "Tax Legislation in Tennessee," *Memphis Law Journal* 1 (1878), 27–32. Heiskell had been a Whig, a Presbyterian, and a prohibitionist; see Hallum, *Diary of an Old Lawyer*, 59–60.

35. H. Shelton Smith, "The Church and the Social Order in the Old South," *Church History* 7 (1938): 115–24. See also Anne C. Loveland, *Southern Evangelicals and the Social Order, 1800–1860* (1980), chap. 4. For a general discussion of the impact of revivalism on Christian theology of this era, see Sidney Mead, *The Lively Experiment* (1963), 123–27. *Baptist Messenger*, 16 Sept., 23 Sept., 28 Oct., and 4 Nov. 1859. Memphis *Presbyterian Sentinel*, 8 Sept. 1869; Nashville *Christian Advocate*, 9 August 1860. This Nashville Methodist newspaper circulated in Memphis, carried Memphis news, and took on the Memphis Baptist and Presbyterian journals in doctrinal controversy. *Baptist Messenger*, 11 October and 12 May 1860.

36. *Christian Advocate*, 16 June 1859; *Appeal*, 1 May 1861; *Presbyterian Sentinel*, 8 Sept. 1859.

37. *Baptist Messenger*, 15 Oct. 1859.

38. For a sampling of the literature on the death of infidels, see *Christian Advocate*, 1 Dec. 1859, *Baptist Messenger*, 30 Sept. 1859, and 3 May 1860. For deathbed scenes of saints, see *Christian Advocate*, 6 Oct. 1859; *Baptist Messenger*, 4 Oct. 1860; *Appeal*, 23 May 1845; Thomas Dwight Witherspoon, *Children of the Covenant* (1867), 3–21; Henry Craft, "Yellow Fever in Holly Springs" (1879), Henry Craft Papers, University of North Carolina, 16.

39. *Baptist Messenger*, 28 Oct. 1859, 20 April 1860; *Christian Advocate*, 8 and 17 June 1858, 13 Jan. 1859; Joseph Henry Borum, *Biographical Sketches of Tennessee Baptist Ministers* (1880), 66–75, 106–13, 230–33, 282–89; J. J. Burnett, *Sketches of Tennessee's Pioneer*

Baptist Preachers (1919), 166–69, 200–7; James I. Vance, ed., *Pioneer Presbyterianism in Tennessee* (1898), 19–35, 55–83; Robert H. Mc-Caslin, *Presbyterianism in Memphis, Tennessee* (1928), 26–63.

40. Hallum, *Diary of an Old Lawyer,* 54; *Christian Advocate,* 17 March 1859, praising the Reverend Martin Clark, one of the pulpit heroes of Tennessee; *Baptist Messenger,* 7 Oct. 1859.

41. "The Diary of the Reverend Nicholas M. Long," 16 Oct. and 17 Nov. 1871, 2 Dec. 1874, Mississippi Valley Collection, Memphis State University.

42. *Baptist Messenger,* 14 Oct. 1859; *Christian Advocate,* 3 Sept. 1857; Henry Craft Diary, 158. For other examples of this kind of guilt, see *Baptist Messenger,* 12 and 19 May 1860. Descriptions of Jesus' love are much more plentiful. For a few rhapsodic examples, see *Baptist Messenger,* 21 Oct. 1859, 2 Feb. 1860.

43. Walter B. Posey, *Baptists in the Lower Mississippi Valley* (1957), 117–18; *Baptist Messenger,* 25 Nov. and 2 Dec. 1859, 15 Mar. 1860; *Christian Advocate,* 18 Oct. 1860; Rev. Eugene Daniel, "Annual Sermon," *Manual of the Presbyterian Church of Memphis, Tennessee* (1876), 14.

44. Patrick H. Mell, D.D., *Corrective Church Discipline* (1860), 1–10; *Baptist Messenger,* 16 Sept. 1859, 17 May 1860, 4 Nov. 1859, 27 Sept. 1860.

45. *Baptist Messenger,* 19 Jan. and 29 Nov. 1860; "R. G. Graves," in Dunn, *Credit Ledgers* 3:147; Rufus Babcock, "Sketches of a Southwestern Tour," *Baptist Memorial* 4 (1845): 16–21, 82–83.

46. Rev. Thomas Oscar Fuller, *The Story of the Church Life Among Negroes in Memphis, Tennessee* (1938), 2; Rev. Thomas Oscar Fuller, *History of Negro Baptists of Tennessee* (1936), 21, 232–33, 299; James H. Robinson, "A Social History of the Negro in Memphis and in Shelby County" (Ph.D. diss., Yale University, 1934), 50, 59–60.

47. Philip M. Hamer, *Tennessee: A History, 1673–1932* (1933), 1:346; *Appeal,* 2 Sept. 1862.

48. *Baptist Messenger,* 30 Sept. and 7 Oct. 1859; Minutes of the First Presbyterian Church, Memphis (1845). Microfilm in Memphis Room, Memphis/Shelby County Public Library; *Baptist Messenger,* 28 Oct. 1859, 12 Apr. 1860.

49. *Appeal,* 30 and 31 July 1861; *Daily Avalanche,* 1 Mar. 1862; *Appeal,* 23 June 1861; *Daily Avalanche,* 1 March 1862; *Appeal,* 24 June 1862; *Daily Avalanche,* 15 June 1861. Many Jewish and Catholic laymen, with much display, flocked to the southern cause.

50. *Whig,* 19 Sept. 1855; *Baptist Messenger,* 15 May 1860; *Presbyterian Sentinel,* 8 Sept. 1859; T. D. Witherspoon, *Romanism* (1881), 37; W. J. Batersby, *The Christian Brothers of Memphis, 1871–1971* (1971), chap. 1; Abraham J. Karp, "Simon Tuska Becomes a Rabbi," *Publications of the American Jewish Historical Society* 50 (Dec. 1960): 89. See also the obituary for Tuska in the *American Israelite* 17 (6 Jan. 1871), 9, and (13 Jan. 1871), 4; *Congregation of Children of Israel* (Memphis), Minute Book, American Jewish Archives, microfilm no. 149; James A.

Wax, "The Jews of Memphis: 1860–1865," *West Tennessee Historical Papers* 3 (1949): 82, 84.

51. *Daily Avalanche*, 26 April 1862; McCaslin, *Presbyterianism in Memphis*, 37; Albert Bruce Cuvey, *History of the Second Presbyterian Church of Memphis, Tennessee* (1936), 11–12.

52. *Appeal*, 4 August 1861; Henry Craft Diary, 156; *Daily Avalanche*, 19 June 1866.

53. Rev. George A. Lofton, *Habitual Drink and its Remedy* (1874). Police Chief Davis listed 50 "houses of ill fame" and 338 whores in 1881, in *History of Police in Memphis*, 44; *Daily Avalanche*, 12 Sept. 1877; Henry Craft, *The Constitutionality of the Sabbath Law* (1880), Craft-Thorne Papers.

54. Phyllis Allen, "Etiological Theory in America prior to the Civil War," *Journal of the History of Medicine* 2 (1947): 489–520; Owsei Temkin, "A Historical Analysis of Infection," *Studies in Intellectual History*, Johns Hopkins University History of Ideas Club (1953), 123–47; George Rosen, *A History of Public Health* (1958), 280–95; Marcus J. Stewart, ed., *History of Medicine in Memphis* (1971), 19–44.

55. Richard H. Shryock, "Empiricism versus Rationalism in American Medicine, 1650–1950," *Proceedings of the American Antiquarian Society*, n.s. 79 (1969), 99–150; Lester S. King, *The Medical World of the Eighteenth Century* (1958); George Daniels, *American Science in the Age of Jackson* (1968), 140–41, 63–85; John Harley Warner, *The Therapeutic Perspective* (1986), 24–27, 39–57.

56. Erwin H. Ackerknecht, "Anticontagionism between 1821 and 1867," *Bulletin of the History of Medicine* 23 (1956):588–93; Stewart, *History of Medicine in Memphis*, 311–15; *Appeal*, 8 Jan. 1847.

57. "Code of Ethics of the Tennessee Medical Association," in *The Centenary History of the Tennessee Medical Association, 1830–1930*, ed. Philip C. Hamer (1931), 516, 517.

58. Howell W. Robards, *Introductory Lecture: A Brief History of the Origin, Progress, and Present Condition of the Science of Medicine and Surgery in the United States* (1853); *Appeal*, 19 March 1847; *Enquirer*, 26 August 1839; *Daily Avalanche*, 18 July 1866.

59. E. W. Sayer to W. H. Morgan, 15 May 1869, Morgan Family Papers, Tennessee State Library and Archives, Nashville, Tennessee. Also in the Morgan Papers: Wm. T. Arrington, 4 and 10 May 1875; F. W. Garkey to W. H. Morgan, 2 Aug. 1866; S. P. Cutler to W. H. Morgan, 30 July 1867, 11 Nov. 1868; Wm. T. Arrington to W. H. Morgan, 10 May 1867, 6 Feb. 1869, 4 and 10 May 1875.

60. *Medical Reformer* 1 (May 1850): 1–5 and (August 1850): 50–53, 106–27; *Memphis Medical Journal of the Progressive Medical and Physical Sciences* 1 (1851): 1–24; *Whig*, 24 Sept. 1855; *Daily Avalanche*, 6 Aug. 1866 and 2 Sept. 1877.

61. *Appeal*, 10 April 1846, 8 Jan. and 1 Sept. 1847; Keating, *History of Memphis*, 1:299; *Journal of Josiah Hinds, April 24, 1839–July 10, 1863*, ed. Newton Haskins James (1938), 241, in the Memphis Room of the Memphis/Shelby County Public Library. Hinds was a self-taught Bo-

tanic doctor. Dr. Ayers Phillips Merrill, *A Public Lecture on Medical Ethics, and the Mutual Relations of Patient and Physician* (1857).

62. Montgomery, "Memoirs" (see n. 29), chap. 24; *Appeal,* 1 Sept. 1847; James Conquest Cross, *Valedictory Address on the Art of Examining the Sick* (1836), 16.

63. Cross, *Valedictory Address,* 18; James Conquest Cross, "An Inaugural Discourse, on the Policy of Establishing a School of Medicine in the City of Memphis, Tennessee," *South-Western Medical Advocate* 1 (1847), 1–47. Simon R. Bruesch, "James Conquest Cross," *Bulletin of the Medical Library Association* 49 (October 1961): 510; *Enquirer,* 16 Sept. 1837; *Daily Avalanche,* 23 Mar. 1878.

64. James Marion Sims, *The Story of My Life* (1888), 245; S. Pollak, M.D., *Autobiography and Reminiscences* (1909), chaps. 2, 3; *Whig,* 3 May 1855; *Memphis Medical Recorder* 3 (April 1855): 36–39, 108–73.

65. *Memphis Medical Recorder* 5 (October 1857): 709–23; William Ragan Stanton, *The Leopard's Spots: Scientific Attitudes toward Race in America, 1815–1859* (1960), 65–72, 119–21.

66. *Appeal,* 11 Jan. 1851 and 28 Oct. 1847.

67. *Appeal,* 11 Jan and 26 Jan. 1851; Charles Todd Quintard, M.D., *A Report on the Health and Mortality of the City of Memphis for the Year 1852* (1853), 21–30; John Millington, "Valedictory Address," *Memphis Medical Recorder* 2 (May 1854): 270–71, 275, 284; *Daily Avalanche,* 18 August 1877.

68. Keating, *History of Memphis,* 1:327; Dr. Ayers Phillips Merrill, *Health and Mortality of Memphis, Tenn.* (1853); Dr. Ayers Phillips Merrill, *Lectures on Fever* (1865), 3–10; *Whig,* 3 May 1855; Stewart, *History of Medicine in Memphis,* 311–15; Dr. Ayers Phillips Merrill, *The City Schools* (1851), 7.

69. Merrill, *City Schools,* 8, 10, 15, 20, 22–23.

70. Keating, *History of Memphis,* 1:327; *Baptist Messenger,* 30 Sept. 1859; *Appeal,* 4 Sept. 1873, and 21 Aug. 1877.

71. *Daily Avalanche,* 18 Aug. 1877; *Appeal,* 11 and 13 Aug. 1878. See also John H. Ellis, "Disease and Destiny," *West Tennessee Historical Society Papers* 28 (1974):23 ff.

72. One of the best descriptions of the yellow fever epidemic is still the contemporary account by John McLeod Keating, *A History of the Yellow Fever: The Yellow Fever Epidemic of 1878 in Memphis, Tennessee* (1879), but it must be supplemented by the version critical of the city's leading classes. See D. A. Quinn, *Heroes and Heroines of Memphis, or Reminiscences of the Yellow Fever Epidemics* (1887). The best recent discussion is Simon R. Bruesch, "Yellow Fever in Tennessee," *Journal of the Tennessee Medical Association* 71 (Dec. 1978): 887–96, (Feb. 1979): 91–104, and (March 1979): 193–205.

73. L. D. Bejach, "The Taxing District of Shelby County," *West Tennessee Historical Society Papers* 4 (1950): 14; Keating, *History of Memphis,* 1:629–30; *Daily Avalanche,* 1, 15, and 19 Jan. 1879; John H. Ellis, "Memphis Sanitary Revolution, 1880–1890," Tennessee Historical Quarterly 23 (March 1914): 59–72; J. M. Keating, "The Value of Sani-

tation from an Economic Standpoint," American Public Health Association, *Papers and Reports* 6 (1880): 268–72.

74. Charles Clotfelter, "Memphis Business Leadership and the Politics of Fiscal Crisis," *West Tennessee Historical Society Papers*, 27 (1973): 33–49; *Daily Avalanche*, 15 July, 4 and 6 Sept., 12 Oct., 16 Dec. 1877, and 3 Jan., 14 Feb. 1878; Robertson Topp Papers (see n. 8), box 12.

75. *Daily Avalanche*, 1, 29 Jan. and 11 Feb. 1879.

76. *Appeal*, 14, 20, 22, Feb., 11 Mar., 16 Apr. 1880; Keating, *History of Memphis*, 1:684–85.

77. Capers, *Biography of a River Town*, 204–09; *New York Times*, 3 Feb. 1879; William M. Farrington, *The Memphis Debt* (1881), 11–12, 14; *Commercial and Financial Chronicle* 36 (24 Feb. 1883): 221 and (14 May 1883): 561.

78. Simon R. Bruesch, "Yellow Fever in Tennessee in 1878," *Tennessee Medical Association Journal* 72 (March 1979): 196, 202–4. Bruesch's numbers included those who died in neighboring towns; J. M. Taylor, "Regulation of the Practice of Medicine," *Mississippi Valley Medical Monthly* 3 (Feb. 1883): 52.

Chapter 5

1. Richard Wade, *The Urban Frontiers: The Rise of Western Cities* (1959), 53–56, 58–59, 80; Henry Clyde Hubbart, *The Older Middle West, 1840–1880* (1936), chap. 4; Vernon David Keeler, *The Commercial Development of Cincinnati to the Year 1860* (1938), 1–2.

2. William A. Mabry, "Ante-bellum Cincinnati and Its Southern Trade," in *American Studies in Honor of William Kenneth Boyd*, ed. David K. Jackson (1940), 60–85; Keeler, *Commercial Development of Cincinnati*, 20; *Cincinnati Lancet and Clinic*, n.s. 1 (5 Oct. 1878): 263.

3. George W. Pierson, *Tocqueville and Beaumont in America* (1938), 553; Keeler, *Commerical Development of Cincinnati*, 12–20, 25–39; Louis Leonard Tucker, "Cincinnati: Athens of the West," *Ohio History* 75 (Winter 1966): 10–25; Irwin F. Flack, "Who Governed Cincinnati? A Comparative Analysis of Government and Social Structure in a Nineteenth-Century River City: 1819–1860" (Ph.D. diss., University of Pittsburgh, 1977), 76, 89–93, 98–99.

4. Charles Cist, *Sketches and Statistics of Cincinnati in 1851* (1851), 45–48; on the race riots, see Charles Theodore Greve, *Centennial History of Cincinnati and Representative Citizens* (1904), 1:592–603.

5. Carl Wittke, "The Germans of Cincinnati," *Bulletin of the Historical and Philosophical Society of Ohio* 20 (1962): 3–14; Edwin H. Zeydel, "The Teaching of German in Cincinnati," *Bulletin of the Historical and Philosophical Society of Ohio* 20 (1962): 29–37; Henry A. Ford and Mrs. Kate B. Ford, *History of Cincinnati, Ohio* (1881), 134–35.

6. Pierson, *Tocqueville and Beaumont*, 553, 556–57. For a careful estimate of the influence of family connections in Cincinnati banking, see Harry R. Stevens, "Bank Enterprise in a Western Town, 1815–1822 [Cincinnati]," *Business History Review* 29 (June 1955): 153–56; see also Alvin F. Harlow, *The Serene Cincinnatians* (1950), chap. 20. How-

ever, the chief reliance for this paragraph comes from the reading of local newspapers.

7. *Cincinnati Enquirer*, 22 December 1845; Lee Shephard, "New England Society of Cincinnati," *Bulletin of the Historical and Philosophical Society of Ohio* 5 (1947): 35–37; Louis L. Tucker, "The New England Society of Cincinnati," *Bulletin of the Historical and Philosophical Society of Ohio* 20 (1962): 216–18; *Cincinnati Enquirer*, 23 November and 27 December 1856; "The Cincinnati Pioneer Association," *Bulletin of the Historical and Philosophical Society of Ohio* 2 (1944): 5–8.

8. "Uber die Gründung Deutscher Pionier-Vereine." *Deutsche Pionier* 1 (1869–70): 319; "Rede des Herrn Carl Rümelin," *Deutsche Pionier* 1 (1869–70): 27 ff.; Carl Rümelin, "Die Zukunft des Deutschtums in Amerika," *Deutsche Pionier* 2 (3 January 1871), 1.

9. Charles Cist, *Cincinnati in 1841: Its Early Annals and Future Prospects* (1841), 102–7; Charles C. Cole, Jr., "Finney's Fight against the Masons," *Ohio Archeological and Historical Quarterly* 59 (July 1950): 283; "From the Anti-Free to the Pious," *Cincinnati Pandect* 1 (17 March 1829): 4; Dwyer Berges, *The Anti-Conspirator; or Infidelity Unmasked, being a development of the principles of Free Masonry, to which is added strictures on slavery* (1832); John M. Goodenow, "Defence of Masonry," [Cincinnati] *Masonic Review* 1 (1845): 49–53; T. M., "A Denial" *Masonic Review* 1 (1846): 190–91; "Ohio and Her Colored Masons," *Memphis Masonic Jewel* 6 (November 1876): 310–11; "The Question of Colored Masons," *Memphis Masonic Jewel* 7 (March 1877): 45–46; Charles H. Wesley, *The History of the Prince Hall Grand Lodge of Free and Accepted Masons of the State of Ohio, 1849–1960* (1961), 33–34, 60–70.

10. "Cincinnati's First Directory," *Bulletin of the Historical and Philosophical Society of Ohio* 3 (March 1945): 6; Charles Cist, *Sketches and Statistics of Cincinnati in 1841* (1841), 49, 99, 102, 136, 143; Walter S. Glazer, "Participation and Power: Voluntary Assocations and the Functional Organization of Cincinnati in 1840," *Historical Methods Newsletter* 5 (September 1972): 152–64; W., "Letters from Ohio," *New England Magazine* 1 (1831): 34; John G. Cawelti, *Apostles of the Self-Made Man* (1965), 43–46.

11. Timothy Walker, "Defence of Mechanical Philosophy," reprinted in *Science in America*, ed. John C. Burnham (1971), 96, from *North American Review* 33 (1831): 122–36. See also Timothy Walker, "Lecture at Lyceum, 1831," in Timothy Walker Collection, Cincinnati Historical Society.

12. Henry D. Shapiro, "Daniel Drake's *Sensorium Commune* and the Organization of the Second American Enlightenment," *Cincinnati Historical Society Bulletin* 27 (Spring 1969): 50.

13. William Henry Channing, ed., *The Memoirs and Writings of James Handasyd Perkins* (1851), 1:171–72; Glazer, "Participation and Power," 152, 161–68; Flack, "Who Governed Cincinnati?" 93, 98, 295–302.

14. Harry N. Scheiber, *The Ohio Canal Era: A Case Study of Govern-*

ment and the Economy, 1820–1861 (1969), 205, 254–55; Harry N. Scheiber, "Entrepreneurship and Western Development: The Case of Micajah T. Williams," *Business History Review* 37 (Winter 1963): 345 ff.; Cist, *Cincinnati in 1841*, 76–93; Isaac Lippincott, *A History of Manufactures in the Ohio Valley* (1914), 130–38, 168, 176–86.

15. Cist, "Cincinnati—Its Destiny," in *Cincinnati in 1851*, 306–20; James Hall, *The West: Its Commerce and Navigation* (1848), 20–25; Greve, *Centennial History*, 1:590–92; Carl Abbott, *Boosters and Businessmen: Popular Economic Thought and Urban Growth in the Antebellum West* (1981), chap. 6; Louis L. Tucker, "The Semi-Colon Club of Cincinnati," *Ohio History* 73 (Winter 1964), 13–26; Walter Theodore Hitchcock, "Timothy Walker: Antebellum Lawyer" (Ph.D. diss., University of Mississippi, 1980), chaps. 2, 3; Emmet Field Horine, *Daniel Drake (1785–1852): Pioneer Physician of the Midwest* (1961), 108, 134–35, 277 ff.

16. On Longworth, see Walter R. Houghton, *Kings of Fortune* (1885), 138–53; Richard W. Pih, "Negro Self-Improvement Efforts in Ante-Bellum Cincinnati, 1836–1850," *Ohio History* 78 (Summer 1969), 186; for Topp, see Paul R. Coppock, *Memphis Memoirs* (1980), 44–45.

17. [Timothy Walker], "View of Ohio," *American Quarterly Review* 13 (March 1833): 119; Cist, *Cincinnati in 1851*, 107–10; Stephan Goldfarb, "Science and Democracy: A History of the Cincinnati Observatory, 1842–1872," *Ohio History* 78 (Summer 1969): 172–78.

18. "The Reception of Mr. Adams," *Western Law Journal* 1 (1843–1844): 148; Timothy Walker, *Introductory Lecture on the Dignity of the Law as a Profession* (1837), 4. See such contradictory sentiments expressed by A. W. G. Carter, *The Old Court House* (1880), 96, 314–15.

19. Timothy Walker, *Introduction to American Law* (1837), 26–33, 67–77, 658; John Handasyd Perkins, *Duties of the Liberal Professions* (1840), 12.

20. Walker, *Introductory Lecture*, 12; "Constitutional Power of the State Legislature to Take Private Property for Public Use," *Western Law Journal* 1 (1843–1844): 371.

21. [Walker], "View of Ohio," 126; *Western Law Journal* 1 (1843–1844): 203; William S. Groesbeck, *An Address on the True Scope of Human Governments* (1855), 23.

22. Walker, *Introduction to American Law*, 29; *Western Law Journal* 1 (1843–1844): 435.

23. "Law Reform in Ohio," *Western Law Journal* 1 (1843): 37; *Western Law Journal* 1 (1844): 437; Walker, *Introduction to American Law*, 58, 60, 648.

24. Hitchcock, "Timothy Walker," chap. 3; "Law School of the Cincinnati College," *Western Law Journal* 9 (1851): 48; Timothy Walker, *Diary*, Cincinnati Historical Society, 20 Sept. 1831, 3 Feb. and 1 Dec. 1839; 6 Oct. and 1 Dec. 1841, 1 Oct. 1844.

25. *A List of Graduates of the Cincinnati Law School* (1904), 3 ff.; H. A. Rattermann, *Johann Bernhardt Stallo: Denkrede gehalten im Deutschen Litterarischen Klub von Cincinnati* (1902), 24–25, 31–44;

Thomas J. McCormack, "John Bernard Stallo, American Citizen, Jurist, and Philosopher," *Open Court* 14 (May 1900): 276–83; "Johann Bernhardt Stallo," *Dictionary of American Biography* 17:496 ff.

26. Walker, *Introduction to American Law*, 451; Timothy Walker, *The Reform Spirit of the Day: An Oration before the Phi Beta Kappa Society of Harvard University, July 18, 1850* (1850), 27; Timothy Walker, *The Legal Rights of Women* (1849); J. B. Stallo, *Reply to Prof. O. A. Brownson's Lecture* (1852), 3 ff.; Bellamy Storer, *The Value of Man* (1848), 12–13. Among the other Cincinnati lawyers active in reform were: Stanley Matthews, later U.S. Supreme Court justice, who took up "the theory of a regenerated social life" with the intention of joining the Fourierist North American Phalanx, and his more cautious friend, Rutherford B. Hayes, later president of the United States, who entered politics on the Cincinnati Workingman's Party ticket. See Stanley Matthews to Minnie Matthews, 7 February 1849, in the Rutherford B. Hayes Papers, Fremont, Ohio; and Walter P. Marchman, "Rutherford B. Hayes, Attorney at Law," *Ohio History* 77 (1968): 31.

27. Groesbeck, *True Scope of Human Government*, 3, 14, 17. For Groesbeck's career see Elizabeth Baer, "William S. Groesbeck," *Bulletin of the Historical and Philosophical Society of Ohio* 20 (1962): 111–22, and *Dictionary of American Biography* 8:13–14. For similar views of another eminent Cincinnati lawyer, see Isaac C. Collins, *Speech of Hon. Isaac C. Collins of Hamilton County against a Uniform Rate of Interest* (1859).

28. This was apparent in the careers of leading Cincinnati lawyers, Democrat and Whig, such as Joseph Cox, Warner M. Bateman, J. B. Stallo, Bellamy Storer, Timothy Walker, Alphonso Taft, W. Y. Gholson, Flamen Ball, Rufus King, and Stanley Matthews. For brief descriptions of these careers, see M. Joblin and Co., compilers, *Cincinnati Past and Present; or Its Industrial History as exhibited in the Life and Labor of Its Leading Men* (1872).

29. J. W. Schuckers, *The Life and Public Services of Salmon Portland Chase* (1874), 62–64; Leo Alilunas, "Fugitive Slave Cases in Ohio Prior to 1850," *Ohio State Archeological and Historical Quarterly* 49 (1940): 179. See also Eric Foner, *Free Soil, Free Labor, Free Men* (1970), chap. 3.

30. *Cincinnati Commercial*, 24 January 1854; *Cincinnati Gazette*, 7 March 1857; *Cincinnati Enquirer*, 8 March 1857. Edward D. Mansfield, clipping from *Cincinnati Gazette*, 29 October 1875, Box 2, Scrapbook 2, 12, in Edward D. Mansfield Papers, Ohio State Historical Society, Columbus, Ohio.

31. Carter, *Old Court House*, 47–48, 270–72, 325–27. See the historical sketch of the Superior Court of Cincinnati in *Bench and Bar of Ohio: A Compendium of History and Biography*, ed. George Irving Reed, vol. 1 (1897), 67–74, and see Evan Haynes, *The Selection and Tenure of Judges* (1944), 125.

32. Timothy Walker, "Ways and Means of Professional Success," *West-*

ern Law Journal 1 (1843–44): 542–49; Timothy Walker, "Advice to Law Students," *Western Law Journal* 1 (1843–1844): 481; Timothy Walker, "The Profession of Law," *Western Law Journal* 2 (1845): 97–113; Charles D. Drake, *Address Delivered May 8, 1878, at the Annual Commencement of the Cincinnati Law School* (1878), 3–18; "Address of Hon. Stanley Matthews before the Convention of the State Bar Association," *The Weekly Cincinnati Law Bulletin* 5 (1880): 473–82; "Remarks of Mr. Dransin Wulsin," in *Bar Meeting to the Memory of James H. Perkins* (1889), 12–13.

33. Walker, *Introduction to American Law*, 115–16, 243–50, 661–62; Walker, *Introductory Lecture*, 19–20; an extraordinary instance of the relationship of authority and dependence that lawyer and client often assumed was the association of Frances Wright, brilliant radical and principled egalitarian, as client, with the lawyer W. Y. Gholson, during Miss Wright's last years, which she spent in Cincinnati. While for her, those were years of physical decline, she remained strong-minded and energetic. That this well-educated, self assertive woman should assume an astonishingly childlike relationship to Gholson is suggestive of some of the uses that privileged communication could be put to with more ordinary clients. Frances Wright to W. Y. Gholson, 7 Feb. 1850, 15 March 1851, 6 June and 30 Oct. 1852 in the Kittredge-Gholson papers, Cincinnati Historical Society.

34. Pierson, *Tocqueville and Beaumont*, 537; Walker, *Introductory Lecture*, 2; Carter, *Old Court House*, 42–43.

35. I have estimated the relative size of these denominations using the number of church buildings as a rough gauge and taking into consideration the judgment of contemporary observers that the individual Methodist churches were the smallest, Presbyterian churches were usually appreciably larger, and Catholic churches had the largest membership per building. *Cincinnati Directory* (1831) and *Williams Cincinnati Directory, City Guide and Business Mirror* (1880). See also "Statistics on Churches and Religious Societies in Cincinnati," *Central Christian Herald*, 14 Feb. 1856.

36. Raymond Lee Hightower, "Joshua L. Wilson, Frontier Controversalist," *Church History* 3 (1934): 306; Joshua Lacey Wilson, *Episcopal Methodisms, or Dagonism Exhibited* (1811). For the history of Presbyterians and Methodists in Cincinnati, see Jesse Halsey, ed., *One Hundred and Fifty Years of Presbyterianism in the Ohio Valley: 1740–1940* (1941), 53–175; E. B. Welsh, ed., *Buckeye Presbyterianism* (1968), 82–132; and John Marshall Barker, *History of Ohio Methodism* (1898). As the Methodists saw it, they "broke through the crust of Calvinism to get at the heart of the people" with "more simple and winning doctrines." R. T. Stevenson, *One Hundred Years of Methodism in Ohio* (1898), 36.

37. For a perspective discussion of the schism in Presbyterianism, see George M. Marsden, *The Evangelical Mind and the New School Presbyterian Experience* (1970), chap. 3. See also Sidney E. Ahlstrom, *A Religious History of the American People* (1975), 1:559–66.

38. Lyman Beecher, *Views of Theology* (1836), 237–38. In the sizable literature about Beecher, Winthrop Hudson's *The Great Tradition of the American Churches* (1953), chap. 4, remains one of the most succinct and penetrating treatments. Also very helpful is Marsden, *The Evangelical Mind*, 20–25.

39. Paul H. Boase, "Let the Men and Women Sit Apart," *Bulletin of the Historical and Philosophical Society of Ohio* 15 (1957): 33–48; William B. Sprague, *Annals of the American Pulpit* 7 (1860): 531; Rev. James Bradley Finley, *Sketches of Western Methodism,* ed. W. P. Strickland (1859), chap. 5.

40. On the 1852 revision, see Boase, "Let the Men and Women Sit Apart," 46–47. Barker, *History of Ohio Methodism,* 338–46. A leading minister explained the church's success as owing to the fact that "Methodism has been, and must be more and more in the future, *adaptation*" (emphasis in the original). Stevenson, *One Hundred Years of Methodism,* 37.

41. "John Baptist Purcell," in *Dictionary of American Biography* 15:266–67. Rev. John H. Lamott, *History of the Archdiocese of Cincinnati, 1821–1921* (1921), 70–83.

42. Joseph Michael White, "Religion and Community among the Cincinnati Germans, 1814–1870" (Ph.D. diss., University of Notre Dame, Department of History, 1980), 160–86. Anthony H. Dye, "Archbishop John Baptist Purcell of Cincinnati: Pre-Civil War Years" (Ph.D. diss., University of Notre Dame, 1959), 170–77.

43. Sister Mary Agnes McGann, *Archbishop Purcell and the Archdiocese of Cincinnati* (1918), 91–94. For Purcell's later troubles, see A. Stritch, "Cincinnati, Archdiocese of,' in *The New Catholic Encyclopedia* (1967), 3:876.

44. For the more restrained Presbyterian revivalism in Cincinnati, see Rev. James Hall Brookes, "Fufilment of the Ministry," in *Original Sermons by Presbyterian Ministers* (1833), 100–107, and for its Methodist counterpart, see Rev. F. G. Hibbard, D.D., *Biography of Rev. Leonidas L. Hamline, D.D.* (1850), chap. 5, and Rev. F. G. Hibbard, D.D., ed., *Works of Rev. Leonidas L. Hamline, D.D.* (1869), 9–27, 150–64, 179–94, 213–49, 366–81; Rev. Samuel W. Lynd, *A Discourse on Spiritual Manifestations* (1853).

45. C[harles] G[randison] Finney, *Revival Fire from C. G. Finney: Letters on Revivals to All Friends, and Especially All Ministers of Our Lord Jesus Christ* (Cincinnati: God's Revivalist Office. n.d.), 9–10, 82, 61; *Central Christian Herald* [Cincinnati], 11 Sept. 1851, 8 April 1852, 15 April 1858.

46. White, "Religion and Community," 274–83; Rev. John V. Mentag, S.J., "Catholic Spiritual Revivals, Parish Missions in the Midwest to 1865" (Ph.D. Diss., Loyola University [Chicago], 1950), 54–85, 152–69, 246–94; Jay P. Dolan, *Catholic Revivalism: The American Experience, 1830–1900* (1978).

47. Frank R. Shivers, Jr., "A Western Chapter in the History of American Transcendentalism," *Bulletin of the Historical and Philosophical*

Society of Ohio 15 (1957): 117–30; *Central Christian Herald*, 27 Jan. 1857.

48. John D'Entrement, *Southern Emancipator: Moncure Conway: The American Years, 1832–1865* (1987), 134; Perkins, *Duties of the Liberal Professions*, 6; Daniel Walker Howe, *The Unitarian Conscience* (1970), 257–58.

49. Stephen G. Mostov, "A 'Jerusalem' on the Ohio: The Social and Economic History of Cincinnati's Jewish Community, 1840–1875" (Ph.D. diss., Brandeis University, 1981), 229–30; Isaac Mayer Wise, "Intelligent Religion" [1854] in Nahum N. Glatzer, *The Judaic Tradition* (1970), 591–92. For a helpful discussion of Wise, see Michael A. Meyer, *Response to Modernity: A History of the Reform Movement in Judaism* (1988), 238–45.

50. Rev. Dudley Ward Rhodes, *Creed and Greed* (1879), 144; Clara Longworth Chambrun, *Cincinnati* (1939), 237, 242–43; Toby Lelyveld, *Shylock on the Stage* (1960), chap. 7. Anti-Semitism surfaced in 1853, when leading businessmen and clergymen uncharacteristically applauded a movement for higher wages on the part of the city's seamstresses, with reference to "usurers" and to a "certain class of the community," and with a direct attack upon "Jew shops." See Abbott, *Boosters and Businessmen*, 158. *Cincinnati Daily Times*, 30 May 1878; "The Saengerfest in Cincinnati," *American Israelite*, 17 June 1870; Isaac Mayer Wise, "Reformation not Deformation: Abstract of a Sermon Delivered in Memphis, Tenn.," *American Israelite*, 11 Feb. 1876.

51. *Central Christian Herald*, 21 Aug. 1851, 15 April 1852, 29 Jan. 1854, 5 June 1856, 9 April and 12 Nov. 1857; *The Central Watchman*, 11 May 1849.

52. *Central Christian Herald*, 3 and 10 Jan., 14 March 1861; McGann, *Archbishop Purcell*, 79; Rev. R. C. Grundy, D.D., *A Sermon Delivered in the Central Presbyterian Church, Cincinnati, Ohio, August 4, 1864, the day appointed by the Congress and President of the United States for National Fasting, Humiliation, and Prayer* (1864), *passim*; Lewis G. Vander Velde, *The Presbyterian Churches and the Federal Union* (1932), 128–29, 158–61, 292–93, 324–25, 500–501.

53. White, "Religion and Community," 326–29; Harold M. Helfman, "The Cincinnati 'Bible War,' 1869–1870," *Ohio State Archaeological and Historical Quarterly* 60 (1951): 369–74; Nancy R. Hamant, "Religion in the Cincinnati Schools, 1830–1900," *Bulletin of the Historical and Philosophical Society of Ohio* 21 (1963): 240–42.

54. Helfman, "The Cincinnati 'Bible War," 381–86; Rutherford B. Hayes to Alphonso Taft, 27 August 1875, Rutherford B. Hayes Papers, Fremont, Ohio; Hamant, "Religion in the Cincinnati Schools," 246–51; Anon, *The Bible in the Public Schools* (1870), *passim* (a complete transcript of the court proceedings).

55. *Cincinnati Commercial*, 10 July 1882; Harry Jebsen, "Cincinnati Protestant Clergy in Social and Political Reform, 1865–1915" (Master's thesis, University of Cincinnati, 1966), 23–35, 51–62.

56. The Reverend James Foster's attack upon the selfishness of Capital

and Labor led him to a rejection of laissez faire and to the advocacy of a return to the notion of just price. *Cincinnati Commercial,* 14 Aug. 1882; "The Minister—His Privileges," *Central Christian Herald,* 7 July 1859.

57. Edward D. Mansfield, *Personal Memories* (1879), 176; Horine, *Daniel Drake* (see n. 15), 38 ff.; 82–83, 117–18.

58. Horine, *Daniel Drake,* 363–67, 393. See the discussion by Henry D. Shapiro and Zane Miller in their edition of *Physician to the West: Selected Writings of Daniel Drake on Science and Society* (1970), 330. After Drake's death two admiring doctors edited his various drafts of volume 2 and published it, without fulfilling Drake's intentions for that volume.

59. Daniel Drake, *An Introductory Lecture on the Necessity and Value of Professional Industry* (1823, reprinted 1937), 3, 8; Daniel Drake, "Introductory Lecture on the Formation of Professional Character," [1835], MS, Health Sciences Library, University of Cincinnati, 16–17; Daniel Drake, "Address" (before a society for the diffusion of knowledge) (1842), MS, Health Sciences Library, University of Cincinnati, 7, 9. For the broader setting of this sort of "Baconism" in American science of the era, see George Daniels, *American Science in the Age of Jackson* (1968).

60. Daniel Drake, "An Introductory Lecture on the Importance of Promoting Literary and Social Concert in the Valley of the Mississippi" (1833) and "An Introductory Lecture on the Means of Promoting the Intellectual Improvement of the Students and Physicians of the Valley of the Mississippi" (1844), in *Physician to the West,* ed. Shapiro and Miller, 223ff. and 295ff. "Western Medical Schools," *Western Journal of Medicine and Physical Science* 9 (January 1836): 610–11, 616; "Medical History of the West," *Western Journal* 9 (January 1836): 680–81; "Western Meterology," *Western Journal,* n.s. 7 (January 1843): 63–64; Daniel Drake, "To the Medical Convention of Ohio," *Proceedings of the Ohio Medical Convention* (1845), 8–9; Daniel Drake, "Diseases of the West," *Boston Medical and Surgical Journal* 28 (May 1843): 308.

61. *Physician to the West,* 331; *Dr. Daniel Drake's Letters on Slavery* [1851], ed Emmet Field Horine (1940), 6–22, 32–36, 38, 54–63; "Miscellaneous Intelligence' (report of paper by Frederick Tiedemann, M.D.), *Western Journal of Medicine and Physical Science* 11 (October 1837): 182 (pages irregular in this issue). For the declining support for colonization proposals in both the North and the South, see Early L. Fox, *The American Colonization Society, 1817–1840* (1919), 124–25, 155, 176–77.

62. Horine, *Daniel Drake,* 162; Otto Juettner, *Daniel Drake and His Followers* (1909), 62.

63. John P. Harrison, M.D., *An Address on the Bonds of Professional Union* (1847), 14, 27; Samuel Hanbury Smith, M.D., *Introductory Address Delivered in the Cincinnati Medical Institute, April 3, 1848* (1848), 21. Armor is quoted in Juettner, *Daniel Drake,* 222.

64. Smith, *Introductory Address,* 9, 10, 16.

65. John Harley Warner, *The Therapeutic Perspective* (1986), chap. 3. Much of Warner's study is based upon Cincinnati materials.

66. Russell M. Jones, "American Doctors and the Parisian Medical World, 1830–1840," *Bulletin of the History of Medicine* 47 (1973): 40–65, and Russell M. Jones, Introduction, *The Parisian Education of an American Surgeon* (1978), 1–69; John Harley Warner, "The Nature Trusting Heresy," *Perspectives in American History* 11 (1977–1978): 291–324, and Max Neuburger, *The Doctrine of the Healing Power of Nature* (1933); William G. Rothstein, *American Physicians in the Nineteenth Century: From Sects to Science* (1972), 125–74, 217–46; Paul Starr, *The Social Transformation of American Medicine* (1982), 30–59; Alex Berman, "The Impact of the Nineteenth-Century Botanic Medical Movement on American Pharmacy and Medicine" (Ph.D. diss., University of Wisconson, 1954), 133–41; Martin Kaufman, *Homeopathy in America* (1971), 63–75, 110–24; Joseph Kett, *The Formation of the American Medical Profession, 1780–1860* (1969), 97–164; Harrison, *Bonds of Professional Union*, 22–25; George Mendenhall, *Professional Success* (1865), 11. Warner, in *Therapeutic Perspective*, 127–29, suggests that Cincinnati doctors returned to more drastic procedures.

67. See comments of John Abernathy, FRS surgeon to St. Bartholomew's and Christ's Hospital on his visit to the United States, *Western Journal of Medicine and Physical Science* 2 (December 1828): 459; Dudley W. Palmer, "Reuben Dimond Mussey, M.D.," *Ohio State Medical Journal* 34 (1938): 1023–25. There were other eminent surgeons in Cincinnati, but Mussey was clearly a cut above the rest. It was not until George Curtis Blackman came to Cincinnati in 1855 that Mussey had a serious rival.

68. Juettner, *Daniel Drake*, 169; Palmer, "Mussey," 1024; Horine, *Daniel Drake*, 392–94.

69. Leonidas M. Lawson, M.D., "The Present Condition and Future Prospects of the Medical Profession," *Western Lancet* 11 (1850): 59–62; Reginald C. McGrane, *The Cincinnati Doctors' Forum* (1957), 3–7 and chap. 4; Alan I. Marcus, "In Sickness and in Health: The Marriage of the Municipal Corporation to the Public Interest and the Problem of Public Health, 1820–1870, the Case of Cincinnati' (Ph.D. diss., University of Cincinnati, 1979), 254–56, 335–36; Jebsen, "Cincinnati Protestant Clergy," 23–24.

70. Annie Fields, *Life and Letters of Harriet Beecher Stowe* (1898), 79. Scattered letters to and from Cincinnati patients and doctors can be found in the papers of Benjaman Parham Aydelott, William H. Dawson, Goodwin Volney Dorsey, Edward Young Kemper, William C. Langdon, James Lakey, Charles Louis Metz, and Charles Wilkins Short, at the Cincinnati Historical Society, and in the Matthew Cook Papers (Cornelius George Comegys) at the Western Reserve Historical Collection in Cleveland. Mendenhall, *Professional Success*, 19.

71. Kett, *Formation of the American Medical Profession*, 130; Dr. George W. L. Bickley, Dr. William Bird Powell, and Dr. John Bunyan Campbell were exemplary figures of this sort.

72. Juettner, *Daniel Drake*, passim, presents an extensive discussion of these various unorthodox therapies in Cincinnati.

73. T. V. Morrow, M.D., *Introductory Address Delivered before the Class of the Eclectic Medical Institute* (1847), 7, 9, 12; Editorial, *Cincinnati Eclectic and Edinburgh Journal* 1 (February 1859): 125–26; "Who Are the Educated Physicians?" *Cincinnati Eclectic and Edinburgh Journal* 1 (September 1859), 566–67; Harvey Wickes Felter, M.D., *History of the Eclectic Medical Institute, Cincinnati, Ohio, 1845–1902* (1902).

74. Frederick C. Waite, "Thomsonianism in Ohio," *Ohio State Archeological and Historical Quarterly* 49 (October–December 1940): 324–31; Lucy Stone Hertzog, M.D., "The Rise of Homeopathy," *Ohio State Archeological and Historical Quarterly* 49 (October–December 1940): 340–42.

75. Juettner, *Daniel Drake*, 89–91; Edward Kremers and George Urdand, *History of Pharmacy*, 3d ed. (1963), 249; Reginald C. McGrane, "The Cincinnati College of Pharmacy," *Bulletin of the Historical and Philosophical Society of Ohio* 13 (1955): 28–29; *Ninth Annual Announcement of the Cincinnati College of Pharmacy, Session 1879–80* (1879), 3–13; Edward C. Mills, "The Taylor Family of Dentists," *Ohio State Archeological and Historical Quarterly*, 56 (1947): 392–95; Edward C. Mills, "Dental Education in Ohio, 1838–1858," *Ohio State Archeological and Historical Quarterly* 51 (1942): 294–312; 52 (1943): 356–72.

76. Jonathan Taft, *Practical Treatise on Operative Dentistry* (1877), chap. 1. The Dental Practice Act of Ohio was passed on 8 May 1868, and Jonathan Taft, who was influential in its passage, served on the Ohio State Dental Board from 1868 to 1892. The act provided for certification of dentists on the basis of examinations administered by a state board of examiners. Taft was also professor and dean at the Ohio College of Dental Surgery. Teachers of dentistry and pharmacy took particular interest in the passage of such practice acts. See B. V. Christianson, "The Teaching of Pharmacy in Ohio," *Ohio State Archeological and Historical Quarterly* 61 (1952): 354–57. On the relation of pharmacists to physicians in Cincinnati, see A. J. Howe, M.D., *Address Delivered at the Commencement Exercise of the Cincinnati College of Pharmacy, March 19, 1879* (1879), *passim.*

77. Alphonso Taft, *Lecture on Cincinnati and Her Rail-Roads* (1850), 7, 18 ,42; Alphonso Taft, *Lecture on the University of Cincinnati* (1872), 10–18; Henry F. Pringle, "Alphonso Taft," *Dictionary of American Biography* (1936), 18: 264–65.

78. Taft, *Cincinnati and Her Rail-Roads*, 11–13.

79. Sherry O. Hessler, "'The Great Disturbing Cause' and the Decline of the Queen City," *Bulletin of the Historical and Philosphical Society of Ohio* 20 (1962): 185; see also Abbott, *Boosters and Businessmen* (see n. 15), chap. 6. Margaret Walsh, *The Rise of the Midwestern Meat Packing Industry* (1982), 47–54, 63–66, 70, 82, 90.

80. Todd Jordan Butler, "The Cincinnati Southern Railway: A City's Response to Relative Commercial Decline" (Ph.D. diss., Ohio State University, 1971), 189, chaps. 5, 6.

81. *Cincinnati Star,* 26 July 1877; *Cincinnati Weekly Gazette,* 1 Aug. 1877. Stephen Joseph Ross, *Workers on the Edge: Work, Leisure, and Politics in Industrializing Cincinnati, 1788–1890* (1985), passim, for a cultural history of Cincinnati workers. James Matthew Morris, "The Road to Trade Unionism: Organized Labor in Cincinnati to 1893" (Ph.D. diss., University of Cincinnati, 1969), provides a trade union history.

82. Greve, *Centennial History* (see n. 4), 1:967; Henry F. Pringle, *The Life and Times of William Howard Taft* (1939), 1:54–55. Irwin S. Rhodes, "The Founding of the Cincinnati Bar Association, 1872," *Cincinnati Historical Society Bulletin* 30 (Summer 1972): 123.

83. W. Laird Kleine, "Anatomy of a Riot," *Bulletin of the Historical and Philosophical Society of Ohio* 20 (October 1962): 235–37; Steven W. Plattner, "Days of Dread," *Queen City Heritage: Journal of the Cincinnati Historical Society* 42 (1984): 36.

84. "The Cincinnati Riots," *Harpers Weekly* (12 April 1884), 241–42; James H. Rodabaugh, "The Cincinnati Riot of 1884," *Museum Echoes: Ohio Historical Society at Ohio State Museum* 326 (December 1959): 19 ff.

85. "The Riot in Cincinnati," *American Israelite,* 4 April 1884; Greve, *Centennial History,* 1:1002. The response to the news was curious, with those farthest from the startling events finding it most possible to be sympathetic. Victor Hugo, at his worst, with predictable grandiloquence, hailed the rioters and compared them with those who had stormed the Bastille. "The rioters of Cincinnati inaugurated the era of glorious revolution; they were champions of justice: they were more than champions; they were heroes. They were more than heroes, they were men. The world says so, France says so—I say so." In reverse order of importance most likely. The editor of *The Spectator* in London wrote, "For once we find ourselves sympathising with rioters." *The Chautauquan's* editor lamented, "It tortures the conscience and the self-respect of honest men." Even *The American Law Review* was equivocal. Hugo quoted in Joseph S. Stern, Jr., "It Was the Best of Times; It Was the Worst of Times," *Queen City Heritage: Journal of the Cincinnati Historical Society* 42 (1984): 11; "The Riots in Cincinnati," *The Spectator* 57 (1884): 433; "Editor's Outlook," *The Chautauquan* 4 (1884): 485; "Criminal Justice in Cincinnati," *American Law Review* 18 (1884): 675.

86. Joseph Salathiel Tunison, *The Cincinnati Riot: Its Causes and Results* (1886), 47–53.

87. Tunison, *Cincinnati Riot,* 15, 17–23, 30, 44–46, 88.

88. Tunison, *Cincinnati Riot,* 18; "Jospeh Salathiel Tunison," *Who's Who In America* (1912–1913), 7: 2129.

Overview of Part III

1. Twain's joke about Cincinnati was taken seriously by local reformers and was quoted repeatedly to argue for change. For the most recent quote see *New York Times,* December 12, 1986, 7.

2. James M. Cox, "Introduction," in *Life on the Mississippi* ([1883] 1984), by Mark Twain, 14–17.

3. This paragraph is based upon chaps. 5–14 of *Life on the Mississippi*. For the "science of piloting," see 115. Plato, *The Republic*, Book IV, sections 488–90. For James Wilson's use of this almost proverbial metaphor see chap. 3 above.

4. *Life on the Mississippi*, 122–23.

5. *Life on the Mississippi*, 137, chap. 15.

6. *Life on the Misisisppi*, 404. Twain returned to this theme in the *Connecticut Yankee in King Arthur's Court* (1889).

7. Alfred D. Chandler, *The Visible Hand* (1977), chaps. 3–5; Michael Robbins, *The Railway Age* (1962), 161.

8. Robert Lichtenberg, *One Tenth of a Nation: National Forces in the Economic Growth of the New York Region* (1960), 20–22; Sidney M. Robbins and Nestor E. Terlecky, *Money Metropolis* (1960), chap. 1; Vincent P. Carosso, *Investment Banking in America: A History* (1970), chap. 2; E. C. Campbell, *The Reorganization of the American Railroad System, 1893–1900* (1938); N. R. Danielian, *AT&T: The Story of Industrial Conquest* (1939), 3–13; Thomas Bender, *New York Intellect* (1987), 191–94; Ferdinand Lundberg, *Imperial Hearst* (1936), chap 3. The growing divergence between high and popular culture in the late nineteenth century is discussed by Lawrence W. Levine, *Highbrow/Lowbrow: The Emergence of Cultural Hierarchy in America* (1988).

9. Hollis B. Cheney, "Patterns of Industrial Growth," *American Economic Review* 50, (1966): 624–54; David A. Wells, *Recent Economic Changes* (1896), 465–66. On industrial production, see Edwin Frickey, *Production in the United States: 1866–1914* (1947), 12, and *Historical Statistics of the United States: Colonial Times to 1957* (1960), 570. For some interesting suggestions on the role of the tariff in American economic growth, see W. Elliot Brownlee, *Dynamics of Ascent*, 239–42. The effect of economies of scale is discussed by Chandler, *Visible Hand*, 365–68; Lee C. Soltow, "Evidence on Income Inequality in the United States, 1866–1965," *Journal of Economic History* 29 (June 1969): 270–86; Sam Bass Warner, Jr., *The Private City* (1968), 111–23; Sam Bass Warner, Jr., *The Urban Wilderness* (1972), chap. 4; Ray Farley, "The Urbanization of Negroes in the United States," *Journal of Social History* 1 (Spring 1968): 241–58; Gerlad N. Grob, "Knights of Labor versus American Federation of Labor," in *The American Labor Movement*, ed. David Brody (1971), 41; Edward Bellamy, *Looking Backward* ([1888] 1967), chaps. 6 and 7.

10. William Dean Burnham, "The Changing Shape of the American Political Universe," *American Political Science Review* 59 (1965), 7–28. For Black disenfranchisement, see C. Vann Woodward, *Origins of the New South* (1951), chap. 12; Leo E. Aylsworth, "The Passing of Alien Suffrage," *American Political Science Review* 25 (1931), 114–16. David Rothman, *Politics and Power: The United States Senate, 1869–1901* (1966), 48–50. 92–98; Nelson W. Polsby, "The Institutionalization of the U.S. House of Representatives," *American Political Science Review* 62 (1968): 144–60. William Warren Sweet, *Revivalism in America* (1944), chap. 8; James Findlay, Jr., *Dwight L. Moody* (1969), 303–7, chap. 10;

John Bates Clark, "The Limits of Competition," *Political Science Quarterly* 2 (1887): 45–61; Simone Sterne, "Monopoly," in *Cyclopedia of Political Science, Political Economy, and of the Political History of the United States,* ed. John J. Lalor, 3 vols. (1883), 2:894–95.

11. Charles Dudley Warner, "Equality," *Atlantic* 45 (1880), 24; Henry Childs Merwin, "The American Notion of Equality," *Atlantic* 80 (1897): 361; William Dean Howells, "Equality as the Basis of Good Society," *Century* 51 (1895): 63–67; Thomas Henry Huxley, "On the Natural Inequality of Men," *Popular Science Monthly* (1890), 761–83; Wallace Evan Davies, *Patriotism on Parade* (1955), 353–58; Henry George, "Chinese Immigration," *Cyclopedia of Political Science* (1881)1:409–14.

12. Woodrow Wilson, *The State* (1889), 660; Arthur Twining Hadley, *Railroad Transportation* (1885), 78–79; Arthur Twining Hadley, "The Relation between Politics and Economics," [1889] and "Economic Theory and Public Morality," [1900], in Arthur Twining Hadley, *The Education of the American Citizen* (1901), 81, 96–99.

13. For the new vitality in the AMA, see Perry H. Millard, "The Propriety and Necessity of State Regulation of Medical Practice," *Journal of the American Medical Association* 9 (1887): 471, and "The Legal Regulation of Medical Practice in the U.S.," *Journal of the American Medical Association* 13 (1889): 471ff. For the ABA, see Edson R. Sunderland, *History of the American Bar Association* (1953), 3–13; Lawrence M. Friedman, *A History of American Law* (1973), 563–66. The increased self-confidence and influence of the Episcopalians is discussed in E. Clowes Chorley, *Men and Movements in the American Episcopal Church* (1950), chap. 9. Daniel H. Calhoun, *The American Civil Engineer: Origins and Conflict* (1960), chap. 8; Monte Calvert, *The Mechanical Engineer in America, 1830–1910* (1967), chap. 2; Edwin J. Layton, *The Revolt of the Engineers* (1971), 3–4, 10, 27–28; Dorothy Fahs Beck, "The Development of the Dental Profession in the United States" (Master's thesis, University of Chicago, 1932), 187–203; Charles R. E. Koch, *History of Dental Surgery* (1909), 1:273–76; Edward Kremers and George Urdang, *History of Pharmacy* (1951), 309–51; Laurence Veysey, *The Emergence of The American University* (1965), 388–91, 418–33; Frederick Rudolph, *The American College and University* (1965), 408–15.

14. J. P. Coughlan, "The Profession of Architecture," *Munsey's Magazine* 25 (1891), 837–40; Henry H. Saylor, *The American Institute of Architects' First Hundred Years* (1957), 36–37; A. D. F. Hamlin, "The Influence of the Ecole dex Beaux Arts," *Columbia Quarterly,* 10 (1907–1908): 14–16; Mardges Bacon, *Ernest Flagg: Beaux-Arts Architect and Urban Reformer* (1895), chap. 3. Paul K. Baker, *Richard Morris Hunt* (1980), 112–17, 327–31; 102–7, 440. The American Institute of Architects helped establish an approved fee of five percent of the total cost of construction as an appropriate remuneration, amid recurrent and probably sincere declarations that the architects' rewards were not primarily pecuniary. American Institute of Architects, *Proceedings of the Eighteenth Annual Convention, 1884* (1885), 3, 12, 16–17, 21, 53, 76; B. M.

Boyle, "Architectural Practice in America," *The Architect: Chapters in the History of a Profession*, ed. S. K. Kostof (1977), 309–44.

15. Marcus Cunliffe, *Soldiers and Civilians: The Martial Spirit in America, 1775–1865* (1973), 412–23; Stephen E. Ambrose, *Duty, Honor, Country: A History of West Point* (1966), chap. 6, 64–65, 69. The use of "solider" as a verb to mean the shirking of work is an Americanism recorded in the *Oxford English Dictionary* (1933). Russell F. Weigley, *Towards an American Army* (1962), 41–43, 55, 76–77, 105; Samuel P. Huntington, *The Soldier and the State* (1957), chap. 9.

16. Robert C. Derbyshire, *Medical Licensure and Discipline in the United States* (1982), chaps. 1 and 2; Samuel L. Baker, "Physician Licensure Laws in the United States, 1865–1915," *Journal of the History of Medicine and Allied Sciences*, 39 (1984): 173–94; William E. Ellis, "Licensing and Registration of Engineers in the United States," *Mining and Metallurgy* 26 (1945): 22–27; William J. Geis, *Dental Education in the United States and Canada* (1926), 37; Kremers and Urdang, *History of Pharmacy*, chap. 9. Thomas Davidson, "Teaching the Mechanical Arts," *Forum* 6 (1888): 382.

17. Dent v. West Virginia, *United States Reports* 129 (1888): 116; Frances DeLancey, *The Licensing of Professions in West Virignia* (1938), chap. 1; John W. Clampitt, "The Police Power of a State," *Cyclopedia of Political Science* (1884), 3:212 ff; Franklin Smith, "Reversions in Modern Industrial Life," *Popular Science Monthly* 51 (1897): 34–43.

18. John S. Billings, "Progress of Medicine in the Nineteenth Century," *The Nineteenth Century: A Review of Progress* (1901), 336–47; William Osler, "Medicine," *Progress of the Century* (1901), 207–14; Guy Carleton Lee, "The Position of the Lawyer in Society," *Green Bag* 8 (1892): 246; Melville M. Bigelow, "Respect for the Law: Responsibility of the Profession," Bar Association of the State of New York Reports (1892), 38–56; William H. Welch, "Some of the Conditions Which Have Influenced the Development of Medicine, Especially During the Last Century," *Johns Hopkins Hospital: Bulletin* 19 (1908), 33 ff.; S. Weir Mitchell, *Doctor and Patient* (1888), and *The Conduct of Medical Life* (1893), 26, 50; Austin Flint, *Medical Ethics and Etiquette* (1883), 35; Barbara Sicherman, "The Uses of a Diagnosis: Doctors, Patients, and Neurasthenia," *Journal of the History of Medicine* 32 (1977): 33–54.

19. Henry Hitchcock, "Law as a Science: Address before the Graduating Class of University of St. Louis Law School, June 1894," in *Henry Hitchcock Papers*, Missouri Historical Society; Edward J. Phelps, "The Relation of Law to Justice," *South Carolina Bar Association Proceedings* (1890), 67ff.; John Shaw Billings, "Medicine as a Career," *Forum* 14 (1893), 733; Welch, "Some of the Conditions Which Have Influenced the Development of Medicine," 40. See also chaps. 6 and 10 in this book.

20. For a brief discussion of the shift from sins to rights, see Herbert W. Schneider, *History of American Philosophy* (1963), 35–76. For some indication of the shift from rights to needs, see Mary Putnam [Jacobi], *The Value of Life* (1879), 211–29; Henry Dwight Chapin, "Social and Physiological Inequality," *Popular Science Monthly* 16 (1887): 757–65;

W. H. Walsh, "Physiology vs. Metaphysics," *Popular Science Monthly,* 25 (1884): 249–58; William Graham Sumner, "Sociological Fallacies," *North American Review,* 138 (1884): 576.

21. [Eugene Fletcher Ware], *Some of the Rhymes of Ironquill,* 10th edition (1900), 11; William James, "Is Life Worth Living?" [1848] in *Essays in Faith and Morals,* ed. Ralph Barton Perry (1962), 16, 28, 24; William James, *Principles of Psychology* [1896], ed., Frederick H. Burkhardt (1981) 2: 1222–26, 1270–79; Oliver Wendell Holmes, Jr., "The Path of the Law" [1897], *Collected Legal Papers* (1952), 200; Dr. Austin Flint, *Medical News* (Philadelphia) 45 (1884): 592; [Jacobi], *The Value of Life,* 84–93, 180–81, 201.

22. Billings, "Medicine as a Career," 743; Edward T. Casswell, *Reform in Medical Education: Address Before the 6th Annual Meeting of the American Academy of Medicine* (1881), 3–6; George M. Gould, M.D., "Is Medicine a Science?" *Forum* 8 (1889), 417–27; Austin Flint, "A Possible Revolution in Medicine," *Forum,* 6 (1888): 361–69; Nathan Smith Davis, "The Present Status of the Medical Profession," *Journal of the American Medical Association,* (1883): 41; Millard, "Propriety and Necessity of State Regulation," 491–93.

23. William Osler, "Address on Medicine," *Medical News* (Philadelphia) 68 (1896): 307; A. L. Loomis, "President's Address," *Transactions of American Congress of Physicians and Surgeons* 3 (1894): 314; Abraham Jacobi, "Medicine and Medical Men in the United States," *Journal of the American Medical Association* 34 (1900): 497–98; H. C. Wood, "The Medical Profession," *New England and Yale Review* 51 (August 1889): 130–34; Clarence John Blake, "The Sociological Status of the Physician," *Science,* n.s. 11 (1900): 772–82; Paul Gibier, "The Physician and the Social Question," *North American Review* 160 (1895): 461–69.

24. N. S. Shaler, "The Sense of Honor in Americans," *North American Review* 149 (1889): 206–7; C. A. Pratt, "The Honor of A Gentleman," *Harpers Weekly* 35 (1891): 914–15; Theodore Dwight Woolsey, *The Relation of Honor to Political Life* (1875): 3–5; Dorman B. Eaton, "The True Significance of the National Civil Service Act," *Unitarian Review* 27 (1887): 297; George Martin, *Causes and Conflicts: The Centennial History of the Association of the Bar of the City of New York, 1870–1970* (1970): 14; Edward Deering Mansfield, *Personal Memories* (1879), 134. Mansfield is quoting Joseph Addison's play, *Cato,* Act IV, Scene 4: "When vice prevails, and impious men bear sway, the post of honor is a private station."

Chapter 6

1. James Porter Hall, "James Bradley Thayer," in *Great American Lawyers* (1909), 351; Joseph B. Warner, "The Responsibilities of the Lawyer," American Bar Association *Reports* 19 (1896): 333ff. (hereafter ABA *Reports*); Rufus King, *The Administration of Justice, and Some of its Obstacles: An Address to the State Bar Association of Ohio . . .* (1883), 4–6. In 1845 John Van Buren, Attorney General for the State of New York, and a "very distinguished opponent," Ambrose L. Jordan,

came to blows in open court in the course of an important public trial. (Both lawyers were imprisoned by the judge for their excesses.)

2. *Great American Lawyers: the Lives and Influence of Judges and Lawyers Who Have Acquired Permanent National Reputation, and Have Developed the Jurisprudence of the United States,* ed. William Draper Lewis, 8 vols. (1907–1909), 8:351–52; Thomas Cooley, "The Bar," in *Cyclopedia of Political Science, Political Economy, and of the Political History of the United States,* ed. John J. Lalor, 3 vols. (1881), 1:265.

3. Theodore Bacon, Esq., "Professional Ethics," American Social Science Association *Proceedings* 2 (1882–1883): 41; George C. Sharswood, *An Essay on Professional Ethics,* 5th ed. (1884), 84–87 (originally published as *A Compend of Lectures on the Aims and Duties of the Profession of the Law, Delivered before the Law Class of the University of Pennsylvania* [1854]); Francis Lieber, *The Character of the Gentleman,* 3d enlarged ed. (1864), 62–63; King, *Administration of Justice,* 20–21.

4. "Lawyers, Clients, Witnesses and the Public," *Littell's Living Age* 24 (1850): 179–90, 230–37, 306–8; 25 (1850): 289–90, 308–11; Cooley, "The Bar," 261; Sharswood, *Essay on Professional Ethics,* 103–7, 183–96; Lieber, *Character of the Gentleman,* 66–74.

5. George F. Hoar, "The Relation of the American Bar as an Order or Brotherhood to the State: Address Before Virginia Bar Association . . . ," *American Law Review* 32 (1898): 643–47; Daniel Dougherty, *Some Reflections on the Bar, Its Integrity and Independence; An Address Delivered before the State Bar Association of New York . . .* (1888), 9–11.

6. "Address Before the Law School of New York University, Dec. 21, 1871," *The Historical Magazine* 1 (1872–1873): 98; Constitution of the Association of the Bar of the City of New York, printed in Association of the Bar of the City of New York *Reports* 1 (1870): 35 (hereafter ABCNY *Reports*).

7. Dorman B. Eaton, "Elective Judiciary," in *Cyclopedia of Political Science,* 2: 641.

8. ABCNY *Reports* 1 (1870): 28.

9. George Martin, *Causes and Conflicts: The Centennial History of the Association of the Bar of the City of New York, 1870–1970* (1970), 87–103, covers the association's quarrels with Field. I have found some errors in his account, but it has much useful information. A. Oakey Hall, "Reminiscences of David Dudley Field," *The Green Bag, A Useless but Entertaining Magazine for Lawyers* 6 (1894): 212; John W. Pratt, "Boss Tweed's Public Welfare Program," *New York Historical Society Quarterly* 45 (1961): 396–411; David Dudley Field, "For Whom Shall I Vote and Why," *Forum* 14 (1892): 405; David Dudley Field, "The Primary: The Pivot of Reform," *Forum* 14 (1892): 192.

10. The *New York Times* (siding with the reformers) complained that any politician apparently could become a lawyer. Boss Tweed "and nearly all his associates down to the lowest ward politician were duly admitted by the Supreme Court as attorneys and counselors at law." *New York Times,* 24 May 1881. For the ideas of the reformers who wished to ele-

vate and restrict the legal profession, see William M. Evarts, ABCNY *Reports* 1 (1870): 28–29, and Henry Nicoll, ibid., 9.

11. Edwards Pierrepont, ABCNY *Reports* 1 (1870): 14–15; George Martin, *Causes and Conflicts*, 43, 358; Dorman B. Eaton, ABCNY *Reports* 1 (1870): 30. The German lawyer was J. C. Langbein, *New York Times*, 14 May 1881, 2.

12. Joseph B. Warner, "The Responsibilities of the Lawyer," ABA *Reports* 19 (1896): 321–23, 340; King, *Administration of Justice*, 22.

13. For one study of the creation of a state bar association, see Margaret F. Sommer, "The Ohio State Bar Association: The First Generation, 1880–1912" (Ph.D. diss., Ohio State University, 1972). See also Alfred Z. Reed, *Training for the Public Profession of the Law* (1921), 206. Accounts of the founding of the American Bar Association include Edson R. Sunderland, *A History of the American Bar Association and Its Work* (1953), 3–13; Jacob Weart, "The American Bar Association: Its History for the First Sixteen Years of Its Existence . . . ," *New Jersey Law Journal* 27 (1904): 292–99, 336–43; Norman Brockman, "The History of the American Bar Association: A Bibliographic Essay," *American Journal of Legal History* 6 (1962): 269–85.

14. John Higham, *Strangers in the Land: Patterns of American Nativism, 1860–1925* (1955), 27–28; Henry G. Smith to Henry Craft, 21 August 1878, in the Craft-Thorne Papers, History of the South Collection, University of North Carolina, Chapel Hill.

15. John Austin Matzko, "The Early Years of the American Bar Association, 1878–1928" (Ph.D. diss., University of Virginia, 1984), 1–36, 78; Wayne K. Hobson, "The American Legal Profession and the Organizational Society, 1890–1930" (Ph.D. diss., Stanford University, 1977), 14.

16. James Willard Hurst, *The Growth of American Law: The Law Makers* (1950), 297–308; Julius Goebel, Jr., and others, eds., *The Law Practice of Alexander Hamilton: Documents and Commentary*, 5 vols. (1964–1981), 2:406.

17. Constitution of the American Bar Assocation, ABA *Reports* 1 (1878): 16.

18. William Blackstone, *Commentaries on the Laws of England* 1: 27; *The Centennial History of the Harvard Law School, 1817–1917* (1918), 345.

19. James C. Carter, "The Provinces of the Written and the Unwritten Law: An Address delivered at the Annual Meeting of the Virginia State Bar Association . . ." (1889), 36; James C. Carter, "The Ideal and the Actual in the Law: The Annual Address delivered at the Thirteenth Annual Meeting [of the American Bar Association] . . ." (1890), 17; James C. Carter, *Law: Its Origins, Growth and Function; being a course of lectures prepared for delivery before the Law School of Harvard University* (1907), 127.

20. Carter, "Idea and Actual in the Law," 21, 8–9.

21. Carter, "Provinces of Written and Unwritten Law," 4, 10.

22. Carter, "Ideal and Actual in the Law," 11; Carter, "Provinces of

Written and Unwritten Law," 11–13, 35, 21, 60; Richard M. Venable, "The Growth or Evolution of Law," ABA *Reports* 23 (1899): 228. See also James Mills Woolworth, "Jurisprudence Considered as a Branch of Social Science," ABA *Reports*, 11 (1888): 229.

23. Charles M. Cook, *The American Codification Movement: A Study of Antebellum Legal Reform* (1981).

24. "Carter on Codification," *The Nation* 49 (1889): 436–38; Carter, "Provinces of Written and Unwritten Law," 53, 58. See also James C. Carter, *The Proposed Codification of Our Common Law: A Paper Prepared at the Request of the Committee of the Bar Association of the City of New York, Appointed to Oppose the Measure* (1884); David Dudley Field, *A Short Response to a Long Discourse: An Answer by Mr. David Dudley Field to Mr. James C. Carter's Pamphlet . . .* (1884).

25. In the name of harmony, some leading members of the association proposed what seemed to be a compromise resolution. "The law itself should be reduced, so far as its substantive principles are settled, to the form of a statute." This passed 58 to 41. However, it was clear from the debate that most discussants thought that much of the law, and even its "substantive principles," changed gradually over time and that codification was therefore inexpedient. Carter recognized the kinship of his approach to that of Langdell. See Carter, "Provinces of Written and Unwritten Law," 49.

26. C. C. Langdell, "Teaching Law as a Science: An After-Dinner Speech," *American Law Review* 21 (1887): 123; Louis D. Brandeis, "The Harvard Law School," *Green Bag* 1 (1889): 19–23; Alexander Hirschberg, "Methods of Legal Study with Reference to Present Conditions of the Law," *Albany Law Journal* 57 (1897): 87; Henry Raymond Fink, "Law and Philosophy: The Rival Schools," *American Law Record* 2 (1888): 79; Arthur E. Sutherland, *The Law at Harvard: A History of Ideas and Men, 1817–1967* (1967), 175–88.

27. Compare C. C. Langdell's address, "Teaching Law as a Science," with the discussion of James Coolidge Carter's ideas in James Barr Ames, *Lectures on Legal History and Miscellaneous Legal Essays* (1913). See also Thomas Grey, "Langdell's Orthodoxy," *University of Pittsburgh Law Review* 45 (1983): 1–53.

28. Oliver Wendell Holmes, Jr., *The Common Law* (1881), 36, 38, 321. For Holmes generally, see Mark De Wolfe Howe, *Justice Oliver Wendell Holmes*, 2 vols. (1957–1963), vol. 2, *The Proving Years, 1870–1882*. Oliver Wendell Holmes, Jr., *Collected Legal Papers* (1920), especially "The Law," 25–28, "The Use of Law Schools," 35–48, "The Path of the Law," 167–202, and "Law in Science and Science in Law," 210–43. See also G. Edward White's discussion, "Looking at Holmes in the Mirror," *Law and History Review* 4 ((Fall 1986): 445.

29. Edward J. Phelps, "The Relation of Law to Justice: An Address before the South Carolina Bar Association . . ." (1981), 7, 10, 14. For another dissent from Carter's views, see King, *Administration of Justice*, 10: "For truth is always simple, and delights neither in darkness nor subtleties."

30. Alfred Russell, "Avoidable Causes of Delay and Uncertainty in Our Courts," ABA *Reports* 14 (1891): 197; Charles C. Lancaster, ABA *Reports* 14 (1891): 41, and ABA *Reports* 4 (1881): 77; King, *Administration of Justice*, 23 ff.; Phelps, "Relation of Law to Justice," 16–17, 26–27. ABA *Reports* 5 (1882): 363–86; ABA *Reports* 14 (1891): 163 ff.; Max Radin, "The Achievement of the A.B.A.," American Bar Association *Journal* 25 (1939): 908; Felix Frankfurter and James Landes, *The Business of the Supreme Court* (1927), 60–69, 72–73, 80–81. The ABA enjoyed similar success in modifying the National Bankruptcy Act. See also Matzko, "Early Years of the American Bar Association," 138.

31. Calvin G. Child, "Shifting Uses, from the Standpoint of the Nineteenth Century," ABA *Reports* 2 (1879): 71–92; Seymour D. Thompson, "More Justice and Less Technicality," *American Law Review* 23 (1889): 22–23; "The Changing Role of the Jury in the Nineteenth Century," *Yale Law Journal* 74 (1964): 170–92; John F. Dillon, "American Institutions and Laws," ABA *Reports* 7 (1884): 219; Joseph H. Choate, "Trial by Jury: Annual Address before the American Bar Association, August 18, 1898," reprinted in Choate, *American Addresses* (1911), 205, 221, 221–22, 238–39.

32. See the discussion of this aim in Jacob Weart, "American Bar Association," *New Jersey Law Journal* 27 (1904): 336–43. Phelps, "Relation of Law to Justice," 12; George A. Mercer, "The Relationship of Law and National Spirit," ABA *Reports* 2 (1879): 143–71; Matzko, "Early Years of the American Bar Association," 130–37, 138–39, 267. Later, in the 1920s, some association members came to view uniform state legislation as a means of forestalling the growth of federal power. See also Lawrence M. Friedman, "Law Reform in Historical Perspective," *St. Louis University Law Journal* 13 (1969), 351–67, for an analysis of such reform.

33. David J. Brewer, "A Better Education the Great Need of the Profession," ABA *Reports* 18 (1895): 441–56; Matzko, "Early Years of the American Bar Association," 505; *American Law Review* 15 (1881): 531; "Report of the Committee on Legal Education and Admission to the Bar," ABA *Reports* 20 (1897): 362–64; 4 (1881): 296; 11 (1888): 244; 18 (1895): 15; 20 (1897): 372; Max Radin, "The Achievement of the A.B.A.," American Bar Association *Journal* 26 (1940): 23. Some of the most eminent law school professors who were also active in the ABA include Henry Hitchcock, St. Louis Law School (Washington University); Simeon Baldwin, Yale; James O. Broadhead, St. Louis Law School (Washington University); William Allen Butler, City College of New York Law School; George Hoadley, University of Cincinnati Law School; Carlton Hunt, University of Louisiana (Tulane); Edward J. Phelps, Yale; George G. Wright, University of Iowa. See Matzko, "Early Years of the American Bar Association," 615.

34. ABA *Reports* 4 (1881): 28–30; 20 (1897): 19–33; 23 (1900): 449, 456; 25 (1902): 736.

35. "Report of the Committee on Legal Education, and Admission to the Bar," ABA *Reports* 20 (1897): 362–64; "Overcrowded Profession,"

Central Law Journal 16 (1883): 221; John J. Wickham, "Are There Too Many Lawyers?" *Pittsburgh Legal Journal* 37 (1889): 155; Robert Treat Platt, "Decadence of Law as a Profession and Its Growth as a Business," *Yale Law Journal* 12 (1903): 441–45; "American Lawyer Crop," *Scientific American* 77 (1897): 186; Reed, *Training for the Public Profession of the Law*, 443. As the second generation of immigrants came to enjoy the benefits of higher standards of living and free public education, the possibility of going on to higher education, once more likely only for the wealthier classes, now became possible for these sons of immigrants; Harry First, "Competition in the Legal Education Industry," *New York University Law Review* 53 (1978): 348. New York and Chicago attracted both the most prominent lawyers and the largest numbers of immigrants. Hobson, "American Legal Profession and Organizational Society," 117–19.

36. Samuel Hand, "Annual Address of the President of the Bar Association of the State of New York," Bar Association of the State of New York *Reports* 3 (1879): 67–87; J. A. M., Jr. [pseud.]. "The Decline of Lawyers," *New Jersey Law Journal* 6 (1883): 36–43, and editorial notes, 66–68; Charles C. Bonney, "Law Reform and the Future of the Legal Profession," Illinois State Bar Association *Proceedings* 6 (1883): 45–53; David B. Hill, "Lawyers and the Profession of Law," Bar Association of the State of New York *Reports* 10 (1887): 38–47; "The Business of the Lawyer," *Albany Law Journal* 48 (July 1893): 55 ff.; Franklin A. Wilson, "Lawyers of Today and of Yesterday: Address by the President," Maine State Bar Association *Proceedings* (1898), 20–33; Zenophon Wheeler, "Law: Decadence of Its Dignity: Address by the President," Tennessee Bar Association *Reports* 4 (1885): 60–78.

37. William Hornblower, "Has the Profession of Law Been Commericalized?" *Forum* 18 (February 1895): 684; C. H. Pickstone, "'One Law for the Rich and Another for the Poor': A Protest," *Michigan Law Journal* 4 (1895): 323–33; Edwin Countryman, *The Ethics of Compensation for Professional Services* (1882). On the danger of the contingent fee, see Joseph B. Warner, "The Responsibilities of the Lawyer," ABA *Reports* 19 (1896): 324–25; Tracy C. Becker, "Contracts for Contingent Compensation for Legal Services, . . . Their Legal Status and Ethical Relations," Bar Association of the State of New York *Reports* 3 (1879): 134–43; Gustave Koerner, "The Doctrine of Punitive Damages and Its Effect on the Ethics of the Profession," ABA *Reports* 5 (1882): 211–20; P. Bliss, "Contingent and Exorbitant Fees," *American Law Review* 22 (1888), 390–402; Robert L. Harmon, "Lawyer and the Shyster," Alabama State Bar Association *Reports* (1897), 39–51.

38. George F. Shelton, "Law as a Business," *Yale Law Journal* 10 (1901): 278, 282. Other lawyers sensed danger, but they were unwilling to concede defeat. David McAdam and others, *Bench and Bar of New York* (1891) 1:1—"It may be that Plutocracy is gradually displacing the Profession of Law. There are signs that point in that direction, but thus far the peril has only been a threat not a reality." R. Tate Irvine, "The

Lawyer of the Future," West Virginia Bar Association *Proceedings* 7 (1900): 201; George Sharswood, *Essay on Professional Ethics* (1854).

39. Even in the leadership of the ABA there were those who believed the contingent fee to be a legitimate legal practice. Simeon Baldwin called it "the only protection for persons having meritorious causes of action to command the aid of competent, counsel"—Matzko, "Early Years of the American Bar Association," 362. Later, Thomas J. Walsh defended the contingent fee. Simeon Baldwin, ABA *Reports* 9 (1886): 498; "Report of the Committee on Delay and Uncertainty in the Law," ABA *Reports* 9 (1886), 355. See also Lawrence M. Friedman, *A History of American Law* (1973), 422–23; Max Radin, "The Achievements of the ABA," American Bar Association *Journal* 26 (1940): 138. Edward Patterson, "The Practical Lawyer," *New York Times*, 15 December 1897. Judge Patterson delivered the speech to the Phi Delta Phi legal fraternity. Philip C. Jessup, *Elihu Root*, 2 vols. (1938), 1:133.

40. For the dangers posed by the "kings of fortune," see Warner, "Responsibilities of the Lawyer (see n. 1)," 339–42; Guy Carleton Lee, "The Position of the Lawyer in Society," *Green Bag* 8 (1896): 246; M. A. Spoonts, "The Divided Allegiance of the Lawyer," Texas Bar Association *Reports* (1897): 105–13; Melville M. Bigelow, "Respect for the Law: Responsibility of the Profession," Bar Association of the State of New York *Reports* (1892), 38–56; Pickstone, "'One Law for the Rich and Another for the Poor'," 323; Joseph W. Errant, "Justice for the Friendless and the Poor," Illinois State Bar Association *Proceedings* (1888), 12.

41. This transition is discussed by Henry W. Taft, *A Century and a Half of the New York Bar* (1938). See also Theron G. Strong, *Landmarks of a Lawyer's Life* (1914), 346.

42. Gerald Carson, *A Good Day at Saratoga* (1978), 46–49; Jacob Weart, "The American Bar Association: Its History for the First Sixteen Years of Its Existence and Its Impress upon the Thought of the Nation," *New Jersey Law Journal* 27 (1904): 292–93; Shelton, "Law as a Business," 277. On Saratoga and its prejudices, see Elizabeth Drexel Lehr, *King Lehr and the Gilded Age* (1935); Henry Collins Brown, *Brownstone Fronts and Saratoga Trunks* (1938); Melvin Leighton Heimer, *Fabulous Bawd: The Story of Saratoga* (1952).

43. G. Edward White, *Tort Law in America* (1955), 3, 16; James Willard Hurst, *The Legitimacy of the Business Corporation in the Law of the United States, 1780–1970* (1970); Robert W. Gordon, "Legal Thought and Legal Practice in the Age of American Enterprise, 1870–1920," in *Professions and Professional Ideologies in America*, ed. Gerald L. Geison (1983), 70, 106–10; Thomas M. Cooley, "Law of Corporations," in *Cyclopedia of Political Science*, 1: 664–89. For the contrasting case in Europe, see Leslie Hannah, "Mergers, Cartels, and Concentrations: Legal Factors in the U.S. and European Experience," in *Recht und Entwicklung der Grossunternehmen im 19. und frühen 20 . . .* , ed. Norbert Horn and Jürgen Kocka (Gottingen, 1979), 306–16;

Jürgen Kocka, "The Rise of Modern Industrial Enterprise in Germany," in *Managerial Hierarchies: Comparative Perspectives on the Rise of the Modern Industrial Enterprise*, ed. Alfred D. Chandler (1980), 106; David S. Landes, "The Structure of Enterprise in the 19th Century: The Case of Britain and Germany," *Rapports du XI Congrès Internationale des Sciences Historiques* 5 (Upsala, 1960): 107–28.

44. White, *Tort Law in America*, 61; Robert A. Silverman, *Law and Urban Growth: Civil Litigation in Boston Trial Courts, 1880–1900* (1981), 114–15, 120. In West Virginia, with a great number of rural jurisdictions and with much of the population holding an older, more fatalistic and stoical attitude toward injury, only five percent of all reported accidents were litigated. However, many of these were apparently won by the plaintiffs, when lodged against large companies. Such companies lost 84 percent of all their cases brought to trial in the state in which they were the defendants. Frank W. Munger, Jr., "Commercial Litigation in West Virginia State and Federal Courts," *American Journal of Legal History* 30 (1986): 336, 346.

45. Hobson, "American Legal Profession and Organizational Society" (see n. 15), 118–21.

46. See First, "Competition in the Legal Education Industry," 347–51, 358–60.

47. Hobson, "American Legal Profession and Organizational Society," 312–13. For incomes of Boston lawyers, see Silverman, *Law and Urban Growth*, 35–36. Litigation in Boston doubled between 1880 and 1900 (Silverman, 11), as did the number of lawyers (30). The number of lawyers in the nation also increased, as did the proportion of lawyers to the total population; U.S. Bureau of the Census, *Sixteenth Census of the United States, 1940; Population; Comparative Occupation Statistics for the United States, 1870–1940* (1943), 111. The market for legal services was created by many forces and factors. Most obvious among them were the decisions of the courts and legislatures as to what was litigable, the propensity of those with possible claims to go to court, the interest of those liable to such claims in legal counseling, the growth and diminishment of conflicts that impelled those claims, and the expense of litigation along with the ability of litigants to meet those expenses. Brewer, "A Better Education, the Great Need of the Profession," 452. One careful study of overcrowding in Wisconsin from 1880 to 1920 found that opportunities for lawyers increased more rapidly than their growth in numbers, and the study suggested that the same pattern was true for the nation as a whole. Lloyd K. Garrison, "A Survey of the Wisconsin Bar," *Wisconsin Law Review* 10 (1934): 133–49; William R. Johnson, *Schooled Lawyers: A Study in the Clash of Professional Cultures* (1978), 170–71.

48. James Elbert Cutler, *Lynch-Law: An Investigation into the History of Lynching in the United States* (1905), 171.

49. Kenneth S. Tollett, "Black Lawyers, Their Education and the Black Community," *Howard Law Journal* 17 (1972): 330–33; D. Augustus Straker, "The Negro in the Profession of Law," *A.M.E. Church Review* 8

(1891): 178–82; Charles Sumner Brown, "The Genesis of the Negro Lawyer in New England," *Negro History Bulletin* 22 (April and May 1959): 147–52, 171–77; Silverman, *Law and Urban Growth*, 24, 31, 146; Roger Lane, *Roots of Violence in Black Philadelphia, 1860–1900* (1986), 27, 33, 153. For Black lawyers in Chicago, see Allan H. Spear, *Black Chicago: The Making of a Negro Ghetto, 1890–1920* (1967), 29–30.

50. Richard Kluger, *Simple Justice: The History of Brown v. Board of Education and Black America's Struggle for Equality* (1976), 132. Another odd exception was the small town of Muskogee, Oklahoma, where more than a dozen Black lawyers served a tiny community of Afro-Indians who had struck it rich in oil; Tollett, "Black Lawyers," 347–48. Dorothy Thomas, "Charlotte E. Ray," in *Notable American Women, 1607–1950*, ed. Edward T. James and others, 3 vols. (1971), 3:121–22; Karen Berger Morello, *The Invisible Bar: The Woman Lawyer in America, 1638 to the Present* (1986), 14. Some women lawyers were more fortunate, however.

51. Beatrice Doerschuk, *Women in the Law* (1920), 62; Eleanor Flexner, *A Century of Struggle: The Woman's Rights Movement in the United States*, rev. ed. (1975), 115–24, 132–33. Nevertheless, most of these pioneer women lawyers were not themselves active in the women's movement. For one analysis of the relation between feminism and professionalism, see Nancy F. Cott, *The Grounding of Modern Feminism* (1987), 215–39. D. Kelly Weisberg, "Barred from the Bar: Women and Legal Education in the United States, 1870–1890," *Journal of Legal Education* 28 (1977): 59; Ada M. Bittenbender, "Women in Law," in *Woman's Work in America*, ed. Annie Nathan Meyer (1891), 227, 243; Martha Strickland, "Women and the Forum," *Green Bag* 3 (1891: 240–45.

52. Morello, *The Invisible Bar*, 31–35; Weisberg, "Barred from the Bar," 486.

53. Weisberg, "Barred from the Bar," 489–93.

54. Weisberg, "Barred from the Bar," 498; Doerschuk, *Women in the Law*, 63.

55. Wayne K. Hobson, "Symbol of the New Profession: Emergence of the Large Law Firm, 1870–1915," in *The New High Priests: Lawyers in Post-Civil War America*, ed. Gerard W. Gewalt (1986), 6.

56. Robert W. Gordon, "Ideals and Actual in Law," in *The New High Priests: Lawyers in Post–Civil War America*, ed. Gerard W. Gawalt (1984), 59.

57. Wilson, "Lawyers of Today and of Yesterday," (see n. 36), 20–33; Shelton, "Law as a Business," (see n. 38), 278; Irvine, "Lawyer of the Future" (see n. 38), 200–201; Hobson, "American Legal Profession and Organizational Society," 157–58, quoting Erwin O. Smigel's study of Wall Street firms, *The Wall Street Lawyer: Professional Organization Man?* (1964).

58. Hobson, "American Legal Profession and Organizational Society," 143–45.

59. Gordon, "Legal Thought and Legal Practice," 73–75; Frederick Pollock, *The Law of Torts* (1887), v.

60. Paul D. Cravath, "The Reorganization of Corporations," in *Some Phases of Corporate Financing, Reorganization and Regulation* (1916), 177–78; Paul D. Cravath, "Gray's Inn," ABA *Journal* 10 (1924): 19–21.

61. Francis Lynde Stetson, *The Lawyer's Livelihood: Address to the New York State Bar Association* . . . (1909).

62. James B. Dill, "The Business Lawyer of Today," *Albany Law Journal* 65 (1903): 111–13.

63. Ralph Stone, "The Mission of State Bar Associations," Bar Association of the State of New York *Reports* 19 (1895): 150.

64. Simeon E. Baldwin, ABA *Reports* 20 (1897): 430; Simeon E. Baldwin, "The Decline of Lawyers," *New Jersey Law Journal* 6 (1883): 37; Thomas Fenton Taylor, "The Practice of Law in New York City," *Harvard Law Review* 10 (1896–1897): 23–45; Stone, "Mission of State Bar Associations," 161–62.

65. John S. Bradway, *The Bar and Public Relations: An Introduction to the Public Relations Field of the Bar* (1934), 50.

66. George D. Watrous, "Torts," in *Two Centuries' Growth of American Law, 1701–1901* (1902), 85–114; Roscoe Pound, *Interpretations of Legal History* (1923), 104–11; Lawrence M. Friedman, *A History of American Law* (1973), 409–27.

67. Walter Barnard Hill, "Bar Associations," Georgia State Bar Association *Proceedings* (1888), 51–88; David Bennett Hill, "Address as President: Lawyers and the Profession of Law," Bar Association of the State of New York *Reports* 10 (1887): 38–47.

68. Stone, "Mission of State Bar Associations," 148–77; Charles C. Bonney, "Law Reform and the Future of the Legal Profession: President's Annual Address . . . ," Illinois State Bar Association *Proceedings* 6 (1883): 45–53.

69. Norman Brockman, "The National Bar Association, 1888–1893: The Failure of Early Bar Federation," *American Journal of Legal History* 10 (1966): 122–27.

70. Thomas M. Cooley quoted in Matzko, "Early Years of the American Bar Association" (see n. 13), 159. See also Courtland Baker, "Address of the President," ABA *Reports* 7 (1884): 174; U. M. Rose, "Trusts and Strikes," ABA *Reports* 16 (1893): 287 ff.; Charles Claflin Allen, "Injunction and Organized Labor," ABA *Reports* 17 (1894): 299 ff.; Richard Wayne Parker, "Tyranny of Free Government," ABA *Reports* 18 (1895): 295 ff.; Joseph B. Warner, "The Responsibilities of the Lawyer," ABA *Reports* 19 (1896): 319–33; Eugene Wambaugh, "The Present Scope of Government," ABA *Reports* 20 (1897): 307 ff. Andrew Alison described this intermediate position as "an inner Republic," ABA *Reports* 7 (1884): 256.

71. Matzko, "Early Years of the American Bar Association," 151–83. See also Allen, "Injunction and Organized Labor," 299 ff.; Parker, "Tyranny of Free Government," 295 ff.; and Henry B. Brown's two suggestive

papers presented to the ABA: "Judicial Independence," ABA *Reports* 12 (1889): 265 ff., and "The Distribution of Property," ABA *Reports* 16 (1893): 213 ff. Gerald G. Eggert, "A Missed Alternative: Federal Courts as Arbiters of Railway Labor Disputes, 1877–1895," *Labor History* 7 (Fall 1966): 287–306; William E. Akin, "Arbitration and Labor Conflict, 1886–1900," *Historian* 29 (1967): 565–87.

72. ABA *Reports* 10 (1887): 29–46; ABA *Reports* 11 (1888): 45–46; John Randolph Tucker, "The Constitution of the United States: The Best Product of Political Science for the Security of Man," Ohio State Bar Association *Proceedings* (1896), 159–95; John Randolph Tucker, "The Constitutional System of the United States . . . Origin, Nature and Tendencies," Mississippi State Bar Association *Proceedings* (1889), 38–55; Lunsford L. Lewis to John Randolph Tucker, 21 May 1886, and Tucker to Lewis, 29 May 1886, in John Randolph Tucker Collection, University of North Carolina, Chapel Hill.

73. "Five Long Hours of Talk," *New York Times*, 5 February 1890.

Chapter 7

1. H.J.M., "The Denominations," *Methodist Quarterly Review* 12 (1892): 313; K. Rayner, "The American Episcopal Church and the Anglican Communion, 1865–1900," *Journal of Religious History* 3 (1964–1965): 158–74; James Bryce, *The American Commonwealth* 2 (1895), 706–7. The classic study is H. Richard Niebuhr, *The Social Sources of Denominationalism* (1940), new ed. For more recent research, see N. J. Demarath, III, *Social Class in American Protestantism* (1965).

2. H.J.M., "The Denominations," 313. Charles Edwin Jones, *Perfectionist Persuasion: The Holiness Movement and American Methodism, 1867–1936* (1974); David Edwin Harrell, Jr., *The Social Sources of Division in the Disciples of Christ, 1865–1900* (1973), especially chaps. 1, 13.

3. Bryce, *American Commonwealth*, 705; Rev. Elijah Lucas, "Shall Liberty Die; or, Patriots to the Front," *Baptist Home Mission Monthly* 20 (1898): 75; H. K. Carroll, "Religious Progress of the Negro," *Forum* 14 (1892–1893): 75–84; V. E. Daniel, "Ritual and Stratification in Chicago Negro Churches," *American Sociological Review* 7 (1942): 352–61.

4. Rt. Rev. A. N. Littlejohn, *The Christian Ministry at the Close of the Nineteenth Century* (1884), 6, 18, 71.

5. Russell H. Conwell, "An Institutional Church," *Homiletic Review* 31 (1896): 264–65; George Willis Cooke, "The Institutional Church," *New England Monthly* 14 (1896): 645–68; R. Q. Mallard and others, "Symposium on the Institutional Church," *Homiletic Review* 33 (1897): 84–89, 154–55, 281–84, 373–77, 472–78. George P. Mains, "Our Special Legislation on Amusement: Honest Doubt as to Its Wisdom," *Methodist Review* 74 (1892): 375–89.

6. M. J. Savage, "The Growth of Secularism," *The Religious Life* (1890), 119–20, 125–29; Rev. F. H. Hedge, "The Church in Modern Society," *Unitarian Review* 18 (1882): 263 ff.; John W. Chadwick, "The Future of Religion," *Unitarian Review* 23 (1885): passim.

7. Phillips Brooks, "The Public School System," in *Essays and Addresses* (1894), 519–29; R. Freeman Butts, *The American Tradition in Religion and Education* (1950), chaps. 4, 5; William K. Dunn, *What Happened to Religious Education?* (1958).

8. See chap. 8 of this work. Robert G. Ingersoll, *Collected Works* 1:517 ff.; 7:226, 400. Robert T. Handy, "The Protestant Quest for a Christian America," *Church History* 21 (March 1952): 13–14; Rev. C. M. Morse, "The Church and the Workingman," *Forum* 6 (1888), 653 ff; Josiah Strong, *The New Era* (1893), chap. 10; Robert F. Bishop, "The Alleged Estrangement of the Masses," *Methodist Review* 76 (1894), 64–75.

9. Rev. E. B. Hulbert, "Home Missions as Related to the Stability and Perpetuity of Our Institutions," *Baptist Home Mission Monthly* 14 (1892): 299, 301. "The Secularization of the Church," *The Nation* 11 (1870): 39–40. Hilary T. Hudson, *The Methodist Armor* (1904): 156–59. Rev. Arthur T. Pierson, "The Three Leavens: Formalism, Rationalism, Secularism," *The Pulpit Treasury* 10 (1892): 567; Frederik A. Norwood, *Church Membership in the Methodist Tradition* (1958), 83–84.

10. For an example of this contrast in views, see Bryce, *American Commonwealth*, 483, and Hulbert, "Home Missions," 299, versus "Impossibility of Unbelief," *American Catholic Review* 6 (1881): 709–27, and Noah Porter, "The Newest Atheism," *Princeton Review* 2, 5th ser. (1886): 359–97.

11. Frank Wakely Gunsaulus, "The Ideal of Culture," *The Chautauquan* 16 (1892): 59–64. Sam Jones, *Sermons* (1886), 319. William C. Wilkinson, *Modern Masters of Pulpit Discourse* (1905), 3:379, 11:57. W. D. Evans, "Preacher and Plutocrat," *Arena* 14 (1895): 228–38. "The Trust Octopus," *Baptist Quarterly Review* 10 (1888): 237. Rev. W. C. Helt, "The Demand of the Hour," *Homiletic Review* 28 (November 1884): 471.

12. H. J. M., "The Denominations," 313. Lyman Abbott, "What Are a Christian Preacher's Functions?" *Forum* 15 (1893): 54.

13. William Jewett Tucker, "The Making and the Unmaking of the Preacher," *The Biblical World* 12 (1898): 183–89; Charles A. Briggs, "Theological Education and Its Needs," *Forum* 21 (1891–1892): 634–45.

14. Rufus B. Spain, *At Ease in Zion: Social History of Southern Baptists, 1865–1900* (1967), chaps. 2, 3, 4. John Henry Barrows, "The World's First Parliament of Religions," *Homiletic Review* 25 (May 1893): 387–89. Rev. S. B. Halliday, *The Church in America and Its Baptism of Fire* (1896): 302.

15. H. K. Carroll, "The Negro in His Relation to the Church," *Independent* 4 (1895): 171. John E. Meeter, ed., *Selected Shorter Writings of Benjamin B. Warfield*, 2 (1973), 216. Briggs, "Theological Education and Its Needs," passim.

16. Borden P. Boune, "Secularism and Christianity," *Methodist Review* 48 (1894): 203–17. Tucker, "Making and Unmaking of the Preacher," 186.

17. B. M. Palmer, "Inter-Professional Responsibilities," *Presbyterian*

Quarterly 4 (1890): 188, 191; W. S. Lilly, "The Pulpit and Progress," *Homiletic Review* 34 (1897): 496–501.

18. Rev. Charles H. Brigham, "The Choice of A Profession," *Unitarian Review* 14 (1886): 162. Joseph Parker, "The Ministry of Christ is Not a Profession but a Vocation," *Homiletic Review* 37 (1894): 5.

19. H. J. Barrymore, "The Ministry: A Paradoxical Profession," *Forum* 29 (1900): 202.

20. Rev. William W. Farris, *Unemployed Ministers and Vacant Churches* (1892).

21. Barrymore, "The Ministry," 191. Noah Porter, "The Christian Ministry as a Profession and a Sacred Calling," *Andover Review* 1 (1884): 346–47.

22. "Who Shall Rule?" *Baptist Home Mission Monthly* 13 (1891): 254–57; Thomas E. Wangler, "The Birth of Americanism," *Harvard Theological Review* 65 (1972): 415–36. Rev. Patrick Corrigan, "What the Catholic Church Most Needs in the United States; or, The Voice of Priests in the Election of Bishops" (1884), 5, 14–15, 36, 79 (sermon at Church of Our Lady of Grace, Hoboken, N.J.).

23. John Tracy Ellis, "The Formation of the American Priest: An Historical Perspective," in *The Catholic Priest in the United States: Historical Investigations,* by John Tracy Ellis (1905), 80 ff. E. Nelson Blake, "What a Businessman Says about Our Duty to the American Baptist Home Mission Society," *Baptist Home Mission Monthly* 14 (1892): 373–74.

24. Wangler, "Birth of Americanism," 415–36.

25. Cardinal James Gibbons, *The Ambassador of Christ* (1896), 169–70. John B. Hogan, *Clerical Studies* (1898), chaps. 1, 2; Rev. John Talbut Smith, *Our Seminaries* (1896), chap. 21. Ellis, "Formation of the American Priest," 80 ff.

26. Edward A. Pace, "Our Theological Seminaries," *Catholic University Bulletin* 1 (1895): 398. Michael V. Gannon, "Before and After Modernism," in *The Catholic Priest,* by Ellis, 303–4. Barrymore, "The Ministry," 10. John Tracy Ellis, "Historical Perspectives," in *The Catholic Priest,* by Ellis, 30.

27. Cardinal Bedini quoted in Ellis, *The Catholic Priest,* 307. J. Sheehy, *Jura Sacerdotum Vindicta. The Rights of the Clergy Vindicated; or, A Plea for Canon Law in the United States, by a Roman Catholic Priest* (1883), 7. Corrigan, "What the Catholic Church Most Needs," 51.

28. Barrymore, "The Ministry," 116, 214; Corrigan, "What the Catholic Church Most Needs," passim.

29. "The Position of American Priests," *Donahue's Magazine* 24 (1890): 329–30.

30. "Vocations to the Priesthood and Our Seminaries," *American Ecclesiastical Review* 3 (1890): 169–77.

31. Kenneth Paul [Rev. Melanchthon Lockwood], *The New Minister* (1893), 108, 123–27, 270–72.

32. Charles S. Bernheimer, "The American Jewish Minister and His

Work," *Godey's (Ladies) Magazine* 136 (1898): 211–14. On the Reform rabbi, more generally, see Michael A. Meyer, *Response to Modernism in the History of the Reform Movements in Judaism* (1988) chaps. 6 and 7; Abraham J. Karp, "New York Chooses a Chief Rabbi," *Publications of the American Jewish Historical Society* (1954), 129–94; Jeffery S. Gurock, "Resisters and Accommodators: Varieties of Orthodox Rabbis in America, 1886–1983," *The American Rabbi: A Century of Continuing and Change, 1883–1983*, ed. Jacob Rader Marcus and Abraham J. Peck (1985). The foremost leader of conservative Judaism was Solomon Schecter. His remark is quoted in the preface.

33. A. L. Phillips, "The Development of the Negro Ministry," *Homiletic Review* 36 (1898): 504. W. E. Burghardt Du Bois, "The Religion of the American Negro," *The New World* 9 (1900): 615. Rev. Matthew Anderson, *Presbyterianism: Its Relation to the Negro* (1897), 123. Booker T. Washington, "The Colored Ministry: Its Defects and Needs," *The Christian Union* 42 (1890): 200.

34. Harvey Johnson, "The Righteous and the Wicked," in *The Negro Baptist Pulpit; A Collection of Sermons and Papers by Colored Baptist Ministers*, ed. Edward M. Brawley ([1890], 1971), 166–74; Edward M. Brawley, "The Duty of Colored Baptists," in *The Negro Baptist Pulpit*, 292, 294; Rev. H. L. Morehouse, "Comment" in *The Negro Baptist Pulpit*, 299. Francis J. Grimké, "A Passing Thought," *Independent* 47 (1985): *passim;* Anderson, *Presbyterianism*, 121–22. Rev. T. G. Steward, *The End of the World; or, Clearing the Way for the Fullness of the Gentiles* (1888), 126; *The Christian Recorder* of the African Methodist Episcopal Church condemned socialism as a pernicious doctrine, but the *AME Church Review* occasionally published articles sympathetic to Christian Socialism. See Philip S. Foner, ed., *Black Socialist Preacher* (1976), 4. A broad discussion can be found in Edward L. Wheeler, *Uplifting the Race: The Black Minister in the New South, 1865–1902* (1986).

35. Rev. J. B. Chenoweth's discussion of the difference between spiritual and fleshly sin is quoted in the diary of Rev. George A. Marston (1884); Bishop B. T. Tanner, "The Colored Ministry," *Independent* 43 (1891): 476. Henry Clay Gray, "Negro Christianity," *Independent* 43 (1891): 481.

36. Rosemary Skinner Keller, "Lay Women in the Protestant Tradition," in *Women and Religion in America*, ed. Rosemary Radford, 1 (1981), 258–93; Francis E. Willard, ed., *Women in the Pulpit* (1881), 97. Rev. Anna Howard Shaw, "Women in the Ministry," *The Chautauquan* 27 (1898): 443, 494–95; see also F. M. Holland, "Our Clergywomen," *Open Court* 5 (1891): 3121–22, and Keller, "Lay Women," 258–93. Rev. W. B. Godbey, *Shall the Women Preach?* (1891).

37. Mary Ewens, "The Leadership of Nuns," *Rueters* (1975), 101. *Secrets of the Convent* quoted in Mary Ewens, *The Role of Nuns in Nineteenth-Century America* (1978), 301. William Dean Howells, *Their Wedding Journey* (1895), 256–57.

38. William Wright Barnes, *The Southern Baptist Convention, 1845–1953* (1954), 148–51. Henry Ward Beecher, *Last Sermons* (1887), 174.

39. Melvin Easterday Dieter, *The Holiness Revival of the Nineteenth Century* (1980), chaps. 5, 6; Jonas Oramel Peck, *The Revival and the Pastor* (1894), chap. 8; B. Fay Mills, "The Evangelist and His Work," *Homiletic Review* 21 (1841): 123–32. Ernest Trice Thompson, *Changing Emphases in American Preaching* (1943), 127. Dwight L. Moody, *The Way to God and How to Find It* (1884).

40. "The Comparative Importance of College and Seminary Courses," *Seminary Magazine* 1 (1888). "A Lawyer's Criticism of Young Preachers," *Western Christian Advocate* (1883): 4. Daniel Curry, "Ministerial Education," *Methodist Review* 68 (1886): 586–90.

41. Benjamin B. Warfield, "Spiritual Culture in the Theological Seminary," in *Selected Shorter Writings* 2:480. Rev. George N. Loftan, "Elective Grace," *Seminary Magazine* 3 (1890): 253. Richard J. Storr, "The Religion Man Needs," *Homiletic Review* 21 (1891): 229.

42. Richard Morgan Cameron, "Boston University School of Theology," *Nexus* 11 (1968): 40. "Princeton Theological Seminary: Professor Paul Van Dyke's Resignation," *Magazine of Christian Literature* 6 (1892): 223–25. Nathan E. Wood, "Baptists," in Albert H. Newman, *A Century of Baptist Achievement* (1901): 428–38.

43. Benjamin B. Warfield, "Recent Reconstruction of Theology: From the Point of View of Systematic Theology," in *Selected Shorter Writings;* Charles A. Briggs, "The Authority of Holy Scripture," Inaugural Address (1891), 33–36, 70–80. Benjamin B. Warfield, "Improvement of Our Theological Seminaries," *Christian Literature* 13 (1895): 137–39; Benjamin B. Warfield, "Theology as a Science," *Bible Student and Teacher* 3 (January 1906): 1–4, reprinted in *Selected Shorter Writings,* 207–12.

44. Briggs, "Authority of Holy Scripture," 7 ff. George Lewis Prentiss, *The Union Theological Seminary in the City of New York: Its Design and Another Decade in Its History* (1899), 14, 21–22, 537.

45. Warfield, "Improvement of Our Theological Seminaries," 138–39; Charles A. Briggs, "Whither? A Theological Question for the Times," *Scribners* 6 (1889): 12–14, 17–19.

46. Robert Price, "Theological Education in Universities," *Presbyterian Quarterly* 7 (1895): 38–48.

47. Howard Henderson, *The Ethics and Etiquette of the Pulpit* (1892), 60. Rev. Charles Sheard, *The Minister Himself* (1900), 120–21. Barrymore, "The Ministry," 195.

48. E. G. Robinson, "That Great Brotherhood of the American Ministry," *Lectures on Preaching* (1895), 76. Henderson, *Ethics and Etiquette,* 60, 91; Sheard, *The Minister Himself,* 102–6, 111–13, 115–16.

49. Phillips Brooks, "The Minister and His People," *Harvard Theological Review* (1908), 228 ff. Storr, "The Religion Man Needs," 239. Barrymore, "The Ministry," 192. F. H. Foster, "Recent Reconstruction in Theology," *Homiletic Review* 35 (1898): 308; Francis G. Peabody, "The Proportion of College-Trained Preachers," *Forum* 18 (1894): 31. E. G. Robinson, *Lectures on Preaching* (1895), 127; see also Bryce, *American Commonwealth* (see n. 1), 3:486.

50. Frederik Palmer, "The Contribution of the Episcopal Church to Modern Religious Life," *Andover Review* 17 (1892): 376–92. Sidney Meal, "The Evangelical Conception of the Ministry in America," in *The Ministry in Historical Perspective,* ed. Helmut Richard Niebuhr (1956), 235.

51. William H. Allison, *Baptist Councils in America: A Historical Study of Their Origin and the Principles of Their Development* (1906), 96–109; "A Ministerial Bureau," *Baptist Quarterly Review* 10 (1888): 511–12. John A. Wright, *People and Preachers in the Methodist Episcopal Church* (1886), chap. 4. Andrew C. Zenes, *Presbyterianism in America* (1937), 123. Thomas G. Apple, "The Lord's Supper and Mystery," *Homiletic Review* 28 (1894): 449–50; J. B. Remensnyder, "The Real Presence," *Homiletic Review* 27 (1894): 500–509; A. A. Muller, "The Episcopal Doctrine of the Eucharist," *Catholic World* 70 (1899): 178–92; Littlejohn, *Christian Ministry at Close of Nineteenth Century* (see n. 4), 390–91.

52. Rev. Dwight Pratt, "Pastoral Psychology," *Homiletic Review* 24 (1892): 118. "Pastoral Visits," *Pulpit Treasury* 10 (1893): 787. Henderson, *Ethics and Etiquette,* 57, 59. Rev. John Watson, *The Cure of Souls* (1896), 240–41; "Psychology for the Pastor," *Methodist Review* 80 (1898): 115–19; Craig B. Cross, "The Pastor as a Physician," *Lutheran Church Review* 18 (1898): 111–17. "Visitation of the Sick," *Pulpit Treasury* 10 (1892): 152–53.

53. Robinson, *Lectures on Preaching,* 40. Tucker, "Making and Unmaking of the Preacher" (see n. 13), 185.

54. Sheard, *The Minister Himself,* 80. Rev. W. G. Blaikie, "The Preacher's Avenues to the Human Soul," *Homiletic Review* 35 (1898): 487–92; Rev. J. Spencer Kennard, *Psychic Power in Preaching* (1901), 131, 144.

55. Rev. William Christ Schaeffer, "Emotion in Religion," *Homiletic Review* 27 (1894): 23. See several essays by Benjamin B. Warfield, in *Selected Shorter Writings,* vol. 2: "Inability and the Demand of Faith," 726; "Authority, Intellect, Heart," 668, 670, 671; "Systematic Theology and Creed," 287, 288; and "The Significance of the Westminster Standard as a Creed," 662. See also W. Benton Green, Jr., "The Function of Reason in Christianity," *Presbyterian and Reformed Review* 6 (1895): 46; C. C. Everett, "Reason in Religion," *New World* 6 (1897): 638–57; J. P. Lilly, "Hypoevangelism," *Presbyterian and Reformed Review* 4 (1893): 222 ff.

56. Watson, *Cure of Souls,* 120–21. Arthur T. Pierson quoted in Timothy P. Weber, *Living in the Shadow of the Second Coming* (1979), 36–37. Howard Crosby, "Exegesis in the Pulpit," *Homiletic Review* 22 (1891): 20–22; A. H. Tuttle, "The Teaching Element in Preaching," *Methodist Review* 80 (1898): 205–12; H. S. Wayland, "Doctrinal and Practical Preaching," *Homiletic Review* 34 (1897): 439–41; "Reason Not Rationalism," *Methodist Review* 11 (1891–92): 423–30.

57. "The Literary Culture of Clergymen," editorial, *Andover Review* 18 (1892): 180–82; Harwood T. Pattison, "The Minister's Literary Culture," *Homiletic Review* 26 (1893): 291–302; J. O. Murray, "Culture in Its Re-

lation to Preaching," *Homiletic Review* 22 (1891): 3–9; Watson, *Cure of Souls*, 125.

58. "The Relation of the Clergy to Conscience," *The Church Eclectic* 22 (1894): 52. Rev. Jesse T. Whitley, "The Nature and Function of Conscience," *Homiletic Review* 20 (1890): 137–42.

59. Charles W. Eliot, *Educational Reform* (1898), 67. Littlejohn, *Christian Ministry at Close of Nineteenth Century*, 421–22.

60. Wilkinson, *Modern Masters of Pulpit Discourse* (see n. 11), 88. John Dyer, "Theological Education in America," *Pennsylvania Monthly* 11 (1880): 600.

61. "Fear," *Homiletic Review* 35 (1898): 340; Rev. Frank H. Foster, "Recent Reconstructions of Theology," *Homiletic Review* 35 (1898): 305. George M. Stone, "The Theme, the Method, and the End of Preaching," *Homiletic Review* 23 (February 1892): 147. Henry Ward Beecher, "Fear or Love," in *Last Sermons* (1887): 175. Rev. John A. Broadus, *A Treatise on the Preparation and Delivery of Sermons* (1891): 239. Alexander MacLaren, "Constraining Love," *Homiletic Review* 20 (1890): 523–5. Rev. Dr. Otto Pini, "The Wonderful World of Eternal Love," *Homiletic Review* 35 (May 1898): 426; Sandra S. Sizer, *Gospel Hymns and Social Religion: The Rhetoric of Nineteenth Century Revivalism* (1978), passim.

62. Jones, *Sermons* (see n. 11), 319; Moody, *The Way to God*, 11, 18. Alexander MacLaren, "Constraining Love," 525.

63. Benjamin B. Warfield, "Dreams and the Moral Life," *Homiletic Review* 20 (1890): 216–18.

64. Charles E. Knox, "Can the Bible Be Wrought More Fully into the Science and the Art of Preaching?" *Homiletic Review* 20 (1890): 102. Henderson, *Ethics and Etiquette*, 26. Sheard, *The Minister Himself*, 184–87.

65. Sheard, *The Minister Himself*, 237–39; Watson, *Cure of Souls*, 73, 219, 227; Robert F. Sample, "Effective Preaching," *Homiletic Review* 23 (1892): 567–68; Paul Van Dyke, *Gospel for an Age of Doubt; the Yale Lectures on Preaching, 1896* (1896), 22–23, 284–85. Tucker, "Making and Unmaking of the Preacher," 186–87; John Worcester, "Sympathy as a Natural Basis of Charity," *New Church Review* 2 (1895): 364–68. Kennard, *Psychic Power in Preaching*, 125, 129; Porter, "The Christian Ministry" (see n. 21), 354, 355, 362.

66. Charles S. Peirce, "The Marriage of Religion and Science," *The Open Court* 8 (1893): 3560. The Catholic and Lutheran stories, though differing sharply from it on the means of redemption, were actually close to the Calvinist story. For a sample of the various Protestant stories see: George J. H. Northcraft, "The Christian Interpretation of Life," *Methodist Review* [South] 48 (1896): 178–202; Anon, "Life's Help: The Presence of God," *Evangelistic Repository* 68 (1891): 365–68; Henry M. Tenney, "Divine Goodness in Severity," *Bibliotheca Sacra* 55 (1898): 485–95; W. B. Carpenter, "The Paradox of Death and Life," *Christian Literature* 3 (1890–91): 40–45; C. Hedge, "Three Views of Life," *Unitarian Review* 34 (1890): 377–89.

Chapter 8

1. For a discussion of pre–Civil War professors, see Laurence Veysey, *The Emergence of the American University* (1965), 6–7; Frederick Rudolph, *The American College and University* (1962), 157–64. For a discussion of engineers in an earlier era, see Raymond Merritt, *Engineers in American Society, 1850–65* (1969).

2. See chaps. 1, 2, and 3 in this book.

3. John C. Trautwine, "The Duty of the Engineer to the Public," *Proceedings of the Engineers' Club of Philadelphia* 18 (1901); Charles F. Thwing, "The Wealth of English Universities and American Colleges," *International Review* 12 (1882), 343.

4. Earl James McGrath, "Evolution of Administrative Offices in Institutions of Higher Learning in the U.S., 1860–1933" (Ph.D. diss., University of Chicago, 1936), chap. 1. By present-day standards most colleges and universities were quite small. Nonetheless they looked to the largest and most rapidly growing schools, particularly to the University of Chicago, as models. It is surprising how quickly even the smaller schools developed bureaucratic forms.

5. Granville Stanley Hall, "Research: The Vital Spirit of Teaching," *Forum* 17 (1894); Veysey, *Emergence of the American University* (1965).

6. Richard J. Storr, *Harper's University: The Beginning* (1966), 183; Hugh Hawkins, "C. W. Eliot, University Reform and Religious Faith in America," *Journal of American History* 51 (1964): 191–213; A. T. Hadley, "New Theology and Optimism," quoted in George W. Pierson, *Yale College: An Educational History, 1871–1921* (1952), 116–17; George S. Morrison, *The New Era* ([1898] 1903), 27.

7. Mark Sibley Severance, *Hammersmith: The Harvard Days* (1878); for a fictional description of the pre–Civil War professor, see especially the description of Dr. Brimblecom, 67–68. Bliss Perry, "College Professors and the Public," *Atlantic Monthly* 89 (1901): 282; Hugo Munsterberg, "Productive Scholarship in America," *Atlantic Monthly* 87 (1901): 630; Veysey, *Emergence of the American University*, 309–11.

8. U.S. Bureau of the Census, *Historical Statistics of U.S. Colonial Times to 1970* (1975), pt. 1, 383; Alan Creutz, "From College Teacher to University Scholar: The Evolution and Professionalization of Academics at the University of Michigan, 1840–1900" (Ph.D. diss., University of Michigan, 1981), passim; F. Ringer, "Higher Education in Germany in the Nineteenth Century," *Journal of Contemporary History* 19 (1967): 125–26; Munsterberg, "Productive Scholarship," 617.

9. Munsterberg, "Productive Scholarship," 619; "Confessions of a College Professor," *Scribners* 22 (1897): 629–34; Bliss Perry, "The Life of a College Professor," *Scribners* 22 (1897): 512–18.

10. Helen Watterson Moody, "The Unquiet Sex: First Paper—The Woman Collegian," *Scribners* 22 (1897): 150–56.

11. Owen Wister, *Philosophy Four* (1903); William James, "The True Harvard," *Memories and Studies* (1903), 353; Winton Solberg, *The University of Illinois, 1867–99* (1968), 354.

12. Charles F. Thwing, *College Administration* (1900), 102–3; James, "The True Harvard," 353.

13. For pre–Civil War origins of scholarly-edifiers, see Rudolph, *American College and University,* 104–6, 394–95. Charles F. Thwing, *Guides, Philosophers, and Friends; Studies of College Men* (1927), 441–42; George Herbert Palmer, "Can Moral Conduct Be Taught in Schools?" *Forum* 14 (1893): 683.

14. John Wright Buckham and George Malcolm Stratton, *George Holmes Howison: Philosopher and Teacher* (1934), 1, 4, 370–79.

15. Thwing, *College Administration,* 79.

16. Pierson, *Yale College,* 276–77; Walter Camp, "Eugene Lamb Richards," *Yale Alumni Weekly* 22 (1912–13), 33–34.

17. For a discussion of the teaching style of some of these iconoclast-priests, see Dickinson S. Miller, "Beloved Psychologist William James," in *Great Teachers,* ed. Houston Peterson (1946), 223–28; Harris E. Starr, *William Graham Sumner* (1925), 380 ff.; "Barrett Wendell," *Harvard Alumni Bulletin* (9 Oct. 1924); Herbert M. Hopkins, *The Torch* (1903), which is based on E. A. Ross; and Joseph Dorfman, *Thorstein Veblen and His America* (1934), 248–52.

18. James, "The True Harvard," 443; Starr, *William Graham Sumner,* 380; "Barrett Wendell."

19. James McCosh, "Discipline in American Colleges," *North American Review* 126 (1878): 432–36; N. S. Shaler, "The Problem of Discipline in Higher Education," *Atlantic Monthly* 64 (July 1889): 24–37; George Herbert Palmer, "Necessary Limitations of the Elective System" [1887], in *The Ideal Teacher* (1908), 240–42.

20. Palmer, "Can Moral Conduct Be Taught in Schools?" 683–85; George Herbert Palmer, *The Ideal Teacher* (1908), 23–24; Helen Lefkowitz Horowitz, *Campus Life* (1987), 41–55.

21. Rudolph, *American College and University,* 148–49; Pierson, *Yale College,* 276–77. George Cunningham Edwards (1852–1931), "the little colonel" of Berkeley, was almost the twin of "Dicky-Bird" Richards at Yale. Edwards taught freshman math but spent much more time on the football practice fields at Berkeley. His loyalty to "the traditions of California enabled him to exert a wide and admirable influence." His final wish for "one more reunion and one more Big Game" on the athletic field dedicated to his honor, sadly enough, was not fulfilled. He died a few days before that historic event. *Oakland Tribune,* 20 November 1930; *The Daily Californian,* 19 November 1930; "George C. Edwards, Some Traditions of California," *Occident* 76 (1936): 97.

22. Charles S. Peirce, "Fixation of Belief," *Popular Science Monthly* 12 (1877): 15; "Sketch of William Graham Sumner," *Popular Science Monthly* 35 (1889): 263; Munsterberg, "Productive Scholarship," 616; John Dewey, "Academic Freedom," *Educational Review* 23 (1902): 14; George Santayana, "The Spirit and Ideals of Harvard University" [1894], in *Santayana's America* (1967), ed. James Ballowe, 59; Starr Jordan, "College Discipline," *North American Review* 165 (1897): 403.

23. Ira Remsen at Johns Hopkins University was clearly a research scholar but not an iconoclast-priest. See B. Harrow, *Eminent Chemists of Our Time* (1927) for a complete biography. Barrett Wendell was not a research scholar but was an iconoclast-priest; Robert Herrick, *The Professor's Chance* (1897), 723–32.

24. Granville Stanley Hall, "Scholarship and the Training of Professors," *Forum* 17 (1894): 484, 568; Charles F. Thwing, *American Colleges* (1888), 18; G. B. Halsted, "Original Research and Creative Authorship," *Science* 1 n.s. (1895): 203–7.

25. Pierson, *Yale College*, 126; Storr, *Harper's University*, 89; Veysey, *Emergence of the American University*, 320–21.

26. Lord Bryce, *The Elective System* (1888), 438; Thwing, *College Administration*, 67; Richard Hofstadter and Walter P. Metzger, *The Development of Academic Freedom in the United States* (1955), 120–21.

27. "The Perplexities of a College President," *Atlantic Monthly* 88 (1900): 483–93; Thwing, *College Administration*, 21, 29–30, 69; Hofstadter and Metzger, *Development of Academic Freedom*, 120–21; Daniel Coit Gilman, "College Controversy," *The Nation* 39 (1884): 49–50.

28. McGrath, "Evolution of Administrative Offices in Institutions of Higher Learning," (see n. 4), 194.

29. Storr, *Harper's University*, 62, 93–94.

30. Professor Giuseppe Allievo, "The Division of Labor in the University," *NEA Proceedings* (1893), 110; Veysey, *Emergence of the American University*, 58, 314; George Herbert Palmer, *Trades and Professions* (1918), 23, 25; "The Status of the American Professor," *Educational Review* 16 (1898): 423.

31. John Dewey, "Academic Freedom," *Educational Review* 23 (1902): 12–13; Palmer, *The Ideal Teacher*, 125; Josiah Royce, "The Freedom of Teaching," *Overland Monthly* (1883), 235–40.

32. Royce, "Freedom of Teaching," 236–37.

33. Royce, "Freedom of Teaching," 237.

34. Dewey, "Academic Freedom," 3.

35. Dewey, "Academic Freedom," 3, 6–8.

36. Martin Kellogg, "Authority," *Overland Monthly* (1883), 637–39, 644.

37. Alton B. Parker, "The Rights of Donors," *Educational Review* 23 (1902): 18, 20; Royce, "Freedom of Teaching," 237.

38. Arthur T. Hadley, "Academic Freedom in Theory and Practice," *Atlantic Monthly* 91 (1903): 152–60, 334–44.

39. Hadley, "Academic Freedom," 158, 159.

40. Hadley, "Academic Freedom," 344.

41. Vincent Buranelli, *Josiah Royce* (1964), 68–69; Merle Curti and Vernon Carstensen, *The University of Wisconsin* (1949), 1:614; Richard Hofstadter and Walter P. Metzger, "Academic Freedom and Big Business," in *Development of Academic Freedom*, 413–67; "Editor's Table," *New England Magazine* 17 (1897): 119–28.

42. Thwing, *College Administration*, 93, 96. Munsterberg, "Productive Scholarship," 636; George Herbert Palmer, "Doubts about Uni-

versity Extension," *Atlantic Monthly* 69 (1892): 370; Pierson, *Yale College*, 126.

43. Parker, "Rights of Donors," 15–21; Dewey, "Academic Freedom," 10.

44. Thwing, *College Administration*, 92–96; Herrick, *The Professor's Chance*, 99.

Chapter 9

1. "Suggestive Seals," *American Engineer* 6 (1882): 229.

2. "Suggestive Seals," 229.

3. James Gregory McGivern, *First Hundred Years of Engineering Education in the United States (1807–1907)* (1960), 97, 103, 117, 123, 128–29, 150. See also Lawrence P. Grayson, "A Brief History of Engineering Education in the United States," *Engineering Education* 68 (1977): 256–57.

4. John Butler Johnson, "Birth of a Profession," *Journal of the Association of Engineering Societies* 12 (1893): 78–87; Raymond H. Merritt, *Engineering in American Society, 1850–1875* (1969), chap. 1. See also Daniel H. Calhoun, *The American Civil Engineer: Origins and Conflict* (1960), 24–53, 206–9.

5. "Graduates from Technical Schools," *American Engineer* 10 (1885): 11–12; George W. Dickie, "Industrial Education," *Journal of the Association of Engineering Societies* 18 (1897): 160–61; "Good Advice to Engineering Graduates," *Engineering News* 29 (1893): 613; "Engineering Ignorance," *American Engineer* 20 (1890): 115; Edgar A. Marburg, "Nineteenth-Century Engineering," *Proceedings of the Engineers' Club of Philadelphia* 18 (1901): 15; "Annual Meeting of A.S.M.E.," *New York Times*, 4 Nov. 1881; Aubrey F. Burstall, *A History of Mechanical Engineering* (1965), 365; George S. Morison, *The New Epoch as Developed by the Manufacture of Power* (1903), 89–92. For the expansion of engineering education after the passage of the Morrill Land Grant Act, see Grayson, "Brief History of Engineering Education," 251.

6. Henry T. Eddy, "An Engineering Education," *Proceedings of the Society for the Promotion of Engineering Education* 5 (1887): 11; "The Ideal Engineering School," *Engineering News* 29 (1893): 419; "The Standing of the Mechanical Engineer," *American Engineer* 4 (1882): 254; George W. Dickie, "Engineering Graduates from Universities," *Cassier's Magazine* 18 (1900): 169–70; Thomas C. Clarke, "The Education of Civil Engineers," *Transactions of the American Society of Civil Engineers* (hereafter *Transactions ASCE*) 3 (1875): 557; McGivern, *First Hundred Years*, 112–14.

7. Frederick W. Taylor's first paper before the American Society of Mechanical Engineers analyzed a conflict between material and commercial efficiencies; Frederick W. Taylor, "The Relative Value of Water Gas and Gas from the Siemens Producer for Melting in the Open-Hearth Furnace," *Transactions of the American Society of Mechanical Engineers* (hereafter *Transactions ASME*) 7 (1886): 669–79. For other aspects of

this conflict, see "The Economics of Engineering," *American Engineer* 4 (1882): 233–34, and "The Standing of the Mechanical Engineer," 254.

8. "Commercial Engineering," *American Engineer* 10 (1885): 71. See also Samuel Haber, *Efficiency and Uplift: Scientific Management in the Progressive Era, 1890–1920* (1964), 11–17.

9. William H. Searles, "The Consulting Engineer in Municipal Affairs," *Journal of the Association of Engineering Societies* 19 (1897): 110, 113; "American Engineering Enterprise," *American Engineer* 9 (1885): 141; Robert H. Thurston, "Our Progress in Mechanical Engineering," *Transactions ASME* 2 (1881): 451.

10. "Speculation and Business," *Bankers' Magazine* 37 (1883): 85; Burton J. Hendrick, *The Life of Andrew Carnegie*, 2 vols. (1932), 1:195–97, 299; 2:67–68; Samuel Whinery, "Ethics for Civil Engineers," *Engineering News* 29 (26 Jan. 1893): 77; "The Real and the Humbug Engineering Discovery," *American Engineer* 8 (1884): 124; "The Bell Telephone Decision by the Supreme Court," *American Engineer* 15 (1888): 131.

11. Morison, *The New Epoch*, 35; William Kent, "The Relation of Engineering to Economics," *Engineering News* 34 (1895): 156–57.

12. Robert H. Thurston, "Functions of Technical Science in Education for Business and the Professions," *Science*, n.s. 17 (19 June 1903): 975; Robert H. Thurston, "Careers," *New York Tribune*, 29 March 1903. See also William Frederick Durand, *Robert Henry Thurston; a Biography, the Record of a Life of Achievement as Engineer, Educator, and Author* (1929), 209; William Kent, "Engineering as a Profession," *American Engineer* 10 (1885): 51; "Technical Education," *American Engineer*, 4 (1882): 263.

13. "Good Advice to Engineering Graduates," *Engineering News* 29 (1893): 613; John Butler Johnson, "The Birth of a Profession," *Journal of the Association of Engineering Societies* (hereafter *JAES*) 12 (1893): 78–87; Alexander C. Humphreys, "Engineering as a Learned Profession," *JAES* 18 (1897): 309; George H. Paine, "Engineering as a Profession," *Munsey's Magazine* 25 (August 1901), 752; Edgar A Marburg, "The Duty of the Engineer to Himself and His Profession," *Proceedings of the Engineers' Club of Philadelphia* 18 (1901): 216–19. George F. Swain, "Status of the Engineer," *Journal of the Association of Engineering Societies* 18 (1897): 187; Edwin T. Layton, Jr., *The Revolt of the Engineers: Social Responsibility and the American Engineering Profession* (1871): 3–4, 10.

14. "Professional Ethics and Etiquette," *Engineering Record* 27 (1892): 1–3; Charles Warren Hunt, *Historical Sketch of the American Society of Civil Engineers* (1897), 44; William Metcalf, "The Engineering Profession," *Transactions ASCE* 28 (1893), 391–95.

15. Benjamin F. Isherwood, "The Engineer and His Work," *Engineering News* 29 (1893): 21–22.

16. Samuel Whinery, "Ethics for Civil Engineers," *Engineering News* 29 (1893): 77; George S. Morison, "Presidential Address," *Engineering News* 33 (1895): 414–15; Morison, *The New Epoch*, 70.

17. There is no scholarly study of the growth of specialization in engineering. This description is derived from a reading of the histories of the four "founder societies."

18. "Specialists," *American Engineer* 3 (1882): 27.

19. George S. Morison, "Address at the Annual Convention . . . ," *Transactions ASCE* 33 (1895): 472–73; Lingan S. Randolph, "Engineering Specialization and Education," *Cassier's Magazine* 8 (1895): 533; William H. Wisely, *The American Civil Engineer, 1852–1974: The History, Traditions, and Development of the American Society of Civil Engineers, Founded 1852* (1974), 36–39.

20. Morison, "Address," 467–84; Randolph, "Engineering Specialization," 533; "Professional Relations of the Engineer: A Symposium," *Journal of the Association of Engineering Societies* 12 (1893), 437–53.

21. Clark C. Spence, *Mining Engineers and the American West: The Lace-Boot Brigade, 1849–1933* (1970), 253–77; Paine, "Engineering as a Profession," 752; Thomas A. Rickard, "Mining Engineering," in *Careers for the Coming Men. Practical and Authoritative Discussions of the Professions and Callings Open to Young Americans* (1904), 114; Samuel B. Christy, "The Growth of American Mining Schools and Their Relation to the Mining Industry," *Transactions, American Institute of Mining Engineers* (hereafter *Transactions AIME*) 23 (1893): 457.

22. Thomas A. Rickard, ed., *Rossiter Worthington Raymond: A Memorial* (1920) 1, 58; Arthur B. Parsons, ed., *Seventy-Five Years of Progress in the Mineral Industry, 1871–1946* (1947), 432; Joe B. Alford, "History of the Institute," in American Institute of Mining, Metallurgical and Petroleum Engineers, *Centennial Volume, 1871–1971* (1971), 239–44; "Engineering Societies," *American Engineer* 8 (1884): 195.

23. Parsons, *Seventy-Five Years of Progress*, 403; "Richard P. Rothwell," *Engineering and Mining Journal* 71 (1901), 486–87; Andrew Bryan, *The Evolution of Health and Safety in Mines* (1975).

24. Harold C. Passer, *The Electrical Manufacturers, 1875–1900: A Study in Competition, Entrepreneurship, Technical Change and Economic Growth* (1953), 343; Robert H. Thurston, "Progress and Tendency of Mechanical Engineering During the Nineteenth Century," *Popular Science Monthly* 59 (1901): 35; Bruce Sinclair, *A Centennial History of the American Society of Mechanical Engineers, 1880–1980* (1981).

25. See Haber, *Efficiency and Uplift*, 1–30.

26. See Haber, *Efficiency and Uplift*, chaps. 2, 3.

27. More attention might be given to Porter and the "industrial betterment" movement. See Holbrook Fitz-John Porter "The Rationale of the Industrial Betterment Movement," *Cassier's Magazine* 30 (1906): 343–47, and his "Higher Law in the Industrial World," *Engineering Magazine* 29 (1905): 641–55.

28. Robert H. Thurston, "Electrical Engineering as a Profession," *New York Evening Post*, 10 Sept. 1898; Thomas C. Martin, "Address to Fellow Members of the Institute," *Transactions of the American Institute of Electrical Engineers* 4 (1887): 124–28; Charles F. Scott, "The Institute's First Half Century," *Electrical Engineering* 53 (May 1934): 647; A. Mi-

chael McMahon, *The Makings of a Profession: A Century of Electrical Engineering* (1984).

29. Alfred O. Tate, *Edison's Open Door: The Life Story of Thomas A. Edison, A Great Individualist* (1938), 278–79.

30. Scott, "The Institute's First Half Century," 645–70.

31. F. B. Crocker, "The Electrical Distribution of Power in Workshops," *Journal of the Franklin Institute* 151 (1901) 1–28; Passer, *The Electrical Manufacturers*, 321–62.

32. "The Status of Engineers and a Proposed Plan for Improvement of It," *Engineering News* 29 (1893): 515; Alexander C. Humphreys, "Engineering as a Learned Profession," *Journal of the Association of Engineering Societies* 18 (1897): 309; "Pay and Standing of Engineers," *Engineering News* 29 (1893): 514. See also Edgar A. Marburg, "The Duty of the Engineer to Himself and His Profession," *Proceedings of the Engineers' Club of Philadelphia* 18 (1901): 217; Mortimer E. Cooley, *Scientific Blacksmith* (1947), 247.

33. For a biographical sketch of the career of William Kent, see the entry in *Dictionary of American Biography* (1933), 10:348–49.

34. Alfred D. Chandler, Jr., *The Visible Hand: The Managerial Revolution in American Business* (1977), 302–14; John B. Rae, "The Engineer as Business Man in American Industry," *Explorations in Entrepreneurial History* 7 (1954): 101–2; L. S. Randolph, "Engineering Specialization and Education," *Cassier's Magazine* 8 (1895): 533.

35. Morison, *The New Epoch*, 44; Robert H. Thurston, "The Work and Policy of the Mechanical Engineer," *Van Nostrand's Eclectic Engineering Magazine* 27 (1882): 482, and Robert H. Thurston, "Progress and Tendency of Mechanical Engineering during the Nineteenth Century," *Popular Science Monthly* 59 (1901): 134, 141.

36. Charles F. Thwing, *College Administration* (1900), 291; William H. Burr, "The Ideal Engineering Education," *Scientific American Supp.*, 36 (1893): 26; Palmer C. Ricketts, "Present Favorable and Unfavorable Tendencies in Engineering Education," *Proceedings, World Engineering Congress* 1 (1893): 72; Humphreys, "Engineering as a Learned Profession," 310; Robert Fletcher, "The Present Status and Tendencies of Engineering Education in the United States," *Proceedings of the Society for the Promotion of Engineering Education* 8 (1900): 189 (hereafter *Proc. SPEE*); Robert H. Thurston, "Mission of Science," *American Engineer* 8 (1884): 151.

37. "Supply and Demand in the Engineering Profession," *Engineering News* 32 (1894): 13; Robert H. Thurston, "Functions of Technical Science in Education for Business and the Professions," *Science*, n.s. 17 (1903): 974; Michael Bezilla, *Engineering Education at Penn State: A Century in the Land-Grant Tradition* (1981), 41, 49; Edgar A. Marburg, "Historical Sketch of the Engineers' Club," *Proceedings, Engineers' Club of Philadelphia* 18 (1901): 63; Henry T. Eddy, "On Engineering Education," *Proc. SPEE* 5 (1887): 16; Ira O. Baker, "Address of the President," *Proc. SPEE* 8 (1900): 26, and his "Engineering Education in the United States at the End of the Century," *Science*, n.s. 12 (1900): 666–

74; W. E. Wickenden, *Report of the Investigation of Engineering Education, 1923–1929* (1930), 1001.

38. W. S. Aldrich, "Engineering Education," *Journal of the Franklin Institute*, 140 (1898): 262; Anson Marston, "Original Investigations by Engineering Schools: A Duty to the Public and the Profession," *Proc. SPEE* 8 (1900): 235; Robert H. Thurston, "Scientific Research," *Science*, n.s. 16 (1902): 449; James Kip Finch, *Trends in Engineering Education: The Columbia Experience* (1948): 18–19; Richard S. Kirby and others, *Engineering in History* (1956), 510; "The Ideal Engineering School," *Engineering News* 29 (1893): 513; *American Engineer* 10 (1885): 41; William Kent, "Engineering as a Profession," *Van Nostrand's Eclectic Engineering Magazine* 33 (1885): 89; Robert H. Thurston, "Functions of Technical Science in Education," 963–65; Charles C. Brown, "The Desirability of Instruction of Undergraduates in the Ethics of the Engineering Profession," *Proc. SPEE* 4 (1886): 242 ff.; John B. Johnson, "The Birth of a Profession," *Journal of the Association of Engineering Societies* 12 (1893): 78–87.

39. Arthur W. Locke, "The Engineer in His Relations to His Clients," *Journal of the Association of Engineering Societies* 2 (1893): 445; Whinery, "Ethics for Civil Engineers," 78; J. C. Bayles, "Professional Ethics," *Transactions AIME* 14 (Feb. 1886): 611; Octave Chanute, "Address," *Transactions ASCE* 24 (1891): 429. See also Octave Chanute, "Annual Address," *Transactions ASCE* 9 (1880): 254, and his "Ethics of Consulting Practice," *Engineering News*, 28 (1892): 444.

40. Morison, *The New Epoch*, 68–69.

41. Kent, "Engineering as a Profession," *Van Nostrand's Eclectic Engineering Magazine* 33 (August 1885): 93; H. G. Prout, "The Engineer and His Country," *Wisconsin Engineer* 3 (1899): 77–78; Morison, *The New Epoch*, 76.

42. Humphreys, "Engineering as a Learned Profession," 307; M. S. Parker, "Engineering Compensation," *Journal of the Association of Engineering Societies* 18 (1897): 100; "Concerning the Status of Engineers," *Engineering News* 29 (1893): 589.

43. Eckley B. Coxe, "The Prospects for Young Engineers," *Engineering News* 32 (1894): 5. "Suggestive Seals" (see n. 1), 229.

44. "Suggestive Seals," 229.

45. "Suggestive Seals," 229; "The Special Apprentice," American Engineering and Railway Journal 77 (April 1903): 140; McGivern, *First Hundred Years* (see n.3), 152–84; J. Shirley Eaton, "Educational Training for Railway Service," in *Report of the Commissioner of Education, 1898–1899* (1900), 875; Ernest Ellis, "Licensing and Registration of Engineers in the United States," *Mining and Metallurgy* 26 (1945): 22–27.

46. Morison, *The New Epoch*, 63, 65; "The Civil Engineer," *Engineering News* 33 (1895): 414–15; G. H. Babcock, "The Engineer, His Commission, and His Achievement," *Transactions of the American Society of Mechanical Engineers* 9 (1888): 23–37.

47. "A 'Close' Profession," *Engineering News* 35 (1896): 224, 226, 274; Stuart Morris, "Stalled Professionalism: The Recruitment of Railway Of-

ficials in the United States, 1885–1940," *Business History Review* 47 (1973): 323–28; "Prestige," *Oxford English Dictionary: Second Edition* (1989): 425–26.

48. "The Prospects for Young Engineers: A Symposium," *Engineering News* 32 (1894): 5–6; "Supply and Demand in the Engineering Profession," *Engineering News* 32 (1894): 13–14.

49. "The Ownership of Employees' Inventions," *Engineering News* 27 (1892): 180; "Engineers as Inventors," *The American Engineer* 19 (1890), 103; "The Faith of Inventors," *The American Engineer* 20 (1890): 257.

50. Brown, "Instruction of Undergraduates," 242; Morison, *The New Epoch*, 65; "Proposed Code of Engineering Ethics," *Engineering News* 30 (1893): 117–18; R. E. McMath, "Engineers: Their Relations and Standing," *Journal of the Association of Engineering Societies* 6 (1887) 78–87.

Chapter 10

1. John Shaw Billings quoted in Fielding H. Garrison, *John Shaw Billings: A Memoir* (1915), 146; Henry Adams, *The Education of Henry Adams* (1931), 248; Stephen Smith, "Civil and Military Surgeons," in *"Doctor in Medicine" and Other Papers on Professional Subjects* ([1872] 1972), 222. For the role of physicians in the Civil War, see John Shaw Billings, "American Inventions and Discoveries in Medicine, Surgery, and Practical Sanitation," *Boston Medical and Surgical Journal* 124 (1891): 351; Harry Miller Lydenberg, *John Shaw Billings, Creator of the National Medical Library and Its Catalogue . . .* (1924), 20; *Medical News* (Philadelphia) 46 (1883): 385, 64 (1894): 43; U.S. Surgeon-General's Office, *Medical and Surgical History of the War of the Rebellion, (1861–1865)* 3 vols. (1870–1888).

2. For Billings's Civil War experiences, see Garrison, *John Shaw Billings*, 19–135. John S. Billings, "The Rights, Duties, and Privileges of the Community in Relation to Those of the Individual in Regard to Public Health," in *Selections from Public Health Reports and Papers Presented at the Meetings of the American Public Health Association (1873–1883)*, ed. Barbara Gutmann Rosenkrantz (1977), 50; John S. Billings, "Medicine as a Career," *Forum* 14 (1893): 725–34.

3. Garrison, *John Shaw Billings*, 136–37; John Shaw Billings, "A Report on Barracks and Hospitals; with Descriptions of Military Posts," U.S. War Department, Surgeon General's Office, *Circular No. 4* (1870) and "A Report on the Hygiene of the United States Army, with Descriptions of Military Posts," U.S. War Department, Surgeon General's Office, *Circular No. 8* (1875).

4. Garrison, *John Shaw Billings*, 161–66, 183–90; John S. Billings, "The Registration of Vital Statistics," *Annual Report of the National Board of Health* (1883), 355–461; Raymond Pearl, "Some Notes on the Contributions of Dr. John Shaw Billings to the Development of Vital Statistics," *Bulletin of the History of Medicine* 6 (1938): 387–97; Alan M. Chesney, *The Johns Hopkins Hospital and the Johns Hopkins Uni-*

versity School of Medicine; a Chronicle . . . 3 vols. (1943), 1:25–33, 46–49, 54–61, 149, 241–55.

5. John S. Billings, "The National Board of Health and National Quarantine," *Transactions of the American Medical Association* 31 (1880): 454–55; Billings, "Rights, Duties, and Privileges," 48–50.

6. John S. Billings, "The Medical College of Ohio Before the War: Address to the Society of the Alumni of the Ohio Medical College . . . ," *Cincinnati Lancet-Clinic* 20 (1888): 297–305; Garrison, *John Shaw Billings,* 8–13.

7. Billings, "Rights, Duties, and Privileges"; *Life and Correspondence of Henry Ingersoll Bowditch,* ed. Vincent Y. Bowditch, 2 vols. (1902), 2:243–45; *Memphis Appeal,* 18 Jan. 1880; Garrison, *John Shaw Billings,* 176–80. See also John M. Toner, "Boards of Health in the United States," in *Selections from Public Health Reports and Papers . . . (1873–1883),* 500; John McLeod Keating, *History of the City of Memphis and Shelby County, Tennessee,* vol 1 (1888); John McLeod Keating, *A History of the Yellow Fever: The Yellow Fever Epidemic of 1878 in Memphis, Tennessee* (1879).

8. John S. Billings, "The Plans and Purposes of the Johns Hopkins Hospital," *Medical News* 54 (1889): 505–10. For Charles W. Eliot, see Thomas F. Harrington, *The Harvard Medical School: A History, Narrative and Documentary, 1782–1905,* 3 vols. (1905), 3:1020–43, 1057. For William Pepper, see Fred B. Rogers, "William Pepper, 1848–1898," *Journal of Medical Education* 34 (1959): 885–89. See also Samuel Haber, "The Professions and Higher Education in America: A Historical View," in *Higher Education and the Labor Market,* ed. Margaret S. Gordon (1974), 264–65.

9. See Billings's playful essay, Dr. Newlenz [pseud.], "Microscopical Memoranda," 21–23, and, more seriously, "The Military Medical Officer at the Opening of the Twentieth Century," 263–69, in *Selected Papers of John Shaw Billings,* ed. Frank B. Rogers (1965). Garrison, *John Shaw Billings,* 270–71, 392; Chesney, *The Johns Hopkins Hospital,* 1:87, 103; Harvey W. Cushing, *The Life of Sir William Osler,* 2 vols. (1940), 1:297; William Osler, "Medicine," in *The Progress of the Century,* ed. Alfred Russel Wallace and others (1901), 176–77.

10. Charles P. Emerson, "Reminiscences of Sir William Osler," 347, and William H. Welch, "Sir William Osler," iii, *International Association of Medical Museums Bulletin* 9 (1926). This entire issue of the *Bulletin* was the "Sir William Osler Memorial Number." See also Willam Osler, *Aequanimitas, with Other Addresses to Medical Students, Nurses, and Practitioners of Medicine* (1905) and *Counsels and Ideals* (1906), 57–64; Chesney, *The Johns Hopkins Hospital,* 103–7.

11. Simon Flexner and James Thomas Flexner, *William Henry Welch and the Heroic Age of American Medicine* (1941), 152; Osler, "Medicine," 176–77; Henry E. Sigerist, *American Medicine* (1934), 124–30, and *The Great Doctors* (1958), 383. See also Cushing, *Life of Sir William Osler,* and Donald Harnish Fleming, *William H. Welch and the Rise of Modern Medicine* (1954).

12. Chesney, *The Johns Hopkins Hospital*, 1:91–95, 150–164; John Shaw Billings, "Hospital Construction and Organization," in *Hospital Plans: Five Essays Relating to the Construction, Organization and Management of Hospitals, Contributed by Their Authors for the Use of the Johns Hopkins Hospital* (1875), 3; Richard H. Shryock, *The Unique Influence of the Johns Hopkins University on American Medicine* (1953). For Welch's analysis of German contributions to medicine, see his introduction to Theodor Billroth, *The Medical Sciences in the German Universities: A Study in the History of Civilization* (1924).

13. Austin Flint, "The Revolution in Medicine," *Forum* 10 (1891): 527–36; Osler, "Medicine," 181–92; Austin Flint, "Address on Some of the Relations of Physiology to the Practice of Medicine," *Transactions of the New York Medical Association* 2 (1885): 220–39; William H. Welch, "Adaptation in Pathological Processes," *Transactions of the Congress of American Physicians and Surgeons*, 4th sess. (1897), 284–310; William Clendenin, "The General Causes of Disease," in *Selections from Public Health Reports and Papers . . . (1873–1883)*, 49–50. See also the review of Claude Bernard's *Rapport sur le progrès et la marche de la physiologie générale en France* in *The North American Review* 107 (1868): 322–28, and, more generally, John E. Lesch, *Science and Medicine in France: The Emergence of Experimental Physiology, 1790–1855* (1984).

14. Donald MacLean, "Presidential Address: A Few Living Issues Affecting the History of Medicine, and What Became of Them," *Journal of the American Medical Association* (hereafter *JAMA*) 24 (1895): 698; Welch, "Adaptation in Pathological Processes," 286, 288–91, 310.

15. William G. Rothstein, *American Physicians in the Nineteenth Century: From Sects to Science* (1972), 261–81; Phyllis Allen Richmond, "American Attitudes toward the Germ Theory of Disease, 1860–1880," *Journal of the History of Medicine* 9 (1954): 428–54. See also T. H. Huxley, "The Connection of the Biological Sciences with Medicine; Address at the International Medical Congress," *Popular Science Monthly* 19 (1881): 807.

16. Osler, "Medicine," 174, 181–92; William H. Welch, "The Johns Hopkins University," in *Papers and Addresses*, ed. William H. Welch, 3 vols. (1920), 3:21–22; John Shaw Billings, "Progress in Medicine in the Nineteenth Century," in *The Nineteenth Century: A Review of Progress* (1901), 336; Chesney, *The Johns Hopkins Hospital*, 1:158–60. Chesney's study of Johns Hopkins in the early years includes brief biographical sketches of the graduates who went on to eminent medical careers.

17. Stephen Smith, "On the Limitations and Modifying Conditions of Human Longevity, the Basis of Sanitary Work," in *Selections from Public Health Reports and Papers . . . (1873–1883)*, 1–17; the quote is from p. 10. For the general background of the creation of the American Public Health Association, see Wilson G. Smillie, *Public Health: Its Promise for the Future; A Chronicle of the Development of Public Health in the United States, 1607–1914* (1955), 296–306.

18. Henry M. Lyman, *Medical Record* (New York), 26 June, 4 Sept.,

and 6 Nov. 1880; Henry M. Lyman, "A Review of the Present State of Exact Knowledge Regarding the Causation of Epidemic Infectious Diseases," in *Selections from Public Health Reports and Papers . . . (1873–1883)*, 88–102. Charles V. Chapin, "Preventive Medicine and Natural Selection," *Journal of Social Science* 41 (1903), 57; Stanford E. Chaillé, "A Consideration of the Objections Urged by Some Evolutionists Against Sanitary Laws, Boards of Health, and the Stamping-Out of Certain Epidemic Diseases" [1880], in *Selections from Public Health Reports and Papers . . . (1873–1883)*, 279–98; Billings, "Rights, Duties, and Privileges," 48–52.

19. John S. Billings, "The Relation of Hospitals to Public Health," *Lend a Hand* 11 (1893): 175. See also Frank B. Rogers, ed., *Selected Papers of John Shaw Billings*, 7.

20. John S. Billings, "The National Board of Health and the National Quarantine," *Transactions of the American Medical Association* 31 (1880): 454; Smillie, *Public Health: Its Promise for the Future*, 331–39; see also Peter W. Bruton, "The National Board of Health" (Ph.D. diss., University of Maryland, 1974).

21. Barbara G. Rosenkrantz, "Cart before Horse: Theory, Practice and Professional Image in Public Health, 1870–1920," *Journal of the History of Medicine* 29 (1974): 62, 66; Billings, "Rights, Duties, and Privileges," 48–49.

22. Stephen Smith, "On the Reciprocal Relation of Efficient Public Health Service and the Highest Educational Qualifications of the Medical Profession," *American Public Health Association Reports, 1874–1875* 2 (1876), 187–200; John Shaw Billings, "Higher Medical Education," *American Journal of Medical Sciences* 76 (1878): 187; Samuel L. Baker, "Physician Licensure Laws in the United States, 1865–1915," *Journal of the History of Medicine and Allied Sciences* 39 (1984): 173–94.

23. Edward T. Caswell, *Reform in Medical Education the Aim of the Academy* (1881), 1–16. See also John Shaw Billings's assessment of the various reasons why men became physicians and his own distaste for purely economic motivations, in "A Century of American Medicine, 1776–1876: Literature and Institutions," in *Selected Papers of John S. Billings*, 72–75; P.S. Conner, "Medical Charities," *The Clinic* (Cincinnati) 14 (1878): 229–32.

24. H. C. Wood, "The Medical Profession, the Medical Sects, and the Law," *New England and Yale Review* 51 (1889): 118 ff.

25. Dent v. West Virginia, *U.S. Reports* 129 (1888): 116; Frances P. DeLancy, *The Licensing of Professionals in West Virginia* (1938), 25; Samuel L. Baker, "Physician Licensure Laws in the United States," 173–94.

26. John Henry Rauch, "Address on State Medicine," *JAMA* 6 (1886): 645–52; George Rosen, *A History of Public Health* (1958), 246–48; James Cassedy, *Charles V. Chapin and the Public Health Movement* (1962), 44–45; F. Garvin Davenport, "John Henry Rauch and Public Health in Illinois, 1877–1891," *Journal of the Illinois State Historical*

Society 44 (1951); K. H. Schnepp, "Medical Licensure in Illinois: A Historical Review," *Illinois Medical Journal* (1976): 147–48.

27. Morris Fishbein, *A History of the American Medical Association, 1847 to 1947* (1947), 19–58; Rothstein, *American Physicians in the Nineteenth Century,* 170–73, 199–200, 299–304, 314–16. John Collins Warren, *Medical Societies: Their Organization and the Nature of Their Work; an Address . . .* (1881), 31–68; Samuel D. Gross, *Autobiography of Samuel D. Gross . . .* , ed. Samuel W. and A. Haller Gross (1887), 1:394; Isaac Newton Danforth, *The Life of Nathan Smith Davis* (1907); Thomas N. Bonner, "Nathan Smith Davis and the Growth of Chicago Medicine," *Bulletin of the History of Medicine* 26 (1952): 370; *Medical News* (Philadelphia) 68 (1896): 533, and 63 (1893): 277; James B. Herrick, "Nathan Smith Davis," *Bulletin of the Society of Medical History of Chicago* 10 (1935): 65.

28. Mary Roth Walsh, *"Doctors Wanted: No Women Need Apply": Sexual Barriers in the Medical Profession, 1835–1975* (1977), 106–46; "Discussion on the Female Physician Question in the American Medical Association," *New England Journal of Medicine* 84 (1871): 350–74; John S. Haller, Jr., "The Physician Versus the Negro: Medical and Anthropological Concepts of Race in the Late 19th Century," *Bulletin of the History of Medicine* 44 (1970): 154–67. See also John S. Haller, Jr., *Outcasts from Evolution: Scientific Attitudes of Racial Inferiority, 1859–1900* (1971), 157–202, and John S. Haller and Robin M. Haller, *The Physician and Sexuality in Victorian America* (1974), 48–61.

29. Herbert M. Morais, *The History of the Negro in Medicine* (1967), 52–58; Samuel C. Busey, *Personal Reminiscences and Recollections of Forty-Six Years' Membership in the Medical Society of the District of Columbia* (1895), 276–77; John B. Blake, "Women and Medicine in Ante-Bellum America," *Bulletin of the History of Medicine* 29 (1965) 113–26; Gloria Moldow, *Women Doctors in Gilded-Age Washington: Race, Gender, and Professionalization* (1987).

30. W. Montague Cobb, *The First Negro Medical Society* (1939), 39.

31. Helen Buckler, *Daniel Hale Williams: Negro Surgeon* (1968); *Who's Who in Colored America,* (1927), 1:221–22.

32. Myles Vandahurst Lynk, *Sixty Years of Medicine; or, The Life and Times of Dr. Myles V. Lynk: An Autobiography* (1951); Morais, *History of the Negro in Medicine,* 59–60.

33. Mary Putnam Jacobi, "Woman in Medicine," in *Woman's Work in America,* ed. Annie Nathan Meyer (1891), 139–205; Madeleine B. Stern, "Lucy Beaman Hobbs Taylor," in *Notable American Women, 1607–1950,* ed. Edward T. James and others, 3 vols. (1971), 3:433–34; Eleanor Flexner, *Century of Struggle: The Woman's Rights Movement in the United States,* rev. ed. (1975), 117–21, 237; Regina Morantz, "The Lady and Her Physician," in *Clio's Consciousness Raised: New Perspectives on the History of Women,* ed. Mary Hartman and Lois W. Banner (1974), 48–50; Jennie G. Drennan, "Sexual Intemperance: Some Explanation of What Is Meant by the Term," *New York Medical Journal* 54 (1901):

70; Jennie G. Drennan, "Sexual Intemperance," *International Record of Medicine* 83 (1901): 19–20; Carol Lopate, *Women in Medicine* (1968), 6.

34. Ruth Putnam, ed., *Life and Letters of Mary Putnam Jacobi* (1925), 169; Gulielma Fell Alsop, *History of the Woman's Medical College, Philadelphia, Pennsylvania, 1850–1950* (1950), 127. See also Jean Carwile Masteller, "The Women Doctors of Howells, Phelps, and Jewett: The Conflict of Marriage and Career," in *Critical Essays on Sarah Orne Jewett*, ed. Gwen L. Nagel (1984), 135–47; Esther P. Lovejoy, *Woman Doctors of the World* (1957), 123.

35. Roy Lubove, "Mary Corinna Putnam Jacobi," in *Notable American Women*, ed. Edward T. James and others, 3 vols. (1971), 2:263–65; Mary Putnam Jacobi, "The Needs and Shortcomings of Woman Physicians," *Boston Medical and Surgical Journal* 133 (1895): 146. See also the discussion of Putnam in Regina Markell Morantz, "Feminism, Professionalism, and Germs," *American Quarterly* 34 (1982): 460–78, and Regina Markell Morantz-Sanchez, *Sympathy and Science* (1985).

36. Edwin R. Bingham, "Bethenia Angelina Owens-Adair," *Notable American Women*, ed. Edward T. James and others, 3 vols. (1971), 2:657–59.

37. My characterization of the division of the profession on this issue comes from a wide reading in the materials of this controversy. For a similar, contemporary appraisal, see *New York Times*, 9 June 1882, 4.

38. Haber, "The Professions and Higher Education in America" (see n. 8), 248–49, 251–52; Fishbein, *History of the American Medical Association*, 19–58.

39. Martin Kaufman, *Homeopathy in America: The Rise and Fall of a Medical Heresy* (1971), 121; Rothstein, *American Physicians in the Nineteenth Century*, 243–46; Richard H. Shryock, *Medical Licensing in America* (1967), 51–52; William Osler, "The License to Practice," *JAMA* 12 (1889): 649–54; see also Harris L. Coulter, *Divided Legacy: The Conflict Between Homeopathy and the American Medical Association: Science and Ethics in American Medicine, 1800–1914* (1973). Frank Hastings Hamilton, *Conversations Between Drs. Warren and Putnam on the Subject of Medical Ethics* (1884), 36.

40. *New York Times*, 14 Feb. and 19 Feb. 1882; Alfred C. Post and others, *An Ethical Symposium; Being a Series of Papers Concerning Medical Ethics and Etiquette from the Liberal Standpoint* (1883), 20, 212; Austin Flint, *Medical Ethics and Etiquette* (1883), 3; Chancey Depew Leake, ed., *Percival's Medical Ethics* (1927), 55; Donald Konold, *A History of American Medical Ethics* (1962), 114.

41. Konold, *History of American Medical Ethics*, 124–26; Leake, *Percival's Medical Ethics*, 55 ff.; Rothstein, *American Physicians in the Nineteenth Century*, 314–16.

42. Garrison, *John Shaw Billings* (see n. 1), 260–63; Busey, *Personal Reminiscences and Recollections*, 237; Rogers, *Selected Papers of John Shaw Billings* (see n. 9), 224–25; Austin Flint, Sr., "Annual Ad-

dress," *Journal of the American Medical Association* 2 (1884): 505–13; *New York Medical Journal* 42 (1885): 44–45; Fishbein, *History of the American Medical Association*, 124.

43. "Why the New Organization of the Congress Should be Repudiated," *Medical News* (Philadelphia) 53 (1888): 96; Cushing, *William Osler* (see n. 9), 1:255; John B. Hamilton, *Transactions of the International Medical Congress: Ninth Session*, 5 vols. (1887), 1:10–16, 5:Appendix, 735–61.

44. *Transactions of the Congress of American Physicians and Surgeons* 1 (1888): xiii-xxv; James Howard Means, *The Association of American Physicians: Its First Seventy-Five Years* (1961), 29; Fishbein, *History of the American Medical Association*, 135; "The Great Medical Congress," *Science* 12 (1888): 146–47.

45. Fishbein, *History of the American Medical Association*, 146–49; Medicus, "The Advertising Question," *JAMA* 22 (1894): 438–39; "Letter to the Editor," *JAMA* (1894): 480–81; *Medical News* (Philadelphia) 64 (28 Apr. 1894): 263.

46. Fishbein, *History of the American Medical Association*, 188–96; Rothstein, *American Physicians in the Nineteenth Century*, 316–22; P. Maxwell Forshay, "The Organization of the Medical Profession," *Forum* 32 (1901): 168.

47. James G. Burrow, *AMA: Voice of American Medicine* (1963), 49–51.

48. George Rosen, *The Specialization of Medicine* (1944). On the rise of "Baconian" thought among American doctors, see George H. Daniels, *American Science in the Age of Jackson* (1968), 140–41. Worthington Hooker and others, "Report of the Committee on Medical Ethics," 501–2, and D. H. Storer, "Address," 55–66, *Transactions of the American Medical Association* 17 (1866). Edwin C. Seguin, "The Cultivation of Specialties in Medicine," *Opera Minora* (1884), 673–83; William Osler, "Remarks on Specialism," *Medical News* (Philadelphia), 60 (1892), 542–44; William H. Welch, "On Some of the Humane Aspects of Medical Science," in *The Papers and Addresses of William Henry Welch* (1920) 3:3–8; W. H. Watney, "Specialism in Medicine," *Medical Register* (Philadelphia) 26 (1887): 36–39; A. W. Herzog, "Specialist and General Practitioner," *New York Medical Journal* 54 (1891): 325.

49. This discussion of the disappearance of the cordwainer in nineteenth-century America is based upon John R. Commons's classic study, "American Shoemakers, 1648–1895," *Quarterly Journal of Economics* 21 (1907): 39–81.

50. Robert T. Morris, *Fifty Years a Surgeon* (1935), 110; John S. Billings, "Literature and Institutions," quoted in Garrison, *John Shaw Billings* (see n. 1), 169–70; W. W. Keen, "Surgery," in *The Progress of the Century* (1901), 217–61; George F. Shrady, "American Achievements in Surgery," *Forum* 18 (1894): 172–78; J. H. Brinton, *The March of Surgery* (1882).

51. Shrady, "American Achievements in Surgery," 176; H. O. Marcy, "Modern Surgical Technique," *Medical Record* (New York) 47 (1895):

257–59; A. E. Bulson, Jr., "The Development of Operative Skill on the Part of the Surgeon," in *A System of Ophthalmic Operations . . .* , ed. Casey Albert Wood, 2 vols. (1911), 1:179–204; R. C. Coffey, "Psychology and Habit in Surgical Technique," *JAMA* 39 (1902): 536–38.

52. J. E. Moore, "The Trend in Modern Surgery," *JAMA* 40 (1903): 953–56; James Ewing Mears, *The Evolution of Surgery* (1904), 1–16; Frederick F. Cartwright, *The Development of Modern Surgery* (1967), 310–12.

53. Morris J. Vogel, "The Transformation of the American Hospital, 1850–1920," in *Health Care in America: Essays in Social History*, ed. Susan Reverby (1979), 108–12; Lewis S. Pilcher, "On the Organization of the Surgical Staff in General Hospitals," *Annals of Surgery* 2 (1885): 399 ff.; E. T. Tappey, "Some Individualities in Surgery," *Transactions of the Michigan Medical Society* 17 (1893): 24–37.

54. *JAMA* 35 (1900): 501. See also George Rosen, "The Hospital: Historical Sociology of a Community Institution," in *From Medical Police to Social Medicine: Essays on the History of Health Care* (1974), 274–303.

55. On laboratories as the center of science in hospitals, see H. H. Hurd, "Laboratories and Hospital Work," *Bulletin of the American Academy of Medicine* 2 (1895–97): 483–95; C. N. B. Camac, "Hospital and Ward Clinical Laboratories," *JAMA* 35 (1900): 219 ff.; W. G. McDonald, "The Relation of the Clinical Laboratory to Modern Surgery," *Medical News* (New York) 76 (1900): 161–64. Edward Kremers and George Urdang, *History of Pharmacy* (1951), 229–51; William J. Gies, *Dental Education in the United States and Canada* (1926), 7, 39–44; Dorothy Fahs Beck, "The Development of the Dental Profession in the United States" (Master's thesis, University of Chicago, 1932), 87–103; L. C. Ingersoll, "Supplemental Report on Education," *American Dental Association Transactions* (1880), 143.

56. Charles R. E. Koch, ed., *History of Dental Surgery*, 2 vols. (1909), 1:101, 173–76; J. Ben Robinson, "Dental History: The Foundations of Professional Dentistry," in *Proceedings, Dental Centenary Celebration . . .* , Maryland State Dental Association, Dental Centenary Committee (1940), 1016–20, 1039–41; Charles William Everest, *The Poets of Connecticut, with Biographical Sketches* (1843), 187–89.

57. J. F. Smithcors, *The American Veterinary Profession: Its Background and Development* (1963), 292–97; James R. Gregg, *The American Optometric Association: A History* (1972), 4–7; Maurice E. Cox, *Optometry, the Profession: Its Antecedents, Birth, and Development* (1957), 31; Charles Prentice, *Legalized Optometry and Memoirs of Its Founders* (1926).

58. Prentice, *Legalized Optometry*, 134, 288; E. L. Patch, *Proceedings of the American Pharmaceutical Association* 41 (1893): 232; "Shall It Be a Profession or a Trade?" *Medical Record* 10 (1875): 682; Edward Kremers and George Urdang, *History of Pharmacy: A Guide and a Survey*, 2d ed. (1951), 247–49; Beck, "Development of the Dental Profession," 180–83; Gies, *Dental Education* 4; Joseph Winters England,

"The Status of Prerequisite Laws and Pharmaceutical Licensure," *American Journal of Pharmacy* 93 (1921): 539; *American Dental Association Transactions* (1889), 242.

59. Beck, "Development of the Dental Profession," 183–85; Cox, *Optometry, the Profession*, 33; Smithcors, *American Veterinary Profession*, 390–93, 497.

60. "The Old and the New Pharmacy," 135–38, "The Purpose of the National Association of Retail Druggists," iv, and "The Needs of the American Pharmaceutical Association," 438, *American Journal of Pharmacy* 72 (1900).

61. "Report of the Special Committee on the History of the Classification of Dentists by the Census Bureau for the Eleventh Census," *Transactions of the American Dental Association* (1895), 150–67.

62. Editorial, *JAMA* 31 (1898): 932–35.

63. "The Physician as a Sociologic Factor," 78, and "The Sweat Shop and Disease," 697, *Medical News* (Philadelphia) 64 (1894). Henry Dwight Chapin, "Social and Physiological Inequality," *Popular Science Monthly* 30 (1887): 761–63; Billings, "Relation of Hospitals to Public Health" (see n. 19), 170–71; J. M. DaCosta, "The Higher Professional Life," *Popular Science Monthly* 23 (1883): 425; Clarence J. Blake, "The Sociological Status of the Physician," *Science*, n.s., 11 (1900): 773; Billings, "Medicine as a Career" (see n. 2), 725–34; Post, *Ethical Symposium*, 20–26; Welch, *Papers and Addresses* (see n. 16), 2:19–22; Rogers, *Selected Papers of John Shaw Billings* (see n. 9), 114. Paul Starr, in the otherwise excellent study *The Social Transformation of American Medicine* (1982), tries to describe the medical profession primarily as an economic interest group. The classic late nineteenth-century statements of the protector/dependent relation were by S. Weir Mitchell: *Two Lectures on the Conduct of Medical Life* (1893) and *Doctor and Patient* (1888), which went through twelve published editions. Leake, *Percival's Medical Ethics*, 214, 225.

64. John S. Billings, "Progress in Medicine in the Nineteenth Century," in *The Nineteenth Century: A Review of Progress* (1901), 346; John S. Billings, "The Effects of His Occupation upon the Physician," *International Journal of Ethics* 4 (1893): 46; William Osler, "Address on Medicine," *Medical News* (Philadelphia) 68 (1896): 507 ff.; A. L. Benedict, "Medicine as a Profession," *Lippincott's Magazine* 54 (1894): 811–14; Henry S. Williams, "A Century's Progress in Scientific Medicine," *Harper's Monthly Magazine* 99 (1899): 52.

65. Rothstein, *American Physicians in the Nineteenth Century*, 272–81. Welch's important paper, "Adaptation in Pathological Processes" (1897), was a turning point that linked interventionist medicine to the newest science; Austin Flint, Jr., *Medical News* (Philadelphia) 45 (1884): 592.

66. Flint, 595; Osler, *Aequanimitas* (see n. 10), 380; Mitchell, *Doctor and Patient*, 31; Austin Flint, *A Treatise on the Principles of Medicine* (1880), 1083; D. W. Cathell, *Book on the Physician Himself* (1889), 92.

67. Mitchell, *Two Lectures on the Conduct of Medical Life*, 50–51.

68. F. W. Hatch, *Address Delivered before the Sacramento Society of Medical Improvement* (1872), 4; Mitchell, *Two Lectures on the Conduct of Medical Life*, 32, 9; John Collins Warren, *Medical Societies: Their Organization and the Nature of Their Work* (1881), 67–68; William B. Atkinson, *Medical Organizations and Their Value* (1877), 8–9.

69. Baker, "Physician Licensure Laws in the United States" (see n. 25), 173–94; Morris J. Vogel, *The Invention of the Modern Hospital: Boston, 1870–1930* (1980), 64–67, 78–96. See also "Shall Physicians, or Shall Lay Trustee Boards of Charity, etc., Decide as to Medical Matters?" *Medical News* (Philadelphia) 65 (1894): 695; George M. Gould, "Hospitalism," *Medical News* (Philadelphia) 66 (1895): 702.

70. Alfred L. Loomis, "The President's Address," *Transactions of the Congress of American Physicians and Surgeons* 3 (1894): 314. For praise of the physician's conduct during epidemics, see Rufus W. Clark, *The Sources of a Physician's Power* (1863), 16–18; Keating, *History of the City of Memphis* (see n. 7), 1: 246–47 (on doctors in the great yellow fever epidemic of 1878), and Charles E. Rosenberg, *The Cholera Years* (1968), 69–70.

71. Cassedy, *Charles V. Chapin* (see n. 26), 30; Lewis A. Sayre, "Address to the American Medical Association," *New York Times*, 2 June 1880; John Walker Harrington, "the Physician and His Fees," *Munsey's Magazine* 25 (July 1901): 586; Williams, "Century's Progress in Scientific Medicine," 38–52; William Osler, "Address on Medicine," *Medical News* (Philadelphia) 69 (1896): 507; Sir James Paget, "The Cultivation of Medical Science," *Popular Science Monthly* 19 (1881): 783–84; William H. Welch, "The Johns Hopkins University," in *Papers and Addresses*, 3:19.

72. The best discussion of these paintings and their impact can be found in Lloyd Goodrich, *Thomas Eakins: His Life and Work*, 2 vols. (1982), 1:123–38, 2:39–51. They both ignited an expected uproar, not because of the heroic treatment of the two doctors, but owing to the realistic depiction of the bloody operations. Genteel art critics of the day thought that young ladies should not be exposed to such brutality. Eakins was called "the butcher." He replied, "all I was trying to do was to picture the soul of a great surgeon," 2:46. However, the critics *did* approve of the depiction of the two doctors; see Gordon Hendricks, *The Life and Works of Thomas Eakins* (1974), 90.

73. Goodrich, *Thomas Eakins*, 50.

74. A candid discussion of the mixed motives of physicians can be found in Flint, *Medical Ethics and Etiquette*, 8–9, 40–41, 76–78. See also Harrington, "The Physician and His Fees," 589; G. F. Shrady, "Pay of Physicians and Surgeons," *Forum* 18 (1894): 68–79; John S. Billings, "Literature and Institutions," in *A Century of American Medicine*, ed. E. H. Clarke (1876), 363–64; John S. Billings, "On Medical Museums," *Transactions of the American Congress of Physicians and Surgeons* 1 (1888): 355. On fee bills, see George Rosen, *Fees and Fee Bills: Some Economic Aspects of Medical Practice in Nineteenth-Century America* (1946).

75. For the ratio of doctors to the general population in the period 1870 to 1900, see U.S. Bureau of the Census, *Sixteenth Census: Population, Comparative Occupation Statistics for the United States . . . ,* ed. Alba M. Edwards (1943), 111. On fee bills becoming customary charges and the difficulties that followed, see Smith, *"Doctor in Medicine"* (see n. 1), 213; Daniel Drake, *Practical Essays on Medical Education and the Medical Profession in the United States* (1952), 100; Rosen, *Fees and Fee Bills,* 55–56; Wilhelm Moll, "Medical Fee Bills," *Virginia Medical Monthly* 93 (1966): 657–64.

76. On medical patents, see Susan Crawford, ed., *Digest of Official Actions: American Medical Association, 1846–1958* (1959), 547–48; Konold, *History of American Medical Ethics,* 20. On advertising, see *New York Times,* 27 Jan. 1878; Crawford, *Digest of Official Actions,* 669–70. "President's Address: Harvard Medical Alumni Association," *Boston Medical and Surgical Journal* 131 (1894): 137.

77. "Introductory Note by the Secretary of the Association," xi–xii, and Stephen Smith, "On the Limitations and Modifying Conditions of Human Longevity, the Basis of Sanitary Work," 1–17, in *Selections from Public Health Records and Papers . . .* (1873–1883). Elisha Harris, "General Health Laws and Local Ordinances, Considered with Reference to State and Local Sanitary Organization," in Elisha Harris *General Health Laws,* 472–82. See also John Duffy, "The American Medical Profession and Public Health," *Bulletin of the History of Medicine* 53 (1979): 1–13.

78. On the Flint family, see the various entries in the *Dictionary of American Biography;* also helpful is Francis J. Heringhaus, "Austin Flint," in *Builders of American Medicine: Being a Collection of Original Papers Read before the Victor C. Vaughan Society of the University of Ann Arbor,* ed. Thomas Findley, Jr. (1932), 109–32.

79. Austin Flint, "Vaccination," *North American Review,* 590–91; Chaillé, "A Consideration of the Objections Urged by Some Evolutionists," 288; Cassedy, *Charles V. Chapin,* 41; Frank J. Billings, "State Medicine," *JAMA* 5 (1885): 313.

80. C. H. Reed, "Why Is the Profession Poor in Purse?" *JAMA* 32 (1899): 977; Billings, "Relation of Hospitals to Public Health," 175; Henry Dwight Chapin, "Child-Study in the Hospital—A Record of Six Hundred Cases," *Forum* 18 (1894): 127.

Epilogue

1. Illustrative of that brief period when many sensed drastic changes in the professions are: Robert Perrucci, "In the Service of Man: Radical Movement in the Professions," in *Professionalization and Social Change* (1973), ed. Paul Halmos, 174–94; Ronald Gross and Paul Osterman, eds., *The New Professionals,* (1972); Joel Gerstle and Glenn Jacobs, eds., *Professions for the People,* (1976).

2. Among the notable studies of American engineers in the twentieth century are: Monte Calvert, *The Mechanical Engineer in America,* (1967); Edwin T. Layton, *The Revolt of the Engineer,* (1971); Robert

Zussman, *Mechanics of the Middle Class* (1985); Robert Perrucci and Joel Gerstle, *Profession Without Community* (1969).

3. Eli Ginzberg, "Service Sector of the U.S. Economy," *Scientific American* 244 (March 1981): 48–51; Ronald K. Shelp, *Service Industries and Economic Development* (1984); N. Gemmell, "Economic Development and Structural Change: The Role of the Service Sector," *Journal of Development Studies* 19 (October 1982): 37–66; Jonathan Hughes, "Industrialization: Economic Impact," *International Encyclopedia of the Social Sciences* (1968), vol. 7, and sources cited there; Richard B. Freeman, "The Evolution of the American Labor market, 1948–80," in *The American Economy in Transition,* ed. Martin Feldstein (1980), 356–63; Juergen Kocka, *White Collar Workers in America, 1890–1940* (1980). The quest of some of these service occupations for professional status is described by Amitai Etzioni, ed., *The Semi-Professions and Their Organization: Teachers, Nurses, Social Workers* (1969). For a perceptive book about librarians, see Dee Garrison, *The Apostles of Culture* (1974). Marxists have been predicting the proletarianization of the professions: *Professionals as Workers: Mental Labor in Advanced Capitalism,* ed. Charles Derber (1982) and Margali S. Larson, "Proletarianization and Educated Labor," *Theory and Society,* 9 (1980): 131–75. The professionals, however, seem to have stubbornly held on to their "false consciousness." See, for example, Joel Seidman, "Engineering Unionism," in Robert Perrucci and Joel Gerstle, *The Engineers and the Social System* (1964), 219–44. Some service workers have turned toward professional organization, others toward labor unions, and yet others toward both. Mark McCulloch, *White Collar Workers in Transition: The Boom Years, 1940–1970* (1983); Seymour Martin Lipset, "White Collar Workers and Professionals—Their Attitudes and Behavior towards Unions," in William H. Faunce, *Readings in Industrial Society* (1967), 525–54.

Acknowledgments

This book has been a long time in the making, and over that span of years I have presented parts of it to many scholarly societies. As a result, some of my ideas may have become familiar in restricted circles, and the chairmen and discussants of those sessions upon reading these pages after so many years might easily think that this book must be somehow a second edition or a reprint. Such are the costs of bruiting about and at the same time holding back.

Over the years, it has been the critical reading and encouragement of my friend and colleague Henry F. May that have helped me the most. He maintained happy expectations when some thought this book would never happen. Many others generously read the manuscript in part or full and offered insightful comments. Among them were David Bailey, Gunther Barth, Cynthia F. Behrman, Steven M. Bundy, Nathan and Ann Hale, Deborah Hardy, David Hollinger, James Kettner, Thomas Leonard, Robert Middlekauff, Kenneth Stampp, and Lawrence Veysey. Ed Dreschel, friend and neighbor, gave me the benefit of an informed layman's perspective. Their criticisms and suggestions, even when conflicting—or, rather, particularly when conflicting—were quite helpful. It is impossible to explain how much I have benefited from the books I have read and the discussions I have joined. Like the professionals I describe in this book, I am keenly aware of the way in which any individual accomplishment rests upon collective achievement.

At various stages of my work I have been aided by research assistants. Among them were Robert Havens, Pauline Jones, Gordon Link, Anne Lipke, and Mary Regan. Barbara Loomis's help was truly extraordinary. When at a late moment the footnotes to four chapters evaporated into the fourth dimension, she constructed and reconstructed most of them from rudimentary materials. Florence C. Myer typed the manuscript with astonishing accuracy and went beyond that to help bring it clarity of expression. Kate Haber and Paul Marcus assisted with the illustrations.

Acknowledgments

I made use of the resources of many libraries. Eleanor McKay of the Mississippi Valley Historical Collection at Memphis State University and Laura L. Chace of the Cincinnati Historical Society Library were helpful. At Berkeley, Aija Kanbergs was especially obliging. The National Endowment for the Humanities, the Davis Center at Princeton, and the Humanities Research Committee at Berkeley supported some of my research and writing.

I have been truly fortunate in my publishers, the University of Chicago Press. Margaret Mahan was efficient and supportive. Anne Eskra helped make my prose proper and precise. Martin L. White worked on the index. Doug Mitchell, the senior editor, was truly firstclass. His wide reading and sharp intelligence made his comments on my manuscript among the most perceptive that I received.

Of course, my wife Jan helped in the most important ways.

Index

ABA. *See* American Bar Association
Abbott, Lyman, 246
Academic departments, 286–87
Academic freedom, 287–92
Acland, Sir Henry, 323
Adair, Bethenia, 335–36
Adams, Henry, 243, 319
Adams, John, 15, 75, 84, 101
Adams, John Quincy, 161–62
Adams, Zabdiel, 31
Adversary system, 77, 79, 80, 129, 167, 203
Advertising, 124, 356
Agassiz, Louis, 299
Agnew Clinic, The (Eakins), 355, 457n.73
AIEE. *See* American Institute of Electrical Engineers
AIME. *See* American Institute of Mining Engineers
AMA. *See* American Medical Association
Amalgam (dental), 108
American Bar Association (ABA): on administration of justice, 219–20; aims of, 213; courtroom versus corporate lawyers in, 203; and Field's Civil Code, 217, 426n.25; founding, 199, 211–12; on legal education, 221–22; and other bar associations, 237–38; and social relations among lawyers, 225–26; on uniformity of legislation, 220–21
American Dental Association, 348
American Engineer, The, 294, 313
American Institute of Architects, 200, 421n.14
American Institute of Electrical Engineers (AIEE), 306–9
American Institute of Mining Engineers (AIME), 303–4, 309

Americanism (Roman Catholicism), 251, 254
Americanizers (Roman Catholicism), 250–51
American Medical Association (AMA): on Blacks and women, 331–33; code of ethics, 350; on irregular physicians, 336–41; *Journal,* 340, 349; late nineteenth-century revival, 199; leadership by laboratory-trained doctors, 203; on medical education, 107; Mussey's selection as president of, 183; Percival's code accepted by, 54; on public health, 356–57, 358; specialties recognized by, 108
American Medical Eclectic College, 330
American Pharmaceutical Association, 349
American Public Health Association, 326, 328, 329, 357
American Revolution: churches affected by, 38–40; lawyers affected by, 78; and Mississippi Valley expansion, 91.
American Society of Civil Engineers (ASCE), 300, 302
American Society of Dental Surgeons, 109
American Society of Mechanical Engineers, 304
Anderson, James A., 151
Andover Theological Seminary, 41, 261, 262, 263
Angel of Bethesda (Mather), 62–63
Anglicanism: American Revolution's effect on, 39; clerical disestablishment, 105, 106; in colonial America, 16–20; and the Great Awakening, 29. *See also* Episcopal Church

Episcopal Church, 39; in Methodism, 171; and priests' rights movement, 253, 254; professional status
in eighteenth-century England, 4, 5
Blackman, George Curtis, 417n.67
Blacks: in American Bar Association,
212; in Cincinnati, 155; Drake's
views on, 179; and late nineteenth-
century religion, 241–42; in legal
profession, 229–30, 431n.50; Masonic lodges in Cincinnati, 158; and
medical profession, 146–47, 332–
34; Memphis influx of, 152; ministers, 137–38, 256–58; and segregation, 247; slavery's effect on, 138
Blackstone, Sir William: *Commentaries*, 79, 82–83, 110, 214; definition
of law, 215; on justice and economic
enterprise, 80; on law's foundation,
17; on legal knowledge's diffusion,
86; and legal science, 214; social
origins of, 7
Bleeding (bloodletting), 52, 56, 57,
184
Bloomfield, Maxwell, 398n.44
Boerhaave, Herman, 50, 51
Boston: Blacks in legal profession in,
229; personal injury cases, 227,
406n.47
Boston University School of Theology,
260, 263
Boswell, James, 47
Botanic medicine, 106–7, 144–45,
337
Boudinot, Elias, 14, 372n.28
Boynton, Charles, 177
Brewer, David, 228
Briggs, Charles A., 247, 262–64
Brigham, Charles H., 248
Brinkley, H. L., 151
Brinkley, Robert C., 120
Brinkley, W. A., 138
Broadhead, James O., 427n.33
Broadus, John A., 271
Brooks, Phillips, 269, 270
Brougham, Lord Henry, 207
Broussais, François, 342
Brown, John, 182
Brown, Robert Fryerson, 145, 147
Brown, Solyman, 346, 347
Brown University, 292
Brunton, Sir Lauder, 323

Bryce, Lord, 285
Burnet, Bishop, 26
Burr, Aaron, 11–12, 372nn. 22, 23
Butler, William Allen, 427n.33

Calvinism: in Cincinnati Presbyterian-
ism, 169; in conservative seminar-
ies, 261; and disestablishment of
the ministry, 106; in late
nineteenth-century world view, 203;
Old Calvinists, 23, 32; preaching,
273; and revivalism, 132; in Warfield's view, 262
Cambridge Ministerial Association, 25
Cambridge Platform, 21
Campbell, Thomas C., 188
Capitalism, market. *See* Market capi-
talism
Carnegie, Andrew, 298, 302
Carter, James C., 214–18, 426n.10
Cartwright, Peter, 94
Case methods, 217, 222, 234
Catholicism: Americanizers and
priests' role, 251–55; in Cincinnati,
168, 170–71, 172–73, 176,
413n.35; in late nineteenth century,
241; in Memphis during Civil War,
139; nuns' role, 259; and social
stratification, 246, 247
Catholic University, 252
Celibacy, in Catholic priesthood, 254
Chandler, Thomas Bradbury, 16–17,
18
Channing, William Henry, 173
Chapin, Charles V., 327, 354
Chapman, William B., 185
Character of the Gentleman, The (Lie-
ber), 99
Charleston (South Carolina), medical
profession in, 60
Chase, Salmon P., 165–66, 168
Chauncy, Charles, 30–31
Chinese immigration, 198
Choate, Joseph H., 212, 220
Christianity, and honor, 9–10. *See
also* Catholicism; Muscular Chris-
tianity; Protestantism
Christian Science, and women preach-
ers, 258
Church and state, separation of. *See*
Separation of church and state
Cincinnati, 154–90; and Billings,

208; and judicial discretion, 80; in judicial process, 215; and natural law, 219

Kellogg, Martin, 290
Kent, William, 308
King, Rufus, 212, 412n.28
King's counsel, 4
Koch, Robert, 325, 328
Know-Nothings, 171

Labor: discipline in factories, 305–6; management responsibilities to, 309; in mining, 304; organized, 239, 309; and right to be commanded, 360
Labor, division of. *See* Division of labor
Laboratories, 345
Land speculation: lawyers' participation in, 79–80, 130, 389n.27
Langdell, C. C., 217–18, 222, 233–34, 426n.10
Laryngology, 107
Laski, R. L., 147
Law: in Cincinnati, 161–68, 186, 188–89; in colonial America, 67–87; egalitarian attack on, 109–12; in eighteenth-century London, 4, 5; independence of lawyers, 274; in late nineteenth century, 206–39; licensing of, 105; medicine's status compared to, 202–3; in Memphis, 124–32; natural, 214–15, 219; status among professions, x; status changes in America, xiii–xiv, 15–16; tort, 227, 236; written and unwritten, 217. *See also* Bar associations; Law schools
Law schools: Blacks in, 229; Cincinnati, 160, 164; in early nineteenth-century America, 103; Harvard, 214, 217, 233; in late nineteenth century, 222; Litchfield, Connecticut, 71, 104; proprietary, 104, 228
Lawyers. *See* Law
Legislation, uniformity of, 220–21
Lehman, Leopold, 129, 130, 131
Liberals (Congregationalist): on conscience, 31; on the Great Awakening, 29, 30; on ministers' calling, 31
Liberty: and the Constitution, 162; in

Howison's teaching, 280; changing meaning, 40, 75–76
Licensing: American professionals' relinquishment of, 113; of early American professions, xii, 9; egalitarian attack on, 105, 107; of kindred medical occupations, 347; of late nineteenth-century American professions, xiii, 201–2; of medicine, 46, 329–30, 331, 353
Lieber, Francis, 99–102
Life of Col. James Gardiner (Doddridge), 10–11, 100, 368n.20
Life on the Mississippi (Twain), 193
Litchfield (Connecticut), law school, 71, 104
Littlejohn, A. N., 242
Livingston, Robert R., 84
Livingston, William, 73
Locke, John, xiv
Lockwood, Belva A., 230
Lockwood, Melanchthon, 255
Lofton, George A., 141
Log Cabin College, 37
Lombard, Solomon, 15
London (England): professions in eighteenth century, 4–6
Long, Nicholas M., 135
Longworth, Nicholas, 160, 168
Loomis, Alfred L., 354
Louis, Pierce, 182
Louisville (Kentucky), Southern Baptist seminary, 261, 262
Love, in preaching, 270–72
Lutherans: in late nineteenth century, 240, 241; ministry, 266; and revivalism, 171, and social stratification, 246, 247
Lyman, Henry M., 327
Lynd, Samuel W., 172
Lynk, Myles Vandahurst, 333

McClean, John R., 188
McClurg, James, 48, 52–53
Madison, James, 7
Management, and engineers, 305, 309
Mansfield, Edward Deering, 205
Manual dexterity, and surgery, 342, 344
Market capitalism: and economic expansion, 197; and egalitarianism, 97; and engineering, 297, 301; and